IVORY

IVORY

A History and Collector's Guide

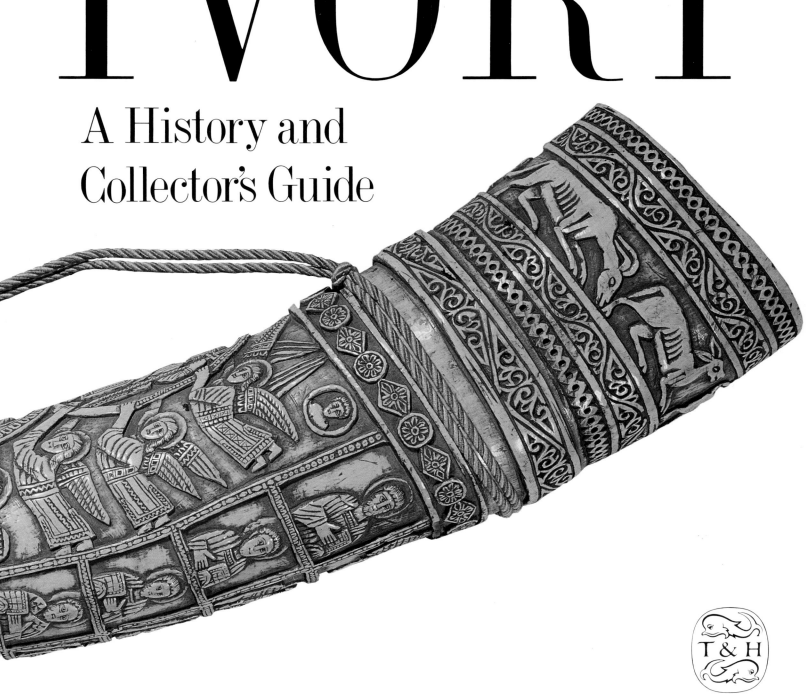

THAMES AND HUDSON

Contributors

MICHAEL VICKERS
Ashmolean Museum, Oxford
Early Civilizations; Rome and the Eastern Empire
(Rome; Rome and Constantinople).

PROFESSOR PETER LASKO CBE
Rome and the Eastern Empire (Late Antique and Early
Byzantine Stylistic Development; Byzantine Empire);
Europe (Early Middle Ages excluding Islamic section).

PAMELA TUDOR-CRAIG (LADY WEDGWOOD)
Professor of Art at Harlaxton College
Europe (Late Middle Ages).

SIMON YATES
Christies, London
Europe (Sixteenth, Seventeenth and Eighteenth
Centuries).

CARSON RITCHIE
Europe (Nineteenth and Twentieth Centuries); The Far
East, South-East Asia (Australasia, Oceania).

NIGEL BARLEY
Museum of Mankind, London
Africa.

CHARLOTTE CHESNEY
The Near East, India (Islam); Europe (Early Middle
Ages: Sicily, Spain).

BRENDAN LYNCH
Sotheby's, London
The Near East, India (India); The Far East, South-East
Asia (Himalayan Countries, South-East Asia).

ROGER KEVERNE
Spink and Son, London
The Far East, South-East Asia (China).

DAVID BATTIE
Sotheby's, London
The Far East, South-East Asia (Japan).

FREDERICK GRUNFELD
North America (excluding Ivory Products in the
United States).

ANTHONY SHELTON
Museum of Mankind, London
Central and South America.

Jacket: Details from the fan shown in colour on pages 252–3; by
courtesy of Spink & Son.
Page 1: Ivory plaque showing Emperor Otto I offering a model of
Magdeburg Cathedral to Christ in Majesty. Tenth-century.
Pages 2–3: Medieval ivory horn.
Opposite: Edenshaw walking-stick; Canada.
Page 6: Ivory wrist rest; China. Eighteenth-century.
Page 7: Workbox from India. Nineteenth-century.
Page 8: Panel from an ivory box; China. Nineteenth-century.
Additional text by Arthur Credland, Matthew Flamm, Ian Barritt
and Charlotte Plimmer.

CREATED AND PRODUCED BY
PHOEBE PHILLIPS EDITIONS

First published in Great Britain in 1987 by
Thames and Hudson Ltd, London

Photoset in Frome, Somerset
by Tradespools Limited
Printed and bound in Belgium
by Offset-Printing van den Bossche N.V.

Edited by Fiona St Aubyn
Designed by Harry Green

Contents

Introduction

Ivory has been treasured for many thousands of years, since the first pendants, beads and bracelets were fashioned from the tusks of mammoths who roamed the European plains in the millennia towards the end of the last ice age. In colours that range from the traditional purest white through pale creams and the dark patina of age – even, occasionally, the brilliant colours that can be found in mammoth ivory – this remarkable substance has been used for objects as diverse as crucifixes and combs, intricately carved boxes and ornamentally inlaid furniture.

Ivory has been designed to reflect this unique material's astonishing range. It opens with a description of different kinds of ivory, and a short survey of the trade in elephant tusks – vicious and bloody, and inextricably linked with the African slave trade, but tightly controlled today by the Convention of International Trade in Endangered Species of Wild Fauna and Flora. A detailed time chart places developments in the use of ivory in a world context, pinpointing every period in its long history.

The first chapter describes how ivory was carved by the early civilizations which flourished between 35,000 and the decline of the Hellenistic world in the first century BC. The following ones cover different geographical areas, sub-divided by period, religion, culture or region. They start with Rome and the Byzantine empire, and then circle the globe through Africa, the Near and Far East and South-East Asia to North America – and Central and South America where bone replaced ivory. Scrimshaw, prisoner-of-war carvings in bone and other associated crafts are included where relevant. The final chapter highlights modern artists who have inherited this ancient tradition of ivory carving.

Ivory contains nearly a hundred colour illustrations, pictorially cross-referenced to relevant parts of the text, as well as hundreds more black-and-white photographs. Measurements – the height of a piece unless otherwise stated, and normally the tallest in a group – have been given in inches and centimetres (where possible; not all museums and collectors have been able to detail these exactly, on request).

An illustrated glossary defines technical terms and is followed by a section on collecting ivory objects – and another on how to care for them. A list of museums with collections of ivory is included, and also a detailed bibliography for further reading.

PHOEBE PHILLIPS EDITIONS

The Story of Ivory

More than three thousand years ago, so the Old Testament records, 'King Solomon made a great throne of ivory' and to him 'came the navy of Tarshish, bringing gold and silver, ivory and apes, and peacocks'. Throughout the ancient world, the carving of ivory was an established art, and even prehistoric man had reacted creatively to its unique qualities.

Over the millennia, this singularly responsive substance with its subtle, glowing colour has been used and appreciated by cultures throughout the world for objects as diverse as religious images and thimbles, furniture and jewellery.

Above: Ivory coffer with fretted decoration, and detail (*opposite*). Tutankhamun's Egypt (*c.*1361–1352 BC). Ivory has always been a luxury, and was imported from Ethiopia to Egypt and Babylon.

Far right: Narwhal ivory cup on a walrus ivory base. Seventeenth-century.

Right: Deposition from the Cross, carved in walrus ivory. *c.*1200–10.

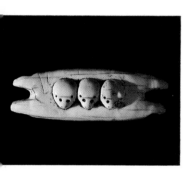

Above: Inuit ivory toggle shown in colour on page 15.

Sensuously appealing to the touch, ivory will take a fine polish and acquires a rich patina with age. Most important, it is tractable. It can be sliced paper-thin, sawed, cut, carved, etched, ground, or worked on a lathe; it can be stained or painted; and it is so flexible that riding whips cut longitudinally along the grain of a tusk are 'as finely tempered as a Toledo sword blade and as supple as a willow switch'.

The Oxford Dictionary defines this beautiful 'hard, white, elastic and fine-grained substance' as 'dentine of exceptional hardness', 'composing the main part of the tusk' of the elephant, mammoth, hippopotamus, walrus and narwhal. All are used artistically and commercially, but only the tooth of the elephant – this includes the extinct mammoth – is regarded as 'true' ivory.

True ivory

The most prized ivory comes from Africa, where the elephant is altogether larger than the Indian species, and both males and females bear long, heavy tusks. In India, females frequently have none at all, and in Sri Lanka, even the males can be tuskless.

The average African tusk weighs about fifty pounds (22.5 kg) and measures some five to six feet (up to 2 m). But male tusks as long as ten feet (over 3 m) and weighing up to 150 pounds (68 kg) have been recorded. The largest pair known, the Kilimanjaro tusks, weighed 460 pounds (207 kg) and measured twenty-four feet (almost 8 m) in length.

Small tusks are not scorned. When they weigh under eighteen pounds (8 kg) – these are usually female, short and straightish – they are dubbed 'scrivelloes' or 'ball scrivelloes' and have been much in demand for billiard balls.

African ivory is not only larger than Indian but also finer grained and richer in tone, though ivory from West Africa is usually harder and less intensely white than that from the east.

The elephant's tusks are the upper front teeth, the incisors rather than the canines, as in all other tusk-bearing creatures. They are not coated with enamel, as are the others, but are covered with a rough, brownish bark. Hollow for about half the length that juts out from the jaw, they are built up from within in layers. The outer layers expand to make room and the ivory retains this elasticity for ever. The tusks are weapons, of course, but are even more valuable as tools. The elephants use them chiefly to burrow among roots and undergrowth and to rip off the tree-bark on which they feed.

'Dead' ivory – taken from a beast that has died of natural causes – traditionally made up about 80 per cent of what reached the world's markets, 'hunted' ivory 20 per cent. The trade today, however, is scrupulously controlled.

The 'true ivory' tusks of the elephant's gigantic prehistoric predecessor, the mammoth, are on average about five times as large, a pair easily weighing up to 500 pounds (226 kg). Great caches used to be 'mined' in the Arctic tundra of Siberia and Alaska, having been embedded over 50,000 years ago. From the seventeenth century on, and especially during the nineteenth, there was a brisk trade in them. Before the First World War, huge consignments were regularly shipped from Moscow to Europe and the Far East, particularly China.

Although mammoth is known as 'fossil' ivory, this is a misnomer, for the intrinsic character of the substance remains unchanged. The tusks are frequently twisted and deformed, but can still be worked just as elephant ivory can. Many, however, have an almost stone-like hardness and are stained in brilliant colours – a beautiful turquoise blue in northern Alaska – as the result of being buried near mineral deposits. Known as odontolite (literally 'tooth-stone', from the Greek), the tusks have been cut as gems and set in costume jewellery.

Other 'ivory'

The Arctic **walrus** is the only native source of ivory in Europe. Most of Scandinavia's early ivory artefacts were carved from morse, as this ivory is sometimes known. Alaskan Inuit (Eskimos) used to slay walrus in enormous numbers and made the two-foot (0.6 m) tusks into tools.

The ivory is less dense than the elephant's and has a distinctive 'damascened' or marbled appearance and a creamier tone. Because the cavity is proportionately larger, there is considerable waste.

Morse has been credited with magical qualities. Medieval Scandinavian warriors believed that rings and weapon hilts of walrus ivory prevented cramps; Muslims, that a walrus dagger hilt could miraculously staunch blood and hasten the healing of a wound; the early Turks and the Chinese, that walrus ivory 'sweated' if it touched a poisoned dish – trade boomed in seventeenth-century China, where walrus chopsticks soared to six times the price of those made of elephant ivory.

The **narwhal**, a fairly rare Arctic whale, is known as the 'sea unicorn' because of its single cylindrical tusk – the left canine – which can grow up to eight feet (2.6 m) long. Valued chiefly as a curiosity, it has never been particularly attractive to carvers. Although it has a smooth surface and a pleasing pale white colour, the cavity is extremely large, and the entire length is grooved spirally, leaving very little workable material. The Japanese used it until fairly recently for netsuke and other small objects.

In medieval times the same marvellous power of poison detection as that of the walrus was

attributed to narwhal ivory and apprehensive potentates commissioned narwhal drinking cups.

The **sperm whale**, known in all the world's oceans, was until recent wildlife preservation measures hunted almost out of existence. It has some forty to fifty teeth in the lower jaw, each up to eight inches (20 cm) long and three inches (7.5 cm) wide. They are indeed a sort of ivory, but the inside colour is dark and unattractive, and half the tooth is hollow, making it fairly useless as a commercial product.

Nineteenth-century whaling men, however, used to while away long hours at sea etching scrimshaw on whole teeth. Extracting them was a lugubrious process. The entire jaw of the beast was hacked out and either towed behind the vessel for a month or so, or left on deck to decompose, which loosened the massive teeth. Even so, sailors often needed a block and tackle to yank them free.

The **hippopotamus**, the vast African 'sea horse', now generally protected, used to be widely slaughtered for meat, oil, hide and ivory-like teeth. Of the six in the lower jaw, two are long and dramatically curved, but do not qualify as tusks because they do not project out of the mouth. The smaller teeth are almost entirely hollow, suitable only for tiny objects. They were used for dentures in ancient Rome, and people

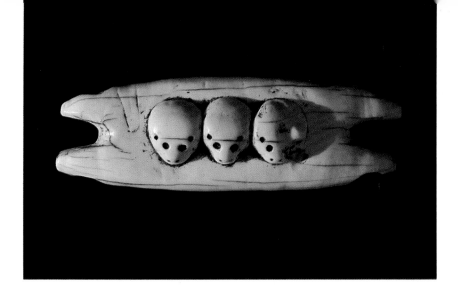

Opposite: Kneeling ivory figure from China, with traces of original pigment. Seventeenth-century; 3 in. (7.6 cm). See also page 18.

Left: Inuit toggle carved from walrus ivory, from Alaska. Nineteenth-century.

Below: Knives and spoons with handles of green-stained ivory. Probably eighteenth-century.

were still having them fitted as late as the eighteenth century; George Washington is said to have had a set.

The ivory is dense, white, strong, fine-grained and non-yellowing, but it is covered with a coating of enamel so hard that it resists even steel tools. The Japanese, who have used it for netsuke and other small curios, soak the teeth in acid to soften the enamel; this, unfortunately, also tends to soften the ivory within.

Carvers elsewhere were reluctant even to tackle the stubborn stuff until the invention of the viciously rasping rotary grindstone early in the nineteenth century.

The **boar** of Africa and Asia, like the **warthog** and other wild pigs, has four fairly large, upward-curving tusks which share many of the characteristics of ivory. They are, however, seldom longer than ten inches (25 cm) and consequently are used mostly in one piece for the handles of cutlery and tankards, the natural shape providing a comfortable grip.

Substitutes

There are various substances, some natural, some man-made, which more or less equate with ivory in texture and density, and have been employed in similar ways.

The casque of the **helmeted hornbill**, an East Indian bird, consists of a solid mass of ivory-like horn that is in itself decorative. Cut in cross-section, it shows a yellow interior with a reddish-orange rim. As long ago as the fourteenth century, it was used not only in the East Indies but also in China and Japan for intricate small objects – brooches, buckles, beads, rings and the like – and, like the walrus and the narwhal, was credited with the power to detect poison; Malayan tribesmen put their faith in the wearing of hornbill rings.

By the turn of this century, the bird was almost extinct, having been slaughtered mercilessly for the sake of its carvable casque.

The horn of both the African and the Asiatic **rhinoceros**, totally unlike ivory in appearance and composition, is the hardened epidermis or cuticle – a toe-nail rather than a tooth. It has, nevertheless, served for carving small decorative objects such as netsuke. In common with the horns or antlers of **rams**, **deer**, **antelope** and so on, it has also been valued since time immemorial for the handles of weapons and mugs, powder-

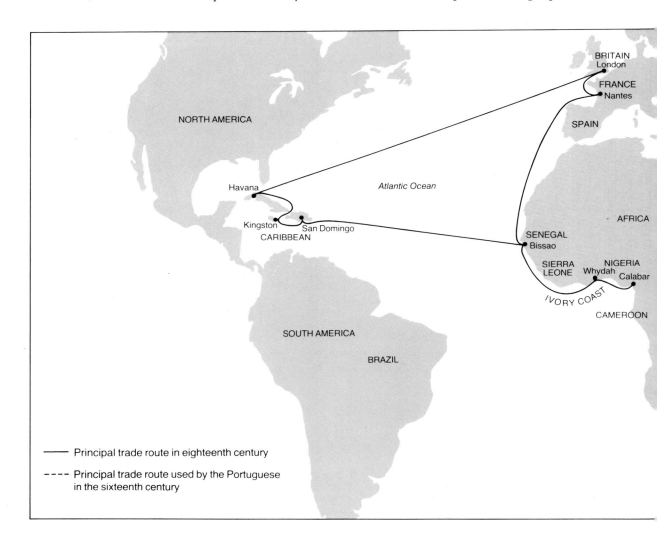

—— Principal trade route in eighteenth century

---- Principal trade route used by the Portuguese in the sixteenth century

horns, spoons, beakers, knobs, buttons and boxes and, of course, as an instrument. The Chinese used pulverized rhino horn in potions, as an aphrodisiac and to promote virility. Until several decades ago, when London was the centre of the world's ivory commerce, rhino horns sometimes turned up on the 'Ivory Floor' at St Katherine's Dock, where the tusks were laid out for viewing before auctions.

Bone – both animal and human – is in a sense the poor man's ivory, an adequate alternative, but without the subtleties and elegance of the real thing. It lacks the handsome graining and the mellow colour; cannot be polished to the same gleaming finish; and, although its outside is hard and completely carvable, the inside looks spongy.

Even so, bone art works can be extremely beautiful, often mistaken for ivory and indeed passed off as such by the unscrupulous. Remarkably fine pieces were carved in Mexico and South America long before the coming of the European traders.

During the Napoleonic wars prisoners evolved a highly specialized and delicate art form – carving bone to make model ships.

Far less costly and easier to come by than elephant tusks, bone has been employed since ancient times for domestic objects – combs, hairpins, buttons, shoehorns, handles, containers, dice – and to inlay furniture.

The seeds – **corozo** – of the South American dwarf palm tree have been an important commercial substitute for ivory since the 1840s, imported in great quantities into America and Europe for the manufacture of utilitarian articles such as buttons, thimbles, knobs and poker chips. When dried, corozo become very hard, take a reasonably good polish and will accept stain or dye. The natural colour, however, is dead white, lacking in depth and mellowness.

The Japanese have used corozo for netsuke, but attempts to substitute it for ivory in major artistic works have failed.

The ever-increasing scarcity of true ivory, with its concomitant soaring prices, has long preoccupied the makers of **synthetics**. The search for a genuinely acceptable alternative has recently become more urgent than ever, with the increasing agitation worldwide over the preservation of wildlife.

As long ago as 1863, Phelander & Collander, America's leading manufacturer of billiard balls, offered a prize of $10,000 (£2,000) – a munificent sum in contemporary terms – for anyone who could invent a practical approximation of ivory. The man who came closest (but not, in the minds of the judges, close enough to merit the money) evolved a substance based on collodion which was later dubbed **Celluloid**. It became popular with the manufacturers of a great variety of domestic objects, from brushes and combs to fountain-pen cases, picture frames, cutlery handles and assorted containers. Competing compounds soon appeared on the market, with such names as **Bonzoline**, **Cellonite** and **Xylonite** and (perhaps to attract customers) even **Ivorine** and **Ivorite**. All have been durable, lightweight and washable, but they are generally too hard to carve; and they feel wrong. Recent refinements have simulated ivory's grainy look, but man's ingenuity has yet to come up with a synthetic that can completely match all of Ivory's unique qualities.

The ivory trade

Ivory, so long a coveted luxury, figured importantly in the earliest known cargoes of exotic goods. In classical times, it was carried – partly by caravan, partly by sea – along the steamy, dangerous trade routes from Ethiopia to Greece and Rome, routes taken by earlier shipments to ancient Egypt and Babylon.

It reached early Christian Europe by way of Nubia, Egypt, Syria and the ports of Cyprus, whose skilled navies may also have carried it to

Below: Map outlining the route used by the Portuguese in the sixteenth century and other Europeans in the eighteenth century. In the nineteenth century, London became the *entrepôt* of the world ivory trade, re-exporting ivory to North America and around the globe.

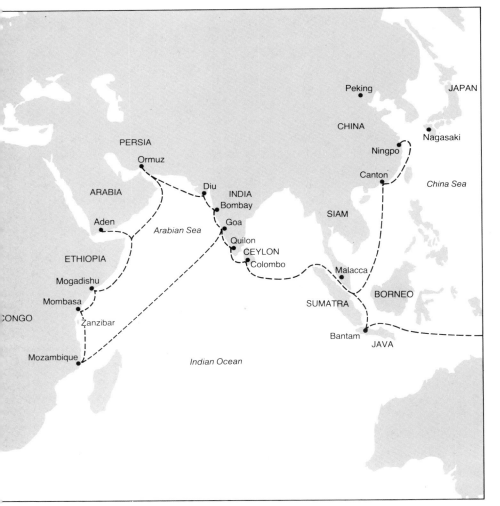

Above: Chinese ivory figure shown in colour on page 14.

Below: African ivory figure of a European holding a bottle. Seventeenth-century.

the Far East. The traffic to Europe was interrupted in the seventh and eighth centuries AD by Islamic conquests (notably of Spain) and for several hundred years morse – the tusk of the walrus – Europe's only native ivory, was used increasingly both for secular and religious carvings. Morse was exported to the Near East and even as far away as China during this period.

The native Chinese elephants had become extinct in the second century BC. When their own supply ran out, the Chinese imported tusks from Siam, India and Burma. Great connoisseurs of ivory, they had recognized, however, as early as the twelfth century, that the African ivory was by far the best.

Arabs on the east coast of Africa were the first to engage in the trade on a large scale. They had a flourishing commerce in ivory, along with ostrich feathers, ebony, spices and slaves, as early as 300 BC. Much of the ivory that reached the rest of the world from India over the centuries was originally African, having come by way of Zanzibar and Mozambique through Bombay.

Not until the sixteenth century did Europeans enter the lucrative trade. The Portuguese, seeking a route to India, pillaged the western coast of Africa, along the Guinea coast, bartering trinkets, knives, tallow, calico and gingham for black slaves, especially in demand when the rapid colonization of the Caribbean began, and for ivory. Their monopoly was brief. Before long, the Dutch, the Swedes, the Danes, the French and the British were competing viciously for control of Guinea's richest strips, the so-called Gold Coast and Ivory Coast.

Trade in finished ivory had begun in a small way with the first souvenir collectors, the crusaders and the early Christian pilgrims. Restraints upon trade were put into effect surprisingly early, especially by the colonizing countries of the New World. In the sixteenth century, for instance, Spain forbade the import into Mexico and South America of ivory objects from the Philippines and elsewhere in Asia.

But this was a mere sideshow to the traffic in raw ivory – 'white gold', as it became known. The sharp competition among Europeans along Africa's west coast ebbed in the mid nineteenth century with the abolition of the British and American slave trade with which it had been symbiotically entwined. This opened the way for the Arabs, still operating from the east coast, to re-enter the business far more aggressively than ever before. Central Africa was already crisscrossed with trade routes, and Arab adventurers, operating mostly out of Zanzibar, began to penetrate the interior. Ivory was part of an African king's regalia, and his power, prestige and efficiency were measured by how much he could accumulate. Rulers built up great hoards, which they now released into the trade.

The appetite for ivory at this time seemed insatiable, and far more for industrial purposes than for artistic, as in the past. Manufacturers in Britain, the United States and Europe were buying voraciously – for piano and organ keys, surgical tools, billiard balls, cutlery and umbrella handles. China took tusks in their thousands, often of inferior quality, for chess sets which were colourfully stained to hide the defects, and then exported to Europe.

On average, some 514 tons a year were being imported into London's international entrepôt. About forty-two tusks make a ton (1000 kg) of ivory. By 1890, a peak year, the figure had soared to 700 tons – about 14,700 elephants. About a quarter came from India, three-quarters from the great herds of Africa, mostly along the Gulf of Guinea; this proportion has always prevailed.

Ivory waste products virtually constituted an industry on their own. The hollow ends of tusks went to India for bangles, a never-ending market (the bangles being buried with their wearers). Small offcuts were bought by furniture makers for decorative inlay. The dust was used as sizing for paper and fabrics; burned to produce indian ink and the artists' colour, ivory black; fed, in India, to female cows and buffalo, in the belief that it helped them produce more milk, and

Above: Guitar made in the United States. Nineteenth-century. Made in 1834. Because of the elaborate design, the guitar was custom-made. It has an ivory bridge and fingerboard.

elsewhere to invalids, in ivory jelly – considered 'nutritious' and medicinal.

As the demand increased and prices soared, the Arab adventurers penetrated ever deeper into the jungle, carving out little kingdoms where they ruled absolutely, imposing taxes and controlling the movement of goods. The native inhabitants, ignorant of the value of ivory, killed the elephant not for gain but for meat, and in self-protection, for the massive marauders could reduce entire districts to famine overnight (as they still occasionally do). Sometimes the villagers, having slain their foraging enemy, would simply toss the tusks away; sometimes they used them as ordinary building material – for fences, stockades or corner supports.

While Zanzibar continued as the hub, a smaller but not insignificant trade operated out of the Sudan. Another grew up with the Boer and British traders and big game hunters in South Africa.

Even though the depletion of the herds, both through sport and for gain, grew ever more grave, the trade in elephant ivory continued on a large scale well into the twentieth century. In 1900, more than 587 tons were imported for auction in London. The figures gradually dwindled over the decades – partly through natural diminution, partly through the efforts of wildlife protection groups – and the highly charged sales are now a thing of the past. The echoing warehouses at St Katherine's Dock which sheltered the 'Ivory Floor' have been turned into luxury flats, and famous merchants like Puddefoote, Bowers and Simonett, long the world's leaders, no longer deal in ivory.

The trade in 'white gold', now made more valuable than ever by its rarity, is today rigorously controlled. The UN organization known as CITES, the Convention of International Trade in Endangered Species of Wild Fauna and Flora, has, since the 1970s, operated a meticulous monitoring system in co-operation with Africa's ivory-producing nations, from Angola through Zimbabwe. (India regulates her own relatively minor export trade, as do the walrus-producing countries.)

All African tusks, including old stock, must be registered and marked with identifying numbers, whether they come from beasts that have died naturally, been culled under supervision or hunted, either legally or illegally. Each country establishes an annual export quota, and buying nations are watched as closely as the sellers. States without elephant populations that have amassed stocks – Singapore, Hong Kong, Portugal, for instance – must also register in order to trade. The traffic in cut pieces and art antiques is scrutinized as well. Unauthorized shipments of any kind are confiscated, no matter where they turn up. The herds of Africa, protected at last, may yet recover their former glory.

Time chart

DATE	EUROPE	NEAR AND MIDDLE EAST
35,000–10,000 BC	**Russia** (Gravettian culture): Mammoth ivory bracelets, decorated with intricate geometric designs. **France** (Magdalenian culture): Ivory figures fashioned.	
10,000–8000 BC		
3600–1500 BC	**Russia** (Gravettian culture): Smooth, stylized figurines for use in fertility rites.	**India** (Harappa culture): Beads, dice, hairpins, kohlsticks, combs, mirror handles, seals, pegs, jewellery made in the Indus valley. A plaque from Mohenjo-Daro was earliest known depiction of the human form in India.
1600–1000 BC	**Greece:** Workshops in Mycenae produced statues, ivory boxes and furniture inlaid with ivory for export to the Greek mainland.	**Egypt** (Reign of Tutankhamun): Ivory used for luxury goods – gaming boards, furniture, chests, head supports and general inlay. **Iraq:** Nimrud ivories produced with their distinctive naïve style, many featured on gaming cups, nude figures forming the handles.
900–680 BC	**Italy:** Etruria imported ivory cups carved with exotic animals from the Phoenicians.	
462–1 BC	**Greece:** Ivory imported from Africa. Athena statue in the Parthenon constructed by Phidias.	**India:** Ivory exported throughout the world.
First Century AD	**Italy:** Ivory figure of a satyr possibly from the household of Verres, the Roman Governor of the province.	
Second Century AD	**Italy:** Ivory statuettes made by Roman craftsmen widely exported. The reliefs from Ephesus also date from this period.	
Third and Fourth Century AD	**Italy:** Brescia casket, the earliest ivory decorated with Christian subjects.	**India** (Gupta period): The red sandstone Sikri Buddhas carved at Sarnath and Mathura. These were the foundation of all subsequent Buddhist imagery in India. Kashmir ivories also featured Buddhas and Bodhisattvas.

Little is known about African ivories before the fifteenth century. Ivory is not durable under hostile environmental conditions and only fragments and decayed remnants remain.

North: Signs of Inuit carving along the Alaskan coast.

Thailand: Ivory necklace beads carved in Udon Thani province.

China (Shang Dynasty): Ivories absorbed the techniques of bronze making. Many artefacts were carved in relief using the taotie figures, bands of masked dragons and animals, for the first time.

Beginning of the African export trade.

China (Zhou Dynasty): Ivory was highly prized and often used for thumb rings, plaques, combs and back-scratchers. The Han Dynasty continued the popularity of ivory and brought humour to the objects carved. Much inlay work was made during this period, together with jewellery. Religious themes in ivory carving became more pronounced and images of the Buddha became frequent subjects for craftsmen.

South: Ivories produced with geometric engravings in Peru.
North: Inuits produced sophisticated harpoon heads and masks in the Hudson Bay region.
North: The Okvik Madonna carved in walrus. Artistically more advanced than later Inuit work.
Central: The Maya used human femurs at Chiapa de Corzo for bone carving.

North: Inuit carved elaborate harpoon heads and socket pieces; Old Bering Sea style.

DATE	EUROPE	NEAR AND MIDDLE EAST
Fifth Century	**Italy:** Boethius diptych carved; one of the last diptychs before the fall of the Roman Empire.	
Sixth Century	**Italy:** Ivory used in the Ravenna throne of Bishop Maximianus. It retained many classical traits through the close link between Ravenna and the Eastern Empire at Constantinople. Iconoclasm took root in Europe.	Islamic ivories followed traditional patterns of incision, carving, inlaid woodwork and mosaic marquetry. One of the first pieces known is a chess piece dating from this period.
Seventh Century		
Eighth Century	**France:** Caskets made with ivory panels, and decorated with scenes from history and the northern sagas. The Dagulf psalter carved for Charlemagne, influenced by late antique which gave the figures a thickset appearance.	
Ninth Century	**France:** Charlemagne founded schools at Metz, Tours and Rheims which began the Carolingian renovation. One notable product was the St Peter throne now in Rome.	
Tenth Century	**Britain:** Golden age of Anglo-Saxon art. Influenced by the Utrecht psalter and the Carolingian schools. Work from this period included a nativity panel and a crucifix carved in the Reims style; known in Britain as the Winchester style. **Italy:** Veroli casket made in Rome. **Germany:** Separate style developed from the late Carolingian during the reign of Otto I. The Ottonian Renaissance was characterized by stunted, square figures with capped hair styles. The Gregory Master carved St Gregory in his study.	Movement away from iconoclasm reflected in an ivory panel representing Christ crowning Constantine. Egyptian craftsmen working in Spain made caskets inlaid with ivory sheets. Cordoba caskets were made in this Hispano-Moresque style. **India:** Kashmiri temple architecture forms the model for shrine altarpieces.
Eleventh Century	**Britain:** Winchester style persisted throughout the century. An *Agnus Dei* in this style was carved at the time of the Conquest.	**India:** Chess pieces and ivoryware exported to the west for the first time.
Twelfth Century	Walrus ivory becoming rare in northern Europe, though ivory work was of high quality, using well-proportioned and rounded forms. **Spain and Italy:** Main centres of carving, producing both secular and religious works. **Germany:** Ivory carved in the 'pricked' style and monumental in composition, with artefacts ranging from a nativity to a Tau crosier.	Oliphants for hunting and drinking made throughout the Near East and in Islamic Spain.

Spread of Islam disrupts the ivory trade with Europe.

Large comb found in the tomb of St Cuthbert in Durham, made from African ivory. ▽

China (Tang Dynasty):   Whalebone sceptres produced for nobility.

North (Thule culture):   Combs and other practical items, rather than ornamental work, on the Alaskan coast of Beaufort Sea.

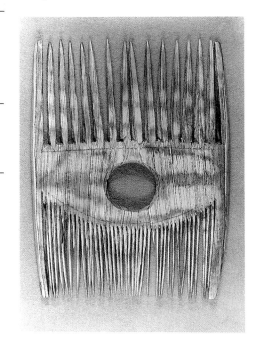

Central: With the end of the Maya culture, bone carving became cruder.

China (Song Dynasty):   Ivory played a special role in cermonies. Used in state carriages and horse fittings, and formed a large part of the tributes paid to court.

North: The Inuit in Greenland adopt some western forms through contact with Norsemen.

South: Incas carved small bone figures in Peru.

China: High-quality jewellery produced in the southern Song capital of Hangzhou.

| --- | --- | --- |
Thirteenth Century	**France:** Dedication of the Ste Chapelle and inclusion of the ivory Virgin, a model for many subsequent carvings. Ivory became a popular material, used for the Soissons diptych; Matthew of Paris took the ivory Herlufsholm crucifix as a gift on a visit to Norway. **Italy:** Centre of crosier manufacturing. Giovanni Pisano created the Virgin and Child altarpiece.	**India:** Ivory carving at Orissa; produced the rampant *gajasimha*. Also ivory bed panels.  **Syria:** Minbar of Hamâh mosque worked with ivory by several Mamluk craftsmen.
Fourteenth Century	**Italy:** With the Pope's transfer to Avignon, French and Italian styles merged. In particular the ivory statuette in St Francesco in Assisi. **Britain:** Some Byzantine influence in the Grandisson ivories at Exeter Cathedral. **Germany:** Soft style emerged, bringing a loose flowing quality to the carving of drapery. The diptychs of Master of Kremsmünster and some figure work display this. **Italy:** Embriachi used hippopotamus bone and tooth as an ivory substitute. Used successfully in the altarpiece at Poissy. ▽	Ivory Koran boxes made in hexagonal shapes. Many other boxes inlaid with ivory.
Fifteenth Century		

China: Official workshop for ivory carving established with a workforce of 150.

Supply of ivory from East Africa controlled by the Islamic Empire.

Australasia: New Zealand Maoris carved whale tooth ornaments.

Central: Aztecs colonized Central American valleys and began carving bone rattles and inlaying skulls.

China: The Ming Dynasty was famous for its jewellery, brush handles, wrist rests, figures and brush pots.

Portuguese traders began trading with Africa.

China: Vasco da Gama opened trading route to China for the Portuguese. This brought western influence to Ming figure carving.

Sixteenth Century

After the Reformation religious carving developed from the monumental to the small scale, with Italian sculpture providing the dominant influence. The work of Leonard Kern is representative of the period.

Seventeenth Century

Use of ivory for *memento mori* became a persistent strain in the northern European tradition. One of the major artists of this period was Christof Harrich.

Ignaz Elhafen and Balthasar Permoser began work after the Thirty Years War in a more decadent style, with classical subjects as themes. Plaques, through the work of Francis van Bossuit, became a common medium for ivory. Another form was the portrait medal; Jean Cavalier carved an equestrian medal of Charles II. Ivory veneer was also widely used for gaming equipment and firearms.

Sri Lanka: Produced quality ivories, especially caskets.

India: Ivory used for decoration in weapons, box panels, inlaid cabinets, especially in Goa; often decorated in a European style.

Tibet: Human bone used for trumpets, and skulls for drinking cups. Handles and amrita vases made in ivory.

Eighteenth Century

Germany: Simon Troger and Wilhelm Kruger took everyday subjects for their figure groups; influenced by porcelain figures.

Ivory used for inlaying furniture throughout the Continent. Pietro Piffetti was one of the foremost exponents; also Angermair, who built the Elizabeth of Lorraine cabinet.

With the expansion of the whaling trade, sperm whale teeth became a prime material for European scrimshaw.

Italy: Giuseppe Maria Bonzanigo carved miniature designs.

Germany: Guild of ivory workers founded at Erbach by Franz I. This produced such artists as Christian Kehrer.

India: East India Company established; much Indian furniture carved to Georgian designs, especially Hepplewhite.

Widescale export of goods to Europe through Portuguese traders. Much African ivoryware made deliberately for the western market. This 'tourist art' remained fairly uniform throughout the Continent, with slight regional variations. The 'Sherbo style' produced pedestal cups which could be transformed into salt-cellars, as well as horns, necklaces and spoons. Objects from the Benin area tended to be heavier and less fluid. Some ivory work was produced only for internal consumption and mainly for ceremonial.   ▽

Yoruba kingdom carved bracelets, ritual swords and figurines.

Philippines: Population taught to carve ivory by European colonists, taking western models and themes as their guide. Later came under influence of Chinese, who set up workshops to trade with South America.

China: Ivory carvers produced religious images for Christian missionaries. Figures of Guanyin.

Japan: Trading with the west.

Japan: Beginning of Edo period.

China: Figure carving especially important, either as simple groups, man and woman embracing, or as medical figures. Greatly influenced by Christian ivories of the Holy Child. Factory established by Emperor Kangxi specialized in western figures and ruyi decorated with ivory.

South-East Asia: Dagger hilts fashioned in Burma.

China: Major centres of Ningguo, Huizhou and Suzhou flourished making fans and wrist rests, also the twelve 'pleasures of the month' panel. Ivory appliqué and white on black technique very popular, the latter used on screens. The export market was furnished with pagodas, snuff bottles and figures.

Japan: Tomotada and Masanao carved netsuke from wild boar tusks.

Thailand: Ivory goods exported from Bangkok.

North: A duck amulet was the first recorded artefact made by the Northwest Coast Indians.

Nineteenth Century

1810s

France: Art school established in 1808 at Dieppe. Pierre-Adrien Graillon worked there, producing his famous portrait of Napoleon III.

Ivory gaming pieces and model ships made by prisoners of war during the Napoleonic wars.

1820s

Germany: Beginning of the Biedermeier style at Erbach resulted in romantic flowers, jewellery and realistically carved animals.

1830s

India: Ivory carvers from Travancore made the throne and footstool for the Great Exhibition. Indian furniture incorporated European, Hindu and Muslim motifs – sometimes mixed together. In eastern India, western furniture was produced. Some Bengali ivories show groups of Europeans. Patiala work was carved using shallow tracery designs.

France: Paris Exhibition in 1834 drew many Dieppe carvers to Paris.

Britain: Nathaniel Cook produced the Staunton design chess set.

1840s

Britain: Benjamin Cheverton developed the ivory sheet veneer machine in 1844.

Britain: Richard Cockle Lucas carried on the classical style with his 'Cupid seated on a rock'.

France: Henri de Triqueti combined ivory with other media for large scale works.

1850s

France: Paris International Exhibition in 1855. Pierre Charles Simart exhibited his replica of Phidias' Athena.

Islam: European-style furniture decorated with ivory inlay.

Britain: Scrimshaw, depicting whaling scenes and portraits, engraved in northern England.

1870s

Russia: 'Palace Art' created liturgical objects and fine furnishings.

India: Art school at Trivandrum established.

Australasia: Whaling fleet established in Van Diemen's Land; whale teeth used for scrimshaw with a pointillist technique.

North: Inuit combined wood and ivory in articles for everyday use. Most carved objects were purely functional, for example toggles for the reins of a dog sledge.

China: Exported chess sets, devil's balls, pastoral scenes on rhino horn, canes and caskets around the world. Haoching particularly famous for carving in the western style. Fans were also produced in great quantities during this period. As the century progressed design tended to become repetitive and lose its ingenious quality.

The Benin carved elephant tusks using animals and Europeans as designs. Ivory was whitened with acid fruit juices. Benin craftsmanship created the composite ivory leopard aquamaniles, made with ivory pieces bound together by metal pins and staples.

North: Indians carved tusks with totemic designs. Ivory also used for ritual objects. By the end of the century this totemic culture became westernized.

Thailand: Ivory work tended to centre on the carving of elephant tusks.

Japan: Ivory used for masks worn during Noh plays and sometimes for naturalistic portraits. These were always signed.

Ivory miniatures produced at Pende, including amuletic wooden face-masks stained with palm oil.

Japan: Two great netsuke carvers, Kaigyokuai Masatsugu and Ohara Mitsuhiro, carved lifelike birds and animals. Mitsuhiro's popular 'animals of the zodiac' was carved at this time.

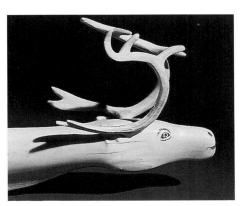

North: Inuit carved souvenirs, cribbage boards for the crews of passing whaling ships.

Japan: Export trade with US stimulated by presence of US navy. Objects included erotic ivories, netsuke and okimono – especially that of the Ogawa school, showing happy peasants.

DATE	EUROPE	NEAR AND MIDDLE EAST
1880s		
		Nepal: Ivory gaming pieces and divinity figures crafted from ivory.
1890s		
	Belgium: Wolfers created first Art Nouveau ivory.	
	Belgium: Brussels Exhibition in 1897. Japanese art was particularly influential, especially in work of Sir William Reynolds Stephens.	

Twentieth Century

DATE	EUROPE	NEAR AND MIDDLE EAST
1910s	**France:** Art Nouveau style combined ivory with other media. Good examples are Clovis Delacour's Andromeda and the jewellery of René Lalique, in particular 'Fairy with Wisterias' pendant.	**Tibet:** Wheels of Life carved. Exhibition of Tibetan art in Delhi. Bone objects were still made, though ivory working mainly discontinued.
	Germany: Ferdinand Preiss' 'Naked Dancers' heralds Art Deco.	
	Britain: Alfred Gilbert and Frank Lynn Jenkins used ivory inlay in their work.	**India:** Many local styles merged; campaigning by Ananda Coomaraswamy to encourage these dying arts. Indian schools of art concentrated on western styles. Wood and soapstone replaced ivory.
1920s	**Britain:** Direct carving technique had short-lived vogue.	
	France: Art Deco gained popularity at the Paris Exhibition and generated mass-produced chryselephantine sculpture, taking dance as their main theme.	
1930s	Ivory carvers much influenced by Art Deco, especially Ludwig Walther and Louis Richard Garbe, who carved 'The Source'. One of Garbe's pupils, Jeanne Bell, was noted for her unusual subjects as in the case of 'Black Ivory'. Other pupils of Garbe included Mary Morton and Alan Durst.	**Nepal:** Ivory carving declined except for jewellery and archaic religious images. **Islam:** Pahlavis revived the *khatam-kar* marquetry technique.
	Germany: The Erbach school continued to flourish until the 1960s with the famous carvers Karl Schmidt-Rottluf, Ludwig Gies, Emy Roeder, Oswald Ammersbach and Eric Kuhn.	
1940s		
	Namba Roy, originally from Jamaica, carved impressive works such as 'Black Albino'.	
1950–		

Congo produced staff heads, sword handles, pendants and whistles. Best known are the small Luba pendants of very hard hippo or warthog ivory, depicting the torso of a woman with a complex hairstyle.

Carved tusks and Lamu chairs exported from East Africa.

Japan: Tokyo School of Art founded under the western influence. The major figure in this movement was Ishikawa Komei.

China: Yu Xiaoxin carved fine-quality miniatures.

Japan: Wearing of swords banned; armourers turned to miniature objects: detailed insects and crustaceans.

North: Scrimshaw of good quality produced by the Yankee whaling fleets.
▽

Japan: Netsuke and okimono work continued to be exported until 1914.

North: William Perry began carving scrimshaw and continued until the 1960s.

The 1920s saw the reopening of the Royal Workshops in Benin, following closure by the British in 1897.

China: Ivory working, interrupted by ravages of 1930s and 1940s, then the Cultural Revolution, was not revived until 1960s. Hong Kong produces mahjong sets, chopsticks and figures based on Japanese characters. Ivory from Hong Kong is often coloured.

North: Earl Mayac continues the Indian tradition with his 'Crouching Hunter' and 'Bear Man'.

Tanzania produces hand-turned candlesticks.

1
Early Civilizations

One of the earliest known habitations of modern man, occupied some thirty-five thousand years ago, was discovered in 1868 at Cro-Magnon in the Dordogne in south-western France. At the back of a rock shelter were found the remains of a small group of people lying among scattered beads of shell and pendants of ivory, which must rank among the earliest known examples of objects used for personal adornment.

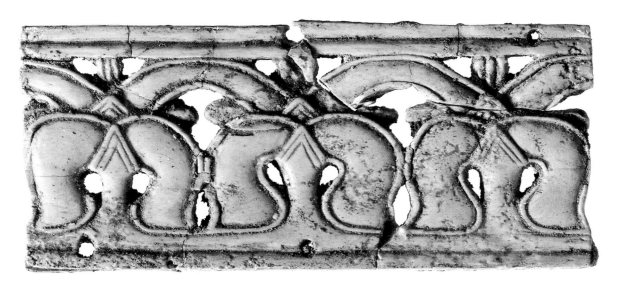

Above and opposite: Ivory panels from Nimrud in Iraq. Eighth-century BC; 3½ × 1½ in. (9 × 4 cm). The detail above shows stylized vegetation in the Phoenician style. The panel opposite was mounted on wood to form part of a bedhead or throne and the detail depicts a warrior in ceremonial dress clasping a climbing plant.

Europe: the Advanced Palaeolithic era

'And the houses of ivory shall perish,' said the Old Testament prophet Amos. In fact, most of the human settlements of ages long past have disappeared virtually without trace. For the earliest period of man's existence in Europe, in the Palaeolithic Age, all we have is the imperfect archaeological record; it is, however, a record rich in ivory objects.

The Palaeolithic Age covered an immense span, *c*. 400,000–10,000 BC, generally divided into three eras: Lower Palaeolithic, *c*. 400,000–110,000 BC; Middle Palaeolithic, *c*. 110,000–35,000 BC; and Upper or Advanced Palaeolithic, *c*. 35,000–10,000 BC, with the appearance of modern man towards the end of the ice ages, about thirty-five thousand years ago.

The ivory used by these early inhabitants of Europe was from the tusk of the mammoth, a creature larger even than the African elephant. A remarkable representation of a mammoth with a high, domed forehead, long, curving tusks and a hairy body was found in an Advanced Palaeolithic cave in south-western France: a miniature fore-runner of the life-sized murals of bison, wild boar and deer which adorn the prehistoric caverns at Altamira and Lascaux, painted some ten to fifteen thousand years ago.

The people of the Gravettian culture, 22,000–18,000 BC, were hunters and gatherers of food. The bones of young mammoths have been found in their middens – rubbish dumps – in eastern Europe, together with those of other game: reindeer, horse, Arctic fox, hare and grouse. They used rocks and mammoth tusks to weigh down the leather walls of their wigwam-like dwellings and even burned mammoth bones as fuel. Theirs was a culture distinguished by the versatility of its craftsmen: workers in clay, flint, bone and antler, and ivory carvers.

Many pieces of ivory jewellery have been preserved thanks to the Gravettian practice of burying their dead fully clothed. Beads and pendants were made of stone, shell, fired clay and deer teeth as well as ivory. There is even one instance of ivory having been carved to resemble deer teeth, which probably indicates that ivory was not then as exotic a material as it was to become later in European history. A bracelet of mammoth ivory from Mezine in southern Russia was made from a cylinder of ivory nearly 1¾ in. (4.5 cm) high, cut down one side and perforated with holes for a fastening. The whole of the surface is decorated with a highly intricate pattern of chevrons and other geometric designs.

Gravettian artists are rather more famous for their representational art. A smooth, stylized profile of a mammoth rendered in mammoth

ivory from Pavlov in Moravia is a masterpiece of simplification. More complex, however, are the figurines of women. The famous 'Venus of Willendorf', a generously endowed woman holding her hands over the top of her breasts, is a Gravettian product. She was made from limestone, but there are several analogous figurines made from mammoth ivory. One such is known from Kostienki in southern Russia. She holds her hands over her belly, but is in most other respects similar to the Willendorf figure: huge hips, no waist to speak of and enormous breasts. From Mezine again, there comes a group of symbolic pregnant female figurines in mammoth ivory the surfaces of which are engraved with geometric designs like those on the bracelet discussed above. The imagery is clearly sexual and the apparent emphasis on pregnancy suggests that they may have been connected with fertility beliefs. Survival and procreation were the two principal concerns of Gravettian society; in this it in no way differed from most societies today.

After the Gravettian period came the Solutrean (18,000–15,000 BC) and then the Magdalenian (15,000–8000 BC) with its superb cave paintings of the animals on which human survival depended: bears, bulls, cows, reindeer and horses – the latter still at this period hunted for food. A mammoth ivory figurine of a horse, found at Lourdes in the Pyrenees, has a large body and a small head with a short, spiky mane and is incised along the length of its body with a double wavy band.

There were Advanced Palaeolithic peoples in Siberia, too, notably in the Angara valley near Lake Baikal. Once again the mammoth figured large among the game that was hunted, and again its secondary products were turned to good use by local craftsmen. The climate was exceptionally severe, as we are reminded by an ivory figurine of an individual dressed from head to foot in a snugly fitting fur garment. The surface of the object is carefully pitted, probably with a flint tool, so as to give the illusion of a furry texture.

The global climatic changes of around 10,000 BC took effect over the next three or four thousand years as the Polar ice cap began to melt and the sea levels rose. The afforestation of much of Europe forced Arctic animals further north. Gone were the mammoths; gone a local supply of ivory. In future, ivory would have to be imported into Europe from Africa or the Near East.

The Fertile Crescent and the eastern Mediterranean

The distribution of elephants in, say, 3000 BC was far wider than it is today and included species which have long since become extinct. In Africa, elephants were to be found as far north as Mauretania and Libya, and in Asia there were

Above: Ivory figure found at Abydos in Egypt. Third-millennium BC; 3¼ in. (9 cm). The lower part is damaged but the head wears the crown of Upper Egypt.

herds in Syria down to about the ninth century BC. The main reason for the extinction of the animal in these areas was the desire for ivory.

Cities, settled communities whose populations could be numbered in tens of thousands, first came into existence in the Fertile Crescent – the area between Egypt and Mesopotamia – during the third millennium BC. A highly organized network of trade grew up between the different urban centres. We occasionally catch glimpses of it in the surviving written records; literacy, too, was a by-product of urbanism. Merchants and middlemen propagated decorative schemes far beyond the centres for which they were originally designed. The widespread practice of hoarding precious objects – gold and silver vessels, rich textiles, furniture made from ivory and exotic woods, ivory boxes and figurines – in palace and temple treasuries, meant that articles could survive over long periods and give rise to the revival of older artistic styles when the occasion arose.

The elucidation of the history of ivory working in Egypt and the Near East is an extremely complex task. One thing, however, is clear: ivory was a luxury item whose use was widespread in the region for several millennia. It was used for inlays, for handles and knobs, for small vessels and boxes, for spoons, sceptres and drinking horns, for statuettes and for the faces, hands and feet of larger statues; and it was frequently stained and gilded, a fact easy to forget when many early ivory articles have either lost their colour or had their gold stripped from them by looters.

Pre-dynastic Egypt (5000–3100 BC) provides the earliest examples of ivory working from the Fertile Crescent. Combs, bangles and pendants are the most common items found in early tombs. A grave of the Garzean period (3500–3100 BC) at

Naqâda produced a quaint little statuette of a stylized, bearded man. The most important surviving artefacts of the Garzean culture, however, are the elaborately carved ivory handles of flint knives. Scenes of hunting predominate. One knife from Abu Zeidan has minute game animals and birds carved along its length: wild goats, cranes, *mouflons*. Another, from Jebel El-Araq, shows on one side men fighting on river boats and on the other hunting dogs, lions and a deity or hero holding two lions in his outstretched hands, a motif which is thought to have originated in western Asia rather than Egypt. It recurs time and again in Near Eastern imagery.

The city of Hierakonpolis ('Falcon Town'), reputedly the seat of the earliest kings of Upper Egypt, is the site of a temple enclosure within which was found, towards the end of the nineteenth century, a large cache of regalia and ivory objects. Nothing was later than the Second Dynasty (2890–2686 BC), and the ivories included fragments of furniture such as chair-legs carved in relief or a support carved in the form of a kneeling captive with his hands tied behind him. There were boats, nude women, and men either dressed in cloaks or virtually naked wearing elaborate penis sheaths.

Above: Ivory comb from Abydos in Egypt, carved with royal and divine symbols. Old Kingdom (3110–2258 BC).

Right and far right: Two ivory haircombs from Pratodynastic Egypt (fourth millennium BC). Combs are among the items most frequently found in the tombs of this period.

Ivory was comparatively scarce in Mesopotamia before the first millennium BC, but there are occasional examples of its use in the third and second millennia. At Mari on the Euphrates, a city so placed that it could exact a tax on all goods passing between lower Mesopotamia and Syria, ivory was used as a kind of mosaic inlay. At least two temples, those of Shamash and of Dagan, have ivory figures inlaid into panels of schist or limestone. The scenes are repetitive groups of priests performing sacrifices. From Kish further to the south comes a charming statuette (c. 2400–2300 BC) of a bull with the head of a smiling, bearded man. The stylized curls of his hair are continued over the shoulders of the beast. This was one of four figures which were part of an unusual wheeled stand. At the time, Mari was subordinate to the kings of Ebla near Aleppo,

Above: From a temple at Mari in Mesopotamia, a stone panel inlaid with ivory. *c.*2400 BC; 6¾ in. (17.1 cm). The panel shows the sacrifice of a ram.

rulers whose empire has only come to light during the past twenty years or so. To date, no ivory has been found at Ebla; there were, however, some wooden reliefs very similar in character to Syrian ivory carving of some fifteen centuries later. Tablets found at Mari, but of Old Babylonian date (1850–1800 BC), record in great detail life within the palace. They include inventories and letters, enabling scholars to reconstruct a remarkably vivid picture of everyday life nearly four thousand years ago. One text lists ivory stands for drinking vessels. They were plated with gold and silver and one was inlaid with two stars of lapis lazuli.

A remarkable ivory box found at Acemhöyük in south-eastern Anatolia (Turkey) in a level dated to the eighteenth century BC exemplifies the problems connected with isolated finds of ivory in the ancient Near East. It is made in the form of a cube and was probably once attached to a stand.

Each side is decorated with prominent studs made of bronze and gold, iron and lapis lazuli, as well as with a large and a small carved relief. These are all highly complex: some show seated rulers with attendants and tribute bearers, others animals of the chase such as lions and deer. Its precise origin, however, is uncertain; it could have come from Syria, but this is only a guess based on a few points of resemblance with motifs on cylinder seals.

In the Egypt of the Eighteenth Dynasty of the New Kingdom (1570–1293 BC) ivory was used on a lavish scale. At this period the pharaohs controlled all the available supplies of ivory within the Fertile Crescent; indeed, it seems that ivory may have been a royal monopoly. In *c.* 1464 BC we hear of an elephant hunt which took place in Syria. The general Amunhotep describes how Thothmes III 'hunted one hundred and twenty elephants for their tusks and . . . I engaged the largest . . . I cut off his trunk while he was alive, before his majesty . . . Then my lord rewarded me with gold . . . and three changes of clothing.' A few decades earlier, *c.* 1500 BC, Queen Hatshepsut had sent an expedition to what is now Somaliland in search of elephant tusks.

Paintings in the tomb chapels of court officials show delegations bearing gold and silver vessels from Crete, wine amphorae from Syria, and exotic animals, ivory and ebony from Africa.

The 'wonderful things' found in 1923 in the tomb of Tutankhamun (*c.* 1334–1325 BC) in the Valley of the Kings at Luxor provide an unparalleled assemblage of luxury items made in Egypt during the centuries of greatest prosperity. The gold mask and the gilded shrine guarded by graceful images of Selket are perhaps the most striking of all, but the ivory contributes greatly to the overall impression of immense wealth. Whether as inlay on chests or gaming boards, claws on lion's-foot supports or tongues of alabaster lions, ivory plays its part as an important decorative material. Perhaps the most effective use of ivory and ebony is a folding stool which appears to be draped with a leopard's skin. The true colours have been reversed and the spots are rendered in a series of irregular ivory patches inlaid into the surface of the black wood. Another impressive object is an ivory headrest: a kneeling figure of the god Shu carries the curved head-support on his upraised hands. On either side crouch two lions who represent the mountains to east and west: in effect, sunrise and sunset.

The most interesting object, however, must be the ornate chest which bears carved and painted ivory reliefs showing on the lid Tutankhamun and his queen Ankhesenamun within a bower, Tutankhamun shooting fish and wildfowl, with his wife crouched charmingly at his feet, and around the sides hounds and cheetahs chasing bulls, calves and ibexes. All the scenes contain exquisite floral patterns and all retain their original colours: blues, blacks, browns, ochres and yellows. It is a superb piece.

The great civilizations of New Kingdom Egypt and Mesopotamia were the exemplars of luxury for the eastern Mediterranean *c.* 1500–1250 BC. Crete was small but its rulers enjoyed many of the trappings of wealth. There was an ivory workshop in the palace at Knossos, the material for which had to be imported from Egypt or Syria. Some of the pieces once attributed to this workshop are now widely held to be modern forgeries. One that is certainly genuine is a spirited representation of a youthful acrobat.

Even mainland Greece, on the edge of the civilized world, provides a delightful group of two women and a girl, probably made in a

Right: Ivory statuette. Reign of Tutankhamun (*c.* 1361–1352 BC); 3¼ in. (8.2 cm). The figure is of a young girl wearing an unguent comb.

Mycenaean workshop in the fifteenth century BC. Roughly contemporary are two ivory boxes (*pyxides*) found in a Mycenaean chamber tomb at Athens. The surface of the smaller one is decorated with sea shells in relief; the larger has reliefs of griffins – creatures with lions' bodies and the heads of birds of prey – attacking deer. Furniture inlaid with ivory is referred to in Linear B tablets from Pylos which date to the thirteenth century BC.

Some of the finest examples of ivory working in the Late Bronze Age, *c.* 1700–1200 BC, come from Cyprus. In 1896, there were found in a tomb at Enkomi in eastern Cyprus three mirror handles, two of which have lions pulling down bulls and the other a heroic figure of a man attacking a griffin, and a remarkable box with a gaming board on the lid and especially vivid hunting scenes on front and back. The more important huntsmen ride in chariots, shooting with bows at the game, wild goats for the most part, which hurtles away from them. Only the wild bull turns to face the onslaught. The prevalence of hunting scenes on ivories is highly appropriate; ivory was a commodity which was firmly part of the luxury trade, and institutionalized hunting, then as now, was largely a prerogative of the rich.

The spectacular ivory objects found at Ugarit (Ras Shamra), a busy, thriving, cosmopolitan centre at the Mediterranean end of trade routes which extended across Syria, via major cities such as Mari and Ashur, to the Gulf and beyond, reflect the activities of Phoenician or Canaanite craftsmen settled there. The most distinctive piece is a small but expressive head of a youth or woman with various features inlaid in other, mostly precious, materials: the hair is made of silver, with gilded lapis lazuli locks at the front; the eyebrows and eyelids are also of lapis, and the eyes of copper. It may have been part of a cult image and demonstrates the great skill of local Syrian ivory carvers.

Two golden bowls were found at Ugarit; one has a scene of a bull hunt from a chariot, highly reminiscent of those on the box from Enkomi, which suggests that it, too, was of Canaanite origin. A local workshop apparently made ivory furniture of the kind listed in the trousseau of Queen Ahat-milku of Ugarit: 'three beds decorated with ivory plaques'. The remains of such a bed found in the excavations at Ras Shamra were in a room with some half-completed furniture, which suggests that it was made on the spot by local craftsmen. The footboard consisted of ivory panels carved with reliefs in a superficially Egyptian style, but many of the details, and certainly the themes represented – the sun goddess suckling two youths, a bowman bearing a stag – are Syrian or Hittite. Such amalgamation of motifs from Egypt and from the western seaboard of the Levant was to be characteristic of Phoenician

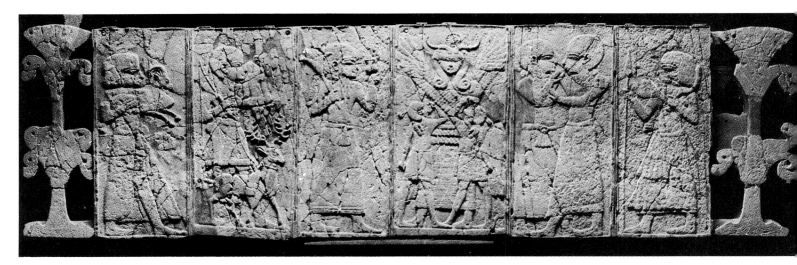

Above: Carved panels from an ivory bed, found at Ugarit (Ras Shamra). Late-fourteenth- or early-thirteenth-century BC; 9½ in. (24 cm). Probably the work of Phoenician craftsmen, the carvings show a queen praying to a naked fertility goddess (*outer panels, top*) and, pregnant, being embraced by the king (*second from the right, above*).

craftsmen in all media, including ivory, during the second millennium.

With the bed was found an ivory flask carved with a female figure, perhaps the fertility goddess Astarte, standing between winged sphinxes. Her hair is done in a typically Hittite manner, a reminder of the powerful empire to the north which had dominated Anatolia since about 1800 BC, and had come to control Syria – and Ugarit – under the Hittite king Suppiluliumas (1380–1355 BC). By the twelfth century BC, however, successive attacks by sea-borne raiders from further north devastated many of the coastal cities of the eastern Mediterranean and even threatened Egypt. Just before this catastrophe overtook the Near East, ivory production flourished at Megiddo in Canaan. It has been suggested that one reason why the large-scale use of ivory should have occurred in this part of the world only at the end of the Bronze Age is that the Egyptian monopoly over the material was weakening. In 1937, some three hundred assorted items of ivory in a great variety of styles were found in a single deposit at

Megiddo; the collection of an eccentric Canaanite prince, suggested the excavator. Subsequent work on similar caches from later contexts in Mesopotamia, however, has convinced scholars that what was found at Megiddo was part of a palace treasury. Ivory in good condition was a valuable commodity though looters sometimes stole the precious metal and left behind the ivory, to be found by archaeologists.

There are in fact indications that the furniture at Megiddo, dated c. 1250–1150 BC, was looted, perhaps in the Late Bronze Age raids. Nevertheless, the Megiddo ivories are sufficiently well preserved to illustrate the tastes, beliefs and customs of the Canaanite aristocracy. Many of the items are concerned with ladies' toilette: combs, fans, mirror handles, unguent bowls and cosmetics boxes. There are also imports of ready-made objects from Egypt and a very important one from Anatolia, a panel illustrating the meeting of two Hittite Great Kings, supported by a large number of Anatolian gods and goddesses, the whole resembling a highly intricate circus act.

Right: Box from Megiddo carved with lions and sphinxes. Late Bronze Age (twelfth–century BC); $2\frac{3}{4} \times 5$ in. (7 × 13.2 cm).

Quite how the panel reached Megiddo is something of a puzzle.

More Syrian in appearance is a fragmentary casket whose sides are carved with lions and winged sphinxes in high relief. The way their heads are turned threateningly towards the spectator strongly implies that they were originally envisaged as playing a protective role over the contents of the box they adorn.

Some of the Megiddo ivories have been classified as 'Mycenaean', that is, as imports from Greece. This, however, probably gives too privileged a position to what are more likely to have been Near Eastern ivories, or ivories made under strong Near Eastern influence, but found in Greek contexts. The elaborate winged griffin on a plaque from Megiddo, for example, does indeed bear a fairly close resemblance to creatures carved on one of the *pyxides* from Athens or on a plaque from Mycenae, but to suggest that the influence went from west to east in this case is to make the tail wag the dog. Moreover, the supposed association of some gaming pieces found at Megiddo with

Mycenaean 'figure of eight shields' is surely fanciful.

The Near East and the eastern Mediterranean

'King Solomon ... also made a great ivory throne, and overlaid it with the finest gold. The throne had six steps, and at the back of the throne was a calf's head, and on each side of the seat were armrests and two lions standing beside the armrests, while twelve lions stood there, one on each end of a step on the six steps. The like of it was never made in any kingdom.' Solomon's Temple and House, described in detail in the first Book of Kings in the Bible, sound extremely lavish, but were not atypical. Many other buildings in the eastern Mediterranean or Mesopotamia would have been just as richly adorned.

The kingdom of Israel was one of the states which arose after the disturbances at the end of the Bronze Age; other peoples who established themselves were the Philistines, who settled in parts of

Canaan c. 1150 BC, and were said to have introduced the use of iron, and the Phoenicians, who lived along what is now the Lebanese coast and were skilled craftsmen – so skilled in fact that they were employed to build Solomon's Temple in Jerusalem. Further north were the Aramaeans, who by the end of the twelfth century BC had spread throughout northern Mesopotamia and Syria, and further east was Assyria, a major force whose rulers reduced the whole of northern Syria to Assyrian provincial status by the end of the eighth century BC. The Assyrian kings, Ashurnasirpal II (reigned 883–859 BC), Shalmanesar III (reigned 858–824 BC) and Sargon II (reigned 721–705 BC), thrust westwards; Ashurnasirpal reached Mount Lebanon and 'washed his weapons' in the Mediterranean, and received 'many tables of ivory and boxwood, whereof the weight could not be computed' from the Aramaean city of Hattina on the Upper Orontes; Shalmanesar took the Aramaean state of Til Barsib and pillaged 'ivory without measure' from Hattina; Sargon sacked a Urartan capital and took away from the palace 'staves of ivory, maple and boxwood, together with their knobs whose inlay was of gold and silver ... eight great *mahrisi* [this word has defeated philologists] and baskets for vegetables, of ivory, maple and boxwood, whose inlay was of gold and silver ... drinking cups of ivory, maple and boxwood, whose inlay was of gold and silver'. He seized an 'ivory couch, a bed of silver, for the repose of his divine majesty; one hundred and thirty-nine ivory staves, ivory vegetable baskets, ivory daggers, poniards of ivory and maple [?] whose inlay was of gold'.

The source of this ivory has been long debated by archaeologists. Many have subscribed to a belief in economically significant herds of Syrian elephants lasting until well into the first millennium, but this is highly doubtful. Recently, indeed, fragments of what had been called 'ivory tusks', some of them scored ready for cutting, found by Sir Leonard Woolley at Al Mina in a late-eighth-century context, were shown to be in fact the cores of buffalo horns. But even had they been ivory, they would not necessarily have indicated local herds, any more than the great nineteenth-century ivory warehouses of Liverpool or London betokened herds of elephant on the Wirral or the Kent marshes. Only hides and tusks – no live elephants – are recorded in the area after the reign of Tiglath Pileser III (reigned 744–727 BC); the five hundred war elephants recorded in Syria centuries later in the Hellenistic period were clearly imported from India.

Al Mina (in effect the successor to Ugarit at the Mediterranean end of the trade route to the east via Mesopotamia and the Gulf) was equally well placed to receive ivory tusks from India or from Egypt. Ugarit had grown wealthy, it seems, primarily from trade in precious metals, acquiring relatively cheap gold from Egypt and cheap silver or other commodities from its eastern contacts. Al Mina may have done likewise and acquired ivory, another luxury item, from both directions.

Most of the ivories found in the Near East in the first millennium BC were discovered well away from their probable places of manufacture. It is, however, possible to identify at least two major schools of ivory carving, the North Syrian and the Phoenician. Comparisons with architectural sculpture at centres such as Tell Halaf, Carchemish and Zincirli have enabled scholars to distinguish elements which are characteristically North Syrian: squat, somewhat plump figures, often represented frontally, a tendency to compress much detail within the space available, and a total avoidance of Egyptian motifs. Phoenician ivories are characterized by the use of a wide range of applied colours and a general borrowing of Egyptian features.

The find spots of North Syrian ivories are for the most part in and around their homeland. They are very rare indeed in Palestine and are totally absent from Cyprus. There are occasional examples from sites in Greece and Italy. Phoenician ivories, by contrast, are very common in Palestine and Cyprus and also occur in Greece, Italy, North Africa and Spain. Assyria regularly plundered both Syrian and Phoenician cities, and the most productive sources of both kinds of ivories have in fact been the treasuries of Assyrian kings and officials. Arslan Tash, the site of the palace of an Assyrian overlord who ruled part of Syria, produced very many Phoenician ivories. But the most important finds of all were made at Nimrud in Iraq, where great numbers of carved ivory fragments have been excavated: the remains of the booty won by Assyrian kings and stored in their palace treasuries.

Ancient documents attest the importance of Nimrud. An inscription of Ashurnasirpal II attributes the city's foundation as a royal Assyrian capital to 'Shalmaneser', but whether it was Shalmaneser I (reigned 1272–1243 BC) or Shalmaneser II (reigned 1030–1019 BC) remains uncertain. Nimrud remained an important centre until it was destroyed by fire, probably in 612 BC when Assyrian authority came to an end. Towards the end of the eighth century BC, Sargon II rebuilt part of the palace and claimed that 'the plunder of cities acquired through the success of my weapons ... I shut up therein and filled it to bursting with luxuries'. A few years earlier Tiglath Pileser III (reigned 744–727 BC) told in much greater detail how he had 'shrewdly used to the best advantage' the skilled artisans: 'The palaces' terraces I constructed, laid their foundations and raised high their towers. The palaces' doorways, of ivory, maple, boxwood, mulberry, cedar ... juniper, tribute of Hittite kings, of the princes of the Aramaeans and of Chaldaea, which I brought to submission to my feet through my valorous heroism I made and richly adorned them.'

Other documents show how Assyria's military power led to its mercantile domination of Syria and Phoenicia. We should not therefore assume that all the ivory at Nimrud and other Assyrian centres was necessarily the direct fruits of conquest; some must have come through trade, but which pieces it is impossible to say. It is highly problematical too whether carvings in a given style were made on the spot by peripatetic craftsmen or were introduced ready-made.

The bulk of the fragments from Nimrud were simply decorative elements of larger objects such as beds or thrones, chests or incense burners, mirrors or fans. The most important group of Syrian ivories was found near the temples of Nabu and Ezida in 1854 but details were only published in 1957. The ivories include fragmentary circular boxes decorated with reliefs of lion-hunting scenes or women playing the double flute and tambourines. The style is distinctive but almost naïve. Handles consist of two, three or four draped male or nude female figures standing rigidly to attention, eyes front and hands by their sides. Hair is rendered in a series of close-set dreadlocks or in two lank curls on either side of the head. The folds of the garments, when worn, are shown by means of shallow striations. Many of these objects would once have been gilded.

Another characteristic form of North Syrian ivory was a bowl apparently held either in the carved human hand attached to it or within the grasp of conjoined lions. An especially fine and intricate example of the latter is known from Nimrud: two lions' heads hang over the bowl, their jaws agape. The animals appear to hug each other with one foreleg and the outside of the bowl

Below and right: Ivory carvings from Nimrud. Eighth-century BC. The 'woman at the window' was possibly a temple prostitute; 3¼ in. (8.2 cm). The clasped hands were once part of a statue. 2½ × 1½ × ⅞ in. (6.3 × 3.8 × 2.25 cm).

with the other. Winged sphinxes wearing pillbox hats (*poloi*) stand forward of the lions, their heads carved in the round, their bodies in low relief, a 'tree of life' between them. The object has all the complexity of an elaborate piece of netsuke.

The cramped stylization of these Syrian sphinxes is a world away from the svelte elegance of their Phoenician counterparts. One example in particular exemplifies this distinction. From Fort Shalmanesar at Nimrud, it must once have been part of the backrest of a throne. The body, seen in profile, is rendered plastically, the frontal face powerfully modelled. Many of the details are wholly Egyptian: the crown, the head-dress, the broad pectoral and the cobra image. The palmettes growing almost organically below and above the creature add another exotic touch. A more or less complete Phoenician ivory throne found in a tomb at Salamis in Cyprus has two such sphinxes supporting each armrest. The same tomb also produced an ivory bed, the headboard decorated with sphinxes in relief.

These Salaminian finds may throw light on some other ivory objects excavated at Nimrud. Nineteen similar pieces of furniture, neatly stored away here, were probably the backs of thrones, and all have relief panels, frequently showing men with their hair and beards in close-set stylized ringlets, dressed in chainmail and apparently attempting to wrestle with a mysterious plant. Others show seated figures, mostly women, who either hold similar plants or have tables piled high with food and dishes. Sometimes the sun symbol appears above. The source of these intriguing ivories is disputed. They stand apart from the Phoenician school of ivory carving and may have been the products of a provincial Syrian workshop, or even come from Anatolia.

The many Phoenician ivories found at Arslan Tash, near Carchemish on the Upper Euphrates, include some which even bear Aramaic and Phoenician inscriptions on their backs. There are more winged sphinxes of the kind found at Nimrud and Salamis, and a wide range of standard Phoenician motifs: kings and goddesses with 'trees of life', goddesses looking out of a window (thought by some to represent temple prostitutes), grazing stags, cows giving suck to their calves. All once decorated the kind of furniture seen on reliefs from the palace of Assurbanipal at Nineveh, now in the British Museum.

Phoenician traders carried luxury goods to the west: to Cyprus, Greece and Italy and to their own colonies at Carthage and in Spain. The foundation of the Carthaginian colonies in western North Africa gave Phoenicia a new and abundant source of ivory independent of Egypt. Homer twice mentions silver wine-mixing bowls made by craftsmen from the Phoenician port of Sidon and his works are full of references to ivory:

Above: An ivory plaque from Nimrud. Eighth-century BC; 5 × 3 in. (12.7 × 7.5 cm). Phoenician work, the plaque shows a winged-headed sphinx walking in a papyrus thicket.

for example, Penelope's throne in the *Odyssey* was adorned with ivory and silver, and in a beautiful simile in the *Iliad* the poet compares the blood flowing from a hero's wounded thigh to the effect created when a dyer stains a horse's ivory cheek-piece with purple.

Silver vessels of eastern Mediterranean type survive in Etruria in Italy, and it is here, thanks to some unusually rich burials, that we can best observe the impact made by oriental luxury imports on a very wealthy western society, *c.* 700–575 BC. The remarkable ivory objects deserve to be more widely appreciated. An ivory cup from Praeneste on a high, conical, fluted foot is similar in shape to many extant ceramic cups made from *bucchero* ware (themselves, however, based on vessels of silver). There is a frieze of truly exotic animals around the bowl – winged lions and goats – and above and below them an oriental cable pattern. Similar animals appear on some highly unusual ivory arms also from

Praeneste. Up to eight narrow bands of reliefs are carved around these strange objects.

In mainland Greece, at Athens, a grave of the eighth or early seventh century BC produced five crude ivory statuettes of nude females, said to have been cut from a single tusk. The *poloi* on their heads imply North Syrian affinities. Sanctuaries are the places where most ivory is found in Greece: small votive seals and plaques and ivory spectacle fibulae (brooches) have been found at the shrine of Artemis Orthia at Sparta. Excavations at Perachora on the Corinthian Gulf have produced a small ivory head of surprising sophistication as well as a crouching sphinx of provincial aspect. Its kinsfolk are to be found in an ivory group of two women in the Metropolitan Museum, New York: one is clothed, but the other has almost lost her attractive dress carved with intricate geometric patterns. Another sanctuary, Delphi, was the source of a splendid ivory statuette of a man holding a spear in one hand and resting the other on the head of an exquisitely carved rampant lion. Among the most attractive early ivory finds from Greek shrines, however, is the lean, belted figure of a kneeling boy from Samos which once supported one branch of a miniature cithara. His Ionian elegance is a feature shared by the numerous small ivory figurines of priests and priestesses from nearby Ephesus on mainland Asia Minor.

In the sixth century BC, so ancient writers tell us, monumental Greek sculpture was born. The 'first to win renown for sculpture in marble', Scyllis and Dipoenus, were natives of Crete and flourished during the middle decades of the sixth century. They were also renowned for their work in ebony and ivory: still extant at Argos in the second century AD was a sculptured group of the Dioscuri, mostly in ebony but with some ivory inlay. Egypt was then enjoying almost unparalleled prosperity under its king Amasis (reigned 568–526 BC); the king, who had made a peace treaty with Nebuchadnezzar of Babylon at the beginning of his reign, strengthened his position by making diplomatic gifts to tyrants and shrines in Greece. These gifts – paintings, textiles and sculpture (including at least one piece commissioned from Scyllis and Dipoenus) – were the major influence in the development of early archaic Greek art, the simple hieratic style of which was described by later writers in antiquity as 'Egyptian'.

Babylon, which had succeeded Assyria as the foremost power in the Near East, fell in 539 BC to Cyrus the Great, founder of the immensely rich Persian Empire, which was to incorporate Egypt in 525 BC. At its greatest this empire extended from the Indus to the Aegean. Towards the end of his reign, Darius the Great (reigned 521–486 BC) began the construction of the Apadana at Persepolis where all his subject peoples were represented. They include an African carrying an ivory tusk; the Ethiopians sent gold, two hundred logs of ebony and twenty ivory tusks every second year.

Classical Greece

The Persian Empire was to serve as the exemplar of great wealth for the best part of two centuries. At the beginning of the fifth century, in 499 BC, the Ionian Greeks attempted to win their freedom from their Persian overlords, but failed to do so. The outbreak of the Ionian Revolt was signalled by an attack on Sardis, the capital of the western satrapy of the Persian Empire, not by the Ionians alone but also by their fellow Greeks from across the Aegean, the Athenians and Eretrians. In 490 a punitive force was sent to deal with the mainland Greeks, but at Marathon the tiny city of Athens won an amazing victory over the mightiest empire the world had yet seen.

Eleven years later the Persians returned with Xerxes, the Great King himself, at their head and were again defeated, this time by a coalition in which the Athenians played a prominent part. Athens, enriched from the war, became the dominant power in the eastern Mediterranean. In addition to campaign booty the Athenians had rich native supplies of silver, doubtless worked all the more easily thanks to the availability of enslaved prisoners of war. Bullion was the key to Athens' prosperity.

Not only did the Athenians take a leaf out of the Persians' book, running their empire as a miniature version of the Achaemenids', with subject peoples bringing annual tribute, but the wealthiest citizens began to enjoy, again on a reduced scale, the luxuries of power. Boom-town conditions prevailed at Athens. Great fortunes paid for the new luxury goods and craftsmen from areas within the Persian Empire where a high level of artistic patronage had traditionally existed had good reason to flock to Athens. The Persian conquests had displaced the craftsmen of Ionia, Egypt and Babylon; traditional religious practices had been stamped out by the conquerors, tribute levied, treasures melted down. Deprived of the means of and motive for employment at home, refugee craftsmen from all quarters helped supply the needs of newly enriched Greeks to commemorate their victories over the Persians in war, or their victories over each other at the games. Some of the major artistic productions of the fifth century BC, which rank among the most important works of art of any period, were of ivory. They have not survived, but their appearance can often be reconstructed from descriptions by writers in antiquity, representations on coins, or even terracotta models and copies.

'The weaving of wreaths is an easy task,' said Pindar in a poem composed early in the fifth

Below: Three views of an elegant ivory figure of a kneeling boy, found at Samos. Seventh- or sixth-century BC; 5¾ in. (14.5 cm). The figure was part of the frame of a lyre.

century to celebrate a victory by Sogenes of Aegina at the Nemean games. 'Lo,' he continued, 'the Muse is welding gold and ivory white in one, with the lily she has stolen from beneath the ocean's dew.' The 'lily' is coral, and the imagery of the Muse weaving together exotic and costly materials well befits verses written by the most highly paid poet of the day for a patron from Aegina, an island whose merchants had permanent trading links with Naucratis, a Greek emporium in the Nile delta.

Naucratis was probably the source of the ivory used in the gold and ivory statues made by pupils of Scyllis and Dipoenus that the Greek traveller Pausanias (*fl.* AD 143–76) saw when he visited the temple of Hera at Olympia in the second century AD. Scyllis and Dipoenus worked in ivory and ebony, and it is likely that the artists to whom they passed on their skills retained some of their Egyptian contacts. The chryselephantine (gold and ivory) statues which Pausanias saw included Themis by Doryclidas, the five daughters of Hesperus by Theocles, and Athena by Medon. All these artists were Laconian – that is, from Sparta – and it is tempting to think that a search for an independent source of ivory was one of the driving forces behind the abortive attempt, led by the Spartan prince Dorieus in the late sixth century BC, to found a Spartan colony in Tripolitania. Other 'very old' chryselephantine statues in the same temple were of Demeter and Persephone, Apollo and Artemis, their mother Leto, Tyche (Good Fortune), Dionysus and a winged Victory.

In the same temple Pausanias saw a 'cedarwood chest with figures on it in ivory and gold, and carvings in the cedarwood itself'; to this object, the so-called 'chest of Cypselus', he devotes three chapters describing its intricate mythological scenes and recording many of the inscriptions, some of which were in verse. The date of this remarkable object is a matter of great current controversy, some preferring the sixth century, others a time between Marathon (490 BC) and Salamis (480 BC). But whatever the date, some fragmentary ivory friezes found at Delphi, the other major shrine in Greece, are roughly contemporary with it. As on the 'chest of Cypselus', parts of the Delphi figures were gilded, and a similarly wide range of mythological scenes must have been present on the object for which they were originally made.

A large hoard of Greek silver coins found in 1969 at Asyût on the Nile, some two hundred miles south of Cairo, seems to have been buried late in the 460s BC. It included coins from all over the Greek world. The bulk, however, were from Aegina and Athens. What were these coins doing so far up the Nile? They may represent bullion sent in payment for another valuable commodity,

ivory. Weight for weight, ivory at this time probably cost about one-tenth the price of silver.

The importing of ivory from Africa to Athens is mentioned in a long list of commodities given in a fragment of a play by Hermippus written not long after 431 BC: 'from Egypt we get rigged sails and papyrus; from Syria, again, frankincense; beautiful Crete sends cypress wood for the gods. Libya supplies much ivory for trade . . . Carthage supplies carpets and multi-coloured pillows.' While Libya can mean Africa in general, it seems that a distinction is being made between Egypt and Libya on the one hand, and Libya and Carthage on the other. Although the Athenians were clearly getting linen and papyrus from Egypt, it could be that the Persians, who controlled the country at the time Hermippus was writing, monopolized the ivory trade and deliberately prevented any that came up through Egypt from falling into foreign hands. In 460 BC the Athenians had supported an Egyptian revolt against the Persians and had held the country, and presumably monopolized the ivory trade, until the Persians succeeded in throwing them out in 454 BC. Such was the Athenians' fright at the resurgence of Persian military power that they persuaded their allies to move the treasury of the Delian League to Athens, an act of unbridled imperialism, as was the subsequent building programme on the Acropolis paid for out of the league's funds. One consequence was the continuation of the Parthenon, begun by the general Cimon in the 460s. The populist leader Pericles, brought to power as a consequence of the revolution of 462/1 BC, began the construction of a new Parthenon aided by his overseer, the sculptor Phidias. Phidias' chief responsibility was the construction of the gold and ivory statue of Athena Parthenos, the colossal cult image the temple was built to house. (A Greek temple was not intended for congregational use; priests performed sacrifices at open-air altars before the open doors through which the cult image could be seen.) Pausanias the traveller describes the Athena figure: 'The statue is made of ivory and gold. In the middle of her helmet is a sphinx, and griffins worked on either side . . . The statue of Athena stands upright in a robe which reaches the feet and on her breast there is the head of Medusa carved in ivory. She has a Victory six feet high, and a spear in her hand. At her feet there is a shield and near the spear is a snake . . . On the base of the statue there is carved the birth of Pandora.'

Far from being made of solid gold, the statue would have been built over a wooden armature, and we know that all the gold parts were removable. It has recently been estimated that the forty talents of gold (1 talent = 57 lb or 26 kg) would have had to cover a surface of at least 240 sq. yd (200 sq. m), counting in all the deep folds on the known copies of the statue. The gold must have been beaten to a thickness of under one sixty-fourth of an inch (0.33 mm).

Quite how the ivory which was used for the flesh was worked is even more problematical. It may have been built up from relatively small pieces, like a Roman period statuette found in the Athenian Agora, or large panels may have been bent into shape. There is a very telling passage in Plutarch's life of Pericles describing how he encouraged employment by means of his grandiose building schemes: 'The different materials used ... would require special artisans for each, such as carpenters, modellers, bronzesmiths, masons, gilders, moulders of ivory, painters, embroiderers and carvers in relief.' The technique of ivory bending was said to have been invented by Democritus of Abdera, born around 460 BC, and two methods are actually described by ancient writers, Plutarch saying 'They soften ivory in beer, and when it is loose, they bend it and form it into shapes', and Pausanias, 'Fire turns the horns of oxen and the tusks of elephants from round to flat, and also into other shapes.' However, the copies we have of Phidias' Athena Parthenos do not allow us to ascertain which, if either, of these techniques was adopted.

Phidias made another colossal statue of gold and ivory: the cult image in the temple of Zeus at Olympia. Judging by the response of those who saw it in antiquity, the Olympian Zeus was an even more magnificent creation than the Athena. Strabo said that although the temple was a very large one, the seated god seemed disproportionately big, 'almost touching the roof with his head, thus creating the impression that should he rise and stand upright he would unroof the temple'. Again the flesh was ivory and the robes and hair of gold.

Pausanias provides us with some fascinating information concerning how the ivory in these major statues was preserved. At Olympia, there was a recess in the pavement 'which keeps in the oil which streams from the statue. For it is oil which is best fitted to preserve the statue at Olympia, and protects the ivory against damage from the marshy atmosphere of the Altis. But in the case of the statue called Parthenos on the Acropolis of Athens it is not oil but water which keeps the ivory sound. For since the Acropolis is dry owing to the great height, the statue, being made of ivory, requires water and the moisture which water gives.' Both these statues survived until late Roman times, and served as a constant reminder of what could be achieved by patrons with a lot of money to spend.

In fifth-century Athens, and well into the fourth century, cylinders of ivory were commonly mounted in silver to serve as oil jars at the cremations of the rich. The oil would help the pyre, usually of olive wood, to burn more fiercely. Such vessels were called LEKYTHOI and many pottery imitations survive. It is possible from these to see how the body and shoulder of an ivory original might be made from two separate pieces of turned ivory fitted together, while the foot and neck would have been of gold and oxidized silver. The bodies of these ivory containers would have been attractively painted – a trade which apparently continued, judging by a reference in Aristophanes' *Ecclesiazusae*, long after the manufacture of the pottery imitations ceased.

A few fragments of decorated Greek ivory have survived from graves in southern Russia, an area colonized by Greeks and which had close trading links with cities such as Athens and Miletus. The quality of the drawing is superior even to that of the very ably painted pots. These ivory plaques, found at Kul Oba in the Crimea, were originally used as panels on timber coffins. One has a chariot-racing scene, another has exquisitely drawn and delicately coloured goddesses. A gold bowl was found in close association with the latter, a reminder that only the wealthiest could afford to use ivory. One of the features of the great luxury enjoyed at Acragas in Sicily during the fifth century BC which aroused comment was the existence there of solid ivory couches.

Below: Model of the gold and ivory statue of Athene Parthenos, commissioned by the Athenians from Phidias. Mid-fifth-century BC; the Victory held in the right hand was 6 ft (1.8 m) high. On the advice of Pericles, Phidias constructed the statue so that the gold, laid over a wooden armature, was removable. When enemies accused him of embezzling some of the gold, the statue was dismantled and the beaten gold weighed, and Phidias was cleared.

The Athenian orator Demosthenes (384–322 BC) spoke of his father's having left 'two factories, in each of which a considerable trade was carried on. One was a sword factory, in which thirty-two or thirty-three slaves were kept at work ... the other was a bed factory, in which were employed twenty slaves ... Besides this, he left ivory and iron, used in the manufacture, and wood for sofas, worth altogether about eighty minas; and gall and copper which he had purchased for seventy minas.' There were sixty minas to the talent, and elsewhere Demosthenes tells us that his father left a talent's worth of ivory; 'one of the factories easily consumed two minas' worth of ivory a month for the couches, while the sword factory required the same amount of ivory and iron besides.' The ivory would have been used for veneers and inlays on the beds and for the handles of the swords, the gall for staining it yellow, a feature which is sometimes picked up by pot-painters when they show ivory couches, boxes or mirror backs.

Temple inventories give us an idea of the wide range of uses to which ivory was put. In the Parthenon, for example, there were 'ivory lyres', 'a table inlaid with ivory' and 'a gilded ivory flute-case'. In the nearby Hecatompedon could be seen 'an ivory and gold palladium [an image of Athena]', 'a little ivory bull', 'three big thrones, unsound, with backs inlaid with ivory', 'a small cup inlaid with ivory', 'a miniature helmet ... with gold cheekpieces and an ivory plume', and 'little ivory animals'. The treasury of the Brauron-ion, also on the Acropolis, contained 'an ivory mirror handle'. In the Heraeum on Samos there was 'an ivory unguent container' and in treasuries on Delos 'an ivory box' and 'the ivory handle of a fly-swatter'.

Macedon and the Hellenistic world

'The Hellenistic world' is an expression used to describe the civilization which existed in the area between Greece in the west and the river Indus and the Himalayas in the east during the centuries following Alexander the Great's conquests between 334 and 323 BC. Alexander came from Macedon, a kingdom which lay to the north of Greece, and which had become progressively, if intermittently, Hellenized. In essence, the kings of Macedon imported the trappings of the sophisticated culture which had developed in the Greek world during the fifth century, and Alexander and his successors then imposed a Hellenic veneer on the lands which the Persians had administered for nearly two centuries: Asia Minor, Egypt, Syria and Palestine, Mesopotamia, Persia itself and Bactria.

The most graphic account of the change which occurred in Macedon during the fourth century comes from a speech which the historian Arrian puts into the mouth of Alexander addressing mutinous troops at Opis in Babylonia in 324. He speaks of his father, Philip II (reigned 359–336 BC), who had united the tribal kingdom, reformed its army and mastered the city-states of mainland Greece, transforming Macedon from a minor kingdom to a great power: 'When Philip took you over, you were nomadic and poor, the majority of you clad in skins and grazing sparse herds on the mountains, putting up a poor fight against [your neighbours]. He gave you cloaks to wear in place of skins. He brought you down the mountains to the plains, making you a match in battle for the neighbouring barbarians, trusting for your salvation no longer in the natural strength of places so much as in your own courage. He made you dwellers in cities and graced your lives with good laws and customs. As to those very barbarians by whom previously you had been constantly plundered and pillaged ... from being slaves and subjects he made you their leaders.'

The archaeological record bears out Alexander's statement concerning the early Macedonian way of life. Numerous small bronze pendants, beads, fibulae, bracelets and hair ornaments have been found throughout this region in contexts which seem to date from the tenth to the fourth century BC. Similar in many respects to the kind of objects which in Greece itself are usually classified as Geometric, they are often mistakenly dated by reference to the Geometric period at Athens (900–750 BC); but a 'peasant continuum' was probably responsible for the persistence of a Geometric or sub-Geometric culture in Macedon long after oriental and classical modes of decoration had supplanted Geometric in the south. Thus, there is scarcely a break between the primitive beads and bangles still worn by poverty-stricken, skin-clad, nomadic herdsmen in Philip's time and the lavish, hyper-Hellenic luxury goods – including some of the most exquisite ivory objects to have survived from antiquity – commissioned by Macedonian nabobs in the later fourth century.

Philip of Macedon learned to appreciate Greek civilization when he was a hostage at Thebes before succeeding to the Macedonian throne in 359 BC. The unity he established in Macedon owed much to his giving the army a national rather than a local role, and to his generous rewarding of loyal service, both features which were among the most notable characteristics of Achaemenid Persia. The introduction of new fighting methods – notably the Greek phalanx – gave Macedon new strength but also meant that the army had to be kept active. Philip had already possessed himself of the rich mineral resources of Thrace (the gold mines of Mount Pangaeus brought in an annual income equivalent to 25½ tons (26 tonnes) of silver), before he turned his attentions south to Greece, a region which was, in the words of Xenophon, 'in confusion and disorder'. Within a few years, he had brought low even Athens and Thebes, garrisoned the Peloponnese and was making preparations for a campaign against the Persians.

On the point of leading a powerful army to attack Persia in 336 BC, Philip was assassinated. Greek archaeologists recently discovered what many think was the tomb of Philip at Vergina, the traditional capital of Macedon. Vaulted chamber tombs were found within a tumulus, and their rich contents – purple textiles, a golden quiver,

Below: An ivory figure depicting a hunchbacked slave, found in Alexandria. 4 in. (10.5 cm).

silver wine vessels and couches adorned with ivory – have surprised archaeologists and public alike by their splendour. One of the chamber tombs contained within a golden casket the cremated bones of a man, from which scientists have succeeded in reconstructing a skull with the physical characteristics which we know Philip possessed: he had lost an eye eighteen years before his death, and is also supposed to have had an emphatically hooked nose.

One of the small ivory heads found in 'Philip's tomb' shows a bearded man in early middle age, with a prominent bridge to his nose and apparently with a scar on his right brow. Few scholars doubt that this miniature ivory masterpiece 1¼ in. (3.2 cm) high with its powerful image of an autocrat is a portrait of the Macedonian king. It seems to have formed part of a frieze on an elaborate wooden couch. Pairs of historical figures, probably members of the Macedonian royal house, were apparently placed along the frieze. Their heads, arms and legs were made from ivory and have largely survived, while the rest of their bodies were made from wood or plaster and have perished.

Other ivory figures, smaller in scale and representing mythical as opposed to historical figures, come from the same couch, though it is still problematical whether they are from the same frieze or another. The fragmentary ivory figures are exquisite and have a beauty and grace almost unparalleled among the ivory objects which have come down to us from the Greek world. A seated Muse plays her seven-stringed lyre and turns her head towards a companion, now lost. On another, more complete, plaque, a youthful nude Dionysus sits – almost reclines – on a rock over which a panther skin is draped. Next to him an old garlanded Silenus extends a hand towards his master. Faces and bodies both contribute to the characterization: Dionysus' skin is smooth and almost feminine, Silenus' flesh hangs loosely from his arm.

A magnificent parade shield from 'Philip's tomb' has been painstakingly put together over several years from numerous fragments of ivory and thin sheets of silver-gilt. Around the circumference of the outer face is a band of gilded ovoli and within them an elaborate pattern in ivory of interlocking meanders between two spiral bands. The blazon consists of an ivory group carved in high relief. It is badly preserved, but seems to represent a warrior threatening a woman who kneels between his legs and looks up at him imploringly. Is she an Amazon? It was well known to the Greeks that the most effective way to annoy a Persian was to call him a woman, hence the frequent allusions in Greek art to battles between Greeks and Amazons – battles which the Greeks always won. Philip of Macedon spent his last years in active preparations for a campaign against the Achaemenids; a defeated Amazon would have been a fitting image to place on a ceremonial shield. A parallel 'speaking' shield blazon is the ivory figure of Eros wielding a thunderbolt, said to have been inlaid on the golden shield of the Athenian general Alcibiades (c. 450–404 BC), a highly appropriate symbol for a notorious womanizer.

The 'magnificence of ivory, gold and purple' was the usual accompaniment to an upper-class Greek funeral. The funeral rites of Macedonian royalty differed only in that the conspicuous consumption extended to the objects that were entombed. In Athens, pottery vessels were felt to be adequate substitutes for silver; precious metal vases remained above ground, for 'the living felt their need was greater'. Even in Macedon, the most precious possessions were kept back: the object Philip most prized in life, a solid gold drinking cup which he even took to bed with him, was not placed in the tomb. Nevertheless, Philip's funeral will have been in keeping with his life: 'He did everything in a reckless manner, whether he was acquiring or giving.' The remains of the funeral pyre suggest that horses, chariots and wooden boxes decorated with ivory were burned together with the king's body, for hundreds of charred fragments of small ivory mouldings were found there.

Not far from 'Philip's tomb' lay another chamber in which the ashes of a youth were buried in a silver jar. A gold crown of oak leaves was placed over the jar and more silver vessels, mostly for the consumption of wine, lay around it. A couch decorated with ivory had been deposited in the tomb as well. One of the groups from it is a superb piece of ivory relief carving. Three figures are represented: a goat-legged faun playing the *auloi* (double flutes); a naked, tipsy, bearded male, perhaps Dionysus, holding a torch; a young woman dressed in *le style empire*. Gold still adheres to their hair and to some of their clothing. For all its fragmentary condition, the group must rank as the finest example of ivory carving from this period.

Alexander succeeded Philip in 336 BC, aged twenty, and used the military machine created by his father to conquer Egypt, the Aegean world and the vast Persian Empire, reaching east to the borders of India. He died, still only thirty-three, in 323 BC. Such great amounts of bullion were sent westwards from the Persian treasuries at Babylon, Susa, Ecbatana and Persepolis, that gold supplanted silver in the Greek temple inventories; and the trappings of the Greek way of life adopted by the Macedonians were carried eastwards. In the east, Alexander and his successors founded cities to house veteran soldiers (Alexandria in Egypt being the most famous). These cities were laid out on up-to-date lines, they had Greek institutions, and their inhabitants spoke Greek. Decoration, whether of architecture, furniture, plate or jewellery, was basically Greek in character, although local styles often continued to exist. The official policy was one of coexistence between conquerors and conquered, but Alexander's empire was quickly divided between warring Macedonian generals, which probably encouraged Hellenization at the expense of local traditions.

The wealth of the Hellenistic kings was considerable. The scale of some of the ceremonial processions in which many objects of gold, ivory and silver were carried before the citizens of the great new metropolises stretched the credulity even of contemporary observers. 'The scene which presented itself to the eyes of the guests' at the procession of Ptolemy Philadelpheus early in the third century BC 'passed belief'. A pavilion prepared for the festivities contained gold and silver plate to the value of nearly 300 tons (300 tonnes) of silver. The procession itself included a huge mobile winepress, a wineskin holding 30,000 gallons (over 136,000 l), 120 men dressed as satyrs and silens, each carrying a gold vessel, an elaborate silver mixing bowl holding 6000 gallons (over 27,000 l) of wine, sixteen silver Panathenaic amphorae, twenty-four chariots drawn by elephants, and 'a gold phallus 180 feet [55 m] long, painted in various colours and bound with fillets of gold [which] had at the extremity a gold star'; a gold effigy of Alexander, richly attended; 400 cartloads of silver vessels, 20 of gold vessels and 800 of spices. Ivory was present in abundance: 'many thrones constructed in ivory and gold', and 'Ethiopian tribute bearers, some of whom brought 600 tusks, others 2000 ebony logs, others 60 mixing bowls full of gold and silver coins and gold dust' – almost the same mixture of goods as Ethiopians had brought to the Great King of Persia centuries earlier, although the quantities involved are immensely greater. It is quite possible that the Hellenistic kings of Alexandria had a royal monopoly of ivory.

Another extraordinary procession was put on by Antiochus Epiphanes, nicknamed 'the Mad', at Daphne near Antioch in Syria during the second century BC. Antioch had become the major city at the Mediterranean end of the trade route across Mesopotamia. The procession was intended to outdo a parade held when the Roman general Aemilius Paullus conquered Macedonia in 167 BC (by no means the last such Roman celebration at the expense of Alexander's successors) and included 1000 slaves carrying silver vessels, 600 royal slaves with gold vessels and no fewer than 800 elephant tusks.

Important finds made further east illustrate some of the uses to which the raw ivory might have been put. In 1977, Soviet archaeologists at the site of Takht-i Sangin (the 'Stone Platform') in Bactria, now in the Tadjik SSR, found a monumental temple (the 'Temple of the Oxus') surrounded by storerooms within which were sealed dumps of votive offerings – including many fine ivory objects – made over several centuries. Among the earliest finds was the ivory sheath of a dagger similar to those being worn by Medes on the Persian reliefs at Persepolis (c. 490–480 BC). The surface of the Takht-i Sangin sheath, which has been dated to the fifth century BC, is carved with a large rampant lion holding a small deer in his front paws. The chape (butt) has a stylized group of a feline and a goat. The ivory hilt of a sword is carved with unusual scenes of Heracles fighting a Silenus-like figure. A third relief once formed the chape of a scabbard and represents a most extraordinary mythical figure: the upper part is a winged female holding a rudder in one hand and a spherical object in the other; below her waist sprout horses' legs in front and a large fishy tail behind. It is a very complex composition, but the boldness of the conception outstrips the quality of the execution. Perhaps the most interesting find of all from Takht-i Sangin is a fragment of a miniature ivory sheath which bears a portrait in relief of Alexander the Great in the guise of his mythical ancestor Heracles. Like Heracles, he wears a lion skin: Heracles killed the Nemean lion with his bare hands; Alexander is supposed to have killed a lion of unusual size with a single blow.

These discoveries were made within the limits of Alexander's empire; another major find of Hellenistic ivories comes from just to the north, from the site of the Parthian city of Nisa in Turkmenistan. Nisa was the traditional burial place of the kings of Parthia, and in 1948 very many ivory drinking vessels of a kind known as rhytons, and fragments of ivory thrones and couches, were found within a large square treasury building there. The excavation was conducted in extremely difficult circumstances; not only were the ivory objects on the point of crumbling to dust, but half the team's workmen died in the catastrophic Ashkhabad earthquake of 1948. Thanks, however, to the great skill and perseverance of the archaeologists and conservators involved, about three dozen rhytons and thirty-three pieces of furniture have been restored.

The couch and throne fragments are mostly legs. They are lathe-turned and have the appearance of a series of elaborate superimposed bobbins with a flaring bell-like member at the bottom. A close parallel has been found at the Hellenistic city of Ai Khanoum in Afghanistan, and the general type is well known on Achaemenid Persian reliefs. One of the Nisa furniture legs shows a Hellenistic development of a traditional Achaemenid form: it incorporates not only a lion's foot but also a small Corinthian capital.

It is the rhytons, however, which have attracted most attention. They are all of different sizes, ranging in height from about 12 in. (30 cm) to 24 in. (60 cm). The largest have an upper diameter of 6.7 in. (17 cm) and could once have contained one-third of a gallon (1.5 l) of wine. Although rhytons bear a superficial resemblance to drinking horns, people did not drink from them directly. The rhyton served rather to aerate the wine, which would spurt from a hole near the base into a cup or shallow dish. It has been suggested that the Nisa rhytons may have been used for purely ceremonial purposes. Their bases are adorned with elaborate terminal figures, some resembling Achaemenid winged, horned lions, while others are more Hellenic in character and look like centaurs (creatures, however, to which the Greeks compared the Persians). One rhyton ends with a winged elephant. The upper parts of the vessels are decorated with friezes of classical figures. Some show the gods of Olympus, others the Muses, or nymphs, or sacrificial scenes. The rims are frequently carved separately as a kind of cornice to which human heads in high relief are attached. Most of the gilding was stripped away in antiquity. A few of these remarkable objects are exhibited in Moscow and Leningrad.

These discoveries may help us to envisage the lavish architectural arrangements in which we hear of ivory being employed, but of which no trace has survived. Ptolemy Philopator (116–108 BC) built two huge ceremonial ships. One, a seagoing vessel, was given painted ornament; the other, a river boat, was decorated with the most costly materials, gold, jewels, exotic woods and marbles – and ivory. The largest cabin, which 'could hold twenty couches', had twenty doors with 'panels of fragrant cedar nicely glued together, with ornamentation in ivory'. The columns had shafts of cypress and Corinthian capitals 'entirely covered with ivory and gold'. 'The whole entablature', moreover, 'was in gold; over it was attached a frieze with striking figures in ivory, more than a cubit [18 in. or 45 cm] high, mediocre in workmanship, but remarkable in their lavish display.' Awnings and sails were of precious purple fabric and the total length of the craft was 300 ft (92 m).

To the west of the immensely wealthy Hellenistic kingdoms a new power was emerging in the first century BC. Rome was originally a small town on the Tiber in central Italy, but during the third and second centuries had extended its influence, defeating the Carthaginians. Some of Rome's citizens had gained a taste for Hellenistic luxury as a consequence of victories won over the cities of southern Italy and Sicily. They were impatient to win the means for more.

2

Rome and the
Eastern Empire

By the late first century BC, Rome had emerged as a power greater even than the
Hellenistic kingdoms. An index of the change from the severe simplicity of Rome's
early centuries was the Senate's decision in 45 BC to honour Julius Caesar with 'an
ivory of him' carried in procession. Little ivory survives from the early centuries AD,
but following the inauguration of Constantinople, capital of the eastern empire, in
330 and its development as an artistic centre came some high-quality ivories, in
particular the diptychs, ceremonial gifts marking the donor's accession to the
consulship, an office of state whose history reached back over a thousand years to the
early republic, founded in 509 BC.

Above: An ivory knife handle from Roman
Egypt. Fourth-century AD or earlier;
2½ in. (6.5 cm). See page 55 for detail.
Opposite: Close-up of a beardless Christ from the
fifth-century Christian *pyxis* on page 62.

Rome

Not until the late third century BC, when the Romans felt the need of a past as glorious as that of their eastern Mediterranean contemporaries, was a history of Rome written. The material available at that time consisted of a few recorded facts (such as lists of magistrates with but a brief indication of their achievements) and many traditions in the form of folk memory preserved in religious customs and myths or in national legends, going back to Romulus, first king and legendary founder of Rome in 753 BC.

By the end of the third century Rome had fought two wars against Carthage (264–241 BC and 218–201 BC) which had had a devastating effect on the people and the landscape, and the earlier struggles against Pyrrhus (c. 280–275 BC) were just within living memory. Also familiar were the distorted outlines of the 'struggles of the Orders' in the fourth and fifth centuries which had resulted in the improved status of the plebeian class, and the laying of the foundation of Roman law in the mid fifth century with publication of the Twelve Tables. Two dramatic events had left their mark: the sack of the Etruscan centre at Veii by the Romans in 396 and the sack of Rome itself by marauding Gauls in 390. There were tales of the expulsion of the last kings of Rome and the removal of official Etruscan influence, more than a century earlier, in the person of Tarquinius Superbus, said by the Roman historian Livy to have sat on 'an ivory throne' in 'a golden crown and purple clothes' carrying 'an ivory sceptre'. After nearly 250 years of monarchy – including a century of Etruscan control – the Roman Republic was created (in 509 BC according to tradition) with its chief magistrates, two annually elected consuls, advised by the Senate.

It is said that the Romans' struggles against the Etruscans, Volsci, Aequi, Gauls and Samnites during the fifth to third centuries left them no leisure to cultivate the arts. Strabo said that they 'cared nothing for beauty, for they were taken up with greater, more necessary things'. The archaeological record tends to reinforce the impression of frugality; private life was austere and ivory was clearly not part of the general scene.

All this changed through Rome's contact with the Hellenistic cities of southern Italy and Sicily during the second war against Carthage. Rich booty was carried in procession through Rome. Gold and silver are most frequently mentioned, but ivory occurs. Scipio Asiaticus returned in triumph from a campaign in Asia Minor against the Hellenistic king Antiochus in 189 BC; his procession included 1231 ivory tusks. 'Captive ivory' – captivum ebur – was the apt phrase employed by the poet Horace as shorthand for the exotic oriental luxuries which had poured into Rome during the second and first centuries BC. Sometimes the greed of colonial administrators was so extreme that it aroused criticism at Rome. Verres, governor of Sicily from 73 to 70 BC, was prosecuted by Cicero on completion of his tour of duty. He had held whole communities to ransom until they were divested of all their wealth. Cicero told of a Hellenistic temple at Syracuse: 'I can assert with a clear conscience ... that more splendid doors, doors more exquisitely wrought in ivory and gold, have never existed in any temple at all ... Upon these doors were various scenes carved in ivory with the utmost care and perfection: Verres wrenched off, and took away, a lovely Gorgon's face encircled with serpents.'

In the Walters Art Gallery, Baltimore, is a carefully modelled figure of a youthful satyr said to come from Sicily and dated to the first century BC, the period in which Verres was active. The extremities have been restored in modern times, but the head, the torso and much of the legs are original. The satyr is shown walking, gesticulating with his right hand and carrying a club in his left. His boyish face is surrounded by unruly curls and he wears a wreath. A deerskin cloak is knotted in front, and around his midriff he wears a kind of kilt made from leaves.

The Roman Empire

By the late first century BC Rome ruled Spain, Gaul, the Rhineland, Illyricum, Macedonia, Greece, most of Asia Minor and the eastern Mediterranean seaboard, Egypt and large parts of North Africa. The old austerity was gone. The dominant cultural influence at Rome was Greek. Augustus, emperor from 31 BC to AD 14, was captivated by things Greek; the Roman poet Horace wrote in 15–14 BC that 'conquered Greece took her rude captor captive and brought the arts to rustic Latium', a none-too-transparent way of saying that Augustus carried off art treasures from Greece, among them the centuries-old ivory statue of Athena Alea from Tegea set up near Augustus's new Forum at Rome.

Augustus claimed to have found Rome a city of brick and left it a city of marble. Marble buildings in the Greek style required the appropriate fittings. It has been plausibly suggested that the doors on the Palatine temple of Apollo dedicated in 28 BC, described by Propertius as 'the noble work of the Libyan tooth' and showing the attack on Delphi by the Gauls in 279 BC, in turn inspired the description of Aeneas' shield in Virgil's *Aeneid* – a work written for the Augustan court. The figures on the shield are to be thought of as being rendered in metal in relief; prominent among them are Gauls being repulsed from the Capitol at Rome in 390. The hair, clothes and neck ornaments of the Gauls are all in gold, but their flesh by contrast is described as 'milky', an adjective frequently associated with ivory in Latin poetry.

The decorative role of ivory in the Roman Empire is well attested: on furniture, thrones, chests, triumphal wagons; as sceptres, sword handles, personal adornment. In the second century AD a Roman of consular rank wore as 'an outward sign of his high birth a crescent-shaped ivory buckle attached to his sandal'. Ivory couches were naturally costly items, and were thus not usually placed in tombs, couches decorated with bone reliefs being used instead. The most elaborate of these was recently restored from a mass of disparate elements. The form of the legs was similar in principle to those from the Achaemenid empire, with a flaring bell below, although the series of turned bobbins above is interrupted by figures of winged goddesses and cupids. The couch itself had a fretwork pattern along the front, reliefs of Apollo the Lyre-Player at the corners, and headrests and footrests adorned with cupids' heads inlaid with glass eyes and pigments.

Below: An ivory satyr from Sicily. First-century BC; 9 in. (22.8 cm).

A rather more exotic ivory object from a Roman context is the Indian figurine found at Pompeii in 1938, in the form of a voluptuous female, possibly of Satavahana workmanship. Pompeii was destroyed in AD 79, so the figurine must have reached Italy before then, probably through the agency of Nabataean traders. There was a colony of these Arab merchants nearby at Pozzuoli, the chief port of entry for goods from Alexandria, and their capital at Petra was a major distribution centre for merchandise coming from India and China either overland or by sea.

An inscription gives us a glimpse of the social life of a group of ivory workers at Rome, members of a fraternity to which the *citrarii*, or makers of citrus-wood tables, also belonged; these tables were fitted with ivory legs and feet. The fraternity had a clubhouse, elected officials, held annual banquets and made regular distributions of presents. But the inscription tells us nothing about how the craft was conducted. We do, however, have some wooden furniture inlaid with ivory from a fourth-century tomb at Qustul in Roman Nubia, just north of the modern frontier between Egypt and the Sudan: a large wooden chest about 3 ft (1 m) in height. The front is elaborately inlaid with ivory decoration and panels painted in red and green. Rows of plaques with incised figure decoration occupy 'windows' around which are intricately inlaid arches. Two rows consist entirely of circular motifs set between vertical panels of stylized bunches of grapes. The circular patterns recall the medieval mosaics of the Cosmati brothers, which often consisted of very small pieces of exotic and costly marble, clearly a device to use up broken fragments. Ivory was too valuable to waste.

Apollonius of Tyana, or rather his biographer Philostratus, tells us something of the ivory trade on the Upper Nile: 'When he reached the borders of Egypt and Ethiopia . . . he found unstamped ingots of gold, flax, ivory, roots, myrrh and spices, all lying unguarded at a fork in the road . . . The Ethiopians bring their native merchandise for sale, and other parties take it up and bring their Egyptian wares of equal value, to the same spot, buying the commodities they want with those they have.' Two ports on the Red Sea were famous for the ivory trade: Muza, now in North Yemen, and Adulis ('Freetown'), now Zula in Eritrea. Ivory would have reached these ports from India and East Africa.

In Greece Phidias' gold and ivory Zeus at Olympia had undergone repairs by the sculptor Damophon during the Hellenistic period 'when its ivory was breaking away'. It was apparently still well looked after in the second century AD, when Pausanias the traveller saw an altar 'to the Worker. This is where Phidias' descendants, who are called the polishers, who were granted by Elis the office of cleaning dust and dirt from Zeus' statue, offer sacrifice before they begin to polish it.' In the second century AD, Apollonius of Tyana criticized the practice of shipping ready-made sculpture around the Roman Empire, saying that in the old days, sculptors 'did not go about from town to town selling their goods. They took with them no stock in trade but their own hands, and their tools for cutting stone and ivory, but had their raw material set down beside them and turned a temple into their workshop.'

The trade in ready-made commodities means that there is no guarantee that a findspot is necessarily the place of making. There are, moreover, surprisingly few surviving Roman ivories of a quality to match those of earlier or later periods. Perhaps the finest is the statuette found in a well near the temple of Hephaestus at Athens. Painstakingly restored from more than two hundred fragments, it represents a languid Apollo with one arm resting on his head and the other ready to hold a lyre or a bow. About 12 in. (30 cm) high, it is thought to be a miniature replica, made in the second or third century AD, of an original from the fourth century BC, which stood in the Lyceum gymnasium at Athens.

Recent excavations at Ephesus have produced more Roman ivories. A relief 9¼ in. (23.4 cm) high shows a scene more familiar in monumental sculpture: the surrender of a barbarian chieftain to a Roman emperor, probably Decebalus and Trajan at the end of the first Dacian War in AD 102. The tale is told more fully on Trajan's Column in Rome; the Ephesian relief (probably part of a longer panel) shows Trajan standing next to his horse, his shield by his feet, and backed by armed soldiers in plumed helmets and chainmail, facing a band of unarmed, bearded, trousered Dacians. Also from Ephesus is a pair of burnt ivory portrait heads, made probably *c.* AD 250, both with the distinctive carved pupils of work of this period.

The Roman city of Aventicum (modern Avenches) in Switzerland has also produced some Roman ivories of more than passing interest. Had it been complete, the recently excavated panel originally measuring some 5 by 11 in. (13 by 28 cm) and representing Bacchus, Diana and other deities, would have been our most important Roman period ivory. As it is, however, the two dozen fragments, many of them scorched, can give only a faint idea of what must once have been a very attractive object, adorning an imposing box.

Many late Roman and Byzantine ivories bear representations of the events in the circus or the amphitheatre, structures specially erected to allow large crowds to watch chariot racing and gladiatorial and animal combats. These institutions were not merely a means to keep the people happy ('bread and circuses') but also provided an accurate gauge of the opinions of the populace. Souvenirs of many kinds were made for gladiators' supporters, occasionally from ivory. A knife handle, again from Aventicum, shows a *secutor* (armed with sword and shield) and a *retiarius* (armed with net and trident) in close combat. The latter is no longer armed, but with his right hand he grasps firmly his opponent's helmet, and with the other attempts to fend off a sword thrust.

Another ivory knife handle, now in Baltimore, but found in Egypt at Hermoupolis Magna on the Nile, is carved in the round and altogether more pacific in character. A little fat boy sits clinging to a bunch of grapes, looking over his shoulder in case anyone might take the fruit away from him.

Below: An ivory Apollo from Athens. Second- or third-century AD; *c.* 12 in. (30 cm).

Above: Detail from the carved ivory knife handle on page 51.

Left: A plaque from Roman Egypt. Late-second- or third-century AD; 8½ × 4½ in. (21.4 × 11.5 cm).

Even though the glass inlay from his eyes has gone, he is an alert little fellow, and very appealing. The general form goes back to a Hellenistic model and recalls such statues as the Boy with a Goose. Although it has been dated to the fourth century AD, it may be as early as the second century. Very many bone carvings, mostly reliefs from caskets or furniture, have come from Roman Egypt; reminders that Egypt was probably the country of transit for much of the ivory used in the Mediterranean over many centuries.

A very fine, Roman period ivory plaque, now in Washington DC, was almost certainly made in Egypt. It shows two figures, one seated and the other standing behind him. An altar decorated with a leafy garland occupies the right foreground. The seated figure wears a tunic, a mantle and a laurel wreath. Bald or shaven headed, he reads from a scroll and has been identified as a *hierogrammateus*, a sacred scribe of Isis, the Egyptian deity whose cult spread throughout the Mediterranean in Hellenistic times. The standing figure has his garment gathered beneath his armpits; parallels are known on a fresco at Herculaneum representing an Isis cult. Part of a draped cloth can be seen in the background, an important element in the ceremonies associated with the Isis ritual. The Egyptian origin is assured by an inscription in the bottom left corner: *Andropoleites*, a reference to an Egyptian administrative district, Andropolis, not far from Alexandria. It was most probably made in the second or third century, but its precise function is uncertain.

Ivory was used for small objects such as dice, theatre tokens (the ancient equivalent of tickets for numbered seats), or gaming pieces, although surviving examples are more frequently bone or antler. A complete Egyptian draughts set was found in a fourth-century cemetery at Qustul in Nubia. There was a wooden gaming board, about half the size of a large backgammon board, marked with inlaid ivory fretwork squares arranged in three rows of twelve with three larger round or segmental places in the middle of each row. It is strengthened at the corners with silver brackets and has a handle attached by silver pins. Within a leather bag were fifteen ivory and fifteen ebony lathe-turned gaming pieces shaped like truncated acorns, five ivory dice with their drill holes filled with red paint, and an ingenious wooden dice-box specially designed to prevent cheating.

Despite the popular, but incorrect, view that Rome fell into decline about the time of the Emperor Nero (AD 54–68), the Roman Empire reached its widest extent a few decades later under Trajan (98–117) and although it was never to be quite as large again, 'decline' is scarcely the word to apply to the reigns of emperors such as Hadrian (117–38) or Septimius Severus (193–212). The

northern and eastern frontiers were admittedly under constant attack from the mid second century onwards, and there were nineteen 'soldier-emperors' between Marcus Aurelius (161–80), who wrote philosophical works while on campaign, and Diocletian (284–305), who retired 'to grow cabbages', but Romanized Europe, North Africa and the Near East enjoyed a degree of prosperity rarely paralleled in history. Rome itself – far from either the northern or eastern frontier – ceased to be an imperial residence. Diocletian built a dozen huge palaces around the empire and himself spent most of his time at Nicomedia on the Sea of Marmara.

Very little ivory survives from the first, second and third centuries, but the situation changes dramatically from the fourth century onwards. Ivory was widely used in the Roman Empire, and Diocletian's price edict of 301 prices ivory at one-fortieth its weight in silver, cheap compared with other imported luxury goods such as silk, and much cheaper than in the fifth century BC when it cost one-tenth of its weight in silver. The difference can probably be put down to the better organization of the ivory trade. Instead of being brought, in effect, overland, up the Nile Valley from Ethiopia and the Sudan, ivory now came by the shipload from East Africa. The comparative rarity of Roman period examples may be put down to the pagan imagery with which ivory was frequently decorated in Roman times. After Christianity became the official religion, many earlier pieces will have been destroyed, or at best not cherished. From its origins in first-century Palestine Christianity spread rapidly during the second and third centuries, especially among the poorer classes in the cities of Asia Minor and North Africa, and despite persecution, gradually penetrated even the senate, the court and the imperial family. The Emperor Gallienus (260–8) granted the first edict of toleration. Diocletian, however, who took over in 284, was extremely conservative in religious matters and a period of intense persecution began in 303, more severe in the east than the west. This finally came to an end when Constantine fought his way to power in 312 having, so he claimed, seen the sign of the Cross in the sky, and ordered his men to paint the Christian Chi-Rho monogram, the *Labarum*, on their shields. The Edict of Milan, drawn up by Constantine and his colleague Licinius in 313, granted toleration to all religions. In 324 the two emperors quarrelled and fought a decisive naval engagement at Chrysopolis near Byzantium, Constantine under an imperial standard bearing the monogram of Christ and Licinius relying on the pagan gods whose symbols his troops carried into battle. Constantine won and celebrated his victory by rebuilding Byzantium and giving it his name: Constantinople.

Rome and Constantinople

Constantine was in fact somewhat ambivalent towards paganism as were many of his subordinate officials. The foundation of Constantinople was accompanied by pagan rites and the city was adorned with statues of pagan divinities: 'a veritable museum of the Greek East'. Formally inaugurated in 330, Constantinople, the 'second Rome', was filled with palaces and churches of great splendour and magnificence. Wealthy residents were attracted to the new imperial capital by land grants; the poor were sustained with free bread, on the old Roman model, and at old Rome's expense. The promotion to high office of those who followed the Christian religion encouraged conversion. The traditional rights and privileges of pagan temples were slowly whittled away, their treasures were seized, their cult images stripped of their gold sheathing. Phidias' Olympian Zeus probably lost its gold at this time, although it kept its ivory.

Dozens of ivory objects, many of high quality, have survived from the centuries after Constantine. The unbroken continuity of the Christian tradition in the west has been largely responsible. Most pieces owe their survival to their having been kept in cathedral or monastic libraries and treasuries, valued all the more when ivory became scarce after the seventh century. The panels of one of the most important fourth-century ivory objects, the reliquary in Brescia, were for centuries mounted in a cross kept in a local church. Only in 1928 was it reconstituted in its original form. Nearly 13 in. (33 cm) across the front and 8½ in. (22 cm) high, it is decorated in relief on the lid and all four sides and constitutes a compendium of Old and New Testament stories. The main panel on the front shows Christ in the Temple at Jerusalem disputing with the Doctors; on either side are Christ healing the Woman with the Issue of Blood and Christ the Good Shepherd guarding his flock from a ravening wolf. Two smaller panels above, flanking the lock, illustrate Jonah swallowed by a sea-monster (which looks nothing like a whale) and Jonah cast ashore after three days and nights in its belly. Below the main panel are Susanna being spied on by the Elders, who play peeping Tom from behind trees, the arrest of Daniel, and Daniel in the lions' den.

The lid and the other three sides are decorated in an equally complex manner, mingling Old and New Testament scenes. The right-hand short side shows the Healing of the Blind Man and the Raising of Lazarus (who stands wrapped in mummy bandages at the entrance to his temple-like tomb); above, scenes from the life of Moses; below, Jacob and Rachel at the well and the fight between David and Goliath. The left-hand short side shows Christ curing the daughter of Jairus; above, the Man of God killed by the lion and guarded by the ass; below, a sacrificial meal before the Golden Calf. The back shows Christ and two apostles on the sea, and Ananias and Sapphira; above, Susanna, Jonah asleep beneath the gourd, and Daniel; below, Moses in the bulrushes, Moses slaying an Egyptian, and the first Passover meal. The lid contains two principal panels: the capture of Christ in the Garden of Gethsemane, and Peter denying his Master, with a cock on a column ready to crow; beneath these scenes, Christ brought before Caiaphas and before Pilate. No inscriptions identify the patron who commissioned the box or give any direct indication of its date. Comparisons with works in other media, such as marble sarcophagi, catacomb frescoes and early Christian gold-glass, suggest that it was the product of a North Italian workshop, although it has been attributed to Antioch and Asia Minor as well.

There is a good deal of scholarly controversy over the centres in which ivory was worked in the fourth and fifth centuries. Most of the relevant extant material is probably of western origin, and Constantinople, despite the aspirations of its founder, was arguably not a leading cultural centre before about AD 500. We lack the material proof, but it seems likely that there was a stylistic *koine* shared by élites in both Italy and Constantinople and that ivories were one way in which motifs travelled between the capitals.

Diptychs

Ceremonial diptychs were arguably a principal medium of artistic interchange between west and east. These were pairs of rectangular plaques, usually ivory (sometimes wood), frequently carved on the outside with elaborate reliefs, and gilded, and hollowed out slightly, with a message on wax, on the inside. They were sent by consuls, and other officials, to their friends and it has been estimated that as many as 100,000 such diptychs were made over a couple of centuries, using up over a hundred tons of ivory. Ivory was clearly still a prestigious material, but one easily available to wealthy members of the governing class.

The consulship, an office of state which went back to the days of the Roman Republic, had been preserved by Augustus and his successors to camouflage their regimes with a cloak of legality. Even when Constantine transferred the seat of the empire to Constantinople and transformed it into a Christian state, consulships were keenly sought after – there were only two a year – and, if not held by the emperors or members of their families, usually went to the old aristocracy. A

Above: Detail from the Brescia casket shown in colour on page 65. Below the lock it depicts Christ and the Doctors in the Temple.

Right and below: Panel from the Lampadiorum diptych and detail from the chariot race. Probably AD 396; 11½ in. (29 cm).

both held the consulship. At the top of the panel are three men in a box at the Circus Maximus in Rome. One is larger – hence more important – than the others and has been identified as Postumius Lampadius, probably suffect consul in 396. Two of the officials hold *mappae* (cloths); the dropping of the *mappa* by a magistrate was the signal to open the starting-gates through which the teams of chariots entered the arena. As many as twelve teams could race at the same time, but these have been reduced to four by artistic shorthand. Each team is driven by a charioteer in a leather costume and a tightly fitting crash helmet. The chariots had to circle the long central barrier seven times, and there were frequently crashes at the turning points. The craftsman has considerably abbreviated the barrier and has greatly reduced the number of monuments on it. The Egyptian obelisk in the centre was brought to Rome by Augustus and reminded the Roman populace that Augustus had brought Egypt, the source of much of the city's grain supply (the other half of 'bread and circuses'), under Roman control. From the numerous recorded statues, only two groups are represented, of military trophies and bound captives. This choice was perhaps intended to recall the victory of the imperial Christian forces over pagan rebels at the river Frigidus in 394. The fact that many of the other statues which adorned the barrier were pagan in character tends to support this hypothesis.

In the long term, the days of paganism were numbered. The Emperor Theodosius (reigned 379–95) had prohibited pagan sacrifices and closed temples to the public in 391. Eighteen months later, the ban was extended to domestic cults, and severe penalties were laid down. The Roman Senate urged the preservation of the altar of Victory, and some senators rallied to the usurper Eugenius. Theodosius died in 395, soon after crushing the Eugenian revolt, leaving two young sons, Arcadius and Honorius, to rule a divided empire. The supreme authority in the west then rested with his chief general, Stilicho.

Stilicho, married to the late emperor's niece Serena, was appointed guardian of Honorius and Arcadius, emperors of west and east, respectively. The greater part of the imperial army was in the western part of the empire under his direct command. He tried unsuccessfully to win the throne for himself but fell from power only in 408. In 396, still very much in command, he issued, probably from his capital Milan, the ceremonial diptych now in Monza. Stilicho is the very image of imperial power, in military dress, with a spear, a shield and an impressive gold fibula. His court propagandist, the poet Claudian, alludes to Stilicho's dynastic ambitions in a description of the figures supposedly woven into his

consul celebrated his accession by sending diptychs to fellow aristocrats and by sponsoring games for the populace. Although the diptychs were made from expensive materials, their cost will have been minimal compared to that of other ceremonial gifts, and fortunes were expended on the games. In 521, for example, Justinian spent 228,000 golden *solidi* to celebrate his accession to the consulship. Rather earlier, in 384, an edict issued at Constantinople discouraged the distribution of diptychs by persons other than consuls, perhaps to limit in the east the kind of flamboyance associated with western aristocracies. This legislation reveals that ivory diptychs, and hence ivory carving, existed at Constantinople before the earliest dated diptychs from the west.

Among the first dated ceremonial diptych panels is one in Brescia whose inscription can be reconstructed: *Lampadiorum*. Its companion piece, once in Novara but now lost, read *Rufiorum*, and it has been plausibly suggested that the diptych was issued to commemorate a marriage between two great fourth-century Roman houses.

The central official sits in a box holding a sceptre, the head of which consists of small images of the emperors of east and west. One is smaller than the other, an indication that he was a minor at the time. The most likely date is 396, when the Emperor Arcadius was nineteen and his brother the Emperor Honorius was twelve, and

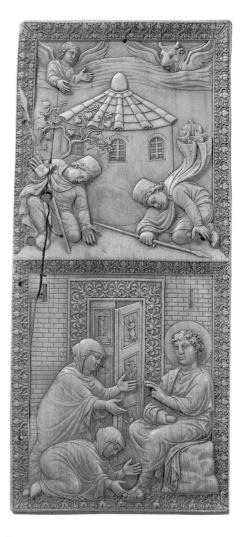

Right: The
Symmachorum panel
formed the right-hand leaf
of a masterly ivory
diptych. *c.*AD 394–402;
11½ × 4¾ in.
(29.5 × 12 cm). The
priestess sprinkles incense
from a *pyxis* on the flames
of the altar fire.

Far right: An ivory plaque
showing the Women at
the Tomb of Christ; 12 in.
(30.7 cm). Probably made
by the same workshop as
the Symmachorum panel
and about the same time.

cloak. The diptych shows no full-length figures
on the cloak, only heads in roundels, but the
pattern is intricate. The occasion for issuing it
seems to have been Stilicho's raising of his young
son Eucherius (whom he hoped to marry to
Theodosius' daughter) to the post of tribune and
notary. Eucherius stands on the other panel, to the
right of his mother Serena, and thus in the centre
of the group. The two emperors on Stilicho's
shield are said to be represented as consuls, and are
differentiated as on the Lampadiorum panel. This
makes a date of 396 certain.

Influential members of the Roman aristocracy
still remained loyal both to the emperors and to
the traditional pagan religion. It was presumably
to pacify this class that two of its members from
the Anicii family had been chosen as consuls for
the previous year, 395.

A famous ivory diptych well illustrates the
tastes and religious predilections of the pagan
circle at Rome at this time. The better preserved
panel, in the Victoria and Albert Museum,
London, is inscribed *Symmachorum* and shows a
priestess sacrificing at an altar. The other panel,
in the Musée de Cluny, Paris, and inscribed
Nicomachorum, represents another priestess hold-

ing lowered torches. It used to be thought that the
diptych was issued to commemorate a marriage
between two prominent pagan Roman aristocratic
families, but the imagery is, if anything, funerary
in character and it has recently been suggested that
it was issued by Memmius Symmachus to commemorate the deaths of his father-in-law
Nicomachus Flavianus (died in disgrace in 394 as
the chief minister of the rebel Eugenius) and of his
father Quintus Aurelius Symmachus (died in 402).

On the Symmachorum panel the left foreground is occupied by an altar hung with a
garland of oak leaves. To the right stands the
priestess wearing a deeply folded tunic and a
cloak, sandals on her feet, bracelets on her wrists,
her hair decorated with ivy. She takes a piece of
incense from a small round box in order to place it
on the fire burning upon the altar. A small
assistant holds up a bowl of fruit and a wine
vessel. In the background is an oak, a tree sacred
to Jupiter, the chief divinity in the Roman pantheon. Ivy recalls the cult of Bacchus, the wine
god. This apparent syncretism of cults was not at
all unusual. Q. Aurelius Symmachus had himself
declared: 'One cannot arrive at such a great secret
by following a single road.'

The Nicomachorum panel alludes to yet more pagan cults. It shows the pine tree, sacred to Cybele as were the cymbals hung on it. Lowered torches allude to Demeter and Persephone, the Eleusinian deities associated with death and rebirth.

The figures on both panels are shown in profile, in sharp contrast to the contemporary frontal norm: classicizing to an extraordinary degree given the period in which they were made.

The diptych was clearly intended to express the traditional values and outlook of a beleaguered class. It is generally assumed that it was made at Rome by the workshop which also produced the Christian ivory plaque formerly in the Trivulzio collection, now in Milan. The almost identical ornamentation of the frame of 'The Women at the Tomb of Christ' makes the association likely, though the arrangement of the narrative and the composition of the scenes are remarkably different. A bull and an angel, symbols of the evangelists Luke and Matthew who relate the biblical story, fill the sky. Beneath them is what is probably intended to be the upper part of a sepulchre, circular in plan. Distraught guards gesture towards what is both another scene with its own frame, and also the lower part of the building. The door of the Tomb (appropriately decorated with reliefs of the Raising of Lazarus) is open, and before it sits a wingless, haloed angel who tells the kneeling women that Christ has risen. The quality of the carving is again very high, but in place of the quiet classical grandeur of the pagan panels, there is an immediacy and vivacity unusual even in other Christian reliefs.

The characteristic frame employed by this workshop occurs on another diptych made in 396. Both panels represent Rufianus Probianus, the Vicar of the City of Rome. The scheme is familiar from the 'Women at the Tomb': a two-part arrangement with the figures in the lower part completely within their own frame. Probianus is shown on both panels seated on a throne within a room whose spatial depth is indicated by means of perspective. Next to him stands an ornament on which can be seen portraits of the emperor-consuls. Officials stand on either side of him, writing on tablets. Probianus' dress differs on each panel, and each time matches the dress of the patricians who acclaim him from below. The composition strongly recalls reliefs on the Arch of Constantine at Rome where the emperor hands out benefactions from a high throne.

Another diptych panel was probably made to commemorate the death of Q. Aurelius Symmachus. It does not, however, share the classicism of the Nicomachorum–Symmachorum reliefs; rather, it obeys the prevailing aesthetic of the time. The Symmachi monogram is inscribed on a small roundel at the top. The diptych is clearly of a funerary nature and pagan into the

bargain. It too is conceived in two parts, but these are not divided into separate frames. In the foreground four elephants, ridden by mahouts carrying goads and loaves of bread ('sticks and carrots'), draw an elaborate carriage bearing a tempietto, within which rides the deceased holding a laurel branch towards a funeral pyre surmounted by a pagan charioteer, before which a pair of eagles, Jupiter's birds, fly upwards – evidence of Symmachan devotion to Jupiter. Two wind gods bear what must now be the soul of the dead man towards five figures who are perhaps his ancestors. The sun god looks on and before him are zodiacal signs – Libra, Scorpio, Sagittarius, Capricorn, Aquarius and Pisces; Symmachus presumably died in the autumn.

The existence of absolutely contemporary pagan reliefs in two completely different styles is of great interest. It is clear, as so often, that content is more important than style; which is not to say that style is not important, simply that it is secondary to the ideological message. It can enhance that message (witness the classicism of the Nicomachorum–Symmachorum reliefs) or even distract from it (as a classicizing Christian scene might create the wrong resonances). Its role, however, remains a subsidiary one.

There are five datable non-consular ceremonial diptychs before the first known consular example: the diptych of Probus, consul at Rome in 406, which bears two different full-length portraits of Honorius, one on each panel. A good deal of pagan imagery in the details is counterbalanced by an explicitly Christian inscription on the standard the emperor carries on the more elaborate panel. This reads (in Latin) 'In the name of Christ you will always be victorious', and is surmounted by the *Labarum*. And yet the orb Honorius holds in his other hand is surmounted by a pagan Victory. An immense victory over the Ostrogoths, won by the Romans at Faesulae in 406, probably accounts for her presence and for the palm and victor's wreath she carries. Iconographically speaking, Victories were at this time in a state of metamorphosis, gradually assuming the canonical image of Christian angels. There is nothing remotely Christian, however, about Honorius' breastplate, for on both panels it bears the head of the gorgon Medusa, a pagan motif in existence for the best part of a thousand years, but which ought in principle to have disappeared by now.

The chryselephantine Zeus

Although surviving ivory from Constantinople datable before *c.* 500 is scanty in the extreme, we are well informed about the Constantinopolitan phase of the most illustrious ivory statue of all, the chryselephantine Zeus from Olympia. At the turn of the fourth and fifth centuries Lausus, a prominent courtier, assembled a great collection of

Greek masterpieces in his palace. The most important piece by far was Phidias' Olympian Zeus; others were Praxiteles' Cnidian Aphrodite, and Lysippus' Eros from Myndos. Lausus first comes to notice in 391; he was the secretary of the imperial bedchamber in 420, and possibly in 436, and this was the only period in which such a collection could have been put together. He probably acquired the pieces when it was enacted in 408 that 'the statues which are still in temples and honoured by pagan rites should be taken from their seats'. He was in the perfect position to do so, for temple estates now belonged to the emperor's privy purse.

The account of Lausus' collection refers to the statue only as 'ivory'. The bullion value had been realized in Constantine's day and what was left was presumably largely redundant. It is true that ivory is itself a high-cost luxury commodity, but at well nigh a thousand years old, its resale value is negligible. Current research has established that Lausus' sculpture was arranged programmatically, with the colossal Zeus firmly differentiated from the rest. The underlying philosophy was fundamentally Christian, and the Zeus conceived of as somehow monotheistic; Lausus was a devout Christian.

Although the palace of Lausus was burned down in 475, the long-term artistic impact of the presence of Phidias' Zeus in the city was immense. It is likely that the image of a bearded, as opposed to beardless, Christ depends directly on Lausus' ivory statue. Its influence was not immediate, but a tale told about a painter in the time of Archbishop Gennadios, Patriarch of Constantinople from 458 to 471, is instructive; this man made an icon 'at the instigation of a pagan, portraying Christ in the likeness of Zeus'; his hand and arm are said to have withered in consequence of his blasphemous act, but he was healed miraculously through the intercession of Gennadios. By the time the image was first employed for Christ the Ruler of All in sixth-century Constantinople, paganism had been thoroughly repressed, but the miracle story suggests that it was not so long after the destruction of the statue itself that its truly majestic appearance could have been forgotten. Phidias' gold and ivory masterpiece thus survived in form, if not in reality, as one of the most important symbols of Christian art.

The Boethius diptych

One of the latest surviving western diptychs was issued by Manlius Boethius on the occasion of his consulship in 487. It is not the latest of all, however, since the Basilius diptych in Florence has been shown to date to 541. At this period we can perhaps truly begin to speak of the Roman Empire in decline. Alaric's Goths had pillaged

Rome in 410 and Odoacer, the Gothic king of Italy, had destroyed the western empire in 483. Even before that, the practice of appointing a western consul had fallen into disuse. Boethius is shown as consul in the east, although he resided in Rome. The emperor in Constantinople, Zeno the Isaurian (474–96), would occasionally appoint a western man as second consul, sometimes even the Gothic king himself, in an attempt to preserve the fictional unity of the Roman Empire. This custom, however, was soon discontinued, not least because the consul found his double allegiance difficult to fulfil. Manlius Boethius' son, Anicius Boethius (sole consul in 510), later suffered as a direct consequence of this; suspected by Theodoric the Great (the Ostrogothic king who defeated and replaced Odoacer) of favouring the Emperor Justin's scheme of reuniting Italy to the empire, he was imprisoned and eventually executed in 524. While awaiting his execution he wrote his famous essay 'On the Consolations of Philosophy'; in Gibbon's words, 'a golden volume not unworthy of the leisure of Plato or Tully'. Until the Renaissance this work was the principal means through which the philosophy of the ancients was known.

Manlius Boethius' diptych is now in Brescia. One leaf shows him seated, the other standing, clad in an elaborately woven cloak. In his right hand he holds a *mappa* and in his left a sceptre surmounted by an eagle. Beneath his feet, shod in ceremonial slippers, are palm branches, money bags and silver vessels – symbols of largesse at the games it was customary for the consul to sponsor.

Pyxides

Although ivory diptychs can be arranged in some kind of sequence, another prolific class of early ivory objects, namely the little boxes known to scholars as *pyxides*, cannot. The craftsmen who made them took advantage of the cylindrical character of the lower part of the elephant's tusk. *Acerra*, 'a casket in which was kept the incense used at sacrifices', and *arca turalis*, 'incense box', are names applied to such containers in antiquity. The sacrificing priestess on the Symmachorum panel actually holds one. Incense was used both in pagan and in Christian ceremonies, which accounts for the wide range of imagery found on *pyxides*. Some pagan *pyxides* were used in the Middle Ages as housel-boxes (for sacramental hosts) or containers for holy relics.

A *pyxis* in Bobbio thus owes its survival to its incorporation into a Gothic reliquary. The subject matter – Orpheus playing to the animals – was in fact employed as an image of universal salvation in early Christian art, but it is clear from the lion and tiger hunt on the reverse of the Bobbio *pyxis*, and of a similar container in Florence, that both were made for secular rather than religious use.

The main zone of the Bobbio piece shows Orpheus playing the lyre to calm the savage beasts surrounding him: birds, stags, goats, a lion, a tiger, a lynx, a horse and a monkey, as well as hybrid animals such as a griffin, a centaur and a goat-legged Pan. In a smaller zone around the top are miniature pastoral scenes. Taken together, the images reflect a view largely lost today: that nature in the raw must be kept under control if agriculture was to exist at all. Hunting was the usual means; the Orpheus represented a yearning for a world of peace and calm in which agriculture could flourish unchallenged. The figures are so deeply undercut that they almost stand free of their background. The closest stylistic parallels are on marble reliefs made in early-sixth-century Constantinople, but there is no certainty that this *pyxis* is eastern in origin or quite as late.

None of the other surviving *pyxides* is as ornate. A roughly contemporary Christian *pyxis* decorated in relief which is almost as high has on the front a beardless Christ enthroned among apostles. The features of each apostle are individualized: Peter, on his Master's right hand, old, balding and bearded; Paul, on his left, with a fuller beard and a more vigorous head of hair. On the reverse is the Sacrifice of Abraham. The infant Isaac with his hands bound behind his back stands before an altar, while his father raises a sword over his head. The Hand of God reaches down from the sky to halt the proceedings and the Angel produces a ram as a substitute victim.

Abraham's sacrifice of his son was symbolic of Christ's sacrificial death on the Cross, and it is likely that this *pyxis* was used as a housel-box to hold consecrated wafers. The proportions of the figures, and indeed the treatment of the drapery, are rather more classical than analogous features on other *pyxides*. Scholars cannot agree whether the piece was made in the east or the west. We are on surer ground with the dated ceremonial diptychs issued at Constantinople after 500, for these splendid productions are certainly eastern.

Late antique and early Byzantine stylistic development

The style developed by the late-fourth-century ivory carvers who achieved an incomparably high standard of excellence, in both Rome and Constantinople, was based on that of the sculptors responsible for such marble sarcophagi as that of the Roman senator Junius Bassus, carved in *c.* 359 with scenes from the Bible, or the one found near Fenari Isa Djami in Asia Minor, carved with two flying angels. They are carved in deep relief with gently modelled yet strong figures, often almost totally released from their background – a superb, idealized kind of naturalism. Their patrons, as the subject matter of the finest sarcophagi proves, were often members of leading Christian families. The rare surviving ivory carvings prove that the craftsmen who made them worked in the same naturalistic style.

Below right: An early Christian ivory *pyxis*. Probably made in western Europe in the sixth century AD; 3½ × 5¾ in. (8 × 14.6 cm). Mounted as the sleeve of a nineteenth-century tankard until its age and rarity were recognized, it is carved with scenes of Christ's miracles, the Christian figures shown in Roman dress.

Below left: Ivory *pyxis*. Probably early-sixth-century; 4¾ in. (12 cm). SS Peter and Paul flank the enthroned Christ. See page 50 for detail.

The tradition set by the fifth-century consular diptychs lasted well into the sixth century, both in Rome and the eastern empire, and for over a century the outlines of the design remain basically unchanged – a dominant major figure, an architectural setting, an inscription above and increasingly elaborate scenes below – but the high quality achieved in Theodosian Rome (379–95) could not be sustained for long. The later panels developed much harsher lines, sharper forms with a strong

emphasis on surface pattern – all intended, it seems, to underline the representational elements, the aristocratic richness of the donor's status, rather than the gentle, well-articulated forms of the Probus diptych issued in 406. The same intentions, although created with the greater skill probably available in Constantinople, can be seen in a massive panel, perhaps showing the Empress Ariadne, probably carved *c.* 500. Far thicker than the Probus diptych, the panel is deeply sculpted, releasing the figure of the empress almost fully from the background, a technique more frequently found in the major sculpture of, admittedly rather earlier, sarcophagi. But the emphasis on ornamental detail is at least as pronounced in this panel as in the far flatter, harder detail of the Boethius diptych – it is just richer.

An almost contemporary leaf of a diptych, much larger and more imposing than is usual, shows the Archangel Michael, with a long sceptre in his left hand and an orb surmounted by a cross in his right, standing on a staircase under a richly decorated archway. It has been suggested that it was presented to the eastern Emperor Justinian (527–65) when attempts were made to reconcile the two halves, eastern and western, of the empire. The quality of the carving is exceptional. There is, for the early sixth century, a surprisingly able handling of naturalistic detail, and only the strange contradictions between the standing figure and the architectural setting prove that the art of antiquity is no longer fully understood. Nevertheless, such a magnificent ivory panel shows that the humanist traditions of the Mediterranean world continued tenaciously at the court of the eastern empire. It is more difficult to be certain that the same is true of the western empire. Much depends on whether a series of so-called five-part diptychs is attributed to western workshops, such as Milan or Rome, or to eastern ones. Among the earliest to survive is one in the treasury of Milan Cathedral, two large panels each assembled from five pieces of ivory, no longer associated with a manuscript, but probably intended to decorate the front and back of a large and prestigious codex. The four evangelist symbols, in laurel wreaths, appear on the upper part of both front and back, with bust portraits of the four evangelists themselves below. Intricate and lively scenes from the life of Christ surround a central panel, decorated with the *Agnus Dei* (the 'Lamb of God' carrying the Cross) on the front and the Cross on the back, both symbols being metalwork and originally set with gems, the only ivory cover enriched in this way. The gem settings and cellwork, typical of northern Italian jewellery of the later fifth and sixth century, strongly support a local origin. The carving is only a little drier than the rich Theodosian naturalism of the early fifth century, and this cover is therefore likely to have been made

Opposite: The Brescia
casket with its rich
mingling of Old and New
Testament scenes.
Fourth-century AD;
9¾ × 12½ in.
(25 × 32 cm). See page 56
for detail.

Above and right: The
Ravenna throne, carved
for Bishop Maximianus.
*c.*547; 59 × 23¾ in.
(150 × 60.5 cm). The
carvings show biblical
scenes from the lives of
Christ, the Virgin and St
Joseph. The borders of
vine scrolls are inhabited
by animals and peacocks.
In the detail (*above*) is St
John the Baptist holding
in his hand the *Agnus Dei*
(the Lamb of God).

*c.*450–500, when a memory of this style still survived.

Another five-part diptych of the same size and structure, known as the Barberini diptych, is the kind given by the emperor to consuls or military commanders on their appointment. On the central panel the emperor rides over a figure symbolizing *Terra*, the earth. Above him is a Victory, behind him a defeated barbarian. The right-hand panel has not survived; and on the left a soldier offers another Victory. Above, a bust of Christ is carried by angels; below, defeated barbarians bear gifts, including an elephant ivory tusk. It is quite possible that the soldier is Belisarius, who recaptured North Africa from the Vandals in 532–5. Although the central panel with the imposing, victorious emperor is carved almost as deeply and with the same high quality as the slightly earlier panel of the Empress Ariadne, those surrounding him are much flatter and cut in a more jagged, rougher style, attributed by scholars to a number of eastern Mediterranean centres, most frequently to Egypt, Syria and Asia Minor. A more typical version is seen in a pair of book-covers from St Lupicinus (Jura). The central panel shows a seated Christ accompanied by SS Peter and Paul, surrounded by the usual four panels: above, two flying angels; right, left and below, scenes from the life of Christ. The back-cover has the Virgin and Child; angels above; scenes from the life of the Virgin to each side; and Christ's Entry into Jerusalem below. The covers were used to decorate a western ninth-century gospel book, splendidly written in silver on purple vellum, which fits their rather broad dimensions so well that it

was probably made to go between them. These ivories relate very closely indeed to the covers of a tenth-century gospel book from the Armenian monastery of Etschmiadzin, which may have been the model. On the latter, the scenes on the 'Virgin' cover all show her life – a more logical programme. Both pairs of covers were carved in the sixth century, and in a style that was in very widespread use in the eastern Mediterranean; it may be typical of work of somewhat lesser quality rather than a style typical of any particular region.

In 535, ordered by Justinian to recapture the western empire by force, Belisarius landed in Sicily and by 540 had penetrated as far north as Ravenna. However, his early successes were soon reversed and only Ravenna remained part of the eastern empire, a constant link between north Italy and the classical traditions so jealously guarded in imperial Constantinople. Among the earliest examples is the famous Ravenna throne of Bishop Maximianus (545–53), whose monogram is carved on the front, in the centre of a decorative border. Below it is a row of saints, St John the Baptist between the four Evangelists, magnificently carved in a style that retains much of the classical tradition, a style not far removed from that of the Archangel Michael carved for Justinian, twenty or thirty years earlier. The throne also has a large number of carvings by various hands with scenes from both the New and the Old Testaments, in the rougher, more vivid, and perhaps more truly contemporary style of the St Lupicinus gospel-covers, and of pieces attributed to Syria, Egypt, or, with even more precision, Alexandria. But it was probably made in Ravenna itself, although no doubt craftsmen from several parts of the eastern empire, including a master from Constantinople, were involved.

The Ravenna throne is also remarkable for the fact that it is a utilitarian object. It is true that ivory was much used in antiquity, as in the Middle Ages, for objects of daily use – although normally within the field of luxurious or spiritual rather than mundane use. Late-antique pyxes are frequently found; those decorated with sacred subjects were probably used for the consecrated wafers, but others, carved with secular scenes, must have had a great variety of uses. In style, they vary from strongly classicizing examples to the more 'eastern'. Other useful objects were no doubt made of ivory, but relatively few survive. Large, double-sided combs, often richly decorated, are fairly common and there survives a very rare, tall, lidded vase, decorated with four vine scrolls inhabited by birds and each including a bust of a nimbed and winged figure in a roundel, difficult to date but most likely carved in the sixth or seventh century; its delicate handling of ornament suggests a centre of some importance, perhaps even Constantinople itself.

The Byzantine Empire

Iconoclasm, the movement that sought to prohibit the worship, and indeed the making, of holy images first made itself felt in the early eighth century. It gained the upper hand during the reign of the Syrian Emperor Leo III (717–41) when after a volcanic eruption in 726, thought to be an expression of God's wrath, the first iconoclast edict ordered the destruction of religious images in churches. Except for a short interlude at the end of the eighth century, when such edicts were rescinded, iconoclasm lasted until its final demise in 843, when Orthodoxy was restored at the Council of Constantinople.

It has yet to be explained why more than a century of iconoclasm did not finally break the links with the classical tradition. Probably the earliest datable ivory after iconoclasm had run its course is the small double-sided carving, thought to be the head of a sceptre, with on one side a bust of Christ between SS Peter and Paul, on the second and fourth sides SS Cosmas and Damian, and on the third side the Virgin crowning the Emperor Leo VI. An inscription reads: 'May you strive [for prosperity?] Lord Emperor Leo and may you succeed!' It was therefore carved soon after 886. The carving is rather damaged and little survives from the ninth century with which it can be compared. The figures are fully rounded, overlapping in the restricted space they occupy, and reminiscent of a late-fourth-century diptych now in Liverpool. Although perhaps a little clumsy in execution, it shows that the late antique tradition is still very much alive. Where did the craftsman receive his training, if iconoclasm was enforced as totally as is believed?

Not until the mid tenth century, however, is the post-iconoclastic style in ivory carving seen in its fully developed form. A panel which shows Christ crowning an emperor, with an inscription identifying him as Constantine VII Porphyrogenitus, 'Autocrat and King of the Romans', must have been carved about 945 when he was the sole ruler of the empire. Both bearded figures are elegant and refined, the emperor in his rich, stiff, gem-studded regalia, Christ in his simple robe – a new style has been created. In another panel, this time showing SS John the Evangelist and Paul, this elegance and simplicity are achieved with even more panache. The relief is deeper, the illusion of depth, giving both figures almost total three-dimensional reality in a box-like frame, makes this an outstanding work of art. Few styles lend themselves so well to the expression of dignity, even divinity. Its restraint, sharply defined elegance and almost ascetic purity make it a totally alien expression of the humanist pre-iconoclastic tradition, from whose classical naturalism it is obviously derived. One finds antecedents only in the monastic arts of the eastern church, in Syria and Egypt, perhaps especially in

Below: One side of a small, double-sided ivory carving, showing the Virgin, with an archangel on her left, crowning the Emperor Leo VI. *c.*AD 886; 6 × 3 in. (15 × 8 cm). The late antique consular diptych (*below right*) was carved nearly five hundred years earlier. 11½ × 4¾ in. (29.4 × 12 cm). It shows three officials watching a stag fight from their box at the games.

Above: The Veroli casket of carved ivory and bone on a wood frame. Early-eleventh-century but drawing on centuries-old tradition; 4¾ × 16⅞ × 6½ in. (11.5 × 40.5 × 15.5 cm). The detail (*top*) shows the rosette borders and the vigour of the classical scenes, with the small, heavily muscled bodies and the well-drawn animals.

such ancient monasteries as Sinai, where works foreshadow the remarkable achievements of the tenth century under the emperors of the Macedonian dynasty.

Ivory carving in the same style dominates the whole of the tenth and most of the eleventh century in religious work. A triptych made for private devotion bears an inscription clearly dating from Constantine VII's reign (912–59). The figures of saints in static rows that surround the *Deesis* (Christ between St John the Baptist and the Virgin) are here a little less elegant, a little more squat in proportion, but have the calm dignity and deep seriousness that characterize all Byzantine ivories of this period. The top of a reliquary shaped like a flat tablet, for a fragment of the True Cross, dated by its inscription to 963–9, shows that the style survived Constantine's death in 959, though the figures are somewhat softer and less sharply defined, while their setting has been much enriched by delicate decorative scrolls.

Very soon after, a new style makes its appearance. Less elegant, far more theatrical in its richly developed narrative, it may have been created in less courtly circles. A late-tenth-century panel showing the Dormition of the Virgin became the centrepiece of a book-cover made for the Holy Roman Emperor Otto III *c.* 1000. It was probably taken to Germany by Otto's mother, the Empress Theophanu, a Byzantine princess. Its use on a book-cover for the imperial family shows how much Byzantine carving was appreciated in the west. The figure drawing still shows linear, sharply defined draperies but instead of presenting the saintly figures in sculptural isolation, it shows them as part of an elaborate illusionistic scene, full of movement and dramatic content. Dark shadows behind the small, vivid figures suggest

infinite distance and the lace-like architectural setting theatrically frames the scene.

A large free-standing figure of the Virgin and Child made in the twelfth century proves that the art of the earlier centuries received additional refinement and sophistication, but not really any new inspiration.

The Byzantine carvers also produced a fine series of quite large caskets, built of wood covered with decorative and figurative thin panels of ivory. Both religious and secular subject matter is found on them, so they no doubt had a wide and varied use, and may well have held Christian relics as well as jewellery. One of the finest of these caskets came from the cathedral of Veroli near Rome. Quite close parallels with illuminations dated to the eleventh century have led to its being attributed to the same date, but its subject matter is drawn from classical mythology and proves close links with much older traditions. On all surviving caskets the figure scenes are surrounded by single rows of rosettes. Here the classical scenes of gods, heroes and centaurs are carved with astonishing skill. Lively figures, almost totally released from their backgrounds, act their parts with immense vigour for such a miniature scale and show an understanding of anatomy unequalled since antiquity. The carvers' classicism is so convincing that one can almost believe that they drew on an unbroken tradition reaching back to the fifth or sixth century. Virtually no firm dates exist for the caskets, and it is not impossible that some of the mythological subjects may have been carved during the century of iconoclasm, thus giving continuity to the craft of ivory carving so richly exploited under the Macedonian dynasty. But this can only be a tempting hypothesis.

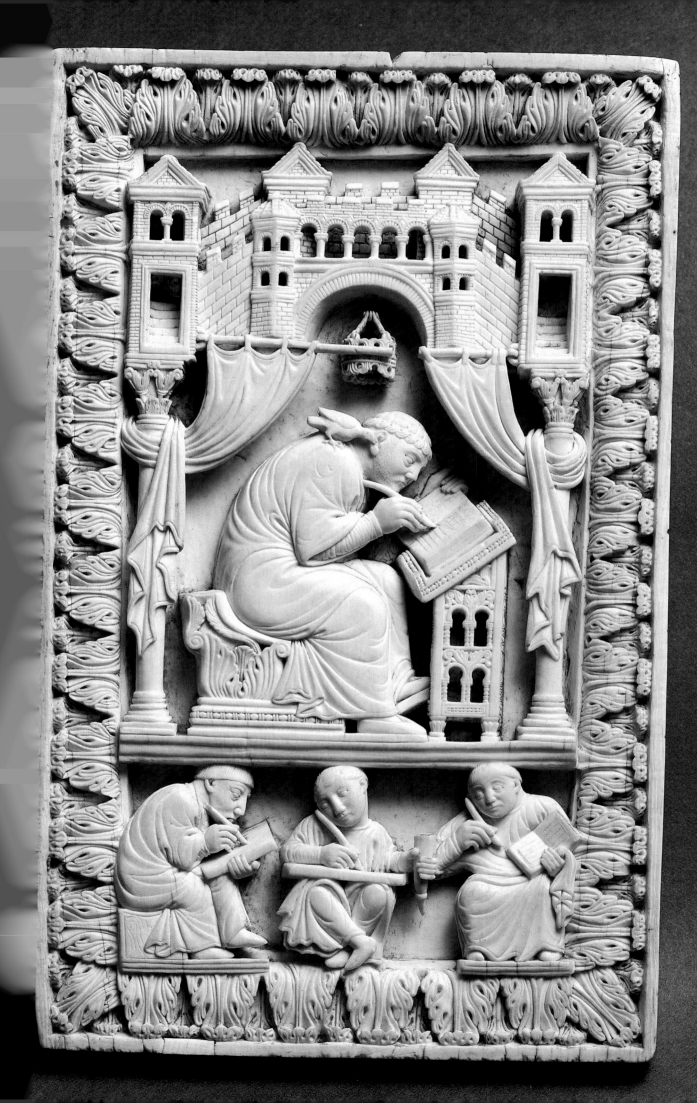

3

Europe

Europe both inherited the classical humanist traditions of the Mediterranean and developed its own ways of working ivory and bone, the disruptions in trade causing the northern craftsmen first to work whalebone, in the flat patterns they favoured, and then to adopt the material that became virtually exclusively theirs, walrus ivory. Shifts in the emphases of patronage took effect, from the superb Carolingian book-covers, often reworking and incorporating late antique diptychs, to the ivory sculptures of medieval France, which culminated in the Virgin of Ste Chapelle. The ivorywork of post-Renaissance and post-Reformation Europe demonstrates an increasingly lively artisanal tradition, in functional and charming folk art, carved in bone, alongside the exuberant baroque and rococo carvings and the soberly elegant neo-classical work, inlaid and veneered with ivory. The nineteenth century's rapid industrialization and its innovative techniques led into the Art Nouveau and Art Deco ivorywork, exemplifying the designer's belief in the pre-eminence of the decorative arts and, by way of Direct Carving, to some masterly modern work, with a renewed stress on the profound importance of the individual artist's cultural roots.

Above: Ivory bracelet with
diamond and onyx decoration. Twentieth-century.
Opposite: Ivory panel, depicting St Gregory.
c. 1000; 8 × 5 in. (20.5 × 12.5 cm).
St Gregory, in his study, is inspired by the Holy Spirit
in the form of a dove, with three scribes below.
See also page 85.

Early Middle Ages

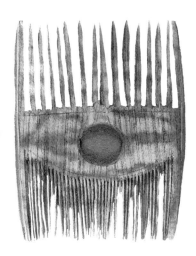

Above: The comb of St Cuthbert, cut from a single slab of ivory. Seventh-century or later; 6⅜ × 4¾ in. (16.3 × 11.9 cm).

Above and far right: The Franks casket in whalebone, found at Auzon. Eighth-century AD; 9 in. (22.9 cm) long. The detail (*right*) shows the Adoration of the Magi, portrayed alongside Roman legend and northern folktale.

With the spread of Islam during the seventh century, the ancient trade routes to Africa and to the east on which Europe depended for so much of its luxury trade were severely interrupted and the supply of ivory itself virtually ceased.

Most unusually, however, an exceptionally large piece of African ivory, a handsome double-sided comb, was found in Durham Cathedral when the tomb of Northumbria's St Cuthbert (*c.* 634–87) was opened in 1821. The craftsman who cut it clearly knew little of the material's potential for miniature sculpture. Possibly it arrived in Northumbria as a finished comb. Quite similar ones have been found in Egypt, where ivory was more readily to hand, and there is evidence of connections between the eastern Mediterranean, where the monastic life originated, and the early monasteries in Celtic Britain. Theodore, Archbishop of Canterbury, who consecrated Cuthbert as Abbot and Bishop of Lindisfarne at York in 685, was a native of Tarsus in Asia Minor and his companion Adrian, who came to England with him, was born in Africa.

In the absence of ivory, northern craftsmen turned to an acceptable substitute – whalebone. The so-called 'Franks casket' is unquestionably the finest piece ever made in it. Presented to the British Museum in 1867 by Sir Wollaston Franks, it was found in Auzon, in France. One end panel became separated and is now in Florence. It is surprisingly large and is best compared in size, shape and elaboration of figural ornament with the Brescia casket from the late fourth century – but how different it is in style! It represents one of the finest achievements of northern craftsmen, whose preoccupations were with flat, often abstract or stylized patterns rather than the late antique naturalism of the Brescia casket. A scene like 'Egil the Archer' defending his home against armed attackers, which forms the central panel of the lid of the Franks casket, shows well the conceptualized abstraction of the artist's view of nature. Egil's house is represented by an arch carried on two pilasters, and the surrounding wall by castellations spread out around it. This is not a naturalistic perspectival representation, but a pictorial statement laid out with great clarity. And yet at least one scene has defied all attempts at identification, the result of a quite extraordinary mixture of sources. The front panel includes a Christian scene, the Adoration of the Magi, and Weyland the Smith; and other scenes are of Egil, from the sagas, and the Sack of Jerusalem and the story of Romulus and Remus from Roman history and legend. It has been convincingly suggested that some universal history compilation was available to the craftsman or his patron.

The casket's date is still uncertain, although the large and splendidly cut runic inscriptions are thought to be eighth century, as are the few elements of Germanic animal ornament, although little convincing comparative material can be found in contemporary manuscripts. But when so little work survives, it is not surprising that some will seem unique.

A fragment of a bone carving, probably the side of a casket about half the size of the Franks casket, was found at Larling in Norfolk. Surprisingly on this fragment too the rare legend of Romulus and Remus is represented. Moreover, it is decorated with a winged biped with an intricately interlaced tail, typical of the period 750–800 in northern Britain, which can be closely paralleled on the Gandersheim casket, in Brunswick. Here very similar ornament, perhaps just a little more precise, almost rigid in handling, is repeated many times over. It is very different in shape and has ornamented bronze mounts, and to be sure of its use is impossible, but the 'house-shaped' form was frequently used for small portable shrines in which relics were reverently preserved. A runic inscription on the base mount was once thought to read: 'Holy Virgin be thou a light to Ely.' But this mount was rather clumsily replaced in modern times, and although the runes were presumably copied from the original, the reading remains uncertain. One might have doubted whether such animal ornament could have been made as far south as East Anglia, but since the discovery of the Larling fragment, it must be thought possible that the casket was the property of Ely before the abbey's destruction by the Danes in 886.

With the diptych from St Martin at Genoelselderen, ivory carvers found a style much

Right and far right:
Thin ivory panels
from the diptych at
Genoels-Elderen. Late-
eighth-century;
12½ × 7½ in.
(30 × 18 cm).
The front leaf shows
Christ treading the Beasts
– 'Thou shalt tread upon
the lion and adder: the
young lion and the dragon
shalt thou trample under
feet'; the back leaf, the
Annunciation and the
Visitation.

Pages 72, 73: Details from
either side of the lock of a
carved, Hispano-
Moresque casket from
Cordoba in Spain.
Eleventh-century. See
also page 79 for a
contemporary casket.

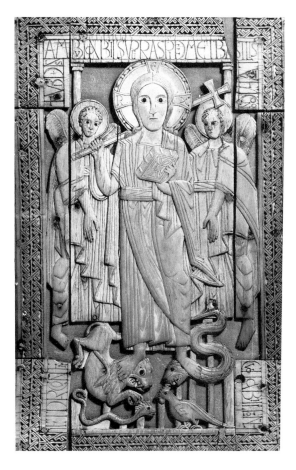

closer to the highest achievements of insular manuscript illuminators who by the early eighth century had so successfully created a compromise between the humanist Mediterranean traditions and the northern preference for flat pattern. The two panels, carved on unusually thin ivory, are assembled from a number of pieces, so the material must still have been in short supply. The design is pierced, which would produce a very rich effect when set against gilt metal or a rich textile. On the front panel is Christ, accompanied by two angels, treading the Beasts (Psalm 91. 13) and on the back the Annunciation appears above the Visitation. The key pattern and the tightly interlaced borders, as well as the palaeographic character of the inscriptions, also point to the strong insular influence already suggested by the figure style. The subject matter, however, was very well known at the court of Charlemagne and it may well be that these panels were made in the Low Countries, where the achievements of the imperial court were known, but by a craftsman working within the earlier insular traditions, so influential on the continent throughout the eighth century.

The Carolingian dynasty

When Charlemagne was crowned Holy Roman Emperor on Christmas Day in 800, he had already spent more than two decades working towards the creation of a new Roman empire in northern Europe centred on his palace at Aachen, to rival both the eastern empire in Constantinople and Rome itself. The revival of the naturalistic classical art of antiquity was an integral and important part of that intention. At first Charlemagne turned to Britain, where a Christian art strongly influenced by Mediterranean traditions had flourished for nearly a hundred years, and in the 780s he called the British scholar Alcuin to lead his newly founded court school. After Alcuin moved in 796 to the abbey of Tours to edit the Vulgate, more direct links with the art of northern Italy were forged by a younger generation of scholars and artists.

Ivory carving was important to that revival of antiquity – the 'Renovatio' as contemporaries called it – by which Charlemagne set out to create a 'second Rome' at Aachen. Although some fine-quality ivory now became available, the bulk of the material may well have been antique pieces reused by Carolingian craftsmen. Evidence is often found on the reverse, in planed-down remnants of earlier carving or the engraved name of a Roman consul. Very simple undecorated diptychs which carried only a name lightly engraved on a quite solid panel were particularly popular, because they allowed deep relief to be carved afresh. The mere fact that so many Carolingian ivories are of the size and shape of

Above: Detail from the Dagulf psalter opposite, showing the delicacy of the work.

consular diptychs, even when there is no obvious evidence of reuse, indicates that a major source of ivory must have been the classical panels themselves. But trade with the Near East also began to revive when Islam retrenched after two major defeats, first at the gates of Constantinople in 717 and 718, and then in France in 732, which finally put an end to its expansion, although the Moors were to establish a western European foothold in Spain.

The production of book-covers for the magnificent manuscripts made in Charlemagne's court scriptorium gave ivory carvers their best opportunities. Perhaps the most outstanding are the two made for the Lorsch gospels in the early ninth century, now unfortunately separated from the manuscript. It is uncertain which was the front and which the back. One shows Christ treading the Beasts, flanked at right and left by two angels bearing long sceptres, with flying angels carrying a jewelled, equal-armed cross above, and the Three Magi, before King Herod, and adoring the Christ Child, below. The other has the Virgin and Child, flanked by St John the Baptist and the Prophet Zacharias, flying angels above carrying a bust of Christ, and the Nativity and the Annunciation to the Shepherds below.

The lower panel of the first cover was cut from a consular diptych, its origin proved by the name of Consul Anastasius, appointed in Constantinople in 517, engraved on the reverse. Moreover, the five-part diptych form itself is clearly derived from the same Byzantine source along with the style, obviously related to the front panels of the throne of Maximianus in Ravenna. But why are the side panels angled at the top on both covers and those of the Virgin and Child cover at the bottom also, when similar panels in antique prototypes are always cut square? It is highly probable that the two top panels with flying angels are sixth-century originals reused by the Carolingian carver. The assembly of five-part diptychs required the cutting of mortise and tenon joints, which weakened the ivory, and in many surviving examples, such as the Barberini diptych, the top panel is damaged at this point at both ends. It seems more than likely that the Carolingian carver planed down these broken edges to cut new, deeper mortises. The inevitable conclusion is that the Magi panel is also a late antique survival, almost certainly from the same diptych that provided the angels. All three reused panels were clearly trimmed for the Carolingian diptych and in the process lost parts of their broad, flat frames and even of their figure decoration.

Although it has always been agreed that more than one hand worked on the Lorsch book-covers, the ten panels display a certain stylistic unity and at first sight it may therefore be difficult to believe that three of the panels are some three

centuries older than the remaining seven. Closer analysis, however, shows that the treatment of the draperies on the large central figure of Christ is far less well understood than that on both flying angel panels. The heads, with their large eyes, broad jawlines and tightly curled hair, do follow a similar pattern throughout the diptychs, but that is precisely why it is highly likely that the Carolingian carvers imitated the angels as exactly as they could. In the case of the lower panel, similarly, the architecture is more crudely fashioned and the figures of the Magi on the Carolingian panel are thicker set and clumsier in detail than those on the Nativity relief that served as its model.

While the Lorsch gospel-covers might almost be called a 'restoration', the cover of a gospel book in Oxford is a more straightforward imitation of a similar model, much smaller in size and carved on a single piece of ivory. The iconography of a number of scenes on it proves that the model was somewhat earlier and of western rather than eastern provenance. The very models probably survive in two panels with three scenes each, one now in Paris, the other in Berlin, which may originally have formed the two side panels of a five-part diptych. The Oxford panel may well belong to the manuscript it covers, a ninth-century gospel book attributed to the abbey of Chelles, near Paris.

The earliest surviving ivory carvings known to have been made at Charlemagne's court are a pair of book-covers, now in Paris, that once decorated the Dagulf psalter, now in Vienna. The manuscript was presented to Pope Hadrian I by Charlemagne and must therefore predate 795, the year the Pope died. The four scenes carved on it, all particularly relevant to the psalms, are praised specifically in the dedicatory verses in the manuscript. The size of the two panels, given that they were once in a golden frame set with precious stones as was customary, is further proof that they belonged to the manuscript. Their style again indicates how important the late antique was to Carolingian carvers. The figures are thickset and broad, and fully fill, indeed rather overcrowd, their frames, which is typical of the compositions on which they are modelled.

With the death of Charlemagne in 814, the empire, now covering almost the whole of Europe, to the Weser in the east and to Rome in the south, only excepting Britain, Ireland and Scandinavia, passed to his only son Louis the Pious (reigned 814–40). Louis did not merely seek to enhance the material splendour of the court and ape the achievements of the Roman emperors, but introduced a vigorous intellectual life. He may also have had less surplus wealth at his disposal than Charlemagne, whose conquests had filled his coffers. Changes in the style of patronage were thus due in part to the very different character of

Above and opposite: Book-covers from the Dagulf psalter. *c.*783–95; 6½ × 3 in. (17 × 8.1 cm) and 6½ × 3 in. (16.8 × 8.2 cm). These are the earliest ivories known to survive from Charlemagne's court school.

Page 76: Anglo-Saxon figure of the crucified Christ. *c.* 1000; 7¾ in. (18.5 cm). It is mounted on a gold cross adorned with gold filigree and *cloisonné* enamels, made in the Rhineland. See also page 82.

Page 77: The Virgin and Child seated on a rainbow. *c.*1000; 5½ × 4½ in. (13.8 × 11.3 cm). An example of the linear Winchester style. See also page 83.

the new emperor and in part to the loosening of the centralized control established by Charlemagne. The result was a much wider acceptance at other centres in the empire of the new humanism introduced at the court, and perhaps a more scholarly understanding of antique sources. There were close connections between Louis' court and Metz, whose bishop was Louis' half-brother, Drogo, and no doubt Reims too, where Ebbo, Louis' friend and librarian, was appointed archbishop in 810. Both centres were to create enormously influential arts.

Central to the activities at Reims was the Utrecht psalter, which is now preserved in Utrecht, in the university library: a most unusual manuscript, written in three columns, in Roman rustic capitals, all accompanied by vivid, unframed pen drawings drawn most modestly in brown bistre only, with not a sign of rich colour, gold or silver. The text is illustrated in the most remarkable, literal fashion. The sources of this style, of such enormous importance to succeeding centuries, have long been debated, but, broadly speaking, by far the most important role in its creation was played by the classical tradition. Indeed, the representation of architecture and the sense of space in the loosely composed scenes find their undoubted ancestors in the painterly, illusionistic wall-paintings of antiquity, like those of Herculaneum. This very manuscript served as a model for a group of ivory carvings; five were reused some fifty years later, in the 860s or 870s, in the scriptorium patronized by Louis' son, Charles the Bald, but must have been carved in

the scriptorium that produced the Utrecht psalter in the 820s. Not only do the scenes on the ivories follow the compositions in the psalter precisely, but the ivories use the same sketchy figure style of the manuscript, executed with remarkable facility, at times in almost free-standing relief, giving the same illusion of infinite space by the subtle use of highlights set against deep shadows; a perfect rendering in three-dimensional form of the manuscript's light touches of penmanship. The panel illustrating Psalm 56, now on the front cover of Charles the Bald's personal psalter, is typical; it interprets the text exactly as the Utrecht psalter does, by 'literal' illustration.

A magnificent large panel, reused, perhaps for the second time, on a book-cover made for the Emperor Henry II in the early eleventh century, was carved in the same workshop, perhaps even by the same hand. It shows a Crucifixion enriched by a number of closely related scenes. As well as the usual Stephaton and Longinus with sponge and spear, and the mourning women, Church is shown twice, once catching Christ's blood in a chalice and once paying homage to the City of Rome, while Synagogue hides her face in her cloak. Above are the Hand of God, angels awaiting the soul of Christ, and chariots with the sun and moon; below, under a great curled serpent, the Three Maries approach the empty Tomb; and below that again, the tombs break open at the Last Judgement, with a classical river god and earth goddess to each side.

Whether this composition combining Christ on the Cross with scenes that underline its cosmic significance is a Carolingian invention, made up out of various elements already in existence – some are certainly in the Utrecht psalter, for example – or whether it reflects a lost early Christian tradition is not certain, but the former seems by far the most likely. Partial early Christian sources were certainly available to the court carvers. Outstanding among them is a panel with a Crucifixion and the Three Maries at the Tomb, not only of the finest quality, but also of great importance because the early Christian model that was imitated by the Carolingian carver has survived. It is a splendid, early-fifth-century panel, now in Munich, with the Three Maries below and the Ascension above, and its lower scene has been copied with more than usual precision. Nothing is known of its provenance or its original use. In style it is different both from the work at Reims and from that at Metz a little later. The splendid quality and the fact that the very best late antique model was available makes a court workshop most likely. The figure of the suffering Christ is not unrelated to the large Utrecht ivory and the combination with the Three Maries scene may also be significant. The work of carvers commissioned by the emperor would almost certainly be

known at Reims. Once the greater composition was created, however, it is not surprising that iconography of such great richness exerted a strong influence on subsequent ivory carvers.

At Metz, a whole series of book-covers based on the large Reims Crucifixion panel was produced in the scriptorium established by Bishop Drogo (823–55). The composition remained popular for at least a generation after it was first introduced in the early 840s. Perhaps the finest cover among them, making fuller use of the elaborate subject matter than most of the later panels, survives in all its splendour, its gold frame set with gems and fine enamels, on a gospel book written at Metz, probably for Drogo himself. It departs, however, from the quick, sketchy touch of Reims in favour of a more solid, almost stolid, figure style, perhaps based on more conventional classical models.

After the death of Louis the Pious in 840, his three surviving sons divided the empire and Europe took on the face we know today. Charles the Bald obtained the western part, France; Louis the German took the eastern part; and the central kingdom, which stretched from the Low Countries to Rome, was inherited by the eldest son Lothair, along with the imperial title, now of little more than formal significance. Under Lothair's rule (840–69) Metz continued to flourish. Imperial patronage now resulted in some outstanding ivory carvings. Perhaps the finest is a pair of book-covers, one of which survives on the front of its original gospel book while its back cover was moved to a later tenth-century manuscript. The centre panel shows the Annunciation above, the Three Magi presenting gifts in the middle and the Massacre of the Innocents below. The whole is surrounded by a broad frame, against a pierced background, carved with an exquisite double vine-scroll of the purest classical tradition. The figure scenes are also pierced and set against a gilt-bronze background, probably original, which enhances the brilliant sparkle and lively touch of the carver – he really has understood the illusionism of the antique.

That the revival of this style was well known at Metz in the late 840s is proved by the painterly style of such manuscripts as, for example, the sacramentary written for Drogo. For this, the ivory carver has managed to translate a flickering, insubstantial, painterly style into a subtle and delicate relief. The golden background adds an illusionistic infinity, very like the aerial perspective employed by late antique painters, and not equalled in art until golden backgrounds were introduced by Byzantine artists.

After Lothair's death in 869, his powerful brothers divided his kingdom, Charles, who already controlled Reims, adding Metz, which from about 825 to 850 had proved itself the most

creative centre of the arts. One of the most important pieces commissioned by Charles, the throne of St Peter, now in Rome, may well have been produced there. The rich ivory inlay is certainly very much in keeping with Metz work, although perhaps not of quite the high standard achieved a decade earlier. The whole chair, however, is only a shadow of its former self. No doubt the wood, inlaid with carved ivory panels, was originally enriched by gilding, if not by sheet silver or gold. The early Christian plaques of the story of Hercules, now mounted rather incongruously on the front, were probably not part of the original decoration. The acanthus scrolls follow the work long established at Metz, but the figure style, what there is of it, is a little heavy, even rather clumsy – the artistic traditions are beginning to decline somewhat. Indeed, in the 870s the output of the scriptorium, so active for more than a generation, almost ceased, and with it the production of ivory book-covers. Only one late Metz object is outstanding: a splendid, hipped-roof, ivory casket, perhaps intended as a reliquary, richly decorated with scenes from the gospels.

Exactly the same Nativity scene, with the Virgin reclining on a bed, a servant arranging her pillow, and Joseph resting his head in his hand, appears in the benedictional of St Aethelwold illuminated at Winchester in the 970s, strongly suggesting that this casket was made available to Anglo-Saxon craftsmen in Wessex towards the end of the tenth century.

Charles the Bald's patronage was apparently concentrated on his court school, which was either at St Denis, just north of Paris, or at Compiègne, his favourite foundation. The extremely sumptuous manuscripts and book-covers, made of gold and silver rather than ivory, which it produced, show that in his taste for ostentatiously rich, almost barbaric splendour, he followed his grandfather rather than his more scholarly father. Among the few ivories which are likely to be products of his school, and which were not reused pieces of earlier date, this desire to enrich the material, even such luxurious material as ivory, is evident. A splendid small Crucifixion has a delicate frame carved with patterns imitating a jewelled border, undoubtedly originally painted and inlaid with gold leaf. The figure style is an interesting amalgam of previous ninth-century styles, with perhaps the light touch and prominent relief of Reims predominant. The same is true of the book-covers which decorate a gospel book in the great royal monastery of St Gall, near Lake Constance. They were carved by Tutilo towards the end of the century. The rich iconography of the front cover, closely linked with the great goldsmith's work that decorates the *Codex Aureus* (a manuscript written in gold on purple vellum) from St Emmeran, a masterpiece produced at Charles's court, shows Christ in Majesty, with the four evangelists accompanied by their symbols. Personifications of the sea god and the earth goddess echo the Utrecht psalter tradition. Perhaps Tutilo received his training at Charles's court school in the 870s.

With the death of Charles the Bald in 877, the last great individual patron of the Carolingian dynasty was lost. What survives from 875 to 900, and there was a marked reduction in output, tends to be scattered throughout the empire and of no great consequence. A number of small carved panels began to show those stylistic tendencies that were to be the source of Ottonian ivory carving.

Spain: the Cordoba Caliphate

The Umayyad caliphs, ruling from Damascus, were the first of the great Muslim dynasties, but within a century they had been superseded by the Abbasids, who moved the seat of power to Baghdad.

One of the Umayyad princes fled from Syria to Spain when the Abbasids took power. His name

Above: End panel of an Islamic casket from Spain. 1049–50. Ivory plaques carved with a fanciful hunting scene are mounted on wood and gilded leather. See pages 72, 73 for details from a contemporary casket.

was Abd er Rahman (756–88) and in southern Spain he established an independent Umayyad line which was to flourish there for nearly three hundred years. By the mid ninth century the court of Cordoba, adopting much of the ceremonial luxury and refinement enjoyed at the court of the Abbasids, the rival dynasty in the east, was renowned as one of the richest and most cultivated known throughout the western world.

A little over a century later, in the 960s, the first of the lavishly decorated 'Hispano-Moresque' ivory boxes, made for the caliphs, princes and dignitaries of the Spanish Umayyad court, were carved in the palace workshops.

It is fairly evident that the motifs decorating these cylindrical and rectangular boxes were initially drawn from Near Eastern textiles, particularly the silks woven in Umayyad Syria, which themselves show the strong influence of earlier Byzantine and Sassanian styles. The designs are closely related to those seen in Spanish Umayyad architectural ornament. The origin of the ivory carving tradition in Spain is more difficult to establish. It is tempting to think that ivory workers emigrated there in the wake of Abd er Rahman, but the gap between the carved ivory boxes attributed to sixth-, seventh- and eighth-century Syria and those of tenth-century Andalusia makes the connection hard to prove. It is known that in the tenth century Egyptian craftsmen set up workshops in al-Mansuriyya near Kairouan (Tunisia) under the patronage of the Fatimid caliphs before they assumed sovereignty in Egypt. Whether the craftsmen who carved the first caskets in Cordoba could have been of Egyptian origin we have no means of telling. An important rectangular casket of wood inlaid with flat sheets of ivory produced at al-Mansuriyya *c.* 970, and now in Madrid, throws no light on the question, for its simple decorative borders are painted rather than carved. The inscription, in the square Arabic script known as *Kufic*, which ornaments its flat lid, is of considerable significance. It tells not only where and for whom the box was made but also the name of the maker, Muhammad al-Khurasani. His surname means 'from Khurasan', the area that is now eastern Iran and Afghanistan; the considerable mobility of Islamic artists and craftsmen at that time is one of the many factors which contributed to the unity of artistic styles and motifs throughout Islam.

Kufic inscriptions with a strongly horizontal base line and the uprights terminating in stylized leaves are a characteristic feature of the carved Spanish caskets. They appear round the vertical edge of the lid, which on cylindrical boxes was domed and on oblong ones flat or sloping. Many bear the date and the name of the person for whom the box was made, others consist solely of blessings on the owner, a distinctive feature on treasured possessions of all kinds in the Islamic world.

The evidence is that the caskets were made in special workshops in the caliphal palaces in Cordoba and in the palatine city built at Madinat al-Zahra near by. Examples which do not live up to the exacting standards of craftsmanship set by those that we know to have been made under royal patronage may be the products of commercial establishments. The intricate carving which covers the entire outer surface is in unusually deep

three-dimensional relief. The most celebrated are those where the profuse foliage inhabited by paired animals and birds acts as a background for lobed or polygonal medallions or arcades containing figural scenes. But perhaps the most beautiful are those ornamented with a purely vegetal arabesque, so sharply carved as to look almost like tracery, held to be earlier both on stylistic grounds and on the basis of dated pieces. An outstanding example is a superb *pyxis* now in New York, signed by an artist named Khalaf whom we know to have worked *c.* 966. Like the other cylindrical caskets and some of the smaller rectangular ones, the body and lid are each carved from a single piece of ivory (larger rectangular ones were constructed of flat sections held together with ivory pins). The symmetrical yet varied design is composed of interlacing scrolling vine-stems, reminiscent of the pre-Islamic 'tree of life', growing from clusters of leaves bearing complete and split palmettes made up of a highly distinctive leaf form which characterizes all the 'Hispano-Moresque' ivories. It has a curled tip and pronounced veining, its edge often punctuated with little holes which must originally have been set with precious stones, as the inscription bears out: 'The sight I offer is the fairest, the firm breast of a delicate girl. Beauty has invested me with splendid raiment, which makes a display of jewels. I am a receptacle for musk, camphor and ambergris.' An inscription treating an object as a metaphor for something else is entirely characteristic of the symbolism which imbues the arts of Islam.

Larger rectangular caskets were probably made to hold jewels. In the cathedral in Pamplona is a masterpiece of this remarkable school of ivory carving. Made in 1005, apparently by a team of carvers, it exemplifies the figural group, showing a series of indoor and outdoor court scenes (of the genre also found on fine-quality inlaid Islamic metalwork of a slightly later date), some of which may portray the royal patrons for whom such caskets were executed. They provide an extraordinarily vivid picture of the life and pastimes of the Andalusian princes – hawking, listening to music, feasting and drinking, giving more formal audiences, or simply sitting beneath a palm tree, watched over by attendants with fans, fly-whisks and scent bottles. The background, both within and without the figural medallions, is filled with profuse scrolling foliage of the kind that provides the sole ornament on the Khalaf box. On the Pamplona casket the arabesque vines bear bunches of grapes and are peopled with curiously compressed cross-legged figures; other examples are adorned with parrots, confronting peacocks and griffons, ibexes, lions and other birds and beasts, real and mythological. Animals and birds in pairs, flanking a palm tree frond, often appear as the principal motif within the medallions; frequent

subjects, too, are lions attacking their prey (a Sassanian theme) and rustic activities such as gathering the date harvest; sometimes there is a single elephant or a person of high rank riding in a palanquin on a camel. As the eleventh century advances, a gradual coarsening in the style of execution is detectable.

After the fall of the caliphate of Cordoba in 1031, the ivory carvers sought asylum under the Dhu'l Nunid kings of Toledo and a group of craftsmen working for them was established in Cuenca. The caskets attributed to Cuenca in the mid eleventh century employ the same motifs – scenes of archery and hunting, paired animals and birds, creatures attacking one another and heart-shaped palmettes – as their Cordoban predecessors, but they are reduced to relentlessly repeating patterns strung out in monotonous horizontal bands. A striking example in Madrid is unusual for being constructed of panels of openwork ivory carving backed on to gilded leather.

Anglo-Saxon ivories

In the second half of the tenth century, under three outstanding churchmen, St Dunstan, Archbishop of Canterbury from 959 to 988, St Aethelwold, Bishop of Winchester from 963 to 984, and St Oswald, Bishop of Worcester from 960 to 972 and Archbishop of York from 972 to 992, the English Church was reformed and the 'Golden Age of Anglo-Saxon Art' was initiated. It is more than usually difficult to separate ivory carving from contemporary manuscript illumination. Anglo-Saxon illuminators became increasingly aware of the great achievements of all the Carolingian schools, first Charlemagne's court school and Metz, and then, towards the end of the century, Reims also. Indeed, by the year 1000 the Utrecht psalter itself had been brought to Canterbury and a first copy made of it. Copied twice more in the next two centuries, it became one of the most influential works of art in Britain for generations to come.

How close ivory carving can be to manuscript illumination is shown by a Nativity panel which closely follows the composition of the same scene in the benedictional of St Aethelwold, a manuscript illuminated at Winchester in the 970s, which in turn had been copied from the late Carolingian Metz casket. The style of carving is closer to the English transformation of the Metz style than to the Carolingian source. The solid, compact figures of the Metz casket are drawn here with a more vigorous line, producing drapery which, at the edges of the bed sheet and the hem of Joseph's garment, looks more fluttering. The drapery on the recumbent Virgin, however, is more tightly stretched with parallel folds, closer to the Metz manner. The Ox and the Ass and the crib with the Christ Child, which on the casket

Opposite: Three of the seventy-eight walrus ivory chessmen – king, bishop, knight – found on Lewis in the Hebrides. *c.* 1135–50; all under 4¼ in. (10.5 cm). Compact and easy to handle, they are carved with vigour and humour, no two alike. See also page 91.

are behind the bed, appear, most unusually, underneath it in the illumination.

It is in the excitement of line, rather than in the tight bandage-like drapery reminiscent of Metz ivories, that English carvers began to excel. The effect was further enhanced by the material they used virtually exclusively – walrus ivory. This may perhaps at first have resulted from the difficulty of obtaining elephant ivory, but once the potential of walrus was recognized, craftsmen made the most of the fine buttery colour and the almost translucent surface. This is also why the carvings are small-scale and why many are miniature sculptures in the round rather than panels, more difficult to cut from the relatively smaller tusks. When larger panels were required, whalebone was used. Walrus and whales had been hunted by Scandinavians since at least the time of the English King Alfred (reigned 871–901) and by the tenth century the Basques of northern Spain hunted them also. Walrus ivory is from now on more common than elephant ivory throughout northern Europe until the thirteenth century.

Two figures of the Virgin and St John, originally part of a Crucifixion, are typical of the way English craftsmen exploited the fine surface of walrus ivory. By the beginning of the eleventh century the influence of the Utrecht psalter had been fully absorbed; the earlier parallelism is replaced by a sketchy touch and an excited network of folds. Tall elongated figures clearly derived from the Reims style almost dance on the swirling ground. An exquisite Anglo-Saxon crucifix figure of the same style is mounted on a finely decorated gold cross, with the four evangelist symbols at the ends of the arms and the titulus at the top, which must have been made in the Rhineland very soon after the figure was carved, c. 1000. Obviously Anglo-Saxon ivories were as greatly appreciated by the discriminating aristo-

cratic patrons of the Ottonian Empire as the much-prized Byzantine ivories.

This predominantly linear style, normally called the 'Winchester' style, remained popular for more than two generations throughout England. Two mandorla-shaped panels, one with a Christ in Majesty enthroned, the other with a Virgin and Child seated on a rainbow, are splendid examples of this style. Both are damaged on the left side (perhaps wrenched off a book-cover?). Although the figures are carved in considerable depth, the sharply engraved drapery tends to obscure their corporeality, rather than emphasizing it. In this respect, Anglo-Saxon artists seem more captivated by Carolingian traditions than their contemporaries on the continent, who were developing a far greater interest in three-dimensional sculptural form. Even in objects that are obviously of solid form, like the head of a Tau crosier, found at Alcester in Warwickshire, the rich ornament, clearly derived from manuscript illumination, is pictorial rather than sculptural in character and tends to obscure the form of the object rather than emphasizing it.

In the period 1025–50, the more sculptural tendencies of the emergent Romanesque on the continent began to be felt in England also. A Virgin and Child panel still shows the same love of vivid surface decoration, even finer indeed in its detail, yet the figures are realized in greater relief and emerge more solidly from the background. There is a real sense of distance. A Baptism of Christ appears to be fully presented as a free-standing group, but pinholes near the base suggest that it was originally mounted on a solid panel. The hunched, bearded St John retains that feature of the Utrecht psalter style but, no longer as slim or as elegant, has its feet planted solidly on the ground and is modelled with a sense of weight. The draperies, still fine in detail, now clearly

Below: The cross shown in colour on page 76. The figure conceals a reliquary.

Below: Anglo-Saxon Tau crosier (so named from the resemblance to the Greek T), from Alcester, Warwickshire. *c.*1030; 1¾ × 5½ in. (4.8 × 14.4 cm).

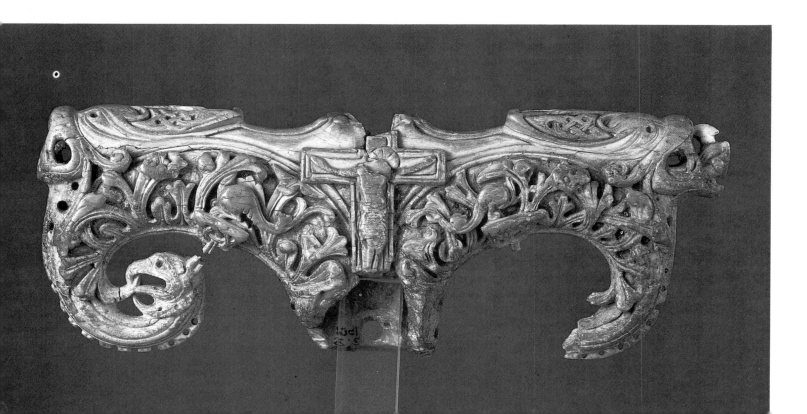

Far right: Two scenes from a late Carolingian ivory panel. Early tenth-century; 6¼ × 4 in. (16 × 10 cm). The top represents the Ascension, the bottom the entry into Jerusalem.

Above: The Winchester-style Virgin and Child shown in colour on page 77.

reveal the figure below the cloth. Even before the Norman Conquest of 1066, Anglo-Saxon carvers, like their contemporaries in northern Europe, were looking for greater realism and monumentality in their figural art.

The Ottonian Empire

Towards the end of the ninth century, Europe suffered unusually turbulent times. The successors of Charles the Bald and Louis the German could not control internal conditions in the western and the eastern kingdoms. The Slavs and Magyars attacked in the east, the Norsemen (who finally settled in what was to become the duchy of Normandy) in the west. The nobles of the eastern kingdom met in 911 and elected Conrad, Duke of Franconia, as their king. His son Henry I (reigned 919–36) really laid the foundations of the revival of the empire. In 929 he defeated the Slavs and in 933 he finally stopped the advance of the Magyars in Thuringia. By the time his son Otto (King of Germany, 936–73) was crowned emperor by the Pope in 962, the empire could once again provide the stable society in which the arts were able to flourish.

While in England Carolingian art had been an import, a fresh and new creative stimulus, in Germany the traditions reaching back into the Carolingian period remained unbroken. Late Carolingian ivories, like the small Metz panel with the Healing of the Leper and the Blind Man, show figures more cramped, compositions more crowded. The panel with the Ascension and the Entry into Jerusalem, one of two that survive, makes even more evident the changes beginning in the early tenth century. The illusionism of Carolingian art is replaced by a far more solid, more sculptural style. The figures are almost stunted, square in outline, with large heads and cap-like hair-styles. These characteristics are fully developed in an important set of ivories commissioned by Otto I, probably between 955 and 968. One of these panels shows the dedication of a church, possibly Magdeburg Cathedral, in the presence of SS Peter, Mauritius and Innocent, the cathedral's patrons, with the emperor himself presenting the model of the church to the enthroned Christ. Another shows the Raising of Lazarus. Sixteen others survive in a number of collections. They are all of the same size and most still have the wide, flat frames that were no doubt originally partly covered by metal frames set with jewels. It has been suggested that they decorated an altar frontal or perhaps a pulpit commissioned by Otto for Magdeburg. The style of the late Carolingian Ascension panel is evidence of the kind of sources available to the craftsmen. The upright, stiff, almost rigid figures, tightly pressed into the frame of the composition, the flat, engraved detail of the drapery, the cap-like hair,

especially the tight curls – all are closely related. What is original is the backgrounds: all richly decorated with foliate scrolls and geometric patterns, all pierced to make use of an underlay, probably of gilt metal, which would have enriched the rather stiff style considerably.

The Magdeburg altar frontal lays the foundations for the great achievements of Ottonian ivory carvers. The severe monumentality that was to be an important part of their contribution seems firmly established, but a little dry and a little lacking in humanity. These qualities, however, were to be found in renewed contact with North Italy and Byzantine art. In 972 Otto II married the Byzantine princess Theophanu, probably a daughter of the Emperor Romanus II. A direct contact with Constantinople was established and the links with the eastern tradition were reinforced. The most obvious example of this new intimacy is the panel showing Otto and Theophanu crowned by Christ. It not only exactly follows the pattern set by Romanus II and Eudocia in an ivory carved in Constantinople *c.* 945, but is even inscribed in Greek.

Another, smaller panel, also carved for the emperor and inscribed *OTTO IMPERATOR*, shows Christ enthroned between St Mauritius and the Virgin, two adoring angels above, the kneeling emperor below to his right, the empress, presenting her infant son to Christ, on his left. It must have been carved shortly before Otto's death

Above: Ivory panel of Christ crowning the Emperor Otto II and his Byzantine wife, Theophanu. Late-tenth-century; 7 × 4 in. (18 × 10.3 cm).

occurred in 983. It is a fine example of the style developed at his court, dependent for the most part on Byzantine sources, with just a little of the northern Carolingian tradition so important in the Magdeburg frontal. The head and beard of St Mauritius do resemble the northern style, but the draperies have the gentle overlapping folds of contemporary Byzantine ivories. A panel like the single figure of St Matthew, now on a modern cover of a manuscript, further underlines this school's dependence on Byzantine models. The stark placing of the figure, sharply outlined against a spacious, utterly plain background, the feet firmly planted, even the pensive look, the looped drapery over the right leg and the stiff upright folds over the standing leg – all follow contemporary Byzantine practice. Compare it, for example, with the panel of SS John and Paul in Venice. Only the rather flat acanthus ornament of the frame is totally within the western tradition.

Perhaps the most outstanding piece from the same workshop is the *situla*, or holy water bucket, now in the cathedral treasury of Milan. It shows the Virgin and Child between the four evangelists, all seated below a solid architectural arcade. An inscription states that Archbishop Godfredus of Milan (975–80) had it made for the reception of the emperor; no doubt it was intended for Otto II's visit to Milan in 980. The superb handle is cast

Right: Holy water bucket from Milan. 690; 6¼ × 4¼– 5 in. (16 × 11– 13 cm). One of only four such ivory *situlae* in existence, it shows scenes of the Passion and the Resurrection.

in silver and gilt. The style of carving closely resembles the pieces that must have been commissioned by the court and it therefore seems more than likely that the workshop was at home in Milan.

Otto II died in Italy in 983 and was buried, most appropriately, in an antique sarcophagus in St Peter's, Rome. The Empress Theophanu became regent for her three-year-old son, Otto III (king of Germany, 983–1002; emperor from 996). Imperial patronage was largely concentrated in Italy but centres of excellence were created north of the Alps by great church dignitaries often closely related to the court, among them Archbishop Gero of Cologne (969–76), Archbishop Egbert of Trier (977–93), who had been the head of the Imperial Chancellery, Abbess Mathilde of Essen, a granddaughter of Otto I, and Bernward of Hildesheim (993–1022), tutor to the young Otto III in Italy from 987 until 993.

Egbert of Trier stands out both as a politician and as a patron of the arts. It was at Trier especially that the 'Ottonian Renaissance' took shape. Western late antique models of *c*. AD 400 were absorbed and adapted to play a new and medieval role. The revival of the late antique here can truly be called a 'rebirth', quite distinct from the influence of contemporary Byzantine art at court. It was Egbert of Trier who first patronized the outstanding illuminator of the late tenth century, called the 'Gregory Master' after two superb paintings that once illustrated a manuscript copy of the letters of St Gregory, now at Chantilly in France.

A group of ivories has also been attributed to the Gregory Master. Among them is a panel showing the Presentation in the Temple, perhaps a side panel from a casket. The rounded figures and smooth drapery can be quite convincingly compared to the Master's illuminations, but it is more likely that both draw on an understanding of the late antique model than that the ivory carver is the Gregory Master himself. The rather flat, broad heads do not look like the Master's refined drawing, and indeed the whole style lacks his elegance. In contrast, the ivory carver emphasizes the weight and mass of the figures and their quite violent movement. Another panel which underlines the relationship with the late antique shows St John the Evangelist, with his symbol and, unusually, a scribe taking dictation, in an illusionistic landscape which translates the painterly qualities of late antique aerial perspective into relief form – a remarkable achievement not unlike the translation of the Utrecht psalter style into ivory reliefs a hundred and fifty years earlier.

Once the late antique style had been fully absorbed, the growing interest in monumentality, established a generation earlier, began to fuse with it. Unfortunately, none of the surviving panels

Above: Part of the ivory panel depicting St Gregory, shown in full on page 68.

Right and below: Ivory panel carved at Metz. *c.*984–1005; 6 × 3½ in. (15.2 × 9.2 cm). The detail shows the bust of Bishop Adalbero II, who commissioned the panel.

that resulted give any clue to their provenance. Perhaps the most impressive of them shows St Gregory hunched over his desk in his study, with three scribes below and a dove, representing the Holy Spirit, whispering into his ear: a handsome and monumental carving indeed.

A panel carved further north at about the same time, at the ancient centre of Metz, proves yet again how long the influence of the Utrecht psalter style was to persist. A donor's inscription proves that it was commissioned by Bishop Adalbero of Metz, almost certainly Adalbero II (bishop from 984 to 1005). The composition surrounding the cross continues the rich programme so often used in Metz throughout the Carolingian period and so close is it to those early models, both in style and iconography, that lacking the inscription one might

date it as ninth century, not late tenth.

After the sudden death of Otto III in Italy in 1002, Henry, Duke of Bavaria, was elected emperor by force of arms and by skilful diplomacy. He disliked Italy almost as much as his predecessors disliked Germany and not until some twelve years later was he crowned emperor by the Pope in Rome. He was an immensely generous patron and enriched Aachen Palace Chapel as well as his favourite foundation of Bamberg. His

personal piety and firm support of church reform led to his canonization in 1146. Ivory was relatively rare among his many commissions, perhaps because the material itself was once again in short supply (it was at this time that walrus ivory began to replace elephant ivory in Britain). On the great pulpit he ordered for Aachen, six large, splendid, deeply carved, late antique ivories were reused, and on the large book-cover he gave to Bamberg the great Crucifixion panel carved in the time of Louis the Pious was used again, probably for the third time, its outstanding quality recognized over some two centuries.

In a book-cover made for the Abbess Theophanu of Essen (1039–56) an ivory with the Crucifixion occupies the centre. The iconography only partially continues the Metz tradition and includes the four evangelists at the corners, the Ascension above and the Nativity below. The crowded detail and small figures do resemble the great Carolingian Crucifixion panel, but in its less sculptural treatment and its squatter, less refined figures, it does not come as close to the Utrecht style as the Adalbero panel.

Another among the relatively rare ivories produced during Henry II's reign is a magnificent carving of the Virgin and Child, now in Mainz. Unfortunately nothing is known of its provenance. The Virgin presents the Child in strict symmetry and frontality and is carved in remarkably high relief, her head totally released from the background. The carving's heavy, rounded forms, with draperies only gently suggested, and its tremendous feeling for monumentality are markedly different from the light touch and delicate form of the Reims tradition still so obvious in the Adalbero plaque. It has been claimed that this style derives from the Gregory Master, and such weight and tendency towards the monumental do remind one of his work. This ivory also closely resembles a wooden cult figure, originally covered in sheet gold, made for Bishop Bernward of Hildesheim. Both works date from about 1010, at least a generation later than the Gregory Master. They carry the tendencies first exploited by the earlier Master to a new level of excellence and foreshadow the feeling for solid, three-dimensional form that was to become a hallmark of Romanesque art.

Towards the end of the Ottonian period, another, more aggressive style, with an astonishing force of expression achieved by controlled distortion and stylization, makes a brief appearance. A Crucifixion made for and mounted centrally in a book-cover for the Empress Theophanu *c.* 990 was reused for the so-called *Codex Aureus* written at the monastery of Echternach, near Trier, between 1053 and 1056. It may be difficult to see this powerful and rough style as contemporary with the comparatively delicate panel of

Right: A Crucifixion carved for the book-cover made for the Empress Theophanu. *c.*990. It was later reused to cover the *Codex Aureus* written at Echternach (near Trier) *c.*1050.

the Theophanu cover in Essen. But it is precisely this diversity that is typical of the Ottonian period in the empire. Instead of the coherent and centralized patronage of the Carolingian period self-consciously promoting an imperial image, the patronage of the Ottonian period, although still largely personal and aristocratic, is nevertheless far more widely diffused. The Ottonian contribution, fragmented and various, is highly creative and sets the scene for the Romanesque to come.

Romanesque and Transitional

Many of the style characteristics of Romanesque, the heavy monumentality and expressive force, a preference for stylized pattern and balanced composition rigidly related to the frame, were already developing by the middle of the eleventh century. But nevertheless changes of considerable importance took place *c.* 1050–1100. Instead of being nurtured mainly by aristocratic and cultured individuals, art now found a far wider base in the expanding economies of wealthy monasteries and growing cities. As a result, patronage became more continuous and regional workshops began to develop.

The major regions in which ivory carving was practised from the later eleventh century onwards were Italy and northern Spain in the Mediterranean area, and Britain, the Rhineland and lower Lorraine – or what became known as the 'Mosan' region centred on the valley of the river Meuse – in northern Europe.

Italy

In Italy a school of carving was established in the late eleventh century at Amalfi near Salerno, which drew on the strong indigenous traditions of its classical past. A retable in the cathedral treasury at Salerno is set with more than thirty ivory panels, carved, even in its incomplete form, with an extensive cycle of over thirty Old and forty New Testament scenes. The rich iconography is very obviously drawn from early Christian sources, but while elements within the scene of the Healing of the Blind Man can be traced back to early-fifth-century models, the style of the carving has been transformed from their painterly illusionism to the much more rigid pattern-making of the late eleventh century. Lacking the understanding of such painted images taught to northern artists by Carolingian and Ottonian classical revivals, these panels indicate that the craftsmen can produce only a pale, and perhaps rather clumsy, reflection of such early sources.

Spain

In Spain the approach is far more creative and positive. The eleventh century saw the continuous expansion of the Christian kingdoms of Leon and Castile, Navarre and Aragon at the expense of the Islamic caliphates. The Leon court's generous patronage and the traditions of the superb Islamic craftsmen of Cordoba established an unmistakable style that spread throughout northern Spain. The earliest and perhaps finest piece to survive, a

cross some 20 in. (50 cm) high, is the first of only three ivory altar crosses to survive from the early Middle Ages. An inscription records the donors, King Fernando and Queen Sancha, and documents prove that they gave it to San Isidore in Leon at its rededication in 1063. The front still has its original corpus, fully carved in three dimensions, a scene with the Risen Christ at the top, and the figure of Adam at the base. Tiny figures are carved along the edges, on one side the elect rising to Paradise, on the other the lost descending into damnation. On the reverse is an *Agnus Dei*, with the four evangelist symbols at the ends of the cross. A rich, thoroughly Romanesque inhabited scroll fills the remainder of the arms of the broad cross. The same workshop produced a splendid casket, decorated with large ivory panels illustrating the Beatitudes each accompanied by an angel, large figures which compare well with the small Risen Christ on the altar cross – the same forceful stylization, the rich surface pattern, broken by vividly organized and well-defined drapery. The powerful heads, with large eyes set with the black glass beads found only in Spanish and English ivories, and the sharply drawn hair-styles, are characteristic of the emergent Romanesque. The style closely resembles such late Ottonian art in Germany as the Crucifixion panel on the cover of the *Codex Aureus* in Nuremberg.

Towards the end of the century, the Leon style developed towards even smoother monumentality in the shrine of St Felix, made for the monastery of San Millan de la Cogolla in Aragon. Only four panels survived the Peninsular war of 1808–14, but they show that the carvers rivalled the achievements by, and may even have provided the models for, the sculptors who were embellishing with life-size figures great cathedral portals in Leon, Toulouse and Santiago de Compostela. Stone masons whose training had been largely restricted to the decorative carving of capitals, only occasionally including rudimentary figure scenes, needed to enlarge their vocabulary from the far more sophisticated sculpture of both goldsmiths and ivory carvers when the end of the century brought an ever-growing demand for elaborate figure decoration. These earliest attempts at 'major' sculpture clearly show the dependence on such models.

The ivory carvers' pre-eminence did not last all that long. Even such large and imposing carvings as the whalebone panel with the Adoration of the Magi no longer provided inspiration to a new generation of mason sculptors. The provenance of this fine carving, in turn attributed to England, Flanders and Spain, remains controversial, although a date *c.* 1100–50 is now generally accepted. The closest parallels do seem to be in Spain, in a stone tympanum at Santa Maria Uncastillo near Zaragoza. The panel's rich sur-

face, architectural detail and crowded composition, a jewel-like decoration replacing the more expressive earlier monumentality, strengthen the argument in favour of Spain.

Northern Europe

The history of ivory carving in Spain is fortunately well documented, but in northern Europe, both Britain and the empire, dating remains highly controversial. In the Mosan region, the date of one ivory is of the utmost significance to any understanding of its development. It is inscribed by the donor, Bishop Notger of Liège, who ruled the see from 971 to 1008. Now mounted on a book-cover, it shows a Christ in Majesty, most delicately carved, surrounded by the four evangelist symbols. Below, in a unique scene, the bishop kneels before an altar in a small chapel, holding a document in his hand. Surprisingly he is shown with a halo. The inscription speaks of a sin for which he is doing penance. Compelling historical arguments date the ivory as early twelfth century rather than in the lifetime of the bishop. The sin is almost certainly the destruction of the castle of Chèvremont, held by opponents of the Emperor Otto III whose loyal supporter he was. The bishop and a number of fellow clerics, armed under their vestments, seized the castle, destroying in the process three chapels, one of them dedicated to St John the Evangelist. Later, Notger endowed a new chapel dedicated to St John in Liège. Long after his death, in a dispute about the

(highly lucrative) baptism rights between the parish church of Notre-Dame in Liège and the chapel of St Adalbert, a dependency of St John's, the latter claimed that the bishop had granted them the right of baptism, and it has been suggested very convincingly that the ivory was carved and mounted on a manuscript that had belonged to Notger to buttress their claim. The dispute lasted from 1101 until 1107. The use of such 'pictorial' evidence in an ecclesiastical inquiry was not uncommon in the twelfth century, and

Far right: The Notger ivory. Probably early-twelfth-century, an example of the difficulties and fascination of dating; 7½ × 4¼ in. (19 × 11 cm).

Above and left: Superb ivory altar cross from northern Spain. 1063; 20 in. (52 cm). The detail shows Christ's head.

bearing in mind the halo, which makes it seem impossible that the panel was carved in the bishop's lifetime, an early-twelfth-century date seems virtually certain. Moreover, it is stylistically convincing. The panel must surely be later than a similar ivory on the cover of an eleventh-century gospel book in the Bodleian Library, Oxford, which is surrounded by an engraved bronze-gilt frame which can also be dated *c*. 1050–75; and it is very convincing to see its strong relief, set against an open flat background framed by a plainly moulded border, as contemporary with a bronze font made in Liège between 1107 and 1118.

To date the Notger ivory before 1008, the year he died, totally destroys the credibility of the development of eleventh-century ivory carving. Having arrived at the 'Small Figure' style in such carvings as the Theophanu book-cover by the mid century, craftsmen became increasingly aware of sculptural values and developed a firmer control of form in the second half of the century. The Oxford book-cover begins to develop from its strong base in the illusionism of Reims towards the more monumental, although it still retains the older tradition of the rich acanthus frame. If we compare the Crucifixion panel in the church of Notre-Dame at Tongeren to the Oxford Christ in Majesty, we see the next stage. Still a little crowded, still making use of deep shadows, the larger figures have gained considerable weight and volume, the background is beginning to act as a flat wall rather than to suggest infinite depth. The earth god, practically identical in both panels, is seen against a dark shadow in the Oxford ivory, but seems to sit in front of a solid background in the Tongeren panel. The large Crucifixion in Brussels, just a little earlier, repeats the iconography of the Theophanu cover precisely, but again the plain background plays a more significant role, and the simple border replaces the earlier acanthus frame. Such panels show, step by step, the development towards the Notger ivory. To date the Notger panel at the end of the tenth century instead of the early twelfth century would therefore make no sense at all.

Much the same development can be traced in Britain, where walrus ivory continued to be exclusively used, but where the consequences of the Norman Conquest in 1066 tend to complicate the understanding of eleventh-century developments. Some historians see the Conquest as a disaster that cut short the full flowering of Anglo-Saxon art; others see it as bringing England back into the mainstream of European development; others again warn convincingly against attributing too much significance to an event that hardly interrupted the life of ordinary Englishmen. Moreover, throughout the early eleventh century Anglo-Saxon art had exerted such a strong influence in both Flanders and Normandy that artists who came to England under the new Norman bishops and abbots installed by William the Conqueror soon after 1066, probably worked in a style totally in harmony with their English brothers. The lively grace and vivid drawing of the Winchester style continued to cast its spell over English, Norman and Flemish artists until at least the early twelfth century. The failure to recognize this obvious fact leads to dating English ivories that bear traces of this style as 'Anglo-Saxon' rather than 'Norman'. Unfortunately the label 'pre-Conquest' is often seen as an accolade of quality among those who believe the Normans put an end to English civilization. Students of architecture tend to a more balanced view and recognize the immense strides made under Norman rule as the striking economic expansion and superior organization that were transforming northern Europe were brought to England. The great English cathedrals and abbeys are evidence of the explosion of creative skills after the Conquest.

Once the underlying continuity of development in English art is understood, and it is accepted that ivories which show signs of the 'Winchester' style may date from the second half of the eleventh century or even the early twelfth century, some of the controversy surrounding individual pieces may finally be settled.

How strong this continuity can be, even reaching back into the tenth century, is proved by a long, narrow penbox with a sliding lid that was originally fitted with a lock. The birds inhabiting

Below: An ivory penbox and a detail (*above*) from the side panel. Late-eleventh-century; 9¼ × 1¼ in. (23.5 × 3.2 cm). The style foreshadows the Romanesque.

a symmetrical design on the lid, which can best be compared to Anglo-Saxon manuscripts of the mid tenth century, the side panel showing a hunting scene that can be paralleled in early-eleventh-century drawings, and another side panel that shows large, rounded and stylized figures attacked by lions, demonstrate how wide a range of reference was at the disposal of the carver. The lion panel, already so close to twelfth-century Romanesque, cannot be earlier than 1150–1200 despite the strong traditional stylistic characteristics of the rest of the decoration.

Even more obviously late-eleventh-century in date is the central fragment of a quatrefoil with the very heavy figure of Christ in Majesty on the front and the *Agnus Dei*, with the symbols of St Luke below and St John above, on the back. Found in St Omer, where the abbey of St Bertin had close connections with Anglo-Saxon England, it is made of walrus ivory; the two pieces originally fixed to each side and carrying the symbols of St Matthew and St Mark on the back are now missing. The draperies still show some of those fluttery edges so popular among 'Winchester' artists, and the frame round the *Agnus Dei* is decorated with some shoots of typical Winchester acanthus foliage, but the sheer bulk of the figure, its sculptural presence and the rigidity of the double-edged broad folds of its main garment are typical of Flemish manuscript illuminations in the later eleventh century, and it was either carved in England or by an English craftsman working in St Omer.

The delicate, small, triangular ivory carved with two flying angels, found in a garden in Winchester, Hampshire, was the side panel from the hipped roof of a small rectangular casket, part of a Christ in Majesty or a Crucifixion composition. Long accepted as Anglo-Saxon, it is normally dated to the late tenth or early eleventh century and compared to the almost life-sized flying angels carved in stone in the church of Bradford-on-Avon, Wiltshire, and the angels that accompany the Christ in Majesty in the charter of New Minster, Winchester. Certainly the deep relief and delicate figure modelling recall the Utrecht psalter style so important *c.* 1000, but the comparisons make the ivory's full sculptural quality all the more pronounced. The continuity of line shown in the draperies, with a thin engraved line along their edges, is very similar to the Christ in Majesty from St Omer and the total absence of the zigzag pattern network that covers early-eleventh-century Anglo-Saxon figures, like the two in St Omer, make the Winchester triangle look much more like post-Conquest carvings. These draperies, and in particular the heads, closely resemble a small oval box, probably a pyx, in the Victoria and Albert Museum. Its subject matter has been much discussed and a very

convincing suggestion is that it represents the medieval drama of the *Visitatio Sepulchri* (the Visit to the Tomb) annually performed at Easter. Stylistically it retains much of the Winchester tradition, but the fully Romanesque details of the architectural settings cannot be pre-Conquest and underline the early-twelfth-century date suggested by the richly narrative subject matter. Closely related to these two carvings is a crosier on one side of which is St John of Beverley, healing a deformed mute. Although the carving is pierced, it is so skilfully designed that the other side shows a parallel scene, St Peter and St John the Evangelist healing the cripple in the Temple. The stem is decorated with an inhabited foliate scroll closely related to manuscript illumination of about 1100, when this fine crosier must have been carved.

Towards the end of the eleventh or at the beginning of the twelfth century, there were close links between the Mosan area and Norman Britain. Architecture had already seen the introduction of the cube-shaped 'cushion' capital, which became the most popular form throughout England. In ivory carving only the reinvigoration of such contacts can explain the appearance of a whole group of sculptures of the highest quality, showing the same classical traditions that had led to the creation of the Notger panel, and which could only have been transmitted to these craftsmen by a knowledge of the Ottonian and even the Carolingian revivals of early Christian antiquity. Their delicacy and subtle naturalism can have no other source.

Two ivory kings, one rather badly damaged, are important examples of this group. They half turn towards each other, and obviously once decorated the same object, probably a reliquary casket or a portable altar. They wear the same short tunics and cloaks fastened on the shoulder; their regalia and the flat arcade and simple capitals in front of which they stand are also typical of the period. The undamaged king wears ankle-length boots and stands on a typical Winchester acanthus leaf, further indications of a date no later than the early twelfth century. The refinement of detail, subtly modelled heads and delicate limbs, are all characteristic of Mosan influence as seen in the Notger panel.

Perhaps the most important ivory monument from the twelfth century is a large altar cross assembled from seven pieces of walrus ivory and nearly 24 in. (60 cm) high, now in the Cloisters Collection in New York. It is decorated with quite exceptional lavishness: on the front is a *Lignum vitae* – the Tree of Life – with its branches lopped off, and Adam and Eve grasping its base (the original corpus is now lost); in the centre, a medallion of swirling forms shows St John, St Peter, the Prophet Isaiah, and Moses with the

Brazen Serpent, the Old Testament prefiguration of the Crucifixion; at the ends, three of the original four scenes survive, with the Deposition on the right, the Three Maries on the left, and the Ascension at the top. On the back is another richly carved medallion carried by two flying angels, which includes the *Agnus Dei*, pierced in the breast by Synagogue, with St John behind. On the cross, framed busts of prophets bear scrolls with quotations from the Old Testament. Three of the evangelist symbols are shown, only St Matthew's being missing. A major inscription is engraved on the front and sides of the cross. Most figures carry scrolls with texts that refer to the Passion and emphasize the prophecies that link the Old with the New Testament, a constant preoccupation of twelfth-century thinkers.

The date remains controversial, ranging from *c*. 1130 to 1180 or even later. Central to the arguments is the so-called 'dampfold' style, introduced to English art by a 'Master Hugo', who illustrated a magnificent Bible for the wealthy abbey of Bury St Edmunds in the early 1130s. It articulates the human figure by outlining the limbs like a rather large, wet, Victorian bathing costume. Once established, this style, fundamentally inspired by Byzantine art, dominated English twelfth-century art. Elements of it can be detected in the altar cross; does it mark the beginnings of the dampfold style, or show its last remnants and therefore belong to the 'Transitional' style of 1175–1200?

Although, taken as a whole, it is a magnificent piece of work enormously rich in content, there are clear signs of some naïvety and lack of sensitivity in detail, which indicate an artist still searching for his style. The refined sophistication of the late twelfth century is totally lacking here. Heads of individual figures are rather large and even clumsy; the eyes, globular and sketchy in execution, bear a remarkable resemblance to those of the Crucifixion plaque in Brussels, dating 1050–1100, and none to the refinement and smoothness of the late pieces. The same is true of the draperies. Above all, the whole composition at the ends of the cross arms shows none of the subtle spatial understanding displayed in the late-twelfth-century works, like the Ascension panel, now in the Victoria and Albert Museum, where a closely packed crowd is far more naturalistically and convincingly realized. Nevertheless, the sheer wealth of carving and rich iconography make the Cloisters Cross one of the masterpieces of the twelfth century.

It has been suggested that a splendid fragmentary figure of the crucified Christ, now in Oslo, carved almost fully in the round from a large piece of walrus ivory, may be the corpus from the Cloisters Cross. Although this is possible, it is certainly not carved by the same craftsman. Not only is it a little later, but the sculptor's background and training were very different, his style, especially in the loin-cloth, based on the school of Roger of Helmarshausen, a goldsmith active in lower Saxony *c*. 1100–25. No trace of this influence can be detected in the Cloisters Cross.

It is difficult to establish the more precise provenance of English ivories. Stylistic evidence does not always agree with the find place. Ivories are small and portable. Thus, the beautifully carved decorative fragment of a figure in a pierced foliage scroll found at St Albans, Hertfordshire, finds its closest parallels in the work of the scriptorium at Canterbury Cathedral, Kent, while the style known at the abbey of St Albans is clearly shown in a double-sided comb, illustrated with many scenes from the New Testament, now in London. No doubt craftsmen of ability travelled extensively, and it is therefore more rewarding to establish where such craftsmen received their training and what sources were available to them.

A carver working for the Danish royal house produced the third altar cross to survive. Only a little smaller than the other two, it was made for the 'daughter of the great King Svein', probably Svein III who ruled from 1152 to 1157. Like the comb in London, its style is very close indeed to that of the so-called 'Alexis Master' who illuminated the famous St Albans psalter, now in Hildesheim. There is another connection in a goldsmith named Anketyl who, after some years in the service of the King of Denmark, became a monk at St Albans and made the major shrine of the abbey's patron saint between 1124 and 1129.

Much the same is true on the continent. A fine panel of the Crucifixion decorates the cover of a gospel book, probably from the church of St Gereon in Cologne. The sharp folds, however, outlined by double lines and the angular movement of the figures, not only in the ivory but also in some of the illustrations that decorate the manuscript, show that both were certainly produced by artists trained in Flanders rather than Cologne.

In the Rhineland, and indeed probably in Cologne, a whole series of ivories was carved in the 'pricked style', so called because small notches nick the lines of the drapery. Among them is a group of large, almost square panels some 6 in. (15 cm) high, made up out of pieces of walrus ivory. Some retain decorated frames that serve to hold the relatively narrow pieces of ivory together. The well-rounded forms and the rather plump faces with large eyes characteristically marked with pupils, seem to continue the Mosan style of earlier in the century – a style ultimately derived from the soft naturalism of early Christian ivories. Compositions are also linked closely with the same source. A Nativity, for example, shows the scene within a walled city, a perspective view

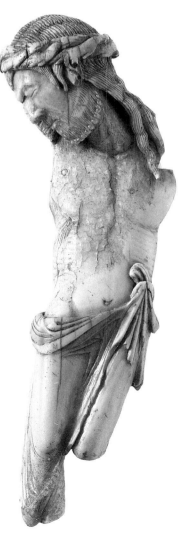

Below: A fine, walrus ivory crucifix figure. *c*. 1125–50; 7³/₅ in. (19.5 cm).

Above: Bishop and two knights from the Lewis chessmen shown in colour on page 80.

Above right: Walrus ivory tableman, or games counter. Twelfth-century; 2½ in. (6.2 cm) diameter. It was carved in Cologne with the scene of Samson as the Philistines' prisoner.

typical of late antique illumination and the Ottonian revivals of it. The weight and monumentality of this style, found also in the other twelfth-century arts, especially in major architectural sculpture, might be called the most typically Romanesque.

In England, too, a similar 'typically Romanesque' style is also found *c.* 1125–50. A Tau crosier, decorated with the Virgin and Child on one side and a Christ in Majesty on the other, both between large and almost dominant inhabited scrolls, is as fully rounded in its forms as the 'pricked' style in the Rhineland. But its far richer treatment and its fleshy foliate vocabulary make attribution to a southern English workshop a certainty. It comes closest to mid-century manuscripts illuminated at Winchester and might be called the fully Romanesque version of traditional Winchester design. Further north, and closely linked with the major sculpture of the West Front of Lincoln Cathedral, four whalebone panels were carved, most probably the sides of a portable altar, a unique English survival if so. Some of the standing figures of the twelve apostles are carved under decoratively pierced domed canopies, which prove that the craftsman responsible must have seen either Byzantine ivories or major architectural sculpture derived from such a source.

One of the most remarkable finds of Romanesque ivories was made in 1831 when seventy-eight chess pieces were discovered in a cave on Lewis in the Outer Hebrides. They clearly do not make up a number of complete sets. None is incompletely carved, so this was not a workshop. They were probably a merchant's stock, perhaps lost by shipwreck. Decoration on the seats of the kings, queens and bishops proves them part of a whole group of carvings, some found in Scandinavia, one in the river at Hamburg. The decorative vocabulary is known in architectural sculpture in eastern Britain and in Scandinavia. Trade along the seaboard of the North Sea is well recorded in the twelfth century. The severe forms and the heavy, strictly controlled pattern of the chessmen climax the High Romanesque in English miniature sculpture.

The Transitional style

In the second half of the twelfth century, the quantity of ivory carving was once more in decline. The appearance of poor-quality bone carvings in Cologne suggests that walrus ivory now became as difficult to get in northern Europe as elephant ivory. Perhaps, also, ivory carving of high quality simply went out of fashion. Certainly the finest work that survives from the period tends to be in gold, silver and enamel – the work of goldsmiths rather than ivory carvers. The few surviving ivories attempt to come to terms with a new style, called 'Transitional', a name in general use but an unfortunate one suggesting that the style forms the bridge from Romanesque to Gothic art, which was to be dominant in northern Europe for at least three centuries. But it does not form a transition; rather it existed alongside Gothic, with its roots in the third quarter of the twelfth century. At the end of the century all art was looking for a direct contact with nature, unknown since the Roman period, and it reacted against the stylization and symbolism of a Romanesque that grew increasingly sterile. The art of antiquity, both in its early Graeco-Roman and its more contemporary Byzantine form, played an important part in this search. In the creation of the 'Gothic' the idealism of antiquity was of the greater importance, while in the 'Transitional' style both Byzantinism and perhaps the imitation of nature – true naturalism – played a more significant role.

Ivory carving played only a minor part but the rare pieces created were often of outstanding quality. Thus, a small but exquisite Ascension has all the soft naturalism that rivals the work of the finest goldsmiths of the period. The Virgin and the hunched and frightened apostles seem to be seen from above, where the figure of Christ is assisted in rising to heaven by two angels. The draperies are thin and fluid, revealing well-understood and moving bodies below them. Rhythmic forms create real space in the tightly confined depth of the relief. Within its frame, the scene is almost as convincing in its naturalism as if it were observed through a window.

A fragmentary Flight into Egypt, with its soft draperies and complicated interplay of fully rounded forms, proves that work of the highest quality and great expressive power could still be produced *c*. 1175–1200.

In the small statuette of a seated Virgin and Child an ivory carver rivalled the achievements of goldsmiths and perhaps even of major architectural sculptors. His free-standing and independent piece of sculpture is probably early thirteenth century. The best works of the 'Transitional' style are 'international' in character; this could have been carved anywhere from England to the Rhineland, or even in the Île de France, where the greatest achievements of the High Gothic were realized *c*. 1200–50. This miniature sculpture seems to combine some of the best elements of the 'Transitional' style with those of the High Gothic. Not until the later thirteenth century did ivory carvers once more attract wealthy patrons and produce the work of high quality which assured their popularity until the end of the Middle Ages.

Sicily

A European Muslim community renowned for its ivories flourished in Sicily in the twelfth and thirteenth centuries. Although Sicily had been conquered by the Normans in 1072, both there and in other parts of southern Italy the Norman rulers made a point of employing Muslim artists and craftsmen, either retaining them or bringing them from Egypt, Syria or Mesopotamia to work on specific projects, as when Roger II of Sicily commissioned Arab artists to paint the ceiling of the Capella Palatina in Palermo.

The great majority of the Siculo-Arabic ivories are painted rather than carved. There are, however, a number of boxes with relief decoration cut in a fairly shallow, flat, two-dimensional technique against a hatched blackened ground, which do not fit the tradition established in Moorish Spain. Their origin is the subject of debate. It seems probable that a group of cylindrical *pyxides* decorated with slender scrolling vines and long-necked animals and birds, which are fitted with the lancet-shaped mounts used on identifiably Sicilian caskets, were also made there. Yet more difficult to attribute with certainty are the rare wooden caskets inlaid with ivory decorated with

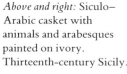

Above and right: Siculo–Arabic casket with animals and arabesques painted on ivory. Thirteenth-century Sicily.

circular medallions or scrolls containing silhouetted human and animal figures strongly reminiscent of those found in Near Eastern silver-inlaid metalwork of the same period. These are generally dated late twelfth or early thirteenth century.

The vast majority of the surviving painted ivories are rectangular or cylindrical caskets, preserved in monasteries and church treasuries. Unlike the Spanish Umayyad caskets, these were not made as exclusive objects for royal patrons but were commercially produced in large quantities. The depiction of figures of saints alongside the Arabic inscriptions and other characteristically Islamic ornamental motifs and the existence of some painted crosiers reveal that these ivories were produced specifically with the Christian market in mind. The inscriptions, in a cursive script, took no account of this, consisting generally of conventional Arabic good wishes to the owner, often with specific allusions to Allah and the Koran, or occasionally of profane verses from *The Thousand and One Nights*. The Christian clientele evidently saw the Arabic script in a purely decorative light, doubtless feeling that it added to the generally luxurious and exotic cachet of the object. Painted ivory combs were also made and were employed by the clergy in liturgical procedures.

Below: An ivory comb with painted decoration, made by Sicilian Muslim craftsmen in Spain for a Christian patron.

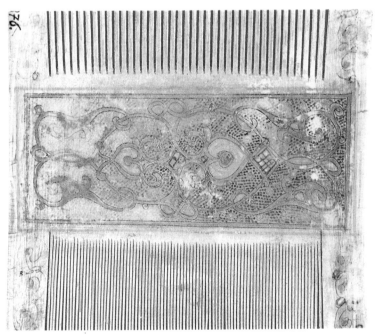

The painted caskets obviously required much less ivory than the carved ones; only thin sheets of it were used, stuck on to a wooden frame and secured with ivory pins and gilt metal braces. The designs of hunting scenes, by now part of the standard decorative repertoire of all the Islamic arts, musicians (particularly harpists), peacocks and other birds standing with their wings folded and looking backwards, hares, hounds, cheetahs and other creatures associated with the chase,

stylized plant forms and linear arabesques are painted in a somewhat cursory manner in a palette of sepia, red, green and, more rarely, blue, outlined in black or grey, sometimes with the addition of painted or leaf gilding. The paint was water-based and has, as a result, often almost completely disappeared. Too strong a design, particularly when combined with heavy gilding, should be regarded with suspicion. When gilding wears away it leaves a dark stain where the ivory discoloured when it was concealed from the light. In sharp contrast to the ivories from the caliphate of Cordoba in Spain, the composition sometimes appears rather undisciplined and the individual motifs, though symmetrically placed, are often broadly spaced and random-looking. Yet the subjects have a spontaneous liveliness lacking in the dignified Cordoban figures. The style of the decoration is quite distinctive and has been related both to the painted ceiling of the Palazzo Reale with its strong Fatimid influence and, more aptly perhaps, to Sicilian painted pottery of the period. Yet there are frequently familiar images from the more easterly reaches of the Islamic world, such as a wide-eyed, typically Seljuk moon-face framed by long, tapering braids of hair.

Sometimes the painted decoration is combined with the patterns of incised dotted and concentric circles filled with coloured pigment used in the earliest Near Eastern Islamic ivories, and occasionally this constitutes the only ornament. Where this is the case the attribution to Sicily rests partly on the similarity of the metal mounts to those used on the painted caskets.

The Sicilian painted ivories went on being produced into the thirteenth century. A small but distinctive group of wooden caskets encrusted with ivory cut into figurative silhouettes showing pairs of affronted hounds and other animals, and a very lavishly decorated example, with sphinxes and scenes of the chase, are also thought by some to have been made in Palermo in the thirteenth century, by others to be Spanish products of this time; they were perhaps both.

When the Muslim community in Sicily was suppressed from the late twelfth century onwards, the craftsmen are believed to have moved across to Spain and some ivory caskets of the Sicilian type, though with the painted decoration consisting of purely geometric devices and occasional inscriptions, have been attributed to the Nasrid kingdom of Granada on the grounds that the designs are characteristic of fourteenth-century Nasrid art. The emphasis on geometry is evident in a minor group of carved ivory boxes also thought to have been made in Spain around the same time, where animal and figural subjects on a ground of repetitious tight spiral scrolls are contained within a framework of intersecting strapwork, creating a pattern of stars and crosses.

Late Middle Ages

The Gothic period

The thirteenth century inherited from the previous hundred years a range of magnificent objects in which ivory was one of a conjunction of precious materials. An assembly, in which the leading parts were played by gold, silver and precious gems, represented an ideal from which the Middle Ages never fully departed. The ivory components of some of these *pièces de résistance* still survive, but the relative scarcity of such *objets d'art* in their complete form reflects the temptation to plunder the more easily adapted gems and metals. Ivory had long been valued as a worthy foil to the blaze of metals and stones, as the most exquisite medium in which to indicate the human form, as the perfect means of suggesting in miniature the marble statues manning the scaled-down City of God. The splendour of the shrines and reliquaries that had been created by 1200 might be said to have saturated the market. Occasions to create a glorious new housing for a relic or a shrine for a major saint were now rare. But the Gothic period did not dismiss the past as easily as has sometimes been supposed. The antiquity of reliquaries was revered as a stamp of authenticity on the contents. Old feretories were not abandoned but further embellished: the head of the statue of St Foy at Conques is of the later Roman period, the figure was made in the ninth century, altered in the tenth century, embellished in the fourteenth century and modified in the sixteenth century and again in the seventeenth. The long extended lifespan of such glorious pieces left little room for a Gothic creation where a more delicate colour range sympathetic to ivory could have played a major part.

By 1200 most high altars were provided with large gospel books or Bibles. Ivory, by natural association with its ancient use in writing tablets, was well established as a fitting medium for their book-covers. The smaller books in monastic and episcopal libraries were shelved in the modern manner and three-dimensional covers are counter-productive when books are stored in this way. After 1200, book-covers studded in hard materials disappear, a feature of the growing non-liturgical reading of books.

So by about 1200 the worker in ivory had lost two of his most conspicuous outlets. At the same time the walrus, the main source of his raw material, had been hunted almost to extinction. Elephant ivory from Africa and India was not readily available before the mid thirteenth century. It follows that the years 1200 to 1250 represented a relatively lean time for ivory sculpture. However, pieces which can be associated with that half-century are outstanding for their originality and, remarkably, an unusual number have been, at one time or another, attributed to English sculptors. This may reflect a strong survival of the craft in England, or may relate to the differences in major stone restoration in England versus the continent during the nineteenth century. Relatively soon after the ravages of the Napoleonic period the portals of the great French cathedrals, such as Amiens and Laon, were systematically repaired, often under the guidance of Viollet-le-Duc. The result was a uniform blandness and gentility of face and draperies. In England, on the other hand, despite the spate of Victorian neo-Gothicism, damage done in the sixteenth-century Reformation and the seventeenth-century Civil War now looked mellow and romantic, and some major groups of early Gothic sculpture, especially that at Wells, did escape the politely 'improving' hand of the nineteenth-century restorer. A handful of ivories has been restored but the body of most genuine pieces is untouched. No wonder they often recall the vitality and eccentricity of English sculpture on a larger scale. The chief difficulty facing a specialist in ivory carving is the lack of localization. The relatively short history of most ivory carvings, which seldom goes back before the heroic nineteenth-century collectors, presents a considerable hurdle. We are driven to using the visual evidence and relating them to major sculpture which still retains its original context, a method of enquiry which cannot be backed up by the customary rigorous examination of circumstantial evidence. Nevertheless, the remarkable unity of art in all media throughout the Gothic period gives some value to this approach.

The sculptor in ivory continued to work within the restricted range of liturgical furnishings, and in the making of chess and gaming pieces.

Crosier heads

The Mosan enameller and the ivory worker were rivals in decorating the crosier head. The inherited subject matter appears to have been confined, at this stage, to the foliate treatment, whereby the crosier becomes a flowering rod, or the dragon treatment, whereby the curved hook becomes the body and neck, as in the dragon crosier at Regensburg. But no surviving ivory shows the dragon's head confronted by a St Michael, as the metalworker was wont to do. There is a tendency to suggest that splendid ivory crosier heads such as the later twelfth-century example in the British Museum, with a cockatrice, a dragon and an eagle, are Italian. An equally vivacious crosier at Oxford, where the dragon confronts the *Agnus*

Dei, has been further embellished by metal trimmings and a figurine of *c.* 1200. In a crosier now in Baltimore, the eagle of St John meeting the dragon has the same superb modelling and rich colour as the British Museum example. The centre of production of this group is believed to have been Sicily, specially favourably placed for the import of ivory. The Baltimore eagle is 6⅛ in. (15.5 cm) across; the tusk must have come from a mighty elephant.

A bishop's crosier is likely to date from the year of his installation and this may enable us to sharpen our knowledge of patronage in ivory carving in the early thirteenth century. There was perhaps a reluctance to bury a fine crosier of precious materials when a bishop died. The opening of the coffins of Archbishop Walter de Grey (1216–55) and Archbishop Geoffrey de Ludham (1258–65) in York Minster in 1967–8 provided a valuable case in point. De Grey was appointed Bishop of Worcester in 1214, surely the year of the making of the simple crosier which was buried in his tomb. Its modest leaf-work is related to the foliage in a Worcester manuscript of the same date. The sculptor of his Purbeck effigy did not copy the actual crosier but devised one in which the confidence of full stiff leaf is allowed full and

most vigorous play. After his installation as Bishop of Worcester, de Grey went to Rome and was there till 1215, when he acquired the archbishopric of York. Did he commission a grander, and possibly Italian, crosier upon that second elevation? If so, the clergy could well have decided against burying it. In 1265 de Ludham was buried at York with a crosier of exquisite workmanship, a filigree of leaves, entirely carried out in wood. A foliate crosier of equal elegance, though not in double filigree work, survives in the church of Maubeuge. It is of silver gilt and is thought to be fourteenth century.

Chess and gaming pieces

Even in the modest field of gaming pieces the early thirteenth century has left some striking work, inaugurated by the splendid group of twenty-five ivory counters from the Horace Walpole collection. They are of fully modelled and vigorous beasts, including apparently the bestiary stories of the lioness who mistook her image in the mirror for a cub, and the elephant and castle. Some – no doubt originally half – of them are stained for differentiation. If they come from one set, and not from an ivory worker's stock, they would not suit the draughts board as we know it, which is designed for twenty-four. Counters are of great antiquity, long predating written literature about draughts. Similar problems beset chessmen. There are three splendid chess pieces of knights, one in Vienna, one in New York and the last in Oxford; their armour and the entwining of the dragons with proto stiff leaf favour an English provenance.

Difficulties arise, however, in the identification of the apparent 'castle' in the Victoria and Albert Museum. The base has heads in roundels and foliate scrolls, comparable with monumental decoration from Peterborough and Canterbury Cathedral, so there is some basis for a claim that this is English work. The drapery, hair-styles and armour all declare the early thirteenth century. However, at this date the castle or the rook was represented by a watchman. There are some fine examples, horn to mouth. This lively piece may in fact be a king.

The Virgin and Child

A carved ivory fragment found in Blackfriars, London, shows the lower half of a draped figure with foliage carving seated on a throne of a type which can be associated with English work of *c.* 1200. Is this a seated king or queen from a chess set, or a Virgin and Child for devotional purposes? Some chess bishops are carved with acolytes around their knees formed from the same block. The same device is used on a not dissimilar scale in an ivory Adoration of the Magi: the Virgin and Child are flanked by Kings bringing gifts, carved within the same block. Despite the loss of the heads, the tenderness of the gesture in which the child turns towards his mother and throws his arms around her neck is still legible. This individualistic treatment is characteristic of the Virgin and Child in all the arts of the thirteenth century. It represents a humanizing of the more rigid *Sedes Sapientiae* ('Throne of Wisdom') type, perhaps derived from the Byzantine icons of the Mother and Child. The fluent drapery of this early-thirteenth-century Virgin relates it to the classic group of the seated Virgin and Child of the same date, now in Hamburg.

The most striking development for the ivory carver *c.* 1200–20 appears to have been the emergence of the free-standing ivory figure of the Virgin and Child, inspired by the growing cult of Our Lady. It was created as a visual focus of worship. As such, ivory is at a disadvantage. It cannot be appreciated at a great distance. Carried in procession by chanting acolytes, it has no sparkle or brilliance to compel the eye in compensation for its small scale. Although some of Europe's most significant ivories are now in cathedral treasuries or religious foundations, their natural home is the aristocrat's private oratory. Where else did the idea of a focus for private prayer originate?

A free-standing ivory of the Virgin and Child now in the Victoria and Albert Museum is a magnificent figure of early-twelfth-century date. It stands 12¾ in. (32.5 cm) high and yet the inclination to accommodate the curve of the tusk is very slight. It must, therefore, have come from an elephant tusk of peculiar magnificence, perhaps looted in the scandalous sack of Constantinople by the Fourth Crusade in 1204. The small diptych or polyptych of the same date, made up of plaques of ivory, must have served as a miniature altarpiece. The novelty, as far as the west was concerned, was not in making relief carvings in ivory of religious subjects, but in creating entire objects so formed as secret altarpieces; not in having a statue of the Virgin but in making one on a miniature scale for private devotion. This new small scale brought the idea within the reach of the ivory carver, but other materials were used too. The early-thirteenth-century wooden Langton Hall Madonna is 18¾ in. (47.5 cm) tall, almost possible in ivory. If the idea of ivory caskets ornamented with romantic subjects probably came from Arab sources, the corresponding provision of exquisite ivory pieces for religious devotion came from the Byzantine world. Both ideas were probably disseminated by the Crusades.

The Île de France school

If the most interesting ivories of 1200–25 frequently hint at an English provenance, those of 1225–50 point in the direction of the Île de France. The *locus classicus* for the development of northern

Above: Broken carved ivory fragment of an enthroned figure. Probably English work. *c.*1200; 1½ in. (4 cm) wide.

Far right: Ivory Adoration of the Magi, carved from a single block. Early-thirteenth-century; 3½ in. (9 cm). Although the Virgin and Child are headless, the pose is the loving one, known as La Glykophilouse, recalling the Song of Songs: 'His left hand is under my head and his right hand embraces me.'

French sculpture is the south jamb of the central doorway of the western portal of Reims Cathedral. The four jamb figures are masterpieces of three discrete figurative styles, which, from their datable appearance in other contexts, may be said to proceed chronologically from the west, or right-hand, end towards the door. They are unlikely to have been planned as a group and were probably brought together towards the end of the building programme, c. 1255. The famous Visitation pair owe most, probably, to the traditional classicism inherited from the metalwork shop of Nicholas of Verdun. The Angel of the Annunciation is a critical landmark of the next stage, but the Virgin Annunciate has a simplicity, a freedom from convention, a slender and calm uprightness contrasting with the rival exaggerations to either side of her. Related figures appear at Villeneuve-l'Archevêque (the west portal, c. 1245) and in the Trumeau St Geneviève (c. 1230) from her church in Paris, and the ivory standing Virgin and Child, now in Baltimore. Her satellites include a Virgin and Child from Aulne-sur-Sambre in Namur. The delicacy, restraint, almond eyes and gentle stance link several outstanding pieces to form one of the finest groups of ivory sculpture, which could be called the Île de France school. There was, without question, at least one workshop producing brilliant ivories in France before 1248.

The fragment of the Deposition from the Cross, now in the Louvre, from the Île de France school is perhaps the most superb surviving sculpture in any medium c. 1230–40. The restraint of the Reims major sculpture is here infused with an elegiac intensity. This ivory was in Italy before 1896 and may be one of the few surviving pieces from which Giovanni Pisano (fl. 1248–1314) could have profited. A comparison has been drawn between the Sibyl's drapery on his Pistoya Pulpit of 1297, and the Virgin's drapery in this group. The Deposition ivory is a fragment 11½ in. (29 cm) high, but must come from a major altarpiece of cathedral status. Pisa Cathedral, which still possesses a Pisano ivory of 1298, is possible. This would account for the less striking but real evidence of French Gothic influence upon the older Nicola Pisano, who was working there from 1260. The central subject of the altarpiece should have been a Crucifixion. Study of such a Crucifixion would explain the harmony between Giovanni Pisano's own rendering of the subject and the later thirteenth-century French Christ on the Cross, now in Florence.

The idea of forming an altarpiece of a series of narrative subjects in ivory, no doubt set in a framework of gilded metal or wood, was apparently short-lived. All the surviving evidence is c. 1200–40. It includes the fine Adoration of the Magi, the related Descent into Limbo, the Three Maries at the Sepulchre and the Resurrection, c. 1250, all in the Copenhagen National Museum. Slightly earlier are a Deposition (the Hunt Collection) and a Morsel of Judas (Victoria and Albert Museum) which could have once belonged to the same ensemble. Almost as important as the great Louvre Deposition are the Two Maries (Victoria and Albert Museum) indicating another altarpiece of the Île de France school.

Above: Standing ivory Virgin and Child. c. 1225–50; 9½ in. (24 cm). Characteristic of the Île de France school. (c. 1225–35).

Right and far right: Deposition from the Cross and detail of the head of Christ. c. 1230–40; 11½ in. (29 cm). This fragment probably comes from an altarpiece showing scenes from the Passion cycle.

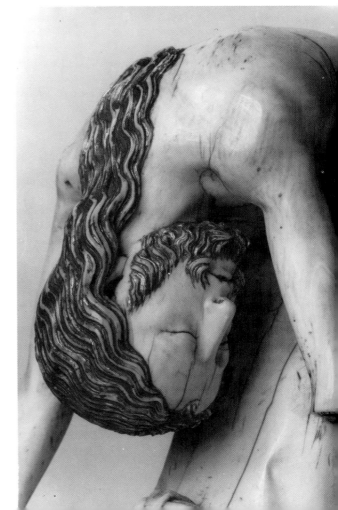

The prodigious quantity of precious ivory needed for an entire altarpiece may have provoked a search for a more practical substitute. Alabaster was to provide it. The carved alabaster altarpiece commissioned in 1367 for the high altar of Windsor Castle Chapel by Edward III, King of England, cost a massive price and, made in ivory a hundred years before, would have been even more expensive. The smallness of scale does not appear to have been regarded as a disadvantage – witness the Westminster retable of 1268, or the narrative panels of the Duccio Maesta of 1311 – but the use of ivory for major retables does appear to have been discontinued just when its use for miniature personal altarpieces flooded the market.

Ivory was ideally suited to one subject where two figures naturally bow towards one another: the Annunciation. The beauty of the group in the Louvre from the Île de France workshop, again allied to the Reims west front, is flawed by a restoration which makes the Angel taller than Our Lady.

The theme of a free-standing Annunciation continued c. 1250–1300 and inspired two of the loveliest pairs to survive, one on loan to the Metropolitan Museum in New York, and the other in the Bargello, Florence. Devotion to the Annunciation was very strong from the later thirteenth century, although the rosary, as known today, waited until 1475. To repeat the Ave Maria 150 times instead of saying the 150 Psalms suited the capacity and education of the laity and lay brethren, at least from the twelfth century, and this devotion was encouraged by a visualization of the original encounter. The Annunciation groups were the prayer, the mantra, of Christianity made visible.

The 1230s saw important developments in the seated Virgin and Child groups. The art historian Danielle Gamborit-Chopin has identified several figures which bear such a striking relationship to one another that they must be the product of a single workshop. The output includes at least one object in relief not carved in the round. There is undoubtedly a close family connection between the Louvre Virgin and the relief head on the reliquary of Balledent. These grave figures are by definition earlier than 1248.

The Anglo-Scandinavian connection
In 1248–9 the English historian Matthew Paris made a visit to Norway. No doubt he took with him a bag of small but precious gifts from Henry III, king of England, to his brother king of Norway (and probably to other suitable recipients). An amazing body of works of art in Scandinavia appear to declare dependence upon English art of the later 1240s. There must have been at least one new crucifix in his luggage. Ivory crucifixes were known in England long before 1248. The torso of a walrus ivory crucifix of c. 1200 was found in Finsbury, London. The corpus in the Metropolitan Museum, New York, has been dated c. 1250 but has far more of the gravity and simplicity of the Chartres north and south portals, or the Amiens Beau Dieu: surely it falls into the c. 1230 group.

On the other hand, it has been suggested that the great crucifix of Herlufsholm is closely linked with Westminster. The loin-cloth of the Herlufsholm crucifix has been matched most convincingly with drapery sculpture at Westminster Abbey, notably that of the south-eastern censing angel from the transept, executed c. 1250–55. The management of the hair and the face also tally very well with the Westminster chapter house angel of c. 1250. At Lincoln Cathedral and Crowland Abbey too the drapery is tied with precisely the same knot as the Herlufsholm loin-cloth. So this exquisite crucifix is likely to represent sculpture of the Westminster school in ivory c. 1250. We may assume that we have here a presentation piece from England, one of the handful of works which were to be studied and repeated with such care in Scandinavia.

Sainte Chapelle and its successors

The Westminster Abbey sculpture and the flowering of sculpture in Scandinavia, inspired by such pieces as the Herlufsholm crucifix, presuppose the style of the Île de France school of c. 1230–40. But the next development stemmed from Paris, though it is declared by the angel in the south-east spandrel of the south wall in Westminster Abbey south transept. It must, therefore, have reached London immediately after 1250, and certainly before 1255. Its impact was as instantaneous and dramatic as Diaghilev's London season of 1928, or Dior's New Look after the Second World War. Thirteenth-century art in any medium falls either before or after the ivory Virgin of the Ste Chapelle in Paris.

Built by St Louix IX, king of France, to house his relics of the Passion, acquired from Constantinople, Ste Chapelle was formally dedicated on 26 April 1248. Its embellishment marks a new, but short-lived, development of bulky and dramatic stone figure sculpture on a large scale, but this very conspicuous novelty made little impact. Everyone's attention was diverted by a remarkable small figure, whose documented association with Ste Chapelle has been fully demonstrated: the ivory Virgin and Child now in the Louvre. Such is the caution of art historians that it is usually allotted a generalized date of 'c. 1250–60', when the actual consecration, a mere twenty-four months earlier, furnishes the natural context for its creation. St Louis left France on crusade in the same year, 1248, and did not return until 1254. The immediate acclaim that greeted this, probably

Above: The Ste Chapelle Virgin and Child. 1248; 16 in. (41 cm). Art in the thirteenth century falls either before or after this figure. It was crowned with gold for feast days (see page 100).

the most influential ivory carving ever executed, is so clearly traceable that to date it after 1254 would be an embarrassment.

The fashion for a swaying stance may be traced through all figurative arts in Europe during the period 1250–75. It has no practical advantage for the worker in stone or marble or the illuminator, but it was forced upon the ivory carver by his medium. The Ste Chapelle Virgin standing 16 in. (41 cm) high is one of the tallest figures ever extracted from an elephant's tusk. As radiography of an early-fourteenth-century statuette of the Virgin and Child sufficiently demonstrates, the carver in ivory was not only confined by the curved limitations of the tusk, but by its pulpy inner core which he must endeavour to pierce in the least conspicuous place. The height at which a fourteenth-century ivory Virgin carries the Child is not only an aspect of balancing the weight – the emergence of the pulpy core is sometimes concealed between the Child and the Virgin's shoulder.

These characteristics can be observed in the stone Virgin of the Trumeau of the north door of Notre-Dame, Paris, of 1250. They are combined with the piquant face of the Ste Chapelle Virgin in the Annunciate Angel from the jamb of Reims central doorway, a gatecrasher in this position. This angel was evidently intended to flank St Remi among the later group in what is now the north doorway. But its winsome ways ousted the calmer Angel of the older master, as its flirtatious fellow angels were to seduce Europe for the next half-century. Setting aside the scale, the pose would again fit into the confines of a curved tusk. The smiling Angel of Reims is the clearest witness to the power of the new fashion set by the Master of the Ste Chapelle Virgin, who deserves one of the most exalted places in the pantheon of Gothic Art. The consequence of his delicious Parisian coquette, with a smile as enigmatic as and a great deal more joyful than that of the Mona Lisa, was a deluge of smiling Angels, smiling Devils, smiling Virgins, smiles appropriate and otherwise, flooding Europe for half a century. The trivial and repetitive sequel has overshadowed the irresistible prototype. After the Virgin of the Ste Chapelle processed the great Virgins of the trumeaux of Reims (central portal) and of Amiens (south transept portal); the smiling Virgins with their tilted hips of St Corneille, Compiègne (now in Compiègne St Jacques) and of Abbeville (now in the Louvre); the smiling Angels of the Westminster transept spandrels. After her trailed the grimacing damned of the Bamberg tympanum of the Last Judgement, the mincing weepers from the tomb of Adelais of Champagne in Dilo Abbey. Resplendent with her encrusted jewels, crowned with real gold, the Virgin of Ste Chapelle probably cost as many francs as a cathedral portal

and focused all eyes. Her influence on major sculpture stretched from Westminster to the Mediterranean and from Regensburg to Cosenza, her power within the field of ivory carving was almost total. She established an inescapable norm which later Virgins had to follow, except in the graver climate of Italy. What is more, the prestige of so outstanding a masterpiece, combined with a new access to a ready supply of elephant tusks, ushered in a century of abundant demand for carvings in ivory.

The immediate offspring of the Ste Chapelle Virgin include three major works of art for which we have a reasonable context. The first is not in ivory at all, but in silver: a book-binding with the Coronation of the Virgin (her face closely corresponding to the Ste Chapelle Virgin) flanked by SS Blaise and Vincent, and below it the Virgin and Child attended by the Blessed Rambert and the Abbot Arnaund who ruled over the monastery of St Blaise from 1247 to 1276. This piece is the art of the inside west front of Reims Cathedral in miniature, a complete vocabulary of architectural and decorative motifs.

The second is the remarkable, if perhaps somewhat repaired, Virgin of the Abbot Bohuslaw (1248–59) in the treasury at Zwettl. The records of Zwettl say that the abbot's gift, placed on the high altar on great feasts, was from northern France and that with it came reliquaries which contained relics of the Virgin and the saints. The figurines from the reliquaries include another Annunciation group, a King from an Adoration, and four half-length angels carrying crowns. The shallow-set eyes and the mischievous smiles declare close association with the Ste Chapelle Virgin throughout the whole group.

The third is the Virgin in the Taft Museum, Cincinnati, who is fully aware of her duty to outshine the Ste Chapelle Madonna. She cannot do it, but it is not for lack of trying. Once a star of the treasury of St Denis, she was there flanked by two candle-bearing angels, which are now part of the reliquary of St Romanus in Rouen. Their upward gaze was presumably directed to a third angel, flying down to place a crown upon the Virgin's head. According to the St Denis inventories of 1505 and 1634 the group included three angels. A third angel coming down from the clouds is a standard feature of Virgins attended by candle-bearing angels in later-thirteenth- and early-fourteenth-century ivories, but such an arrangement depends upon the architectural framework of a tabernacle. The account book of Jehan le Scelleur of Paris lists: '1325 – Pour une ymaige de Notre Dame d'ivire a tabanacle XIX L' (1325 – For an image of Our Lady in ivory in tabernacle, 19 livres). A number of the Virgins still reposing in their tabernacles are in fact carved in the round, so we must assume that many of those which now

Right and far right: Ivory triptych from St Sulpice de Tarn. Fourteenth-century; 12½ × 11⅔ in. (32 × 29 cm). The detail (*right*) shows the figure of the Virgin.

Right: Seated ivory Virgin and Child. *c.*1320–30; 16 in. (40 cm). The pose accommodates the curve of the tusk.

Far right: French ivory statue of the Virgin and Child. Mid-thirteenth-century. The smiling Virgin is clearly related to the Ste Chapelle masterpiece.

Opposite: The Ste Chapelle Virgin and Child. Mid-fourteenth-century. Crowned with gold and adorned with jewels, the ivory was set on the Virgin's altar on feast days.

Right: The smiling Angel of the Annunciation from Reims Cathedral, carved in stone. Before 1255. The resemblance between her face and that of the Ste Chapelle Virgin is unmistakable proof of the latter's influence on contemporary carvers.

stand in isolation were originally so framed. These tabernacles, usually furnished with four hinged wings for protection, are among the glories of the major museums. The central theme of the Virgin supported by two candle-bearing angels reflects the liturgical practice of two candle-bearing acolytes accompanying the priest at High Mass, when he goes to preach the Gospel. In the play of *La Nonne qui Laisse son Abbaie*, which was performed outside the cathedral of Notre-Dame in Paris in 1345, the Virgin processes attended by two candle-bearing acolytes, the archangels Gabriel and Michael, who sing a rondel as they go. The tabernacles presenting this subject are among the loveliest things to survive from the Middle Ages, and frequently among the most complete. As they are generally displayed open we lose something of the sense of disclosure that must have enchanted their owners as they knelt and opened the doors to ask the Virgin to intercede for them. They range from the simplest disposition, with just the Virgin and Child and her two angels, to polyptychs as complicated as the standing Virgin with wings devoted to scenes of the Infancy of Christ. This kind of polyptych shades off into the triptych where the central group of the Virgin attended by angels on the lower tier is surrounded by scenes from the New Testament. In a prime example from the Musée de Cluny, Paris, typically the central group is linked to the Three Kings, forming an Adoration of the Magi, and leads to the Presentation in the Temple (a frequent choice because of its association with the Nunc Dimittis) in the same register on the right-hand side. The Visitation, another popular choice, illustrates in its turn the Magnificat. Above the three joyful scenes are the three sorrowful ones of the Crucifixion flanked by the Carrying of the Cross and the Deposition. The choice of secondary subjects in the wings of a tabernacle or a triptych depended more on the taste of the patron than on the workshop. The selection in the Musée de Cluny triptych might suggest that the patron was an old man: the oldest of the Three Kings (who always takes pride of place) presents myrrh for burial; Simeon declares the Nunc Dimittis ('Now lettest thou thy servant depart in peace'); an elderly bearded version of Longinus raises his spear as a preliminary to his acknowledgement, 'This indeed was the Son of God'; and an aged Joseph of Arimathea receives the body of the dead Christ in his arms.

It seems almost as if the standing Virgin was absorbed into her tabernacle and ultimately surrounded by these little scenes. But the seated Virgin, the *Sedes Sapientiae*, of such great importance as a large free-standing figure in the twelfth century, was not so easily absorbed into a miniature altarpiece, though there are examples of this usage. Two ivories survive where she remains free-standing; in one the back of her throne is richly carved with a scene of two fighting animals placed above an architectural design that could serve for a mid-thirteenth-century clerestory, in the other her throne is actually octagonal. A third example is a drawing published in the *Archaeological Journal* in 1861: an ivory of the Virgin seated upon a throne ornamented with figures, perhaps of the three Theological Virtues, fairly accurately dated to about 1280. This ivory and the famous embroidered Syon Cope were given to the Earl of Shrewsbury by the Nuns of Syon after the Order, originally founded by Henry V of England, returned to Britain in 1809. Nothing about the design would lead one to suspect that it was not a perfectly genuine piece, though the fruited staff might have been replaced. The 1861 engraving includes naturalistic leaves on the capitals of the base, which confirms a date *c.* 1250–1300, which is borne out by every feature of this fine seated figure. Where is it now?

The ivory workers and their fields of activity

So considerable was the prosperity of ivory carving in Paris by the mid thirteenth century that statutes were drawn up in the *Livre des métiers* of Etienne Boileau. The ivory workers were officially divided into specialized groups: some among those 'who paint and carve images', others among those who carve crucifixes and knife handles. These two corporations were reunited in the later fourteenth century. There were further subdivisions among the makers of secular pieces: the comb and lantern makers went together (no doubt they both used very thin slices of the material); the makers of writing tablets; the makers of dice; the makers of paternosters (early rosaries). Boileau's statutes appear to have classified according to the type of article produced, irrespective of the medium used. The conjunction of crucifixes and knife handles is not so strange as it may at first seem. Both require long slender pieces of ivory. They could be made from the pointed end of a tusk after the wider part had been used for a figure or laminated for tablets. The arms of a crucified Christ were carved separately and then attached. Assuming that the feet were worked at the tip of the tusk, and the arms from slivers, the Herlufsholm crucifix, for instance, could have been carved from a very slender tusk indeed.

The omission of crosier heads from the Boileau list could point to an Italian monopoly, which was undoubtedly broken further north, but which the Parisians, around 1250, may have had no wish to challenge, though they were to do so within twenty years. The Bargello in Florence possesses a very fine crosier, certainly Parisian, which may be assumed to have been made by the 1270s. It represents a new idea. Instead of the combat between dragons and the powers of good, we

have the Virgin and Child with attendant angels on one side and a Crucifixion with the Virgin and St John on the other. Some twenty crosiers survive with this basic iconography, plus several with variations; previously dated to the mid fourteenth century or even later. The freshly observed naturalism of the foliage on some of the best suggests a date not later than the 1270s, and many of them probably date *c.* 1270–1320.

Boileau's omission of makers of tabernacles, or miniature altarpieces, suggests that in 1250 these fields of activity had not yet been seriously explored by the ivory workers, though this is the realm in which the bulk of Gothic ivory sculpture now survives. Countless surviving triptychs, polyptychs and diptychs of 1250–1350 are nearly always lovely, and frequently exquisite. Scholarly attention has been directed to analysing the various workshops that can be isolated, and to dating the actual figurines. Not so much attention has been paid to the architectural elements of their framing, which should provide an equally valid criterion in considering both tabernacles and the relatively low-relief polyptychs, some of which have no central subjects, but offer a narrow range of scenes from the Infancy and Passion cycles.

The character of miniature private altarpieces is well illustrated by one of the most famous, the Soissons diptych, now in the Victoria and Albert Museum. Raymond Koechlin made this diptych the focus of a group, nine in all, with another four in the penumbra. It is traditionally believed to come from the church of St Jean des Vignes, Soissons, which in no way denies the probability that it was carved in Paris. One of its quixotic elements is a cavalier approach to the sequence of subjects. In the Soissons prototype and in an ivory diptych now in Leningrad, the Harrowing of Hell is placed *after* the Resurrection. The architecture of the Leningrad example reappears in a Vatican diptych, in which the scenes start at the bottom and work upwards, as they do in an example in Berlin. The prototype reads from the bottom upwards, but the first register reads from left to right, the second from right to left, and the uppermost from left to right again. This approach appears to be characteristic of this workshop, whose master owes his eminence to his eccentricity. He shows outstanding skill in the disposition of the architectural framework, which is based on a series of prominent gables. The mid thirteenth century saw a sudden emphasis on the gable, from a nominal roofing of the entrance portals at Amiens Cathedral *c.* 1225, through the five essays in gable ornament of the Bourges façade of *c.* 1240–60, to the fantasy of Reims and the final stalactites of Strasburg in the 1270s and 1280s. The west front of Bourges, perhaps 1250–60, is about the closest to the Soissons diptych. A useful criterion in examining the architectural idiom of ivory polyptychs is not only the ogee arch – unlikely to appear before the 1290s – but the type of crocket running up the gables. The floriated crocket appears on the St Blaise book-binding, made before 1276, and on the Chasse de St Taurin at Evreux, made from 1240 to 1255: precocious examples in which the metal worker set the pace for all the other arts. The floriated crocket was used in conjunction with the comma crocket, which had been in full use since the 1220s and was not ousted at Westminster until at least the 1270s. The Soissons diptych master and other ivory carvers working *c.* 1250–75 are still using the comma crocket, even though the naturalistic leaf appears to form a decorative frieze.

The Coronation of the Virgin

By the end of the thirteenth century the Coronation of the Virgin had become an alternative climax to the iconographic schemes of Christian imagery, a more joyful option than the Christ of Judgement. Her Coronation, rapturously described in the *Golden Legend* and reflected in Dante's *Paradiso*, replaced the terrible representation of divine righteousness and justice with a vision of 'the Love which moved the sun and the other stars'.

At Notre-Dame the porte rouge of *c.* 1260 showed the Coronation of the Virgin attended by a kneeling king and queen, surely St Louis IX of France and Margaret of Provence. The angelic crowning of the Virgin is a standard feature of tabernacle Virgins. Just as the figure of a king coming to adore in the wings of these tabernacles implies a double iconography referring to the Adoration of the Magi, so the flying angel bearing the crown suggests the Coronation of the Virgin, even though the Christ who will be King of Heaven is still the Child within her arms. The present disposition of the Reims gables, where the Coronation of the Virgin has taken pride of place over the central doorway, ousting the Christ in Majesty to the southern gable, may well represent a change of scheme during building.

Eleanor of Castile, Queen of England, had a Dominican confessor, an Order with a special devotion to the Virgin. Among the decorative emblems painted on the vestments in an ivory of the Coronation of the Virgin, now in the Louvre, are the fleurs-de-lis of France and the towers of Castile. Eleanor was in France in 1264–5, which is about right as a date for this peerless ivory. After 1878, two angels of the same period were added to the Coronation. They are carved in the round but the Coronation pair, being plain on the back, were originally placed in a tabernacle. Whenever the subject appears, in ivory, metalwork or major sculpture, in the following half-century, in either England or France, it seems but a pale reflection of this noble group.

Giovanni Pisano (c. 1248–1314/19)

It took a great sculptor to escape the spell of the mignonne Virgin of the Ste Chapelle, and that sculptor was Giovanni Pisano, whose Pisa Cathedral ivory of the Virgin and Child is associated with the cathedral chapter's payment to him of 25 livres on 5 June 1298. It has been thought that Pisano's work at this date indicates that he had visited France. Alternatively, he may have studied a number of French ivories. The Pisa Cathedral inventory of 1369 suggests that by that date the high altar was richly supplied with imagery: it lists the ivory Virgin between her two attendant angels forming part of a gilt wooden tabernacle or ciborium.

An inventory of 1433 specifies that the angels had gilt wings and that the 'ymaginibus' of 1369 were scenes of the Passion, perhaps models for Pisano's Crucifixion panel at Pistoya. It may be that only the Virgin on the Pisa altarpiece was Giovanni's work. Perhaps the figure replaced the model that he studied.

The art historian Sir John Pope-Hennessy claimed the poignant marble figure of the Christ Crucified, now in the Victoria and Albert Museum, as a work of the same date by Giovanni Pisano and speculated whether it was part of one of the Passion scenes flanking the Virgin and Child on the high altar of Pisa Cathedral. It seems more likely that it was once attached to a cross as part of a free-standing crucifix. The back of the figure is entirely modelled, and there is an attachment at the base which would hold it to the support. Whether it belonged to Pisa, or occupied a more isolated position, it testifies to the highest achievement of ivory sculpture. The subject of Christ on the Cross has fittingly drawn from the sculptor the best that he could achieve.

The late-thirteenth-century French Christ on the Cross, now in the Bargello, could have provided a model for Giovanni Pisano. Both works dispose the figure as sunk into a practically seated position, and the loin-cloth again reaches the knees.

No one else is in Pisano's league, but a late-thirteenth-century Christ shares his concept of the dead torso stretched to maximum length, as the legs are no longer attempting to keep the lungs open. This figure suggests that there was some fine ivory carving in England *c.* 1300, a thesis supported by the seated Virgin who can hardly come from a Coronation, since she turns to the right (a Coronation Virgin is invariably placed on Christ's right hand), perhaps to play with the Child, supported by her missing right hand. Both she and the marvellous seated Virgin, now in the Cloisters Collection, have been claimed as English, partly by association with the figurines of the voussoirs of the Judgement porch at Lincoln Cathedral.

Above: Figure of Christ Crucified, attributed to Giovanni Pisano. *c.*1300; 6 in. (15.5 cm).

Later Gothic ivories

Groups of ivories

A considerable bulk of charming folding altar-pieces from the early fourteenth century at first sight appear to be very similar to one another. However, careful observation has marked out several distinct types, and within these, hands of varying virtues. One such group, characterized by deliciously rounded faces and pointed noses, large floriated crockets and dome centres to the trefoil openings in the spandrels, is called 'the Berlin group', after a triptych with a seated Virgin and Child in the centre, now in the Berlin Museum. It is represented by a fine diptych of the Virgin and Child with angels and Crucifixion in the Walters Art Gallery, a diptych in the Louvre and a single leaf in Houston. The work of the Berlin triptych master is thought to stretch into the period 1350–75 and he is perhaps of German origin.

Another group, which stands apart very clearly, eschews architectural borders and encases the religious scenes in simple rectangular frames ornamented with rosettes. Such rosettes appeared on the enriched metalwork of the mid thirteenth century and within the architectural vocabulary of the Westminster Abbey north transept, but the idea of framing an ivory scene in these terms was a bold simplification in an age of over-elaboration. Moreover, a masterpiece of 'the Rose group' reveals a similar restraint in a minimal number of slender angular figures dramatically placed against the once-painted background. One half of this diptych has been known since 1897; the other was found in 1942 in a seaside shop. There are now thirty-six known diptychs of the Rose group.

One more group centres on the Virgin and Crucifixion diptych from the Mège Collection, now in the Louvre. It includes the centre of a triptych of the Coronation of the Virgin, also in the Louvre; a Virgin and Child with angels and SS Catherine and Clare; and possibly the centre part of a triptych showing Christ crucified between the two thieves. It is even possible to speak of the Mège Master, so tight-knit and interlocked are the group's characteristics. First, the faces are very clearly characterized, with exceptionally long upper eyelids, wide mouths and prominent chins. Secondly, the Mège Master cuts back his panels to a dangerously thin membrane for the background (in the Louvre diptych this has led to structural cracking). Thirdly, he uses the old-fashioned comma crocket, even though the pieces are evidently later than 1300, and fourthly, he has a trick of treating the recess behind the quatrefoils in the spandrels of his upper border with a series of little domed protuberances, like those of the Berlin master. By way of compensation, the Mège Master varies his compositions in a very lively manner. But it is perhaps surprising that an artist

with so many old-fashioned idiosyncrasies should be thought to have worked in Paris. The St Clare might point to a Franciscan connection (the facial features are strongly Italianate). After 1309, when the pope took up residence in Avignon, Italian influence was disseminated across southern France.

The Franco-Italian connection

The interchange between France and Italy, seen in the work of Giovanni Pisano, continued in a superb group of seated Virgins with Child. The keys are the Virgin still preserved in the treasury of Villeneuve-les-Avignon, originally owned by Cardinal Arnaud de Via, who died in 1335, and the statuette preserved in the treasury of San Francesco in Assisi, mentioned in an inventory of the basilica in 1430. We do not know when Simone Martini painted his cycle of the Life of St Martin in the basilica, but when he created his first dated masterpiece, his Maesta in the town hall of Siena in 1315, unlike his predecessors, Giotto, Duccio and Cimabue, who had painted the Christ Child seated upon his mother's knee, Martini showed the Child standing, as French Gothic ivories, and indeed more specifically the French Gothic ivory in the treasury at Assisi, all do. A more conventional dating for the Assisi Virgin would be *c.* 1320, but there are no hard facts to preclude its being in Assisi by 1312. It stretches to a remarkable width – the Child leans away from his mother – so its height, 8 in. (20 cm), is amazing. The other examples of this brilliant group also push the tusk's capacity to its limits: 10¾ in. (27.3 cm) tall, 9¹/₁₀ in. (23.3 cm) tall, 12⅓ in. (31.4 cm) tall, and one now in the Victoria

Above: Leaf of an ivory diptych, showing the Flagellation and the Crucifixion. Fourteenth-century; 7¾ × 4¼ in. (20 × 10.5 cm). Its restraint is characteristic of the Rose group.

Far right: The Assisi Virgin and Child, in ivory with painted decoration. Probably before 1312; 8 in. (20 cm). Its height is remarkable in view of the span from the Child's right hand to the Virgin's shoulder.

and Albert Museum, nearly 16 in. (40.6 cm) tall, including the base. The struggle fully to exploit the material's possibilities led in some cases to employing a wedge below the group to make it approximately upright. The pose and something of the simplicity of the fall of the drapery of these marvellous Virgins, the cream of Parisian work of the early fourteenth century, could well have influenced Simone Martini. They in their turn reflect something of Italian art. The elongated, slender faces with their prolonged upper eyelids, long straight noses, and small mouths and chins are Byzantine out of Pietro Lorenzetti.

The Grandisson ivories and the Salting diptych

Three of the most fully documented English ivories carry the arms of John Grandisson, Bishop of Exeter from 1327 to 1369:

1) a triptych with the Coronation of the Virgin above the Crucifixion, flanked by SS Peter, Stephen, Paul and Thomas of Canterbury
2) one leaf of a diptych with the Annunciation and St John the Baptist (now in the British Museum) and the other leaf with the Coronation of the Virgin and St John the Evangelist (now in the Louvre)
3) a triptych with a large bust of the Virgin and Child, above it the Crucifixion, and on the wings SS Peter, Paul, John the Baptist and probably Thomas à Becket.

Grandisson came to his see from Avignon and is known to have returned there in 1333. Apart from the enlarged Virgin and Child in the third example, the ivories are self-evidently rooted in the lively sculpture of Exeter Cathedral and in his particular interests and devotions (for instance, he wrote a biography of Becket). Nothing is out of key here but the Virgin of the third piece.

The model behind this foreign intrusion could have been a small panel painting from Avignon or, my own feeling, a Byzantine ivory like the tenth-century triptych from Alt-Otting in Upper Bavaria. The rounded arch, the different scale, the hair-style, the facial features and the veil are all comparable. The use of an ivory prototype in low relief would explain the very flat relief adopted in the Grandisson ivory, and the facial characteristics of the Grandisson Virgin are closer to the Byzantine ivory than to any Siennese panel painting. This, the last of the Grandisson altarpieces, could well have been intended for his own chantry chapel at Exeter Cathedral, where the extremely damaged carvings behind the altar represent two scenes involving the Virgin, each with an angel to her left. In both groups the figures are seated.

A feature of the first two Grandisson ivories, agreed to have been made before Grandisson's second visit to Avignon and, therefore, dated 1327–33, and probably the beginning of that period, is the extravagant use of thick pieces of ivory. The Mège Master would have carved two ivories out of each of them. The same can be said of another English ivory, usually dated to the very early thirteenth century, the Salting diptych of Christ Blessing and the Virgin and Child. This piece has been associated with Westminster work and comparison between the face of the Virgin and William Torel's effigy of Eleanor of Castile, died 1291, in Westminster Abbey, is very persuasive. However, this ivory shares with the Grandisson pieces the very clumsy and mechanical crocketed gabling. Its framing suggests a date later than the exquisite figures within it. The stone sculpture at Exeter reached its climax in about 1315 and it is just possible that the diptych is actually Exeter work, made immediately before Grandisson's time. The facial features and the hair are all compatible with Exeter detail in stone sculpture, and elements in the Grandisson ivories are hauntingly similar to those in the Salting diptych. If this wonderful ivory had a relatively provincial origin, there must surely have been a fine ivory workshop in Grandisson's reach.

The Salting diptych is a work of great quality designed very specifically for a patron of importance. It may be the private altarpiece of Bishop Walter de Stapelton, who died in 1326. Lord High Treasurer to Edward II, he had access to the finest craftsmen in England. His predecessor, Thomas Bitten, who died in 1307, had two ivory tabernacles in his private chapel.

Romance motifs

A conspicuous rarity, now in the British Museum, is the Tristan casket, carved in bone with scenes of love, music and war, and perhaps made in Cologne c. 1200. It anticipated by a century the production of many such caskets ornamented with subjects drawn from the romances and appears to be related to a tradition, perhaps largely oral, going back beyond known literary sources. Some of the scenes refer undoubtedly to Tristan and Isolde. Felicitously the actual lock of the casket is incorporated into the design so that the keyholes become the windows

Far right: The Tristan casket, carved in bone, probably from Cologne. c. 1200; 3¾ × 5¾ in. (9.5 × 14.6 cm). The use of such caskets to house small valued items may well derive from the Arab world.

Above: Ivory mirror case. Early-fourteenth-century; 4¼ in. (10.5 cm) diameter. Tristan and Isolde playing chess.

Below: Lid of a Franco-German ivory casket. *c.*1300–50; 5⅛ × 10¼ in. (13 × 26.5 cm). The central scene of the joust is flanked on the right by the Siege of the Castle of Love and on the left by the Siege's conclusion.

above the entrance to the castle in which the lovers meet and endlessly part again.

The romantic language of the Tristan casket did not become common currency until the early fourteenth century, when there was a prodigious expansion of the market for secular pieces. The wardrobe accounts of Edward I, King of England, for 1299–1300 include an ivory coffer with a metal lock signed by Walter de Langton, his treasurer and keeper of the royal wardrobe. It was full of little things 'for the king's private delight' – seals, rings, precious stones, purses and other such items omitted from the main inventory. The will of Humphrey de Bohun, Earl of Hereford and Essex, 1319–22, mentions 'ij broches dargent pur mauntel en un petit case d'yvor' (two gold brooches for the mantle, in a little ivory case), illustrating the natural and most common use of ivory caskets as jewel cases.

Such caskets for 'private delight' were or-namented, like the earlier Tristan casket, with illustrations from the romances, indicating that the stories were more widely, and sooner, known than surviving texts would suggest. For what is the use of an illustration if you do not know the story? A series of seven caskets studied by William D. Wixom with special reference to one in the Cleveland Museum, Ohio, offer no iconographic mysteries. Their subject matter was derived from the *Roman d'Alexander*, written by Alexander de Paris, *c.* 1180, perhaps from the updated *Roman de Fauvel* by Gervais du Bus of the early fourteenth century, Fournival's *Bestaire d'Amour*, the twelfth-century *Fableau du Dieu d'amours* and the thir-teenth-century *Roman de la Rose*, plus Guillaume de Machaut's *Dit du Verger* and, of course, the

Arthurian material from Chrétien de Troyes' *Perceval* or the thirteenth-century prose *Lancelot*. A crash course in medieval romance is clearly indicated for anyone aspiring to pick up the references in these crowded little scenes. It is not necessary, however, to suppose that the ivory carvers themselves read all the stories. The same incidents are illustrated repeatedly. The sculptors may have worked from models, from sketches, or even from casts (a terracotta cast from a French fourteenth-century Presentation in the Temple, from an ivory box in Toulouse, was found in a river in Paris). One of the caskets is devoted to the prominent source of the *Chatelaine de Vergi;* a boss in the Angel Choir at Lincoln, of before 1280, may illustrate an incident from the same story. The most conspicuous single scene on romance caskets, and frequently on mirror backs, is the Assault on the Castle of Love. The spread of this imagery, staged in mock battles at festivals, argues a strong vernacular tradition that would have been common currency in Europe and beyond.

It is sometimes difficult to decide whether the scenes of exchanges between pairs of lovers are entirely generalized, or refer to specific romances, favourite among them the story of Tristan and Isolde. The lovers are frequently shown playing chess, the gentleman's hand often placed around the pillar behind them. In the story, Tristan and Isolde played chess on board ship. An early-sixteenth-century silver nef has a little fourteenth-century silver plaque of the chessplayers propped against the mainmast. If the pillar behind the lovers was in fact the mainmast of a ship, Tristan's gesture is explained.

The Embriachi

On 4 February 1378 Jean, Duke of Berri, bought in Paris a beautiful ivory mirror, some combs in leather cases and six bone candlesticks to hold wax candles 'for reading romances' – all from the same ivory worker. He and his brother, Philippe, Duke of Burgundy, were also great patrons of the Italian bone carver Baldassare degli Embriachi (*fl.* late fourteenth/early fifteenth century). In 1393 two large triptychs were given to the abbey of Champmol by the Duke of Burgundy, as part

Above: Two of the Apostles from the altarpiece by Baldassare degli Embriachi for the abbey of Poissy. *c.*1400; 105 × 93 in. (268 × 236 cm). Fragments of hippopotamus bone or tooth replace the flowing tusk of the Gothic ivories.

of the great visual assembly to which the sculptors Claus Sluter and Claus de Werve and the painters Jacques de Baërze and Melchior Broederlam contributed. Jean de Marville had bought twenty-four pounds of ivory for the Duke of Burgundy in Paris in 1377. In such company, what did the Duke want with Baldassare degli Embriachi, founding father of the Embriachi workshop? The connoisseur Duke of Berri also went to Baldassare degli Embriachi for an altarpiece for the abbey of Poissy. The little figures of apostles in their inlaid settings around the altarpiece may cause a slight shudder, but when the guild church of Orsan-michele in Florence was in its first youth, did the external tabernacling look very different? The Embriachi had hit upon a solution to the problem of diminishing supplies of elephant ivory: the bone or tooth of the hippopotamus. The units of their altarpieces and lavish caskets were tiny – 1¼ by 4¼ in. (3.1 by 10.5 cm) – but they could be multiplied indefinitely. There were 250 elements in the altarpiece of sixty-five reliefs and subsidiary figures which Embriachi supplied for the Certosa

at Pavia between 1400 and 1409. The framework could be made to carry a load of geometric inlays in bright contrasted stained woods, relieved with fragments of bone or mother-of-pearl. The little half-convex sections of bone allowed for only the most sedate and superficial treatment of the figures, which were, therefore, redolent of the Giottesque simplicity which the north expected of Italy. But the whole complex met the real taste for luxurious busywork that was curbed only in Florence, and not all the time even there, during the fifteenth century. The ultimate inheritors of the Embriachi were the makers of Renaissance 'pastiglia boxes'.

The north Italians had already made a particularly lively contribution to casket work *c.* 1350–1400 with the novel pierced panels, laid over a rich foil on the exteriors of caskets.

The 'soft style'

A major artist emerged *c.* 1350–1400. The Master of Kremsmünster was probably German, called after a diptych in the abbey there. Recognized by the ultimate in frilly drapery, contorted poses and 'characterized faces', he was responding to the new, fluent, fluttering drapery of the 'soft style' in all the arts of northern Europe – as demonstrated, for example, by Cologne panel painting of about 1400. His lyrical potential is revealed in a single standing figure of the Virgin and Child, now in the British Museum.

Several freshly observed Virgins with Child were created *c.* 1400, and here 'observed' probably means observed from real mothers and babies. In one ivory the Child is about to take the breast and in an idyllic statuette the Child at the breast is suckling. In the same happy vein is the Mother playing with her Child, now in Baltimore, which stems from the family of Canon Sauve of Laval Cathedral, and another Rouen ivory, the Virgin of Valmont. These very large ivories do not appear to have been restricted by the problems of curvature, as their earlier sisters were. This may suggest a new supply of even larger tusks.

★

Later medieval reliefs show a sad decline, which is of a piece with the general reduction in standards over northern Europe throughout the fifteenth century. But there is still much good fun to be derived from the ornamentation of combs and saddles, or the splendid gaming boards, and the least ivory knife handle has an individuality and loving care beyond that of most of the things we make today. In 1353 Thomas de Fienvillier provided for the King of France a pair of knife handles of ivory garnished with rings and 'ting-lettes' (studs?) of silver gilt and enamelled with the royal arms for the season of Lent, and another pair for the feast of Easter, for a total of 16 livres. What would we offer for them today?

Sixteenth, Seventeenth and Eighteenth Centuries

Change and development

Several centuries of comparative stability in Europe allowed Gothic ivory carving to reach a zenith of coherent style and form; a type which is readily identifiable. The sixteenth-century traumas of renaissance and reformation forced dramatic change to the two major categories: stylized icons and precious secular objects. Ivory carving became a self-conscious art, often the creation of an individual artist with the authority of a signature.

The traditional distinction between art and artefact remains essential in the catalogue of baroque and rococo work but there is now a third and important category: applied or decorative art, increasingly relevant in a world of courtly fashion. The accessibility of the printed word and the engraving enabled the carvers to keep abreast of the rapid changes in court taste inspired first from Italy and later from France. The rate of change increased dramatically during the sixteenth, seventeenth and eighteenth centuries: it took about a hundred years for the baroque to permeate from the Italy of Lorenzo Bernini (1598–1680) to southern Germany; the rococo was universally evident by 1750, but by 1780 had been eclipsed by neo-classicism in all but Germany.

Geographical changes, particularly the accessibility of Africa and the Orient, increased the supply of large good-quality tusks, as trade routes were consolidated in the sixteenth and seventeenth centuries. Plaques, medallions and panels for caskets became larger, groups and figures more fluent.

By the sixteenth century the creative focus had moved convincingly to the Renaissance centres of the south. English sculpture had become primarily monumental or funereal, the ivory output being insignificant. Modern ideas spread northward, accelerated in 1685 when Louis XIV of France repealed the Edict of Nantes; deprived of religious freedom, highly trained Huguenots sought refuge in the parliamentarian state of England and enriched its now domestic carving industry. There the growing merchant class and the traditional aristocracy sponsored the émigré artists; ivory portraiture soon became preferred to the larger editions of bronze commemorative plaques. The impact of the Huguenot masters, well versed in the prevalent artistic conventions of the time, was made greater by their rapid social penetration.

The move from bone to ivory in the sixteenth and seventeenth centuries is counterbalanced by the move from ivory to bone in the eighteenth century when European wars disrupted supplies and the Industrial Revolution introduced substitutes, particularly porcelain, which were colourful and economical. The artisanal tradition of functional folkloric bone products continued, however, often with considerable humble charm. The craftsmen operated a pragmatic ethic but show a sensitivity to the medium and an imaginative homespun repertoire reminiscent of the late Gothic workshops.

The prevalent decorative style of severe neo-classicism did not lend itself to ivory sculpture though veneering of small items did occur and the continental production of figurines and boxes continued. The move from the artistic in the seventeenth century to the practical in the late eighteenth is merely a cycle. The skill is ever present.

The decline of religious art carving in the sixteenth century

The traditional view holds that ivory carving peaked between the thirteenth and fifteenth centuries and thereafter lapsed into the trivial and profane, relieved only by a few major figures. In 1983 a French ivory crosier head dating from the period 1350–1400, sold for a substantial figure, was outstripped by an early Île-de-France Gothic ivory casket. In the same sale the closest comparable price for a post-Renaissance œuvre, a ten-figure Crucifixion signed by Jaillot (rarer, in its way, than either of the Gothic pieces), was less than a quarter of the casket price, and a French eighteenth-century figure of Diana the Huntress less than a twentieth – distinctly parvenu.

Unashamed reverence for the past and respect for the church have been closely questioned in the last five decades, curiously reflecting the changes which at the beginning of the sixteenth century led to an arresting decline in the output of significant religious ivories for almost a century: the Reformation.

In 1509 Henry VIII of England married Catherine of Aragon. After close on twenty years of marriage, it became clear that Catherine was unlikely to produce a male heir; the Pope would not legitimize a second marriage; in Europe, Luther and his followers were rejecting Catholicism on many grounds including papal corruption; Henry divorced Catherine and founded his own church, allowing him to remarry and eventually produce the male heir. A little expeditious asset-stripping involved dissolving the monasteries, which were a major source of religious art, and generally decreasing the influence of the church, which in the thirteenth, fourteenth and fifteenth centuries had been an integral part of everyday life. The medieval monastery played a crucial role in industry and agriculture as well as piety. The monks often had the monopoly on literacy. The church indirectly controlled the demand for religious artefacts. Public worship involved the use of the elaborate pyx, the pax and the crosier, but there was also a great demand for tokens of private devotion. This demand was partly endemic and partly nurtured by the monastic system; supply was certainly cultivated by the monks and indeed they produced some of the finest objects themselves. Mannius, the eleventh-century Abbot of Evesham, was skilled in the arts, especially goldsmithing and carving. The records of Monte Cassino, Italy, describe painting, embroidery, carving in wood and ivory. The Rule of St Benedict (written *c.* 530–40) expressly encourages arts of this kind, but perhaps explains one of the most crucial differences between pre- and post-Renaissance carving; the complete lack of artists' names. 'If there be artists in the monastery, let them exercise their crafts with all humility and reverence ... But if any of them be proud of the skill he has in his craft ... let him be removed from it and not exercise it again, unless after humbling himself the Abbot shall permit him.'

The Reformation and the dissolution of the monasteries were therefore the sixteenth-century terminus of the great period of religious carving. Mainstream ivory production then divided: the Gothic legacy continued the old practices in adapted forms with more secular emphasis, and the continental Renaissance had particular influence on figure and relief carving.

Combs and mirrors

Although the double-edged liturgical comb belongs essentially to the Gothic era, it is interesting to note later references to its use. Formerly of some practical value to the clergy, in spite of their limited tonsure, it soon became of primarily ceremonial value. By 1623, the pontifical of Clement VIII and of Urban VIII considered 'a ring with a stone to be blessed, a comb of ivory and two candles' essential accessories. At this time the combs were so large that their use might well have been ostentatious rather than cosmetic.

Domestic combs, having more practical applications, made a genuine transition to the sixteenth century. Initially, the design remained the same, though the decoration might change from stylized biblical narratives to more secular pleasures. There is a good example of a double-toothed comb on whose central panel a couple meet and join hands between two battlemented houses; it is therefore thought to commemorate a marriage. Mirror cases pass through a similar change, from

Gothic romance decoration to, say, one sixteenth-century example, which is shield-shaped rather than having a circular glass in a rectangular frame; it has a handle reminiscent of the modern form, and the back is carved with ladies and gentlemen in Louis XII costume (1498–1515).

Figures and groups

Of all the categories of ivory use considered here, carved figures are unique because they belong to a category which is undeniably art; in those who have experienced a scientific education the mere word provokes mixed feelings.

It may be useful to outline the world in which the carvers lived and to relate their production across temporal and national or generic boundaries, the former because 'sculpture' is more susceptible to contemporary thought than practical artefacts and the latter because the extent of production is an unequivocal arbiter of taste.

There is a traditional distinction between northern and southern Europe which often in practice compares Italy with Germany and the Low Countries (France moving towards the southern group with time, and England emergent towards the end of the seventeenth century). It is a useful division because Italy produced little of interest in ivory until the end of the eighteenth century. There is a major difference between the attitude in the south, where an ivory carving might be considered useful evidence of an artist's virtuosity but not a mainstream sculptural skill, and in the north, where an artist may be first a carver. This is not to belittle the importance of Italian ivories in the sixteenth and seventeenth centuries or to ignore the competent works of Pozzo or Leoni but it justifies exploring in more depth the world of northern Europe.

Italy: the sixteenth century

First, though, it may be worth considering the reason for the apparent dearth of Italian carvings during the sixteenth century, when a sculptural boom, in the wake of the seminal Renaissance, saw such figures as Giambologna (1529–1608) and Bernini (1598–1680) producing works of towering artistic importance. Sculpture and its patronage was a public philosophical and demonstrative medium as important as painting and rhetoric and was seriously promoted by the commentators of the time as being one of the manifestations of the virtues of humanism; that is, a product of the aesthetic choice of the artist. In the north the preoccupation with the individual and the personal world of the senses was considerably less fashionable and it is arguable whether the Renaissance spirit was significantly absorbed into the mainstream until the late seventeenth century. Although southern sculpture was more public in its applications and intentions, there was a small-scale format, Kleinplastik, for the private appreciation of the cognoscenti. Thus, the great Renaissance casts were exported from Italy throughout Europe. They tended to be bronze partly because the lost wax method made mass production relatively easy, partly in emulation of antique bronze statuettes and partly to harness the respectability inherited from the great bronze commissions of the previous century, notably Ghiberti's Baptistery doors, a concrete metaphor of civic pride, and Donatello's great cycles of bronzes.

Germany and north-west Europe: the sixteenth and seventeenth centuries

In sixteenth-century Germany, contemporary life was very different, not only from ours now but also from Italian then. In Italy the pleasures of the senses, whether naked sculptural allegories or religious erotic monuments, were acceptable to the norm. In Nuremberg at the same time society was so normative that a young girl's neckline must not fall more than two fingers' breadth below her collar bone by order of the government. The Reformation had a drastic effect upon the sculpture of northern Europe. After the late Gothic flowering of ivory art in diptych, pax and crosier, the period 1475–1550 saw carved limewood sculpture at its height. The prevailing mood of the reformers caused such a drastic destruction of images and such a shortfall of commissions that the guildworkers, who were restricted by their charters from working as joiners or carpenters, were complaining at the lack of regular employment.

Such was the decline of northern sculpture in the sixteenth century; there was a continuation of large-scale retable altarpieces, as of Gothic devotional ivories, though of less quantity and quality. One of the results of the declining market in public sculpture was the promotion of small-scale private works; a result partly of native carving tradition and partly of the influence of those who travelled to Rome and Italy. Leonard Kern (1588–1662) of the Swabian school was born and died in Germany but lived for several years in Rome absorbing influences clearly traceable in his single individual figures and small groups. He worked in marble, wood and ivory and though his monogrammed works are rare the body of work attributable to him has a distinctive quality. His works clearly belong to the tradition of Kleinplastik in scale (examples of Diana and her hounds in both boxwood and ivory are less than 9 in. (23 cm) high) and they range in subject from the classically allegorical to the 'fleshly devotional'. There is an ivory relief of Adam and Eve, now in Berlin, in which the figures are nude with contemporary characteristics. They are highly finished in the spirit of the finely chiselled and patinated bronzes which they may have

accompanied in the connoisseur's collection and, perhaps most importantly, they are desirable; desirable as a source of tactile satisfaction and desirable because they are self-contained and finished works of art, uncluttered by the paraphernalia of swirling drapes and angels or iconographic attributes.

There are a number of artists who bridge the sixteenth and seventeenth centuries and represent a transition, a combination of northern and southern styles. François Duquesnoy (1594–1643), known as Fiammingo from his Flemish origins, was noted for his carved plaques. Born in Brussels, he studied in Rome (where he was heavily influenced by Titian) and his work had considerable sculptural influence on his native Flanders. He produced fine bronzes and life-sized marbles as well as ivories. His characteristically chubby putti are prototypes for generations of artists though his quality may easily be inferred from his other work. Christof Angermair (1580–1633) is best known for his celebrated coin cabinet but also carved transitional figures as court turner to Maximilian I, Elector of Bavaria. Jorg Petel (died 1634), who again studied in Rome, was another Bavarian sculptor and worked in both

Right: Ivory of Adam and Eve by Leonard Kern. Mid-seventeenth-century; 9 in. (23 cm). The group combines the ideal human form with individuality of expression.

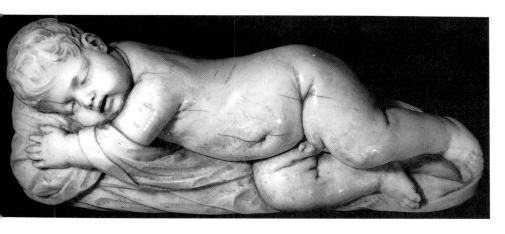

Above: 'Child Asleep', attributed to François Duquesnoy (Fiammingo). Seventeenth-century; 6 in. (15 cm).

Right: Elegant carving of Orpheus and Eurydice by Johann Baur. Eighteenth-century; 9 in. (23 cm).

wood and ivory at Augsburg. His figures have a soft, rounded, silky quality similar to those of Kern though he used a more pronouncedly classical vocabulary. He carved some fine tankards decorated with bacchanalian reliefs; some are mounted with excellent Augsburg silversmith's work.

The Reformation was accompanied by iconoclasm, both implicit in the fall in demand and fashion for public sculpture and explicit in the sense of statue-smashing of the kind in which the puritans indulged a century later in England. The carvers survived partly on the inferior commissions offered by towns which were still positively Catholic (Luther being more tolerant than Zwingli) and partly by developing non-public art in the form of boxwood and ivory statuettes, often of exquisite quality. In the mid seventeenth century three major changes revived artistic and sculptural interest. In France Louis XIV (reigned 1643–1715) became secure as absolute monarch and in the early 1660s began his plans for Versailles, which epitomized the French style and taste that were to be exported throughout Europe; his reign saw the achievement of a centrally controlled academy heralding the prevalence of international conformity and therefore the constraint of national styles. In England the restoration of the monarchy in 1660 brought peace and stability. In Germany and the empire the Thirty Years War ended in 1648 and Protestants and Catholics could divide and indulge their divergent sculptural tastes with more vigour.

The German artist Ignaz Elhafen (1658–1715), a native of Bavaria, worked in Rome and Vienna carving exceptionally fine plaques, tankards and figures in an elegant and more confident southern style, from his years studying with Leoni and probably with the school of Bernini. His pair of statuettes of Bacchus and Venus epitomize this forward-looking southern style, a generation later than Kern and Petel, retaining the same polished 'ideal' effect, but with more elongated elegance and shape, a greater mastery of the mythological rhetoric of garland and putti, and a more subtle erotic language. Unlike the figures of van Bossuit

with their incised genitalia, Elhafen's cupid playfully grasps the dangling bunch with which Bacchus smilingly teases him, all under the guise of the 'concealing' figleaf convention; Venus stands by watching, portrayed as an innocent in her teens rather than a woman in her thirties, one breast covered, the other tensed but hanging free. Both figures stand with their lips parted, implying communication with each other or with the spectator, which logically precedes activity perhaps of a pleasant kind.

Balthasar Permoser (1651–1732), a direct product of the sculptural revival, travelled to Florence, Berlin and Dresden carving in stone on a public scale. His were the vivacious supporting satyrs for the Zwinger in Dresden, his the wood and ivory Triumph of the Cross on a miniature devotional scale. The image of Christ nailed in a glorious burst of light, with cherubim flapping overhead and Death and the Antichrist writhing below, makes frank allusions to Bernini and Legros. The late seventeenth and early eighteenth centuries produced other competent artists: Johann Baur of Augsburg (died 1760); Magnus Berg (born in Norway in the 1660s, died in Copenhagen in 1738) who carved groups of statuettes, and also

Right: Pair of beggars by Simon Troger. Early-eighteenth-century; woman 15 in. (38 cm), man 15¾ in. (40 cm). Troger here combines ivory and fruitwood.

Opposite: A rare Austrian or South German ivory group of Cain slaying Abel, from the circle of Simon Troger. Eighteenth-century; 13½ in. (34.5 cm). More examples of ivory figures are on pages 116, 117 and 120.

profiles, drawing on his training as a painter; Van Opstal (1605–68) who worked in France, and Cavalier and Le Marchand in England (described below).

Germany: the eighteenth century

Germany still had the strongest native carving tradition and with the end of the War of the Austrian Succession in 1711 there was a remarkable revival of Catholic sculpture as the rococo took hold. The momentum in Germany continued throughout the eighteenth century, unrestrained by the stark neo-classical style of 1750–1800, and still has a profound effect on the decorative arts and sculpture. It was difficult for ivory carving, defined by scale, to match these elaborate achievements. Simon Troger (1683–1768) continued in Permoser's vein of combining wood and ivory, often with jewelled eyes giving a combination of colour and life which is rococo in spirit, particularly in an active subject with asymmetry and movement such as his Judgement of Solomon; the more relaxed and adventurous spirit allowed subjects other than the purely religious or classical. Troger's genre groups are in their way innovative and seem to legitimize everyday life as a bona fide carving subject. Wilhelm Kruger (active *c.* 1700–50) was noted for his peasants and beggars; and his view is not unsympathetic, which perhaps explains the adoption of these models as stereotypes for similar production in Germany and Dieppe beyond the end of the century.

It is worth noting the pervasive power of the models carved at this period. For example, one of Kruger's models was reproduced in porcelain at the Furstenberg factory. The development of porcelain, the new darling of the mid eighteenth century, probably helped in the demise of ivory carving towards the end of the century. As porcelain manufacture was perfected, towards the 1750s, it competed with ivory statuettes. Johann Lücke (1703–80), from a family of ivory carvers, spent much of his errant life modelling for the Dresden and Vienna porcelain factories. An interesting relief signed by him, dated 1736, shows the damned in Hell and may parallel the agony of a man trapped in and periodically sacked from the rather precious porcelain workshops. Other groups of figure types translate easily from ivory into porcelain: Harlequin from the commedia dell'arte, beggars, lovers, the Rape of Europa, many of them taken in turn from marble classical originals.

There are original works in ivory which can never be reproduced in any other medium; the early-seventeenth-century Fury by the unknown Furienmeister is a nightmare image whose grotesque violent power is conveyed by the unreal gloss of the white tusk contrasting with the flailing limbs of this vision of hell. There could be no greater contrast than the late-eighteenth-century Dieppe figures of Jean-Antoine Belleteste in which demure, restrained but nevertheless naked allegories stand politely on their plinths, as if the original models never needed even to answer nature's call. But both use ivory well. They are high achievements by capable artists whose material augments its subject. They reflect not only the history of their respective ages but also the hand and eye of the artist.

'Morbid' ivory

A curious German forte was 'morbid' ivory: carvings which illustrate a morbid preoccupation with death. There are three main categories. Christof Harrich (died *c.* 1630), who worked in Nuremberg in the sixteenth century, specialized in morbidity, particularly *memento mori*. These often take the form of human skulls, accurately carved to represent partial decay and adorned with worms and serpents coiled through sockets and around jaws. They theoretically remind the spectator of his mortality but clearly revel in the aesthetic sensuous kick which they deliver. They are related to rosary beads made up of double- or treble-sided death's-heads. There is also a scientific purpose; the celebrated family of Stephan Zick of Nuremberg produced anatomical figures in ivory, generally of corpses or naked pregnant models; limbs or parts of the thorax and abdomen could be removed to reveal the internal organs in gaudy polychrome. These are in turn related to the *tödlein* figures of the living death, which involve walking emaciated skeletons often in ivory, the wasted rags being wood; there is an excellent example in the manner of Troger, known as the Dance of Death.

Plaques

Although the majority of ivory plaques of this period are erotic or religious, and sometimes both, about 20 per cent show other subjects and more than half of them apparently originate from Germany or the Low Countries.

Though not the greatest relief carver, perhaps the best known is Francis van Bossuit (1635–92), who was born in Brussels and studied and worked in Rome. His work, almost entirely 'after the antique', is recorded in a book published in 1727. The fifty-five plates vary from sober scenes of Christ on the Cross or a macabre David with Goliath's decapitated head impaled on his sword, to an overtly orgiastic Nymph being abducted by three satyrs; forty-eight of them show women, only three dressed in any more than tantalizing drapes, in scenes of bestiality (Leda and the Swan), incest (Lot and both of his daughters), mass rape (of the Sabine women), voyeurism and adultery (David and Bathsheba), not to mention infanticide (the Massacre of the Innocents) and paralytic drunkenness (the Triumph of Silenus). The carving is good, in high relief with crisp details, often conveying drama and charm.

In spite of similarity of subject the plaque carvers are often reputable and their styles distinct. François Duquesnoy (Fiammingo) has already been mentioned. His plaques illustrate his feeling for and response to Titian and are distinguished by the skill of the carving rather than the originality of subject. Lucas Fayd'herbe (1617–97) was another carver of plaques but also a great craftsman, having trained in Rubens's studio and been given a certificate by the painter claiming a piece of his work had a 'beauté ravissante'. Indeed, there were several of his ivories at the studio sale after the death of the painter in 1641. It is not difficult to see Rubens's influence in the chubby boys of the bacchanal processions, and it was once said that he carved them as Rubens models. Gerard van Opstal (1605–68) is one of the most distinctive plaque carvers; born in Antwerp he worked for the court of Louis XIII at the invitation of the statesman Richelieu, in marble and bronze. His plaques are often silhouettes, with the background ivory cut out, and may have a floral border. Again, the chubby boys are Rubenesque but his figures are much more realistic. Less ideal than most plaques, they are sometimes bad-tempered and fumbling with windswept hair, northern versions of what is essentially a southern and classical subject.

In contrast Ignaz Elhafen (1658–1715), whose figures were described above, looks forward into the eighteenth century with more elegant figures, younger and more nubile girls, the mothers and grandmothers of Clodion's interminable nymphs; they recline and rotate among classical urns beneath leafy glades in high relief. The influence of

Above: Bacchanalian scene carved in ivory, shown in colour on page 121.

Elhafen's years in Rome is apparent in the lyrical and individual modelling, whether on the sides of the fine silver-mounted tankard carved with the Rape of the Sabines, which bears his signature, or on the plaque of Pan teaching a Nymph to play the pipes, taken from an engraving by the Italian Castiglione, but given a more sophisticated composition and a subtle air of understated intimacy sharply distinct from the bawdy busty Bossuit models, who perhaps belong more to the Bavarian *Bierkeller* than the French court. The central cameo of Pan is both realistic in the portrayal of him as a mature teacher and sympathetic to the tutorial relationship; even in this southern format Elhafen retains his northern spirit.

Antonio Leoni, who worked in Venice and northern Europe *c.* 1700–20, is perhaps most typically 'Italian' in style and content; his subjects tend to be taken from the formal classical set-pieces, such as the Sacrifice of Iphigenia or the Judgement of Paris. Breadth and space give an airy atmosphere in which the elegant ladies recline among the architectural props of contemporary artistic vocabulary: they are clearly inspired by the spirit of such painters as Poussin. The religious counterpart of these painterly secular scenes is Leoni's Conversion of St Paul; a painting in all but size and colour, following faithfully in the tradition of the Renaissance and baroque bronze artists, it is even signed in the lower right-hand corner. In the north Angermair worked in a similar vein *c.* 1600–33, but never with such apparent ease. This may be attributable to his earlier date but perhaps shows evidence of a different tradition, of carving rather than painting. In the north, especially in Germany and the Low Countries, the development from Gothic ivories to baroque continued unbroken. Journeying masters of the fifteenth and sixteenth centuries set up workshops and formed guilds relatively untouched by notions of Renaissance humanism. The Gothic attention to detail and reality only slowly supersedes form, and many ivory carvings are very close in style to carved oak reliefs of Flanders and Germany of the same period.

In the south, ivory reliefs were influenced less by native schools of carving than by the revolutionary artistic events and figures of the time. It is perhaps therefore not surprising that ivory carvers followed the new Renaissance styles.

Northern plaques tend to show the mythological and religious but with a constant accompaniment of folkloric themes, particularly the stag hunt and the boar hunt, which appear as decoration on weapons and powderflasks but also on plaques *per se*, tavern scenes are common, especially on less courtly objects such as snuffrasps; battle and love are often shown in contemporary costume. A most original plaque is a satirical relief which apparently emulates a cartoon of the mid

Page 116: The nightmare
image of a fury from hell,
by an unknown master.
Early-seventeenth-
century; 20 in. (51 cm).

Page 117 (above): The
Four Seasons by the
Dieppe *ivoirier* Jean-
Antoine Belleteste. Late-
eighteenth-century; 7 in.
(18 cm), with pedestal.

Page 117 (below): Six
ivory sheaths for
smelling-salts bottles,
Dieppe. Eighteenth-
century. Pierced designs
using courtly motifs were
a feature of the Dieppe
school, as mentioned in
the text on page 129.

Below and far right:
Examples of a turned
ivory cup (*below*) and of a
table ornament (*right*),
typical of the Zick family
of Nuremberg.

eighteenth century: an eccentric preacher named
Orator Henley, self-indulgent, extravagant and
vulgar, is shown wearing a fox's head, standing
on a barrel and preaching to a bizarre and grotesque audience which includes a dancing bear; the
inscription reads *Let those not calumniate who cannot
confute.*

Such a range of subjects and styles from the
cartoon satire characteristic of everyday political
life to the representations of vogue classicism in
the bacchanal and mythological reliefs, demonstrates that plaques are not as trivial as they may
first appear; the medium could enhance the subject and accomplished sculptors used it to adapt
and innovate within the disciplines of the tusk.

Kabinettkunst

Kabinettkunst, literally 'cabinet art', encompasses
almost any small, valuable object worthy of
collection; statues and plaques (already described),
objects with relief decoration and examples of
turning. The cabinets themselves also merit attention.

Relief decoration

Perhaps the epitome of relief-carved continental
ivory cabinet art is the massive tankard; its
cylindrical body is formed by the tusk section and
mounted at foot and rim in silver or silver gilt, or
occasionally gold, the applied handle and lid being
either ivory or metal. Lucas Fayd'herbe, noted for
his plaques, is associated with the finest seventeenth-century tankards though it is difficult to
make a definite attribution. One of the finest is
mounted in the contemporary style of the Augsburg silversmiths; the footrim and domed, stepped, bun-shaped lid are decorated with repoussé
fruiting vine, the strap handle is in the shape of a
broad double scroll. The drum itself is freely
carved with a bold, particularly Rubenesque
design, showing Silenus the wine philosopher,
draped in vine garlands and lurching along supported by followers, while nymphs dance around
the bowl gathering more grapes; the modelling is
realistically northern but the whole is fluid with
Italian influence. One critic suggests the pig lying
in the mud at his feet is 'typical of his condition'.
The cups and covers from the same period are
similar examples of the Teutonic celebration of
hydromel. Their quality and novelty were de-
valued by nineteenth-century copies, very
common, whose carving is generally crude and
stiff, the facial expression poor and the details of
the hair and hands untextured. Even the fine
revival examples at the Great Exhibition of 1851
lack the robust baroque spirit.

Relief-carved ceremonial vessels are relatively
scarcer than tankards and, highly elaborate, are
superb examples of craftsmanship. Johann
Michael Maucher was from the South German

Swabian school (active *c.* 1650–1700). His vessels,
from vast oval game dishes and elaborate ewers to
an ivory helmet (formerly attributed to Le Marchand), are fundamentally constructed of carved
plaques pinned together, each framing typically a
mythological scene. His famous game dish is
oval, the rim and centre a continuous series of
scenes from Ovid's *Metamorphoses*, which in the
centre are framed by classical columns, to reflect
contemporary Italian taste. The purist will find
little of the clarity of Renaissance spirit in this
work, and it can scarcely be considered mainstream artistic endeavour, but there is nevertheless
high quality, an expression of aspiration, and it
must have given much pleasure to the owner.

Examples of turning

During the great second period of ivory carving,
the seventeenth and eighteenth centuries, turning
was a major domestic art form practised by the
aristocracy, comparable perhaps with embroidery. The tradition dates back to the sixteenth and
seventeenth centuries when ivory turning was
patronized by royalty. Christof Angermair (1580–
1633) was court turner to Maximilian, Elector of
Bavaria, and the fact that he married into the
noble family reflects the esteem in which his work
was held. The range of items resulting encompasses fantastic baroque and rococo goblets and
covers, supported by putti, with lobes, globes,
steps, castellations and architectural motifs of

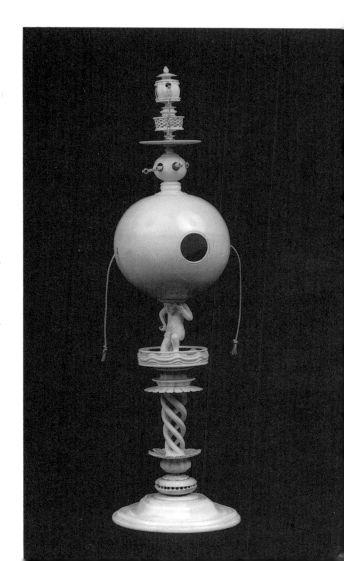

Above: South German cabinet shown in colour on page 124.

Below: Ivory portrait medallion by Jean Cavalier of Charles II of England. 1684.

amazing variety; slender Chinese-style table ornaments supporting concentric balls and encrusted with coils, springs and chains, typical of the Nuremberg Zick family; and, most commonly, everyday objects such as snuffboxes and patch-boxes or toothpick cases, often with a miniature portrait mounted in silver or a precious metals inlay, to adorn the boudoirs and libraries of eighteenth-century gentlefolk. Turning is probably the most common form of working ivory and its popularity waned only with the sophisticated and cheaper casting techniques of the nineteenth century.

Caskets and cabinets

Ivory caskets were abundant. Three great examples should be mentioned. First is the casket made for Marie de Medici, Queen of France (1573–1642), for the oval drawing-room at Fontainebleau; it is truly neo-classical in spirit, being covered in severe geometric panels relieved only by decoration on the framing columns, and conveys a monumental sense of weight. The second is the collector's cabinet made for the 'enamels and miniatures' collected by the English antiquarian Horace Walpole (1717–97). It is of kingwood with carved ivory plaques and finials to Walpole's design. The third is the coin cabinet by Angermair, carved for Elizabeth of Lorraine, wife of

Maximilian I, Elector of Bavaria. It is arguably one of the finest, containing twenty-two drawers concealed behind folding doors, all richly applied with heavy, late Renaissance, relief sculpture. It is very rich, but the detail does not obscure the clarity of its design.

The Huguenot revival: France and England

Religious intolerance, arguably the most destructive blow dealt to the Gothic ivory industry, was eventually to produce the greatest stimulus to English carving in the seventeenth century.

The Reformation had brought Gothic monastic life to an end and had greatly decreased interest in the paraphernalia of devotion, replaced by the Renaissance interest in art *per se* which legitimized secular carving. The religious struggles in France were partially resolved by the signing of the Edict of Nantes in 1598, when Henri IV guaranteed the Huguenots freedom of worship. In 1685 Louis XIV revoked it. William III of England offered royal protection for 'French Protestants . . . that shall seek refuge in our Kingdom', an act which attracted approximately 40,000 refugees, many of them skilled craftsmen, including, most significantly, Jean Cavalier and David Le Marchand, the two great portraitists of the late seventeenth and early eighteenth centuries.

Portrait medallists

Jean Cavalier (fl. 1684–96)

Little is known of Cavalier's wandering life. An equestrian portrait of Charles II of England is one of his earliest known works, inscribed on the reverse *I Cavalier F[ecit] 1684*. Clearly he at some time worked under the influence of a master, possibly Michel Mollart (1641–1713), carver and

Page 120: The Dance of Death, circle of David Heschler of Ulm. Seventeenth-century.

Page 121: Bacchanalian scene, carved in ivory, once owned by Madame de Pompadour (died 1764). See also page 114.

medallist at the French court, who provided an apartment for him in the Louvre, giving him the necessary access to contemporary convention and exposure to the ferocious baroque. Mollart's own rectangular profile of Louis XIV shows the Sun King with explosive curls and wearing fantastic armour adorned with a medallion of his mother, Anne of Austria, over his ear, and an epaulette of his grandmother, Marie de Medici, all beneath an embossed helmet surmounted by Apollo riding in the sun chariot; among which trappings Louis was all but concealed.

Cavalier's Charles shows a more neo-classical style with a less encumbered subject. Although it is in the tradition of monumental equestrian statue portraits, one of the refreshing appeals of this original ivory is the very northern emphasis on detail rather than form – the chiselled saddlecloth, the ribbon-tied flashing tail and knee-length mane, even the pathway strewn with flowers. Critics argue that Charles's billowing cloak is unnaturally still and the posture static, though this appears to be a youthful exaggerated linearity. More importantly, the head and face are sensitively modelled, alive and expressive though stern and intelligent. The details imply political statements: while the king is armoured, referring to his military prowess, he is 'helmeted' with only a laurel wreath suggesting a cerebral inclination towards peace, and extends a baton (intellect) rather than a sword (might). This anglicization of classical motifs is in itself a sculptural acknowledgement of Britain as a rising imperial power in small-scale art; in the macro-sculptural schemes of the early eighteenth century classical gods and British worthies may dominate a parkland side by side.

Cavalier's development is made clearly visible by a comparison of his portrait medallions of Mary II of England in 1686 and of the diarist and government official Samuel Pepys in 1688. The earlier work shows the familiar attention to line; the profile is somewhat harsh and descriptive, the hair piled high like sculptured meringue, and the dress a flat display of gathered swags rather than a three-dimensional ample corsage. Pepys is very different: bold, realistic features, catching a lively expression tempered with depth of character, fluid and flexible hair, glossy as the lacy cravat, and simple folds of drapery that contrast with rather than distracting from the head.

The confident and dashing portrait of William III confirms this trend towards Cavalier's mature style, and is dated 1690. His fees reflect the esteem in which he was held (20 guineas for a pair of ivory portraits in 1690 as against £50 paid to Grinling Gibbons for a life-sized marble of Queen Mary in 1685). By 1693 Cavalier is recorded in Copenhagen and three years later in Sweden. He is known to have travelled extensively and his death is thought to have occurred during a voyage to Russia and Persia: fittingly, little is known of this highly talented but enigmatic character.

David Le Marchand (1674–1726)

Cavalier's medium is extremely limited: the formal portrait roundel, normally in the form of a medal. David Le Marchand enjoyed the artistic latitude of the next generation and benefited from his background. His father painted biblical scenes for the church of St Jacques and the local convents in his home town, Dieppe, an established centre for ivory carving for more than a century since the enterprising merchants had initiated regular trade with Africa, and already known for portraits in horn, such as the pressed relief profiles produced by another Huguenot family, the Obrissets, who also emigrated to London. An early plaque by Le Marchand, a rectangular relief of the Miracle of the Man with the Withered Hand, combines painterly composition and the traditional format. Of his early years little is known. As a refugee he is first recorded as working in Edinburgh in 1696. His name appears in the registers of the French Church in London between 1705 and 1709 and he probably lived there until his death in the French hospital, La Providence, in 1726. He carved over sixty portraits, of which half are now in London museums.

Although Le Marchand's range is broader than Cavalier's, including busts 'in the round', a crucifix and classical figures, the main body of his work is, like Cavalier's, the formal medallion. Why did he choose so tight a discipline? Probably because he needed a patron. The church was now a much less useful source of funds for the carver. On the continent an established tradition of patronage was championed by the nobles who were amateur turners; there was also a plentiful supply of allegorical figures and mythological plaques. In England the appreciation of sculpture had been much less, until the mid-seventeenth-century influx of continental sculptors. The roundel form was part of the classical revival, to the somewhat parochial English it implied the classical fashions of the French court, and it had the authority of antiquity.

The popularity of ivory portraits was such that they were emulated even in their own time. Gosset (1707–85), another Huguenot, carved portraits in white wax, often after other sculptors (coincidentally with a variety of ivory tools still owned by his descendants), issuing small editions. Vertue wrote that the 'ingenious Mr Gosset who even had his Majestyes setting to him' sold the original for four guineas and the copies 'in oval frame for a guinea apeece', 'which imitate ivory'. There is evidence too that Le Marchand's appeal lasted well into the eighteenth century. Wedgwood, the china firm, acquired from many

Below and left: Portrait medallions of William III of England by Jean Cavalier. 1690.

sources subjects for their ceramic medallions and in 1773–4 bought two moulds 'from Ivery'; these were never cast, but modern versions show marked similarity to Le Marchand's work, and the mould bore the name of the Raper family, his greatest patrons and close friends. A glass paste medallion of the same patron was named on the reverse *Matthew Raper Esqre Senior* and still bore traces of the characteristic signature beneath the bust section, though the originals have been lost. The Rapers even commissioned a portrait in oils of Le Marchand holding the famous bust of Sir Isaac Newton which they later gave to the British Museum. The long association also produced his most original work, an ivory portrait of Matthew Raper III, probably carved in 1720. Matthew Raper II was a silk merchant from Buckinghamshire who rose to be Governor of the Bank of England, and in his son's pose we see the aspiration of the bourgeois father. He is portrayed at the age of fifteen, quill in hand, standing in a library demonstrating a proposition in geometry. The room is given depth by the book-lined walls, retreating floorboards and mid-ground furniture, reminiscent both of northern interior painting and, especially, of the intellectual portraits of Louis XIV's court.

The interest in perspective evident even in Le Marchand's earliest works led to achievements beyond Cavalier's and preceded some striking busts. John Churchill, first Duke of Marlborough, is depicted in profile but in quite high relief so that the shoulder stands proud to the viewer and the soft folds of drapery are distanced from the face. In a stunning portrait more immediate than its precedent, the profile, Sir Thomas Guy, founder of London's Guy's Hospital, looks directly out at the viewer. A medallion of Newton known only from a sale catalogue of 1864 shows an imposing sitter turning to his left but glancing slightly to his right, giving a lively motive effect. Le Marchand's portraits today may command five-figure sums.

The few busts by Le Marchand demonstrate his virtuosity and his social penetration. The Bust of an Unknown Lady, made in 1701 when he was only twenty-one, demonstrates a strength of modelling difficult to achieve in a full-sized bust and shows her tantalizing vivacity, with turning head and bright eyes framed by textured curling hair falling on to a sensuous breast draped in generous folds. The unfastened shirt and casual air could not contrast more sharply with Cavalier's early work. Earlier still is a bust of the philosopher John Locke, lost but known from museum photographs, which is Le Marchand's first known work and shows exceptional bravura and verve.

On 11 July 1722 the antiquary William Stukeley 'sat to Mr Marchand cutting my profile in Bass relievo in ivory'. This is his last known work. In June 1726 Stukeley records the death of his intimate friend, 'the famous cutter in ivory Monsr. Marchand who cut my profile'.

Other portrait medallists

Each European country can claim its own medallists, not only at the height of the art but almost continuously until the classical revival of the nineteenth century: in Italy, the prolific Francesco Francelli, in the late seventeenth century; in France and the Low Countries, Mansel, who had a cosmopolitan clientele, and others, including Rombout Verhulst (1624–98); in France again, Mollart (1641–1713) and Mauger (died 1722); in Germany, the Steudners and the Hennens. The initial purpose of portrait medallions seems clear, to present the likeness framed and glazed; others, however, are applied to caskets and furniture such as the eighteenth-century Langlois commodes, often with other exotic materials, and some were presumably collected by the cognoscenti. An engaging intimacy in the uniqueness of the ivory medallion perhaps reflects the bond between patron and artist. The texture can give it the quality of a painting, though rarely constrained by the same formality. It has an enduring fascination.

Scientific instruments

The sixteenth century saw an increase in ivory's application as a purely functional material which

Above: Portrait medallion of John Churchill, Duke of Marlborough, by David Le Marchand.

Far right: An ivory diptych dial by Leonhart Miller. Mid-seventeenth-century; 4 × 2½ in. (10.5 × 6.5 cm). A compass is inset in the lower face and twenty-two European cities are listed on the upper inner face. Seventeenth-century scientific instruments were as handsome as they were functional.

competed with brass, steel and boxwood for use in precision instruments, particularly for navigational purposes.

The Age of Discovery, with Columbus landing in the New World in 1493, da Gama reaching India from the west in 1498 and Magellan reaching Asia from the east in 1521, and their fellow adventurers following up their explorations, initiated the desire to trade, to colonize, to discover, and created a new need for practical portable astronomical instruments and a new interest in the Renaissance pursuit of knowledge *per se*.

Navigation and surveying involved complicated and lengthy calculations, both multiplication and division. The Scots mathematician John Napier (1550–1617) devised logarithms, which considerably simplified the task, and in 1614 published his tables, with the instructions in Latin and therefore not universally accessible. However, he also invented a sophisticated and more workable calculator, 'Napier's bones', first issued in 1617; versions were still being manufactured in the eighteenth century. Rods inscribed with numbers were calibrated with horizontal and diagonal lines and were arranged vertically to allow a swift and simple calculation. The rods were contained in a box frame. Another version utilized cylindrical rods which could be turned in their box. The number of 'bones' varied from less than twelve to more than twenty-four. They were manufactured in ivory or boxwood, and are as picturesque now as they were practical then.

The properties of ivory, not only its pure whiteness but also its durability and the relative ease of engraving it, compared with metal, were ideal for the production of small instruments such as diptych dials. 'Diptych' simply means composed of two leaves hinged together and 'dial' any calibrated measure. Gnomonics is the science of dials and their construction, the gnomon being the horizontal or inclined member whose shadow the sun casts on to some form of scale. A popular form in the sixteenth and seventeenth centuries was the string gnomon, a diptych dial whose two leaves of ivory are joined by a string connecting their two outer edges. When the leaves are opened at right angles to one another, the taut string casts a shadow, weather permitting, on a scale which gives the time. It often incorporates a glazed compass so that the dial can be set to the correct direction. Such dials are often signed and dated. Although something is known of the great makers, such as Paul Reinman of Nuremberg, and Jakob Kearner who characteristically signed his work with the numeral 3, they were instrument makers rather than ivory carvers. The dials are often as decorative as they are scientific. An elaborate dial will be incised with numerous scales, stained in red, green and black, adorned with lunar volvelles, Julian and Gregorian calendars, latitudes for various European towns, fixing points for the string gnomon at four different places, gnomon dials for Italian and Babylonian hours, a compartment at the side for tails of the optional wind vane, and engravings of the nativity and the resurrection applied with embossed, gilt metal mounts depicting amorini, scrolling strapwork and clasps *en suite*. Such a dial is not only a workaday watch; it is a riotous indulgence in baroque rhetoric, an exuberant display of intellectualism.

A more sober-looking instrument with a more serious purpose is the cross-staff. Diptych dials are so latitude dependent that one can calculate their place of origin from their inaccuracy when used elsewhere; clearly they are therefore land based. (Interestingly, the astrolabe, used to take the altitude of the sun or the stars, was known in the tenth century but was not adapted for maritime use until the sixteenth; it was often carried at sea but used only on dry land.) The cross-staff was first described in the early fourteenth century by Levi ben Gerson, a French astronomer. It was used to measure the angles between two stars or between the sun and the horizon. It consisted of a square sectioned stave, about 30 in. (76 cm) long, calibrated on all four sides and fitted with one or more sliding cross-pieces. (It was sometimes known as the arbalista, from the French term for crossbow, which it resembles visually.) The user sighted the sun along the staff and moved the cross-piece until its tips touched the points to be measured; the altitude could then be read from the scale on the staff. Cross-staffs had very short lives, owing to the exposed conditions, and the scales are therefore often of bone or ivory rather than the tightly grained boxwood. In 1497–8, on Vasco da Gama's voyage from Portugal to India, his Arab pilot used a cross-staff; Dutch sailors were still using them in the nineteenth century. The explorer John Davis, who voyaged around Canada in the late sixteenth century, first documents the back-staff, an essentially similar instrument, generally made of lignum vitae. The user turned his back to the sun, with obvious advantage. Extremely popular and used all over the world for two centuries, the back-staff was made almost exclusively in Britain, unlike the cross-staff of which very few English examples are known. This parochial attitude towards innovative designs is surpassed perhaps only by the conservatism with which they were received. Although the sextant was developed in the second half of the eighteenth century it was not until 1920 that sextants became naval issue.

Owing to its fibrous nature ivory tends to warp and crack when planed to a flat surface, a particular drawback in the arc-shaped dials integral to the back-staff and the sextant. Ivory was phased out from the early eighteenth century onwards. Its

Top: South German cabinet for Kabinettkunst, in ebony, ivory and bone, with details (*above, left and right*) of two ivory reliefs showing Adam and Eve. 1690; 30¾ × 40¼ × 15¾ in. (76.85 × 102 × 38.75 cm). Ivory reliefs of Eden and the Fall, and Cain and Abel, are applied to the front drawers and the Mocking of Christ and the Entombment are on the central bottom drawer. On the central door, which opens to reveal the inner drawers, are ivory figures of the Risen Christ, with soldiers and angels. See also page 118.

Right: Enamel and ivory counter box. 1800.

Below: , French ivory snuffbox (*top left*) carved with figures, birds and masks. 1720; *top right*, Louis XV silver-mounted ivory box with piqué point decoration, 1717–22; *bottom left*, George III ivory toothpick case with gold piqué point decoration, 1790; *bottom right*, eighteenth-century ivory toothpick case.

continued use as inset scales and detailing on precision instruments results perhaps from its legibility and cosmetic appeal. From the mid eighteenth century onwards and throughout the nineteenth, carved and turned ivory was used in monocular telescopes and simple microscopes of the Wilson screw-barrel or Withering type, and for talc boxes, surgical instrument handles and other quasi-scientific paraphernalia.

Domestic cutlery

In the medieval world the banquet was a structural event rather than a meal. The utensils were fairly basic, the diners eating primarily roast meats in various sauces from flat wooden platters lined with stale trencher bread to catch the drips. The role of carver at a royal feast was an honoured one, for carving was an art. The only significant eating implements were the two carving knives, the presentoir, a broad-bladed knife used to serve the meat to important guests (the others would serve themselves) and the personal knives which the diners brought with them, cutting up the meat and then eating it with the fingers. The presentoirs and personal knives surviving from the early sixteenth century often have ivory, bone or horn handles, sometimes inscribed ('Better it is a poor house to hold than to lye in prison with fetters of gold').

The philosopher Erasmus, writing in 1530, says that the Italians were displeased if a guest arrived without his own knife, the Germans became positively angry, yet the French seemed to manage with only two or three shared in common. 'If someone offers you something out of a cake or a pie receive it with your piece of bread,' he writes, but if offered a fluid dish, 'eat it and return the spoon but not without wiping it on your napkin first.' There is an unusually fine, early-seventeenth-century Netherlandish spoon from Hever Castle in Kent, which is carved in ivory, the handle being a siren wearing a helmet, the rounded bowl held in the teeth of a marine monster. Silver and base metal spoons, however, are more common from this period.

The Italians were enjoying pasta during the Middle Ages and appear to have first taken to the fork. The Worshipful Company of Cutlers in London owns a fine, early Italian knife and fork set from the mid seventeenth century, the handles depicting Adam and Eve after the Fall, standing against the tree with fruit and foliage over their heads, a curious theme for eating aids. This period represents the zenith of elaboration in eating and such figural sets were relatively common. At best they are crisply carved with charming topical subjects; another Cutlers Company fork has a handle carved with William III of England and his wife Mary II embracing. The carved subjects vary from a pair in staghorn, depicting a bishop and a fool, through the allegorical and mythological, to the rather decadent, weak, stereotyped carving of the mid eighteenth century with endless heaps of tumbling putti.

These elaborate sets appear at the height of the vogue for personalized cutlery epitomized by the habit of the groom presenting the bride with a pair of wedding knives or a knife and fork set. There are many literary allusions to this practice ('Both fitted into the one sheath'). The lady wore them at her waist, on show, which justifies or perhaps encourages the elaborate decoration in almost every material at this period.

By the late seventeenth century the French were paving the way for smaller suppers and a range of dishes which necessitated more sophisticated cutlery. The host would provide knives and forks for a dozen guests himself; no longer items of personal display, they were ordered in large matching canteens. The dinner party, for better or worse, was born.

By 1750 the demand for finely carved handles was extinct. Orders for canteens in the neoclassical post-rococo taste brought simple and severe designs, perhaps the shape of a pistol grip but little more elaborate. Carved ivory handles disappear towards the end of the century, apart from anachronistic revival of figural desk knives and other precious items favoured in Europe where there was a stronger carving tradition. Porcelain and enamel knife handles were cheaper and more colourful; the ivory handle was regularly used throughout the eighteenth and nine-

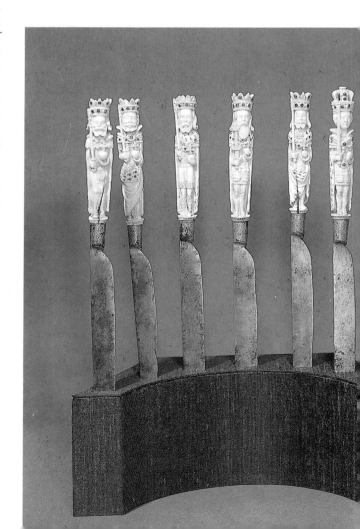

Far right: French ivory snuffrasp. Seventeenth-century; 6½ in. (16.4 cm). An eighteenth-century snuffbox is shown, in colour, on page 125.

teenth centuries for functional, plain, rounded, faceted grips (commonly stained green in the mid eighteenth century). In essence it has changed little up to the present day, except that in the last two decades an ivory substitute has been introduced to preserve endangered species.

Although little remains of the former glory of the carved handle there was a revival in the mid nineteenth century of carved figural handles, particularly on carving sets; these tend to be of high quality although limited artistically. The dirk is still worn with Scottish dress and there is still some tradition attached to the Sunday joint.

Snuff tobacco and gentlemen's paraphernalia

During the seventeenth and early eighteenth centuries, snuff, which is essentially treated tobacco leaf, arrived from the New World in moist blocks tied with string. To convert it into powder it was rubbed along a rasp of perforated metal and the fine grains were funnelled via a conical receptacle – arriving fresh, aromatic and potent.

These snuffrasps, rappoirs or tabakrasps were made of many materials, including wood, enamel, pottery and porcelain, but the finest and most durable are carved in ivory. The conical shape and curved section of the tusk forms an ideal chute, the end being carved to form a spout; one end is sometimes compartmented with a sliding lid to store any surplus. The exterior became well rubbed, giving a bright, deep patina,

Below: Set of fourteen table knives with ivory handles. *c.*1604.

ideally accentuating the low-relief decoration on the panel, which varied from 6 to 12 in. (15 to 30 cm) in length and was a few inches wide. The proportions approximated the human form so it was often carved with an appropriate silhouette. More commonly the design was framed within an architectural cartouche decorated by prevalent baroque or rococo motifs. The charming, often rather naïve designs can perfectly blend art and everyday social history in a pleasing object.

Snuffrasps were sometimes known as 'Grivois', named apparently after the soldiers of bad character who used them, but the practice was also common among the leisured classes.

Decorative techniques

The one consistent application of ivory throughout the sixteenth, seventeenth and eighteenth centuries was as a means of decoration of precious objects, primarily as veneer or inlay, each being sometimes engraved to enhance the effect, generally following the stylistic fashion of the time.

Veneer involves slicing the tusk into thin layers, from ½ to ¹/₁₆ in. (12 to 1.5 mm) thick, which are then glued to the carcase of wood. Until the end of the eighteenth century the veneer is generally

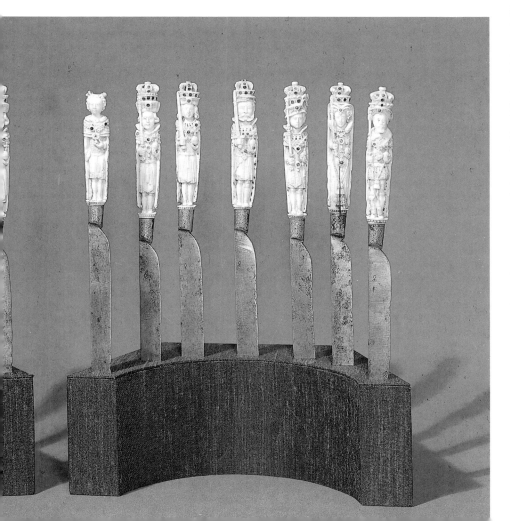

Opposite: Pair of wheel-lock holster pistols (*below*) with walnut stocks inlaid with staghorn and ivory, from Germany. *c.*1610. After designs by Theodor de Bry. The detail (*left*) shows the intricate inlay and carving.

hand cut and therefore rarely larger than the tusk section; larger pieces, formed by cutting continuously round, appear not earlier than the nineteenth century. An elegant lute from Hever Castle in Kent is German sixteenth-century; strips of ivory separated by strips of ebony are applied to the oval bowl, the first and second neck and the pegbox; other lutes have chequered necks, as do theorbos; their shining brightness is still striking. The veneering of instruments did not continue much past the seventeenth century, but it was revived in the nineteenth, for technical reasons of resonance as much as changes in taste, though

solid plaques, through the intermediate round boxes of 1700–50, to the severe veneered ovals and rectangles of 1775–1800. Each nation enjoyed its individual taste: in Germany, rococo dominated the eighteenth century; in France, the Dieppe school (which declined dramatically after 1685) favoured pierced designs reworking the formal courtly scenes; in England, the neo-classical was accepted much earlier.

Games paraphernalia

As domestic life became more civilized, games boxes were veneered to hold cards, counters and

Above: Two caddies, both of polygonal section. Eighteenth-century. The one on the left, in tortoiseshell, is the simpler. That on the right, in gold and ivory, has an oval miniature of a mythological scene, with tortoiseshell border and stringing. The restrained elegance is typical of the neo-classical. Ivory is combined with enamel in a counter box shown in colour on page 125.

there are recorders and other small wind instruments made from turned tusks in the eighteenth century.

The baroque and rococo tendency towards more sculptural, shaped, scrolling decoration in the seventeenth and eighteenth centuries was marked by an increasing use of inlay rather than plain veneer. The strong influence of the neo-classical revival typified by Adam and Chippendale in the 1760s and 1770s sobered the frivolous bands of strapwork and shell paterae into severely geometric and undecorated rectangular surfaces ideal for veneering. The boxes, caskets and tea caddies of George III's reign (1760–1820) are small and discreet with no greater concession to polychrome than ebony stringing, tortoiseshell borders which enhance the purity of the ivory, or perhaps a silver escutcheon. Smaller boxes for cosmetics, snuff or toothpicks followed a similar trend, from the seventeenth-century versions carved with mythological scenes in relief or on

other paraphernalia, often with delicate, incised and stained decoration. The sixteenth and seventeenth centuries produced the most elaborate chess sets, commemorating monarchs, for example, or great battles and wars, often of high sculptural quality, the boards with alternating squares of ebony and fruitwood and inlaid borders (often with backgammon or Nine Men's Morris on the back). One box board from the Mentmore collection was formed from alternate squares of opaque and clear amber, with ivory silhouettes revealed beneath the latter, and represents the heights of sumptuous effect to which post-Renaissance Europe aspired.

A Conventional decree in the French Revolution replaced the chess king with a flag, the queen with an adjutant, the knight with a dragoon, the rook with a cannon, the bishop with a volunteer, the pawn with a soldier of the line. The most famous of all French designs, the 'Directoire' chess set, predates the French Revolutionary

Below: The Danish throne at Rosenborg Castle, made by Bendix Grodtschilling, from pieces of narwhal tusk, to striking effect; 1662–5. The figures were added later.

government of October 1795 to November 1799, after which it was named. Directoire pieces were possibly the most beautiful ever made. Their tall stems, marked by annular ornament, rose from a substantial turned unit that was often bulbous or cup-shaped. The knight was distinguished from the bishop by a rounded, sloping collar, as the bell-shaped tops of the two pieces were very similar. In spite of the decree, the king still wore his crown. The tall, spindly, major pieces were graduated in size according to their importance. They were so much alike that it was possible in the intense concentration on the game to play the king or the bishop in mistake for the knight. The Directoire design survived the French Revolution and it was to prove very popular, both in Britain and in America, during the early nineteenth century.

Arms and powderflasks

A compact history of ivory decoration can be traced through the changes in style of arms generally, and powderflasks specifically, during these three centuries. Crossbows, the natural precursors of firearms, are often richly decorated with bone and ivory panels of relevant scenes, sporting weapons showing the hunt, and military weapons for aristocrats showing battle scenes. During the seventeenth and eighteenth centuries the decorators ran amok with relief scenes inlaid on to the wooden gunstocks, plaques let in with incised decoration in turn inlaid with gold and silver. There is even a Dutch pistol, the entire stock of which is carved ivory, a classical helmeted head forming the butt.

The less self-conscious and more utilitarian powderflasks represent more personal art and have less stereotyped application; in the earlier circular type, each side of a cushion-shaped flask is often carved in high relief with hounds and their prey intertwined lyrically as they race through a frieze of ferns and trees, each stag, boar and fox naturalistically carved. The other characteristic form is of the fork of a reindeer antler, the interior hollowed and the ends plugged to contain the dry powder, the exterior incised with simple scenes from nature.

Furnishings and furniture

The decoration of furnishings and furniture similarly follows art historical lines, sometimes regardless of the item adorned, but often with striking effect. The casket for jewels and small but precious things follows the Embriachi tradition, and the table cabinet derives from the small-scale Renaissance writing chests and the more extensive Spanish *vargueno*, both often showing Islamic influence in their marquetry decoration; their absorption into the western European tradition of rococo and baroque motifs, in the sixteenth and seventeenth centuries, produced a diversity of styles, shapes and colour combinations.

Continental furniture of the eighteenth century employed designs into which ivory inlay was frequently integrated to contrast with different woods. Pietro Piffetti (1700–77), who worked in Turin, is famous for his original and elaborate designs and Reisener, Roentgen and Langlois are also known for their marquetry, sometimes using plaques and *pietra dura* to enhance the overall effect.

Nineteenth and Twentieth Centuries

Nineteenth-century France

In the early nineteenth century there were more ivory carvers at work in France than in any other European country. Their standing, always high, was enhanced when Napoleon's client kings and nobles flocked to Paris to consume French goods. Paris rapidly attracted ivory workers from other countries.

The aged Giuseppe Maria Bonzanigo (1744–1820) had worked all his life in Turin, Italy, which Napoleon added to the French Empire. He was noted for his miniature carvings in ivory of flowers and fruit, his 'allegorical and emblematic designs' and his boxes.

At the request of Napoleon's second empress, Marie Louise, Bonzanigo constructed a coin cabinet, now in the Louvre, of ebony and ivory, ornamented with a portrait of the empress, imperial emblems and allegorical figures. A frieze of ivory sculpture runs round the base. Whether Bonzanigo left Turin for Paris is not known, but the tradition of carving in ivory in Italy has been said to come to an end with Bonzanigo and his pupils, so perhaps the latter did so.

No new centres of ivory working seem to have been formed in France during the nineteenth century and some of those already existing may have had to struggle to survive, but ivory workers were much more spread out over the whole country than is sometimes realized. The *département* of Oise was noted for its production of fancy ware, buttons, fans and other articles in ivory, bone and mother-of-pearl. Méru was a particularly important centre in Oise and its Friday market must have attracted many customers. Oyonnax, in the *département* of Ain, was noted for its ivories, particularly combs. Its subsidiary industries in horn and wood may have helped it to survive. St-Claude in the Jura, a centre of pilgrimage, and hence souvenirs, until a disastrous fire in 1799, was famous for its fancy articles in ivory, horn, tortoiseshell and wood. But the most notable centres in France were Paris and Dieppe, both of which must have contained large numbers of workers in ivory. .

The French ivory carver benefited from having a recognized place in the hierarchy of art workers. *Ivoirerie*, the craft of ivory carving, was part of *tabletterie*, and the *tabletier*, according to Chambaud's Dictionary, was 'he who makes and sells chessboards, chessmen, draughts, billiard balls, and other works of ivory, ebony, etc., a toy-man or woman, one that keeps a toyshop'. 'Toyshop' is used in its eighteenth-century sense, as a store for the sale of expensive luxury items for grown-ups, not children. The *ivoirier* also made the plates of purses, covers of wedding albums, spoon and knife handles, salad servers, door handles, combs, statues, particularly religious ones such as crucifixes, holy water stoups, fans, particularly the outside leaves or *maîtresse branches*, and everything for the lady's workbox, including the *navette* or spindle, an item so popular that many carvers must have made it their speciality.

Paradoxically, though, French ivory carving was on the decline throughout the nineteenth century. It must be said, straightaway, that this decline was a relative one. It did not involve the abandonment of the highest possible artistic standards on the part of the best craftsmen. Time and time again an ivory figure will appear in the modern saleroom, a figure which has no signature, no known provenance, but is so exquisite in taste and execution that the verdict must be: 'French, possibly Dieppe, nineteenth century.'

Dieppe ivory carving

Yet nowhere was the nineteenth-century decline more evident than in the very heart of production, Dieppe, with its long history of ivorywork. The 'toyshop' men and women sold the ivories in their shops in the *Grande Rue*, without the intermission of the middlemen who had helped to keep down the English ivory worker, and either kept studios themselves or bought from those who did. An eminent and successful shopkeeper-carver would have several pupils, sometimes as many as a dozen, working to the designs he provided and under his supervision, though there was always the danger that once their instruction was complete they would set up by themselves or go to another *ivoirier*. There were also piece-workers available.

As for the patrons, Dieppe was both a seaport and a watering place, and visitors usually arrived regularly every summer. When Napoleon and Josephine visited Dieppe in 1802. she was given an ivory ship, he a snuffbox decorated with a plan of the town and the motto, in Latin, 'He came and I recovered strength.' On a subsequent visit, in 1810, with his second wife, Marie Louise, he bought from Le Painteur two medallions, a snuffbox and a flagon, ornamented with gold, and from Louis-Charles-Vincent Belletête an ivory ship. Dieppe was suffering from the British blockade, which had interrupted supplies of ivory from Senegal, and from the absence of English visitors. The changed distribution of wealth in France had also affected the carvers very much. Up until twenty-five years earlier, before the French Revolution, the church had been the wealthiest institution in France and had ordered the most sumptuous ivories. A holy water stoup such as that made by Lefebvre in 1779, with the perforated background called *mosaique* by the Dieppois, must have provided weeks of work for a whole team of carvers. Now Napoleon had confirmed the complete confiscation of the church's wealth. The Dieppois continued to make religious objects, especially crucifixes, but these were often totally lacking in merit – *christs en grosse*.

An art school was set up in Dieppe in 1808. Its director, Marie-Joseph Flouest, though an inspiring teacher, had been born in 1747 and was a disciple of *ancien régime* artists such as Florian and Houdon. He was faced with finding subjects that would appeal to the new rich. The carvers tried topical subjects – 'The Passage of the St Bernard by Napoleon', by Boulais, 'The Night before Austerlitz', 'Soldier Defending a Wounded Comrade', even 'Soldier Burying a Dead Comrade' – but none of these new departures elicited any enthusiasm from the patrons. Carvers had to keep going as best they could by making snuffboxes, reduced figures from the antique, *bonbonnières* and fans.

In 1815 Napoleon was exiled and the Bourbon dynasty reinstated. Instantly everything royalist became fashionable. Busts of Napoleon were put aside to be sold to the English tourists, now crowding back to the town, and the *ivoiriers* began work on subjects which would appeal to supporters of the Bourbons, such as 'A View of the Ruins of the Château d'Arques' (where Henri IV had won a famous victory) or a ship called *Le Bon Roi Henri*. Many of the carvings also feature seabathing, a new fashion in France, and the newly built Dieppois bathing establishment.

The sprightly Princesse de Berri became a regular visitor. Born Marie Caroline, the daughter of the King and Queen of Naples, she married her cousin, Charles Ferdinand, Duc de Berri, the heir to the French throne, in 1816. He was assassinated in 1820, but his widow gave birth to a posthumous daughter. The princess captivated the Dieppois and won their hearts. She gave certificates 'By Royal Command' for the best work both in ivory and in lace, and she made many purchases of ivories. Even after her departure, due to another change of dynasty in 1830, French royalty continued to patronize the ivory workers. Louis Philippe of Orleans, the 'citizen king' (reigned 1830–48), made some truly royal purchases: the two 'Medici' vases, one showing the Birth of Bacchus, the other the Triumph of Bacchus and Ariadne, made by Adrien-Nicolas Clemence, were bought by the king in 1833 for 4000 francs.

The connection between the French rulers and the Dieppe carvers ended only with the fall of the Emperor Napoleon III in 1870. In 1853 he had presented Pierre-Adrien Graillon (1807–72), one of the greatest and most original carvers, with the Legion of Honour, in recognition of his talented figurine portrait of the emperor. In the same year the emperor and his wife Eugénie bought numerous cups, candlesticks, coffrets and mirror frames from Pierre-Jacques-Théodore Blard (1822–1902).

The Dieppe dynasties of ivory workers, such as the Belletêtes, the Flamands, the Blards, the Nicolles, the Clemences, the Graillons, the Bignards, the Souillards and the Farge Hébert Garcins, provided a continuity in the art which is paralleled only in Erbach, in Germany. Father taught son, brother brother. Family secrets, notably detailed measurements for special kinds of work, such as crucifixes, plaster models and drawings, were conserved from one generation to another. A master ivory worker might own and bequeath a private gallery of old master carvings or books on ivory. The master–pupil relationship supplemented and extended the family network.

Jacques Blard took as pupil a poor shoemaker, Pierre Graillon. Starting him off with ship models made in wood, wholesale, he then taught him to carve ivory. Graillon proved himself a gifted carver who could work in any medium. He went to study in Paris but returned to Dieppe and made

Above: Detail of the carved ivory wreath shown in colour on page 145. It frames a portrait in ivory of Napoleon III and the Empress Eugenie.

Far right: Ivory plaque of a beggar by Pierre Graillon. 1854; 8¼ × 4½ in. (21.3 × 11.5 cm).

a speciality of carvings of poor people, sailors, fishwives, beggars and the hangers-on of the quays. He had a talent for tackling the most difficult pieces of raw material. Out of the hollow of an elephant tusk he would fashion a convention of beggars, meeting on the skirts of a forest. A whale's tooth (too intractable for most) would become a human head crowned with a bonnet.

In 1824 Blard acquired the services of Adrien-Nicolas Clemence (1798–1828), the best pupil of Louis-Charles-Antoine Belletête, who sold up, in consequence. Also recruited outside the circle of hereditary ivory carvers, Clemence had been brought up to the sea. He had made a name for himself under Belletête by making statues of the Virgin for wholesale export, and then the celebrated 'Medici' vases, already mentioned, an equestrian statuette of Henri IV, and bas reliefs of Virgil's *Eclogues*, now in the Louvre.

The noted worker Auguste Philibert Meugniot (1802–42) was a sturdy individualist of the Graillon stamp. His masterpiece, now in the Louvre, is 'The Old Man Dying'. Full of unsparing realism, it attracted the attention of the Princesse de Berri and was the last Dieppe ivory she bought. She had already refused to accept Meugniot's portrait medallion of her in high relief. He was famous for the speed with which he could dash off these medallions, spending only a day on them and selling them for 100, 150 or even 200 francs. It may be that the portrait was not sufficiently flattering.

In 1821 there were six master ivory carvers at work in Dieppe. The figure rose to nine in 1824, ten in 1835, thirteen in 1849, then eighteen, its highest, from 1854 to 1873. In 1883 it was down to fifteen, in 1892 to eleven, and at the end of the century to eight. Many of the younger carvers had been drawn away to Paris, especially after the 1834 Exhibition there. From the mid century onwards imitation ivories made of celluloid and other substitutes discouraged customers from buying, for fear of fakes. It had become increasingly difficult for carvers to fit in their commitments at the workshop with the hours of instruction at the school of art that would have given them a real sculptor's training, while training in modelling had disappeared altogether. Some Parisians felt Dieppe work was a little rustic – the taste of Dieppe and the capital were now far apart. Critics complained that purchasers could no longer get the old Dieppe *mosaique*; the new work was too regular, too mechanical. In answer one Dieppe carver, Antoine-François-Victoire Nicolle (1807–83), argued in 1851 that present-day sculpture at Dieppe was superior to that made in the past ('Flowers and ornaments surpass former work in their taste and delicacy'), though figurines left something to be desired.

More than one Dieppe carver had died in

extreme misery and want. Meugniot had killed himself in a Rouen asylum. Poitevin, the creator of *Le Bon Roi Henri* and other ivory ships, had gone blind and had been forced to beg his bread. Pierre-Modeste Buisson (1795–1844), believed to have organized the resurgence of religious carvings following the Bourbon restoration in 1815, died in the workhouse.

During the boom in ivory carving, workshops had multiplied and too many apprentices were taken on, sometimes by master carvers who had little or no artistic training. Many ivory workers hesitated to send their work to the exhibitions in Paris where they might have gained an artistic reputation as well as a useful second income, and failed to get themselves an education in art, even though they had an art school in the port. These omissions put them in a fatal position of inferiority when it came to bargaining with the shopkeepers, who combined to drive down wages. Between 1840 and 1870 the price of ivory had doubled and, unlike in England, customs duty had to be paid on it.

By 1900 there were barely forty carvers left and the turners, formerly numerous, had disappeared. The great days were over. But what an artistic triumph the nineteenth century had been! The Dieppois were masters of certain types of carving:

Above: Detail of the sails and rigging of an ivory ship from Dieppe.

Far right: French ship rigged and armed in ivory. 5½ in. (14 cm) high, 6½ in. (17 cm) long. Ship models were a speciality of the Dieppe carvers.

ship models, flowers of all sorts (there were still twenty-one *fleuristes* as late as 1900) and statuettes, often portraits of fishermen and fishwives (maritime subjects always abounded in Dieppe), figurines portraying Napoleon, Henri IV and Louis XIV, popular religious subjects – Christ on the Cross, the *Ecce Homo* ('Behold the Man'), the Virgin, and the saints – the gods and goddesses of pagan antiquity, and for the English visitors such historical personages as Charles I, Mary Queen of Scots, and Queen Elizabeth's favourite, the Earl of Leicester.

Innumerable minor works poured out of the

workshops: a huge range of handles, trinkets, ornaments, vases and clocks. Much of this work is difficult to identify because it is usually unsigned, even by a monogram, but the best has the indefinable quality that shows it is Dieppe.

Combination sculpture

Emigrants from Dieppe to Paris settled to producing *articles de Paris* or aiding, as *practiciens*, the experiments in combination sculpture. To catch the eye of the mid- and late-nineteenth-century exhibition juries, ivory had to escape from the *bibelot* scale and stand forth in works of larger dimensions. It could do this only if combined with other materials. The great Parisian goldsmith François-Désiré Froment-Meurice (1802–55) commissioned from Henri de Triqueti an all-ivory sculpture, 'Nymph pursued by Cupid', which was exhibited at the Crystal Palace in 1851.

Triqueti's main contribution to combination sculpture was a vase in which ivory and bronze flowed, as it were, on different levels. Between the bronze fitments – handles, base and mouth – was a hollow cylinder of ivory, covered with a continuous frieze of low-relief sculptures and resembling a drum from a sculptured Roman column (this connection with antiquity was reinforced by numerous inscriptions between the sculpted figures). The joins between the pieces of ivory were shown quite openly, without any covering of bronze, and suggested the fitted stones that would make up a sculpted column.

The most important of all combination sculptures was made for the Paris International Exhibition of 1855 by the sculptor Pierre Charles Simart (1806–57) to the order of the Duc de Luynes. It was nothing less than a reproduction of the famous statue of Athene made by Phidias. Though considerably smaller than the original, Simart's statue was none the less the largest ivory work seen in modern times, down to the present day. It towered over 9 ft (3 m) high and dazzled the beholder by its combination of different surfaces.

The undraped portions of the statue were of ivory, as were the head of Medusa and the Victory which formed part of the work. The lance, helmet and serpent were of bronze, the tunic and shield of several tones of silver, repoussé and chased. Froment-Meurice carried out the goldsmith's work. It had a most important influence on European ivory carving, for it was hailed as the first modern 'chryselephantine' statue.

Simart's Athene was imitated by other ivory carvers on a much smaller scale. The statuette 'Lady Reading' by Ernest Carrier Belleuse (1824–87) stands some 10½ in. (27 cm) high, including the base, and can be dated *c.* 1870–80. In the Gothic taste and a good example of what the Germans call Kleinplastik, 'miniature sculpture', the gold and ivory statuette is a bridge between the early- and mid-nineteenth-century combination sculpture and the late-nineteenth-century Art Nouveau sculpture which was to lead straight in to Art Deco.

French sculptors also tried to solve the problem of combining pieces of ivory to make a large composition, by carving them to fit and pegging them with dowels or pins. Louis Lautz created a number of impressive tankards of very large size. He worked in Paris, and exhibited in the French section of the 1851 Great Exhibition, but his work shows some affinity with contemporary German tankards. But the happiest results in combining large pieces of ivory were to be achieved in Germany, by the Erbachers.

Prisoner-of-war carving

Among the particular forms of ivory carving popularized by the Dieppe carvers was the ivory ship, a *genre* acclimatized and made famous by the Dieppois but not invented by them. In 1620 the Elector of Saxony had asked the Dutch ivory carver Jacob Zeller to make him an ivory ship, complete in every detail, on the model of those made by the Chinese and often used by them as wedding presents (marriage being a ship, captained by the husband who had the right to unswerving obedience from the crew – that is, the wife). Zeller fulfilled his commission by making a European ship, based on the contemporary *fregata*, and this model must have attracted a good deal of attention. By the eighteenth century the ship model had become one of the most popular products of Dieppe. A ship model presented by the Dieppois to Napoleon's second wife, Marie Louise, still survives in the Château Museum in

Below: Detail of the box for gaming counters shown in colour on page 148.

Above: French fan carved from ivory. 11 in. (28 cm) when open. Many fans, made by prisoners-of-war, were bone and not ivory.

trade card printed: 'James Francis Neau. Derby Street, Leek. Sells straw hats, ivory, and bone articles made by the French prisoners.'

Those British customers who could afford to do so brought expensive materials such as ivory, tortoiseshell, or mahogany, to the prisons to be worked up by the prison craftsmen. In this way a very few British patrons acquired ships made entirely of ivory. One good example is a 14-gun ship, made entirely from ivory, rigging as well as hull; it is only 3½ in. (9 cm) long and the detail is faultless. These prisoner-of-war ivories are extremely rare. They include some of the finest ivories ever made.

Imprisoned Dieppois craftsmen, and the American prisoners who were to learn their skills from them, became adept at using the invariable substitute for ivory, bone. Forton, near Gosport in Hampshire, was famous for the bone ships made there by American prisoners. One of them, writing under the pseudonym of 'The Green-horn', describes how a model was made. Two American seamen began with just a clasp knife and a needle, filed into a point to serve as a drill. To acquire tools, they sold their prison rations – half a pound of meat a day, costing the British taxpayer sixpence three-farthings per pound but selling at a penny a portion – and eventually got together a file, a pair of pliers, a small saw, glue, silk for the rigging, brass wire for pinning the planks and thicker wire for the guns. They cut a wooden hull and planked it using beef and mutton bones bought from fellow prisoners, sawn into strips, scraped and polished, drilled and pinned in place. The 'planks' were only 3/16 in. (4.7 mm) wide. One medium-sized model used 3021 pins. The completed hull looked as smooth as if it had been cut from a solid tusk. Every deck fitting was correctly proportioned and placed. The capstan, wheel and rudder worked. The guns could be run in and out. The rigging was completely authentic. The model was enlivened with discreet touches of paint: the insides of the gunports were painted red, the name picked out in gilt.

These ship models were so expensive that many were raffled, not sold. To tempt the casual visitor, the prisoners made an enormous number of tiny knick-knacks: dominoes, skittles, chessmen, playing cards, cribbage boards, fans, tobacco stoppers, snuffboxes, salad tongs, apple scoops, seals, knitting needles, lace bobbins and thimbles – all made from bone.

Another Forton prisoner, a Frenchman, Germain Lamy, told his foster brother, Doisy de Villargennes, that he and his comrade had produced a model of a 74-gun ship of the line, made of bone and rigged with human hair. It had taken them six months. Lamy proved so successful as a modeller that at the end of the war he had enough money to buy a little farm.

Dieppe. It is made from large sections of ivory put together without planking, and the sails and even the rigging are made from ivory.

The Château Museum also contains a watch-stand, topped with the British lion and unicorn, presumably the work of a French prisoner held in Britain during the Napoleonic wars. The prison hulks and camps often held thousands of prisoners, of many nationalities; in the late eighteenth century they had been kept under constant scrutiny, and sometimes had been raided when the prison carvers were producing improper automata and erotic items. More than 60,000 French prisoners were held in confinement between 1803 and 1814. These French prisoners were joined, after 1812, by many American prisoners. Among the prisoners were men from Dieppe, ivory craftsmen from Amsterdam, French ormolu workers, craftsmen in tortoiseshell, jet carvers, and probably fan makers, button makers, cutlers, whalebone workers and other craftsmen as well. The British Government gave the prisoners every encouragement to earn money from craft work, so long as they did not compete unfairly with British workers. The better organized and more prosperous British craftsmen, such as the straw-plait makers, successfully complained about competition from prisoners' plait, but there is no record that British ivory workers ever did so. One Liverpool ivory worker was even charged with assisting a French prisoner to escape; the Englishman may have supplied the prisoner with ivory or sold his work for him. A French privateer officer living in Leek, Staffordshire, on parole, had a

Above: From a 32-piece chess set made at Dieppe. 1800–50; tallest piece 3½ in. (9 cm). Dieppe sets were among the most beautiful in France.

In one particular commission, some English ladies, captured at sea by the famous French privateer Surcouf (1773–1827) who treated them very well and released them, commissioned from prison craftsmen a model of his ship. It is quite likely that among the prisoners were men who had sailed with him and could give technical advice. Such a commission was a faithful replica of a particular vessel; others were merely fantasy models.

Every art form is a product of its time. The prison craftsmen lived in a world where there were no interruptions from work save for an occasional roll-call or meal times. The export of grown-up 'toys' from Europe had been interrupted by the continental blockade. These were to some extent supplied by the prison craftsmen. To the purchaser the bone ship might symbolize Britain's stand against Napoleon; to the craftsman, his hope of eventual freedom.

Chess carvers in France and Britain

Partly because of their attractive appearance, partly because they were a delight to handle as well as look at, ivory chessmen were preferred by those nineteenth-century chess players who could afford to indulge their taste. Sometimes the whole set would be made from ivory, with the coloured men stained red, green or black. Sometimes the coloured pieces would be made from some natural hardwood, such as ebony.

An astonishing variety of designs was available at the start of the nineteenth century. In England, for example, 'Barleycorn' pieces were so called from their design, based on a stylized ear of barley, and the barley leaves carved on them. In the 'Upright' design all the pieces except the pawns had tall, pillar-like shapes. 'Maltese' chessmen originated in Malta where there was an ivory carving school set up by the Knights of St John; there was a Maltese cross on the king and the bishop's mitre sprouted into a delightful tulip-like form.

Fine chessmen were made in England throughout the nineteenth century and beyond. Messrs Calvert of Fleet Street, London, marketed sets with the most elaborate kings and queens like flowers topped by tall stamens which had burst from elongated bulbs. Charles Hastilow, who exhibited at the Great Exhibition of 1851, made the most intricately carved kings surmounted by Maltese crosses, queens topped with fleurs-de-lis, and tall rooks with billowing standards that seemed to tower above all the other pieces. Three generations of the Hastilow family made sets between 1830 and 1904.

The mark of a really good English chess set is the superior quality of the pawns (usually carved by the apprentice but sometimes by the master) and the 'hallmark' of the vendor's name. An old-established firm, such as Calvert, Lund, Pringle, or Toy Brothers of London, would have its name engraved on the pieces by the Sheffield chasers, whose engraving was superlative.

English chess sets incorporated more turning than carving, and the bulk of this turning was done by piece-work turners in small workshops in London or Birmingham. These 'small masters', often too poor to afford an apprentice or a journeyman, were reduced to slave rates of labour. They faced very powerful competition from imported sets, both at the top and the bottom of the market.

Dieppe, Paris, Oyonnax and Méru were the centres of French chess manufactory. The greatest French rival was the cheap bone chess set. The Dieppois were past masters at the art of bleaching bone (ox, horse, sheep) and many of their bone sets were as finely carved as the ivory ones. They were lavishly decorated with colours and gilding or silvering, which served to make the bone look whiter while at the same time hiding the tell-tale surface signs that betrayed its real raw material.

A characteristic Dieppe design made both in bone and in ivory was the *pique sable* figure – the 'stick in the sand' chessman, bold, original and reminiscent of the pegged gaming pieces which the Norsemen had used with a pierced board while at sea.

The higher-priced Dieppe sets were often more attractive still. The demand was stimulated by the Napoleonic wars and the fashion for pursuing scientific studies – there is no more scientific game than chess. Napoleon was considered a very gifted player.

Dieppe carvers created beautiful sets, often based on designs current in the previous century, which usually achieve a very happy mixture of carving and turning. In the pilaster-and-bust type an urn-shaped pedestal is surmounted by a miniature bust. The kings and queens were often portraits, Napoleon and Josephine opposing Henri IV and Marie de Medici. The most expensive and elaborate chess sets did away with turning altogether and presented two files of full-length statuettes: William III of England confronted Louis XIV, George III faced Louix XV, and Wellington was ranged against Napoleon, with all the supporting pieces of the proper period. Thus, in the Battle of Waterloo set the bishops were Berthier and Massena and the pawns the Old Guard.

Nineteenth-century chess sets showed marked regional variations. The turners and carvers had now created so many new designs, just to tempt the customer, that they seemed to endanger the role of chess as an international game.

In 1835 Nathaniel Cook produced a design which was called after Howard Staunton (1810–74), an internationally famous chess champion and writer on chess. Staunton patented the design in 1849 and Jaques of Leather Lane, London, put it into production. The white pieces were made from the best African ivory, the black from ebony (heavily weighted so that both sets would handle in the same way). Two sizes were made, the 3½-inch and the 4½-inch, which were used for friendly games and competition play, respectively. While differentiating each man clearly, Cook cleverly incorporated much that was familiar and well loved in former sets: the king's crown was surmounted by a Maltese cross, the queen wore a coronet, the rook was a simple castle, the bishop had a mitre, the knight was a horse's head, the pawn was marked by a simple ball as its finial. All the pieces rose from wide bases on sturdy stems.

The Staunton design put the game on a scientific footing, but removed it completely from the realm of fancy. To please the connoisseurs French ivory workers continued to produce sets made in the Gothic or neo-classical style, one French set *c.* 1850 even arraying all the Assyrian deities as major pieces, others depicting rival politicians.

The Great Exhibition: 1851

The Great Exhibition, held in the Crystal Palace, Hyde Park, London, in 1851, brought together many of the themes of European ivory carving during the nineteenth century.

Elephant tusks and other hunting trophies had been sent in by Roualeyn Gordon-Cumming (1820–66). The young Scots baronet's son had just published a bestseller, *Five Years of a Hunter's Life*, describing his travels in Central Africa in search of elephants. His trophies included a pair of tusks weighing a total of 325 lb (147 kg), from an elephant shot near Lake Ngami. Other tusks on show consisted of ivory from the Gabon river, the Cape, Zanzibar, Dahomey, India and Ceylon, as well as narwhal, walrus and hippopotamus tusks.

There were not many ivory carvers in England in 1851. Kelly had flourished around 1818 and made miniature busts, William Ewing had been active in the 1820s and made profile portraits in high relief, but the only prominent figure in 1851 was Richard Cockle Lucas, who was not merely an ivory carver, but a distinguished sculptor in other media as well.

Richard Cockle Lucas (1800–83)

Lucas was that most admired of artists of the time – a working man who had become a professional artist through his own endeavours, not through family connection or influence. He had begun life working as an apprentice for a cutler in Winchester, shaping the ivory handles for knives, but decided that he wanted to become a sculptor.

Lucas worked in the neo-classical style that was fashionable at the time. Often his inspiration for a work was derived from classical prototypes, such

Above: 'Cupid Seated on a Rock, Breaking his Bow': ivory sculpture by Richard Cockle Lucas. (1800–83). One of the most admired sculptors of the nineteenth century, much of Lucas' work was inspired by classical art.

as coins. His group of Cupid and Psyche, 5 in. (12.7 cm) high, was made in 1828, the year he entered the Royal Academy schools. Very similar in inspiration is the work that is probably his masterpiece: 'Cupid Seated on a Rock, Breaking his Bow'.

Lucas's miniature busts, such as his portrait bust of Thomas Slingsby Duncombe, MP, show a sturdy Victorian realism. He would begin by making a model of the subject in wax (many of his wax studies were sold by his son in 1909). Lucas was a very adept modeller, so much so that one of his wax busts, 'Flora', was bought by the Kaiser Friedrich Museum in Berlin in the belief that it was the work of Leonardo da Vinci.

Besides eighteen ivories, Lucas exhibited 'imitation bronzes' at the Great Exhibition. The judges' reaction, however, was distinctly lukewarm. His copies of celebrated antique works, 'executed with great fidelity', won only a bronze medal, though an anonymous continental ivory carver, for Wittich, Kemmel & Co. of Geislingen in Germany, received a Prize Medal for 'upwards of two hundred bone and ivory small wares ... very small and exquisite models of furniture in which there is much minute piercing and carving'.

Some years later, in 1865, Lucas decided to try to exchange his ivories and collection of antiques for a Civil List pension of £150 a year. He had continued to win fame as a sculptor, in spite of his set-down by the juries in 1851. The statesman Lord Palmerston, for whom he had an admiration amounting to obsession, wrote on his behalf to Earl Granville: 'His works are really very good, though of course I cannot say whether they are worth the sums at which he values them, but if I made the arrangement he proposes, will you accept the gift he engages to make to the Kensington Museum?'

The ivory exhibits

At the Great Exhibition the ivories were scattered throughout the building. An art ivory might be classified under material, like the carvings shown in 'Manufactures from Animal and Vegetable Substances', or in a national section, such as the 'Colonial Department, Indian Section', where the Indian carvings were on view, or by genre, like an ivory fan exhibited alongside fans made of fabric, paper, etc.

Bundled into an industrial section, the ivory carver had no chance of being judged by his peers. The exhibitors of ivories, L. Bigotti of Tuscany, Michael Hagen of Bavaria, C. W. Heyl of Hesse, C. G. Klingsley of Denmark, and J. Lautz of France, were received with less than acclaim.

The label 'industrial' was affixed to carved ivories, and it was going to stick. The carver's work would go on show alongside brushware, basketware and leatherwork, or billiard balls and hair brushes, items which were quite likely to be made of ivory. A distinguished French ivory sculptor, Augustin Moreau-Vauthier, might find himself on a jury judging meerschaum pipes, while his ivories were being judged by a specialist in decoratively sewn boots.

'Chryselephantine' combination sculpture

The most important, and portentous, ivory exhibit was the Matifat coffret. This was a jewel box of ivory and bronze. The bronze legs were attached to the corners of the box; they were extended upwards to form four candlesticks and downwards to form animal feet. On the front was a polychrome painting of women and children at play. The painting, the metal fittings, the carved ornament, were neo-classical, while on top of the box was a sculptured ivory group in the same style. It showed a mother playing with a child, with their hands clasped together. The mother's gold bracelets concealed the join between the two pieces of ivory from which the figures had been carved.

This heavy and ill-designed exhibit was the work not so much of an artist as a committee: designed by M. G. Dieterle, principal designer to the Sèvres Porcelain Manufactory in France, and well known for his theatrical scenery designs; supervised by Matifat, an artistic entrepreneur; and carved by Vechte, a professional sculptor and chaser in metals. This kind of collaboration was to become increasingly popular in France as the century wore on. Sometimes a fourth person would be involved, the *practicien* or sculptor's assistant who actually carved the ivory. This constituted a completely new departure in ivory sculpture. Carvers had often worked from artist's designs before, or from plaster models, but the designer had not stood over them and told them what to do.

The coffret was a combination of materials as well. This technique was to persist through all 'combination sculpture' of the nineteenth century, notably Lynn Jenkins's 'Spirit of British Commerce', and to carry on into the twentieth century in the Art Deco figurines.

The Victorian critic H. Digby Wyatt hailed the coffret as 'a charming specimen of the art known to the ancients as chryselephantine, that is, one in which the sculptor produces his effect by the combination of ivory with gold and other metals'. But in reality what took place in the 1850s was not a revival of a classical type of ivory sculpture but a completely new departure. The Minoan statuettes had been figures carved from ivory, with attached arms, but no attempt had been made to hide the shoulder joint, though the figurines were decked in clothes of thin gold; there seems every reason to believe that this procedure was followed with much bigger works as well.

Combination sculpture, then, was not an art revived but an art discovered, though to contemporaries the combination of materials seemed a reform, bringing ivory carving back into the correct classical line.

Artificial ivories and mass production

The Great Exhibition juries rewarded not art but commerce, particularly British commerce, not real ivory but imitation ivories, not hand-made craftsmanship but what could be made by machine, not unique works of sculpture but what could be mass-produced. The semi-official publication *History and Description of the Crystal Palace*, for instance, dismissed the Chinese ivory exhibits with the words: 'The Chinese are capable of wasting any amount of time upon any triviality', though it did lavish praise on the Indian exhibits.

Imitation ivories also came in for praise. Cheverton's 'artificial ivory' procured a prize, and Henry Brown was given a medal for his invention of 'British ivory', a plastic composition. The *Reports of the Juries* called 'vegetable ivory', made from the inner seed of the nuts of the ivory-palm tree, *Phytelephas macrocarpa*, 'a good substitute for ivory where appearance and durability are not principal objects. Its whiteness soon becomes tarnished, and it wears when used for articles where much friction is required.' The seeds were not large, and the most that could be made from them were small objects such as buttons, thimbles, and perhaps chessmen. Benjamin Taylor received a prize medal for 'a number of objects turned with great skill' from this material. Judging by the illustrations, he must have built them up from several separate turnings joined together.

Machines for making ivory products were warmly received by the juries. Cheverton's reducing machine (described below) was hailed as 'a most valuable and original invention'. Julius Pratt showed an up-and-down saw for cutting ivory veneers from a rotating tusk.

Other exhibits included Charles Holtzapfel's masterly set of chessmen, which had been carved by machinery. The turner Dr W. D. Hemphill, an Irish designer and manufacturer, had sent in a cup 'covered with intricate tracery, and yet so miraculously thin in texture as to be quite transparent, standing upon a stem reduced to the slenderness of a knitting needle, a hyacinth stalk, with its pendant flowers and leaves carved into a delicate and web-like tissue that appeared absolutely evanescent, and a vase of Hippopotamus ivory, perforated, containing a white single hyacinth and jonquil, standing on a fluted pillar of walrus tooth'. Oscar Smith exhibited 'a unique specimen of ivory turning; a solid piece, the form of an egg, hollowed out to the thickness of the natural shell from a perforation of a twelfth part of an inch'.

The Great Exhibition was a microcosm of European ivory carving during the nineteenth century. The great interest taken by the jurors in artificial ivories stimulated inventors, particularly Americans, to produce plastic materials which were more and more like the real thing. In 1865, after Phelan & Collender, the biggest manufacturers of billiard balls in the United States, offered a $10,000 prize for a successful substitute for scarce and expensive tusk ivory, John Hyatt of New York invented the substance which two years later was renamed 'Celluloid'.

The new synthetics and the carving machines cut the cost of production, but eliminated the charm of the hand-made that every good ivory should have.

Industrial ivories

One of the most striking features of the nineteenth century was the rise of factory-made ivory products. In the early years of the century, workers concerned with ivory were often 'small masters'

Below: The Juno cabinet, in ebony inlaid with ivory and various woods; it was designed by B.J. Talbert and made by Jackson & Graham in England. The cabinet was shown at the Paris Exhibition, 1878. 1870s. A detail is shown in colour on page 149.

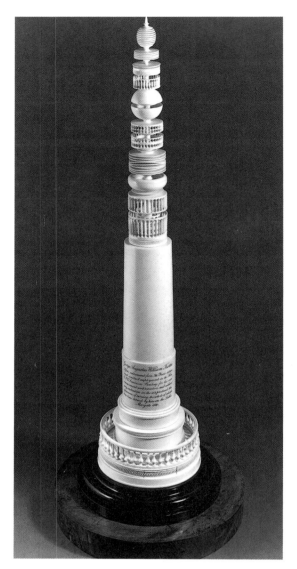

Right and below: Turned ivory column. 1860; 28 in. (67.2 cm). The inscription (*below*), says it was made by Mr Trotter 'without any instruction in the art'.

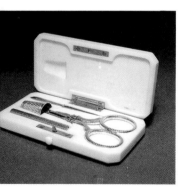

Above: French ivory sewing *nécessaire* shown in colour on page 152.

gammon men, shaving-brush handles, picture frames and lining-pen handles.

Comb making also involved ivory. Having selected a suitable piece of ivory, the maker would saw it up, leave it to season, and then cut blanks for combs. One was fixed into a clamp with a long handle on which the workman sat, turning himself into a kind of human vice. He then sawed out the teeth with a double-bladed saw, like a cabinet maker's, smoothed them with a series of files and finally used a rasp to give the ends of the teeth a small bevel and remove any roughness from their sides. The comb was then polished with rotten stone and oil, put on with a piece of buff leather.

Comb making was obviously a very laborious business, so it is not surprising that here industrialization began early. Around 1808 a Mr Bundy of Camden Town took out a patent for a comb-cutting machine. Others followed, and by 1851, with the aid of machines such as these, comb making had become completely industrialized in Aberdeen, Scotland. At the works of Stewart, Rowell & Co., a disciplined workforce of 600 men worked the machines for a ten-hour day. The only exception to this machine work was the finishing department, where a small workforce carved elaborate chain ornament on braid combs.

Throughout the nineteenth century industrialists sought ways of replacing the craftsman by the machine completely. They were not always successful. The Chinese worked ivory fan leaves into openwork patterns with a drill and a piercing saw, fine as gossamer and light as well as beautiful. Attempts made in Birmingham in the early part of the nineteenth century to imitate this *ajouré* style of decoration by machinery failed.

Yet a much more ambitious attempt to work ivory by means of machinery was to meet with complete success. In 1828 Benjamin Cheverton (1794–1876) of London invented an 'aid to the carver' with which he was able to reduce three-dimensional models to miniature proportions, so that full-sized statues could be reduced to figurines, with no loss.

Cheverton had originally used his machine to make small figurines in wood, but after the arrival of Thomas Brown Jordan's wood-carving machine, patented in 1845, he confined himself to ivory, alabaster, metal or marble. His statuettes, busts and bas reliefs in ivory and marble were not even finished by hand. The machine was a complicated one and when it went on exhibition there were scientists who were prepared to say in public that his process was impossible. In essence it was a kind of three-dimensional lathe. Upwards of fifty different rotary files could be used for different types of cut. Just changing the file must have been quite a task. A sitter could have his portrait made and a dozen reproductions sculpted for presents to

with one or two apprentices, or single craftsmen who were often self-exploiting piece-workers.

One important ivory worker was the turner. Labouring away in his tiny workshop, with the raw materials of his trade – horns, ivory tusks, boxwood, ebony – piled on the floor, he would lay his chisel against the prop of the lathe and press his foot on the treadle, removing minute shavings from the object he was turning. He might be called on to produce anything in circular form: an eyepiece for a telescope or an adjustment screw for a microscope; ivory rings for woodwind instruments or ivory inlays for, say, the stops of a flute; and a great list of other items, including buttons, napkin rings, magnifying glasses, puzzle-balls or puzzle-rings, knitting needles, bracelets, beads (sometimes given a black trim for mourning use), bodkins, basting-thread removal pins, darning eggs, thread spools and barrels, thimbles, billiard balls, pestles and mortars, dice cups, the knobs for canes, umbrellas and parasols, pillboxes, cosmetics containers, door knobs, whistles, draughts pieces and back-

Right: Presentation casket in ivory, with sphinxes and elephants. 1883; 9 × 4 × 4½ in. (3.5 × 1.5 × 1.7 cm).

Above: Victorian thimble cases shown in colour on page 148. The egg-shaped and barrel-shaped ones (centre) are ivory.

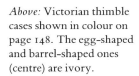

give his friends, at a cost about equal to that which the original portrait fee would have been. The judges at the Great Exhibition declared that 'the cheapness with which the noblest works of art can be multiplied by these means cannot but tend to the more general development of a feeling for the beautiful'. The busts are charming, though whether they would have gained or lost if cut by hand is difficult to say.

An enormous demand for ivory slips for piano keys resulted from the invention of the modern upright pianoforte by an Englishman, John Isaac Hawkins, in 1800. Almost overnight, the piano became the most popular instrument of the nineteenth century, creating a vast market for new instruments. The early nineteenth-century instruments had short ivory head-pieces (the part touched by the fingers) and ivory tail-pieces (running up between the black keys) after the fashion of the older spinets and harpsichords, but undue wear on the front edge of the keys brought about rearrangement and lengthening.

The resulting demand for veneer led to new

mechanical ivory-cutting methods being devised. Cheverton invented one in 1844. H. Pape already had one on the market and in 1834 had displayed a sheet of ivory veneer, 30 by 150 in. (76 by 380 cm), in London. Such a size could only be achieved by rotating a section of tusk and cutting it so that a sheet of ivory was unrolled, like unwrapping a scroll. Benjamin Stedman and Fenner Bush, two American inventors, created the best-known of all veneer cutters for the Pratt ivory products factory in Connecticut, and at the Great Exhibition Julius Pratt suspended from the dome of the Crystal Palace a sheet 14 in. (35 cm) wide and 52 ft (15.8 m) long.

One other product demanded ivory on a scale similar to that of the piano key, and that was the billiard ball. Only ivory could supply a ball with sufficient elasticity. This elasticity was soon lost in play so the demand for replacements was considerable. Only three fine-quality balls could be cut from the tusk, called a 'billiard ball scrivelloe'. It was cut into sections and turned under a machine lathe, while a jet of water was sprayed on

Below: Cameo portrait in ivory, shown in colour on page 160.

Below: An assortment of ivory handles for canes and walking-sticks. They include a segmented cane with a dog's head.

it to prevent its overheating and cracking. The rounded end of the blank would next be placed in a wooden chuck, shaped to fit it, and the process repeated.

Every class of Victorian England demanded more and more ivory for industrial products throughout the nineteenth century. Billiards was universally popular in aristocratic houses, clubs, cigar divans and public houses. Another item was the walking stick. An ivory-handled walking cane would make an extremely useful weapon against thieves. First bulbous knobs were in vogue, then L-shaped handles, then around the 1870s octagonal-shaped knobs swelling to a smooth convex top. Alongside the regular shapes went more unusual forms: dogs' or horses' heads, pistol grips, dice, even a woman's leg, complete with boot and garter. Dowagers apart, women did not usually carry walking sticks until Edwardian times but their riding crops usually had L-shaped handles.

One last outlet for ivory production on an industrial scale deserves notice, the umbrella. 'In the highest class of umbrellas and parasols,' said the *Report of the Juries*, 'France undoubtedly stands pre-eminent. The tasteful designs and sharp and excellent carving of the ivory handles . . . give to the French manufacturer a decided superiority.'

Britain did what it could to establish a place in the production of cheaper umbrellas, relying on the advantage of duty-free imports of the basic materials, whalebone, ivory and horn. The 1330 umbrella makers who worked in London in 1851 could also feel that the British climate was on their side.

It was the demand for industrial ivory, not sculpture, that brought about the enormous expansion of the ivory import trade in nineteenth-century Britain.

Germany and Biedermeier

At the start of the nineteenth century two towns in Germany were particularly noted for ivory carving. One was Geislingen, a small town on the Thierbach in the kingdom of Württemberg, the other Erbach in Hesse, in the middle of the Odenwald, which was to inspire its carvers with forest themes.

The ivory industry of Erbach owed its existence to Count Franz I (1754–1823), who became ruler of the little state in 1775. His mother, the dowager Countess, had given him a very careful upbringing which had culminated in a tour of Europe undertaken between 1769 and 1775. Franz I studied for a year at Lausanne, where he made the acquaintance of Rousseau and Voltaire, and matriculated at Strasburg University. He had already displayed his artistic bent by becoming a devotee of the works of Winkelmann, and beginning to collect Greek and Roman coins. His Grand Tour took him to Paris, London and Brussels, Amsterdam, the Hague and Kassel. 'He visits the most notable collections,' his tutor wrote home, 'shares his pleasure with me, and shows great attention.'

When Franz returned from his Grand Tour, his already strong taste for every form of classical art had been confirmed, but he had also acquired a new interest – ivory carving. The monarchs he had met were mercantilist economists, who showed him that a country should produce its own luxury products which could be sold abroad for much-needed foreign gold.

The Count decided to introduce the inhabitants of Erbach to ivory carving and turning. Under the direction of Johann Tobias Arzt, a master from the near-by town of Michelstadt, he became an expert turner. In 1783 he founded a guild of ivory workers, with himself as president; two journeymen and two apprentices, one called Count von Furstenau, were admitted to the guild, with Arzt and seven master carvers.

Franz I was a master of design. His round box in the museum at Erbach is about a hundred and fifty years ahead of its time. It could easily have come from a Bauhaus exhibition. The only decoration the turner has permitted himself is a thin line

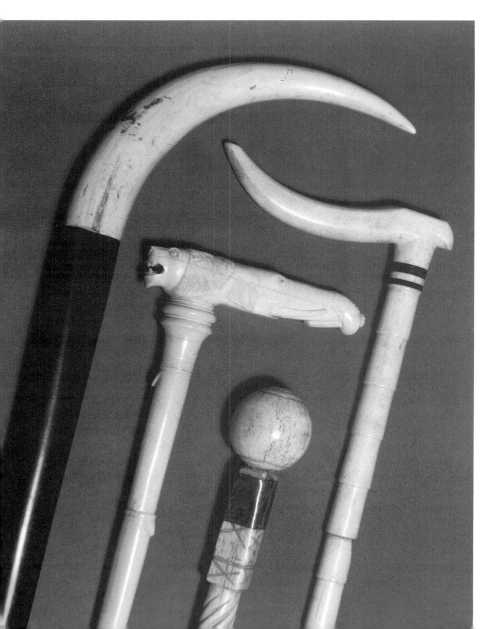

round the extremity of the lid, and where the lid joins the rest of the box. Other turned work of his includes billiard balls and a chess set, and his carving includes *cachepots* in ivory and tortoiseshell and an ivory and staghorn candlestick.

Franz I introduced to Erbach Christian Kehrer (1770–1869), an artist who designed the stags which were to appear on so much Erbach work. Christian was in turn succeeded by his son Eduard, who began a Sunday Art School for the carvers, the forerunner of the *Fachschule* for ivory and wood carving, set up in 1892, and still in existence.

When Franz I died in 1823, the direction that carving at Erbach was going to take during the rest of the century had already been laid down: alongside purely artistic works, more utilitarian and immediately saleable works; alongside ivory carving and turning, work in the cheaper staghorn and wood; carving to be naturalistic, neo-classical or sentimental, without the grim realism characteristic of a Meugniot.

Throughout the nineteenth century, the Erbachers were successful. The prevailing style from 1820 till 1860 was 'Biedermeier', a title taken from a fictional character supposed to embody all the middle-class attributes of opulence and philistinism. The style throve on carved detail, exaggerated curves, realistically carved animals and decorative flower and fruit ornamentation. Erbach ivory carving was never so opulent as to become vulgar. The workers produced backcombs and hairpins, parasol handles and elaborately worked fans.

The great triumph of Erbach Biedermeier, however, is the romantically inspired flower jewellery. By the second half of the nineteenth century, ivory had become the most romantic of materials, and the 'language of flowers', by which lovers could communicate secretly merely by exchanging bouquets in which the flowers spelled out a message, had become an international craze. It was small wonder, then, that *Handbroschen* flourished at Erbach. These delicate ladies' hands, often terminated in a frilly ruff, held sprigs of grapes, vine-leaves, ears of corn, lilies of the valley, lilac, or chrysanthemums, which in the language of flowers meant 'I love you.'

Single flowers appear in increasing numbers as the century progresses. The most famous of these was the Erbach rose, an idea brought to Erbach from Dieppe by Johann Michel, who had travelled round Europe looking for new inspiration. Rose jewellery was to make the artistic fortune of Erbach. Whether in full bloom or with tightly gathered petals, seen in profile or combined with lilies of the valley (as in Franz Wilhelm Wegel's beautiful brooch of 1878), it was the most successful design in romantic jewellery.

The Erbachers invented the hart brooch, or *Hirschebroche*, for themselves, from Christian Kehrer's original designs. His son, Eduard Kehrer (1812–63), was to give the *Hirschebroche* its definitive form, in 1840. In these brooches, stags pace delicately through a woodland scene. The foliage which surrounds them is shown in the greatest detail by means of the piercing saw, till the whole composition seems made from the most delicate ivory lacework.

Alongside jewellery of international appeal Germany kept up a steady flow of serious academic carvings, works such as Friedrich Hartmann's elaborate goblets, *Stein* by Lebricht Wilhelm Schulze, portrait medallions by Norbert Schrödl, busts by Gottfried Schadow and other exhibition pieces. Philipp Willmann specialized in portrait studies of historical figures and copies from the antique.

The Erbachers also made large flagons and bowls combining sizeable pieces of ivory, neatly jointed together with handsome silver figures. One bowl by Otto Glenz, showing a Bacchic celebration, proved so popular that it was repeated again and again.

Meanwhile, alongside these exhibition pieces, work in what might be called 'the Erbach style' continued unabated. This consisted of works influenced by Biedermeier with its emphasis on realistically carved animals, but with a local flavour that only Erbach could impart. These carvings of squirrels, hunters and their hounds, boars rooting up the ground with their tusks, stags about to engage in mortal combat, all distil that sentiment of the forest that is so typically German.

European scrimshaw

Scrimshaw is typically the manufacture of naïve keepsakes by sailors using sea ivory, either whales' teeth, whalebone, or, less commonly, narwhal horn, which they decorate with designs, incised and stained. The most common form is a whale's tooth carved with a ship in full sail, often titled and dated, perhaps decorated on the reverse with a commemoration of a battle, a cameo scene of a courting couple or the name of a loved one, with a sentimental message attached. (Rarer scenes depict intimate comforts desired by sailors.) It may also take the form of walking sticks, corset stays or any household item from an industrious souvenir industry, especially in the whaling fleets of the late nineteenth century. This charming bona fide form of naïve art is highly collectable.

Owing to the essentially naïve input, scrimshaw is sometimes confused with prisoner-of-war work, which is in turn often indistinguishable from the bone carvings of the late-eighteenth-century Dieppe workshops, and incised decoration is a frequent addition to all three. Scrimshaw

Opposite: Portrait in ivory of Napoleon III and the Empress Eugenie by the French *ivoirier* Pierre Graillon. 1854; 5½ × 4 in. (14 × 10 cm). See page 132 for detail.

Right: Stay busk made from sperm whale jawbone. British scrimshaw. 14⅜ in. (36.6 cm) long. The incised decoration is coloured in black, red, blue and green. Details are shown in colour on page 153.

inferior quality would have been available to seamen for their simple craftwork. Two tobacco boxes survive, inlaid with walrus ivory and engraved *1665* and *1712* (but were these scrimshaw?); in general, however, identifiable walrus scrimshaw does not predate the nineteenth century. Whalebone, or baleen, was different. The European maritime nations hunted whale in the northern seas until the end of the nineteenth century and although whalebone was valuable commercially, there were up to 600 pieces of varying lengths removed from each whale, leaving plenty for sailors to make useful or ornamental items.

Many of the most skilled seamen of the Dutch and German vessels came from the Frisian Islands or Hallingen. As well as wooden items they made elegant little ditty-boxes of whalebone. A fine example, now in Hamburg, is inscribed *JACOB FLOER ANNO 1661* and is decorated with a simple incised representation of a church, trees and geometric designs. From England there are eighteenth-century stay busks of whalebone, cut with chip-carved geometric patterns like their wooden counterparts, but these may well have been made by shore-based carvers. In the nineteenth century, however, these busks were the favourite gift of the whaler to his wife or sweetheart and were invariably decorated with simple incised lines and cross-hatching. A rare contemporary European source referring to scrimshaw work, though not by that name, is the memoir of Christopher Thomson, carpenter's mate aboard a Hull whaleship in 1820, who describes cutting initials, decorative borders and ornament on whalebone.

The European whaling trade expanded into the southern hemisphere in the eighteenth century and there is little doubt that the carving and decoration of sperm whale teeth began almost immediately, but it is difficult to pinpoint authentic survivals. It is impossible to date scrimshaw on purely stylistic grounds and only the occasional example actually bears a date – which may well not be the date on which the decoration was actually applied. A tooth now in the Castle Museum, York, has an inscription, *Success to Whalers 1790 N.B.*, which is probably spurious.

The British whaling trade declined throughout the nineteenth century as the whales became fewer. By 1869, for example, Hull, on the east coast of Yorkshire, had only one ship in the trade, the *Diana*, and when she was lost the Hull trade ended. But the surviving whalers, converting from sail to steam, began to hunt seal as well and the crews found they could trade for walrus tusks with the Eskimo; and there were still supplies of sperm whale teeth from the southern whaling fishery.

European scrimshaw techniques have been handed down to twentieth-century scrimshanders

and prisoner-of-war work are the art forms of isolated men with common backgrounds of sea adventure and a common longing for home; with minimal materials they produced a most coherent style and a clear identity.

Because walrus tusks were greatly sought after and valuable, being a very infrequent source of ivory in Europe, only fragments or pieces of

such as Captain Spencer Johnson and Captain E. C. Parkes.

'Regarding your inquiry about sperm whale's teeth,' Captain Parkes wrote. 'These had first to be sandpapered, as they were very rough, then polished properly. Then a piece of transparent paper was placed over the tooth, then a cutting from some paper, magazine or book was placed over that, and numerous pricks were made with a pin [reproducing] the illustration in minute holes on the tooth. Then Indian ink was used to fill in all the holes . . . When the ink was quite dry, another gentle polish was given to the tooth.'

Captain Spencer Johnson wrote: 'My father, a Cape Horner, taught me scrimshaw over 50 years ago. It takes two to four months to get used to the [sperm whale] tooth, less for a killer whale. It's in your pocket the whole time, daily work on and off watch on deck . . . scraping and polishing with china clay and whale oil.' Homeward bound, there came the day to complete the scrimshaw. 'Fine weather, north of 45°, a good needle, and a pad of lampblack, and a peaceful mind (happy ship). Then to make the leather bag and it stays in your pocket until required for currency. Ninety per cent of the old 'real' USA scrimshaw was sold to get home to Dundee, Whitby or Lynn . . . Today passages are too short. One tooth took three months of very hard work and two days of scrimshaw.'

Sharkskin could be used instead of sandpaper and some workers outlined the illustration with a

Below: Scrimshaw. A ship in full sail is one of the most popular motifs.

jack-knife before etching the finest lines with a 'pickwick', a heavy sailcloth needle. The tooth was buffed and polished with damp wood ash, applied with much vigour, and the drawing coloured with Indian ink (Captain Parkes), lamp-black (Captain Spencer Johnson) or tobacco juice. Some scrimshanders made up their own designs, perhaps doing the preliminary sketches on the woodwork of their bunks. James Lamont, an amateur walrus hunter writing in 1861, remarked of the cabin: 'The beams and boarding is . . . of a very light and soft description, eminently adapted for whittling and engraving, and in these intellec-tual and scientific occupations we find a great resource.'

The subjects for British scrimshaw were whal-ing scenes, portraits of seamen, patriotic and symbolic emblems, and women, often ladies in the latest fashions. This fondness for female portraits reflects the fact that scrimshaw was a commercial art. The teeth were engraved as ornaments, usually for the mantelpiece, and such a picture would be as acceptable to the lady of the house as a fashionplate illustration.

Is it possible to distinguish American work from British? Sometimes a piece of scrimshaw is provided with unimpeachable authentication: one example, sent home to his sweetheart by a dying seaman, was cherished for many years and eventually passed by her to a collector. Sometimes a tooth will contain evidence about where it was made: a pair illustrated in Flayderman's *Scrimshaw*

Below: Art Nouveau plaque shown in colour on page 167.

and Scrimshanders figures HMS *Iris* and the royal coat of arms on one tooth, with a portrait of Iris, messenger of the gods, and an iris flower on the other. HMS *Iris* was built in 1840 and disposed of in 1869. The scrimshander was presumably sailing under the White Ensign. Portraits of prominent Britons probably also suggest a British provenance.

National emblems may indicate origin: Highland lassies, for example, Scottish lions, thistles and castles flying the Union flag, all suggest a Scottish connection. It also seems reasonable to suppose that teeth ornamented with patriotic British emblems, such as HMS *Victory* flying the Royal Standard, Union Jacks, Britannias and the like, are British work.

Outside these narrow limits it would be dangerous to dogmatize. Scrimshaw always had a very international flavour. In some distinctively Scottish scenes the 'olive branch' pattern found on so much American scrimshaw appears alongside the thistle. Much British scrimshaw was apparently made for sale to foreigners. Some teeth, now in British collections, bear legends in a foreign language, and were perhaps made for a foreign market but brought back, unsold, by the maker to England.

British scrimshaw is often very well made and is rarer than American because there were far fewer whalers flying the Red Ensign. Its Britishness may lead to some conclusions about its age and where it was made. A pair of teeth showing cartoons of a sailor and his lass on one and a sailor sitting smoking with a friend on the other carry the words:

> *'Where shall I tell her to write to you Jack?'*
> *'Say Sebastopol or Petersburg, I shall be at*
> *one or the other by that time.'*

This surely indicates the Crimean War of 1853–6, and probably early in the war, judging by the optimistic comment. Another tooth shows a sailor and his sweetheart with the legend *Back from India* and may mark a safe return from the Indian Mutiny, in which many sailors served. Fighting ended in November 1858.

Scrimshaw which bears distinctly British allusions or devices is almost certainly authentic; forgeries aimed at American collectors would surely carry spread eagles and Stars and Stripes.

Art Nouveau

So far as ivory carving is concerned, modern times may be said to begin at the Brussels Exhibition of 1897, in a Europe dominated by what was to be known as Art Nouveau, Jugendstil, or 'Modern Style'. The effect made by the carvings on show at Brussels was to be reinforced by those at the Paris Exhibition of 1900.

There were several reasons why Art Nouveau ivory sculpture should first become prominent in Belgium. The tradition of ivory carving had not died out there, as it had in some other countries. Alphonse van Beurden (born 1854) had been trained in the Antwerp Academy and exhibited work regularly in the Royal Academy in London. He was to show a beautiful bust there, 'The Young Singer', just a year after the Brussels Exhibition. Belgian carvers were famous for a genre, apparently attempted nowhere else at this time, which was related to the 'beggar' figures made in Dieppe in the early part of the century: groups of poverty-stricken or tipsy musicians, playing different instruments.

With a view to exploiting Belgian carvers' potential, the Belgian Secretary of State for the Congo Free State suggested that the king place at the disposal of forty leading sculptors some of the ivory which the Congolese had been accumulating for decades. This exercise in public relations produced very mixed artistic results. Franz Juygelen and Alfred Courtens treated the ivory as though it were any other sculptural material. They put blocks of it together and produced busts apparently constructed from large ivory bricks.

Other sculptors rose to the occasion and created works falling within the natural limits of the tusk. Floris de Cuyper produced a charming medallion made from ivory alone. Constantin Meunier (1831–1905) also created all-ivory sculpture. But most of the exhibitors showed the new 'chryselephantine work', which had become part of the Modern Style staple.

Julien Dillens (1849–1904) made his allegorical figure 'Glory' from the ivory and gilt bronze to which the term 'chryselephantine' now by convention refers. Charles van der Stappen (1843–1910) created 'Silent Sphinx', which had an ivory face and bust, with silver gilt helmet and armour. Fernand Knopff, under the influence of symbolist trends, presented an ivory mask with bronze wreaths and flanking wings surely incapable of raising it from the ground. It was exactly this feeling of unease and imbalance that so much Art Nouveau ivory sculpture was intended to convey.

The star of the show was Philippe Wolfers (1858–1929). The great sculptor and jeweller was the son of a Brussels goldsmith, who had taught him his craft. He had studied at the Académie Royale des Beaux Arts and in 1873 visited the International Exhibition at Vienna, where he was deeply impressed by the Japanese exhibits.

The influence of Japanese art on many Art Nouveau sculptors and jewellers was indeed profound, as Alfred Maskell pointed out in 1905. 'Their use of the inlay and combination with ivory of gold and silver, coral and mother-of-pearl, of using ivory and further adorning it with enamels and precious metals, is, it can scarcely be doubted, a following of Japanese tastes and ideas.'

Right: Victorian thimble cases. The egg-shaped and barrel-shaped examples are ivory. See also page 141.

Opposite: Detail from the Juno Cabinet. See also page 139.

Below: A counter box and its original counters, made by prisoners-of-war. 1795; 8½ × 7¼ in. (21.6 × 18.4 cm) by 2½ in. (6.4 cm) deep. See page 134 for detail.

Above: Beech armchair by Baillie Scott, the back inlaid with mother-of-pearl and bone. *c.*1900–1; 33½ in. (85 cm). Probably made at the Pyghtlie Works, Bedford.

It was Wolfers who had introduced ivory to Art Nouveau jewellery, in 1893. Ivory in combination with precious metals, stones and enamels was a completely new idea. It gave the soft gleam, even texture, creamy appearance and hue that Modern Style jewellers wanted. Nor was it merely a new colour in the jeweller's palette. Wolfers must have been well aware that it was extremely tough and robust, compared with some of the other, very fragile materials used in the new jewellery, such as horn and enamels. Ivory, the colour of life, was also the ideal material from which to construct the female faces and bodies which appear in so much Art Nouveau jewellery. The combination of gold and ivory in female-form jewellery had in fact been the discovery, not of Wolfers but of François Désiré Froment-Meurice, who had designed a bracelet in 1841 showing two voluptuous, half-naked females.

By 1897 Wolfers had set up his own workshop and was using a reducing machine, similar no doubt to that introduced by Cheverton, to make statuary and jewellery from ivory. His sculpture owed as much to his talents as a goldsmith as to those of a sculptor.

His 'Fairy with a Peacock' shows a female nude, with a head-dress made in the shape of a peacock, holding in one hand a live peacock and in the other a fan made from peacock feathers. Light from the polished ivory was reflected on to the silver gilt, translucent enamels and precious stones. In another statue, 'The First Jewel', Wolfers is content to allow the theme of voluptuous femininity to dominate. Cut from the confines of a tusk, the beautifully posed nude girl contemplates a jewel, which is here the only decorative element.

The lessons of the Modern Style learned at Brussels were to be repeated at Paris in 1900. Notable exhibits at this exhibition were two candelabra designed by Egide Rombaux, the silver parts of which were made by Franz Hoosmans. In the centre of each candelabra is a languorous nude girl, caught, as it were, in the tangles of the silver plant forms which surround her. One of the two figures seems to swoon ecstatically into the thorny branches, the other struggles desperately to free herself from their enlacement.

A similar sense of *Schadenfreude* is present in at least one other carving, Jean Dampt's 'Raymondin and Melusine', in which the knight, in silver armour, draws the almost naked ivory-and-diamond Melusine closer to him with his steel-gloved hands.

The same skilful, yet disquieting, mixture of materials is to be found in 'Salammbô before Matho', by Théodore Rivière. The bronze African mercenary has fallen at the feet of the ivory Carthaginian princess. Everyone who had read Gustave Flaubert's novel *Salammbô* would know that the heroine gave herself to the mercenary in order to persuade him to spare Carthage, and then died of shame.

Rivière's statuette heralded the Art Deco figure. It was made from bronze and ivory, enhanced with paint and with attached gold and jewellery work. At least two replicas survive. One, shown at Dresden in 1901, has a round verd-antique base and a much simpler array of jewellery. All that distinguishes 'Salammbô before Matho' from an Art Deco figure is the fact that it was an expensive piece of exhibition sculpture, intended for the wealthy connoisseur, and was not put into mass production.

Other pieces of about the same time also suggest Art Deco. They include Clovis Delacour's 'Andromeda', exhibited in 1901, in which the central figure, made of ivory and goldsmith's work, is chained to a granite rock and menaced by a bronze dragon rising from an onyx sea. Much more pleasing is E. Barrias's 'Nature Unveiling Herself to Science'. The ivory arms, head and bosom of Nature emerge from gracefully modelled drapery of silver gilt that flows down to a lapis lazuli base. A ribbon of goldsmith's work, tied to the left arm, indicates the junction of a separately carved segment and the ivory torso. Like 'Salammbô', 'Nature' was produced in several different versions.

A decade or so earlier, visitors would have been shocked by this mixture of brightly coloured materials, so different from the 'white sculpture' of the earlier nineteenth century. The vogue for

Below: St Elizabeth of Hungary by Alfred Gilbert. 1899; 21 in. (53.3 cm). The polychromed bronze figure has an ivory face; insets are gemstones and mother-of-pearl.

collecting Japanese netsuke displaying a wide variety of decorative materials – ivory, tortoiseshell, gold, coral, precious stones and so forth – and tsuba displaying brightly hued alloys and interesting patinations may have influenced public acceptance.

These Japanese elements were taken up by the English school of Art Nouveau sculptors, the 'Decorative Sculptors' as they are sometimes called. Their themes, completely different from those of the French and Belgians, were Arthurian, or at least medieval.

Sir William Reynolds Stephens (1862–1943), a British sculptor though born in Detroit, won fame with an Arthurian group in which ivory figured. 'Lancelot and the Nestling' was exhibited in 1899. 'It was this statue,' wrote the critic Marion Spielmann, 'in which the artist began his delightful use of various coloured metals, ivory, gems, and the like, with pretty symbolism in the base.' Even more successful was the companion statue, 'Guinevere and the Nestling'. Reynolds Stephens uses comparatively little ivory, and that mostly for face and hands, perhaps because of the difficulty of getting a good assistant to work it. This may have been the case with other sculptors of the school as well. Reynolds Stephens had possibly been drawn to ivory partly because he was very interested in new methods – some of his bronze work, for example, was done by the electro-deposit process – and also because of the influence of Gilbert.

Alfred Gilbert (1854–1934), later knighted, was the most distinguished English sculptor of his day. At the Royal Academy schools he worked as an assistant to J. E. Boehm, later studying under P. J. Cavalier at the École des Beaux Arts in Paris. He executed many statuettes as well as large compositions and designed goldsmith's work as well as medals. An artistic leader of enormous influence, he was impractical about money and unhappy in his relations with his patrons. His most famous statue was the aluminium Eros in London's Piccadilly Circus. He used ivory, rather sparingly, for his 'St George' in the parish church of Sandringham, Norfolk, and for the face of his polychrome bronze 'Virgin with Roses' on the Duke of Clarence's tomb in the Albert Memorial Chapel, Windsor Castle.

Sir George Frampton (1860–1928) was another decorative sculptor who worked in ivory, and was well known as a leader of the Arts and Crafts Movement. His 'Lamia' is a bust of a lady with a medieval head-dress and hair-style; the bronze dress is slashed to reveal three quite small patches of ivory flesh, the chin is divided by a rather unexpected strap.

The most enterprising use of ivory by a decorative sculptor was by Frank Lynn Jenkins (born in 1870). At Lloyds Registry, in London's Fenchurch

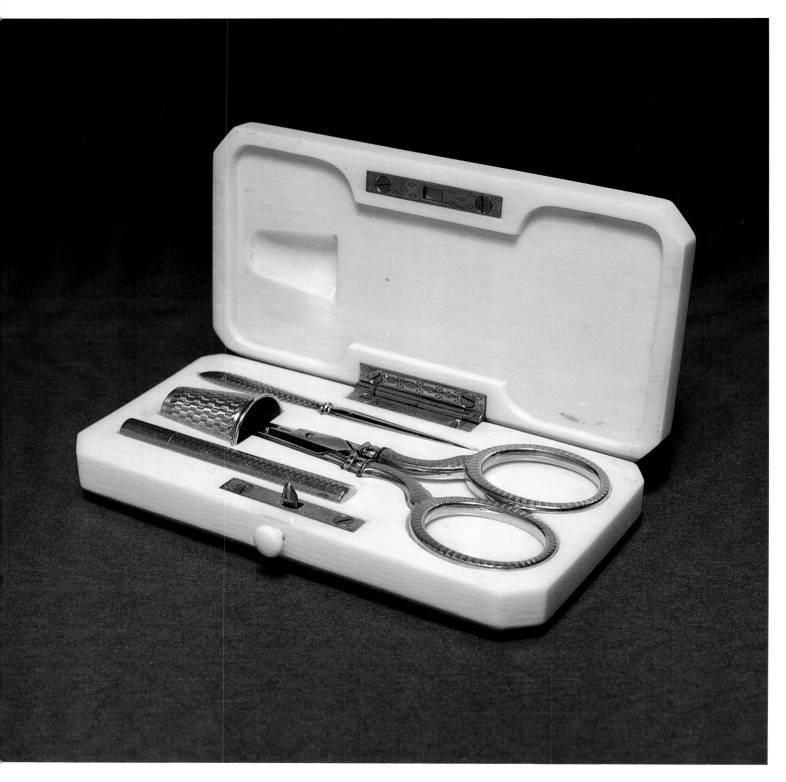

Above: A French ivory sewing *nécessaire* fitted with gold
implements. 1840. See also page 140.

Opposite: Details from the decoration on the British
scrimshaw stay busk shown on page 144: *above right,* a
cottage; *below right,* hearts fixed by an
arrow; *above and below far right,* pots of flowers.

Street, in an Art Nouveau building designed by Thomas Edward Colcutt, is a quite remarkable composition by him.

Round the first-floor vestibule runs a dado frieze of 'Galleys'. Panels depicting Arthurian ships alternate with allegorical bronze figures – some with outstretched hands, some holding a globe, a palm, a sword, a scroll, a lighthouse, a sextant. The faces, hands and accessories are made of ivory. Some of the coral cabochons which ornamented the frieze are still in place. The shell inlay, which mostly depicts the sails, has lost its iridescence, the patinas on the bronze have darkened, and part of the ivory has cracked. The allegorical ladies are carefully muffled up to the chin. Is this Victorian prudery, or difficulty in getting the right assistant carver? Surely at least one nude figure would have been allowable in a frieze depicting the sea.

At the top of the stairs is a bronze galley, with an enigmatic winged female figure, 'The Spirit of British Commerce', at the helm. Her head and bosom are cut from a substantial piece of ivory. A fold of bronze drapery laps over her arm to conceal a join. The work was done in 1903.

Art Nouveau jewellery

Only one English Art Nouveau artist, A. C. C. Jahn, made jewellery in which ivory played an important part. Many of the prominent continental jewellers, on the other hand, made considerable use of ivory. The greatest of them, René Lalique (1860–1945), began painting and selling miniature flowers in gouache on thin ivory plaques, while still at school. He made skilful use of the new material. In one of his brooches, for example, sculpted writhing female figures surround two nephrite cabochons and the ivory plays the part of the framework for the whole piece, instead of gold. The larger part of a corsage ornament is an oblong panel of carved ivory, depicting two girls struggling against the waves. Perhaps his most ambitious use was an ivory orchid set in gold enamelled leaves for a corsage ornament. Lalique carved his ivory mechanically by a *tour à reduire*, which enabled him to make a small ivory carving from a larger master model of plaster or wax.

Lalique's work was very influential in European jewellery and he returned again and again to ivory: in carved orchids on combs, in full-sized figures such as his pendant 'Fairy with Wisterias', in which a nude girl is surrounded by wisterias in gold, enamelled green and purple, and in plaques and busts, also set with gold and enamel and rose diamonds with baroque pearls, often incorporating plant motifs.

Where Lalique led, everyone followed. Lucien Gaillard (born 1861) created a beautiful yet very simple comb with two tines, made from wood and adorned with two apple blossoms carved in ivory, their stamens formed from gold and diamonds. Paul Vever (1851–1915) and his brother Henri (1854–1942) delighted in female figures carved from ivory, set in gold and enamel ornamented with diamonds, and with a baroque pearl at the feet.

Among the motifs for which ivory proved particularly suitable was the mask, which appears in the sculptures of symbolists like Knopff, and is used very extensively in jewellery. Philippe Wolfers's 'Medusa' pendant is the best-known

example. The ivory face of the gorgon, framed in writhing snakes of enamelled gold, glares balefully with opal eyes. Below, a pendant opal is held by a snake which frames the face.

Closely related to the mask is the girl's face theme. It can appear smiling and gracious as in the work of Emmanuel Jules Joë Descomps (1872–1948), one of the Art Deco figurine carvers, or in androgynous guise, framed in pine-cones or jester's garb by Lalique; or be given bat wings, or surrounded by wind-blown hair; or be set in profile and backed up by goldwork, as in the work of Lucien Gautrait.

Although some Art Nouveau jewellers may have imitated Wolfers and Lalique and used a reducing machine, it seems likely that much work was done by hand, especially in countries with a strong tradition of ivory carving, like Germany.

Art Deco

The Art Deco style placed particular emphasis on the 'decorative arts', handicraft and industrial design. It put great faith in progress and equated the beauty of an industrial artefact, such as a ship, with the beauty of Venus. Although it is usually dated to the 1920s and 1930s and takes its name

from a 1925 exhibition in Paris, the Exposition internationale des arts decoratifs et industriels modernes, its beginnings may be traced a generation earlier.

The advent of Art Deco 'chryselephantine sculptures', mass-produced statuettes incorporating ivory with cast bronze elements which were silvered or gilded, had been forecast by Christian Scherer (1902) and Alfred Maskell (1905). 'In the

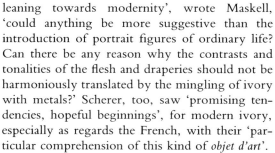

Above: Ivory travelling clock. 1920s. An example of how Art Deco combined function with style.

leaning towards modernity', wrote Maskell, 'could anything be more suggestive than the introduction of portrait figures of ordinary life? Can there be any reason why the contrasts and tonalities of the flesh and draperies should not be harmoniously translated by the mingling of ivory with metals?' Scherer, too, saw 'promising tendencies, hopeful beginnings', for modern ivory, especially as regards the French, with their 'particular comprehension of this kind of *objet d'art*'.

Following on from the quite large figures of bronze and ivory combined, such as Pierre Charles Simart's 'Athene', made for the Paris Exhibition of 1855, ivory sculptors had begun developing a new version of 'chryselephantine' work, the current vogue, but at an affordable price, which meant in a smaller size.

Bridging pieces such as Albert Belleuse's 'Reading Woman' had begun to appear during the 1870s and 1880s, and the exhibitions of Antwerp, 1894, Brussels, 1897, and Paris, 1900, had nurtured what was to become the most international of all ivory carving styles: small ivories, like 'Salammbô', which stood 15¼ in. (38.7 cm) high, on bases of semi-precious stone which raised them up and compensated for the lack of inches.

Though Art Deco figurines were a natural development from nineteenth-century ivory carving, their emergence depended on the time. There were plenty of skilled carvers trained in repetitive work and purchasing power had spread to the middle classes, who were looking for something not too modern, not too expensive, and on sale not at an exhibition, but where they did their shopping for the home, a big store.

The metallic parts of the statuette were cast from a model, made by the designer, and a great variety of patination, gilding, silvering or cold enamelling was then applied to the bronze portions, sometimes to a special order, to tone in with a particular colour scheme. Further decoration could take place, such as encrusting with gems. Meanwhile, the ivory portions of the figure were being carved, once more from the master model, and probably by carvers used to producing identical items of sculpture, like the makers of the *christs en grosse* of Dieppe. The figure would then be assembled, first legs to torso, then arms to torso, and finally head to torso. The ivory portions were attached to the body by long threaded screws, protected by washers, which pushed into them. Some Art Deco figures might be made entirely from ivory.

Once finished, the figurine would be packed up and despatched to the point of sale – perhaps a large department store in Paris, Berlin or Vienna, where many of the ivories were made, or perhaps abroad, in Britain or America, for example. They would be brought before a wider public by exhibitions, in the capital and the provinces, and

by catalogues. At the *Daily Mail* Ideal Home Exhibition of 1931 was a selection of Art Deco figures from the continent. Prominently on display was an academic figure by the greatest of the Art Deco sculptors, Ferdinand Preiss. Carved from a single piece of ivory, it was only 8 in. (20 cm) high and showed St George slaying the Dragon.

Little is known about many of the carvers, who were, after all, merely members of a team whose dominant partner would sign the piece – if it was signed at all. But much is now known about the single most important artist, Ferdinand Preiss. He came from the mainstream of German ivory carving and was descended from carvers on both sides of his family.

Ferdinand Preiss (1882–1943)

Johann Philipp Ferdinand Preiss was born on 13 February 1882 in Erbach im Odenwald, in the family home, the Hotel Preiss. His father numbered among his ancestors Johann Philipp Preiss, a renowned ivory sculptor who had been born in Erbach in 1605. His mother's two brothers were Erbach ivory carvers. The choice of a name for the baby Preiss seems to have indicated his parents' expectations. Both died when he was fifteen, and their children were brought up by relatives and friends. Ferdinand passed into the family of Philipp Wilhelm Willmann, an ivory carver whose apprentice he became. He travelled to Baden Baden, where he worked at Carl Haebler's workshop, and later to Milan, where he worked for a time as a modeller for the firm of Ghidini. At Haebler's he met fellow ivory carvers – Kuchler, Lenz, Trumpfheller and Walther, who were Erbach men – and his future business partner Arthur Kassler, from Berlin. In 1906 they formed the workshop in Berlin which was to become world-famous for its trademark: 'P.K.'

In 1910, after obtaining Prussian citizenship, Preiss took on Louis Kuchler and Ludwig Walther, carvers of outstanding ability. With their co-operation he now launched his first important multiple statue, one inspired by the classical ideas he had brought back from Italy, a naked female dancer on a base of green onyx: the real beginning of the Art Deco figure. The introduction into the P.K. firm of Robert Kionser from the Berlin Gladenbach foundry made it possible to put into production bronze as well as ivory statuettes, such as the statuette 'Carmen', one of the very first ventures in this genre.

Following the First World War Philip Lenz, a carver of great ability, and another carver, Adam Amend from Schonnen near Erbach, joined the firm. Kuchler and Walther set up independently. The P.K. firm moved to the Oranienstrasse in Berlin. While the bronze portions of the statuettes demanded considerable technique, the artistic part

Above: Statuettes shown in colour on page 166.

Below: Figure by Preiss, shown in colour with other figures on pages 162–3.

of the whole concern was the ivory carving. This was done by hand (in spite of what has been said to the contrary) and it demanded all the skill of Preiss, an outstanding carver, and his co-workers, some of the finest Erbach sculptors. The hand-made portions of the statuettes were thus of a guaranteed quality. The standards of P.K. work ensured that Berlin became the centre of Art Deco. In 1943 Preiss died of a brain tumour and the firm came to an end. Almost all his Kabinett-plastik figures were designed, and to some extent carved, by himself.

Preiss's only possible rival in the carving of ivory was Dimitri Chiparus, a Rumanian who came to study and exhibit in Paris, before turning to the production of figures. A further eighty-nine artists of some note have been listed by Bryan Catley. They came from Germany, Austria, France, Russia, Belgium, Switzerland, Poland, Hungary, Rumania, Luxemburg and Britain. The names of Mme Claire Jeanne Robert Colinet, Henri Fugere, Joë Descomps, Pierre Le Faguays, Marcel Bouraine and B. Chabrol are well known to those who collect French and Belgian figures. Professor Otto Poertzel and Bruno Zach are famous German sculptors; Roland Paris and K. Lorenzl equally notable Austrian artists.

According to Alfred Maskell 'a statuette in ivory, a foot or so in height' could cost as much to make as a life-sized statue. Costs of the mass-produced statuettes were cut by using cast elements in bronze, but Preiss was an ivory carver as well as a modeller and he had a team of skilled carvers to help him. So in his figures ivory played a major part.

Art Deco figures

The brightly coloured base and the lacquered bronze portions of Art Deco figures contrasted with the ivory limbs and face. All-ivory statuettes, like Joë Descomps's 'Nude with Scarf and Roses', often seem to lose by this lack of colour contrast.

The preponderance of female figures is striking. A count of Bryan Catley's illustrations, ignoring some categories of figures, such as book-ends, shows 674 female figures, 200 children, 24 couples but only 139 male figures. The figures may have been calculated to appeal to women purchasers, an important manifestation of emancipated female taste if so.

Moreover, the dance was the principal motif of Art Deco and a majority of dancers were women. The 1920s and 1930s saw Isadora Duncan's fame, the foundation of the famous School of Dance in Dresden, and the introduction of dance exercises and musical gymnastics in schools.

Other 1920s motifs were subsumed into the dance theme: the Russian Ballet, the *Folies Bergères*, George White's 'Scandals', the Ziegfeld Follies and the Alcazar Dancers. So were the Egyptian-inspired figures suggested by the discovery of Tutankhamun's tomb in 1922–3, and the Cabaret dancers. It is these Cabaret figures, notably Bruno Zach's partly clad, whip-carrying girl, and B. Chabrol's 'Cabaret Dancer', who wears one stocking, one glove and what appears to be a swimming costume, that earned the epithet *pervers erotischem*. Chabrol's figure must have cost a lot less in ivory and workmanship than Preiss's very chaste 'Con Brio' dancer with her crooked left knee, which must have taken the whole tip of a tusk, and her bare arms, legs and midriff.

The themes of Art Deco figurines encapsulate the 1920s and 1930s. Individual portraits have been pointed out in the figures, such as flier Amy Johnson and actress Brigitte Helm in *Metropolis*, and perhaps sportswomen and sportsmen, and fashion models, while in the wind-blown, stream-lined figures which reflect the last phase of Art Deco I sometimes feel I can detect likenesses to the famous American photographer, Walter Bird, and his most noted model, Rosemary Andrée.

Though produced in such numbers as to be mass-produced masterpieces, Art Deco figures are now in short supply and record prices are being paid for them. In 1931 Preiss's 'The Hoop Girl' would have been sold for very little and her companion, 'Sonny Boy', for the same. Nowadays a group in good condition would fetch a considerable figure. The rarity of the figures probably reflects the way in which they were treated by their owners. Retailers suggested that the figures should be set in niches lighted by a hidden globe, or mounted upon 'hollowed out marble, in which is placed a small electric bulb'. Treatment of this sort would undoubtedly have shortened the lives of many of the figures and set up cracks in the ivory. These cracks can be seen in some of the figures. Black and unsightly, they were certainly not there when the figurine was carved.

The craze for such figures passed. Preiss and his fellow workers had done an honest job for the patrons, but many of his competitors, despairing of achieving the same effects in ivory, worked in composition instead or used inferior metals or colouring. Then came the Second World War. The work of Preiss and his fellows was abruptly dismissed.

In about 1970 collectors interested in Art Deco craftsmanship began to look for the figures. It was a dramatic reversal of taste. Unfortunately, only one famous carver, Adam Amend, lived to see the rehabilitation of his work.

Art Deco jewellery

Art Deco had never succeeded in launching a vogue for ivory jewellery, even in the spirit of the movement, and it must be admitted that those pieces made in ivory are not always as interesting as what was done in precious metals.

Opposite: Cameo portrait in ivory. Nineteenth-century; 4¼ in. (10.5 cm). See also page 142.

In France, Clement Mere (born *c.* 1870) made ivory rings carved with stylized flowers, which were sold in boxes of carved and stained ivory. In Erbach, Georg Frölich created jewellery which faithfully mirrored contemporary ideas of design. One of his brooches might even be taken for a theme which was supposed to haunt design concepts at this time, an Aztec temple, with its stepped sides, rearing itself from the jungle.

Europe after World War II

German carvers

Modern German carving had been invigorated by the impetus given to it by the Art Deco movement. Some of the exhibition figures made at this time drew on Art Deco inspiration. A case in point was Ludwig Walther's 'Dancer', carved in 1930. This female nude, made completely from ivory, resembles the figures that Walther made for Preiss, when he was his helper, and afterwards made when he went into business with Kuchler. 'Dancer' has arms made from two pieces of ivory, disguised by a simple ivory bracelet, a contemporary hair-style and, like many of the figures, tinted eyes. What sets her apart from the mass-production figures is her very high pedestal of ivory. Another figure of Walther's, carved in 1932, 'Girl Crouching', though set on an onyx pedestal, ends in an ivory base carved from the tusk. This seems to me much more an exhibition figure than a type for mass production. Walther's Art Deco figures led, with very little variation of style, to the works of his later years, such as 'Horses' or his fine 'St George Fighting the Dragon'.

Karl Schmidt-Rottluf, Ludwig Gies, Emy Roeder, Oswald Ammersbach, Erich Kuhn, Kurt Schwippert, Georg Frölich, Wilhelm Wegel, Albrecht Glenz, Jan Holschuh and Georg Schwinn, all these artists were to add weight to the Erbach school from the 1900s into the 1960s. But the greatest element of continuity between the Jugendstil, German Art Nouveau, and the present day was veteran carver Otto Glenz among the other Erbachers.

After flirting with Art Nouveau in a work such as his 'Elfe', Glenz had gone on to show just what fine ivories could be created by picking up and adorning the traditional Erbach themes. In his 'Stags' he had revitalized the old animal carvings. His 'Venus and Cupid' and 'The Tall Girl Bathing' were very much in the Erbach neo-classical style, while 'The Shell' (1920) is, I feel, possibly the finest of all German ivory carvings.

Christian Wegel, too, continued the neo-classical tradition, though by no means as successfully as Glenz, while Max Frenzl has continued animal and bird carvings down to the present day. Even a neo-classical and naturalistic sculptor like Wegel, however, might feel the urge to carve in a

Page 162: Art Deco figures. 1930. On the left, Chiparus bronze and ivory group of Pierrot and Partner; on the right, Colinet figure in gilt and bronze and ivory.

Page 163: Bronze and ivory tennis player by Ferdinand Preiss. 1930. See also page 159.

different style, and to make ivory carving a means of expressing something entirely different from the sculpture of naturalism and the craft tradition.

The work of Hildegard Domizlaff had an expressionism that approached abstract art. Calling in the help of a goldsmith, she carved crucifixes, reliquaries, chalices and crosiers.

Wilhelm Wegel, too, followed this trend, if not towards abstract form, at least to extreme stylization, though he did reach complete abstraction in some of his jewellery.

It is difficult to construct a sculpture which will make a strong statement of expressionism in the narrow dimensions imposed by an ivory tusk. Kurt Degen, moreover, has argued plausibly that 'it seems as though an organic substance such as ivory is by definition incompatible with a non-figurative conception of forms'.

Jan Holschuh sought for the abstract in the form of the ivory itself. Disdaining to saw the ivory into slices or blocks, he began to attack it just under the skin of the tusk. Out of tusks which were half-rotted away, either those of mammoths imperfectly preserved in the Arctic ice, or elephant tusks which had weathered in the 'virgin forest', he began to construct sculptures in a material which anyone else would have disdained. In his 'Sermon on the Mount', the rough cleavages of the mammoth ivory have been skilfully utilized to represent a mountain, against which Jesus and his disciples stand out, mere abstract clothes-peg men but impressive in their grouping. In his 'Holy Ghost', the disciples have semi-abstract faces and wholly abstract bodies, while the Dove of the Holy Spirit is also very stylized. Once again, Holschuh has been led by the form of the piece of ivory into the decision of what his sculpture should be.

Possibly his most ingenious use of apparently intractable material is 'Man Calling Out', in which a slice of tusk has been turned into a face. Black cracks round the sides add to the interest of the carving.

Erbach's charm persists, thanks to its skilful blend of the old and the new. Visitors can buy the kind of animal carvings for which the town has always been famous, and also its excellent jewellery. Twentieth-century models include Christian Theodor Mayer's 'Chrysanthemum', first designed in 1910, and Christian Wegel's 'Narcissus', another splendid prototype put into serial production.

The ivory workshops produce the skilfully designed boxes and containers for which Erbach has been famous ever since Franz I, religious ivories and that great standby, chessmen.

British and British Commonwealth carvers

The work of twentieth-century British ivory carvers is eminently collectable and much of it has

Below: Statuette by Louis Richard Garbe. Twentieth-century; 11½ in. (29 cm). The figure, carved in relief, follows the curve of the tusk.

disappeared into private collections. Apart from ecclesiastics who buy ivories for church furniture or ceremonial use, most buyers are probably primarily ivory collectors rather than collectors of sculpture in general. The late Jeanne Bell, who tried to keep all her sculpture within the limitation of the natural tusk, though that made it more difficult to think of fresh designs, felt that 'the reason why ivory is more difficult to sell than some other sculpture is very probably the price, which has to be high, owing to the scarcity of the material, and the skill, time and patience required to carve it'.

There are no ivory carver dynasties in Britain, as in some continental countries, nor do British ivory carvers seem to take pupils.

The twentieth-century English school has attempted to return to the mainstream of traditional ivory work by what was called 'Direct Carving'. This involves the designer's doing all the carving, not relying on a *practicien* to transpose the lines of the model on to an ivory carving.

The arrival of the Direct Carving school was made all the more easy in that the Art Nouveau fashion for decorative sculpture had begun to die out, even before the First World War. Lynn Jenkins, after his Lloyds Registry frieze, seems to have given up ivory completely and devoted himself to bronze. Meanwhile, an interest in another organic material, wood, made it easier for sculptors to attract attention by carving just in ivory.

The foremost British ivory carver of the early twentieth century was Louis Richard Garbe (1876–1957), son of a craftsman in ivory and tortoiseshell.

Garbe first exhibited at the Royal Academy in 1898 and continued to do so for most of his long life. He was an all-round sculptor who made works in bronze, marble and even lacquered wood. He was praised for the vigour and 'rugged power' of his work in other media.

Although prominent in other media, Garbe was a very prolific and hard-working ivory carver. He made carvings in low relief, triptychs, masks and statuettes. It was not unknown for him to exhibit a whole case of ivory carvings at the Royal Academy, as in 1924, while in 1936 he exhibited no fewer than twelve. These works, which perhaps represented the accumulation of several years, included a mammoth ivory carving called 'Renaissance', two heads, a half-length and pieces called 'The Source' (a theme to which he may have returned in 1951), 'Proserpine', 'Naiad', 'Cupid and Goose', 'Resurgo', 'Java' and 'The Waterman'. He did not show an ivory every year, however, and when he did, was often the only ivory carver to be on exhibition.

Garbe's work was very diversified. He carved figures that followed the curving line of the tusk, which gives them the appearance of swaying slightly in the breeze, and sawed up ivory to make low-relief carvings or heads. 'I have carved figures that conformed to the curves of the tusk,' he wrote, 'and as these lines are in themselves expressive and fine I have incorporated them into the composition.'

Page 166: Three ivory figures, from France. 1880; 10½ in. (26.6 cm). The figure standing on the winged wheel is Fortune. See page 158 for detail.

Page 167: Plaque showing the head of a nymph. c.1900; 5¾ in. (14.6 cm). It was once attached to a piece of furniture. See also page 147.

Jeanne Bell was Garbe's pupil at London's Central School of Arts and Crafts. 'He was always very kind to me and interested in my work, though he said I was "too independent for him" because I would not let him work on anything I was doing. He believed very strongly in doing most of the work with the chisel and scraper, and using files as little as possible. As a sculptor he advised me to concentrate on the figure, human or animal, and to do only what I could ask a good price for.'

Another pupil of Garbe's was Mary Morton. Like Jeanne Bell she liked to carve from the whole tusk, and she showed great ingenuity in getting a whole group out of a tusk, as in her 'Nature's Tribute to Beauty'. Whereas Jeanne Bell had looked for themes which were rather unusual at the time, such as the Negro subjects of 'Pastoral' and 'Black Ivory', Mary Morton, like Garbe himself, was closer to the neo-classical tradition.

A final pupil of Garbe's was Alan Durst, who began his artistic studies at the age of thirty, first studying stained glass at the Central School, then ivory carving under Garbe.

Serving in the First World War, in the Royal Marines, he visited West African ports where ebony and ivory lay stacked on the quayside and could be had for the asking. He began carving aboard ship, making a tea caddy and a biscuit barrel as a present for his wife. His first show was held in 1930 at the Leicester Galleries. His statuette 'Prophet' was exhibited at the Royal Academy in 1938. In between carving ivories he did many statues for churches. Whatever he carved, whether a religious work, such as his crucifix for Marlborough College, or one of his delightful animals, was done in masterly fashion. Alan Durst's work spans more than sixty years, from the Arts and Crafts Movement, whose traditions Direct Carving inherited, to modern times.

Ivory carving in the British Commonwealth today comprises both souvenir carvings, for tourists, and exhibition carvings by trained sculptors.

Malawi, in Central Africa, has a National Craft School at Kota Kota where pupils can train in ivory carving and work to exhibition standard, while outside in the street with their wares spread out about them, are the representatives of folk art tradition.

Fine work, deeply influenced by Maori tradition, is being done in New Zealand, where the nucleus of an Owen Mapp collection has now been begun both by Canterbury and Auckland Art Galleries.

The work of Namba Roy (1910–61) must have stimulated and interested many who had become convinced that in Britain, ivory carving was a lost art and that nobody still carved in the complete tusk. Born Nathan Roy Atkins, a Maroon from the Cockpit Country at Accompong in Jamaica,

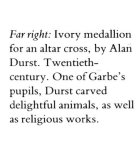

Far right: Ivory medallion for an altar cross, by Alan Durst. Twentieth-century. One of Garbe's pupils, Durst carved delightful animals, as well as religious works.

he was taught carving by his father, who had in turn learned it from Roy's grandfather, the traditional carver of their Caribbean village. The family was of African descent, from the Congo.

Roy settled in Britain after the Second World War, married and became a factory worker. In the early mornings and late evenings and on Sundays he did all his creative work. He wrote and painted but his real love was sculpture. When he could afford nothing else he used plastic wood and metal alloy; when his resources permitted he bought the traditional materials he preferred, wood, ebony and ivory. According to his daughter, 'the shapes of these would suggest the form the finished carving would take. He used the whole ivory tusk and often said that the figures he used were already present – all he had to do was to free them.'

Sometimes Roy painted the ivory. To illustrate his novel, *Black Albino*, he carved Kisanka and Tamba, a black woman with her albino son. It remains one of his most effective pieces.

The work is strongly African and nearly always has a spiritual theme. He seemed to place equal emphasis on Christianity and ancient African beliefs and his biblical figures are primitive with African features. The head is often disproportionately large for it contains the spirit.

Roy saw himself as an offshoot of a tree of artists rooted in the Congo forests. 'At my first exhibition here in London in 1952,' he wrote, 'my purely Negro style caused many of my people to feel embarrassed, remembering how the word "primitive" has been used for political purposes.'

But it was impossible for him to hide his primitivism and carve in a Western idiom. 'The art of my forefathers was always crying to come out.'

His work, all the more impressive in that his time was short and his carvings were monumental, is a reminder of the importance of cultural roots.

Russia

Ivory carving became established in Russia by the early Middle Ages when settlers moving from Novgorod to Pomoroye in the tenth century brought the skills with them.

Novgorod, Ryazan Vyshorod and Moscow were all centres of medieval bone carving and archaeological work has revealed workshops in Moscow from the eleventh century.

Few artefacts have survived.

Although excavations on the southern part of the Novgorod Kremlin have revealed dragon and mermaid carvings in bone, most ivorywork was

Right: Beaker made with ivory panels. 4½ in. (11.4 cm). The quality of Russian ivories varied from amateurish to superb.

Below: Russo-Greek triptych. Late-seventeenth-century ivory plaque; 4½ × 3 in. (11.4 × 7.6 cm). This is one of several splendid examples of ivorywork that have survived from this date.

figures, combs, rings, powderhorns, boxes and knife handles.

Yakut work was fretted, pierced and sawed into a background pattern like Dieppe *mosaique*, but in Yakut art this more resembled netting. *Mosaique* very like that done in Dieppe was also made by Russians, probably in imitation of French work, and looked like lace patterns.

Besides influences from the Yakuts, Russian carvers imitated the Byzantine ivory coffrets which formed part of many church treasures (and their work was imitated by prisoners of war in England).

At the beginning of the nineteenth century an imposing school of 'Palace Art' was still carving ivory. The great master, Nikolay Stephanovich Vereschagin (1770–1814), was at work in St Petersburg, making vases and incense burners of incredibly delicate fretwork. Large dressing-table mirrors and mirror frames were also made. Other work included low-relief icons with fretted frames, portrait medallions set in *mosaique*, portraits, also with frame borders, pincushions, workboxes, coffrets, even chests of drawers made up from single fretted ivory panels, which were surely the largest ivory carvings ever to be produced in Europe.

There is an enormous range of quality in the ivories preserved in various Russian museums. Some may be imported; the Russians and the English were the best customers the Dieppe artists had. A portrait medallion of Tsar Alexander I, set in flawless *mosaique* and surrounded by a garland of flowers, may well be the work of some Dieppe carver. There are some very capable and vigorous carvings which are obviously Russian in their style and subject. But there are many others which are amateurish and totally unsuccessful.

By about 1830, Russian ivory carving had seen its best days, though religious ivories continued to be made.

Possibly the most satisfying nineteenth-century Russian ivory genre is the chess set, in which the ship, called *ladya* after the Greek *lameda*, does duty as the rook. Most chessmen appear to have been carved rather than turned, and have ridged and fluted bases. Even those pieces which show traditional turned shapes have apparently been carved by hand.

Numbers of twentieth-century carvers are now settled in the village of Lomonosov, on an island not far from Kholmogory. The craft work being made here and in other Russian carving centres is in bone, not ivory.

Either the supply of fossil ivory has run out or, more likely, the price of mammoth ivory is now so high that it would be impossible to sell the finished work abroad.

destroyed by the Tartar invasions of the four-teenth century.

Much of this would have been liturgical accessories such as *panagia*, the flat circular box, containing the host, worn round the neck of priests visiting the poor. Ivory was also carved for staff heads and the tiny plaques used as personal icons.

Ivory was still used mainly for liturgical purposes during the sixteenth and seventeenth centuries, and many works have survived from this time. *Panagia*, plaques and staff heads are carved with microscopic detail, but little is known about their history.

Nineteenth-century Russia

Nineteenth-century Russia had the benefit of the vast supplies of mammoth and mastodon tusks, preserved in the frozen shores and offshore islands of Siberia. In Russian the same word, *kost*, does duty both for ivory and bone, a semantic difficulty which may produce references to 'bone carving' in translations when 'ivory carving' was meant.

Certainly the nomad Yakuts or Koryaks who roamed Siberia never showed any inclination to carve bone when they could obtain the much more consistent fossil ivory. The Yakuts were still carving a wide range of objects in the nineteenth century: realistic models of encampments, charm

Africa

Africa is well attested as a source of ivory for the classical world but little is known of the ivories that must have been made south of the Sahara at that time. Because ivory is not durable under hostile environmental conditions, swelling and contracting, cracking and flaking, the yield of carved ivories from ancient African sites is limited to fragments and decayed remnants. Sure knowledge of African ivory working begins with the fifteenth-century European traders. Their arrival on the west coast led both to the preservation of late medieval African ivories and to the influence of European tastes and preferences on African traditions over the next five hundred years.

Above: An ivory spoon from West Africa.
Opposite: Two carved ivory armlets in the Yoruba style, brought from Dahomey for a German merchant. *c.*1659. See also page 178.

Above: An 'Afro-Portuguese' ivory spoon, made by Sherbro craftsmen for export to Portugal. Probably late-fifteenth- or early-sixteenth-century; 13⅓ in. (34 cm) long.

Far right: A Sherbro horn in ivory decorated in high relief with figures of women and of animals. 28½ in. (72.5 cm) long. At the tip, a seated figure with his dog at his feet.

African ivories in the sixteenth, seventeenth and eighteenth centuries

Ivories were among the first goods sent back to Europe from Africa by the fifteenth-century adventurers. Whereas the Africans and Europeans apparently valued gold and copper somewhat differently, they seem to have held ivory in equal estimation. It figures largely in diplomatic exchanges between rulers of the two continents. The association between the secular ruler and his natural counterpart, the elephant, is very old indeed. It is largely from ivory works shipped to Europe during the early years of contact and preserved in the cabinets and royal collections, and later the museums, of Europe, that our knowledge of medieval African craftsmanship in ivory is derived.

Foremost among these works are the so-called 'Afro-Portuguese' ivories. These were, above all, luxury items – salt-cellars, carved spoons, ornate dagger handles, hunting horns – imported into Portugal in large numbers owing to the Portuguese official monopoly of African trade at that time. For a long time, these were something of an academic mystery. They were variously considered to have been made in Turkey, or in India, or by Africans in Europe. Their wholly African origin now seems clear.

Produced in a relatively short period between the late fifteenth and early sixteenth centuries, these carved ivories are the first manifestation of an impulse seen the length and breadth of Africa today: they are tourist art, export ware made by African carvers but calculated to appeal to European tastes, blending both traditions. Three principal sources have to be considered – Sherbro, Benin and the kingdom of the Congo.

Sherbro

Sherbro is the name of an island just off the coast of modern-day Sierra Leone; European traders favoured the setting-up of coastal entrepôts in such locations for convenience and security. But it is also one name of a people – known also as the Bullom – so it seems likely that the 'Sherbro style' refers to works originating over a large part of the coast. The most lasting artistic expression of the first interactions between Europeans and Africans is to be found in the pedestal cups imported into Europe as *salieri*, salt-cellars, in large numbers. The Sherbro style is perhaps the most delicate of all, being characterized by flowing lines, minute working of surface details and a certain artistic wit that has lost none of its force in the intervening years. A variety of forms shows animals and human figures from both continents, Christian symbols and serpents, madonnas and monsters, all blended together in an exotic mix. The salt-

cellars have two basic forms: a lidded pedestal cup supported on a conical base with much swirling scrollwork linking the various components, and a lidded cup supported by carved human figures. Within this broad framework, variation is enormous and the artist probably had great scope for the free play of his imagination. To this day, however, it remains unclear precisely what models were offered to the carvers. The sixteenth-century chronicler Valentim Fernandes notes of the coastal peoples of Sierra Leone: 'The people of this country are negroes who are very skilful with their hands; they make ivory salt-cellars and spoons. And also whatever work you draw for them, they carve it in ivory.'

It may well be that drawings and woodcuts were the source of the hunting scenes that decorate the ivory horns brought back from this area. Customs records in Lisbon reveal that such a horn, for all its value today, was assessed at about the price of a linen shirt.

The refinement of the carved ivories of Sherbro suggests that a tradition supplying similar works for local needs already existed. Indeed, Duarte Pecheco Pereira, another chronicler of the period, records: 'In this country they make ivory spoons of better design and better workmanship than in

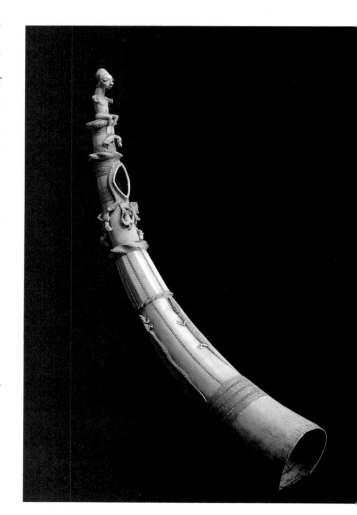

Far right: An 'Afro-Portuguese' ivory salt-cellar, with Portuguese grandees. Probably sixteenth-century; 11½ in. (29 cm). It consists of two separate vessels.

any other part.' Few of these works got into European collections. Their nature is only suggested by the wooden spoons and pedestal cups of the Bijogo, the ivory horns of the Mende and the stone figurines or *nomoli* made by sixteenth-century Bullom carvers and thus closely resembling the figures of the Sherbro ivories.

Benin

The second major source of the Afro-Portuguese ivories lay in the kingdom of Benin, situated in the swampy forests of southern Nigeria. Here, because the kingdom maintained its traditions until the British annexation of 1897, we know a great deal more about the circumstances in which ivories were carved and how they were used.

Carved ivories were produced exclusively by the guild of carvers, the Igbesanmwan, who also worked in wood, under royal supervision in Benin City. It is important to distinguish two classes of works produced by them, the Afro-Portuguese ivories that were intended for a foreign market and the regalia destined for use by the royal court. Whereas hundreds of the former were exported to Europe, the ivory royal regalia were unknown in the West until the annexation of the kingdom. Indeed, elephant ivory was a royal prerogative within the realm, its use being tightly controlled and old works carefully preserved.

Among the first class, we again find spoons, horns and salt-cellars. The salt-cellars are quite different from those of Sherbro, however, in that they possess two chambers, arranged vertically, instead of one. Stylistically, too, the differences are clear. Benin pieces are much heavier and more massive, less fluid than the works from Sierra Leone, which are sometimes so thin as to be translucent.

Of foremost importance, however, is that Benin craftsmen were working within a tightly controlled guild system that set no value by mere innovation. Benin artworks have a stereotyped, static quality that sought to reproduce received models rather than develop new ones and works were subject to censure and refusal by senior guild members.

The salt-cellars from Benin are, again, of two basic designs, a group of standing Portuguese grandees facing outwards from the central chambers, or a set of equestrian figures, incorporating a naked angel, riding around the central vessels. These designs rapidly became fixed and variations between two versions of the 'same' design are minimal. These are not unique pieces after the European notion of 'artworks' but they provide an excellent opportunity to study different carvers tackling the same subject.

When approaching alien subjects through their own visual vocabulary, African carvers were often called upon to interpret the unfamiliar. The

Right: Carved ivory box from Benin. 6¼ in. (16 cm) long. The lid shows two Portuguese soldiers fighting; beside them, a slaughtered reptile. See page 176 for detail.

Opposite: An ivory pectoral mask from Benin, with coral beadwork. 7¾ in. (19.5 cm). It shows the powerful face of the Queen Mother Idia. See also page 177.

Below: Benin carved ivory bracelets. Eighteenth-century. See page 176 for detail.

Above: Detail from the carved ivory box on page 174, showing how the Benin craftsmen visualized European faces.

naked angel seems to have particularly exercised their imagination, being reduced at times to an almost geometric motif. Faces of Europeans hardly vary. Depiction centres on the portrayal of their long hair and beards and big, hooked noses.

It must be stressed that the mass production of stereotyped forms, under almost factory conditions, with minimal variation and with an iconography that signifies rather than represents, is wholly in keeping with the traditional ways in which such works were created in a centralized kingdom. The most astonishing thing about the Benin Afro-Portuguese ivories is that their quality remains of the highest technical order.

The Benin horns similarly differ from their Sherbro counterparts in style and solidity. Like the Sherbro horns made for Europeans, they usually have the aperture at the narrow end of the tusk. (As a rule, horns made for Africans have the aperture at the side. Benin horns are unusual in having the aperture on the *convex* curve, a fact that makes them readily identifiable.) They often also incorporate suspension loops, which would be unusual in ivories carved for Africans. The most common mark of an Afro-Portuguese work, however, is the incorporation of designs such as astrolabes and the coat of arms of the Portuguese royal house.

The royal monopoly of ivory in Benin was an important part of the ritual and economic position of the Oba (the king). One tusk of each elephant slain within his domains had to be presented to him and the other offered to him for purchase. This enabled him to build up large stocks for trade with Europeans and to supply objects for ritual and court use. The absence of competition greatly strengthened his hand when fixing the price with European traders and the European market must have been a welcome outlet for an otherwise embarrassing excess of royal material.

Below: Detail from the carved ivory bracelets shown on page 174. A Benin notable waves a ritual sword.

The ivories made for use within the Benin Kingdom were produced by the same carvers, the Igbesanmwan. Their products included bracelets – carved or inlaid with copper or giltwork – bowls, boxes, combs, sword handles, rattle staffs for the royal altars, staffs, gongs, horns, carved figures and huge carved tusks to be set on the brass ancestral heads of the altars.

Datings of royal regalia raise problems not encountered with export ware, where a few well-documented pieces may fix dates for the rest. Normally, these works are dated on the basis of oral tradition, stylistic comparisons with dated export ivories and brass artefacts, or patination. All these factors, however, are inherently unreliable.

The vagaries of oral tradition will be obvious enough, especially following such an interregnum as occurred after the colonization of Benin. Export pieces were made for a short period only and we have no way of dating what happened afterwards. Since brass and ivory were worked by different guilds there is no reason why stylistic developments in one medium should go hand in hand with those in another. Large collections of Benin ivories sometimes reveal pieces of similar form, by the same hand, but with totally different surface appearance.

Possibly the most striking works made for internal use were the ivory pectoral masks in the form of the Queen Mother Idia. A small number of these is known, thought to date from the sixteenth century – evidence that African centralized kingdoms were well able to preserve

Left: Ivory pectoral mask in the form of the Queen Mother. Sixteenth-century. It is fringed with miniature Portuguese heads and inlaid with copper wire. Another example is shown in colour on page 175.

· *Below:* A Benin waist ornament of ivory with copper studs.

Far below: A pair of Benin ivory leopards. Probably early-nineteenth-century; 32¾ in. (83 cm) and 32 in. (81 cm) long. Each is made from five separate tusks. The copper 'spots' tapped into undercut depressions are percussion caps from rifle bullets. The leopard's courage, strength and cunning made it the symbol of kingship. See page 182 for detail.

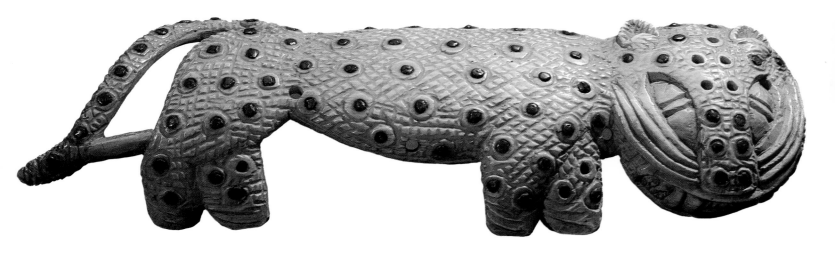

ancient ivories of ritual or political importance. All show a powerful face with the scarification typical of Benin females, fringed above and below with a selection of mudfish, Portuguese heads and 'thunderbolts' (neolithic stone axes thought in much of West Africa to be the material expression of thunder). At either side are suspension loops suggesting that these ivories were originally worn dangling at the breast like the well-known brass mask of the Atta of Idah. Nowadays, the Oba wears the modern equivalents at his hip when he purifies the city of evil influences, but originally they were probably worn at rites commemorating the Queen Mother.

Below: A double bell from Benin. 14½ in. (36.8 cm). It is said to have been struck to signify the Oba's approval.

Not surprisingly, these masks share certain features with the Afro-Portuguese ivories, produced by the same guild and even by the same hands – the use of Portuguese figures, guilloche patterning, etc. – yet here we are aware of a tighter iconography. Ivory, in Benin, had its place in a hierarchy of materials, each of which had strong associations in religious thought. Its colour was of foremost importance in this ranking. Ivory regalia are said to have been bleached or rubbed with chalk to enhance their whiteness, the colour of the god Olokun who brought wealth, children and foreign trade and who was held to live across the water – an association of these ideas neatly matching the Bini experience of white-faced seafarers who dealt in ivory. Europeans supplied guns and gunpowder. At one time there were even European mercenaries in the Benin army. It is small wonder, then, that European faces should appear so widely on ivory regalia, just as complete soldier figures were cast in brass for the royal altars and wooden carvings of armed Portuguese were mounted on the roof of the royal palace. The modern production of tourist objects does not occur in isolation; it affects more traditional pieces.

The mudfish, too, are important as messengers of Olokun, mediators between land and water, creatures that survive the drought by self-inhumation and emerge to make sterile pools suddenly boil with life, effective markers of the Oba's divinity and power since he was identified in one aspect with Olokun. Opposed to this aspect was the red brass that signified the dangerous and ambivalent features of royal power. Ivory, prominent in purification rituals, might be changed from white to red by the application of palm oil.

A largely unresolved question is the importance of the neighbouring Yoruba kingdoms in the development of Benin ivory carving. For considerable periods, Benin influence was strong – especially in Owo. It has been argued that many features found in Benin ivory carving but not in brass casting, such as the bulging eyes and pouting lips, are of Yoruba origin and explicable by the importation of Yoruba carvers from vassal cities into the Benin carvers' guild. In the absence of evidence, this must remain pure speculation. However, a vigorous and early tradition of ivory carving is documented for the Yoruba areas of modern-day Nigeria and Dahomey (Republic of Benin), a number of carvings from this area figuring among the earliest African works preserved in European *cabinets de curiosités*. Whereas we have no record of heavily sculptural pedestal cups in Benin, other than as export ware, the Yoruba kingdoms *do* seem to have carved such pieces for local use. Similarly, bracelets, ritual swords, ivory tappers – used in divination at the Ifa oracle – and figurines, exist in substantial numbers. Once again, the dating of these pieces is very problematical unless the carvings have found their way into European collections which provide evidence for such ivory working at least from the seventeenth century.

The Congo

Numerically less important, but artistically not inferior, are the carved ivories from the Congo. As usual, early travellers bring back objects such as horns that are more or less closely related to local models. It is again safe to assume that features such as suspension hoops and the placing of the aperture at the end as opposed to the side, derive from European influence. Some of these are very plain, others have simple geometric ornamentation, others still are richly carved. One such piece had already made its way into the Medici collection by 1553 and recalls Kuba motifs that we know from much later wood carvings.

Early chroniclers and missionaries give a certain amount of information on these works, declaring with unusual unanimity that they were owned only by the nobility and were used to announce the presence or declare the passing of those of high rank, to rouse soldiers in battle and to mark the moment of transubstantiation during the Mass.

Other carving traditions

Early knowledge of African ivory carving, then, centres on areas of the west coast that were visited by Europeans whose museum collections and documentation have resisted the ravages of time better than ivories in Africa. Only in Benin have we a sufficient continuity of dynastic authority to preserve royal objects and traditions concerning their creation. Even here, however, dating is difficult. It is increasingly clear that our knowledge represents only the tip of an iceberg. Archaeological remains, historical records, the vigour of later carving traditions, all show that ivory carving is both ancient and widespread in Africa. Were it not for a chance sketch of an Ibibio (South Nigerian) horn produced by an Italian artist of the seventeenth century, for example, we might think ivory carving here a relatively recent phenomenon. Were it not for relatively recent finds of small ivories in East African archaeological contexts, we might think ivory carving a neglected art in this area.

The association of ivory objects with royalty and prestige seems a standard theme of Africa as in Europe. Versions of everyday objects were often made in ivory to mark the special status of their possessors. We must remember, however, that huge areas of Africa that display important ivory carving traditions at a later date are unrepresented in the early records and that everyday objects do not endure as does royal regalia. Beneath the sumptuous luxury goods made for foreigners and the display objects commissioned by local rulers there may lurk many unknown carving traditions whose trace is clear only in later centuries.

Nineteenth-century African ivories

The nineteenth century showed a progressive determination on the part of Europeans to penetrate the hinterland instead of merely dealing through voracious and unpredictable middlemen on the coast. By the end of the century, the demands of trade, nationalist rivalry and military insecurity had led to a fundamental change. Colonialism was in full expansion.

All this undermined traditional social and political groupings, sapped local religious belief and exposed African craftsmen to a withering series of new influences and demands. Exports of African 'art' objects had greatly declined from the heady days of the 'Afro-Portuguese' trade. Africa served now as a source of raw material for foreign craftsmen. Yet the new European presence revealed ivory carving traditions that had been hitherto unknown and, in the old carving centres such as Benin, awoke an awareness of works made for purely local use. By the end of the century, Africans had begun to produce for the tourist trade curios that sought to reflect an 'exotic' picture of Africa as conceived by Europe.

Many objects are difficult to date precisely. Owing to the extreme conservatism of many areas, we cannot be entirely sure that some works assigned a nineteenth-century date were not earlier.

Benin

The workshops of the Benin Kingdom continued to cater for the royal altars and the court. The carved tusks are the largest of the nineteenth-century ivory works and bear eloquent testimony to the abundance of mature ivory at that time. Sometimes standing six feet or more in height, they were the most exposed of the ritual paraphernalia, fixed by means of double-headed stakes to the tops of the large brass heads on the ancestral altars and only partly sheltered from the weather by the courtyard roof. They doubtless needed to be replaced at regular intervals as they weathered. Since acid fruit juices and chalk were applied to enhance their whiteness in the face of the pervasive red laterite dust, their surfaces must have abraded fairly quickly.

The Benin tusks are highly stereotyped and come in a number of different basic designs. These presumably relate to the different shrines to which they were assigned but all attempts to 'read' the tusks have proved fragmentary. We know that the figures carved all over their surfaces – Obas, animals, Europeans, retainers – were executed from the base to the tip in parallel bands

Above: Detail from the lower of the two Yoruba armlets shown in colour on page 170.

Page 180: Benin carved ivory pendant. Late-seventeenth- or early-eighteenth-century; 5 in. (12.7 cm). Probably worn on the hip, it shows the Oba and two attendants.

Page 181: A Kongo maternity figure showing bodily scarification.

and are presumably to be read in the same direction. The most plausible suggestion thus far is that they depict major events of a ruler's life mingled with standard statements of power and legitimacy such as the depiction of an Oba in the image of the god of wealth and fertility, Olokun.

The motifs of the carved tusks stand out in low relief and skilful use is made of the natural shape of the ivory in locating images.

African ivory workers, like wood carvers, tend to work within the formal constraints of their raw material. The joining together of different sections within a complex whole is unusual in both media and found only where there has been strong European influence. For this reason, the technique is normally attributed to outside stimuli and is taken as a mark of relatively recent date. A number of striking works of this kind occur in the Benin corpus; for example, the large lidded vessels and pedestal cups. In these, several sections of ivory are joined together with metal pins and staples. An inlay of copper wire dramatically highlights the incised designs that are drawn from the normal Benin repertoire but also serves to bind the complex whole together: a neat simultaneous resolution of technical and aesthetic problems that demonstrates mastery of the medium.

But perhaps the most famous of the composite ivories are the leopard aquamaniles (water containers used in the royal ablutions). Each of the

Right: Ivory horseman from the Yoruba kingdom. It is believed to relate to the Ogboni cult, which worshipped Onile, goddess of the earth, but also had important secular powers connected with kingship.

Far right: Yoruba ivory bracelets. 4¼ × 4½ in. (21.1 × 11.5 cm).

paired leopards consists of five major sections of ivory socketed together and fixed with metal pins. They are reliably datable as an integral part of the surface decoration is composed of copper percussion caps used in nineteenth-century firearms.

This jointing technique enabled Benin craftsmen to construct much larger ivory carvings than the constraints of a single tusk would have permitted. But another striking feature is that the leopard aquamaniles could never have held water. Indeed, they have only mock apertures and must have been used simply for display.

The Yoruba kingdoms

The carving in ivory of objects normally made in other materials is something of a theme in Africa and not limited to the Bini. The neighbouring Yoruba kingdoms of Nigeria, for example, produced non-functional ivory swords for the use of dignitaries. It may indeed have been the Yoruba kingdoms that produced the most accomplished ivory carvings of the nineteenth century. There are major problems of dating but this was the period when many beautiful pieces were brought to the West. Especially fine are the double bracelets, one inside the other, carved from a single tusk so that the inner cylinder serves as a delicate filigree background for the openwork figures of the outer. Often these are adorned with ivory versions of small metal bells – again function has been sacrificed to display.

The ivory lidded cups from the Yoruba seem to demonstrate great constancy through time. Some are clearly of considerable antiquity, dating back at least to the seventeenth century. Yet others, very similar, incorporate the motif of a European in shorts with a rifle and were doubtless carved in the nineteenth century, simply substituting a new motif for an old one in the same overall design.

Cameroon

The nineteenth century found a major new carving area in the western Grasslands area of Cameroon, where the elephant is a powerful symbol of royalty – the ruler being thought able to transform himself into an elephant at will. Important warriors are allowed access to an elephant society whose masked figures are often assigned wide powers of socially sanctioned destruction. Not surprisingly, tusks are here associated with kingship, being used as footrests by the enthroned monarch and often buried with him. Tusks may often be carved in the round with figures of 'royal' animals – leopards, elephants, chameleons – and depictions of court retainers. Cameroonian carving technique produces works where figures stand out from the surface in low relief and are arranged in parallel bands. Often, they will be coloured a deep amber by the regular application of palm oil. It is unclear whether the reddish colour is preferred for aesthetic reasons, whether the oil is held to prevent cracking or whether the glossiness of the anointed tusks is admired.

Smoking tobacco has important connotations of fertility in the Grasslands and pipes may be both items of display and ritual objects. The bowl will be of cast brass or carved clay – usually in the form of a human or animal figure. The stem will be brass, wood or, for wealthy individuals, ornate ivory. It features hierarchically arranged bands of figures – often in postures of submission – and geometric motifs such as occur elsewhere in wood and bead working. The stems become penetrated over time with a mixture of oil, smoke and sweat that creates rich patination and abrades the sharpness of the design. Unusually, it is the ivory

Right: Hand-turned ivory candlesticks from Tanzania. Twentieth-century; 10 in. (25.5 cm).

object that is generally made to be used; much larger versions in wood and brass may be for display only and seldom if ever lit.

The Congo

The Congo area remained important for the production of ivory artefacts in the nineteenth century though many unworked tusks were traded with Europeans. The small but finely worked ivories associated with this area include staff finials, sword handles and especially pendants and whistles.

The best known are perhaps the small Luba pendants of very hard hippo or warthog ivory, usually depicting the torso of a woman with a complex hair-style. These are generally curved, following the dimensions of the natural tusk, the upper part swelling to a bulbous head. The fine grain of these ivories lends itself to delicate surface working of the face and limbs, the hands often cupping the breasts in an act of submission. They are said to depict deceased relatives and are pierced to allow them to be worn on a belt or an arm or even hidden in the armpit.

Other African ivories

Among the most accomplished ivory miniatures of important ritual objects are the small *ikhoko* ivories of the Pende, often only a few inches high. These are amuletic renditions of the carved wooden face-masks worn at male circumcision, whose narrow chins, bulbous eyes and flared nostrils they simulate (possibly, indeed, carved by the same master craftsmen). Only occasionally do complete figures occur. The amulets are held to have a prophylactic or curative function in the handling of disease and are worn only by men. Wood or seed versions are carved for the use of women and children. These amulets often take on a dark red patina as they absorb palm oil rubbed on to the wearer's skin.

Rather more geometric figurines are carved by the Lega in both bone and ivory. A whole range of these occurs. They are valuable properties passed on from generation to generation by the officials of the Bwami cult, important in the context of male initiation, each evoking series of moral precepts that constitute the lore passed on to men as they are promoted through the cult. They are a powerful evocation of the forces of social control and moral enforcement.

Only at the end of the century does tourist ivory art reappear. The Loango area of Angola is the source of the carved tusks made as souvenirs. They are readily identifiable with their spiral thread of naturalistic figures, often depicting scenes of warfare and enslavement, consciously evoking an exoticism that would appeal to a European market.

Southern Africa was a source of many small,

technically accomplished ivory carvings during the nineteenth century. These are principally objects of personal ornamentation, especially ornate combs and carved snuff spoons of elegant sculptural form, the two functions being often combined in a long, thin comb to be worn in the hair, but incorporating a tiny spoon at the free end.

The Mangbetu of eastern Zaire pushed hair adornment to its most extreme form. Not only did they deliberately deform and elongate the heads of their babies but also ornamented their complex coiffures with sinuously carved ivory hairpins some 15 in. (38 cm) long.

A unique development of East Africa in the nineteenth century were the wooden Lamu chairs of the Swahili coast, named after the island with which they are chiefly associated. There has evidently been heavy Arab or Indian influence – possibly a mixture of both. The chairs are typically constructed of dark wood with arms and footrest, woven rattan back and seat, and ivory inlay in geometric designs.

Ivory in Africa

In Africa ivory is a mark of wealth: among the Ibo, high-status women painfully insinuated their arms and legs into the heaviest and largest sections of ivory available and wore them as portable marks of their husbands' wealth. It is a valuable commodity; broken ornaments may be recut into smaller carvings as among the Dinka of the Sudan.

It is a mark of who one is and whom one resembles. Hence, the Mangbetu notable – like the Benin man-killer – may wear a necklace of leopard's teeth. Indeed, the Mangbetu of Zaire carve elephant ivory to resemble leopard's teeth for necklets or use the human ivory of their victims for this purpose.

It is a material that absorbs patina from its wearers and handlers and so may act as a medium linking one generation with another as in the wisdom passed via the Bwami cult of the Lega or the spiritual force held to inhere in the ivory pendants of the Gurunsi. Different cultures may thus home in on quite different characteristics of this versatile material – seeing it as durable or mutable, permanent or adaptable.

It is an article of trade, worked for export or local consumption, to provide accessories for relatively new fashions such as snuff-taking or traditional uses such as lip plugs and penis sheaths.

Ivory is many things in Africa.

Right: Two Bambala ivory figures from Zaire-Kinshasha, representing hermaphroditism.

5

The Near East, India

From its heartlands, the Arabian Peninsula, Islam reached west through Africa and
east into Asia and India. Islamic ivorywork shows the unity of style throughout the
Muslim world, in Spain and Sicily in Europe, as well as in the Near East, and the
profound influence of the arts. The early craftsmen all used elephant ivory from East
Africa and drew on strong pre-Islamic traditions of ivory carving, making it hard to
believe that surviving examples can represent the volume of what was produced. This
view is supported by the great diversity of what survives and the extraordinarily high
quality of some of it, from the carved ivory panels of Fatimid Egypt to the
sumptuous carved and inlaid ivorywork of the high Ottoman style.
The Muslim courts established in sixteenth-century India by the Mughals, and famed
for their splendour, were adorned with ivories from India's ancient craft centres,
whose traditions reached back to the carved ivory thrones of medieval Orissa, the
plaques of the Begram hoard, the figures and amulets of the pre-Christian Buddhist
and Hindu civilizations. With the arrival of European traders and colonizers, India's
craftsmen adapted their skills to the production of ivory-veneered, Georgian-style
furniture and, ultimately, to a mingling of European, Muslim, Buddhist, Hindu,
which absorbs and re-creates all styles in ivories that are characteristically Indian.

Above: Egyptian or Persian chess piece.
Ninth- to eleventh-century; 1¾ in. (4.8 cm).
Opposite: Indian ivory cabinet with
gold, silver and pearls. *c.*1670.
See page 214 for detail.

Islam

Although a distinctive Islamic style was to evolve very quickly in the arts of the Near East following the foundation of Islam in AD 622, there was no abrupt break with earlier traditions. The techniques and motifs of Byzantium and Sassanian Persia were redeployed in the formation of a new aesthetic in which decoration was exalted to the same level as the figurative representational arts elsewhere. Because Arabic script was identified with the revelation of the Koran, calligraphy is pre-eminent. Geometry and a sense of perfect form are crucial elements. Nowhere is this more evident than in the arabesque: traditional vegetal designs worked into regular yet essentially organic patterns of intersecting stems and characterized by palmette foliage. In Islam figurative art is excluded from the religious domain, but the strictness of this prohibition is often over-emphasized; the most brilliantly animated representations of human figures, animals and birds were to occur in medieval ivory carvings, though excepting chessmen there is an absence of sculpture in the round.

The Islamic ivorywork that remains from the seventh, eighth and early ninth centuries AD, though limited in quantity and rather disparate, demonstrates all the principal techniques: linear incision, carving, encrustation, inlaid woodwork and mosaic marquetry.

It is quite possible that the earliest Islamic ivories were chessmen. Chess, like falconry, was one of the principal pastimes of the Near Eastern courts so much admired and emulated in the West. Ivory chess sets appear to have found their way into European collections from an early date (though now on the whole only isolated pieces remain), but the strong conventions observed both in form and decoration often make dating difficult.

One distinctive group is decorated with incised concentric and dotted circles and parallel lines, often filled in with black or red pigment. This style of ornament recurs as a primitive form of ivory decoration, and particularly on chessmen, throughout the Muslim world and persists in India to the present day. A whole series of objects has been attributed not only to the early Islamic period but specifically to southern Arabia on the basis of a single piece ornamented in this manner, a cylindrical box preserved in the treasury of St Gereon in Cologne. Its conical lid bears an inscription telling us that it was made for an amir in Aden in the mid eighth century. But was it actually produced in southern Arabia? The form of the chessmen decorated in the same style follows a model found in a set of rock crystal pieces which was certainly made in Egypt.

Further early ivory chess pieces, some of them stained green, have been excavated at Nishapur in north-eastern Iran and can be dated to the early ninth century.

As with the Egyptian pieces, the horses and elephants (knights and bishops in the west) are of highly stylized but recognizably figural form. But here the decoration consists simply of faceting and carved vertical grooves. On the other hand, in Florence there is an enchanting, naturalistically modelled elephant, its back carved with palmette scrolls, which has been attributed to tenth-century Mesopotamia.

The most famous Islamic chess piece is the complex statuette of an elephant swarming with human figures, long believed to have belonged to a set given to the Emperor Charlemagne (742–814) by the Caliph Harun Al-Rashid, and manifestly Indian in appearance. It is now accepted that, in spite of the artist's name in Arabic on the base, it was made in north-west India between the tenth and fifteenth centuries.

A distinct group of carved ivory boxes has been attributed to seventh- and eighth-century Syria. These relatively numerous *pyxides* are all very similar with bulging sides and cupola-shaped lids (now usually missing). Their decoration, fairly crudely executed in low relief, consists of vine-scrolls bearing trefoil leaves and sometimes bunches of grapes, often growing from a vase, spreading out to form a regular pattern over the entire exterior surface. The same design is found carved in bone and the type seems to have been executed both by Muslim craftsmen in Umayyad Syria (661–750) and by Coptic craftsmen in Egypt, providing a continuous link between the pre-Islamic ivory carving tradition of the eastern Mediterranean and Fatimid Egypt (969–1171).

In the decoration of woodwork there are isolated examples of elaborate architectural designs in mosaic marquetry. They show strong Byzantine influence, incorporating the distinctive wing-shaped fronded leaf taken from Sassanian ornament, and again are attributed to Umayyad Syria. A unique piece, now in Cairo, demonstrates the encrustation technique of applying ivory cut into a two-dimensional openwork design of scrolls, arabesques and inscriptions. Small fragments suggest they must have been inlays in furniture and just enough remains overall for us to be able to piece together a continuous ivory-working tradition.

Ivory in the Near East

The legacy of Islamic ivory from the early Middle Ages is remarkably rich. None the less, despite the considerable number of carved and painted ivories that remain, it is probably unrepresentative of the quantity produced. The great majority of the works extant, predominantly caskets, survives in western collections, often in church treasuries, having served as reliquaries. Some were specifically made for Christian patrons. Many come from the European Islamic centres in Spain and Sicily.

Dated to the eleventh, twelfth and early thirteenth centuries and variously attributed to Syria, Mesopotamia, Egypt, Sicily and other parts of southern Italy is an important series of carved elephants' tusks, known as oliphants, together with a few caskets and crosiers decorated in the same highly distinctive style. The impressive oliphants were used as hunting and drinking horns (figures blowing oliphants appear on some of the Cordoban ivories made in Islamic Spain) and in military contexts, becoming symbols of feudal authority in Europe. Like so many other ivory containers, they were adopted by the medieval church and given a place in the Christian sanctuary as reliquaries; as a result a considerable number has been preserved.

The most striking characteristic of their decoration, rather sharply carved in relief but with a flat surface, which contrasts with the sculptural three-dimensional quality of Islamic Spanish ivories, is the repeated use of adjacent roundels formed by the intertwining stems of a highly stylized scrolling vine, each filled with the figure of a single animal or bird. The repertoire is enormous, including lions, bears, eagles, harpies, hares, foxes and many other characteristic Islamic motifs. The rendering is lively, an odd hind-leg or tail often spilling out of the frame. Human figures do occur, as do pairs of animals, but are much less common. Round the top and bottom of the horn, divided from the rest of the surface area by horizontal bands of foliate scroll, are friezes of similar design, sometimes divided into rectangular panels. A less usual type has bands of animals and scrolling running the length of the tusk. The total absence of inscriptions might militate against a Near Eastern provenance, but this feature is shared by the unmistakably Arab carvings previously attributed to Mesopotamia or Syria but now accepted as being the products of Fatimid Egypt.

Right and below: Ivory oliphant, and detail, from southern Italy. Eleventh-century; 23⅛ in. (58.7 cm) long. Oliphants employ the characteristic Islamic motifs that were brought from the Near East to the western Mediterranean by Muslim craftsmen.

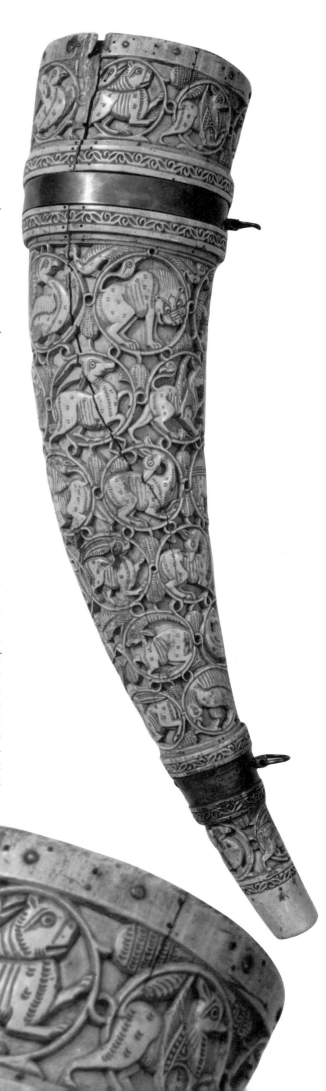

Right and far right: Carved ivory plaque, and detail; from Fatimid Egypt. 14¼ × 16 × 2¼ in. (36.1 × 40.6 × 5.8 cm). The lively scenes of hunting and court life are characteristic of Fatimid ivorywork.

Opposite: Wood table set with an Isnik tile and veneered with ebony, ivory and mother-of-pearl. *c.*1550–1600; 24 in. (61 cm) diameter. An opulent piece of furniture from the Ottoman Empire. See page 196 for detail.

Fatimid Egypt

Arguably the finest of all Islamic ivories of the medieval period are the tantalizingly few carved panels, of which there are important examples in West Berlin and Florence, and related fragments in Paris and Cairo. The principal evidence for classifying these pieces (which look as though they must have been made to decorate wood panelling, perhaps in furniture) as the work of Fatimid craftsmen working in Egypt in the eleventh and twelfth centuries is the existence of comparable wood carvings taken from one of the Fatimid palaces. Though some pieces are related in subject matter, the scant remains of Fatimid and earlier carved ivory found in the ruins of Fustat are too crude to provide a useful point of comparison.

Carved in very high relief, sometimes with an openwork background that heightens the sculptural effect and with details picked out in reddish brown, these long, narrow plaques show familiar scenes of the chase and other courtly pleasures. But here the figures are portrayed with an exuberant vitality quite unmatched elsewhere. The carving is in two registers with the background of foliate scroll on a lower plane than that of the figural decoration, yet the two interact, with the scrolls framing the seated figures but at the same time lending an additional sense of movement to the more animated riders and carousers, in a manner that is the very essence of Islamic art. Details are lovingly observed: a musician puffs out his cheeks as he blows on his pipe, the well-rounded legs of a dancing girl show through her patterned dress, a turbaned reveller, cup in hand, lolls against the vine scroll that contains him, with a realism brilliantly evocative of a medieval Islamic court.

The European and Near Eastern traditions

The history of Islamic ivory in the early medieval period is dominated by caskets decorated with animals and figural scenes made in the outlying areas of Muslim influence in western Europe; examples are illustrated in the section on early medieval European ivory.

In the later medieval period there is both a geographical shift of emphasis back to the heartlands of the Muslim faith and a marked change in the way in which ivory is usually employed and decorated. Carving remained the most popular way of decorating ivory itself, but the material was now predominantly used to embellish woodwork rather than as a medium on its own. Inevitably our knowledge is restricted by what material evidence remains and it is the ivory used in the inlay of extant or recorded mosque furniture that provides us with the basis of our view of the Islamic ivorywork produced in the later Middle Ages. The avoidance of figural or animal subject matter in the carved designs, now more absolutely dominated by the typically Islamic ornamental repertoire of calligraphy, abstract geometry and organic foliate designs stylized into formal scrolls and arabesques, may be partly accounted for by the fact that virtually all the extant ivories of this period were designed to play a part in the decoration of religious establishments.

To say that there are perceptible changes is not to imply that the previous traditions of carved and painted ivory caskets came to an abrupt halt or that there was no precedent for wood panelling decorated with ivory, for the techniques of encrustation and intarsia date back to pre-Islamic times.

Mamluk Egypt

After the fall of the Fatimid dynasty in AD 1171, Egypt and Syria came under the rule of the Ayyubids, who remained in power until 1250 when they were ousted by the Mamluks, an élite corps stationed in Cairo, whose military genius soon secured them an empire which made them the supreme power in the Near East, ruling Egypt, Syria, Palestine and the west coast of Arabia. Besides being able soldiers, statesmen and traders (ivory from East Africa was an important export to Europe), they were great patrons of the arts, imposing their own characteristically bold taste on the geometry and flowing calligraphy that are the hallmarks of Muslim art to create a Saracenic style which dominated the western lands of Islam and had considerable influence on Europe during this period.

The Mamluks were prodigious architects and they equipped their new mosques and other religious buildings with suitably sumptuous furniture inlaid with precious woods and carved ivory. The pre-Islamic intarsia technique had been preserved in Egypt, though apparently practised principally by Coptic rather than Muslim craftsmen. What is perhaps the best-known single article of inlaid mosque furniture, the *minbar* (pulpit) of the Aqsa Mosque in Jerusalem, is probably one of the first of its kind to employ ivory inlay; it was made in Aleppo *c.* 1150–1200. The widespread use of ivory combined with

ebony and teak to create a strikingly bold chromatic effect was, however, a largely Mamluk development. Besides *minbars* there were *mihrabs* (prayer niches), folding lecterns, *kursis* (small tables of rectangular or hexagonal form on which to place the Koran), large balustraded platforms for the repetitors at prayer, screens, doors, window shutters and cupboards. Undoubtedly palatial domestic interiors were similarly embellished but, predictably, the mosque furniture and fittings had the best chance of surviving more or less intact. Unfortunately the carved ivory inlays, easily prised out of their wooden settings, often proved an irresistible temptation and numerous examples are to be found in museums and private collections in the west.

The various items of furniture were all constructed in the same way from quadrangular wooden panels. Each of these was made up of smaller interlocking tongued-and-grooved pieces cut into a variety of shapes and sizes and fitted together to produce a wide range of geometric patterns. The most common were those based on a star of from six to twelve pointed segments from which radiate myriad polygonal and wedge-shaped elements. Other schemes were based more simply on juxtaposed squares and oblongs or hexagons and triangles. The Arabic tradition of constructing panels out of small pieces of wood both satisfied the Islamic taste for richly patterned surfaces and intricate geometric effects and had

Below and right: An example of inlaid mosque furniture, from Mamluk Egypt. *Minbar* (pulpit), and detail. Late-fifteenth-century.

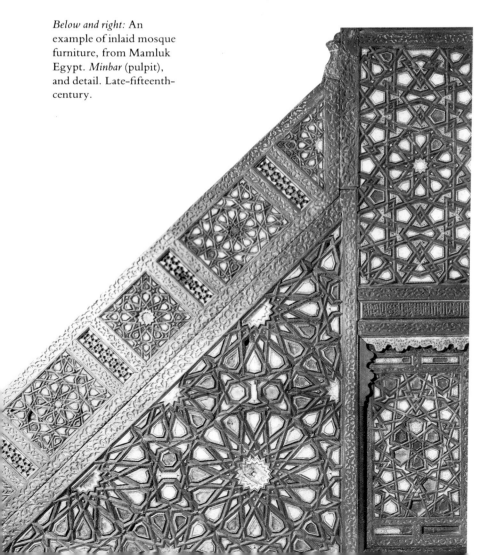

the practical advantage of preventing the panels from warping in the hot climate.

When ivory decoration was used, the inlay was countersunk into a recessed central area; the basic principle of the intarsia technique. The most common shape for the ivory insets is a pointed hexagon; a ring of these measuring some 3 to 5 in. (7.5 to 12.5 cm) long formed the outer perimeter of the star designs while the centre of the star was also highlighted in ivory. Usually the ivory was carved, generally with a sinuous organic arabesque, the principal stems of which bear fronded and ribbed split-palmette leaves and form intersecting heart-shapes in a manner not unrelated to the designs found on the Islamic caskets made in Spain three or four hundred years earlier. The quality of the carving varies greatly and is in some cases very crude, especially when bone was substituted for the more expensive ivory, as happened increasingly towards the end of the period, when the Mamluk state suffered economic decline.

Sometimes a very simple motif such as a quatrefoil rosette or an S-scroll was used and in certain instances the ivory was left quite plain. The latter was used to particularly striking effect when combined with elements of the same shape filled with a geometric mosaic of ivory and ebony tesserae. This mosaic technique is generally associated with the later Mamluk period and given a late-fourteenth- or fifteenth-century date; large areas were sometimes decorated in this way. Thin strips of ivory were also let in round the edge of the wooden segments to outline the composition.

Along the top and bottom of the made-up panels there were often rectangular ivory plaques larger than those incorporated in the geometric pattern. Besides the usual foliate arabesques, these were frequently carved with a single line of inscription, written in the characteristic cursive script of the Mamluks, known as Thuluth, which grows progressively bolder towards the end of the period. The inscriptions are cut in flat relief against a background of scrolling tendrils and veined leaves in only slightly lower relief. Alongside conventional Arabic good wishes, which take on distinctly militaristic overtones under the Mamluks, are the names of patrons and sometimes of artists. The various signatures on a *minbar* commissioned for the Great Mosque at Hamâh in Syria by Sultan Kitbugha (1294–6) show that different artists were responsible for the carving, the inlay and the decoration. Other favourite ornamental motifs were heraldic blazons which identified the sultans and the households of the Mamluk amirs who held specific administrative positions, but these were more often carved in wood than in ivory. A particularly splendid composite blazon incorporating the scimitar of the arms-bearer, the goblet of the cup-bearer and

the penbox of the secretary is inlaid in ivory and wood on a folding Koran lectern, made *c.* 1500, at the end of the Mamluk era.

The same technique of mosaic marquetry, using tiny triangles, lozenges, pentagons and other geometrically cut shapes of ebony and ivory stuck together, carried out on a grander scale and employing different coloured woods and stained bone as well as ivory, was also used to cover most of the surface area on pieces of furniture and extended over long stretches of wood panelling. Very little has survived, but two pieces, a tall hexagonal *kursi* and a hexagonal Koran box, in Cairo, were both made for a *madrasa*, the school attached to a large mosque, built by the mother of one of the Mamluk sultans and completed in 1368–9. Like the earlier eighth- and ninth-century examples, the designs echo the sumptuous architectural mosaics that they were intended to complement, but where patterns composed of square and lozenge-shaped tesserae predominated before, the accent is now on complex stellar formations, arcading is still an essential feature but the arches are squatter. Bands of trefoil lambrequins in silhouette against an ivory ground recall the ornamental pediments found in Mamluk woodwork and stonework.

Although under the Mamluks carved ivory was used mainly as an embellishment for woodwork, there is a distinctive, though small, group of ivory boxes attributable to mid-fourteenth-century Cairo (though some scholars date them as early as the twelfth century and give them a Spanish provenance) as one of the pieces bears an inscription round the lid giving the name and titles of Sultan Salih who ruled between 1351 and 1354. All the examples are remarkably similar, being essentially cylindrical, the sides tapering slightly towards the top in some cases, presumably following the original shape of the tusk. A sharp quatrefoil fretwork formed by overlapping circular polygons creating an overall pattern, generally pierced through, forms the principal decoration with narrower borders of braiding, guilloche, or cursive inscription on a ground broken by small circles.

The Timurid courts: Samarkand, Persia, Anatolia

In the late fourteenth century, Persia, Anatolia and present-day Iraq fell under the sway of the Mongol hordes and the allied Turkic tribes from Central Asia. In spite of the devastation wreaked by Genghis Khan and his redoubtable successors, the Mongol conquests were to culminate in a period of outstanding artistic achievement. The great conqueror Tamberlaine (Timur Leng) (1336–1404) had made his capital in Samarkand and inaugurated an Islamic cultural renaissance in

Above: Koran box with ivory intarsia, from Turkey. Seventeenth-century.

Above: Detail from the Ottoman table shown in colour on page 192.

the East. The Timurid period (1378–1506) is renowned for its breathtakingly beautiful architecture and exquisite schools of miniature painting.

It is difficult to believe that the Timurid courts did not have carved ivory objects executed in the distinctive style shown by their carved jades, but it seems that nothing remains that can be securely attributed to Timurid Persia. There is, however, an ivory plaque, now in the Louvre, that has been tentatively ascribed to fourteenth-century Samarkand. Like many Mamluk examples of this period, the decoration consists of foliate arabesques, although here there is more emphasis on the geometry of the intersecting tendrils which extend from the quatrefoils that provide the main focus of the design to form a diamond lattice in between. The scrolling stems are generally more delicate, presenting a sharp-edged relief surface, and the leaves do not have the fleshy vitality of the exuberant vegetal designs of the Mamluks. Furthermore, the background area is painted blue creating an effect reminiscent of Central Asian architectural ornament of this period. In the past there was a tendency to designate the vast majority of extant carved ivory plaques and inlay fragments as Mamluk, but some may well be Anatolian or Persian, the general similarity of the arabesque employed throughout the Muslim world making it difficult to tell them apart.

Timurid painting provides fairly clear evidence that mosaic marquetry was extensively used in furniture decoration. Miniatures show Genghis Khan preaching from a mosaic pattern *minbar* (1397) and a *minbar* inlaid in the intarsia technique (1485), throne seats, footstools and caskets. An intricately carved wooden box made for Ulugh Beg Gurgani in Samarkand, *c.* 1400–50, has borders of fine ivory inlay incorporated in a particularly minute mosaic pattern using the technique still known in Persian as *khatam-kar* and revived in the twentieth century.

Turkey and the Ottoman Empire

The Byzantine capital of Constantinople finally fell to the Ottoman Turks in 1453. Renamed Istanbul, within the next hundred years it became the centre of an immense and supremely powerful empire stretching from Morocco to the Persian Gulf and from Budapest to the southernmost tip of Arabia. The Topkapi Palace in Istanbul housed design studios and workshops and a homogeneous court style permeated all the decorative arts.

The technique of ivory intarsia was adopted from the Mamluks. In Egypt and Syria, which became Ottoman provinces in 1517, the tradition carried on unchanged but in Istanbul ivory was employed on a much more extravagant scale. A pointed polygonal Koran box dated 1505–6 is

decorated with numerous inlaid ivory plaques, carved with Koranic inscriptions, arabesques and scrolls in relief against a green-painted ground, arranged in a severe geometric formation. By the second half of the sixteenth century undecorated ivory inlay is also being used. The textural effects of relief carving are subordinated to a stunning chromatic display of sleek polished surfaces of ebony or walnut inlaid with ivory cut into delicate ribbon-cloud scrolls, full-blown palmettes or striking patterns of chevrons. Typically Ottoman motifs such as crescents, triple balls, tiger stripes and rosettes of overlapping circles join the rich repertoire of Islamic geometric and foliate ornament. Inscriptions, often inlaid rather than carved, are in a magnificent strong cursive script or sometimes in square Kufic rendered in a mosaic technique.

Large-scale items of mosque furniture were constructed of stone or marble but smaller transportable pieces, especially domed Koran boxes, as well as non-religious objects such as thrones and low tables, were inlaid in a sumptuous manner, not only with ivory and different woods but also with mother-of-pearl and tortoiseshell. Sometimes the ivory was set with precious stones and when it was carved the background was often painted or gilded. Towards the end of the sixteenth century a preference for mother-of-pearl becomes noticeable and by the seventeenth century the predominant inlay materials, often covering the entire surface, were mother-of-pearl and tortoiseshell, ivory being confined to outlines and narrow strips of mosaic. The effect becomes increasingly ostentatious, a particularly dramatic example being the floral and scale pattern embellishment of the galley of Sultan Mehmed (1648–87) still preserved in Istanbul.

The workmanship found in the best-quality Ottoman carved ivory produced in the sixteenth century is quite outstanding. Apart from the rosette- and lozenge-shaped plaques set into inlaid furniture, carved ivory was used for personal articles such as hand mirrors, belts and buckles, and sword and dagger handles. Walrus was used as well as elephant ivory partly because of the accessibility of the Baltic Sea to Turkey and partly because of its reputed magic properties.

The carved decoration consists of floral and foliate motifs usually incorporated in an arabesque formation of scrolling stems, often with the addition of undulating cloud scrolls. Here we find the characteristic composite blossoms, rosettes and swirling serrated *saz* leaves of Ottoman floral ornament. Usually the carving is in relief but one of the belts in the Topkapi Sarayi museum has a finely incised design following what is known as the 'Golden Horn' pattern of delicate spiral scrolls bearing tiny florets and leaves, filled with mastic; over this is superimposed a deeper cut gold scroll

Right: Detail of the lavish decoration from the kiosk of a sultanate galley, believed to have been owned by Sultan Mehmed IV (1648–87).

Below: An Islamic sword hilt, carved in ivory. Sixteenth-century.

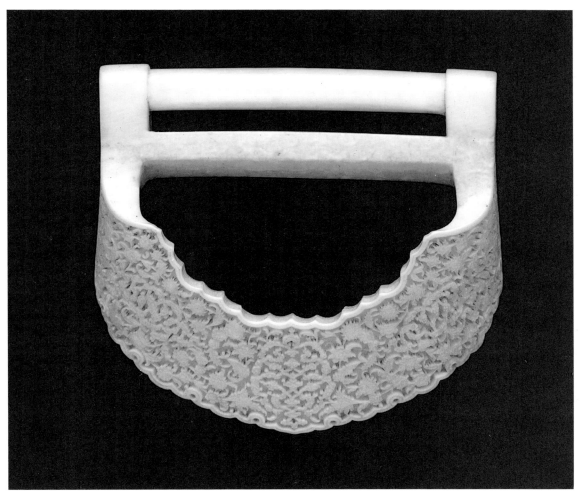

Right: Walrus ivory Ottoman belt buckle. Mid-sixteenth-century; 2¼ in. (5.7 cm).

with rosettes set with emeralds and rubies. In the more intricate relief-carved ivories, sometimes executed in that minute degree of detail more often associated with the Far East, are the same superimposed scrolls that are so distinctive of the court style of Suleyman I (1520–66) and his immediate successors.

A number of superb examples of ivorywork, both carved and inlaid, executed in the high Ottoman style are preserved in Istanbul but they are otherwise exceedingly rare. Ivory hilts datable to the seventeenth and eighteenth centuries are more common but a good deal of confusion surrounds their precise dating and attribution. Terms such as 'Saracenic', 'Persian' or 'Hispano-Moresque' have been used as a generic designation for any arms with identifiably Islamic decoration or inscriptions in Arabic characters. Blades that can be accurately dated have often been fitted with hilts of an earlier or later period and from a different part of the Muslim world. Mughal Indian ivory hilts and powderhorns were popular in both Ottoman Turkey and Safavid Persia.

In the eighteenth century the Ottomans became increasingly receptive to European aesthetic influences and there evolved the Ottoman rococo style. Many of the best domestic interiors decorated in this taste are to be found in Syria. There the cupboard doors and shutters, lining the walls of rooms painted with garlands and bowls of fruit, are sometimes inlaid with arabesque scrolls cut out of flat pieces of camel bone in what is clearly a continuation of the tradition of ivory intarsia.

Many small ivory artefacts such as cosmetics containers and Koranic bookmarks carved into baroque scrollwork or open filigree, and spoons made of ivory or bone, tortoiseshell and coral, are optimistically dated to the eighteenth century, though most surviving examples are likely to be nineteenth century. However, an unusual penbox of ivory, carved with leafy volutes and inscriptions, now in London, was made, according to its inscription, by a Cairene craftsman in 1672 – a surprisingly early date. The shape, with a bulbous ink container attached to the end of the long, flat pencase, is copied from a model which is common in silver or brass from the eighteenth century onwards.

Chests with floral inlay in ivory and mother-of-pearl, popular throughout the Arab world, probably originate at the end of this period. The style of decoration shows strong Mughal influence and the original pieces were probably Indian imports.

The Safavids of Persia

The Ottomans' arch-enemies, the Safavids, dominated Persia and much of Mesopotamia from 1506 to 1722 and in terms of patronage of the arts their empire was if anything more glorious than the Ottoman. Regrettably very little in the way of ivorywork remains. Considerable quantities of Indian ivory, in the form of sword and dagger hilts, powderhorns and furniture inlay, were imported into Persia during the seventeenth and eighteenth centuries and much now described as 'Persian' is in fact Mughal. But a series of openwork plaques, made to decorate the tomb of Shah Ismail (1502–24) in the famous Ardebil shrine, provides a tantalizing glimpse of the Safavid craftsmen's skill in this field. Each is carved with a Nashki inscription on a ground of delicate spiral scrolls bearing small flowers and trefoil and split-palmette leaves, characteristic of the exquisite refinement and elegance that distinguish Safavid decoration at its best.

The nineteenth century

By the nineteenth century the Ottoman Empire was crumbling. The craft of inlaying wood with

Below: An ivory penbox made, according to its inscription, by an Egyptian craftsman in 1672. Attached to one end is an ink holder.

ivory and mother-of-pearl seems to have been carried on in a crude form. Everyday objects decorated in this manner include chests and caskets, the *hammam* slippers worn by women in Turkish baths, drums, folding stands for food trays and gunstocks. The designs are composed of simple geometric elements and are generally rather static though not unpleasing.

The North African guns used throughout the Arab world were decorated with rosettes and chevrons in ivory, mother-of-pearl, coral and brass wire arranged in striking stylized vegetal patterns. In Syria and Turkey firearms were more likely to be decorated with ivory-inlaid flowers or strips of minute mosaic marquetry.

Until this time the Muslim world had used carpets and cushions, with thrones and folding seats for persons of exalted rank, but no chairs and no permanent free-standing pieces of furniture. Now European models were adopted and inlaid in the 'oriental' fashion. Some pieces have considerable charm but the designs, whether of flowers and scrolls or geometric patterns, become increasingly fussy as opposed to imaginative. French and British involvement in Syria, North Africa and Egypt encouraged the European taste for the exotic to take a Near Eastern turn. In the second half of the nineteenth century the vogue for orientalism resulted in a number of books on the traditional decorative or 'industrial' arts of the Arab world, describing the ivory-inlaid furniture of the towns and villages around Mocha, Shiraz muskets decorated with rings of coloured ivory and brass mosaic, and ivory penboxes similarly ornamented. Craftsmen were inlaying secretaires, chests of drawers and armchairs, and making skilful reproductions of earlier Ottoman furniture, doubtless with the keen European collector in mind.

Ivory chess pieces generally follow a conventional form and are thus very difficult to date. After the medieval period, outside India, even the most stylized figural forms are abandoned and a symmetrical baluster or spool shape is the norm. However, in nineteenth-century Turkey elegant stemmed chessmen carved with leaves and petals were also produced.

Except in Mughal India, figurative designs had vanished from the standard decorative repertoire of Islamic carved ivory after the thirteenth and fourteenth centuries. They now reappeared in Persia under the Qajars who had taken over from the Safavids in 1722.

Elaborately though not always very meticulously carved knife hilts portray Persian heroes of the pre-Islamic era, bearded dervishes and European figures, both male and female, copied from prints and drawings imported from the West, who appear bizarrely profane by contrast. Although a few, particularly those decorated

with flowers and birds, may be earlier, most date from the nineteenth century.

Ivorywork in the modern Near East

Catering more and more to colonial taste and the tourist trade, the designs found on carved ivory objects, such as cigarette cases and paper-knives, and in wood with ivory inlay have become increasingly monotonous. The inventive adaptation of complex Islamic architectural ornament to, say, a rolltop bureau or a sideboard is entertaining but owes little to the intrinsic sense of harmony characteristic of Islamic decoration.

In the great bazaars the traditional craft of inlay, though with resinous material or bone now almost always substituted for ivory, is still actively employed in the decoration of an interminable round of mosaic backgammon boards, cigar boxes and containers for Turkish delight. The patterns are generally composed of rhomboids, squares and triangles which though complex appear simplistic by comparison with the compelling geometry found in previous periods. Only rarely is a satisfying composition achieved. The cost of skilled labour means that the work is usually executed in great haste. In Egypt the technique is incongruously employed in the manufacture of pharaonic souvenirs as well. In Damascus a single object passes through a number of workshops, each specializing in cutting out and sticking on one of the materials that make up the mosaic inlay. Recently the growing concern to preserve Syrian inlaid furniture of the eighteenth and nineteenth centuries and the awareness of an international market for it, has involved skilled craftsmen in restoration.

In the twentieth century the Pahlavis revived the particularly minute mosaic marquetry technique known as *khatam-kar*, in which Iran has specialized since the late medieval period. Ivory, stained bone, horn, different coloured woods and strips of metal are cut into long narrow rods with a triangular cross-section and carefully secured in bundles to form a regular star pattern; thin slices from different bundles make up a minutely intricate geometric mosaic. The Pahlavis had entire rooms panelled in *khatam* with furniture of European design decorated to match. It was difficult to maintain a high quality of workmanship over such a large area but the technique has been continued more conventionally to embellish musical instruments and other small objects.

The miniatures painted on ivory commercially produced in Iran in the late nineteenth and twentieth centuries bear only the most tenuous connection to the great tradition of Islamic miniature painting and have even less to do with traditional Islamic ivorywork.

India

In 1921, under the direction of the Archaeological Survey of India, work began at the archaeological site of Harappa (in present-day north-eastern Pakistan), and in 1922 excavations began at Mohenjo-Daro (in Sind, some 250 miles from the mouth of the Indus), leading to the discovery of a hitherto unknown and highly developed 'Harappa Culture' or 'Indus Valley Civilization' covering the period *c.* 2500–1750 BC.

At its height, between about 2300–2000 BC, the Harappan culture flourished throughout most of modern Pakistan, extending to the Punjab and beyond Delhi to Uttar Pradesh as well as Rajasthan and Gujarat. The three main cities were Harappa, Mohenjo-Daro and the more recently discovered Kalibangan near the Pakistan border in Rajasthan. The success of the Harappan culture was based on a thriving agricultural system and on trade with the village culture of Baluchistan. Silver, turquoise and lapis lazuli were imported from Persia and Afghanistan, copper from Rajasthan (or Persia), conch shell and various types of stone from the Deccan and Saurashtra.

Apart from pottery, the Harappans are known for their distinctive seals, some of which have been found in contemporaneous excavations at Sumer, suggesting trade links with Mesopotamia. Usually of steatite, and square or rectangular in form, they often depict an animal – the bull, most frequently, but also the buffalo, goat, tiger, rhinoceros and elephant – or an emblem, with a short inscription above. The script, however, has not yet been decoded. Terracotta figurines of naturalistic animals or the so-called mother-goddesses were also produced and one of the few bronze objects excavated at Mohenjo-Daro is the famous figure of a dancing girl, naked except for bangles and a necklace.

Despite the known existence of elephants in Harappan culture, testified not only by appearances on seals and as terracotta figures but also by the finding of tusks and skeletal remains at Mohenjo-Daro, relatively few ivory objects have been excavated. However, the most frequently encountered ivory objects from Indus Valley sites include beads, dice, hairpins, kohl-sticks, combs, mirror handles, cylinder-seals, small vessels, pegs, batons, pierced rods, small animal figures, miniature fish and inlay fragments. Jewellery was popular for its decorative and amuletic properties and beads made of gold, silver, copper, faience, steatite, terracotta, ivory, shell and semi-precious stones have been found. They were disc-shaped, cylindrical, round or square, sometimes being coloured and decorated with linear incisions or circle-dot motifs. Dice were frequently of terracotta but ivory gaming-sticks were also known,

including three of rectangular form decorated with linear incisions, cross-hatching and circle-dot motifs indicating the values. Ivory hairpins and kohl-sticks found at Harappan sites are very similar to those excavated from contemporary sites in Iran and Iraq and are usually of plain form, occasionally with animal finials. Ivory cylinder-seals from Mohenjo-Daro are of a type found in Mesopotamia, but unlike the square steatite seals, are inscribed but not decorated. Ivory combs have been found at almost every Harappan site; they are often decorated with the ubiquitous circle-dot motif. Numerous small ivory fish discovered at Mohenjo-Daro are thought to have been used either in religious rituals or as gaming pieces. Each is of flat form with an incised eye and cross-hatching on either side of the body; some show traces of red and black pigment in the hatching, others of white or yellow, but almost all are shiny from constant use. The most significant Harappan ivory is a fragmentary plaque from Mohenjo-Daro, depicting a standing male figure, hands on hips, wearing a loin-cloth, a spear or quiver (?) projecting above the left shoulder; it is the earliest known Indian ivory to depict a human figure.

At the beginning of the second millennium BC semi-nomadic barbarians, the Aryans, attacked the Harappan villages, first in Baluchistan, then in Sind and the Punjab, and eventually overcame the great cities of the Indus Valley civilization. With the arrival of a new non-urban people, the city culture declined. There is little archaeological evidence from the following centuries.

During the various neolithic (*c.* 2375–650 BC) and chalcolithic (*c.* 2000–1100 BC) periods, when first stone and then copper were in use, few ivory objects were made. Bone appears to have been widely used for such purposes as tool- and weapon-making; some bone jewellery has also been excavated.

India during and after the rise of Rome

With the use of written historical records commencing in about the sixth century BC, a wealth of epigraphical and literary references to ivory begins to emerge.

The great Hindu epic poem in Sanskrit, the *Ramayana*, thought to date not prior to 1000 BC but with continuous subsequent alterations and additions, mentions a guild of ivory carvers. The other great epic, the *Mahabharata* (*c.* 200 BC–AD 200) refers to ivory court objects such as the spokes of the royal umbrella, sword hilts and furniture including thrones and sedan chairs.

That India was exporting ivory as early as the

sixth century BC is confirmed by an inscription at the palace of Suza, built by Darius I of Iran (reigned *c.* 522–486 BC), which mentions that the ivory worked at Suza was brought from Ethiopia, Sind and Arachosia. An inscription at the great *stupa* (Buddhist tumulus and reliquary) at Sanchi, near Bhopal in central India, which probably dates from the second century BC, records that the figurative decoration on the southern gateposts was executed by the ivory carvers of Vidisa, whose fame was subsequently reported and spread by foreign travellers.

Various minor ivories and bone carvings dating from the eighth, seventh and sixth centuries BC have been found at sites in northern and north-eastern India. One of the most interesting is an ivory female figure from Champanagar, Bihar, of naturalistic form and carved in sections; similar Egyptian and western Asiatic wood figures from earlier periods are known. In contrast, a group of highly stylized ivory female figures excavated at Prabhasa, Gujarat, and thought to date *c.* 600–200 BC, are mostly of flat form decorated with linear incisions and circle-dot motifs to indicate features; possibly a continuation of the Harappan mother-goddess cult. Similar figures have been unearthed at Taxila, Nagda, Ujjain and Avra, along with the more common terracotta figures of the mother-goddesses. As these figures have also been found at Suza in Persia, the prototype may have originated in Palestine (as opposed to Harappa) and passed through Mesopotamia and Persia to India.

During the Mauryan period of the fourth, third and second centuries BC, bone and ivory objects continued to be produced, but do not on the whole reflect any particularly distinctive style. Apart from the usual seals, bone arrowheads, antimony rods and other utilitarian objects, a small figure of an elephant was discovered, and at Bhir Mound, Taxila, a standing male figure, carved in the round and wearing a long tunic and necklace. A small, fossil ivory profile head of a ram which possibly formed part of a dagger hilt, also found at this site, establishes ancient links between India and Siberia, as this material was particular to the latter area.

In the spring of 326 BC Alexander the Great crossed the river Indus, in his bold, and ultimately vain, attempt to form a Greek empire in India. Despite Greek garrisons in the newly conquered territories, the local tribes reasserted themselves after Alexander's army moved on. His sudden death in 323 BC brought to an end any hope of a Macedonian empire in India but Greek colonies remained in Bactria, Afghanistan and north-west India. Disorder in the annexed areas saw the rise to power of the first Mauryan king, Candragupta (reigned *c.* 322–298 BC). His empire flourished under his son Bindusara (reigned *c.* 298–273 BC), but reached its zenith under his grandson, the

great Buddhist emperor Asoka (reigned *c.* 269–232 BC). Asoka's empire covered most of the length and breadth of the subcontinent. He established Buddhism so securely that it was to be adopted by successive empires, despite the gradual emergence of Hinduism, until the demise of the Gupta kings in the mid sixth century AD. After his death the succession was disputed and the empire declined; during the short-lived Sunga Empire, founded *c.* 183 BC, the great Buddhist monuments at Bharut, Sanchi and Bodhgaya were constructed, where human figurative sculpture was used for the first time. Various ivory and bone carvings which can be attributed to the second and first centuries BC are known. Three bone fragments depicting female figures, from Mathura and Ahichchhatra (Uttar Pradesh) and Ter (Maharashtra), share similar features such as broad body, angular face, linear incisions on jewellery, collar-like necklace falling between the breasts, and rows of anklets or bracelets. A headless ivory figure of a soldier, found at Patna, is thought to date from the second century BC. This piece is comparable to soldiers carved on the stone railings both at Bharhut and Sanchi, which seems to confirm this dating. An interesting ivory comb-section, of a type which recurs frequently later, depicting an amorous couple and a fragmentary female figure amid plantain leaves, now in London, is attributed to Malwa, Rajasthan, probably first century BC.

Little is known about India's foreign trade prior to the first century AD but there were probably trade routes by sea to Mesopotamia and South-East Asia. With the arrival of the Roman period in Egypt in 30 BC, the demand for spices, perfume, jewels, textiles, ivory, live animals and birds – such as monkeys, parrots, peacocks, tigers and elephants – increased throughout the Roman Empire. Ports on the west coast such as Supara near Bombay flourished and were soon followed by others in the south. Roman 'Arettine ware' pottery from Arezzo in Tuscany was found at the important Roman trading station of Arikamedu near Pondicherry on the Coromandel coast, dating from the first century BC. Elephants, used by the Romans mostly for entertainments, were usually accompanied overland by their mahouts, via the trading city of Palmyra in the Syrian desert. Ivory was exported both carved and uncarved. An ivory female figure 10 in. (24 cm) high, found at Pompeii and probably originally a mirror handle, depicts a young woman standing cross-legged, nude except for long rows of narrow bracelets and anklets, a bead-edged girdle, a thick collar-like necklace and hatched earrings. The centrally parted hair has elaborate foliate braids at the back. The right hand touches the braids, the left hand the earring (a gesture depicted in a number of contemporary ivories). Two standing female attendants hold toilet requisites. The suggested places of origin are Mathura, Ujjain and Vidisa, the latter perhaps being most likely because of its famous guild of ivory carvers. However, a closely related, fragmentary female figure, also flanked by two attendants and standing cross-legged, was recently excavated at Bhokardan, Maharashtra. This figure has been dated to the second century BC, whereas the Pompeii figure has been variously dated between 100 BC and AD 79 (when Pompeii was destroyed).

Another ivory female figure, from Ter in Maharashtra, also thought to have been conceived as a mirror handle, is dated by scholars c. AD 1–150. The development of the style and the increasing Roman influence can clearly be seen, particularly if this figure is compared with both the Pompeii ivory and the fragmentary bone figure from Ter. The pose is more elegant, the jewellery more refined, though the figure retains its distinctive Indian voluptuousness. Again, one hand is raised to an earring. The figure is carved in the round, the rear details including a long plait, girdle-sashes and waistband with incisions. Ter was one of the two most important trading towns of the Deccan and had numerous contacts with the Roman world. It was connected with Broach (or Barygaza) in the Gulf of Cambay, from which port ivory was exported, and may itself have been a centre of ivory production. Two other well-known female figures from Ter, one of bone and one of ivory, are of interest. The former is fragmentary, the ample body wearing a necklace, earrings, a centrally pleated dhoti or robe and a filet with rosettes; the graphic angular facial features seem archaic, but the fullness of the carving as compared with the fragmentary bone figure from Ter would appear to contradict this; it has variously been dated to the first or second century AD. The ivory is a slender nude figure, carved more naturalistically; it may have been clothed separately and has been attributed to the fifth century AD, though also exhibited as first or second century AD.

The rule of the Kushan kings, from the early first century to the late fourth century, introduced a period of high artistic output, with the widespread adoption of the Buddha image for the first time. Although Asoka had established Buddhism some four centuries earlier, up until now depictions of the Buddha had been largely confined to symbolic representations such as the princely turban, the footprints, the vacant throne, the pipal tree (under which he achieved enlightenment) or the wheel (recalling his first sermon). Under the third and most famous Kushan king, Kanishka (reigned c. AD 78–144), Buddhism regained popularity and a great centre of art was established at Mathura, Uttar Pradesh. The Kushans eventually ruled most of northern India and had dominions in Central Asia. The ancient state of Gandhara, now part of the North-West Frontier Province of Pakistan, which prospered under them, is famous for its grey schist shrines and monasteries, elaborately carved with façades of Buddhas, Bodhisattvas and *jatakas* (legendary scenes from the life of the Buddha). The style is at first glance almost totally classical in conception: figures in robes reminiscent of the Roman toga, often flanked by 'Indo-Corinthian' columns with cornices of acanthus or vines above. Indigenous Indian motifs were successfully incorporated though Persian influences and Scythian and Central Asian elements can also be easily discerned. This hybrid 'Graeco-Buddhist' or 'Indo-Greek' style is thought to have evolved through increasing trade links with the Roman Empire rather than through the adoption of Buddhism by Alexander's Greek colonies in the third century BC and subsequently.

Although some bone and ivory carvings have been excavated at Taxila, their style appears more indigenously Kushan (as at Mathura) than Gandharan. Bone mirror handles carved with semi-nude female figures follow in the tradition of those previously discussed. Two notable ivory combs, their teeth missing, have been found; the smaller is incised with a male and a female bust on one side and a duck on the other; the larger depicts a reclining female figure wearing jewellery and a long diaphanous lower garment, a crouching dwarf with an offering above her head, and on the reverse a lion and an elephant flanked by two auspicious emblems. The female figure is particularly reminiscent of the type found in stone at Mathura, Amaravati and Nagarjunakonda, and it has even been suggested that a guild of ivory carvers may have come from Mathura to Taxila to propagate their art, hence the similarity of style. Other contemporary combs of this type, from Kausambi, simply decorated with rosettes of circle-dots, are known.

An interesting ivory roundel with distinct classical characteristics, now in New York, said to be a Gandharan find and dated to about the fourth century AD, depicts a male bust with long curling hair in a recess with beaded border, the raised outer band carved with a wreath, four of five pierced lugs remaining below. A small ovoid ivory bead, decorated with cross-hatching and probably from a necklace, is also from Gandhara.

The Begram ivories: Afghanistan

One of the most significant discoveries of Indian archaeology, and without doubt the most important discovery of ivories, was made by Professor Joseph and Madame Hackin at Begram (modern Kapisa) near Kabul in Afghanistan in 1937–9, excavating at the summer palace of the Kushan kings. A hoard of about 600 ivory plaques was found, most originally applied to furniture. Ladies are charmingly depicted at various everyday pursuits: arranging the hair, applying cosmetics, looking in a mirror, putting on jewellery, suckling a child, dancing, standing at a doorway or a gate, reclining on a couch or stool, riding – usually on an elephant or a horse – and playing with parrots, peacocks or ducks. They wear jewellery, elaborate head-dresses and diaphanous dhotis, usually incised with narrow wavering bands. The jewellery corresponds with that found on sculptures at Mathura: rows of narrow bracelets, thick double ropework anklets, broad beaded girdles, narrow armlets (if any), beaded necklaces, rosette-shaped or large granulated earrings. The head-dresses range from simple filets to braided and knotted tresses decorated with jewels.

The techniques employed vary from whole plaques of deftly incised figures to others carved in relief, numerous smaller figures elaborately carved and surrounded by areas of piercing to heighten the relief, still others carved in recess. Other figures were carved in the round, such as the woman riding a rampant leogryph issuing from the mouth of a *makara* (a mythical sea-monster), apparently part of a chair-back. Three standing female figures have ample sensuous bodies still following the Mathura prototype, complete with pleated dhotis, sashes and thick anklets, but with slender refined faces and short curly hair distinctly classical in appearance. Each is standing on the head of a *makara*, an indigenous Indian motif, but one seems to have been intended as a caryatid, a classical innovation, to judge from what appears to be a column-base on her head.

The absence of male figures, excepting huntsmen, dwarf-like attendants, two rajahs, is somewhat explained by the fact that in ancient India men were not normally allowed to visit the female apartments. How then were the carvings done? One theory, that the women were courtesans, is certainly supported by their generally flirtatious and sensual appearance, as well as their apparent preoccupation with cosmetics, music and frivolous pastimes.

Above: Ivory plaque from Begram, Afghanistan. Probably first- or second-century AD. The languorous female figures have great visual appeal.

The Begram ivories are notably similar, in theme as well as style, to the stone sculptures at the Buddhist sites of Mathura, Amaravati, Nagarjunakonda, Sanchi and Bharhut. Figurative scenes, everyday objects, numerous decorative motifs, all bear favourable comparison and are often almost identical. The architectural details depicted at Begram are also invaluable, particularly with reference to dating, and numerous gateways of the Sanchi type are shown in miniature. The ivories are generally not thought to be earlier than the first or second centuries AD. Most are now in Kabul, some in Paris, and two fragments in Berlin.

Furniture

A revered and expensive commodity, ivory was used in the carving or inlaying of furniture from the early centuries AD. Thrones, palanquins and bedsteads were the main items, though sedan chairs (*yanani*), couches and stools were also used. The Begram ivories depict various styles of beds, tables, stools and couches. Among the ivories found were entire chair-backs, one composed of two curving horizontal registers, with figurative plaques alternating with equal areas of vertical rods; the upper border consists of a plain ivory band projecting at either side, applied with metal bosses and with linear incisions on the upper edge, the lower borders of two narrow bands carved with foliate scrolls enclosing, respectively, animals and a row of vase-shaped beads. The plaques depict two bejewelled, semi-nude female figures variously occupied at their toilet, seated, standing cross-legged, embracing or holding parrots. Both the pierced openwork panels and the incised plaques from Begram depict further luxuriant female figures seated on low stools or couches with squat bulbous legs and cross-hatched seats, the latter possibly representing caning or woven materials. The traditional couch-bed, which remains ubiquitous in modern India, was described *c.* AD 1350 as four staves laid on four conical legs, with ribbons plaited between them. Figures seated on hive-shaped stools decorated with bands of hatching and wavering foliate motifs are found in ivory at Begram, in stone at Amaravati and in the cave murals at Ajanta, showing that stools of this type were popular – at least at court – in the early centuries AD. A stone cosmetics tray from Taxila, Gandharan, and first century BC, depicts a lady reclining on a rectangular couch with high bulbous legs, but the style of this couch and others in late Gandharan reliefs derives directly from the classical tradition and, along with many other Gandharan motifs, escapes Indianization.

The early Middle Ages

The ascent to power of Candra Gupta in about AD 320 marked the birth of an empire which achieved

Above: A seated Bodhisattva from the group of miniature Kashmir ivories. Eighth-or ninth-century. The crowned Bodhisattva, surrounded by diminutive figures, is set in a frame of carved wood.

a period of political stability and artistic perfection such as India has not known since. The Gupta period of the fourth, fifth and sixth centuries is regarded as the classic period of Indian art, when the Buddha figure introduced under the Kushans was perfected by the development of a physically refined, more human yet deeply esoteric image. The famous red sandstone or mottled *sikri* Buddha figures produced at Sarnath and Mathura, with their sinuous yet rigid bodies, line-pleated diaphanous robes, slender webbed fingers, exquisitely curled hair, pouting lips and heavily lidded eyes, epitomize the 'ideal image' to such an extent that this style influenced almost all subsequent Buddhist imagery in India and the Himalayas. The Gupta Empire expanded to control most of northern India from Assam to the borders of the Punjab under Samudra Gupta (reigned *c.* 335–76) and reached its zenith under the third Gupta king, Candra Gupta II (reigned *c.* 376–415), in an era of peace and prosperity.

In the middle of the fifth century, however, a series of attacks by the Turko-Mongol White Huns began; a century later they brought down the last of the Gupta kings, although another line continued to rule parts of the empire until the eighth century. Northern India was not to be united again until after the coming of the Muslims.

Unfortunately few ivories of the Gupta or post-Gupta period have been found, other than the usual utilitarian objects such as seals, rods and kohl-sticks. However, an interesting group of miniature Kashmir ivories and a bone reliquary have appeared, mostly dating from the eighth and ninth centuries, in the last couple of decades. They are now scattered in museums and private collections worldwide. The ivories are carved in exquisite detail, some with traces of red and black paint like those on the Begram ivories. Most measure less than 5½ in. (14 cm) in height. The subjects depicted include a seated Buddha alone; a seated Buddha in meditation flanked by two Bodhisattvas and numerous devotees; a standing Buddha surrounded by five Bodhisattvas (two examples); a seated crowned Bodhisattva and a seated Buddha receiving the visit of Indra, both surrounded by diminutive figures, both in carved wooden frames; a seated Buddha being attacked by the forces of Mara, the Evil One; two standing female *chauri*-bearers; the Descent of Buddha from the Trayastrimsat Heaven; a standing Buddha surrounded by six figures, one with a parasol; Indra's visit to the Buddha at the Indrasala cave; a seated Buddha flanked by Indra, Panchasika and others; a standing Buddha with two attendants, his beard painted; a standing, crowned Manjusri with three attendants; a standing Avalokiteśvara with two attendants; a fragment showing Mara's attendants. The similar but rather more extensively carved bone reliquary (?) has been dated to the ninth or tenth century. It is three-sided, principally depicting a crowned, bejewelled Buddha seated on a throne supported by animals, his hands in the preaching position (*dharmacakra mudra*), numerous smaller figures surrounding him. The two remaining sides respectively depict the Birth of the Buddha and the Temptation of Siddharta. Most of the ivory plaques and figures are carved as complete entities and most if not all of them were probably mounted in carved (baroque-style) wooden frames, like those mentioned. It is thought that these wooden panels set with ivory centrepieces formed part of portable shrines, modelled after Kashmiri temple architecture. The first framed example has traces of blue, brown, black and green pigments, both on the ivory plaque and the surrounding wooden panel, suggesting that these shrines – like most ancient Indian temples – were embellished with paint. Stone shrines of this kind are also known. A tenth- or eleventh-century wooden panel depicting the goddess Tara shares similar architectural characteristics with these wooden shrine-panels of the eighth century and shows the development of the idiom from the 'baroque', post-Gupta style of plump, indulgent-faced *ghandarvas* holding garlands to a more regimented, less cramped elegance.

Two of the most important ivories of the period are a diptych found in Gansu, the most north-westerly state of China, and an eleventh- or twelfth-century chess piece, once thought to have belonged to the Emperor Charlemagne (742–814). The exterior of the 'Gansu Ivory' depicts an elephant standing on a plain base carved around the sides with recessed cartouches; on his back sits a heavily draped and bejewelled princely figure holding a *stupa* (a Buddhist reliquary). Various diminutive figures including a mahout and armed soldiers surround the elephant. It may show the Distribution of the Buddha's Relics. The hinged diptych opens to show two sections, each with twenty-seven subdivisions minutely carved with scenes from the Life of the Buddha. A *stupa* (inside the *stupa* carved on the exterior), devotees, standing Buddhas and sprigs of foliage are also depicted. The general style brings to mind the architectural reliefs from Gandhara, but it also betrays affinities with Kashmiri sculpture and is particularly comparable with the small eighth-century ivories. The two standing Buddha figures flanking the interior, though retaining Gandharan and Gupta characteristics, may suggest a slightly later date with their elongated attenuated bodies. It has been attributed to north-west India, Kashmir or a neighbouring kingdom, and dated to the seventh or eighth century.

The ivory chess piece depicting a nobleman riding an elephant surrounded by soldiers on

Right: One of a pair of ivory throne-legs from north-east India or Nepal. Twelfth-century (Pala-Sena dynasty); 7 in. (17.8 cm).

horseback must rank as one of the earliest documented Indian ivories in the west. Mentioned in the 1505 inventory of the abbey of St Denis, Paris, it was published first in 1625, mentioned in 1645 and catalogued in 1858. The elephant stands on an ovoid base with a double band of beading around the sides, surrounded by four soldiers on horseback, each horse wearing trappings, each rider wearing a plumed helmet and holding a sword or an axe. The elephant's trunk encircles a further horseman, his hands clasping those of the mahout (?) who sprawls in an X-shape over the face of the elephant. The nobleman in the howdah wears jewellery and a decorated turban or crown. The sides of the howdah are carved with standing warriors. On the underside of the base is an Arabic inscription in Kufic script: *From the work of Yusuf al-Bahlili.* Despite this there seems little doubt that the workmanship is Indian. The association with Charlemagne seems to have arisen because the next item in the inventory listed a chess set which *did* belong to Charlemagne. Datings vary from ninth century to fifteenth. 'Sultanate, from north-western India, late eleventh/early twelfth century' seems satisfactorily to resolve the apparent incongruities of style and inscription.

A pair of ivory throne-legs or supports carved in the form of seated lions has been attributed to the Pala-Sena dynasty, *c.* twelfth century, from north-east India or Nepal. They are carved with great strength and vigour: powerful limbs, exuberantly scrolling manes and grotesque *kirttimukha*-like faces. Each head carries a plain turned support in the form of a capital; each base has a dedicatory inscription, the exact meaning of which is not apparent. Guardian lions of this type are an enduring theme in Buddhism, frequently depicted as throne-supports in Gandharan art (first to sixth centuries), and appear in differing forms in later periods virtually throughout Buddhist Asia. Other Pala ivories include a fragmentary seated female deity from the twelfth century and the lower portions of a miniature *stupa* dated to the tenth century, carved with three registers of Buddhas and Bodhisattvas with dwarf- and animal-supports, respectively.

Muslim invasion of northern India brought the long-established Buddhist culture to an end in the late twelfth century. Following their sweeping victory at Tarain in 1192, the Muslims set up a Turkish sultanate in Delhi, annexed Bihar and sacked the great monasteries that had been the seedbeds of Buddhist art and scholarship for five hundred years.

The late Middle Ages

After the building of the great Sun Temple at Konarak, Orissa, in 1238–64, a great tradition of ivory carving emerged, which continued until the nineteenth century. There are earlier references to the ivory carvers of Orissa; little seems to have survived prior to the thirteenth century, but it is clear that a centuries-old tradition of carving ivory furniture existed in eastern India, particularly Orissa. Royal beds, chariots, palanquins, couches, chairs, sedan chairs, thrones, throne-legs, bed-legs, door handles, caskets, columns, pavilions, balconies and lion-headed conduits are among the ivory (or ivory-inlaid) objects mentioned. The famous Jagannath Temple (*c.* 1198) at Puri, Orissa, has an inscription which records the gift of eight ivory thrones from King Purushottamdeva (1467–97).

The surviving ivories of this period in Orissa consist largely of throne-legs and small bed-panels, though other ivory objects of less clear purpose are known. The best-known throne-leg, 13¾ in. (35 cm) in height, dating from the thirteenth century, depicts a rampant *gajasimha* (elephant-headed lion) on a circular base, encircled by lotus petals and clasping an inverted warrior with his trunk and paws. His head and scrolling tail support a flat square platform. Below his legs is an area of cavernous rocks and scrolling foliage enclosing diminutive figures. The bearded, plump-bodied victim has a terrified expression. The carving and style of this figure closely resemble a similar figure held in the trunk of one of the monumental guardian elephants at the Sun Temple, Konarak.

Four Orissan throne-legs, arguably from the same throne, measuring about 12 in. (30 cm) each and dating from the fifteenth or sixteenth century, depict fully armed warriors riding rampant horses, on waisted lotus pedestals. Below are hunters and animals in combat, above a flaring shaft carved with a *kirttimukha* eating foliage.

Slightly later but still in the *gajasimha* tradition are six further Orissan ivory throne-legs, four of which form a set. They are predominantly carved with lions' bodies and elephants' heads with scrolling trunks; below are hunters on horseback and standing female figures. They measure about 15¾ in. (40 cm) each and have been dated to the sixteenth or seventeenth century.

An important Orissan ivory figure of Ganesha, dated to the fourteenth or fifteenth century, and measuring 7¼ in. (18.5 cm) in height, depicts the four-armed, elephant-headed god seated on a waisted lotus throne. The primary hands hold part of the broken left tusk and a pot of sweet-meats, whilst the upper hands hold an elephant-goad (*ankusa*) and mace (*gada*). The large pot-belly makes the decorated dhoti visible only from the rear. The jewellery, tiered tassels and head orna-ments all find parallels in the stone sculptures at Konarak, though the overlapping lotus leaves on the base and the general formality suggest a date somewhat later than the thirteenth century.

Above: Ivory throne-leg from Orissa, shown in colour on page 209.

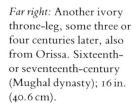

Far right: Another ivory throne-leg, some three or four centuries later, also from Orissa. Sixteenth- or seventeenth-century (Mughal dynasty); 16 in. (40.6 cm).

Below: An erotic ivory panel from Orissa, for a bed. Probably carved between the thirteenth and seventeenth centuries; *c.* 4 in. (10 cm).

Far right: Pair of Indian ivory finials. *c.*1770; 4 in. (10 cm).

An unusual ivory throne-section (?) depicting a huntress supporting a rampant antelope has also been attributed to Orissa, probably thirteenth century. Its size – only 5¼ in. (13.5 cm) – and its projections argue against its being a throne-leg. The tribal huntress wears a leaf-skirt and the antelope's forefeet rest above her shoulders, its head turned round to touch its tail. Flanking the huntress are two figures with legs flexed under the weight of the prey on their shoulders; behind her is a barking dog.

Most of the early Orissan ivory bed-panels measure about 4 in. (10 cm) in height and date from the thirteenth or fourteenth century. This type continued until at least the seventeenth century, though the angularity was lost and the design became increasingly elaborate. Each plaque has one projection above and two below and is carved with a couple embracing within an arched openwork pavilion, usually on a couch, with vessels forming baluster-like supports. Below this is a lotus-petal border with narrow beaded bands; the arch above is similarly carved and has tiered finial and *makara* terminals at either side. The couple wear simple beaded jewellery and short dhotis. Other examples depict similar couples in acrobatic positions of love-making. Examples dating from the sixteenth or seventeenth century are in private and public collections.

The sixteenth, seventeenth and eighteenth centuries

India and the Mughals

In 1526, at the head of his invading Afghan armies, Babur, a Muslim prince from Ferghana (now in Russian Turkistan) who was descended from the two great Central Asian vanquishers, Genghis Khan and Tamburlaine, established himself as ruler of India at Delhi and quelled any hope of a resurgence of Hindu predominance in northern India. After his death in 1530, much of his empire was lost by his son Humayun (reigned 1530–56), but his grandson Akbar (reigned 1556–1605) was the third and mightiest Mughal emperor. Under Akbar, the wealth and splendour of the Mughal Empire became famous in contemporary Europe. Akbar ruled most of northern India from Kabul to the Deccan and from Bengal to Gujarat. He made alliances with the Rajput chiefs and introduced a sophisticated administrative system, of which he maintained ultimate control. At court, miniature painting in Persian style flourished, along with the manufacture of elaborate princely clothing, jewelled daggers, jewellery and *objets de vertu*.

Akbar's son and successor Jahangir (reigned 1605–28) appreciated and greatly encouraged the arts while maintaining the empire he had inherited from his formidable father. His own son Shah Jahan (reigned 1628–58), politically more ambitious, succeeded in expanding his territories in the Deccan and is immortalized as builder of the Taj Mahal (1630–52) at Agra.

Shah Jahan was deposed by his ambitious third son, Aurangzeb (reigned 1658–1707), who waged numerous expensive – though ultimately successful – military campaigns in the Deccan. Under the self-indulgent Muhammad Shah (reigned 1719–48), Mughal power was further weakened and in 1739 the Persian Kuli Khan, Nadir Shah, sacked Delhi. During the second half of the eighteenth century, northern India suffered endless strife. Gradually the British began to take control, though the last Mughal emperor, Bahadur Shah (reigned 1837–58), was not finally deposed and exiled until 1858.

During the Mughal period ivory was used quite extensively for court objects: fly-whisk or fan handles, sword and dagger hilts, boxes and caskets, jewellery, powderhorns, combs and mirror frames, chess and pachesi sets; miniature figures,

too, and under European influence, from the mid eighteenth century on, furniture. A good example of a Deccani fly-whisk handle, dating from the late seventeenth or early eighteenth century, is about 16 in. (40 cm) in length, with a deep, cup-shaped mouthpiece, the sides carved with alternating poppies and cypresses, in low relief; the slender, tapering ropework handle carved similarly around the top has a pineapple terminal. At Sylhet, Bengal (now in Bangladesh), an ancient craft centre, round or crescent-shaped fans were woven of flat strips of ivory, coloured or interwoven with silver thread, and attached to slender ivory handles, often with bud finials. Miniature paintings show that daggers were worn at court in the early period. A fine, early-seventeenth-century Deccani dagger (*khanjar*) has an ivory hilt which is carved with floral arabesques on a black-stained ground. Animal-headed dagger hilts, more commonly found in jade, were also executed in ivory. Walrus or hippopotamus ivory

Opposite: Ivory throne-leg from Orissa. Thirteenth-century; 16 in. (40.6 cm). The elephant-headed lion has a long mane, in layers of curls, a scrolling tail and beaded jewellery. See also page 206.

Far right: Ivory depicting two lovers on a terrace. Seventeenth-century or earlier; 6⅞ × 5⅜ in. (17.5 × 16.4 cm).

Below: Carved ivory primer with animal-head finial, decorated with creatures of the chase. Seventeenth-century; 12 in. (30 cm).

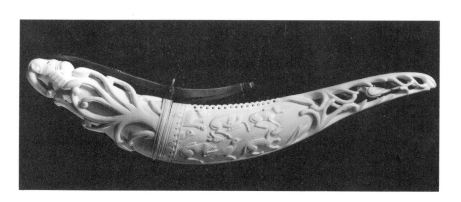

was often used for dagger hilts; drier than elephant ivory, it gives a better grip. During the seventeenth and eighteenth centuries, ivory was used for a variety of other weapons such as matchlock muskets (the stock often with floral inlay), arrowheads (sometimes carved as deer heads), elephant-goad handles and spear handles, as well as for powderhorns and primers. A group of primers showing variations of a specific seventeenth-century type are of particular interest. Of curving form, carved in two pieces and tapering to an animal-head finial at either end with metal stopper attached, these sometimes take the form of an antelope, complete with legs, but more usually have an antelope-head mouthpiece with a body of numerous composite animals, each issuing from the mouth of the next. The central section is sometimes carved with human figures, animals, birds or decorative designs, but hunting remains the basic theme.

A narwhal or walrus ivory archer's ring, carved with European-inspired motifs and dating from the Jahangir period (1605–28), is carved with a bearded head of Christ (?) flanked by two angels. Archery was a popular sport during the Mughal period and these rings – more commonly of jade – were worn on the thumb for protection from the retracting bow-string. Jahangir took great interest in collecting unusual materials such as meteorite, jade and various types of ivory, from which dagger hilts, vessels, rings and other objects were exquisitely modelled by his leading craftsmen. In his autobiography, Jahangir frequently praises his master-craftsmen and mentions several ivory carvers by name, one of whom received, among other gifts, an elephant.

Ivory caskets and boxes, very popular for small valuables, were often square or rectangular, carved of separate panels of flowers and foliage, perhaps with gilt-metal hinges, mounts and handles. In the Deccan during the seventeenth and eighteenth centuries, boxes of this type were carved in low relief with royal lovers, sedate courtiers – perhaps holding a flower or a *huqqa* – animals, flowers and other decorative motifs, perhaps enclosed by a cusped medallion or circle-dot border. An unusual ivory casket, which is

exceptionally fine and probably late-seventeenth- or early-eighteenth-century, is of deep ovoid form, the lid and body narrowly fluted, the top carved with an oval medallion of poppy-heads and scrolling leaves, either side painted with red, green and gilt flowers, the border of split-palmettes.

In Orissa, the great medieval tradition of ivory carving endured, though by the seventeenth century the style has become more elaborate, the figures more languid. Carved box-panels with courtly scenes survive. Two free-standing Orissan figures of Radha and Krishna also date from the seventeenth century.

In western India ivory throne-backs seem to have been popular. One of the best examples measures 26 by 10¼ in. (66 by 26 cm) and is of cusped arched form with scrolling foliate and ropework borders; two identical scenes depict Krishna the Cowherd hunting three bemused-looking cows and two suckling calves, the whole on a ground of foliage. It has been dated to the eighteenth century. Bed- and charpoy-legs were also carved of ivory, in differing forms, sometimes painted or gilded; or carved with erotic couples. A set of unusual ivory charpoy-legs has elaborate incised decoration heightened in black. These are from the Deccan, possibly Hyderabad, and are probably eighteenth-century.

In the south, the main centres of ivory carving were at Madras, Mysore and Madurai; there were numerous smaller centres. Elephants are native to Kerala and Karnathaka on the south-west coast and consequently ivory was – and still is – readily available. A seventeenth-century box-panel, carved with four arched figurative panels on a foliate ground with floral borders, is one of the finest ivories of this period. Another carving,

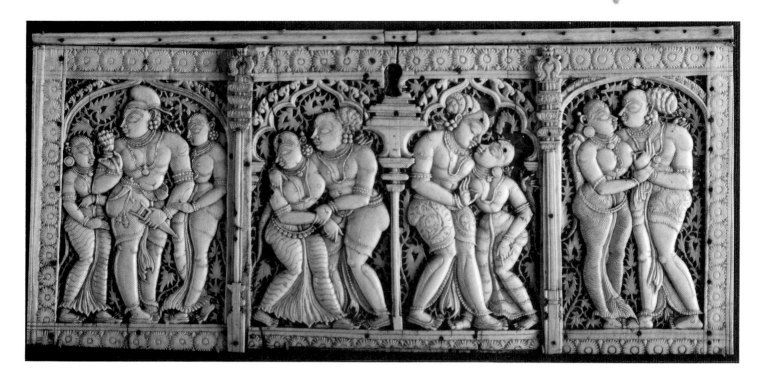

Above: Ivory panel from a cosmetics box, South India. Seventeenth-century; 6 × 12⅜ in. (15.2 × 31.4 cm). One of the highest-quality ivories of its period. A detail is shown in colour on page 212.

thought to be from Srirangam, depicts a standing princely couple embracing and dates from the eighteenth century. A fine pierced ivory box-panel, attributed to the eighteenth century, from Mysore, shows two vigorously dancing female figures flanked by a male drummer and a cymbalist, with a row of lions below. Other Mysore ivories include a fluting Krishna, a pair of figures representing a courtly couple and a bejewelled nobleman with traces of polychrome, all dating from the seventeenth or eighteenth century. A sixteenth- or seventeenth-century casket, carved with four pairs of female dancers wearing pleated skirts and garlands, with a band of peacocks above and foliage below, is attributed to Karnathaka. A fine South Indian polychrome-painted figure of the Child Krishna, with two butter-balls in his outstretched hands, has been dated to the sixteenth century and measures 7½ in. (19 cm). A dancing Balarama, holding a dagger and trumpet, and a figure of a tribal woman wearing a palm-leaf skirt, with a kneeling attendant removing something from the sole of her foot, measure 7½ in. (19 cm) and have been attributed to seventeenth-century Madras. An ivory plaque dated 1766 which apparently formed part of a casket from Tamil Nadu depicts the Marriage of Siva and Parvati, both wearing long pleated dhotis and elaborate jewellery. It displays the increasingly elaborate style of carving favoured in the south in the later period. Combs decorated with Vishna-vite or Sivaite figures were also popular.

Goa

When the Portuguese took the colony of Goa on the south-west coast of India in the sixteenth century a curious hybrid of Indian and western culture produced the Goanese ivory, presumably the result of the Portuguese commissioning carvings to their taste from a land of cheap raw materials and labour.

Goanese ivory comes in a variety of forms. Carved madonnas, saints and angels all have similar characteristics: the hair and flesh details tend to be incised and stained; the folds of the garments are graphic in detail but not plastic in effect. Overall the work is curiously appealing and often quite charming. The most characteristic form is the 'Mountain of Life' or 'Christ the Good Shepherd': a young boy seated on a pyramid of fantastic symbols, often snoozing on his elbow, perhaps holding a lamb or with one perched on his shoulder rather like a bird. The 'mountain', on the scale of a suburban rockery, is usually made up of three or more tiers displaying scenes from the Bible or related subjects; perhaps a stream or spring, with lambs or exotic birds drinking, possibly flanked by saints; maybe a nativity scene or any other device. The carving is essentially one-sided but stray animals may wander round the back as if in an attempt to show that it is round and real. These charming humble figures are difficult to date but were probably made during the seventeenth and eighteenth centuries.

Goa is also associated with the ivory-inlaid wooden cabinets, with drawers concealed by a frontal flap, produced in western India in the seventeenth and eighteenth centuries and often called 'Indo-Portuguese'. They are thought to have been originally produced to Portuguese orders, perhaps at Goa. One fantastically elaborate example, of stout rectangular form, standing

Above: Detail of the carving on an ivory casket decorated with jewels, shown in colour on page 216; *c.* 1540.

Far right: Serene ivory Buddha from Ceylon. Eighteenth-century; 5¼ in. (14.5 cm). Buddhas were in high demand in the Kandy period.

Page 212: Detail from the seventeenth-century cosmetics-box panel opposite.

Page 213: Goanese ivory, depicting the Holy Trinity. Seventeenth-century. The pedestal is reminiscent of 'Mountain of Life' scenes.

on caryatid legs with lion feet, has been specifically attributed to the Goa region in the late seventeenth century.

Sri Lanka

Ceylon, now Sri Lanka, has produced some of the finest ivory carving in the subcontinent, nurtured and influenced by the country's Portuguese, Dutch and British colonists. The carving is marked by the exuberance of its scrolling foliage – an ubiquitous motif in Sinhalese ivory carving – which is often coloured with black and sealing-wax red pigments. In the sixteenth century a particularly fine group of ivory caskets was made in the kingdom of Kotte as diplomatic gifts to the Portuguese. One of the finest, *c.* 1540, mounted with gold, rubies and sapphires, is of rectangular form decorated with panels. At the front, the left-hand panel depicts the King of Ceylon presenting a statue (?) to the King of Portugal; the right-hand panel, the King of Portugal placing a Buddhist crown on the head of the statue; and the central panel two Portuguese guards, each clasping a staff, with above each a lion, the symbol of Ceylon. The other panels are filled with similar figurative carving, with vigorous scrolling and borders of lions, beading and interlacing.

As the tradition of casket carving continued, various different styles emerged. A seventeenth-century box, now in Copenhagen, is of rectangular form with a curving hinged lid; the decoration comprises vigorously intertwining leafy scrolls with two human masks, from whose mouths issue scrolls. An ivory cabinet carved with panels depicting Adam and Eve with the serpent, *c.* 1700, has elaborate silver corner-braces, handles and hinges, and is predominantly carved with delicate scrolling foliage enclosing birds, in low relief.

In 1592 the capital had moved to Kandy, where the arts flourished; ivory carving ranked as one of the highest crafts during the 'Kandy period', particularly under the patronage of the last great Buddhist king of Ceylon, Kirti Sri Raja Simha (reigned 1747–80). A superb Buddha which typifies the style of the Kandy period stands on a waisted circular throne, with the right hand raised in *vitarka mudra* and with the left hand pendant

Below: Detail from the ivory cabinet shown in colour on page 188.

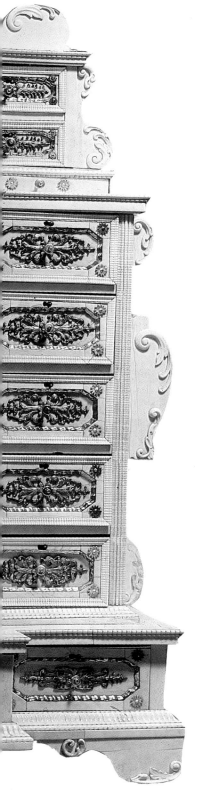

against the long robe of narrow wavering pleats. The benevolent face has spiralling *urna* (forehead markings) and traces of red paint. The tightly curled hair is painted black; the palms are carved with auspicious flower-heads. Other eighteenth-century figures include noblemen and their wives dressed in voluminous Kandyan robes and jewellery and a courtly palanquin-bearer with traces of gilding and polychrome.

Numerous ivory combs also survive from this period and are usually double-sided, carved with a central figurative panel and rows of teeth above and below.

Furniture

Despite the evidence of earlier centuries, there seems no doubt that furniture found little place in the Muslim courts of Delhi and the Deccan, or in the Hindu forts and palaces of Rajasthan. Thrones were the one exception. Elaborately carved ivory legs, particularly those carved in Orissa, described above, seem to have continued popular from the twelfth to the seventeenth century. Mughal thrones, as documented in numerous court miniature paintings of the seventeenth and eighteenth centuries, usually took the form of a square or octagonal dais often covered by a carpet, on which the monarch knelt or sat with legs folded, under a canopy. The ruler was supported by richly covered bolsters. A painting entitled *Shah Jahan Enthroned* is thought to show the illustrious peacock throne, completed in 1634 (and eventually carried off to Persia in 1739). An allegorical portrait of Jahangir, *c.* 1625, shows an elaborate hour-glass throne with intertwining foliate supports and borders inlaid with precious stones. Another miniature, *The Birth of a Prince*, *c.* 1605-10, shows a slender upright gilt armchair, apparently set with precious stones.

Some of the first items of furniture made in India under European influence were the so-called 'Indo-Portuguese', ivory-inlaid wooden boxes, which in the seventeenth century were mostly produced in western India, particularly at Tata in Sind (now Pakistan) and Surat in Gujarat, the latter an important trading port where ships would stop on the way home. They may originally derive from the medieval Near East and be related to the work produced in the Muslim centres in Spain and Sicily, although it is possible that an independent Muslim tradition of wood-inlaying may have existed in India. The Portuguese were commissioning cabinets of exactly this type – rectangular form with frontal flap opening to reveal drawers – in Japan from about 1580. A cabinet now in Bombay is the figurative type, inlaid with ivory courtiers wearing Deccani-style dress, lions flanking profuse trees, Persian-style vases, tigers chasing antelopes and two female figures seated on a couch beneath a tree, on a ground of polished teak banding. Examples, sometimes on European-made mahogany or other stands, are still quite common in Europe, and particularly in England. An interesting elaboration, the form apparently based on an Italian prototype, the inlay in ivory and bone attributed to Sind, now in London, stands on a table with cross-stretcher and two inlaid drawers; above is the usual cabinet section with two doors each profusely inlaid with a bold geometric star motif, ten small drawers with smaller star motifs within; the eaved upper section has six drawers inlaid with courtly figures in Jahangir-style robes against a ground of foliate sprigs. It has been dated to the early seventeenth century, as has another Sind ivory-inlaid cabinet, said to be of German inspiration, of rectangular form with frontal flap concealing eleven drawers, the decoration formalized and restrained, with loose scrolls, rosettes, stars and sprigs, an almost architectural pediment and columns dominating the central drawer. An interesting cabinet attributed to the Deccan, *c.* 1700, has two doors opening to reveal a regimental array of drawers, each inlaid with two or more courtly figures, one with pairs of wrestlers; the inner side of each door is also inlaid with figures and trees; the wide borders depict interlacing foliage. Other cabinets of this form include one, possibly from Surat, *c.* 1650-1700, inlaid with bold poppies and other plants, and on a later English lacquered *chinoiserie* stand. A large Mass or credence table-top, of rosewood inlaid with ebony, ivory, bone and lac, from western India, early seventeenth century, measures 3 ft 6 in. (1.06 m) by 2 ft 8½ in. (0.82 m). A predominant central medallion depicts angels surrounding a monstrance, with a Latin inscription encircling the border, but below is a row of nine courtly figures against a ground of foliate sprigs.

With the successful establishment of the East India Company in Bengal by the mid eighteenth century, particularly in the Murshidabad area, the demand for European-style furniture was established and the traditional ivory carvers of Berhampur and Kasimbazaar soon adapted their skills to the appropriate Georgian designs. One of a set of four Hepplewhite-style, carved and veneered ivory chairs survives, with oval back, tapering legs and carved beading, late eighteenth century, probably from Berhampur, whence comes an exquisitely carved, Adam-style, ivory-veneered sandalwood work-table, *c.* 1800. The victory of Robert Clive (1725-74) at Plassey, near Calcutta, in 1757, firmly established British supremacy in Bengal. In 1784, a nawab's widow presented Clive's successor, Warren Hastings (1732-1818), with a set of elaborately carved ivory sofas, footstools and chairs, made at Murshidabad, a number of which survive, though the provenance is not always certain.

Below, right: Ivory coffer-shaped workbox, with silvered paw feet and lions' heads, from Vizagapatam. 1820; 13 × 8½ × 7 in. (33 × 21.6 × 17.8 cm).

Below: Sandalwood chair veneered with ivory, made in Madras. *c.*1770; 39⅛ × 24½ × 22⅛ in. (99.4 × 62.3 × 56.2 cm).

The ivory-veneered furniture inlaid with black lac floral motifs, and later with European-inspired architectural motifs, made at the south-eastern coastal town of Vizagapatam, is perhaps best known in Europe. Examples include a revolving armchair with caned seat, human-head finials and six paw feet joined by stretchers (late seventeenth or early eighteenth century) and a single armchair of early Georgian design, profusely decorated with floral and foliate ivory inlay (*c.* 1725–50), acquired in Spain as part of a set of six armchairs, six side-chairs, a settee and a table. Towards the end of the eighteenth century, furniture was produced in great quantities at Vizagapatam, with flower designs and architectural motifs copied from European prints: cabinets with grandiose

Georgian broken pediments and cabriole legs, Hepplewhite-style armchairs with shield backs and meandering foliate inlay in black lac, and mirror-cabinets, cosmetics boxes and writing-boxes in various sizes and designs, often combining with a table or additional section to form a larger piece. Rosewood was mostly used, though by the early nineteenth century ivory veneer predominated and the larger items lost favour.

A mid-eighteenth-century Vizagapatam dressing-table, inlaid with elaborate ivory flowers and foliage, was brought home by Warren Hastings; a similarly inlaid rosewood dressing-table, with matching mirror-cabinet, is in the Clive of India Collection at Powis Castle, Wales (inventoried in 1774). Other ivory furniture at Powis, mostly

collected by the second Lord Clive (1754–1839), Governor of Madras 1798–1802, is of particular interest as some was commissioned and most is inventoried. It includes an ivory box with bamboo garland borders and a central medallion on the lid, an ivory table, probably late eighteenth century from Vizagapatam, decorated with lac-inlaid floral garlands surrounding a central cartouche, an ivory-inlaid writing-box, a tortoiseshell and ivory-banded casket and backgammon and chess sets decorated with lac-inlaid borders of delicate meandering foliage.

The nineteenth century

The arrival of the nineteenth century saw the British established with centres at Calcutta, Madras and Lucknow. By 1825 they had taken the Deccan; Delhi and Agra followed, and political agents were successfully established in most of the powerful Rajput kingdoms of Rajasthan. Modernization began with an official system of education, the banning of practices such as widow-burning, the controlling of crime and the arrival of the railway. The last Mughal emperor was exiled after the Mutiny of 1857, the Honourable

217   *The Near East, India: India*

Page 216: Detail from carved presentation casket, in ivory mounted with gold, rubies and sapphires. *c.*1540. A Portuguese nobleman and his lady at table. See also page 211.

Page 217: Ivory throne, made for Queen Victoria by the ivory carvers of Travancore. 1840s; 63¼ × 38¼ × 34 in. (160.7 × 97.2 × 86.4 cm).

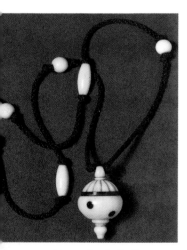

Above: Anglo-Indian ivory pomander.

Far right: Indian necklace of hand-turned and hand-carved ivory. Nineteenth-century.

East India Company relinquished its powers to the Crown, and in 1877 Queen Victoria was proclaimed Empress of India.

Although the changing political climate had not had any immediate effect on the arts during the greater part of the eighteenth century, as declining Mughal patronage was replaced – to some extent – by that of the Europeans in India, the Rajput courts of Rajasthan, relatively unaffected, continued to employ court craftsmen in the long-established tradition, and the established centres of ivory carving, such as Murshidabad and Berhampur in Bengal, Surat in Gujarat and Vizagapatam on the south-east coast, were already producing European-style furniture and related material. Within the first few decades of the nineteenth century, the demand increased and a new form of patronage began to emerge. Whereas in the eighteenth century more or less faithful copies of, for example, Sheraton and Hepplewhite furniture designs were made, notably at Murshidabad, in the nineteenth century an often bizarre, hybrid style emerged, incorporating European, Hindu and Muslim motifs. John Lockwood Kipling in 1885 wrote that an elaborate ivory from Murshidabad, showing the goddess Durga and the Buffalo Demon, showed 'the grotesque tastelessness peculiar to modern Bengal, where pseudo-classic [*sic*] architectural forms frame the many-armed creatures of Hindu fantasy'.

Political skirmishes, border disputes, murders, famines and a series of savage local wars were among the many problems the British encountered in trying to unify the subcontinent. However, the introduction of direct government with the arrival of the first viceroy in 1858 led to the total reorganization of the administration and the establishment of a system which lasted until Independence in 1947.

Encouragement of the 'industrial arts' by the British, both at home and in India, initially for displays at the Great Exhibition of 1851, ensured the survival of traditional Indian arts and crafts, in decline since the demise of Mughal power in the eighteenth century. Exhibitions, displays and publications stimulated both interest and production.

One of the cynosures of the Great Exhibition of 1851 is an elaborate ivory throne and footstool made by the famous ivory carvers of Travancore in the 1840s. The throne stands on four stout curving legs with lion paws. Each arm is divided into eleven panels arranged in two registers, variously depicting eagles, putti, lions, winged griffins, a goddess issuing from scrolls, a nude child wearing a garland, a prowling lion and a standing angel with a foliate bow; the finial is a lion's head, the side and borders are secured with gilt lotus-bud knops. The back of the throne is

carved with three rows comprising fifteen panels in all, containing similar motifs but also including a lion and a unicorn flanking an arch, two sphinxes, rampant griffins and fluting angels; the finial depicts two snouted lions flanking a conch shell; below it is a single curving band of panels, again similar.

At a Simla exhibition in 1881 an elaborate South Indian carved ivory frame was contributed by the Diwan of Travancore, decorated with architectural motifs and a *kirttimukha* finial, and another frame in this style, containing a photograph of Lord Curzon at the Coronation Durbar, Delhi, 1903, is even more elaborate. They exemplify the skill of the Travancore ivory carvers, whose School of Art at Trivandrum was established in 1873. A similar throne, thought to date from the eighteenth century, at the Ranga Vilasom Palace, Trivandrum, is apparently exceptional.

Travancore and Mysore have long been two of the most important centres of ivory production in India and the quality of objects produced there is consistently good, unlike that of most other ivory carvers, as surviving examples and illustrations make evident.

Ivories carved in Kerala frequently depict Hindu subjects such as Radha and Krishna on a swing, or the goddess Durga slaying the Buffalo Demon. The ivory workers of Vizagapatam went

cabinets, it now produced geometric mosaicwork and marquetry boxes, inlaid or banded with ivory, often on a sandalwood base. Similar 'Bombay boxes' display the technique of inlaying with minute pieces of silver, green-stained ivory, ebony, silver wire, staghorn, tin and glass, thought to have been brought to Bombay by the Parsees (descendants of the eighth-century Zoroastrian refugees from Persia), though one historian said in 1880 that the technique originally came from Shiraz to Sind 'about 100 years ago', and a traveller in 1655 mentioned the great skill of the Indian craftsmen in making 'cabinets, boxes, trunks and stand dishes, curiously wrought within and without; inlaid with elephant's teeth or mother-of-pearl, ebony, tortoiseshell and wire'.

In northern India the main centres of ivory carving were Amritsar, Delhi, Patiala, Shahpur, Multan, Lahore, Hoshiarpur, Benares (Varanasi) and Lucknow. Most of them produced utilitarian objects such as bangles, combs, chessmen or *chaupar* pieces, boxes, mirror frames, religious images and charpoy-legs, plus objects for European use where there was a demand. The British bought exotic Indian chess sets with camel-mounted knights, juggernaut cars, snarling tigers and the kings, elephant-mounted, in canopied howdahs. The miniatures on ivory at Delhi developed in response to demand from European

Above: Indian ivory box with erotic designs. Late-eighteenth/early-nineteenth-century; 10¾ × 10¾ × 10½ in. (27.2 × 27.2 × 26.5 cm).

Far right: Indian ivory and ebony games table, with drawers, from Kashmir. 1850; inlaid with cut steel and paste beads.

Pages 220–1: Ivory chess set from India. Twentieth century; each piece 5 in. (12.8 cm) or smaller. See page 225 for detail.

on producing their veneered and lac-decorated furniture throughout the nineteenth century, but through mass production the quality diminished. A tortoiseshell-veneered box might be bound with ivory, the latter perhaps decorated with black lac scrolling. 'Delhi-type' miniature ivory paintings, painted in water-colour, were produced at Trichinopoly.

One of the most common ivory objects found in nineteenth-century India was the *churi* or bangle, worn by most Hindu and Muslim women, in particular by Hindu brides for the first year of marriage. They were usually of plain form, though some were stained red, green or black and others decorated with incisions. Most were made in the ancient town of Pali, near Jodhpur, in graduating sizes; a whole set would cover the arm from wrist to shoulder. Ivory matting and children's toys were also made at Pali.

The ivory comb, produced in India since ancient times, was particularly sought after by the Sikhs, the main centres of production consequently being Delhi and Amritsar in the Punjab. The ivory inlayers of Hushiarpur and the cutters of Bhera and Sialkot came to Amritsar to buy fragments of ivory from the comb-makers. Another important centre north of Bombay was Surat in Gujarat, one of the first ports European ships stopped at; earlier famous for its ivory-inlaid

tourists and were painted in water-colour, sometimes set in elaborately carved ebony frames. The most popular subjects were the Mughal emperors and their wives, or famous Mughal monuments such as the Taj Mahal, Agra, the Red Fort, Delhi,

Above: Painted ivory *ganjifa* cards, from India, from a set of ninety-six. Nineteenth-century; 1⅞ in. (4.7 cm) diameter.

or the Qutb Minar. Mir Muhammad Hussain Khan, one of the better-known Delhi miniature-painters, exhibited at the Delhi Exhibition of 1903. Miniatures were also produced at Jaipur and at Benares where a Hindu, Chuni Lal, painted mythological subjects gilded and coloured like an illuminated manuscript. Twelve of his pictures, sent to the Calcutta Exhibition in 1883, were then highly valued.

Patiala was known for its shallow surface tracery, minutely decorated with elaborate floral designs. A howdah at the palace of Patiala is said to be one of the finest examples of this technique. A large ivory-appliqué carriage, the sides decorated with rectangular ivory plaques, with rows of ten elephants and lions carved in relief on the upper border of each side and wheels inlaid with bands of floral motifs, dating from the nineteenth century, is attributed to Rajasthan.

Hoshiarpur is famous for its ivory- and bone-inlaid wooden objects, all in the same style of dense scrolling foliage. The technique, like the early mother-of-pearl inlaid furniture from Gujarat, and other Indian mosaic and inlaid work, is thought to have originated in Persia.

In eastern India the main ivory carving centres were Murshidabad, Rungpur, Dacca, Tipperah,

Chittagong, Berhampur, Sylhet, Monghyr, Patna, Calcutta, Dumraon and Durbhanga. Murshidabad, Monghyr and Berhampur had earlier produced ivory furniture in the European taste, but by the second half of the nineteenth century became famous for their Hindu images, particularly the large ivory shrines depicting the goddess Durga slaying the Buffalo Demon. One example, shown at the Great Exhibition, measures 19½ by 16 in. (49.7 by 41 cm) and depicts the goddess atop the slain Buffalo Demon, flanked by Lakshmi, Sarasvati, Ganesha and Kartikeya; above her head is a semi-circular, fan-shaped arch with swagged border, supported by columns and with four lunettes below. It was apparently made by members of the Bhaskara caste at Berhampur. By the end of the century copy shrines were being made in Delhi and Patiala. Sir George Watt, in the catalogue of the Delhi Exhibition of 1903 at which a version was shown, called it 'a modern abomination' typical of Bengal, 'where a distorted conception of Doric architecture has passed current as indigenous art for at least half a century'. His comment was made eighteen years after John Lockwood Kipling's forceful dismissal of this type of image from Murshidabad.

Some of the most popular Bengali ivories were small processional groups depicting a rajah riding in a howdah on an elephant surrounded by attendants, or in a palanquin. Others include carved ivory models of the passenger boats used on the rivers in Bengal, of elongated form containing numerous oarsmen, carved with foliage and *makara* finials. Two unusual Bengali ivory groups respectively depicted, first, an Englishman with painted mutton-chop whiskers, seated on a Regency-style chair, wearing a top hat and holding a *huqqa*-snake, his Bengali servant beside him, and the *huqqa*-bottle standing on a painted, speckled-red *huqqa*-mat; and second, a strolling lady and gentleman, standing on a plain base, she wearing bonnet, shawl and dress, he attired in top hat, spats and orange-painted waistcoat; they probably date *c.* 1830–50.

Tipperah and Sylhet, although ancient centres of ivory carving, were known for their ivory mat- and fan-weaving in the nineteenth century, the

Above: Bengali ivory group, unusual in that it depicts a European couple. Probably 1830–50; 3⅛ in. (8 cm). Another group is shown in colour on page 224.

scrolling foliage; the third, the infant Krishna holding his toe to his mouth.

Ivory carving in Rajasthan continued the tradition of the seventeenth and eighteenth centuries, with penboxes, cups, dagger hilts, chess sets, staffs, archers' rings, howdahs, *chaupar* sets, powderhorns and other items, mostly in late Mughal style. Ivory boxes were inlaid with coloured lac in linear or circle-dot arrangements; wooden boxes with ivory stylized animals or foliate motifs. There are some handsome inlaid powderflasks from Kota. Other Rajasthan ivory objects include paper-knives, rattles and syringes for squirting coloured water during the festival of Holi.

Ivorywork in modern India

The Exhibition of Indian Art held at Delhi in 1903 was a milestone in the encouragement of Indian arts and crafts, or 'industrial arts' as they were still popularly known. The illustrated catalogue by Sir George Watt mentioned, but rarely dated, older ivories, as well as the then modern ivories largely under discussion. It laments the lack, first, of ivory objects in both temple and palace, and second, of 'antique examples', and names Delhi, Murshidabad, Mysore and Travancore as the most famous centres of ivory carving in India at that time.

These centres and others – Amritsar, Patiala, Benares (Varanasi), Lucknow, Surat, Ahmedabad, Sattara, Vizagapatam, Vizanagram and Coorg – have continued their separate traditions into modern times. However, despite nuances of local style and technique, the twentieth century has seen a merging of certain styles and subject matter which rarely produces a satisfactory result. The breaking-down of regional traditions is a direct result of the social upheaval instituted by the empire-builders whose measures contributed to the loss of a traditional way of life. By the early twentieth century, many of the maharajahs were abandoning their ivory or silver carriages in favour of motor-cars, their sumptuous robes or *pajama* for western-style suits, and their Victorian palaces filled with bric-à-brac for modernistic buildings with Art Deco furniture. The process of westernization, at least in one stratum of Indian society, was almost complete.

The case for the reversion to ancient Indian traditions and the restoration of the dying arts and crafts led to the establishment of schools of art in most large cities and towns, where local arts and crafts were encouraged, as well as the principles of western art being taught. Ananda Coomaraswamy, a campaigner against the westernization of Indian art, urged them in 1909 'to gather up and revitalize the broken threads of Indian tradition, to build up the idea of Indian Art as an integral part of the national culture, and to relate the work of Indian craftsmen to the life and thought of the

latter being particularly associated with ivory fans.

Cuttack, Puri and Paralakinedi were the main Orissan centres of ivory carving in the nineteenth century, though not many examples survive. Three Orissan ivories of outstanding quality, exhibited at the Delhi Exhibition, 1903, were said to be about fifty years old and carved by Gobind Ratan, Prince of Nayagurh. The first is a tortoise, naturalistically carved in four sections, about 8 in. (20.5 cm) in length. It holds a foliate scroll in its mouth. The shell, which is removable, is carved with four concentric bands surrounding a central oval medallion, and the whole is intricately carved with delicate interlacing foliage. The second is a standing, cross-legged, fluting Krishna, on a waisted lotus base, similarly decorated with fine

Opposite: Unusual carved and painted Bengali ivory group depicting an Englishman and his servant. *c.*1830–50; 2½ in. (6.5 cm). The Englishman holds a *huqqa*-snake, and the *huqqa*-bottle stands beside him on a red mat.

Right: One of the kings from the ivory chess set shown in colour on pages 220–1.

Indian people'. He criticized the Bombay School of Art as 'so entirely un-Indian as to explain at once the dullness of the results'.

Although the schools of art continue in modern India, they are still heavily influenced by western art. Those centres that produce ivory carvings in a traditional manner are largely involved in supplying the tourist trade. Ivories are generally either utilitarian objects, such as boxes, and various ornaments, or stereotyped Hindu religious images, unremarkable in quality. Ivory- and bone-inlaid furniture is still produced at Hoshiarpur, miniatures on ivory at Delhi, inlaid and marquetry boxes at Bombay, images of Durga at Murshidabad, and various decorative objects and images at Travancore and Mysore. Few ivory carvings are now made in Orissa, where the cutters at Parlakimedi and Cuttack carve animal figures, combs, vases, ashtrays and pen-stands from buffalo or bison horn, but rarely from ivory. Wood, stone and soapstone seem to have replaced ivory, as buffalo and bison horn have also become expensive.

Sir George Watt's comment in 1903 that 'the modern work has absorbed all styles and become mainly Hindu' is as relevant today as it was then.

6

The Far East and South-East Asia

In the ancient civilization of China, ivory was used for ritual objects: for the neolithic bi and yuan discs, associated with the rites of death and burial; for the austere hu tablets carried by Tang officials during imperial ceremonies. Highly prized and used for small treasured artefacts – jewellery, chess pieces, combs – it became one of the luxury materials at the imperial courts, for fine Ming figures, a court fan with carved floral sprays on interlaced ivory, a Qing screen of pierced ivory with backgrounds of jade and agate, ivory-inlaid palanquins, intricate miniature boats and other imperial toys. To the purist, ivory was identified with such luxuries and unfit for the scholar's desk, but ivory mounts and terminals for scrolls and ivory seals, deepened and mellowed by handling, pleased even the intellectuals. In eighteenth-century Japan, the seal and the netsuke became works of art, compact ivory masterpieces. With the coming of westernization they lost their function and joined the ever-growing stream of commercial attractions, like the wares of Canton and Hong Kong and the Philippines. Ivory was rare in the Himalayan kingdoms and the South Sea islands, but the ritual artefacts of Tibet, carved in human bone, the Maori whale's tooth *tiki*, the Marquesan carved ear plugs, have their own richness and power.

Opposite: Ivory card case carved in relief with figures in pavilions and landscapes, from China. Qinq Dynasty (nineteenth-century); 4¼ in. (10.7 cm) long. A vast range of ivory cases, boxes, caskets and other items was produced for the expanding European export trade.
Above: Netsuke depicting a tiger, one of the twelve animals of the Japanese zodiac; signed Tomotada.

China

Neolithic Chinese ivories

A most exciting group of ivories was excavated recently from the site at Hemudu, Zhejiang province, about seventy miles from the city of Hangzhou. This site dates to about 5000 BC, and carvings in bone, wood and ivory have been unearthed. More than twenty ivory items were found. One of the most interesting of these is a drilled plaque decorated with a design of two birds' heads confronting a flaming sphere, possibly representing the sun. Others relate to bone carvings and one group in particular, a variety of perforated plaques, was found in wood and stone as well.

The Shang Dynasty: c. 1600–1030 BC

Early ivories, found at neolithic sites in the Shang Dynasty (c. 1600–1030 BC), are very rare. Many of the artefacts found or excavated, which were previously thought to be ivory, have been reclassified as bone, and those of bone outnumber ivory examples. Remains of the neolithic cultures of China have been found in Gansu and Henan provinces. These societies produced both painted and black polished pottery and based their economies on millet, goats, pigs and dogs.

The Shang ruled central China for approximately five hundred years. Anyang, north of the Yellow River, became the capital of the Shang kings c. 1400 BC. It remained so until the Shang were overthrown by the Zhou in about 1100 BC.

The Shang are famous for the remarkable quality and technical skills found in their bronzes. They were slave-owning, and practised human sacrifice. They consulted oracles by inscribing and heating or burning animal bones. Our knowledge of early Chinese culture is based on neolithic and Shang burial sites, and several rare and notable artefacts of ivory have been found there. Objects most frequently found are finials, hairpins, sword pommels, fish hooks, rings, plaques, mounts and fittings, and sections of bowls, and most interesting of all is a certain type of slender beaker, discovered in the tomb of Lady Hao in Anyang. The designs carved on these slightly waisted, elegant vessels bear a close resemblance to similar designs on archaic bronzes, and are also closely paralleled in jade examples. The softer nature of ivory, however, allowed the carver to introduce a more detailed design into his medium. He carved, in relief, bands of small dragons, cicada and bird motifs, with animal-mask designs known as taotie. The taotie was a theme of Shang and Zhou ornament, and its features are usually bovine or feline. It splits into two animals in profile, the two parts forming a confronting mask, which frequently has a ferocious expression and has been referred to as a 'glutton mask'. The difference between the representation of the taotie in bronze, and that in ivory, is noted by the author James Watt, who observes that ivory masks usually have human eyes adapted to the form of the oracle bone characters for *mu* (eye) rather than the alternative convention of a rectangle with rounded corners and a central slit.

The Zhou Dynasty: c. 1100–220 BC

The Zhou Dynasty followed the downfall of the Shang, but there are few examples of ivory which can be definitely and accurately dated to this period. A handle in the Musée Guimet in Paris is very close in design to a jade in the British Museum which can be dated to the tenth century BC. The Guimet ivory is a finely carved example with vigorously portrayed, interlocking and curling dragons. It is reminiscent of the kind of style called Huai which became popular between the seventh century and the first century BC. This style was used mainly on bronzes and, in particular, to decorate mirrors. The characteristics of this design were prominent-eyed, gaping-jawed dragons which interlock and intertwine in a geometric, overlapping pattern.

At Zhou burial sites, decorative ivories have been discovered, most of them small and intended for personal ornament. Thumb rings, belt hooks, beads, plaques, combs and remarkably detailed back-scratchers in the form of human hands have also been unearthed. References and information suggest that ivory was highly valued during the time of the Zhou, and that the source of material was in the south, with the probability of additional imports through trade. It is therefore very likely that by the time the Zhou fell and the Han Dynasty established itself, in 206 BC, ivory was becoming rarer.

Under the Shang and Zhou dynasties, the basic and enduring pattern of Chinese society was set: at the head the king or emperor, who delegated power to vassal lords; below him the nobility, who governed the people and collected the taxes; below them the common people, the taxpayers; and at the bottom the slave classes. The ruler was the Son of Heaven, entrusted with ensuring the peaceful and harmonious life of the population; the service rendered to society by the governing class, whose members had attained their noble position because of their personal merits and those of their ancestors, was regarded as indispensable.

The Han Dynasty: 206 BC–AD 220

The Han period has been regarded with considerable respect by later generations. Politically it was a relatively stable time, when significant cultural and material advances were made. The economy became increasingly prosperous and the population expanded, and a gentry class arose, as did a class of wealthy merchants, providing a stimulus for the production of superior consumer goods and generating new ideas.

Historical records note the transfer of elephants and ivory from southern regions in the form of tribute but little else is noted about ivory at this time.

The Han showed an intuitive and natural skill when producing representations of the domestic and everyday objects they observed around them, such as animals, farms and human beings, and their treatment of these subjects conveyed a delightful sense of play and humour.

The graves and burial sites of officials and landowners of the Han Dynasty tended to include objects of all types. The mourners even placed bamboo slips, giving inventories of the contents of graves, inside the tombs with their much-respected dead. The most common Han burial wares were artefacts of bronze, lacquer and pottery. Vessels, clothes, incense burners, knives and other practical objects were also included, and there were many ornaments. Pendants, beads of opal, jade, amber, gold, quartz and marble were interred, and some rare ornaments made in ivory.

From a Han tomb near Nanchang, Jiangxi province, some ivory scabbard fittings have been excavated, and these relate to similar objects in jade. It is likely that the Han used ivory for inlay work, jewellery fittings and mounts, and there is a reference to 'elephant teeth mats' (none of which have survived) being disapproved of as symbols of luxury. These mats may possibly have been similar to latter-day fans from India, which are woven from split ivory filaments.

Also in Jiangxi province, at a tomb near Nanchang, five objects made of ivory were discovered, four bi and one yuan. These are flat discs, each with a central cavity. The difference between the yuan disc and the bi is the size of this central cavity, which is larger in the case of the yuan. The rare example is the yuan; most examples found to date are made of jade. These discs date from the neolithic period, and various ideas and theories on their use or meaning have been suggested. However, no historical records explain their use, and the best and safest category in which to list them is that of the symbols associated with burial and death. The Han period offers us some help with its examples; and the compiler of ritual texts, who used ancient sources for his work, describes the bi as a symbol of the sky. It was apparently used by the emperor in the performing of sacrifices to heaven. The bi in the Nanchang tomb are plain on one side and have a 'grain' pattern on the other.

Other items unearthed in this group include a scabbard slide and a scabbard chape, and a pendant of a dancing figure. The relationship between these ivories and other materials is once again re-emphasized as they all have counterparts in jade. The pendant of the dancer, for example, relates to a jade example now in the Avery Brundage Collection, San Francisco.

The relative stability of the Han Dynasty gave way in about AD 220 to a long period of disunity and disturbance, with the warlords of three powerful states engaged in permanent hostility, large armies to support, and incessant conflict which led to considerable loss of life and disturbance. The ordinary peasant and his family struggled to survive in conditions of severe depression in this feudal society. Inevitably, many turned to religion as a source of comfort. Daoism was a major philosophy and belief in the China of the Han Dynasty, and in the third century AD Buddhism spread from India into China, where it met receptive ground. Buddhist attitudes offered a way of accepting life in a period when there seemed little or no hope for a future.

It is likely that ivory was still used in the inlay of chariots and furniture, and for jewellery and personal adornment, but its vulnerability has left us with few examples from these troubled times.

Inevitably, there must have been some transport of ivory to China as trade continued with other areas of Asia, and the teachings and artistic influences of the wandering Buddhist monks must have manifested themselves with some representations of the Buddha in ivory, as well as in other materials such as stone and marble.

The third to seventh centuries in China

An ivory group, now in the Charles B. Hoyt Collection in Boston, was in all probability made in the Six Dynasties (AD 221–589). This carving is a female figure, naked from the waist upwards, riding on a tortoise. The art historian Soame Jenyns, writing in 1953, suggested it was Tang period (AD 618–906), but more recent work by James Watt indicates an earlier period, as the hairstyle relates to that of certain pottery figures excavated in tombs in the Nanjing area. The figure has lost its arms, and suffered some considerable distress, but the features of the face are still reasonably clear. Faint traces of a blue paste suggest it was decorated, as we know many ivories were. The tortoise is unusual; it was generally depicted with a stele central to its back, a combination frequently found at burial sites.

Ivories from the intervening years between the Han period, ending in AD 220, and the Tang period, beginning in AD 618, are scarce in number, or may not have been placed accurately in their period. The present methods of dating carvings in ivory are, first, archaeological and in relation to objects found in the same tomb and at similar levels, and, second, stylistic, similar to the approach employed in dating jades. Jade is, however, in greater supply, for it is extremely resilient and resistant to decay. Pottery can now be dated by the thermoluminescence method, but this test has not proved successful with ivory. It appears that there is as yet no scientific technique which can be employed to date ivory accurately. Radiocarbon and similar tests may indicate the dates of certain pieces, but the test requires the destruction of a certain amount of the material, and can only be employed very sparingly and specifically.

Towards the end of the sixth century, the various states and kingdoms of China were reunified under the Sui (581–618), whose waterway projects improved the connection between the north and south, but this was a short-lived dynasty. Military disasters led to its downfall, and it was followed by the golden period of the Tang.

The Tang Dynasty: AD 618–907

It is frustrating that so little ivory survives from this time. A tradition of sculpture was established, flowered and matured during the succeeding centuries. The temptation to imagine the kind of ivory carvings produced under the Tang is reinforced by the existence of a fine example of Buddhist sculpture in ivory, now in the Cleveland Museum of Art. This is a stand or pedestal, circular in form with bands of beading and variously modelled and carved lotus petals. The centre is occupied by four figures below a naturally depicted umbrella-like lotus leaf, separated by shaped and beaded columns. The figures are particularly well carved, rounded and detailed, and can be related to other Chinese figures and, more importantly, to those from other cultures.

Many of the features are similar to Chinese sculpture in stone, and the lotus petal bands and the beading, which relate to Sassanian art, are to be found in Chinese cave sculptures of the late sixth century. The figures themselves bear a close resemblance to the pottery figures of tomb guardians, known as Lokapalas. They also seem to be related to atlantid figures, particularly those produced in Gandhara, in north-west India, the home of Graeco-Bactrian art from the first century BC, and to the figures found at the great Buddhist *stupa* in Sanchi, Madhya Pradesh, who are grouped in fours on the West Gate and stand with their arms raised, short and corpulent, with sashes, ribbons and long earrings. The four figures on the pedestal are associated with the earth, abundance and wealth and are representatives of the four Lokapalas.

The petals carved on the ivory pedestal indicate a sixth-century or seventh-century date. This figure recurs frequently in the Chinese repertoire.

It is found as a supporter of incense burners, ice pails and all manner of other vessels, lasting in modified form even to the seventeenth or eighteenth century.

No one would dispute the importance of the Tang people and their creative energy in what was to be one of the great periods of aesthetic excellence in China, and indeed all Asia. The dynasty was founded in 618 by one of the most famous figures in Chinese history, Li Shih-min, who first placed his father on the throne, fought a civil war for about a decade and assumed the throne himself in 627. His reign was dynamic, cosmopolitan and intellectually enlightened. The ideas and material artefacts of other cultures were of particular interest to the Chinese of the Tang times and inevitably one of the precious rare materials that was transported into China was ivory. There are numerous references to its desirability and to the fact that it was imported both as trade goods and as tribute.

The government systems and bureaucracies of China have frequently been plagued with corruption and the pillaging of state property. The eunuchs were probably the most rapacious and infamous group in this respect. One official is recorded as sending his family pearls and endless boxes of ivory.

By the seventh and eighth centuries the capital of Tang China, Chang-an (modern-day Sian), had become the largest and most cosmopolitan city in the world. It encompassed a vast area and approximately two million people occupied its buildings and suburbs. All religions were tolerated, and trade was so popular that it continued into the night. Amid the jade, agate, crystal, glass and other luxury goods, ivory was traded, always popular as fittings and jewellery, and for personal adornment.

The Tang emperors lived in the Imperial City, which was forbidden to ordinary people. They must have had their own supply of ivory as trained elephants were sent to Chang-an during the second half of the seventh century and the early eighth century. Later in the early ninth century General Zhang Zhou recaptured two Annamese towns. His booty included various war elephants. The Chinese were particularly interested in foreign animals and the importing of 'fire-breathing' horses had affected their military capabilities dramatically in earlier times. Although they were aware of the use of elephants by the Indians in war the Chinese never employed them for this purpose themselves, preferring to exhibit them in the Imperial Palace environs as curiosities and to use them in entertainment and ceremony. Elephants at the Tang court were taught to dance and bow, and in 705 the Emperor Zhongzong watched a stage-managed battle at the southern gate of Luoyang.

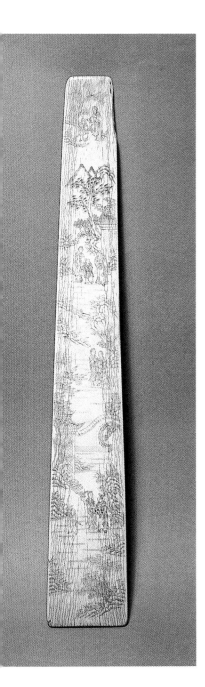

Legends and stories about unusual or magically endowed elephants became prevalent at the courts of the Tang emperors. It is often difficult to separate fact from fiction in Chinese writings and these accounts are no exception. The Cambodian kings were said to have thousands of war elephants, which they handled with regal authority. A Sanskrit inscription of 909 tells of the King of Champa who shone by his splendour in the battlefield 'in the four regions of which the sounds of war drums were drowned by the roars of gigantic beautiful elephants'. Descriptions of the king say that he was surrounded by elephants when he made public appearances, which must have been impressive. An official mission to Yunnan expressed surprise to find that aristocratic families owned elephants and used them as beasts of burden, like cattle and horses in China. The people of the Malay peninsula, the Thais and the Burmese were known for their use of the elephant and they supplied much of the ivory used by the carvers in Chang-an, but some domestic consignments would still have been supplied from the Chinese southern provinces. Legends of elephants motionless with fear at the sound of barking dogs emerge from the ranks of these southern ivory hunters. Trained elephants also came, more rarely, from Sumatra and in 746 an arrival from Iran is recorded.

Elephants sent as tribute to the imperial courts were kept in the stables, fed on beans and rice, and clothed in the winter with felt blankets and sheepskins. Occasionally an emperor would be gripped by a desire to economize; it is said that Dezong, who assumed the imperial position in 780, commanded that thirty-two Cambodian elephants be released.

Although examples of ivory from the Tang and earlier periods are not abundant we are aware of what carvers produced and clients commissioned. There was a tendency towards the production of small delicate artefacts. Jewellery was always favoured and hairpins and comb backs were popular. Chopsticks are obvious. One of the greatest uses was the inlay of ivory into other works of art and furniture. The carriages and palanquins of officials and the royal household were made from a variety of exotic materials such as jade, leather, wood, gold and ivory. The imperial carriages were said to have been decorated with a symbolic blue dragon and equipped with an embroidered blue umbrella in three tiers, surmounted by a universal mountain, and for a normal progress an ivory carriage was employed.

The hu

One ivory artefact whose dating has been the subject of much uncertainty is the 'hu'. Made throughout several centuries, admired for its shape, purity and colour, it is associated both with the Forbidden City and with the so-called 'scholar's taste'. The restrained qualities inherent in the hu have gained new admirers recently. An ivory tablet that can be formed in a variety of shapes and sizes, it is usually entirely plain and often has an attractive curve. Hus are referred to in various Tang texts but examples were made throughout continuing dynasties and the interest in things ancient and old led the Chinese to reproduce, copy, and style much of their later art on earlier examples, inspired by respect for the great works of art made in supposedly illustrious dynasties.

The hu was used by senior officials during imperial ceremonies. Only officials of the fifth rank and over were allowed to have ivory hus, other ranks had to use examples made of wood and bamboo. Privy councillors apparently picked up the ritual tablets from a rack at the doorways of the basilica whereas lesser officials generally kept theirs in bags carried by flunkeys (it was an offence to retain them but by the later Ming period (1368–1644) this control had become slack). One heir to the Tang throne, at the age of twenty, in a kingly robe and crown, and girded with a jade-finished sword, is recorded carrying an ivory tablet decorated with gold. Surviving examples confirm Tang dynasty descriptions of those carried by officials as being rounded at the top and square at the base.

Occasionally hus were inscribed with a poem, a symbol or an official's category. They are particularly pleasing to handle and view, and as works of art they usually rely entirely on their form, shape, colour and texture to please the aesthetic senses.

Tang sculpture

An ivory statue which has been offered as an example of Tang sculpture is that of a figure with a child suckling. If it *is* of the Tang period, it is the only example yet known. It does bear a strong resemblance to Tang dynasty sculpture completed in other materials. The subject is Hariti, an ogress who devoured children but who was reformed by the Buddha and became an image of mother love in Indian statuary. This figure, which is without its head, stands on a circular lotus base, is enveloped in a robe and sways to one side with its hips and leg leaning forward, all features to be found in genuine Tang sculpture.

Ivories in the Shoso-in

The most important and useful groups of Chinese works of art, datable to the Tang period and containing objects made from ivory, are in Japan, in the celebrated Shoso-in at Nara. The Japanese were strongly influenced by the artistic and intellectual developments on the Chinese mainland, particularly in the eighth century. Islamic and Indian works of art and artistic styles that affected the Chinese were carried to Japan by merchants and Buddhist priests, by students and ambassadors, causing much attention. Chinese works of art were treated with particular respect. Many were retained by the imperial Japanese court.

In 751 at Nara, the capital of Japan, the great temple monastery of Todai-ji was completed. As well as various pagodas and halls, it had approximately fifty warehouses for Buddhist paraphernalia and regalia. The Shoso-in was the most important of these.

After the Emperor Shomu died on 2 May 756, his widow, the Empress Komyo, handed over his household and personal possessions to be dedicated at the Todai-ji and stored in the Shoso-in. The dedication is poetic but in one tract usefully specific: 'For the sake of the late Emperor, the various articles which he handled, the girdles, ivory sceptres, bows and arrows, collection of calligraphy, musical instruments and the rest, which are in truth rare national treasures, I donate to the Todai-ji.'

So the Shoso-in is a unique repository of works of art gathered from many cultures at that time and fortunately containing examples of ivories carved in China. Its ivories are the most important group to survive from the Tang period. They were stored in excellent conditions, and have suffered very little disturbance. Virtually intact, the group is a major landmark for the dating of Tang antiques.

In addition to the emperor's flat ivory and whalebone sceptres, rhinoceros horn and gold and ivory sections inlaid with coloured stones combine in a priest's staff to form a beautiful and elegant object. The ivory fittings are of remarkably high quality, some pierced and carved in the form of overlapping leaves. Two confronting birds, with wings outstretched and leaves in their beaks, balanced on curling leaves, form the main section. This staff is a *tour de force* of very high quality.

The Song Dynasty: 960–1279

For nearly three centuries the Tang Dynasty prospered. Its cosmopolitan attitudes led refugees from other lands to seek shelter in China. There was a great flowering of artistic achievement. But the dynasty ended dramatically: legend relates that the last Tang emperor became infatuated with his son's wife, Yang Guifei, and the capital was sacked by rebel armies. China entered another period of disrupted rule and a series of short-lived emperors who followed each other in rapid succession. In 960 China was at last reunited under General Zhao Kuangyin. He founded the Song Dynasty, which was characterized by intense nationalism and an assertion of traditional values, in marked contrast to the reflective attitudes of the Tang.

Ivory came to the Song court as tribute, and records were kept of the weight and quantity of tusks shipped. One interesting source of tribute ivory was the city of Khotan, near the Kunlun mountain range, which is historically better known for its shipments of jade.

State carriages were ornamented with ivory, so were horse-fittings, and it is known that pomanders were made from it. A workshop under the office of Wensi Yuan was noted as producing ivory, and thirty-one other workshops were employed in the production of artefacts for ceremonial and for everyday use in the palace. Regrettably, no single object can be dated with certainty to the Song period. One of the possible candidates for Song attribution is the celebrated plaque, now in the Metropolitan Museum of Art, New York, which is decorated with long-necked, curling dragons; however, it is more probably late Yuan (*c.*1300–68) or early Ming (*c.*1368–1450), or even a mid Ming revival (*c.*1450–1550).

During the time of the Song, there was a gradual but constant movement of population from the countryside into the towns. Industries

Below: Ivory and whalebone sceptres which belonged to the Emperor of Japan and were given to the temple monastery of Todai-ji following his death in AD 756. *c.*11 in. (28 cm) long.

such as metallurgy, mining and silk weaving expanded considerably.

Constant invasions and land disputes in the north culminated in 1127 in an invasion by a group of Tartars, formerly allied with the Chinese, who seized the capital. This resulted in the period of the Southern Song (1127–1279) and the dramatic expansion of Hangzhou into the Southern Song's capital. Sufficient evidence remains to show us a life of great luxury and wealth, with the upper and middle strata of society devoted to pleasure and the pursuit of artistic interests, and the emperor riding in procession to the ritual purification, led by decorated and adorned elephants, while the earth shook to the sound of drums and trumpets.

Hangzhou became celebrated for its manufacture of jewellery, combs, necklaces and pendants, and shops in the city sold 'ivory combs at Fei's, folding fans and painted fans at the Coal Bridge'.

Meanwhile, in the north the Liao Dynasty had established itself. Due to its military strength and mobility, this dynasty quickly encompassed most of the resident Chinese population. Metal workers, potters, and other Chinese possessing agricultural and artistic skills, were encouraged to pursue their livelihood, and the Liao continued the practice of using state carriages. Very little ivory can be dated to the period of the Liao's domination, but it is reported that an ivory comb was found at a Liao tomb excavation in 1980.

The Yuan Dynasty: 1276–1368

The conflicts in the north of China continued as the nomadic tribes fought amongst themselves, until Genghis Khan unified the warring factions and his Mongols, the Golden Horde, spread swiftly west and south, as far as Hungary, Russia and Persia. The descendants of Genghis Khan eventually completed the conquest of the whole of China, and one of them, Kubla Khan, was visited in the late thirteenth century by the traveller Marco Polo.

This Mongol dynasty was called the Yuan. Its leaders had no relevant experience to enable them to control and organize a country the size of China, and so they sought the assistance of native Chinese scholars as administrators. Trade routes were made safer, canal-works improved and the arts encouraged. The technique of painting in underglaze blue on porcelain was perfected at this time, and resulted in some remarkable and innovative decoration.

It is known that the Yuan used ivory, and Berthold Laufer, the American sinologist, refers to 'a bureau for carvings on ivory and rhinoceros horn' established in 1263, with a workforce of 150, where 'couches, tables, implements and general ornaments inlaid with ivory and horn, were turned out for the imperial household'. If this statement is correct, and such a quantity of ivorywork was produced, either this has perished or items have not been correctly identified. Writers and scholars have attempted to guess, by making comparisons with other datable materials, what Yuan ivories might be, but few are accepted by present-day scholars.

In 1321, the Emperor Yingzong ordered some fine carriages, and at least one of these was completed, made primarily from jade. Dragonhead finials were a popular motif of the time, often carved from ivory, and we know of a Yuan design for a carriage which bore ivory chairs, but for the most part we must content ourselves with imaginative speculation. Personal items such as belt plaques and jewellery were certainly made, as they were during other times. There is seldom a complete break in traditions, and influences move from one era to the next.

The Yuan Mongols ruled China for nearly a hundred years, but the strength and vigour which characterized the earlier years of conquest soon gave way to debauchery and decadence. The last

Below: Two large ivory sculptures. Almost certainly pre-Ming, perhaps late Song or Yuan; 10 in. (25.5 cm). Stylistically, these are very close to an ivory Buddha dated AD 1107. The right-hand figure holds the 'wish-granting' jewel in the right hand and a lotus stem in the left. The swastikas on their breast symbolize *Wan* (ten thousand years).

Yuan ruler was described in Chinese annals as being extremely depraved, and though Chinese historians tended to ascribe most disasters to depravity and corruption, in many cases this may indeed be correct.

Groups of scholarly Chinese nobles urged the reinstitution of the state examination systems. These men, previously occupied in government and bureaucracy, had turned more and more to writing poetry, novels and drama. Confucianism, recognized as the state religion under the Han, and now revived, became more and more popular, and secret societies proliferated. A group called the Red Turbans drew its support and leaders from the merchants, artisans and peasant classes.

The Yuan were eventually absorbed by the people they had conquered. They had had an invigorating effect on the Chinese nation, opened up routes to the west and injected new ideas into the decorative arts; and it has recently been recognized that their contribution in these areas was far greater than had been formerly acknowledged.

The Ming Dynasty: 1368–1644

In 1356, Nanking fell to the forces led by Zhu Yuanzhang, a former peasant and Buddhist monk. He succeeded in pushing the Mongols northwards and in 1368 assumed imperial status as Hongwu, the first emperor of the Ming Dynasty.

Hongwu, known as the Beggar King, was deeply suspicious of his advisers and ministers. He modelled his government on the Tang system, which concentrated power in the hands of the emperor. The Ming was the most ambitious of all the Chinese dynasties and its rule was a time of dynamic energy and progress. Maritime exploration expanded, which led to increased importation of ivory in the form of tusks. Foreign traders arrived at China's ports. Admiral Zheng, in the first quarter of the fifteenth century, led an expedition which reached the African coast, and among other treasures brought zebras, giraffes and ostriches back to the Chinese mainland. Although there is no mention of ivory, it is highly likely that some would have been included. Ma Huan, the chronicler of the voyage, refers to ivory being found in Vietnam in abundance, and mentions Thailand as an additional source. Unfortunately a considerable amount of information was destroyed by the official class, who were very deeply suspicious of overseas trade and any resulting foreign influence.

No doubt partly because of their deeply ingrained suspicion of foreigners and the West, the Chinese seldom travelled by sea as other races did, and this reinforced their insular and inward-looking attitude. At the same time, it resulted in stronger maritime powers being able to impose their will, first on the China Seas, then on China's trading ports, and eventually on the centre of government.

During the Ming period, Asian seamen, such as Indians, Thais and Malays, brought to China the luxuries and trade goods that China did not itself possess. The Arabs were an early source of African ivory. The *Ge gu yao lun*, 'The Essential Criteria of Antiques' (1388), remarks that the tusks obtained from the Barbarians were superior, longer and thicker than those from domestic sources.

An interesting reference in 1589 concerns goods passing through the port of Quanzhou. Ivory 'made up into utensils is taxed at 1 silver liang per 100 jin. That not made up into utensils pays 5 silver qian per 100 jin.' What these utensils were we are left, frustrated, to imagine.

We know that ivory continued as a desirable luxury and was used for items such as jewellery and toys during the early Ming period (c. 1368–1450), a time which was politically and economically stable. The capital was moved from Nanking to Beijing at this time, and a considerable amount of building work took place. This was a time of introspection and revival of traditional values and habits, but foreigners were accepted to a limited extent, and the Portuguese, who succeeded the Arabs as traders on the China coast, became influential in the ivory trade and played an important role in the style and form which subsequent ivory carving adopted.

At this time, when the Ming were enjoying a period of restoration and traditionalism, western cultures were competing fiercely in a dynamic explosion of conflict and expansion. Romantic stories of far-off civilizations and untold wealth proliferated in Europe. The possibilities of riches, trade, knowledge and cultural benefits prompted monarchs and merchants to finance journeys of exploration. For many centuries China had held a fascination for the West. The sea route was a considerable prize fiercely competed for by the dominant naval powers such as Portugal, Spain, England and France.

The Portuguese Vasco da Gama braved the route round the Cape of Good Hope in 1497. Other explorers and traders were to follow. Many Portuguese expeditions sailing to the east at this time stopped off in Africa and India, major sources of ivory. The Portuguese established important bases on the trade route to China at Orissa, Malacca and Goa, the latter two being the main trading bases and the most important for the passage of ivory. They initiated their dealings with the Chinese by sending military forces under the leadership of Simao de Andrade, and after their capture of Tunmen were conceded, c. 1565, rights to settle on the island of Macao, at the mouth of the Pearl River, in the South China Sea.

In 1580, the Spanish united with the Portuguese

Below: Ivory seals. Seventeenth- and eighteenth-century; the one at top left, carved with a deer and a lingxi spray, is 2 in. (5 cm) tall. From left to right, top to bottom, the second is a gnarled trunk carved with prunus, the fourth inscribed with a single character, the eighth in the form of a Wangmen coin, the eleventh an elephant, the twelfth a horse whose seal reads 'Yufu'.

under one Iberian crown. They struck a bargain: Portugal would keep Macao, Spain take the Philippines. Their influence on the subjects and styles adopted by the Chinese ivory carvers emanated mostly from their Philippine trading operations.

In China at this time, we can trace domestic production through the office of the Yu yong jian, organized by the imperial eunuchs: 'They acquire and manage all screens, ornaments and utensils used in the Imperial Presence. There is a Buddha workshop, and other workshops. They manufacture [*zaoban*] all hardwood couches, tables, cupboards, and shelves set in the Imperial Presence, as well as dice, chess pieces, dominoes, and combs of ivory, huali, baitan, zitan, ebony, jichimu, and dishes, boxes and fan handles of inlaid and incised and carved lacquer.'

Little had changed in hundreds of years. The traditional use of ivory for small and delicate productions such as jewellery, gaming pieces and combs, explains its position as a luxury material during the mid Ming period. The supply of ivory was undoubtedly fairly limited; it was always a luxury material, and the carver must have tried to stretch it to the full and to produce as many articles as possible from the tusk.

'Scholar's taste'

Some works of art in the so-called 'scholar's taste', to be used by the intellectual or kept on his desk, must have been produced, but ivory seems to have been somewhat 'tainted', in the eyes of the purist, due to its use as a luxury material. Wen Zenheng's 'Treatise on Things that Matter' says of brush trays: 'One can use zitan wood, ebony, or finely inlaid bamboo, only they must not be made of jade or ivory.' The same author dismisses fans made of ivory in similar terms.

Works of art made for the imperial court, throughout China's history, have usually been very much more luxurious than those appreciated

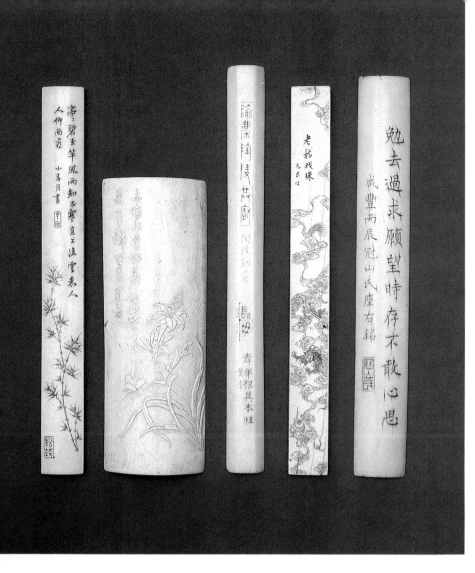

Above: Four scroll weights and (*second left*) a wrist rest. Qing Dynasty (1644–1912); 10¼ in. (25.9 cm) long (weight, *far left*). This first weight is inscribed with a poem, calligraphic seals and bamboo sprays; the second with calligraphy; the third with dragons and flaming pearls; the fourth with calligraphy. The wrist rest is carved in low relief with a lily spray and a butterfly below a poem, and is signed Mei Gong Bai.

by the literati, who also condemned the domestic novelties and artefacts made for the merchant and gentry classes. Ivory does appear to have been acceptable to the Chinese 'scholar's taste' as mounts on the ends of scroll rollers, and terminals on some scrolls exhibit the most pleasing depth of colour and such tactile qualities as can be found only in ivory which has been left undecorated but extensively handled over many years. Another area for the use of ivory acceptable to some scholars was that of seals, and this is another very suitable application. Chinese carvers exhibited remarkable talent and ability to elicit from these smaller works of art that same quality and monumentality inherent in larger sculptures. They sometimes carved figures but their best work is often seen in the little animals crouching on top of the seals. The sculptural qualities and the fact that these seals were handled in close proximity to painting and writing materials gave the best of them a mellow patina and well-worn effect.

Gao Lian's 'Eight Discourses on the Art of Living', written in 1591, lists carvers of an earlier period, compares their abilities and indicates ivory's appropriateness for small artefacts. The carvers worked in horn, incense wood, zitan wood and ivory, and the objects produced varied

from small cases, fan pendants, hairpins and incense boxes, to toggles. In Gao Shiqui's 'Notes Made During Court Recesses', he comments on historical customs and actions in the Imperial Palace. He notes that the Emperor Jiajing (1522–67) was in the habit of making gifts to his favourite officials, and that 'fan pendants in the shape of Immortals, in crystal or ivory' were among them.

Utensils essential to the Chinese poet-scholar were his brushes. Again, these were made from many different materials, the humblest being bamboo, and jade probably the most sophisticated and luxurious. Good mid Ming lacquer examples are known. An existing example in ivory, carved with a design similar to lacquer examples, can be dated to the later Ming. However, the Ming connoisseur Xiang Yuanbian is dismissive of ivory for brush handles (he considered bamboo best for this purpose), and Zhaozhe, in his 'Fine Collected Miscellanies', similarly disapproves.

The wrist rest, an object which was originally formed from a split-bamboo brush pot to support the artist's wrist while he worked, was probably, again, considered decadent by the purist scholar, and if produced in the Ming period would almost certainly have been plain in form. A wrist rest owned by Sir Percival David bears the signature of and a poem by Wen Feng, who lived between 1498 and 1573, and the seal of Xiang Yuan Lian, a well-known collector and connoisseur of porcelain and paintings; but this rest, decorated on the underside with sharply carved lotus, crayfish and geese, is a Qing creation, dating to the eighteenth or nineteenth century. Because of the lack of definite, datable material, it is all too easy to accept signatures or hints of antiquity at their face value.

The brush pot was a cylindrical vessel used to hold the artist's brushes. Were we in a position to date any, with confidence, as Ming, they would tend to be plain, and slimmer than their bamboo relatives, due to the slender tusks used.

Ivory-inlaid furniture

The traditional use of ivory for inlay work in furniture decoration was noted by Gaspar de Cruz in 1556. Visiting Canton, he observed a 'very riche' testered bed, 'made and wrought with ivory and of a sweet wood which they call Cayolaque, and of sandalwood, that was priced at four hundred crowns'.

We have no surviving examples of ivory-inlaid furniture from the Ming period and can only speculate that the decoration used would have been similar to that used on other works of art such as lacquer. A pair of dragon plaques, now in the British Museum, likely to be Ming, were probably used on a panel or screen, or in a piece of furniture.

Ming figure carvings

Of all the ivory products of the Ming period, the most numerous, and in many cases those exhibiting the finest qualities of workmanship, are the figure carvings.

Little exists prior to the mid Ming period, when the Chinese carvers began to produce a quantity of figures for domestic purposes, and other examples for the foreigners who had played a major part in stimulating the whole industry.

Foreign influence emanated from the Spanish-controlled Philippine islands, and the Spanish commissioned religious figures, particularly those depicting the Virgin and Child, from the Chinese carvers of this time. Zhangzhou, situated on the Fujian coast, was a city where these carvings proliferated. It was very much a free port and had a nobility and a merchant class who acted independently of the central government. These influential groups were devoted to trade and entrepreneurial activities, and in such a cosmopolitan and lively environment the carvers were encouraged to produce the different religious subjects which various clients commissioned. Buddhist, Daoist and Christian subjects were all produced in quantity at Zhangzhou.

For several centuries the Chinese had varied their preferences for different religions, but gradually the faiths began to merge and the old conflicts and struggles were lost in a single, popular, all-encompassing religion. Buddhism, Daoism and Confucianism, which had often been in strident opposition, somehow found common ground. This compromise resulted in certain deities being commonly adopted, and one popular figure depicted in ivory is Laozi, the legendary

Below: Chinese god of longevity. Ming Dynasty (sixteenth-century); 7½ × 3⅞ × 3⅝ in. (19.2 × 9.9 × 9.2 cm). The elongation of the skull is characteristic.

founder of Daoism. Other Daoist divinities and related deities proved popular subjects for the carvers when producing ivories for their domestic market. Daoism bases its philosophy on the study and acceptance of the natural order of things; striving to alter situations was considered undesirable. Inaction and a relaxed attitude to the flow of life are appropriate. In time the religion assumed mystical qualities and became closely linked with long life and immortality. Many of the related deities emphasize this aspect of the faith. The longevity figures are a favourite subject, and when skilfully carved they display the features most pleasing in an ivory figure, particularly when they are intelligently combined with the curve of the tusk. These figures invariably have a large cranium (this exaggeration has sometimes been interpreted as phallic). The bearded sage often holds a staff of gnarled wood and sometimes another symbol of long life, the peach. Sometimes a deer curls around his legs like a domestic dog, and young attendants with offerings may be included. The figures usually have a most pleasing expression, and smile beneficiently in a peaceful and contented way. The best of them have assumed the worn and mellow tone associated with frequent handling.

Other longevity figures hold fans, or peach sprays, and may sometimes be depicted seated. A beautiful example, now in New York, is a masterpiece among small sculptures. It captures the stillness and peace of its subject in ivory which has attained a fine mellow brown tone. Various figures carry peaches, some in groups and some singly. The goddess Xi Wang Mu, the Queen Mother of the West, dwelt in a paradise in the Kunlun Mountains, where peaches that ripened only once in every three thousand years would bestow immortality on those fortunate enough to eat them. In paintings, she is usually depicted as a beautiful Chinese princess, but in ivory carvings her attendants, holding trays or branches of peaches, seem to outnumber representations of the goddess herself.

The fertile mythology of the Daoist sect gave the fourteenth-century carvers other interesting subjects in the Eight Immortals, who were said to have lived at various periods and to have acquired immortality through their studies of nature's secrets. Possessing all kinds of talents and eccentricities, each represents a condition of life.

The most exaggeratedly posed figure is usually that of Li Tiekuai, a sage who one day took up residence in the body of a recently deceased beggar. The Chinese carver produces an actively posed individual holding a crutch and a pilgrim's gourd, his head raised and carved in a caricature-like manner with open mouth and wide bulging eyes. In total contrast, He Xiangu is generally portrayed as a passive, sweet-faced girl with the minimum of decorative detail. Her body is usually clad in a long flowing robe, and she holds a pestle and mortar in her hands. She emphasizes the Daoist predilection for alchemy, as the drug in her mortar, crushed mica, gave her the power of flight. Modelled in a similar style is the slender male figure, Han Xiangzi. The Chinese carver, here again, invariably uses the natural shape of the tusk to impart a swaying pose to the young man, who usually has a passive expression and holds a flute to his lips. Han Xiangzi was the patron of musicians and his flute was said to attract birds and even beasts of prey by its sweet sounds. He had little understanding of the value of money and would scatter any that he had on the ground.

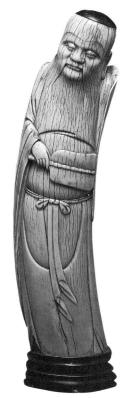

Above: An ivory figure of the Immortal Zhongli Quan. Further examples are shown in colour, with other Immortals, on pages 244–5.

Right: He Xiangu with her pestle and mortar, and another female Immortal swathed in a robe. Both Ming Dynasty; 11 in. (28 cm) and 10½ in. (26.7 cm) high respectively.

Far right: An ivory figure of Guandi with his attendants Guanping and Zhou Cang. Ming Dynasty; 5½ in. (14 cm).

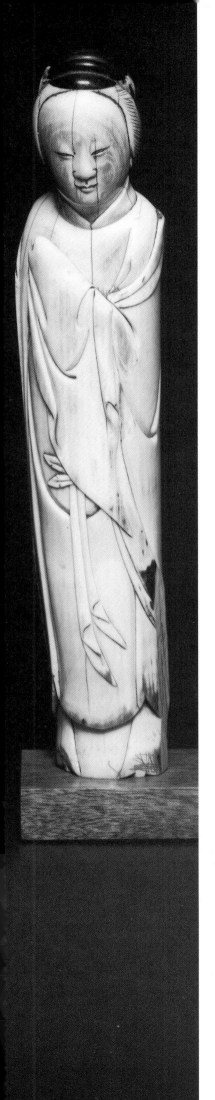

The Daoist standing figures depicting the Eight Immortals are usually positioned in a set pose, and if there is a suggestion of movement or activity, seem to assume a modelled position. Other Daoist figures seem to possess, in contrast, a more natural posture and facial expression. There are Daoist Immortals positioning hairpins, adjusting their caps, turning to smile, or in the act of walking. As many Daoists lived in the mountains as rustics, they are often attired in finely carved and detailed clothes made from leaves or feathers, giving the Ming carver a chance to display his technical virtuosity in handling detail. These Ming carvers had the ability to produce finely detailed and intricate work, but resisted doing so where plainness and form were sufficient to make their statement, which is to their credit, although to please some patrons, particularly Europeans, they sometimes embellished when they might have preferred simplicity.

The repertoire of the carver working for patrons who required Daoist subjects was greater than that of the carver who worked on Buddhist examples. Two figures common to both religions are Wen Chang and Guandi.

Wen Chang, patron god of the literati, is usually depicted in the calm serene pose of a scholar and an examiner of candidates for official positions, and his support was sought by those taking the official examinations. The paleness of one of the most successful figures of Wen Chang, now in Stockholm, effectively emphasizes the scholarly and reclusive character of the subject.

Totally different was Guandi, a figure based on the military hero Guan (died AD 219) and equivalent to Mars, the god of war in classical mythology. He proved to be one of the most popular Chinese gods, honoured in the Buddhist monastery, worshipped in temples dedicated to him and in the home, adopted by various trade and merchant professions, and regarded as the tutelary deity of money-making enterprises and good luck in business. He was also sometimes revered as a god of literature.

Guandi was originally worshipped in connection with the Confucian ideas on ancestral respect, and his intercession was sought by the living to influence the affairs of state; he was finally deified by the Ming emperor Wanli in 1594.

With Guandi as his subject the ivory carver has the opportunity to portray a figure full of masculine vigour, often posed with his leg raised, arm uplifted and forehead creased, a stern expression on his face. A finely patinated, mellow example, now in the Avery Brundage Collection, San Francisco, is a good example of a Ming ivory: a full-bodied Guandi, seated in a hoop-backed chair, the pose animated, the expression forceful, the detail and robes depicted naturally. In another good example shown in a British Museum exhibition, Guandi was accompanied by his attendants, Guanping and Zhou Cang. Sets of ivory figures are often split and it is always fortunate as well as rare when such a set remains intact.

Opposite: An ivory pestle and mortar. 1650–75; 7 in. (18 cm) long (pestle). This was among the earliest Chinese works of art taken to Europe by Danish seamen. See also page 243.

Above: Guanyin, the goddess of Mercy, holding a child. Ming Dynasty; 7½ in. (19 cm). Another statuette of Guanyin is shown in colour on page 244.

Remarkably few figures of the Buddha himself survive in ivory. Because ivory was always a luxury material, it may have been considered, in the Ming period, unsuitable for use in depicting such a serious and important figure. The Buddhist religion was concerned with the after-life and with rebirth, whereas Daoist ivory figures in the home could be begged for assistance and rewards here and now. The exception is the fine and peacefully portrayed Buddha, formerly in the Spencer Churchill Collection, which sits with legs crossed and hands lightly touching, an expression of gentle meditation on its face. Several age cracks do not disturb its appeal, and its colour is yellow to golden brown, with darker areas at the edges of its clothing and robes, suggesting these were emphasized at one time by the possible use of paint or lacquer.

One of the most popular subjects for Buddhist ivory figures was Guanyin, the Chinese goddess of mercy. She corresponds to the Bodhisattva Avalokiteśvara, one of the most important creations to emerge from Buddhist mythology and in some cases worshipped as an equal to the Buddha himself. Bodhisattvas 'looked down with compassion' on earth's creatures. Until the twelfth century Avalokiteśvara was depicted as a male in Chinese figures, thereafter as a female.

Various personifications of Guanyin found favour in Chinese art. The water-moon or *shuiyue* Guanyin observes the moon reflected in water and uses it as an image to emphasize the lack of substance in the material world; the white-robed Guanyin was introduced from Tibet in the eighth century. The Guanyin figure in China was very much a personification of compassion. Those wishing to bear children would seek the help of the goddess 'who hears the sounds or prayers of the world'.

Some mid Ming ivories of Guanyin are reduced but close representations of the large wood figures seated in temples and dating to the Song and Yuan periods (thirteenth to fifteenth centuries). The ivory figures assume the position of royal ease. This relaxed pose indicates a princely and worldly nature. In addition to long flowing robes they are invariably decked out with strands of princely jewellery. The figures are often of a mellow dark brown colour and frequently, due to their pose and high head-dress, remind western observers of European Gothic carvings of the Madonna.

The Chinese ivory carvers were ideally placed to produce religious images for the churches established by Portuguese missionaries in the mid and late sixteenth century. Figures of the crucified Christ, the Infant Jesus and the Madonna were commissioned. Some of these ivories may have been produced in Macao but another likely source is Canton, where export art was later to blossom into a great industry.

The Jesuit missionaries who arrived in and after 1581 were to play a fascinating role at the courts of the Chinese emperors; they provided useful and interesting historical records of their years in Beijing. The Spanish commissioned a variety of wares from the Chinese communities, both in the Philippines (where there was a large community) and on the mainland. In 1590 Bishop Salazar wrote to Philip II of Spain:

'The handicrafts pursued by the Spaniards have all died out because people buy their clothes and shoes from the Sangleys [the term used by the Spanish to describe the Chinese] who are very good craftsmen in Spanish fashion, and make everything at a very low cost. They are so skilful and clever that as soon as they see any object made by a Spanish workman, they reproduce it with exactness . . . When I arrived no Sangley knew how to paint anything, but now . . . they have produced marvellous work with both the brush and chisel, and I think that nothing more perfect could be produced than some of their ivory statues of the Child Jesus which I have seen. The churches are beginning to be finished with the images which the Sangleys made and which were greatly lacked before.'

Examples of these Christian ivories carved by the Chinese survive to this day, many in Mexican collections as well as Spanish and Portuguese. The Christ Child is usually depicted in two forms: standing with one hand raised in blessing, and sometimes holding an orb in the other hand; or recumbent with one hand supporting his head. If the child has hair, it is usually curly. Some of these carvings may represent the young St John the Baptist.

In 1591 Gao Lian writes: 'In Fujian, ivory is carved into human form, the workmanship of which is fine and artful; however, one cannot put them anywhere, or give them as a decent present.' This statement reinforces the idea that ivory figures were objects of luxury, although the quotes usually come from scholars and reflect their cultural snobbery. Works of art made in cloisonné enamel were also considered decadent, and described by one scholar as being fit only for women's bedrooms.

The Chinese versions of the Virgin Mary must be examined closely to differentiate between them and those carved in the west. It is even more difficult to separate them from Goanese works. There is frequently a certain stiffness about the pose of the Chinese Virgin, the arms are sometimes a little rigid, the eyes are often almond-shaped, and although the carvers endeavoured to give it the wider European shape, the eyelid is still depicted with an oriental breadth. This giveaway is found in other oriental portrayals of Europeans, and the eyes betray the origin even when all other details are faithfully reproduced. The Virgin's face

Above: An ivory of a praying Madonna from the Portuguese colony of Goa. Seventeenth-century; 7 in. (18 cm). From 1600 on, the Portuguese imported ivory from Goa into China and the Chinese carvers rapidly adapted their repertoire to a new Christian clientele.

often has an expression of doll-like intensity, and another clue to an oriental origin may be traces of lacquer or paint most readily detectable on the edges or corners of the garments. The characteristic stiffness and doll-like pose may be attributable to the carver's using a woodblock print as his model.

The cross-currents running through the Chinese carver's repertoire were to manifest themselves with a version of the Guanyin, posed with a child and based on the European image of the Virgin and the Infant Jesus. The child accompanying the Guanyin sometimes holds a leaf or a scroll, or may reach out an empty hand, or hold an edge of the Guanyin's robes. He is depicted in a more natural and realistic form than is the Christ Child. Rosary beads are retained in the Guanyin groups, but without a cross, and the robes are draped and tied in the Chinese manner. The goddess's face is entirely oriental in mien, and round the shoulders is often a high swirling scarf that curves in an arch – a feature of the Bodhisattva's dress which can be traced back to the figurative sculptures of the third century AD. Other attributes of Guanyin are scrolls, lotus sprays and, in later periods, the long curved ruyi sceptres with their characteristic heads.

There was, of course, a marked difference between the intended customers for whom these differing figures were made. The Virgin and Christ Child groups were for religious devotion among a foreign population; the Guanyin and Child groups were a curiosity, a novelty, for Chinese homes which could afford such luxuries.

The relationship of ivories to other works of art has to be considered, for many models in other materials were prototypes or inspirations to the ivory carver, as were the large temple figures of the Bodhisattvas. Pottery and porcelain figures provided inspiration, as did those in wood and soapstone, but some of the closest comparisons can be made with Ming bronzes, where the head of a standing figure may be turned to the same angle, the robes of a seated Guandi flow in the same folds.

One of the most fascinating relationships is between carved ivories and the white porcelain made at Dehua, still called by its nineteenth-century French name, *blanc de Chine*. Dehua and Zhangzhou (the site of much of the ivory figure production) are both in Fujian province. Early *blanc de Chine* sometimes has a mellow, yellowish white tone, bearing a close resemblance to ivory. The manufacture of porcelain began at Dehua in the Ming dynasty, probably *c.* 1500–1644. Figures were a popular subject, one of the most favoured being the Guanyin, which was similarly popular in ivory. Many of the figures in ivory can be closely compared with those in *blanc de Chine*, and details and particular charac-

teristics correspond. Some authorities feel that the *blanc de Chine* figures were made to resemble those in ivory.

Other sources of ideas were woodblock prints, many of which were reproduced in romantic novels and plays. We know that bamboo carvers sought inspiration among these prints, particularly in the seventeenth century, and Jianyang in Fujian province was famous for its printing. Clear line drawings of figures would have been ideal as subjects to be copied in other mediums.

The early seventeenth century saw the Ming Dynasty begin to decline after nearly three hundred years. Signs of weakness appeared. The debauched Emperor Wanli (1573–1619) lived in fear of assassination, surrounded by his eunuchs in the inner recesses of the Imperial Palace. There was a dramatic increase in taxation, accompanied by corruption in many areas of political and civil life.

The historian Chao I (1727–1814) wrote that 'the people were not only taxed out of existence by the local officials . . . but were also regarded as easy prey by most of the members of the educated class . . . Officials above, and privileged non-officials below, protected and covered up for each other.' In the late 1620s, famine became prevalent. While various rebel Chinese armies fought for the control of northern China, Manchurian horsemen waited for an opportune moment.

Then the last Ming emperor committed suicide, and Wu Sangui, a Chinese commander, asked the Manchus for military assistance. Once they had arrived, he was unable to get rid of them again. Various Chinese leaders endeavoured to overthrow them but in 1659 the last Ming pretenders were destroyed and the Manchu began to consolidate their hold on China.

The Qing Dynasty: 1644–1912
Sino-European trading relationships
The Jesuits maintained and consolidated their position under the Qing Dynasty established by the Manchus. Their artistic abilities and their knowledge of mathematics and astronomy won imperial favour and their influence was to reach its height in the late seventeenth century, when the European trading nations, particularly Portugal, Holland and England, were making approaches to China. These moves started slowly with diplomacy, blossomed into an expansion of trade in the eighteenth and nineteenth centuries and finally culminated in the Europeans extracting concessions from the Chinese in the late nineteenth century by force of arms.

In the seventeenth century the Europeans were trading elephant tusks for Chinese porcelain. The Portuguese transported ivory between Goa and China and the Dutch offered fine ivory carvings as gifts to the Emperor Kangxi in 1685. These shipments, however, were probably minimal

Pages 244–5: Eight Chinese ivories. Ming Dynasty; varying heights from the fifth figure, an Immortal (13 in./33 cm), to the second, another Immortal (7¾ in./20 cm). The first and third figures depict the Immortal Zhongli Quan, holding the fan with which he revives the souls of the dead. The fourth, Guanyin, with her child and rosary, bears a strong resemblance to a European Madonna. The rare matching pair of Immortals hold staffs and fans and the eighth figure, another Immortal, has a peach spray. See also page 238 for another figure of Zhongli Quan, and page 241 for Guanyin.

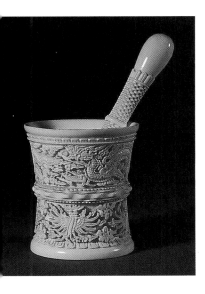

Above: The carved ivory pestle and mortar shown in colour on page 241.

compared to those of the Asian seamen and traders (the Thais were the main source and they also provided tame elephants), probably because the trade was not profitable enough to sustain European interest. A reference in 1628, in the area of Zhangzhou, reads: 'Elephant ivory can no longer be found in the prefecture, and is wholly traded by those who come into the port markets. Zhang people carve it into Immortals and that sort of thing, supplying them for the purpose of providing pleasure. Their ears, eyes, limbs and torso are all life-like. Exceptionally skilful work comes from Haicheng. Ivory chopsticks, ivory cups, ivory belt plaques and ivory fans are also to be had.'

An interesting early reference to ivory works of an erotic nature is made by Shen Defu (1578–1645), a Ming scholar, who writes that Fujian ivory carvers 'made small figures of pairs in sexual congress which were of high artistic quality'. A less explicit example is noted in a European collection. In the late Qing period this type of representation became more common and popular.

It is often virtually impossible to differentiate between late Ming and early Qing ivories. Such figures are best dated 'late sixteenth or early seventeenth century'. Tall, slender ladies were popular on underglaze blue and white porcelain and on bamboo brush pots. It is possible that ivory groups of slender females with hair-styles reminiscent of the European short-cropped medieval type are seventeenth-century; similar types in *blanc de Chine* porcelain are known and can be dated to this period.

The growing interest of European traders during this time has left us some ivories which can be definitely dated to the seventeenth century. One of the best groups of these is in Copenhagen. The first Denmark–China run by a Danish vessel was completed between 1730 and 1732, but some Danish ships had ventured to China in the late seventeenth century from their base in India. They brought back ivories which fascinated Europeans and gave stimulus to the taste for chinoiserie, that exotic idea of the romantic East which captured the European imagination. Some of the works of art and curios that found their way to Copenhagen are now in the National Archives. The collection was inventoried in the seventeenth and eighteenth centuries, and a small group of ivories is included in the seventeenth-century inventories.

A small but technically good figure is that of an Immortal in a recumbent posture, picking his ear, his bearded face with a smiling expression. As in the other figures completed in bronze, soapstone and jade, his robes are open to reveal a large, well-rounded belly. This seemingly gross character is in fact made attractive by his size (2⅓ in./6 cm)

and by the quality of the carving. Recorded in the inventory of 1674, it is described as 'a small east Indian idol of ivory', and in 1690 as 'a small seated idol of ivory'. The words 'Indian' or 'Indies' were used very broadly by all Europeans at this time, to describe works of art that came from the east, including China.

A group inventoried on several occasions (1654, 1674, 1690, 1737) is that of a man and woman embracing. In 1654 it is described as: 'Statue of ivory, five inches [12.7 cm] high, made in China, showing a man in Chinese attire embracing a woman of the same nationality. She raises one hand as if to box him on the ear. With regard to head-dress, clothing, shoes and faces it is quite a skilful rendering of Chinese.' This group is a remarkable depiction of early eroticism, as the figures smile provocatively at the observer, the man closely clinging to the woman.

The last figural group of interest is that of five figures of Immortals. Inventoried in 1690 as 'India idols of ivory', they are in fact made of bone. Their resemblance to ivory is close but the low-relief carving differs from the more sharply defined and higher relief ivory examples. The faces have a variety of expressions, two caricatured like examples of Li Tiekuai.

Three ivory vessels included in inventories are therefore proven products of the seventeenth century: 'an ivory mortar, carved, and a pestle' (1674); 'two cups of ivory with screw covers made in India' (1674); 'two East India covered ivory cups' (1689). These shaped and lobed vessels are very skilfully carved in relief with dragons and mythical beasts, and possess some of the stylistic and decorative elements associated with some Tibetan works of art. Tibet was under Chinese control at various times and Tibetan artists were known to have worked in Beijing as the Tibetan form of Buddhism was in imperial favour during part of the Qing period. It is therefore quite often possible to discern cross-currents of influence between the two cultures.

Types of figures or figure groups which can possibly be dated to the seventeenth century are those on octagonal pedestal bases. The bases often have panels cut in low relief, with bracket shapes and feet to the lower parts, and occasionally a terrace to the top. They are often depicted with more animation than other earlier figures, and a good example is the group of Liu Hai, a mythological figure dating back to the tenth century, with his three-legged toad and string of cash, accompanied by a demon, now in San Francisco. Combined with the animation is a sharper definition and crisper edging, robes, ribbons and facial details all attracting the detailed attention of the carver. The Liu Hai and Toad groups are thought to be beneficial to commercial success and money-making.

Ivories from the imperial workshops

Kangxi, son of the first Qing emperor, Shun Chih, ascended the throne in 1661 at the age of eight, and reigned until 1722. His reign, despite problems, is regarded as being one of considerable achievement and success. He never allowed his position as 'Son of Heaven' to blind him to his responsibilities, as so many of his predecessors, isolated in the Imperial Palace, had undoubtedly done. He interested himself in cartography, medicine, mathematics, music and other cultural pursuits, collected animals, birds and plants, and stimulated the production of works of art, painting and calligraphy, which was to continue and evolve long after his death.

It was formerly thought that Kangxi established in 1680 a group of factories, one of which specialized in ivory carving. This date has been challenged, but the workshops' existence is confirmed by a reference in 1693: 'the office of manufacture [*zaobanchu*] established workshops'. The desire to trace and establish an imperial style tempts many to classify particularly fine or exotic works of art as having been made for the palace; but the best evidence of imperial origin is provided by comparison with genuine signed and dated examples and with similar works of art in imperial collections.

It is likely that the ivory carver who worked in the palace workshops was not confined to ivory as a medium. Bamboo, wood and other materials no doubt proved attractive and a variety of different works of art in varying substances emerged from the same ateliers.

The level of skill attained by the ivory carver in the second half of the seventeenth century can be seen in the pair of Dutchmen, now in the Mottahedeh Collection, which are superbly carved. The clothes, partly Chinese and partly Dutch, date *c.* 1660–70. Their Chinese origin is immediately apparent in the narrow eyes and squat chubby form, and a comparison with the way the orientals chose to depict playful children is possible. These figures were no doubt made for the Chinese domestic market, its curiosity stimulated by the presence of Dutch seamen. Much of the original lightly coloured pigment has been worn away, revealing a not unsatisfactory, toned-down ivory surface.

Much skill and many decorative elements were bestowed on the ruyi, a long sceptre which usually curved and ended in a broad flattish head formed stylistically to resemble a lingxi fungus. The majority of these are made of jade, wood inlaid with jade, bamboo, gilt bronze and cloisonné enamel, but very fine examples were made in ivory, one pierced and carved with an extensive growth of gourds and leaves. The inspiration and origin of the ruyi is thought to be the back-scratcher, which developed into a symbol of office and evolved, rather like the hu, into a decorative form. The shape and ornamentation illustrated the expression 'As You Wish'. By the eighteenth century they were popular as gifts. Heshen, prime minister to the Emperor Qianlong (reigned 1735–96), owned 9000 solid gold ruyi sceptres, 507 sceptres, some with original poems by Qianlong, and 3411 small jade sceptres. Auspicious emblems ornament the ruyis: symbols for long life, such as pine and cypress, bats, cranes and deer; symbols for weddings, such as twin fish for conjugal felicity, butterflies and the pomegranate for fertility.

After Kangxi's death in 1722, the succession was disputed. Yongzheng eventually disposed of several rivals and assumed the throne. His reign was short but he endeavoured to reign wisely and certain areas of the arts flourished. During this period, indeed, some of the finest and most delicate porcelains were manufactured. After his death China was blessed with another great emperor, Qianlong (reigned 1735–96).

Qianlong had a keen and active interest in the arts and continued the imperial tradition of patronizing workshops in the Forbidden City, established by Kangxi. He himself produced much calligraphy and wrote thousands of poems. His habit of inscribing favoured works of art with his poems and other thoughts has been termed vandalism by some purists, but the dated inscriptions prove useful as landmarks in the evolution of the eighteenth-century style, and 195 of his poems were said to have been inspired by works of art. His favourite private apartments, full of jades, jewellery, ceramics and flowers, were his haven where he studied and examined works of art, painted and wrote, with his writing materials and books and the accoutrements of the scholar-painter ranged all around him.

The relative peace of his reign allowed the building of palaces, pavilions and pleasure gardens, filled with his collection of works of art, including contemporary artefacts alongside the old and antique. Courtiers and wealthy individuals followed his example.

The idea of an imperial style has recently been challenged and works of art formerly given imperial status now find their pedigree less secure. Some information on the type of ivorywork produced within the Forbidden City does exist and examples survive which can be taken as indications of the type of ivories favoured at court. In 1758, forty-two workshops were counted as part of the Imperial Household Department, and one is stated as being an ivory workshop. In the same year, the workshops contracted, but expanded again in 1783. The author Zhou Nanquan refers to the existence, between 1731 and 1790, of twenty-one ivory carvers of the Imperial Household Department, and to Huan Zhenxiao from Canton, who began working for the department in 1739. The connection with Canton is emphasized with a reference to the ivory carver Yang Honqing, who entered the imperial service in 1731 and died there in 1790; his son Yang Xin had to leave Canton and take his father's place. Clearly the Canton ivory carvers continued to produce the type and quality of work which had brought them to imperial notice and it is impossible to differentiate between what was made in Beijing and what came out of Canton. The emperor's interest in painting on enamel, a technique introduced to him by the Jesuits, led to his ordering works of art in enamel both from the workshops in the imperial ateliers and from those in Canton.

Another artistic centre, famous for its jades and snuffbottles in particular, was Suzhou, a source of carved works of art. Qian Yong emphasizes this in a most informative statement: 'Although the craft of carving exists everywhere, it is most flourishing and most ingenious in Ningguo, Huizhou and Suzhou. In the Qianlong period, the Emperor Qianlong made six southern progresses, and travelling palaces were built at all the famous cities of Jiangsu and Zhejiang, all filled with ornaments, carved screens or stands of ivory, zitan or huali woods, bronze bibelots, ceramic or jade vessels decorated with dragons and phoenixes, clouds and waves, patterns both archaic and foreign, all so curiously wrought that each piece involved hundreds and hundreds of craftsmen. It was said that carving flourished ever increasingly from this time.'

Of the ivories still in the palace at Beijing, one of the most sophisticated technically, and probably made in Canton, is a court fan; shaped so that it broadens to the top, it has been delicately made of thin strips of ivory threaded together like the finest bamboo carving. Secured with copper threads to the surface of this matting are a phoenix in flight above chrysanthemum and floral sprays, all carved in low relief and painted. The frame combines shell and wood, and the handle is made of painted enamel inlaid with semi-precious stones.

Another ivory in Beijing, still of high technical level but altogether more restrained in its approach, is a wrist rest carved with the Bodhidarma, founder of Zen Buddhism, who was said to have introduced his sect to China in AD 522. On the convex side of the ivory rest, he is seated as a lohan with shaved head and ringed ear, his body enveloped in a long, flowing robe. The carver has here endeavoured to express himself with a minimum of detail. The relief is very low and the incense from the ding placed before the Bodhidarma rises in a vertical line on the plain surface until it curls and forms a cloud in which rests a pavilion. The concave underside is deliberately contrasted; a complicated group of lohans and animals twist and turn amid swirls of cloud or waves. The carver has shown his full virtuosity and his mastery of subject and material.

One of the great treasures in Beijing is a set of twelve panels called 'Pleasure of the Month for Court Ladies'. The principal medium is ivory, thinly cut and pierced, and of a white tone emphasized with highlights of paint. The ivory sections are set against backgrounds of jade, agate and semi-precious stones. Commissioned by the emperor and dated to 1741, the set also has lacquer panels inset with mother-of-pearl calligraphy of poems composed by the emperor.

During the eighteenth century the imperial taste for decorative panels inset with ivory and other relief work inspired some fine examples. There is no doubt that the finest ivory appliqués combine technical excellence with intelligent portrayal of the subjects, and some of the most delightful are of ivory combined with other materials, such as cloisonné enamel, bronze and agate.

Right: An ivory ruyi sceptre. Qing Dynasty (nineteenth-century); 13¾ in. (35 cm) long. Carved with flowers and birds.

Far right: An erotic figure of a lady. Qing Dynasty (eighteenth-century); 4½ in. (11.5 cm) long. Figures like this were once thought to be doctors' models, used by Chinese women to indicate the region of a complaint. See also page 257.

Far right, below: A set of Chinese ivory chessmen. Qing Dynasty (nineteenth-century). Made for the export trade. See also page 260.

Below: A rare ivory group of an elephant and rider, with chain. Qing Dynasty (eighteenth-century); 2¼ in. (5.6 cm) long.

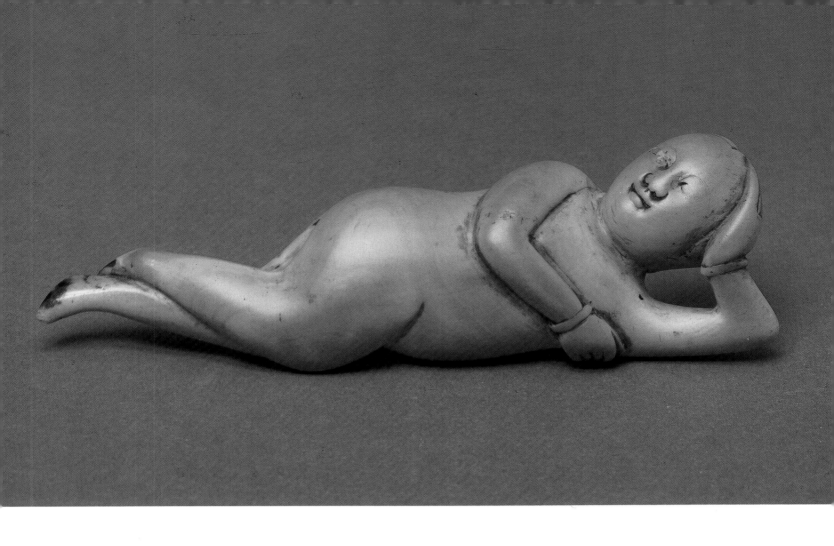

Also in Beijing is an ivory box and cover in the form of a quail. Here the features of the bird are naturalistically observed and the feathers stained and coloured. It is a rare example as this type of quail box is more frequently seen in jade and usually carved in pairs. A hardwood screen with a basket of flowers (a favoured Qing subject) is another *tour de force* of carving; the leaves and flower-heads overlap and are decorated in pale colours. In the same style is a lantern with panels of interlaced ivory decorated with floral reliefs; the whole design is similar to that of the fan described above and parts of the reliefs are again painted. In addition the upper and lower sections have bat motifs in bamboo, symbolizing happiness and longevity. The carvers were in the true sense carvers of all media.

Many of the works of art produced for the palace in the eighteenth century were eccentricities of a highly refined and delicate nature, in many cases toy-like. Many connoisseurs regard Qing works of art as somewhat decadent, imperial toys not to be taken too seriously. However, their technical virtuosity is undeniable.

Below: Log boat, carved in relief, with three figures, under an overhanging branch. Qing Dynasty (eighteenth-century); 9 in. (23 cm).

A Beijing example is an ivory vessel, called a yu, generally seen in jade and rarely in ivory. The yu shape, whose origins date to the Shang and early Zhou periods (*c.* 1550–1000 BC), varies a great deal but is characterized by a wide belly below a waisted flaring body, and a swing handle above the cover. In the Beijing example the body is pierced with an interlocking geometric design, the cover is also pierced, and suspended above it a pierced chain and yoke form the handle. In the National Palace Museum, Taiwan, are some cylindrical, pierced ivory boxes, the ultimate in intricacy, which open to reveal long chains, with monkeys and gourds as the section terminals to further tributary chains, all attached to the interior and carved from a single tusk. Miniature landscapes were popular and two remarkable models, carved to a high degree of detail, somehow exhibit the monumentality of a mountain landscape despite measuring 1¾ in. (4.5 cm). Both have incised inscriptions and the signatures of Huang Chen-hsiao and Gen Chi.

The ultimate 'toy' must be the miniature boat. One example is a dragon boat, with a double-horned dragon's head forming the prow, his long body and tail the vessel. The deck is filled with a pierced pavilion-like building, which has doors that open, and is surmounted by a court parasol, flags fully extended. The whole piece is contained in a lacquer box modelled in the form of a crested cockerel. The boat measures a mere 2 in. (5 cm). Another example, approximately the same size, has a scene of figures taking tea in the boat and is contained in a well-modelled jade box with a cover, in the form of a long-eared rabbit.

Other delicately carved and pierced ivories are a series of boxes whose surfaces retain much of their original brilliant colouring, with strong yellows, reds, greens and browns combining to create a vivid impression. The shapes are those of fruit: an orange, a lychee, a gourd and a finger citron. The finger citron, a theme favoured by Chinese artists, was sometimes called the Buddha Hand, and could either symbolize wealth or suggest money-grasping.

The emphasis on delicacy and detail is seen again in a tripart box (these boxes are also known in jade, and one has the emperor's seal on the base), comprising two small boxes with covers that fit into a further larger box. The cover is carved in bold relief with lingxi fungus, another favourite decorative element, particularly in commissions for the emperor and those in exposed positions, as it was mythologically the plant of immortality, said to have blossomed when a virtuous ruler was to assume the throne, and invariably seen with other life-bestowing Immortals and with the deer, thought by the Chinese to live to a venerable old age.

One type of ivory occasionally seen is the

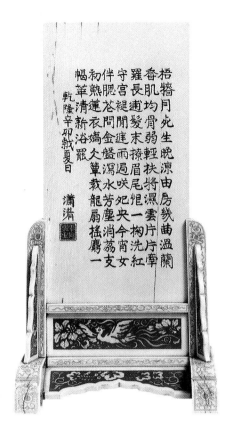

Far right: The back of an ivory table screen incised with a poem and the date 1771. 9 in. (23 cm). On the front is a scene of lakeside pavilions, with ladies on a bridge, superbly decorated in white-on-black. The stand is also decorated in white, on a red lacquer ground.

shaped tray. One in Taiwan is cleverly modelled in the form of a shell and carved in relief with a fish, a crab and a variety of small shells, the pigment remarkably well preserved. There are also two small boxes carved of the finest ivory, one with a spray of peaches on the top, and the other in the form of a melon with intricately curling and interlaced leaves, a lingxi spray and a butterfly.

Of the ivories in the imperial collections one of the most popular subjects was the wrist rest. Here the carver seemed to grasp his greatest opportunity to display his skill. Three in Taiwan offer varying themes and subjects: one has a sage and his young attendant observing the sun amid clouds; another on its concave underside has a 'busy' scene of lohans and animals, and on its convex upperside groups of small boys flying kites, the majority of the surface being left plain to exploit the quality and texture of the material; and the third has figures in a rocky landscape on the underside, and ducks amid reeds on the upperside. These last two wrist rests relate to an example, now in London, which uses themes of lohans and ducks, and was carved by Xianglin. The designs and compositions are so similar that the use of a printed or established design is obvious. The manner in which the wrist rests, and the stands that sometimes accompany them, are carved supports the idea that unlike earlier examples they were very ornamental in character, not so much for use as for display, like screens, a fashion we know was popular with the imperial court.

'Scholar's taste' and the connoisseur

During the Qing period, and particularly the eighteenth century, works of art in the so-called 'scholar's taste' style were made in ivory. The purist no doubt frowned on this, but it was a relatively calm time, when trade expanded and the leisured and increasingly prosperous upper classes could follow the emperor's lead in pursuing an interest in the arts. The principal objects in a scholar's studio, and reproduced in 'scholar's taste', were connected with the desk, and with the pursuit of calligraphy and painting: wrist rests, brushes, brush pots, screens, seals, boxes, inkstick rests, brush washers.

Wrist rests in ivory are relatively common, whereas brush handles in ivory are not. Perhaps the simple bamboo held its own in this case.

Brush pots in ivory were relatively popular, although the plain ones whose surface has a rich, mellow golden patina, due to handling and the passage of time, are not so common. An example now in San Francisco shows a favourite theme: philosophers at the site of the Red Cliff. The boat, cliffs and trees are carved in the lowest of relief with much of the surface left plain. The cyclical date is early Qing, either 1647 or 1707.

Above: An ivory brush pot with incised decoration. Late-seventeenth- or early-eighteenth-century; 5½ in. (14 cm). The entire vocabulary of the ivory worker's skill was used on brush pots.

A highly ornamented, pierced, openwork brush pot decorated with figures, now in Taiwan, has a separate base, similarly carved and pierced. It can be compared with a similar example in the Victoria and Albert Museum, London. Most brush pots in ivory are cylindrical and slender, due to the natural shape of the tusk. A rare example of rectangular tapering form has recessed panels carved with floral sprays.

It is likely that many brush pots started their lives in plain cylindrical form, and were later incised with poems and seals. A decorative element which is rare but seems to be employed skilfully and to great advantage on brush pots is the white-on-black technique. Here, the background is inked in, leaving the design painted or incised. The contrast between the two extremes gives a dramatic effect. A particularly fine screen, now in the Ashmolean, Oxford, is decorated in the white-on-black technique. This style obviously relates to Tang period ivories ornamented in the bachiru style, a form of decoration generally regarded as a Qing revival and part of the increased decorative repertoire developed at this time.

The screen itself is superb, with a boat, ladies on a bridge and ladies in a pavilion, the whole surrounded by a cloudy outer frame. It is held in a sophisticated bracketed stand, which is decorated in white reserved and incised on a red lacquer ground, with phoenixes and floral scrolls. The reverse has a poem, the signature Yiaomen, and the date 1771, a useful landmark.

Small table screens were popular in the late seventeenth and early eighteenth centuries, and

Right: Fine ivory moon/cockade fan, scissor-end guards. Qing Dynasty (late-eighteenth-century); 10½ in. (27 cm) long. See also page 263.

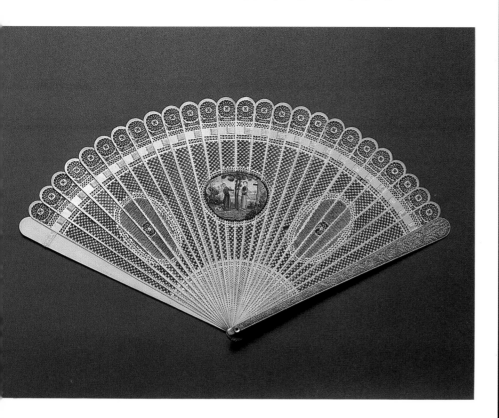

Above (top): Ivory brisé fan. Qing Dynasty (late-eighteenth-century); 9½ in. (24 cm). *Above:* Paper-and-ivory folding fan painted in gouache. Qing Dynasty (early-nineteenth-century); 10 in. (27.5 cm) long. See also page 263.

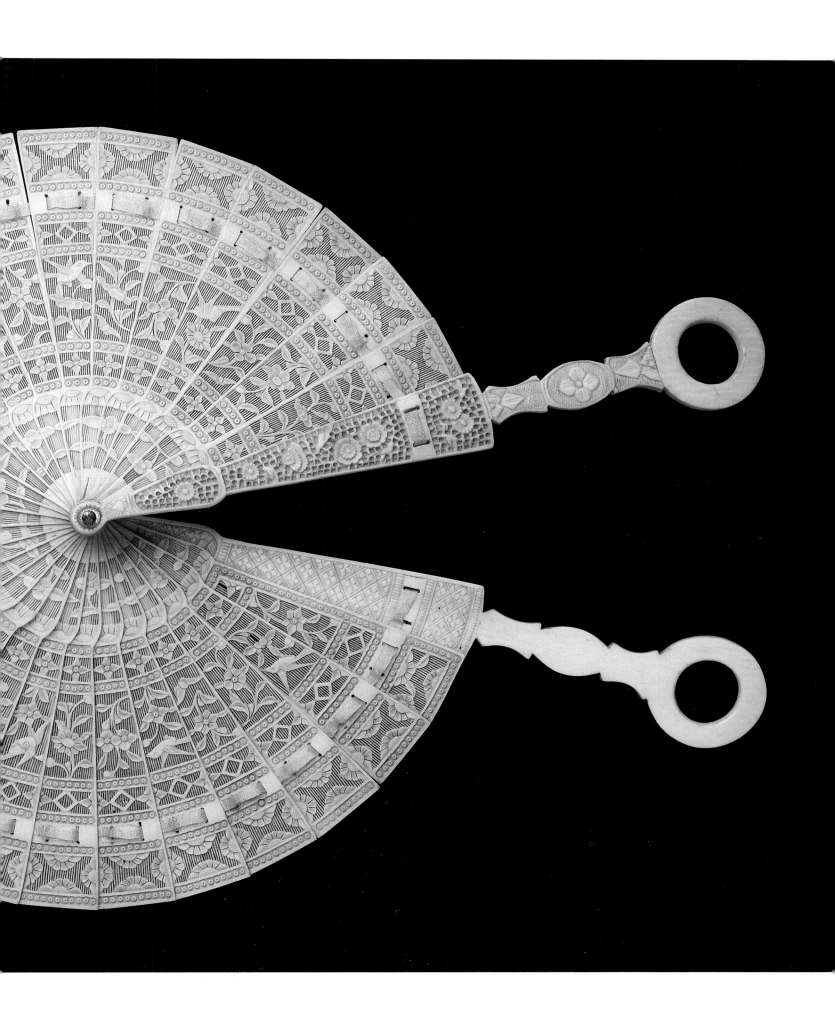

Above: Three ivory belt fittings. Qing Dynasty (eighteenth-century); 2⁴/₅ in. (7.3 cm) long (central buckle). The buckle is flanked by ring-handle plaques. Carved in high relief with dragons pursuing pearls amid swirling waves.

there is a group carved with the relief work proud of the surface, with the theme of elderly scholars in a landscape. Screens incised with landscapes in exactly the same manner as brush pots are known, and another group has very shallow relief stained brown to contrast with the white background.

Like other oriental artefacts, the seal is found in a variety of materials. Ivory seals when skilfully carved demonstrate the most remarkable sculpture in miniature. A favourite subject for the knop on a seal was the dragon, invariably portrayed with its teeth bared. Dogs of Fo or Buddhist lions were also favourites in the Qing period, and the elephant motif was sometimes used. Some knops portray animals the Chinese carver would have observed around him, in everyday life, such as goats, horses and rabbits. Others, more difficult to define, are usually described as mythical beasts. The best animals on seals are not necessarily those which are minutely and sharply detailed, but rather those where the emphasis is laid on the eyes and claws, the spine is subtly developed and the features are combined in a well-balanced manner. The seal was usually handled more than other articles and many seals exhibit the mellow patina associated with fine ivories.

As far as imperial seals for state documents are concerned, silver and jade were the principal

materials. An ivory seal could be used on informal occasions.

There is a variety of small boxes found in ivory and dating to the Qing period. Their surface provided an opportunity for numerous designs and patterns, but some of the most attractive examples are left unornamented, and depend simply on the harmony of their shape and dimensions for their visual appeal. Some of these small boxes belonged on the scholar's desk and would have contained wax for the seal impressions; others were intended for domestic purposes, such as cosmetics. Following the theme of the scholar's desk, a rare box with cover, made to contain an inkstone, is displayed in the Sassoon Collection. This box is of a rounded rectangular form, carved with a geometric scroll design similar to that used on jade and bronzes in the Qing period. The inkstone used by the painter-calligrapher in China was a slab on which to grind the solid inkstick, made from soot, lampblack, glue and a variety of other ingredients, and mix it with water. A charming group of ivories, now in the Palace Museum, Taiwan, comprises the small rectangular stands made as rests to support the inksticks. These are made in the shape of low tables, decorated with chrysanthemums, roses, insects, squirrels, bats and clouds. The usual attention to

detail and quality is displayed in these examples, as in a slim rectangular paper or scroll weight in the same collection. It is rare to see this type of object made in ivory; the more commonly found types were made of heavier materials, like jade, bronze and cloisonné enamel.

Ivory was unlikely to be used for the brush washer as it absorbs and yields moisture, depending on the humidity of its surroundings, and shrinks and swells alternately, eventually warping and cracking.

An unusual small article worn and collected by connoisseurs and men of 'taste', was the squat, cylindrical thumb ring, derived from the archer's ring of the Manchu nomadic hunters and warriors. It is common in jade but rare in ivory, and most examples that do exist are plain, or have a poetic inscription. A rare thumb ring, now in the British Museum, is incised with scholars in a landscape and dates *c.* 1700–50, a useful example of the kind of incised decoration being done at this time.

The technique of incised ornament is also seen on a group of small vases made during the eighteenth century. The favourite theme is scholars and their attendants in a landscape. These vases usually have long necks; occasionally waisted, they are invariably cylindrical and flare to rounded squat bodies. Sometimes they are lobed in sections, and can be found in a variety of tones and depths of colours.

Artistic indulgence and compromise

The eighteenth century saw traditional respect for the past observed in a reverence for the antique and manifested in the reproduction of ivory vessels modelled in the manner of archaic bronzes. Similar examples are known in jade, and rare ones in bamboo. Not many are known in ivory, and ivory reproductions are not particularly successful. One of the more successful reproductions in ivory is an archaic bronze water ewer called a yi, which bears a strong resemblance to an English Georgian silver sauceboat. The handle, usually shaped like a loop, terminates in a dragon's head gripping the body of the vessel with its jaws. Purists might criticize such experiments but the eighteenth century was a time when artistic indulgences were encouraged.

An eighteenth-century, peach-shaped ivory cup is carved in relief with bats, insects and Buddhist emblems. Its interior is lacquered gold. This kind of cup is known in lacquer, the stalk handle carved in exactly the same manner, the interior lacquered in gold as well. It is likely that the lacquer types were made in the seventeenth and eighteenth centuries, the ivory examples dating to the mid or late eighteenth century.

The Chinese taste in art in many cases ran concurrently with that of 'export' art for Europeans, and in the middle ground were some compromise artefacts which combined ideas and themes.

Right: An ivory thumb ring used in archery by noblemen to draw back the bow-string without damaging the thumb. Qing Dynasty (*c.*1700–50); 1¼ in. (3 cm). Incised with scholars in a landscape.

Far right: A rare ivory case in which to display a watch. Qing Dynasty (nineteenth-century); 8½ in. (25 cm). Richly carved with animals and birds, figures and flower-heads. Many ivory cases were made for the export trade, including the card case on page 226.

Opposite: An ivory plaque pierced and carved with a portrayal of a western woman in a decolleté gown. Qing Dynasty (eighteenth-century); 3⅛ in. (8 cm). The plaque is finely painted in the famille rose palette. See also page 258.

An early-nineteenth-century reference illuminates the type of ornamentation called 'zhou' work by the Chinese. Qian Yong in 1838 writes: 'The method of zhou work is unique to Yangzhou ... Gold, silver, gemstones, pearls, coral, dark green jade, fecui jade, crystal, agate, tortoiseshell, clam shell, lead, coloured pine, mother-of-pearl, ivory, secret wax and sinking incense ... are carved into landscapes, figures, trees, pavilions, flowers, birds and animals, then inlaid into objects of zitan wood, huali wood or lacquer. Small ones include brush rests, tea utensils, inkstone cases and book caskets.' The jumble of colours was said to beggar description.

Zhou Zhu, the inventor of the technique of inlaying semi-precious stones into other materials, ivory and wood being two of the most popular, gave his name to this type of work in the late sixteenth century. Only the best inlay or zhou work tends to be satisfactory. There is nothing worse than a vulgar and ostentatious heap of coloured materials – an increasing tendency during the late nineteenth century.

Snuff accessories

A European custom which found favour at the Emperor Kangxi's court was taking snuff. The Chinese readily adopted the snuffbox as yet another decorative item. By 1705 the palace workshops in Beijing were producing snuff-bottles for the court. Their products were smoother surfaced than those of Canton and Shanghai and also tended to be simpler in form and design. Even when the Beijing carver produced more complex compositions, the quality, proportion and balance of the design were maintained.

Some ivory snuffbottles which can be identified as being of imperial origin are the confronting dragon type. A double-horned dragon curls vigorously in pursuit of a flaming pearl. The background is usually a formalized wave design. This type of bottle is found with the incised seal marks of the Emperor Qianlong (1735–96) and his successor Jiajing (1796–1820). Other types show twin fish carved formally, or Buddhist lions pursuing brocade balls, again on a formalized wave ground, or figures on terraces and in landscapes.

Canton school ivory bottles are characterized by their intricacy and technical skill. A group of bottles was produced in porcelain imitating the ivory ones. A favourite subject for decorating these bottles was groups of lohans.

Walrus ivory was a favourite for snuffbottles. The carvers in Beijing acquired most of the supplies, dyeing the material green in imitation of jade. When carved, walrus ivory exhibits a distinctive marbled effect. It was also favoured for 'scholar's desk' items, snuff-taking accessories such as shallow trays, and opium pipes.

Above: Detail of the erotic figure shown in colour on page 249.

'Medical figures'

Western influence is seen in the 'medical figure' or 'doctor's model'. The story that these were used by Chinese ladies to indicate to doctors the region of their complaint, as they were too modest to show themselves naked, is now considered to be an invention. The ladies are usually depicted in languorous poses, resting the head on one hand, invariably with a smile or a passive expression on the face. They are usually completely naked, other than their feet, which are bound, according to Chinese tradition. The Chinese dealer's pretence of modesty, and his reluctance to show the westerner such a supposedly sensitive subject, no doubt made the potential purchaser all the more eager, and when the figure was eventually revealed, its undoubtedly erotic nature was displayed to full advantage.

The ladies' pose was the same as that of 'Christian' ivories which depicted the Holy Child. The position of the legs, arms and head, and even the facial expressions, resemble those in certain examples made in Goa and the Philippines. Changing a boy into a woman would not have troubled the Chinese carver.

The most attractive of the 'medical' figures are usually the seventeenth-century examples, relying as ever on their roundness and mellow colour for effect. Their form and subject prove enticing and tactile. The Danish national archives inventoried in 1737 a partially clothed female figure lying with her feet bound, head resting on an openwork pillow, traces of colour still remaining: 'From Canton ... a small ivory image in a box, which shows how the Chinese women sleep. Same was brought from China in 1732.'

Other Qing ivories

The Danish collection usefully emphasizes that styles and types of carving were maintained over a longer period than was previously assumed.

A group of small vases, rather crudely pierced and chip-carved, decorated with dragons, are described in 1772 as 'from the estate of Queen Sophia Magdalena' and in 1775 as 'six openwork flower pots of ivory'. Two round, pierced, covered baskets which were traditionally assumed to be nineteenth-century export types are described in 1775 as 'two round openwork flower baskets, on the top is a knob with two balls, everything most delicately made of ivory'. A framed plaque of a bunch of flowers is noted in 1785 as 'from Christiansborg Castle' and in 1807 as 'Chinese made'.

The Dutch were particularly active in the China trade and most of the rare ivory figures of westerners that do exist seem to be of Dutchmen. One standing figure of a Dutchman holding a staff is even more interesting due to the medal that hangs round his neck. It is carved in relief with a

Above: Carved ivory plaque shown in colour on page 256.

triple-masted ship and may indicate the man's position as an official of the Dutch East India Company. Two other European figure groups show a kneeling man holding a vase and a family of man, woman, baby and dog. Careful attention is paid to the clothes and even more to the hairstyles with frizzled curls. Perhaps the European curls held a special interest for a carver from a nation with straight black hair. Ivory plaques depicting Europeans are known; a rare example shows three Dutchmen loading bales and large porcelain vases into a longboat which still bears the remains of blue and red paint, the colours of the Dutch flag. The curling hair is again particularly noticeable.

A plaque from the Ionides Collection shows a young European sitting on a mound and holding a potted plant in a blue tapering vessel. His curling hair is topped by a wide-brimmed hat, and traces of the colouring used on the whole plaque are still clearly in evidence.

The most dramatic group of figures using ivory and depicting Europeans is a set of eight figures of carved and painted wood with ivory hands and heads (a combination known from earlier periods). This set dates 1750–1800 and shows westerners, kneeling on one knee, holding aloft the eight precious emblems of Buddhism, which are made from cloisonné or Canton enamel. The

figures themselves wear Chinese-style belted robes, boots and mitre-like hats. The ivory heads are doll-like, their features similarly depicted with broad noses and staring eyes; at the sides of the heads and base of the necks are well-detailed and incised wig curls.

In the same style are two ivory boys, hands held forward, kneeling on one knee. The heads are modelled in a style similar to the group of eight, and although they are doll-like, the blank expressions are mitigated by gently smiling lips. A strong palette of blue and pink has been used and survives with only minor chips and scratches.

By the beginning of the nineteenth century, skilful ivory carving was applied to a vast range of subjects, including cricket cages. These were rarely manufactured entirely in ivory, but the fittings were frequently ivory. The cricket appealed to the Chinese both for its fighting qualities and for its song. It was usually kept in a certain type of gourd with a top which was often made from ivory. Once again, the carver displayed his talents with detailed and pierced work, and favourite subjects included landscapes, flowers, confronting dragons, and occasionally figures and animals. Often a central panel of pierced tortoiseshell was included and inset.

Some of the finest work was used for stands or supports for other objects, such as jades, even

Right: Picnic basket with lid and handle. Qing Dynasty (eighteenth-century); 8¼ × 11½ × 10¾ in. (21 × 29 × 27 cm).

Far right: An ivory pagoda. Qing Dynasty (eighteenth-century); 36¾ in. (93 cm). Nine storeys rest on a base of wood, ivory and tortoiseshell. Pagodas particularly intrigued Europeans and were popular for export.

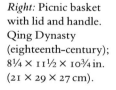

though most of the intricate work on the stand would be concealed by the object it bore. The best ivory stands are stained green, possibly in imitation of jade.

Chinese exports in Europe

During the eighteenth century the Chinese contained, to a reasonable degree, the incursions of the Europeans while trading with the European nations, including Britain, France, Holland and Sweden. Swedish sources give further information on ivory works of art exported to the west. In 1753, Adolf Fredrik, King of Sweden, gave his wife, Louisa Ulrica, a birthday present: the pavilion at Drottningholm. A new 'China' pavilion was built less than ten years later, in the 'Chinese taste'. French-inspired chinoiserie was mixed with Swedish rococo and a variety of curios brought from China.

Of special interest to Europeans were the tall multi-storeyed pagodas, both in gardens and as models. All kinds of materials were utilized in their construction. Two in Drottningholm are hexagonal in form, and are made principally of ivory and mother-of-pearl. Accurately copied from actual pagodas, they are particularly interesting because of their early date; they are noted in the Drottningholm inventory of 1744.

More models can be found in other museum collections. A group of Buddhist temples, now in the Victoria and Albert Museum, London, is constructed of ivory, mother-of-pearl and semi-precious stones. An ivory model of a boat in the same museum was brought to England in 1803 from Canton. It is intricately carved, pierced and set with figures who hold oars to the sides of the craft. A similar ivory boat with oarsmen can be seen in Beijing.

Copenhagen provides a delightful model of a summerhouse, principally lacquer, soapstone and ivory, the figures, plants, roofs, balustrades, ridge-tiles and details all of ivory, some details stained green. This particular example is inventoried in 1762, and again in 1775 as 'a Chinese pagoda or idol's temple of ivory, with four floors ... furnished with lanterns and bells. On the ground floor an erect figure of soapstone beats on the kettledrum, on the first floor are six pleasure crafts on a disc, on the second, six musicians, and on the third, five dancers. All this is to be set in motion by clockwork, and stands on a black lacquered foot.'

Other vessels inventoried in 1732 and 1807 are described variously as 'a model of a Chinese merchant's barque called a gondola' and 'a Chinese pleasure sampan of ivory', and a 'small Chinese pleasure junk like the ones on which the Chinese mandarins or foreign masters will divert themselves ... very subtly carved out of ivory and is 7½ in. [19 cm] long resting on a base,

Opposite: Devil's balls. 12¼ in. (31 cm). First mentioned in 1388, these balls fascinated Europeans and were popular items in the nineteenth-century export trade.

Above: Detail of the chess set shown in colour on page 249.

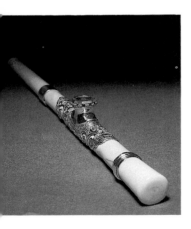

Above: Ivory opium pipe. Qing Dynasty (early-nineteenth-century); 19½ in. (49.5 cm) long. In an effort to check the opium trade a Chinese commissioner in 1839 destroyed over 2.5 million pounds (nearly 1.2 million kilos) of opium.

likewise of ivory, and was brought from China in 1732'.

Two small, so-called 'houses' were inventoried in 1772, one particularly interesting for its depiction of the figures as Europeans.

A major import into Europe was tea, which gained in popularity throughout the eighteenth century. Caskets for tea (and other precious materials) were made in the late eighteenth century and increasingly so in the nineteenth. A rectangular casket, now in the Ionides Collection, is a useful landmark for dating the styles of carving. It is carved and painted with figures and floral sprays, has silver feet and interior caddies, decorated with repoussé floral garlands in the rococo style, and is datable to the year 1742. Two other boxes are also of high quality, one a rectangular example, the interior painted with a scene of Boca Tigris on the Pearl River, the other of quatrefoil form with an interior silver-gilt lining made by James England of Dublin, and dated 1808.

The European trade

The contacts with Europe in the eighteenth and nineteenth centuries also provide important eye-witness observations. The diarist William Hickey visited Canton in 1768 and wrote of 'the painters upon glass, the fan makers, workers in ivory, japanners, jewellers, and all the artificers of Canton'. Adjoining the English factory were 'two rows of native houses, called the new and old China Street, where foreigners might ramble and purchase trinkets'.

The frustration encountered by the English in their attempts to deal with the inflexible and introverted attitudes of the Chinese, inspired the Macartney Embassy in 1792–3. However, the imperial court accepted the embassy's gifts from George III of Britain as 'tributes' and as a gesture of *his* loyalty. The embassy produced a series of detailed drawings by its official draughtsman, and *Travels in China* by John Barrow, Lord Macartney's private secretary (1804). He paid particular attention to ivory production: 'Of all the mechanical arts that in which they seem to have attained the highest degree of perfection is the cutting of ivory. Nothing can be more exquisitely beautiful than the fine openwork displayed in a Chinese fan, the sticks of which would seem to be singly cut by the hand. In short, all kinds of toys for children and other trinkets and trifles are executed in a similar manner and for less money in China than in any other part of the world.'

Trade relations between China and England were relatively calm at the beginning of the nineteenth century, but storm clouds were gathering. China's attitude is well encapsulated in the words of the Emperor Qianlong in 1793: 'The productions of our empire are manifold, and in

great abundance; nor do we stand in the least need of the produce of other countries.'

During the eighteenth century the trading companies had started to ship opium to China, hoping that by introducing a commodity which China would need in great quantity they would facilitate their dealings with the Chinese. They expanded this trade during the nineteenth century. The Chinese authorities tried to check the expansion, and the Opium Wars of 1840–2 and 1860 'opened up' China to the western traders and gave rise directly to artefacts made for the Europeans, and in the European style, by the Chinese. A considerable amount of ivory was employed in these items.

Canton, the greatest centre of production, was full of shops. A large proportion of the clientele were sailors, and baubles, jewellery and toys were very popular. The streets were crowded, the river packed with shipping and boats, the air filled with cries of hawkers, entertainers, porters and traders. The main city was estimated as having at least a million inhabitants. The foreign factories were situated to the west of Canton. The foreign merchants lived in great splendour.

The Europeans were not the only customers for ivory. The United States of America had entered the China trade in 1785 and North American merchants and seamen provide useful documentary evidence of their purchases. In 1816 Benjamin Shreve of Salem, Massachusetts, purchased for his wife an ivory screw pincushion and twelve pieces of ivory on which to wind silk, four barrels to contain thread, and three seals. His most expensive purchase, which was made in 1820, was a set of ivory chessmen. Most Chinese ivory chessmen are nineteenth-century and made for the export trade. Unlike the inscribed counters used in the native Chinese game, such a set consisted of king, queen, two priests or mandarins, two horsemen, two castles (elephants with flags on their backs) and eight soldiers on each side, commonly representing Chinese on one side and Mongols on the other.

One European commission from Canton was for Napoleon, who in 1815 had ordered that a wounded British officer, Captain Elphinstone, should be cared for. In gratitude the Elphinstone family ordered 'a magnificent Chinese set of exquisitely carved ivory, marked with eagles, and the initial *N* surmounted by the imperial crown', to send to the exiled emperor on St Helena (the British governor refused to allow the gift).

The standard chess set was usually carved in the form of Chinese figures in armour, standing on concentric balls. One side is white, the other side is stained red. Some sets were of Europeans, particularly kings and queens, and figures of Napoleon himself are known.

In New York in 1832, 120 chess sets were

offered for sale. 'A set which brings twenty or thirty dollars in the United States,' said Osmond Tiffany in 1844, 'may be obtained in China for eight to ten, and from this one may judge the magnificence of the set which was in the possession of Mouchong Gouqua, and for which he asked one hundred and fifty dollars. The men were as usual white and red, all clothed in the ancient dress of China, one half in position and attitude of attack, the others standing in the defensive. The largest pieces were a foot [30 cm] high, and every one was carved in the most wonderful manner.' He noted the carving done with great patience and skill and he observed fans, counters, boxes, ivory boats and inevitably the carved devil's balls.

The *Ge gu yao lun* ('The Essential Criteria of Antiques') makes reference to 'devil's work balls', or *gui gong qui*, in 1388. These concentric spheres comprise a series of ivory globes carved and wholly independent of one another but contained within each other in ever-decreasing sizes. According to the *Ge gu yao lun*, it was sometimes possible to carve more than ten. It is unlikely that any from the early Ming period have survived, and most of those in existence are considered to be the products of Canton, and can be dated to the nineteenth century, but the fact that they were being made in the eighteenth century, and were not merely revived in the nineteenth for the western visitors, is shown by an item in the Danish archives, recorded as being purchased in 1790 and inventoried in 1807: 'a ball turned of ivory, 4 inches [10 cm] in diameter, in which are 12 other loose balls one inside the other, all out of one piece, and all openwork *à la grecque* – the same is a chain likewise of ivory and all the links are out of one piece – this object was manufactured in China.'

There are examples in the Peabody Museum, Salem, one of twenty spheres, acquired in 1830, and the other of twelve spheres donated in 1826. Walter Medhurst, a printer sent to China by the London Missionary Society, observed in 1838: 'The celebrated Chinese balls, one in the other, to the amount of seven or nine, all exquisitely carved, have puzzled many of our English friends, who have been at a loss to know whether they were cut out of a solid piece, or cunningly introduced by some imperceptible opening, one within the other. There can be no doubt, however, of their having been originally but one piece, and cut underneath from the various apertures, which the balls contain, until one after another is dislodged and turned and then carved like the first.' These devil's balls held as much, if not more, fascination for westerners in China as more serious works of art. The introverted attitude of the Chinese restricted westerners to a superficial and shallow knowledge of their culture. The oldest civilization in the world was so poorly understood by the West that ivory 'toys' were all most westerners knew of Chinese art.

Boats were still popular, more detailed and elaborate than before. They were delicately pierced and carved, and sometimes placed on a wooden stand carved with a representation of waves.

The rhinoceros horn had long been a favourite medium for Chinese carvers. The Tang and Song dynasties favoured it in a relatively plain form, but the Qing taste for elaboration preferred tall pierced carvings in large wooden stands. Ivory tusks carved in a similar manner are surprisingly rare, but a large and magnificent example was taken to America in 1850. Every part of this tusk is pierced and carved with a landscape composition of rocks, trees, pavilions and figures, and the large wood base is again elaborately carved.

The small items produced in the workshops of Canton covered an extensive range from letter-openers, canes and parasol handles to purely ornamental figures. A charming seal, formerly the property of David Macfarland, a ship's officer, is carved as a nude woman and has an engraving of his ship, *Nightingale*, on the base. Other seal tops are formed as fruit, and one as a clenched fist.

The demand for boxes and caskets of all sizes was quite considerable. There were large tea containers; silk-lined lacquer boxes to hold puzzles or ladies' sewing implements made of ivory; smaller ivory boxes lined in silk and filled with mother-of-pearl gaming counters, with the owner's initials or monogram incised on them; card cases, with removable covers, made for visiting cards, very much in vogue, and often decorated with figures and pavilions in a landscape. They show the carver's skill in the precision with which sections are joined and slid together. An unusual type of card case depicts Napoleon's tomb and his home on alternate sides.

The workshops also carved the same designs on other materials; mother-of-pearl was popular, as were tortoiseshell and sandalwood. A favourite decorative motif, twin dragons, can be seen on a number of ivory letter racks. Jewellery boxes, glove stretchers, napkin rings, cribbage boards, hat stands and a rare watch case are all to be found in ivory. Paper-thin baskets and vases were formed from thinly sliced and pierced panels framed and supported by slightly thicker ribs; silk-lined, wooden boxes protected them. Some of these boxes have trade labels stuck inside.

These trade labels are usually of a rudimentary kind. Chinese manufacturers and workers were normally anonymous. The nation rarely celebrated the work of individual artists or artisans other than certain poets, calligraphers or painters.

The name of Haoching is famous in the selling of works of art made to please western tastes. A card case marked with this name, housed in its original box, was made in 1823. The name is associated with a large silversmithing business of good reputation, noted in guidebooks of 1867 and 1875; it is well known to collectors of Chinese export silver, but the shop was primarily concerned with the sale of ivory carvings and jewellery. Haoching was most probably the maker of the very fine boat shown at the 1876 Centennial International Exhibition in Philadelphia. His label indicates that he dealt in ivory, tortoiseshell, mother-of-pearl and sandalwood.

Chongshing was another who exhibited at Philadelphia. His label, 'Chongshing, mother-of-pearl, ivory and silks, tortoiseshell carver, New Street No. 5', is to be found on a backgammon set.

Another famous name from the records of the export trade is that of Leeching, a jewellery trader, whose work stands out as high quality. The small ivory plaques he used are carved to an extraordinary degree of relief and detail, and the brooches which tend to be the most dramatic of his jewellery pieces frequently depict figures conversing or sitting around a table, in gold frames of the finest-quality filigree work. The fitted boxes which Leeching produced for his jewellery are often made from ivory, of rectangular plain form with small cartouches of figures on the outer cover. Their simplicity, at a time when ivory was ornamented to a frequently exaggerated degree, may have been deliberate, to contrast with the highly ornamented contents displayed when the lid was raised.

Chinese carvers and merchants of this time appear to have developed a fairly uniform method of accommodating the western requirements. An advertisement for Sanxing, a company established in 1840, describes their activities as 'gold and silversmiths, jewellers, engravers of stamps and seals, dealers in silk dresses and lacquered ivory and China wares, mother-of-pearl, sandalwood. Curiosities, ornaments, etc.'

Chinese fans

One of the most delicately carved ivories to emerge from the nineteenth-century trade fashions as a favourite of western admirers was the fan. It had a long tradition in China.

Woven bamboo fans which date to the second century BC have been excavated in Hunan province. In Chinese mythology Zhongli Quan, the Immortal, could revive the souls of the dead with his fan.

The court or ceremonial fan was usually rigid, with the material stretched over a frame.

Everyday fans were used by men and women alike but at court the type of fan used was regulated by the occasion and the rank of the user.

The folding ivory fan was introduced later than the rigid type or the court fan. It is possible that the first folding fans may have become fashionable among prostitutes in the coastal areas of Zhejiang, as items introduced from Japan.

Early fans made of ivory were rare – the majority were bamboo and sandalwood – but by the beginning of the eighteenth century those fans made for the western market were almost predominantly in ivory and can be distinguished by certain features. They tend to be of a wedge-shape, the angle made by the guards is approximately 90°, and they are small in size, to abide by the current European fashion. Furthermore, they are painted, and the designs used are the same as those on contemporary Chinese porcelain and Canton enamels. An ivory fan dated to the early eighteenth century has floral motifs and mythical beasts around a central panel, showing a seated European, with servants carrying game. An ivory-ribbed, painted paper fan shows figures

Below: Detail of a superb ivory fan. *c.*1780; 8¾ in. (22.5 cm) long. The pierced lattice-work is interspersed with circular and flower-shaped cartouches. A man in Chinese dress is painted on the central cartouche. See pages 252–3 for more fans, in colour.

Above: Detail of an ivory brisé fan made for export. Qing Dynasty (late-eighteenth-century); 10¾ in. (27 cm) long. The centres of the sticks are carved with hunting scenes, the ends with animals, some of them mythical. The guards are carved in relief with floral designs.

posed in an extensive landscape before a small temple-like building. Early brisé fans were often pierced with diaper designs, and lattice and trellis patterns were popular. In the early fans, the outer ivory guards are plain; there are no pierced guards until the mid eighteenth century. As the eighteenth century progressed, the size began to increase, until by the mid nineteenth century an angle of 180° was possible. Ivory fans were not always ornamented on both sides. Towards the end of the eighteenth century the neo-classical designs popular in Europe began to be used by the Chinese carvers. At the same time, the delicate lace-like piercing, which was to increase in favour during the nineteenth century, was combined with neo-classical garlands, shields and monograms and mixed with oriental baskets of flowers, figures and Chinese pagodas. Some of the most attractive fans of this period are those with a central shield painted in vivid colours, contrasting with the rest of the fan, which relies on its quiet colour and fine carving for effect.

Later fans often carry a larger central monogram and one large, late, ivory fan which is decorated with scenes of Chinese figures has at the top the somewhat strange figure of an apparently European lady leaning on an anchor, possibly Britannia. Floral decoration was more popular in the eighteenth century, but in the nineteenth century the guards tended to be carved with figures and dragons.

Some rare fitted silk and lacquer boxes fashioned to contain ivory fans bear makers' names, among them Kuenchen, Haoching and Lauching.

As the nineteenth century progressed, carving and piercing became repetitive and standardized in design, and the appealing quality and liveliness of earlier fans seem lost.

Ivory inlays

Ivory continued to be used as an inlay material throughout the nineteenth century. At Durham Museum is an inlaid bed, associated with a prominent early-nineteenth-century merchant, which is an attractive example of this type of work and its application.

According to Fortune's *Three Years' Wandering in the Northern Provinces of China* (1847), 'there were beds, chairs, tables, washing stands, cabinets and presses, all peculiarly Chinese in their form, and beautifully inlaid with different kinds of wood and ivory, representing the people and customs of the country . . . They seem peculiar to Ningpo, and are not met with at any other of the five ports.' (Canton, Amoy, Fuzhou, Ningpo and Shanghai were the five treaty ports at this time.)

Tables of Ningpo manufacture are known: square in form, with shaped rectangular legs, the whole inlaid with both ivory and ebony.

Miniature ivories

An exception to the lack of inspiration and the prevalence of stereotyped wares in the late nineteenth century is the development and refinement of fine incising and engraving. Many of the best examples were produced in the twentieth century. Well-known specialist miniaturists are Wa Nan-yu and Chang Chih-yu, but one of the most famous was Yu Xiaoxin, born in 1873, most of whose work seems to date 1913–35.

Yu Xiaoxin was a painter and calligrapher, and a follower of the Qing artist Wang Su (1794–1817). A bamboo fan frame, dated 1897, is accredited to him, but he is probably best known for small ivory plaques, miniature desk screens, seals and fan frames. There are snuffbottles bearing his signature, but these may well be copies, as they are usually less fine than his normal work. His minuscule calligraphic engraving, readable only by microscope, was said to be a manifestation of his divine skill. His popularity illustrates the taste for infinitesimal carving, and although the late Ming and early Qing lavished praise on craftsmen who could carve the entire Red Cliff boating scene on a peach nut, with hinged doors and windows, not until the late nineteenth and early twentieth centuries was technical proficiency in such detail fully developed.

Yu Xiaoxin carved on an ivory frame three-tenths of an inch (7.5 mm) wide thirty or forty lines of hsing-Kai script in characters as fine as flies' heads, and produced a miniature desk screen only 3 in. (7.5 cm) square, with the entire text of Qu Yuan's *Li sao* engraved on one side. On yet another screen, he finely engraved and ink-etched, in a manner freer than his usual work, a scene of a meditating sage poised among waving fronds of foliage on the rocky shore and a fisherman perched on his punt, oar in hand. The broad-grained ivory is engraved with a long poem in the most minute characters, which are barely legible, a date in 1909, and the signature. The reverse is left plain.

Some collectors and purists regard miniature incised ivories as trickery, contrived, not worthy of the appreciation bestowed on earlier and more important ivories. However, these ivories take their natural place within the evolution of ivory carving, even if regarded solely as the refinement of a technique taken to its limits.

Twentieth-century Chinese ivories

Unfortunately there is not much documentary evidence and knowledge of the work of carvers in the late nineteenth and early twentieth century, though Soame Jenyns gives us an interesting insight into Canton in the 1920s in his *Chinese Carvings in Elephant Ivory*: 'The ivory carvers' shops, which were all next door to each other in one street, were run by a Guild as they would have been in medieval Europe. The hours of work were long, and there were no holidays except the public festivals, but ... all their shops were on excellent visiting terms and devoid of the competitive western commercial spirit ... a happy simple community of craftsmen possessing a co-operative spirit lost to the west, and with rare exceptions all their work was anonymous.'

The ravages of the 1930s and 1940s were followed by a period of isolation and then by the Cultural Revolution, when art, as it had been traditionally and historically regarded, came under attack. Ivory carving has since been re-sumed, and Beijing, Canton, Shanghai and Fuzhou are the principal centres.

During the 1960s and into the 1970s, the subject matter and the stimulus derived from the political and social trends prevalent at the time. It is not easy to differentiate between the figures carved in Beijing and those carved in Canton, although the Chinese claim these are two distinct schools. Canton groups usually have more detail and pierced work and are more elaborate.

Traditional folk and historical subjects re-mained in the carvers' repertoire, particularly when a patriot or noble historical figure could be depicted as a precursor of the socialist revolution. An ivory tusk, over 6 ft (2 m) long, carved in openwork and relief, is called 'Crossing Rivers and Mountains' and depicts scenes from the Long March of Mao Tse-tung and his followers. Another Beijing group, of two young girls carry-ing a lamb in the snow and wind, is described variously as 'Sisters of the Grasslands' and 'Heroic Sisters'. China's ethnic minorities were encour-aged by scenes depicting the new life of the Tibetan autonomous region.

At the same time ornamental wares were being made, which included incense burners, vases, dressing-table sets, jewellery boxes, and bird and flower groups. Work produced in mainland China inclines towards sweet-faced individuals, such as maiden Immortals with their faces painted as if for a stage appearance, children, and flower groups. Today it is still the rather sentimental or elaborate groups which are made for sale to the western buyer.

Modern Hong Kong

In one particular carving factory in Hong Kong in the 1970s, 300 craftsmen were employed, but complaints had already started and today they are rife. People complained that the time required to learn the skill was too long for contemporary youngsters, and few were attracted to the work. This same firm was importing about 120 lb (54 kg) of tusks a year from Africa, some 100 in. (2.5 m) in length. Fifteen per cent of this ivory was lost in wastage during the carving process.

Apprenticeship is a long, slow, three to five years, and work is carried out in small family factories. Few girls are employed. The apprentice carvers are first taught the techniques of soaking the ivory, cutting it into blocks, and polishing. Their first jobs are carving characters on mahjong sets and making chopsticks. The primary carving is usually done by machinery, to speed the process along (many carvers now favour using a dentist's drill), but the final carving and detail work can only be completed with traditional hand tools, such as simple wire-cutters and chisels. Most of the finishing and polishing is carried out by hand, using fine sandpaper and dried leaves.

The shape, colour and texture of the material influence the design, but Guanyin is a favourite, as is a Japanese character, 'the Drunken Indecent Gambler', and bridges are popular. Some new styles have been introduced, and many of these are stained and brightly coloured. They include lurid vegetables. These ideas have been brought to Hong Kong by mainland carvers and have yet to find much favour with the resident carvers on the island. A list of what a Hong Kong carver offers today reads: King and Queen, Warrior Riding on Horse, Old Man and Beauty (assorted), Guanyin, the Eight Immortals, Figure in Boat, Incense Burner, Incense Burner Pagoda, Warrior, groups of figurines.

Most ivory is bleached before carving begins, as the carvers believe the market favours 'white ivory'. The common belief that customers seek ivories where a high degree of skill and intricacy is apparent leads to over-elaboration and decoration for the sake of decoration.

Due to the nature of modern Hong Kong society, and the increasing scarcity of ivory, skilled carvers are declining in numbers. The art and skill of the ivory carver may be at a new crossroads.

Japan

Early ivories

The history of the arts of Japan is inextricably entwined with that of China. There was traffic with Korea before the first century AD, when holy images and other religious articles were imported, along with the various craftsmen. During Japan's Asuka period (AD 552–645) the Chinese Buddhist influence was strong and indigenous wood and bronze sculpture was made. It was during the Chinese Tang dynasty (AD 618–907) that civilized Japan adopted the Chinese way of life almost to the exclusion of native culture. The arts, architecture, city planning and literature were Chinese, as was the language of the court.

In AD 753 the Shoso-in, the chief repository of objects used in religious ceremonies, was completed. It was built of wood behind the hall of the Great Buddha in Nara, the capital, and its survival, given the numerous wars, fires and earthquakes which have periodically swept Japan, is in itself a miracle. That the contents, tens of thousands of objects, should also have come down to us almost intact is quite extraordinary. They provide a brilliant picture of life in Japan twelve hundred years ago and the sophistication of the fabrics, the lacquer, musical instruments and arms and armour is remarkable. Precious materials such as gold, silver, tortoiseshell, horn and ivory are used for inlays in designs that are obviously influenced by contemporary China, but on objects that are peculiarly Japanese. Ivory and gold appear as inlays on an armrest. A *go* board has ivory stringing forming the squares and geometric decoration of ivory, deerhorn and various woods. Another board game, *sugoroku*, roughly equivalent to backgammon, has a similarly decorated board. Perhaps the most interesting of the pieces are six ivory rules belonging to the Emperor Shomu (reigned 724–56). Their length averages 12 in. (30 cm) but varies, which suggests that they may have been intended more as scroll weights than for measurement. They are engraved with birds, beasts and rosettes and two are stained red with coloured details. The Tang influence is very strong, but different enough to suggest indigenous work.

Other ivories are known from the period, including a number of figures, but their conception and execution are too close to Chinese to be sure that they are actually Japanese.

Very few other articles with ivory inlay or decoration survive from medieval Japan and it is not until the introduction of the netsuke in the seventeenth century that the material seems to have found much favour with carvers. Meanwhile, however, a Japanese culture took root and developed.

Although Buddhist monasteries and temples were built throughout Japan, Buddhism did not completely supplant Shintoism, the faith in which the indigenous population believed. The Japanese had a continuing deep respect for natural materials and for the spirit in nature, a respect inherent in the Shinto belief. A flourishing industry produced considerable quantities of carvings and decorations for the temples and other buildings, at first in entirely Chinese style, but from the ninth century onwards Chinese dominance waned and Japanese culture took over. Wood carving, fine metalwork, particularly for swords and armour, and the technique that Japan was to bring to perfection, lacquer, all flourished.

Seventeenth- and eighteenth-century Japan

Japan was a strongly stratified society with a *shōgun* dominating the hereditary warrior class, the samurai, who ensured his survival, down through peasants and fishermen to the lowest levels of craftsmen, merchants and the handlers of dead bodies. This traditional hierarchy was upset during the Momoyama period (1568–1615) when power began to devolve to the wealthy merchants. It was in the mid sixteenth century that the Portuguese, followed by the Dutch, the English and others, arrived in Japan and began trading. With the Portuguese came Catholic priests.

By the beginning of the Edo period (1615–1868) the priests had begun to overreach themselves and after a revolt in which the Christians were heavily involved, Christianity was banned and all barbarians, as the Europeans were dubbed,

Above: Three ivory netsuke. Eighteenth-century; 4 to 4⅛ in. (10.2 to 10.3 cm).

Far left: Ivory rules owned by the Emperor Shomu who died in AD 756. 12 in. (30 cm) long. Engraved in bachiru technique, with coloured details.

were banished. The only exception was the port of Nagasaki where the Chinese and the Dutch continued to trade. It was another two hundred years before Japan opened its doors to any western influence. Christianity did not die out, however, but went underground.

The history of ivory carving in Japan, as opposed to inlay work, is not of any antiquity. However, it is likely that the material had already arrived in finished form as the ends of scroll rollers or as seals from the Chinese merchants during the Tang period (AD 618–907). Although both China and Japan recognize calligraphy as one of the highest forms of art and consider the inscription of a poem or title on a scroll painting as an integral part of the subject matter, the artist's signature is secondary to his seal. Likewise, no legal document is valid if unsealed. Seal making has therefore been an important craft for at least a

millennium, the carver's materials ranging from wood to stone and including all forms of ivory.

But the best-known of all eighteenth-century ivory carvings are netsuke, small toggles by means of which a pouch, a pipe or a small nest of boxes, called an *inrō*, was suspended from the obi (a waistband worn by men and women alike) round the pocketless kimono. *Inrō* means 'seal basket' and it was originally used as a seal box.

One side of the seal, with its reversed, usually archaic characters, called for considerable but conventional skill, whereas the top or handle could suit the fancy of the owner. A number of combined netsuke/seals are known and much of the range of pure netsuke art can be found in these pieces. Because the seal already bears the 'signature' of the owner, it is rarely, if ever, signed by the carver. As wood tends to wear quickly, wooden seals may be found with ivory characters.

Apart from seals and netsuke, ivory was sometimes used for a pipe bowl in the form of an animal or a figure or even doubling as a netsuke, but these are rare. The risks of cracking and staining are great but ivory is not as unlikely a choice as might at first appear, as it does not burn readily. Pipe holders and pouches, *inrō*, musical instruments such as the *biwa* and *samisen*, the latter's plectrum, the lid of the tea jar from the tea ceremony, table screens and small images of Buddha for personal use might be wholly or partly made of ivory.

Netsuke and their carvers
The best carvers would probably produce a dozen to twenty netsuke a year but the studio system could increase this. A considerable time was expended on the polishing stage to ensure the right patination, which was often aided by staining and dyeing. This patina, which time has enhanced, is one of the most reliable guides to the genuine netsuke (there are numerous forgeries on the market). Netsuke were functional objects in everyday use and although a wealthy man might own several, selecting which to wear much as today we select a tie or a scarf, they inevitably suffered from wear. This can enhance the appearance of an old netsuke, softening the sharp edges, but too much can seriously detract. The cord holes (*himotoshi*) also suffer wear.

Ivory played a major part in other forms of netsuke. The *manju* gets its name from its resemblance to a small rice cake like a flattened bun. The decoration is usually in low relief lying proud of the surface or sunken in intaglio, and may include other materials. Alternatively, the ivory may be inlaid into lacquer or metal. Large numbers were produced and many are of fine quality, the flat surface leading the carver to 'paint' rather than 'sculpt' it. There are either two cord holes or a loop carved on the back.

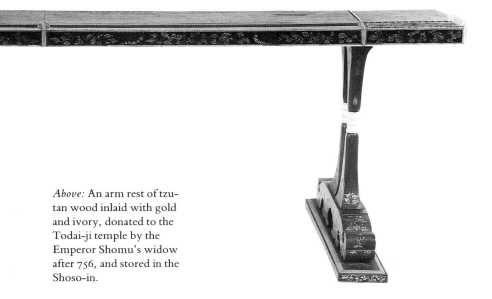

Above: An arm rest of tzu-tan wood inlaid with gold and ivory, donated to the Todai-ji temple by the Emperor Shomu's widow after 756, and stored in the Shoso-in.

  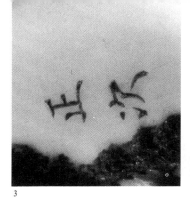 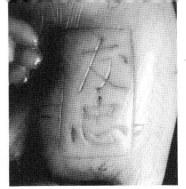 

1   2   3   4   5

Above: Carvers' signatures on netsuke shown in colour on page 276.
1. On a dragon *manju* in staghorn, Shiratama.
2. On a monkey's back, Kaigyokusai Masatsugu.
3. On a sleeping boar, Masatsugu.
4. On fighting tigers, Masanao.
5. On a goat, Sato Masayoshi (1819–65).
6. On an oni and a rat, Masaka.
7. On an octopus and a diver, Mintani.
8. On a figure of a boy, Ryo.

Similar in form to the *manju* is the *kagamibuta*. Here a disc, usually of metal, either chased or inlaid with other metals, sits in an undecorated ivory dish. The cord holes are similar to the *manju*.

The *ryusa* is a *manju* netsuke, the decoration being left against a pierced ground. The removal of much of the background makes the netsuke lighter in weight and very suitable for use with a lacquer *inrō* where a *manju* would normally be too heavy. Many *ryusa* make use of the inferior walrus ivory as its granular core is here easily disguised.

The *sashi* is thin and of elongated form. The pouch or *inrō* is suspended from the hole at the top and the *sashi* pushed under the obi; the main emphasis of the carving is therefore usually at the top where the netsuke is exposed. A variant, the *obihasimi*, based on a Chinese belt hook, has a hook at the lower end for added security. Both these forms are uncommon.

In the eighteenth century as many netsuke were carved in wood as in ivory, and a small number in staghorn, bone, lacquer and other materials. Only in the nineteenth century, probably as much because of supply as demand or inclination, did ivory begin to predominate.

The eighteenth-century netsuke carver was a craftsman, not an artist, an important distinction, for the former led a hand-to-mouth existence and was a long way down the social scale. He may well have been working on netsuke as a sideline, either buying the raw material from a dealer and selling the finished work back to him, or, as was frequently the case, being given the ivory by a dealer in *tabakire* (tobacco pouches), carving it and returning the finished netsuke. The ivory was weighed before and after being worked on and the carver was under an obligation to remove as little ivory as possible. The raw material came in the form of discs about 2 in. (5 cm) thick, cut from the tusk; the disc was then cut into triangular pieces, like a cake, for the carver to work on. When completed they were delivered back to the dealer for sale. As weight could be the determining factor in the price, the triangular form of the original piece, together with the functional compactness, explains the form of many netsuke. The dealer dictated the subject matter, according to what was currently popular, and the style of carving. Only major carvers were free to work on what they wanted and be sure of a ready sale.

Such a carver might take up production full time and possibly employ an apprentice, who would begin by sweeping the floor and running errands before he was allowed near the ivory. One of the simplest forms to start on is the mask or face, which can be considered as almost two-dimensional. It also makes a satisfactory netsuke and can be quick to carve. Large numbers were therefore produced and range from reproductions in miniature of the masks worn in Noh and kyogen plays to animals both real and legendary, ghosts and demons. From about 1850 onwards there are also naturalistic portraits, presumably special orders. The comical characteristics of face-pulling are fully explored. The apprentice might strike out on his own, his work probably retaining hints of the master's style, or be retained in the studio to put finishing touches to each piece and to sign them. This is why we occasionally find carvings with genuine signatures on widely differing subjects. No deception was intended, the master/pupil/studio relationship was accepted; only now are we presented with an almost insoluble problem of who did what.

The master might use his full signature, if he had produced the entire piece, or an abbreviated or different signature, or might leave it unsigned. The Japanese inherits a surname from his father, which is written first, as well as a given name. Unfortunately, he usually adopts a professional name, his *gō*, and this is often changed. The master might also add and drop names throughout his professional life. An apprentice might take the master's name or adopt one character from it and add one of his own. An individual could identify himself by adding a *kakihan*, a scrolling character which is usually unreadable, or a character in archaic or seal style, occasionally staining this red. He might also add biographical details such as his age, his abode or the date of carving. The signature may be badly formed (superb carvers might be illiterate), or free-floating, or enclosed within a rectangle, oval or gourd shape, and these may help to identify a school or locality. There are over 2500 recorded signatures so a firm attribution is not easy. Contemporary forgers in many cases copied the signature as well. Thus there are eighteenth-century forgeries of contemporary netsuke with all the natural wear and patination of the original.

The low status of the professional netsuke

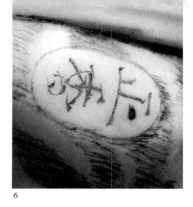 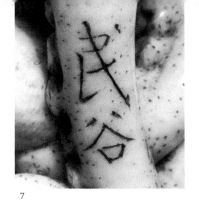 

6   7   8

carver (apart from scholars for whom carving was a diversion) meant that in the struggle for day-to-day existence standards would slip. Today it is impossible to differentiate between hurried or poorer work from a good carver and the best work of a second-rate carver excelling himself on a special commission. This means that many good carvings by major artists are downgraded to copies or attributed to lesser carvers. Equally, although each carver worked in a distinctive style – the subject, the scale, the placing of the *himotoshi* – an inventive artist will continually innovate and there are undoubtedly many fine carvings outside an artist's normal *oeuvre* which have not been attributed to him. As research continues, so once-regarded major pieces are downgraded and unrecognized masterpieces come to light. This, compounded with the fact that there is almost no contemporary documentation, means that netsuke are very much evaluated on the quality of the piece rather than definite attribution, as an example may show.

The earliest reference to carvers of netsuke and *ojime* (the bead fastening) in Japanese literature is in the *Soken Kishō* (1781), a seven-volume work on swords and fittings, the last volume of which listed fifty-four carvers with short notes on them. Most of them were living and working around Osaka and Kyoto, the area known to the author. Among the occupations listed for them were those of carvers of Buddhist images, which would have been in wood, not ivory, of panels for houses and temples and of false teeth. Others were recorded as working for pleasure. One note reads: 'Tomotada from the capital Kyoto. He calls himself Izumiya Shichiemon. He is a genius at carving cattle. His netsuke are highly praised and admired, especially in the Kanto [Tokyo] area. As this is the case, there may be hundreds of imitations. However, the originals are extraordinarily fine in workmanship.' We will never know on what examples the writer based his praise, or if they were even genuine. Tomotada signatures are so prolific that no one man could have carved the output, nor is it likely given the variation of quality that they even emanate from one studio.

The best we can say of a given netsuke showing one of Tomotada's best-known subjects, the ox, is that it is certainly eighteenth-century, finely carved in the style we believe Tomotada worked in and bearing a signature generally supposed to be his. His animals (oxen, tigers, goats, boars) display great strength as if caught in a movement which will continue once the watcher's eyes have strayed. He engraved the hair marking with care and took great trouble with the hidden parts, such as the feet.

Other major carvers from Kyoto are Yamaguchi Okatomo, a pupil of Tomotada, and Masanao. Okatoma developed a group of quail on millet, renowned both today and in his lifetime, witness the numerous copies. While his work bears affinity to that of Tomotada it does not have the muscular power; the animals are more refined and delicate, his mice and monkeys having an almost feminine quality. Masanao is also mentioned in the *Soken Kishō* and considered to be one of the greatest netsuke carvers of all. His work has typical eighteenth-century power and covers a range of real and imaginary beasts and other groups. There were a large number of carvers with the same name and the signature is not a guarantee of attribution.

Certain parts of Japan specialized in the eighteenth century in particular subjects and styles, enabling us at least to narrow down the possibilities to one area or school. The region of Osaka and Kyoto specialized in Chinese subjects but it was also a cattle-raising area – hence Tomotada's subject matter; Tokyo tackled genre subjects; Nagoya chose natural history. But the demarcation was by no means hard and fast.

Netsuke from Iwami province in the southwest of Honshu island, a distant and remote area uninfluenced by the mainstream of Japanese art, stand apart. Probably because of the difficulty of obtaining elephant ivory the local carvers took to wild boars' tusks, which were abundant in the region. Because of the curving form and the narrow nature the netsuke are normally a length of tusk on which sit or crawl insects of every sort, sea life and occasionally birds or animals. In addition the carver frequently records in great detail the date and place of carving, his age and other biographical data, in finely engraved black characters of minuscule size. The area also developed a curious technique of signing wood netsuke in low-relief *ukibori* and in very rare instances these appear on ivory. It is not known how Tomiharu, the first exponent of the feat, achieved the result but he must have used a resist, such as wax, drawn on the tusk which was then etched away with acid. Polishing would then leave the background smooth and lower than the characters.

When the carvers of Buddhist images turned to making netsuke, the Buddhist myths and legends naturally provided subject matter and Chinese subjects are a prevalent theme.

There runs through much of Japanese art a delight in the ridiculous. Response to a personal disaster which makes the sufferer absurd is more likely to provoke gales of laughter than sympathy – the blind are therefore most amusing and are often depicted in groups discovering an elephant. Foreigners, at the time the Dutch, are of course hysterically funny – reincarnated as enormous in size, immensely hairy with green or blue eyes, and lacking the complex social skills that dominated Japanese life. Most would have heard of the Dutch but very few indeed would have set eyes on a Dutchman, confined to his port of Nagasaki. Undoubtedly there was a flourishing trade in the area where travellers could buy netsuke in the form of this semi-mythical being, portrayed with over-large nose, bulging eyes, full wig or curly hair and ridiculous hat, and of exaggerated height. His many-buttoned frock coat is carefully copied, but the original brocade has been transmuted into waves as a clue to his overseas origin.

Although Christianity survived underground, netsuke with Christian iconography are very rare. To display one would have been courting disaster, but examples exist incorporating a cross as part of the design. Figures of priests with curly beards and hair could be either Christian or Buddhist, the latter much more likely. What do not seem to have been produced are any ivory figures of Christian significance.

Nineteenth-century Japan

Later netsuke

The turn of the century saw the netsuke gaining rapidly in popularity and most of the highly regarded netsuke carvers were at work in the first half of the nineteenth century. From the elongated Chinese and European figures and the mythical beasts, the netsuke became more compact and naturalistic. The animals showed a gradual shift in emphasis from the rugged power of the eighteenth century to a more delicate approach. The loss of strength was replaced by greater detail and more complex groups appeared. Ivory began to predominate over wood.

Perhaps the greatest of the netsuke carvers of the early nineteenth century is Kaigyokuai Masatsugu, a perfectionist who chose the finest ivory, rarely used stain (where he did, it was only slight) and carved anatomically correct, perfectly balanced birds and animals, with details, such as the hair, carved in relief rather than incised which was quicker. The figure is often so carved that a leg

forms the *himotoshi*, obviating the need for disfiguring holes.

Among the foremost is Ohara Mitsuhiro, who lived between 1810 and 1875 in Onomichi and Osaka. Much of his work looks surprisingly modern as he stylized animals, particularly birds, refining the outlines and eliminating unnecessary detail. He was skilled also in simulating one material in another, ivory roughened to copy a roof-tile, for example, and he expended considerable time and effort to produce the highest-quality staining and polishing. This, together with such details as the placing of the *himotoshi*, and the overall conception of the design, should enable the numerous copies bearing his signature to be eliminated.

The tiger, not indigenous to Japan, illustrates well the change from the ferocious beast of the eighteenth century to the overgrown cat, trying to look cross, in the nineteenth century. It is one of the twelve signs of the oriental zodiac, given to the months and hours of the clock (in twos) and the years. The others are the rat, ox, hare, dragon, snake, horse, goat, ape, cock, dog and hog, and all are popular subjects. Exceptions to the peaceful tiger are those by Otoman and Kyushu; the latter's animals appear particularly bad-tempered. For greater effect he inlays the eyes with horn and paints the stripes.

As the century progressed, and certainly after the country opened its doors to the west in 1853, netsuke became more and more meretricious rather than meritorious. There was growing emphasis on technical artistry, with the carver displaying marvellously detailed carving of, say, the pattern on a kimono. Inlays of horn, tortoiseshell, glass, metals, coral, etc., had from the mid eighteenth century been used for small details, such as eyes; now their use spread to other details, and in the hands of a mid century artist such as Tokoku could play a significant part in the design. Taste and demand, largely from the west, dictated more and more colourful inlay, to the detriment of the integrity of the piece.

Like most island races, the Japanese had developed a close relationship with the sea. It plays a large part in their art, including the netsuke, ranging from the simple depiction of fish and shells, to the *takarabune*, or Treasure Ship, with the Seven Gods of Good Fortune, and to Ashinaga and Tennaga, the long-legged and long-armed fishermen. Staghorn, a harder material than ivory but relatively thin, available to netsuke carvers as the deer is indigenous to Japan, and cheap, lent itself to netsuke of *kappa* heads. The *kappa* is a mythical beast of unsurpassed nastiness and these netsuke are often green-stained and occasionally found with movable lower jaws.

The Japanese regard western attitudes to sexual matters somewhat askance – surely nothing can be wrong with anything so basic and natural? Sex can be a target for poking fun. Netsuke of outwardly innocent appearance open to reveal scenes of erotic embrace, but these were probably made for the European market. There is no tradition of the female nude in Japanese art and even when wholly abandoned a woman is usually only depicted with a parted kimono. Fungi, either naturalistically but suggestively carved, or being fingered by a beautiful girl, are common subjects, and so, similarly, are mask noses, vegetables and clams, often accompanied by a girl tittering behind her hand at their suggestive appearance. The *ama* (female diver) in her grass skirt (which is occasionally removable) may be locked in the embrace of an octopus whose tentacles and elongated head are suggestive in themselves. The mask continued in popularity throughout the nineteenth century and in the second half sets of miniature examples, too small to function as netsuke, were sold in boxes for export. The signature is usually found on one only or split between two of the set, the rest being unsigned. The boxes often provide much additional information on the carver.

The entry into Yokohama harbour by Commodore Perry of the United States Navy in 1853 was to have a profound effect on Japanese society. After two hundred years of feudalism the change was extraordinarily far-reaching and rapid. Far from being overwhelmed the Japanese enthusiastically adapted their skills to western demand. Men began to adopt western dress and the pockets made the *inrō* and pouch, and with them the netsuke, unnecessary. In 1868 the first netsuke were exported to the west as amusing souvenirs and seemed to appeal immediately – they reflected an exotic way of life, made ideal small presents and were absurdly cheap. By the end of the century, they were sold by volume in two different qualities.

Japan and the western market

The traditional Japanese wood and paper house, constructed to mitigate the damage from earthquakes, had no shelves and almost no furniture. There might be a corner in which hung a scroll painting, possibly with a flower vase beneath it. The tea-house in the garden for the tea ceremony would be utterly plain, nothing to distract the mind, but for a perfectly chosen painting and a single flower spray. The idea of displaying objects lined up on shelves was alien. It was only western ideas that led to the introduction of the *okimono*, an object for display.

Western applied art of the second half of the nineteenth century was concerned with a display of complexity, ingenuity and unparalleled craftsmanship. The netsuke had been moving in the same direction since the eighteenth century and, as in the west, at the expense of strength. Painting in Europe was narrative, every painting had to tell a story, and this too had echoes in Japan. The result was a demand in the west for ivory groups of figures or animals which described the Japanese way of life with extreme realism and exceptional craftsmanship. Although the study of these pieces is in its infancy a few major schools are identifiable, that of Ogawa being the most prolific. The groups are constructed from a number of separately carved pieces assembled on a thin disc of ivory raised on four short legs. The ivory, selected with care, is of the best, the carving is meticulous and the finest pieces have movement and a realistic display of expression. Farmers, poulterers, street entertainers, makers of fans, rush mats, swords, dolls and baskets, and various merchants provide a better picture of contemporary Japan than the photograph albums do. One figure above all others sums them up: the basket seller. The sandal-shod or barefoot peasant, staggering under the weight of numerous baskets, sieves, hats and toys but, and very important this, *smiling*, would have struck an immediate chord with the financier or industrialist who bought the figure. Basket sellers are not among the best carvings; they are impressive in their complexity and the rehearsal of intricate piercing and engraving, but lack the breath of life that suffuses the best sculpture.

Groups illustrating various legends were also carved and in every case the interpretation had to be universal; the western buyer needed no knowledge of the source. However, such was the interest in Japan at this time that the legends were

Below: Ivory *okimono* of rice sellers, signed by Sei. *c*.1900; *c*. 5¾ in. (14.5 cm).

translated, printed with woodblock illustrations and shipped abroad in large numbers.

In 1878 the catalogue of the Paris Exhibition gave guarded, if convoluted, approval to Japanese ivory carvings: 'Uniformity is utterly discarded, and repetition most decidedly, there are no parallel lines and balanced parts – all is free and fanciful. It is in a sense realistic, for the beautiful forms of nature, animal and vegetable, are reproduced with unsurpassed, we had almost said unequalled, exactitude; every leaf, every vein, is studied with admirable art; but the art appears in the beautiful adaptation of the work and its position and the skilful combinations of the parts of the design.'

Although the western buyer would be unable to read a Japanese signature, it added to the aura of the mysterious east and was obviously a bonus. Signatures therefore became more prominent. The red lacquer reserve, perhaps because of a subconscious connection with the sealing-wax seal on documents, seems to have become a symbol of quality. The Ogawa school used large rectangular lacquer insets in the base, with the characters meticulously engraved in typographical style. Occasionally there are two plaques for the two halves of the name. A red lacquer signature by no means guarantees that the piece is a fine one.

Japan had easy access to walrus tusks, which it began to import in vast quantities towards the end of the nineteenth century. Because the granular core is disfiguring on small groups, the tusks are usually left full length with a minimum of carving round them to produce a logical group. The most common is a fruit-picking scene with a farmer at the base of a tree while several children pick and throw down fruit from the branches. Any subject suited to an elongated format was used: an Immortal with a boy on his back, a street entertainer supporting a boy, a *sarumawashi* (monkey entertainer) with an eagle alighting on the

monkey – in every case the form of the tusk has dictated the finished carving and they rarely have any merit.

Elephant ivory was used in the construction of boxes, *kodansu* (small cabinets), vases and screens with varying degrees of success. Thin slices of tusk are prone to warping and may split, although the latter problem is surprisingly uncommon. The sheets were set into thicker frames, in the hope, often unsuccessful, of preventing this. The edges were carved with scrolling flowers, clouds, birds or other designs in low relief. The panels themselves could either be similarly carved with figure subjects, landscapes or wildlife, with varying degrees of skill (and many of the latter are dreadful), or inlaid with mother-of-pearl, stained ivory, hardstones, coconut shell, horn and so on in a technique known as Shibayama, after Shibayama Dosho who introduced in the eighteenth century the technique of using various inlays into ivory. Various members of the family are recorded, including Naoyuki, Senzo, Soichi, Yasumasa, Yasunobu, Yekisei, Yekishin and Yekishu, and *inrō*, screens and *kodansu* simply signed Shibayama appear not infrequently. There is no guarantee that they were produced by the family although some are attributable with some certainty. This inlay displays the extraordinary Japanese skill in handling minute pieces of different materials, all exactly fitting into shallow recesses carved in the ivory ground. As so often with these late works, however, their innate sense of design and balance is lost in a display of vulgar opulence and technical virtuosity to pander to western taste. Among the most decorative are the ivory elephants caparisoned and saddleclothed with flowers and beads and usually supporting a carved lotus flower on which rests a glass ball.

Parallel with these were thousands of appallingly carved tigers, lions, elephants, rhinoceroses, crocodiles and other beasts, usually not indigenous to Japan and often locked in unlikely battles. The details and fur markings are often coloured.

The armourers of Japan were accustomed to working in minute detail, making *tsuba* (sword guards) and other sword and sheath fittings. After the wearing of swords was banned in 1876, many turned to making vases, screens and boxes, finely inlaid in gold, silver and exotic alloys, and meticulously detailed, articulated studies of crayfish, crabs, insects and so on, mostly in iron. These proved very popular in the west and the ivory carvers followed suit, the results being among the most awe-inspiring of all the commercial carvings. Elaborately mounted swords found a ready market in the west and new blades of no merit were sheathed in ivory scabbards, unknown before the mid nineteenth century. The carving is rarely of high standard and while the work displays a certain skill in wielding the knife it has

the lack of restraint in design that typifies most late work. Demand soon outstripped supply and an industry developed carving extremely crude scabbards, usually with squatting warriors, the details picked out in black. The majority are bone, made up in short sections, the joints covered by stamped metal bands, the ends commonly offcuts of ivory.

There was a flourishing trade with Japan for small carvings, with or without inlay, which were mounted on arrival in Europe in an enormous range of goods. These included cane and umbrella handles, cutlery handles, magnifying-glass frames, dressing-table sets of brushes, combs and mirrors, brooches, studs, buttons, paper-knives, hairpins, games counters, photograph frames, book covers, *aides-mémoire*, card cases, opera glasses and trays.

The Tokyo School of Art

Amid all this degeneration there was founded in 1887, under western influence, the Tokyo School of Art at which sculpture, but not netsuke carving, was one of the courses. One of the tenets of the ivory carvers was that, as far as was possible, the figure would be carved from a single section of tusk; only an outstretched arm, say, would be inset. The figures were mostly above 10 in. (25 cm) tall and extremely realistic, depicting a range of occupations from the lowest peasant to

the samurai class. Instead of the finely finished surface required by the export market, in which every mark of the graver was sanded away, the chisel marks, albeit barely visible, were left to remain. These too proved popular in the west and today there are far more examples in the western world than in Japan. An additional conceit was to leave the original rough and brown-stained surface of the tusk showing round the base. Signatures were usually engraved on the underside of the base and not on a lacquer reserve.

The major artist at the school was Ishikawa Komei whose best work is of exceptional quality and stands comparison with the greatest sculptors. His range is from netsuke to large figures and with a considerable variety of subjects, but either he also turned out poor, commercial work or his signature was copied, as it can be found on paper-knives and netsuke of little merit.

Two other carvers whose work was of a high standard are Yoshida Homei and Hirasaka Hobun, the latter specializing in old men.

The twentieth century

Until the beginning of the First World War the production of ivory carvings, both netsuke and *okimono*, for the export market continued undiminished or, if anything, increased. The war stopped any imports of raw ivory, and the post-war depression and the design revolution, which

centred on an uncluttered look, greatly reduced the demand for carvings. Those that were made were generally of far poorer quality. There were exceptions; the Japan Ivory Sculptors Association fought to maintain standards and a few carvers taught their skills to a new generation. Yoshida Yoshiaki (at work in 1911) was a student of Shimura Toshiro, also a carver of *okimono*, whose *gō* was Toshiaki. The carver Yoshida Homei married Yoshiaki's daughter and the contemporary carver Masatoshi is related to Shimura. This linkage by blood, studio, adoption or friendship runs strongly through most Japanese ivory carving. The carvers of today are undoubtedly skilled but there is considerable debate among collectors over what it is that they are producing. They are making miniature sculpture whose function has vanished; the netsuke is no more. Not only do the growing number of collectors interested in the modern carvers argue whether the *himotoshi* should be retained but so do the carvers. The dividing line between netsuke and *okimono* is no longer clear.

A great deal of unimaginative hack-work is being produced which is expensive but is readily absorbed by the west. These carvings are almost without exception naturalistic in the extreme and often with a sickly sentimentality. The major revolutions in twentieth-century art have passed them by, and only a few carvers have moved into the area of abstraction. Strangely enough, stylized subjects taken from toys, such as the good luck sparrow, and the technique of *ikkibori* (one-stroke carving) dating from the nineteenth century, have a very definite modern feel, but their influence has been absorbed by few carvers.

The time-consuming process of polishing is usually skimped, particularly in the areas of undercutting, which, when stained, has a disfiguring roughness. The modern stains are never as subtle as the early ones, taking an unpleasant sepia-grey or pinkish tinge which is wiped away on proud surfaces leaving too great a contrast of tone. To mitigate this, many carvers have taken to a greater use of colour, often covering large areas of, say, a kimono, in brilliant blue and gilding, to hideous effect.

Apart from these 'collector's' carvings, large numbers of tourist-quality netsuke are still being turned out for souvenir shops, hotel lobbies and 'antique' shops the world over. They vary in quality but the studios that make them (some in Hong Kong) have a few best-selling lines, such as *sumo* wrestlers, figures with revolving faces and simple animal shapes, and the collector should have no difficulty in identifying them. More of a problem, as they are realistic in weight and colour, are the resin copies made from flexible moulds which pick up every minute line of the original.

Right: Ivory and wood figure of a flower arranger, signed by Ryoko tō. *c.* 1900; 12¼ in. (31 cm) wide.

Opposite: Netsuke. *Top:* Sleeping boar by Masatsugu; tigers (Masanao); goat (Masayoshi); monkeys (Masatsugu); dragon (Shiratama). *Below:* Ama with octopus (Mintani); kyohime, oni (Masaka). See pages 268–9 for signatures. Boar: 1¾ in. (4.4 cm) long.

Below: Sage with blowing hat (Ishikawa Komei); man and boy (unsigned) and egg tester (Hobun), Tokyo School; woodsman (Roun); poulterer (Okawa Shizumune). From 6 in. (15 cm) (poulterer) to 13¾ in. (35 cm) tall (man and boy). See also page 274.

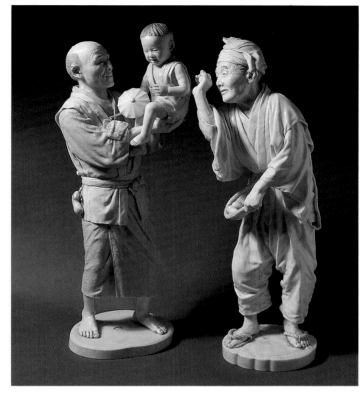

Himalayan Countries

Ivory was not easily available in the Himalayan countries, although some ivory images, both from Nepal and Tibet, are found. On the whole, however, metal was favoured for image making; wood, stone, terracotta and various hardstones were sometimes used.

The elephant was known of in Tibet but knowledge of it was slight, as is evident from primitive and inaccurate depictions in Tibetan painting, both early and late. Images of the elephant-headed Hindu god Ganesha, the son of Siva and Parvati and sometime god of wisdom and good fortune, painted on cotton (*pata*) and rendered in metal, proliferate in Nepal, but his Buddhist counterpart, Vinayaka, is not frequently encountered in Tibet, where he is usually depicted prostrate on a lotus throne, beneath the feet of the ferocious tutelary deity, Mahakala. Stylized elephants or elephant heads often appear in elaborate aureoles (*prabha*) along with mythological beasts and scrolling foliage.

Though rare in Tibet, ivory does not appear to have been prized above other non-indigenous materials such as turquoise, coral, amber and conch shell. The Tibetan practice of carving human or animal bone artefacts may have acted as a substitute. The fashion for bone ritual objects did not spread to Nepal, where ritual, though of great importance, has not the same significance, though in Nepal ivory carvings are even rarer than in Tibet.

Nepal

Although the twelfth-century ivory throne-supports described earlier, vigorously carved as seated lions, are generally regarded as being Pala-Sena work from north-east India, they have sometimes been attributed to Nepal. The stylistic similarity between Pala, Tibetan and Nepalese art at this period is such that neither attribution has yet been proved conclusively, though loosely comparable Nepalese sculptures in stone, and to a lesser extent in bronze, can be found.

Largely through the Newar artists of the Nepal Valley, famous primarily for their metal casting and for their architectural wood carving, an indigenous Nepalese style emerged under the Thakuri and early Malla kings (*c.* 750–1480), continued under the later Mallas (1480–1768) and emerged into modern times under the Gurkhas and Ranas (1768–1951).

Few ivories appear to have survived from the earlier period but a figure of Bhringin, an attendant of Siva, dating from the sixteenth or seventeenth century, vividly encapsulates the later Malla style. The ferocious-faced god, 9½ in. (24 cm) tall, stands dancing on a lotus throne,

flanked by two mischievous-looking attendants, one holding a snake. He wears an arched foliate crown, necklaces of human skulls and of snakes, floral earrings and chain sashes with bell terminals. A drum carved in relief in front of the stomach was probably held in the primary hands. Each of the eight arms is missing below the elbow-joint, where separately carved forearms were originally attached with pegs.

A cylindrical ivory mirror handle with bell-metal mirror, now in the Nepal Museum, was an offering from a barber to Ratnesvara, 'Lord of Jewels', in AD 1733. It is carved on one side with Lakshmi-Narayana (the Hindu god Vishnu and his consort Lakshmi), supported by the winged bird god Garuda, with Krishna fluting in woods below; on the other with Uma-Mahesvara (Siva and his consort Parvati), above a dancing milkmaid, a *gopi* (an attendant of Krishna). Two further *gopis* decorate the sides. The pommel is carved with overlapping lotus petals.

By 1888, according to the catalogue of the Glasgow International Exhibition, ivory carving was carried on in Nepal 'to a limited extent as the raw material is scarce and expensive. The articles made are figures of divinities, combs, dice, dominoes, chopsticks and *kukri* dagger handles.' The latter – the knives still carried by Gurkhas today – were also made with horn hilts, sometimes silver-mounted. The dominoes and chopsticks were exported to Tibet. A small, nineteenth-century ivory box and lid, now in London, mounted with gilt-bronze repoussé decoration and set with turquoises and other stones, is thought to have been inspired by similar boxes made in Rajasthan.

In the twentieth century, ivory carving has declined further in Nepal, though jewellery and archaizing religious images are still produced.

Tibet

Perhaps the earliest known ivory from Tibet is a standing Bodhisattva in the Kashmiri style, possibly tenth- or eleventh-century. Now handless, it wears a diaphanous dhoti and zigzagging sash, with a fragmentary further sash sweeping almost to the ankles, and simple beaded jewellery. The slender elongated body is carved with pronounced musculature. The figure is obviously closely related to the group of eighth- or ninth-century miniature Buddhist ivories, described above, but may have been carved by a Kashmiri craftsman in Tibet, possibly in the temple at Mangnang, where Kashmiri artists are known to have been employed between 958 and 1055.

Between the eighth and the twelfth centuries, Buddhist art, and latterly Hindu art, flourished under the Pala and Sena kings of Bihar and Bengal

Above: Nepalese Lamaist ivory of the Bodhisattva Maitreya. Probably seventeenth- or eighteenth-century.

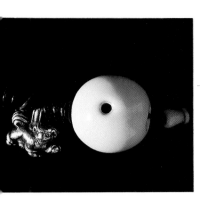

Above: Tibetan rosary shown in colour on page 281.

Above: Tibetan bowl shown in colour on page 280.

and this, the last flowering of Buddhist art in India, was the basis from which Tibetan Buddhist art evolved, the styles of painting and image making being brought to Tibet by monks, scholars and mystics, cross-pollinated with Nepalese influences *en route*. In 1192, following the battle of Tarain, Muslim rule was firmly established in Bengal, Bihar was annexed, and India's great Buddhist monasteries were destroyed. Tibet's submission to the Mongol leader Genghis Khan (1162–1227) further isolated the country. The basic style of Pala-Sena art became subject to Mongol and ultimately to Chinese influences, although Tibet eventually regained its independence under the Great Fifth Dalai Lama (reigned 1642–82).

Although ivory was sometimes used for utilitarian objects such as food bowls, ritual vessels, prayer-wheels, water- or powderflasks, and most commonly chopsticks, Tibetan ivory images seldom display styles as indigenous as those found in comparable bronze images. A fine Sino-Tibetan ivory figure of Daka (*Za-byed*), wearing a ferocious expression, dates from the sixteenth century. This god is associated with fire rituals and incense, his image in bronze sometimes forming the lid of a censer. Another ivory, now in Los Angeles like the Daka, is a seventeenth-century figure of Padmasambhava, 'the Lotus Born', an eighth-century Indian guru who taught the Tibetans Tantric Buddhism and who is known in Tibet as Gu-ru Rin-po-che, 'the Precious Teacher'.

One of the most commonly found ritual objects in Tibet is the *phur-bu*, the ritual dagger, used for the exorcizing of evil spirits, and an example in ivory, now in Los Angeles, dates from the seventeenth century and is elaborately carved with ferocious faces, skulls and snakes. An unusual Tibetan amrita vase, with a fluted vase-shaped body, probably seventeenth-century Mughal, and four turquoise-inset silver mounts and a rock crystal *stupa* finial dating from the eighteenth or nineteenth century, is interesting; the reuse of an Indian object within Tibetan mounts shows that ivory was rare in Tibet, and furthermore its use within a sacred amrita vase, said to contain the elixir of life, shows that it was greatly revered. Although Tibetan amulets are rarely of ivory, rectangular plaques depicting the 'Wheel of Life' were produced in the nineteenth and early twentieth centuries. These usually depict the monster-headed god Bhavacakramudra holding the Wheel in his claws. The Wheel is usually divided into numerous subsections containing various good and evil emblems arranged in concentric bands; the central medallion often depicts the three cardinal sins, lust (the red cockerel), hatred (the green snake) and ignorance (the black pig). The reverse may be incised with *mantras* (prayers) and

with sacred emblems. The Wheel is most often depicted in *thang-Kas* (scroll paintings) and is thought to be one of the oldest Tibetan traditions, originating with diagrams brought by itinerant preachers from Buddhist India. Other Tibetan ivory images dating from the sixteenth, seventeenth and eighteenth centuries include the standing, eleven-headed, multi-armed Avalokitésvara, god of mercy and 'patron saint' of Tibet, but these rarely survive intact.

The carving of human bone in Tibet by far exceeds that of ivory and may be an ancient tradition with shamanistic origins. A Flemish Franciscan, William of Rubruk, heard about the Tibetan custom of using human crania as skull-bowls when he visited the court of Genghis Khan in 1253. A Portuguese Jesuit who visited Tibet in 1624 recorded trumpets and rosaries of human bone, as well as the tradition of making the skulls of the dead into drinking-cups or *kapala*. The skull of a later missionary priest, Fr Brieux, was apparently so treated, some years after his death in 1881.

Skulls were often lined with bronze, copper or silver and set with borders of semi-precious stones such as coral and turquoise, the centre of the interior sometimes being set with a single stone encased in a metal boss. A particularly elaborate example of a *kapala*, with gilt-bronze liner, lid and triangular stand, with a skull at each corner, displayed extremely fine gilding, chasing and repoussé decoration, incorporating motifs such as stylized mountains, scrolls, miniature *vajras*, flames and lotus petals. What was especially interesting was a four-character Qianlong reignmark on the stand, dating it to the eighteenth century. The interior of the skull was painted with red inscriptions, minute sacred emblems and *mantras*.

Human thigh-bones were hollowed and mounted in a similar way with leather, copper, gilt-bronze or silver, perhaps set with semi-precious stones, to make ritual trumpets. Bone beads, sometimes carved in the form of grotesque skulls, were used for rosaries (*mala*); latterly yak bone has been used in place of human bone. Pairs of skulls were made into ritual hand-drums (*damaru*) by joining the two at the crown and binding the open sides with animal skin; brocade streamers, perhaps embroidered with sacred emblems, were attached. Human and animal bones are also used for elaborate plaques depicting various deities (usually tantric), ritual objects and sacred emblems, joined by strings of bone beads to make an apron and usually mounted on silk or cotton for wearing during ritual dances or necromantic rites.

Bone ritual objects continue to be produced in Tibet in the twentieth century, whereas ivory carving has been largely discontinued.

Above: Tibetan bowl in ivory. 4 in. (10 cm). See also page 279. Ivory was used for a variety of objects, from bowls like this one to prayer-wheels, flasks for water or powder, and chopsticks.

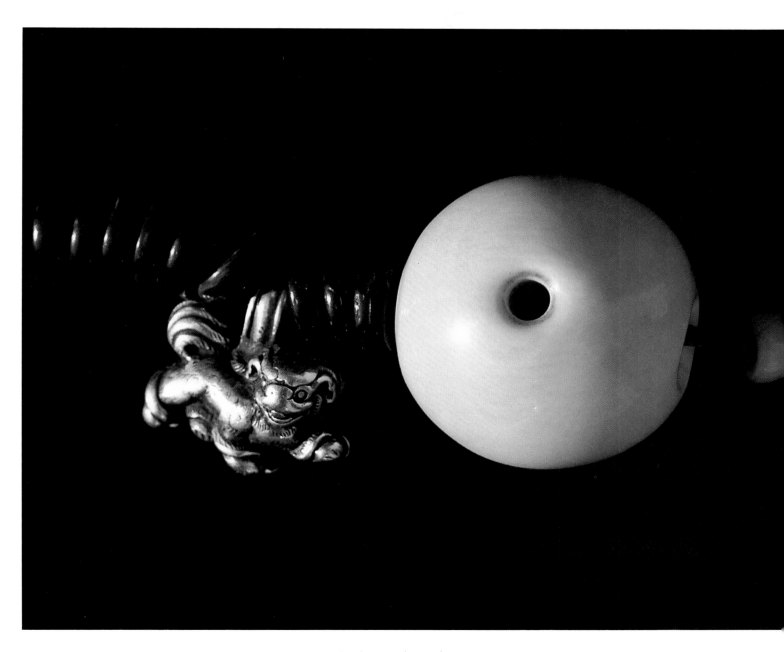

Above: Tibetan *mala* or rosary, made of ivory, silver and
human bone. Eighteenth-century. See also page 279.
Human bone was used more often than ivory for
drinking-cups (made from skulls) as well as rosaries.

South-East Asia

Ivory is used in south-east Asia for a variety of purposes, such as mountings on dagger hilts, jewellery or spice, *pan* or betel-nut boxes, although it is not as common as in India.

Burma

Early Burmese images of Buddha are extremely rare but one interesting small ivory of Gautama Buddha, which is nearly 5 in. (12.5 cm) in height, portrays him seated cross-legged on a waisted lotus throne, the right hand displaying the 'touching the earth' gesture (*bhumisparsa*), the left in the lap in the *dhyana mudra* gesture, and this has been attributed to Burma or southern Tibet, twelfth or thirteenth century. Some small ivory images of Buddha were produced during the eighteenth and nineteenth centuries but few survive.

Ivory was often used for carved and pierced dagger hilts in the Shan states, where elaborate hilts and tusks are carved with ferocious intertwining dragons or anthropomorphic warriors amid elaborate scrolling foliage. One dagger of this type, with silver mounts and carved bone hilt, has been dated to the eighteenth century.

Carved tusks, depicting rows of Buddhas enclosed by foliage, were produced in the nineteenth and early twentieth centuries. Ivory objects in Anglo-Indian style were produced in the nineteenth century at Moulmein, Pyinmana and Rangoon and included chessmen and paper-cutters, picture frames, decorative items and furniture.

Thailand

During the 1960s and 1970s various prehistoric sites in Thailand were excavated, the most important being that of Ban Chiang, Amphoe Nong Harn, in Udon Thani province. Spanning the period 3600–200 BC, and famous for its distinctive buff pottery, this site has produced numerous bronze ornaments from the later period, and necklaces of semi-precious stones among which bone and ivory beads have been found. Undecorated ivory bracelets were also found at Ban Phak Tob, in the same province.

Thailand seems to have produced many more Buddha images than Burma in the eighteenth and nineteenth centuries. One eighteenth-century Thai ivory standing Buddha, 15 in. (38.5 cm) high, has the hands raised in reassurance (*abhaya mudra*) and wears a plain monastic robe with a flamiform finial in the gilded hair.

A small ivory throne, of low square form with an arched back, probably eighteenth- or early-nineteenth-century, and a fine ivory howdah, carved and pierced with foliate motifs and probably dating from the nineteenth century, are both in Bangkok.

Above: Jewelled elephant shown in colour on page 284.

Elephant tusks carved with registers of Buddhas were also carved in Thailand, while uncarved tusks were frequently used as gong stands. Ivory was also used to decorate musical instruments and for fan handles, fly-whisk handles, reliquaries in the form of *stupas* and other small items.

Indonesia

The head-hunting tribes of the islands of south-east Asia are famous for their use of carved reindeer antler, particularly the Dyaks of Borneo. Their deerbone sword hilts attain an orange-yellow patina and are carved with elaborate scrolls. The swords are also bound with rattan and hung with white, black and dark red hair. The Dyaks also carve hornbill, into earrings, for example, again using complex intertwining scrolls, and apply wild boar tusks, uncarved, to skull-hooks with rattan bindings.

The tribes of the Lesser Sunda Islands, the Nias west of Sumatra and the Batak north of Sumatra, all carve boxes and other items from buffalo bone and horn, tortoiseshell and other related materials.

In Java and Bali, ivory is most commonly used for elaborate *kris* handles, usually carved in the form of anthropomorphic creatures and sometimes set with precious or semi-precious stones.

The Philippines

The explorer Ferdinand Magellan, a Portuguese in the service of Spain, discovered the Philippine archipelago in 1521. Further expeditions followed but effective control of the islands was not gained until 1564 when Miguel Lopez de Legazpi led an expedition from Acapulco, Mexico, and founded Manila. From 1565 to 1815 galleon ships from Veracruz and Acapulco traded with the Philippines. The Manila galleon took between three and seven months on the voyage, bringing silver bullion and coin to the Philippines and taking ivories, silks, ceramics, spices and perfumes back to Acapulco, where part of the cargo was sold to merchants and the rest shipped from Veracruz to Spain.

The Philippines had long had successful trade relations with Java, Borneo, China, Cambodia and Indo-China, whose peoples and religions had infiltrated Philippine society. There have reputedly been Hindus in the Philippines since the fourth century BC but the Muslims did not arrive until the fifteenth century AD, coming from the Molucca islands. The Muslims fought the Spanish and largely resisted conversion to Christianity for over three hundred years. However, church building went ahead from the late sixteenth century onwards, the Spaniards at first employing Chinese sculptors for their religious images. Subsequently they brought Spanish artists to the

Above: Balinese *kris* handles in the form of grotesque figures. Nineteenth-century; 4⅛ in. (10.5 cm) on left. The handles on the left and right are ivory.

Philippines to teach Christian carving. To this end, wood and ivory sculptures from Spain and northern Europe were brought to the Philippines and in consequence heavily influenced future Christian carving there and also at Zhangzhou on the Chinese coast north of Canton, the important centre of ivory carving which supplied Christian images to the Philippines during the late sixteenth and seventeenth centuries. At the end of the sixteenth century the Spanish crown imposed restrictive practices on the Pacific trade, decreeing that all oriental commercial activities destined for South America must be channelled through the Philippines. Some Chinese craftsmen moved to the Philippines, the better to participate in the lucrative trade, and taught the techniques of ivory carving to the Filipinos, establishing workshops which specialized in works for South America.

Standing or reclining nude figures of the Christ Child were very popular in the Philippines. An ivory figure of this type, from Flanders, is said to have been brought to the islands by Magellan in 1521. Later examples, mostly seventeenth- or eighteenth-century, are now in Manila and in Mexico. Other saints depicted in ivory, dating from the same period, including St John the Baptist, St Joseph, St Anthony of Padua, St Sebastian and St Francis of Assisi, were shipped to Mexico on the Manila galleon. One of the most famous images of the Virgin, as Our Lady of the Rosary, popularly known as 'La Naval', is in the

St Domingo Church, Manila. The wood figure has an ivory face and hands and is dressed in elaborate robes set with precious stones. It was commissioned in 1593 by Governor Luis Perez Dasmarinas and was apparently 'carved by a pagan Chinese craftsman from Ilocos under the direction of a Spanish captain'. Crucifixes of ivory were also made in the Philippines and generally depict Christ as a passive victim, the head bowed, the well-defined body limp, but with painted and gilt details.

The most popular subjects produced for the South American market, both for the Catholic churches and for the chapels of noble households, were the Holy Family and Christ on the Cross. These were copied from contemporary prints and engravings but are easily identified as of Asiatic manufacture by physical traits, such as slanted eyes, and characteristically Asian poses. For the most part, the Philippine workshops produced only ivory faces and hands for South American commissions (these would sometimes be coloured); they were shipped to Mexico, where native craftsmen carved bodies out of wood, to which suitable vestments were attached.

Despite numerous attacks by the Dutch during the first half of the seventeenth century, and revolts by the large Chinese population during the seventeenth and eighteenth centuries, Spanish rule was not ended until 1898 with a revolution demanding independence for the Philippines.

Above: Jewelled ivory elephant from Thailand. Twentieth-century. See also page 282. The combination of jewels and ivory creates a richly decorative effect.

Opposite: 'La Naval', the image of Our Lady of the Rosary from Manila. Sixteenth-century; 16 in. (40 cm) long (the child). One of the earliest ivory statues from the Philippines, it was commissioned by the Spanish governor in 1593 and carved by a Chinese sculptor. The Christ Child is made entirely of ivory. The Virgin's face and hands are ivory, mounted on a wooden frame; the sculptor has given her slanting eyes and high, oriental cheekbones.

Australasia, Oceania

Long before the first white men entered the Pacific in the sixteenth century the inhabitants of Oceania had discovered the secret of working that most precious of all South Sea materials, whale's teeth. Indeed it is not too much to say that they succeeded in processing it in a way unequalled anywhere else. They were not merely able to carve the tip of the tooth, but also to mould the root. There are only about forty to fifty teeth on the lower jaw of the sperm whale, and it was rare for such a whale to become embayed or drift ashore dead. Accordingly whale's teeth were the prerogative of royalty and could only be owned or worn by those of the highest birth.

The arrival of the whalers in the South Pacific in the late eighteenth century meant that the supply of teeth was very much increased. One whaler, William B. Whitecar, Jr, in the late 1850s and early 1860s, found that whale's teeth would buy all the provisions required for the ship. They were in fact desirable merchandise all over the Pacific. In 1847 John B. Williams, of Salem, wrote: 'Whale's teeth are the most valuable articles in the Feejees . . . for twenty teeth about 200 gallons of coconut oil may be obtained.'

Elsewhere in the Pacific, Whitecar commented on the *kris*, or short swords, worn by the far-ranging Malays, with handles 'of ivory, beautifully carved and ornamented', the work not of the Malay but of the Chinese, who were eager to purchase whale's teeth – 'their hardness and the superior whiteness of the ivory rendering them peculiarly applicable for this purpose'.

The tusks of the Pacific walrus, larger than those of the Atlantic variety, were brought by whalermen to the South Sea islands. Walrus tusks formed the raw material for a whole range of carvings, many of them in forms which had become sacrosanct through traditional usage, intended for use by the aristocracy of the islands.

Long before the whalermen put in to New Zealand in the eighteenth century, the Maori were using *rei puta*, whale's tooth ornaments. Excavations on a fourteenth-century site have revealed an intriguing pendant of figures back to back, ornamented by an edging of crochets down the side. These 'chevrons', as they are called, are supposed to have been suggested by human legs. Multiple legs, or arms, also appear on another chevron pendant, of equivalent or perhaps even earlier date. It also shows human features at the top of the pendant. Another pendant, which looks like a stylized Irish harp, is supposed to symbolize a *taniwha* or *karara*, a protective monster of reptilian form.

Not all Maori jewellery was so elaborately carved. One medieval pendant is a beautifully simple divided sphere, like a Gouda cheese with a slice taken out. It is apparently related to the double testicle pendants worn in the Austral Isles. Other *rei* develop the *tiki*, or totem figure, which runs through the whole of Maori art. Sometimes it is carved with great economy, at other times indicated lightly with stylized incisions, and sometimes merely suggested with lines for eyes and nose. For some reason, possibly the growing popularity of jade, *tiki rei* become less popular after the eighteenth century.

Tonga ivory carvings are stylized, large-headed, brooding female figures worn suspended as pendants round the neck. They are supposed to have been fertility charms and, though not realistic, they are far more representational than ivory carvings on many other islands. Much more stylized are Marquesan carvings. Ear plugs consist of a disc and a spike. On the end of the spike, looking as though it has just sat down for a rest, is a tiny *tiki* figure, its enormous eyes staring, its hands clasped on its stomach. The same motif is repeated twice on the handle of a pandanus fibre fan, separated by bands of ornament, on what is possibly the most impressive of all Oceanic ivory carvings. The Marquesans were undoubtedly masters of ivory and bone carving, and of the group Hiva has provided the most interesting examples: *tiki* toggle figures for pendants or attachments to the top of staffs. They are closely related to the fan handle, also from Hiva. Sometimes multiple *tiki* were carved, and the plug became so heavy as to require support.

Every major centre of Oceanic carving had its typical forms of ivory beads, sometimes testicle-shaped like those of Rarotonga, sometimes reel-shaped like those of New Zealand, sometimes the miniature teeth of Hawaii.

One final ivory figure may be mentioned, from Fiji. Of ancestral *tiki* form, it has a positively Inuit (Eskimo) appearance on account of its round face and collar. Though the artistic convention is traditional, the material is comparatively modern walrus ivory, so it must date from some time in the nineteenth century: a good example of how recognition of the type of ivory used for a carving can help to give it an approximate date.

Australia and New Zealand

When the Australian colony of Van Diemen's Land, later to become Tasmania, was established in 1803, right whales were plentiful in the harbour of the principal settlement, Hobart Town.

Local bay whaling began almost at once and continued until the 1830s. By then the right whale had ceased to frequent Van Diemen's Land waters but whaling for sperm whales had begun in 1828 when the first Hobart Town high seas whaler, the

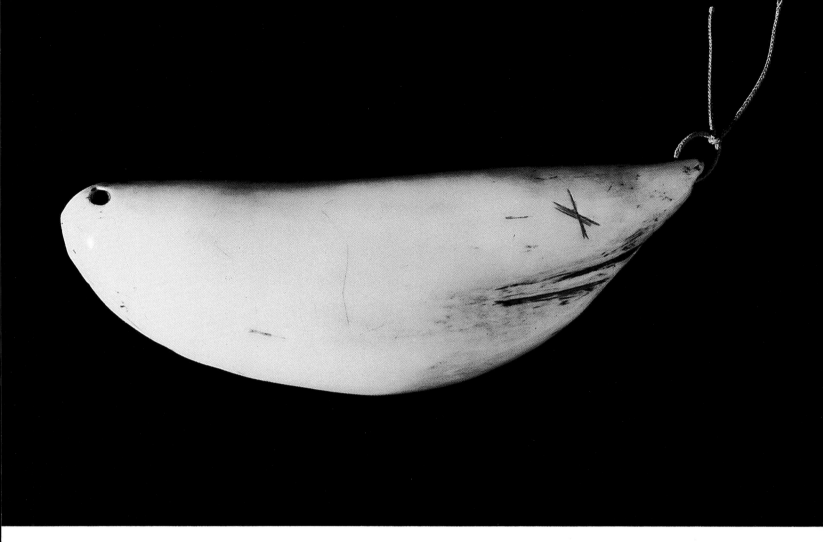

Caroline, set sail for the Pacific. By 1848 there were three full-rigged ships operating from Hobart Town, the *Pacific,* the *Jane* and the *Offley*.

Successful hunts would end with the decapitation of the whale and the hoisting aboard of the head to obtain the spermacetti oil. The Tasmanian scrimshaw collector Sir William Crowther wrote: 'The teeth were divided among the crew for scrimshaw [and] valued above all, as they were gradually brought to a high ivory finish by polishing, and were greatly appreciated as ornaments.'

R. Tilbrook of South Australia described how the engraved ornament was added, using the *pointillist* technique (scrimshoners seem to have worked either in dotted lines or in rather deeply engraved sweeping ones): 'Scraps from books were pasted on to the whale's teeth, and the outline was impressed with a sharp pointed object about 1/64 [0.015 mm] to 1/32 [0.03 mm] pitch centres. From this outline, under magnifying glasses, the whalers bisected these points with lines. Various oil-based ochres were rubbed into these lines, and hence the various colours.'

Australasian designs for engravings are very similar to those in use on British and American scrimshaw. Ladies in crinolines, whalers and whaleboats, and a variety of patterned designs, such as the 'olive branch', are common.

Teeth might be turned out as mantelpiece ornaments, or a pair could be combined with a matching pincushion on a whalebone base. Australian whalers also made cribbage boards, 'jogging wheels' for crimping pastry, 'swifts' for winding wool, carved fids for unpicking knots, sailmakers' rubbers, parasol handles, workboxes, needles, studs, inkstands, pincushions, cuff-links, pegs, walking-stick handles and knife handles. Captain Charles Bayley (1812–75), who had a lathe aboard his whaler, made turned work, such as eggcups. Australian whalers also used whale jaw-pan for large flat pictures, scalloped at the top, of whalers under sail.

Whalers put in to New Zealand from the late eighteenth century onwards and began to establish themselves on the north-east coast in the Bay of Islands. Russell, the whaling settlement there, became one of the most flourishing whaling ports of the islands and a representative collection of New Zealand scrimshaw is preserved there.

7

North America

From earliest times all the indigenous peoples of North America – the Inuit, the Aleuts, the Indians of the Northwest Coast – have made the most of marine ivory, whether for such functional purposes as sled runners and harpoon points, or for ritual objects such as amulets, fetishes and 'soul-catchers'; and the folk artists of a later tradition, America's whalemen, whiled away the long voyages making scrimshaw that was both ingenious and intimate. Accordingly, North America has produced some magnificent pieces of 'primitive' ivory carving, which, like some of the finest African ivories, are instantly recognizable as belonging to a great sculptural tradition.

Above: Inuit polar bears. Fourteenth- or fifteenth-
century; 3½ in. (8.6 cm) and 4 in. (10 cm) long. They
were possibly handles for drag lines. See also page 295.
Opposite: Inuit spirit mask of mammoth ivory.
Nineteenth-century; 3 in. (8 cm). See also page 294.

Marine ivory is a precious and utilitarian commodity both among the Inuit (previously known as Eskimos) of the far north and the Northwest Coast American Indians.

The vast herds of walruses that formerly inhabited the northern coasts of the American continent furnished the main source of Inuit and Northwest Indian ivory.

The narwhal, or 'sea unicorn', was a far more unusual and difficult quarry, and its fluted, hollow tusk 6 to 8 ft (1.8 to 2.4 m) long was better suited for lances and harpoon shafts than for ornamental carving. Sperm whales – the most significant ivory-producing whales – preferred the warmer waters of the Pacific, but their teeth were traded in relays up the west coast of America and constituted valuable articles of primitive commerce.

The Aleuts of the Aleutian Islands and the Inuit of western Alaska had access to another important source of ivory – the so-called 'fossil' ivory of extinct mammoths, the Pleistocene forebears of the elephant, whose remains were found in abundance along the Siberian coast between the mouth of the Obi and Bering Strait, especially on the offshore islands.

Mammoth ivory turns brown or grey after 30,000 years in the frozen Arctic soil, but it does not, in fact, fossilize. Instead, the laminated layers of the giant tusks separate into their constituent rings, usually only an inch or two thick (2.5 to 5 cm) so that Eskimo artists can use mammoth ivory only to carve bracelets or small animals, or such implements as fat scrapers.

Occasionally, trade with Siberia also yielded the still older ivory that came from the extinct mastodons, the Pliocene and Miocene forerunners of the elephant.

Right: Ipiutak skull, North Alaska. *c.*AD 400– 750. Eyes, nose plugs and mouth cover are ivory.

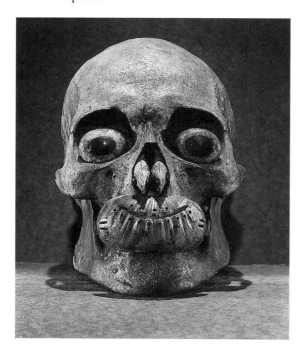

The Inuit

The material evidence concerning the origins of the Inuit remains fragmentary and inconclusive. It is generally assumed that the first migrants came in successive waves to America from Asia across the Bering Land Bridge, perhaps as long as 30,000 years ago, and that the ancestors of the American Indian gradually moved south and east. The last group of migrants, however, remained in Alaska, which was then free of ice but cut off from the rest of the continent by immense icefields. In about the eighth millennium BC they established a recognizable Inuit culture along the Alaskan coast and then spread eastwards along the Polar rim of the continent. The Inuit now rank as the world's most far-flung tribe: some 105,000 of them inhabit about a million square miles along the Arctic shore from Bering Strait to Labrador and Greenland, a distance of more than 4000 miles. Even so, they share a common cultural and biological heritage and speak a series of related languages. Anthropologists have grouped them by regions, into Greenlanders, Canadian Inuit, North Alaskan Inuit, Bering Sea Inuit and North Pacific Inuit.

The Aleuts of the Aleutian Islands in the North Pacific are closely related culturally and ethnically but speak a different language.

Before the advent of the white explorers and their successors in the eighteenth century, all these groups shared similar patterns of survival and adaptation to an extremely difficult, often hostile environment, and of belief in a shamanistic world in which every living thing had a spirit, or *inua*, capable of assuming a variety of physical forms. The art of the Inuit was thus always closely linked to the *inua* of animals and men, relating the artist to his environment (in the past, ivory carving was traditionally man's work) and expressing a hunter-magician's view of the cosmos.

Ivory carvings play an important role in the earliest known phases of Inuit culture. These have been named after the sites at which they were first identified – sites usually centred on 'kitchen middens', or mounds of debris, that developed as succeeding generations lived on the same spot.

The Okvik culture

The oldest known Inuit civilization is the Okvik culture, covering the period 450 BC to AD 900, which was first excavated in the early 1930s on the most northerly of the three Punuk Islands off the coast of St Lawrence Island in the Bering Sea, about 240 miles south of the Arctic Circle.

The name Okvik, suggested for the site by St Lawrence Island Inuit, means 'place where many walrus haul up', and indeed its middens were liberally sprinkled with ivory implements. Of a total of 1404 objects recovered by a team of

Page 292: The Okvik
Madonna from St
Lawrence Island. Two
thousand years old;
c. 6½ in. (17 cm) high. A
figure of a woman
holding a child, carved in
walrus ivory.

Page 293: A miniature
ivory mask, from the
prehistoric Dorset
culture. Radio-carbon-
dated to 720 BC; 1⅜ in.
(3.5 cm). It may have been
a shaman's prop for
winter entertainment. See
also page 294.

Below: A socketed, ivory
shaft head for a harpoon.
Old Bering Sea culture,
c. AD 200; *c.* 8¼ in.
(21 cm) long.

archaeologists, no fewer than 1026 were ivory artefacts, illustrating 'a great dependence on walrus meat for food as well as upon walrus ivory for the manufacture of technical apparatus'.

More than a third of them are elaborately engraved with smooth curvilinear designs combined with circle-and-dot motifs and acute angles. Frequently the entire surface of an object is covered with thick lines, sometimes doubled, that finish in slanting spurs. These geometric designs resemble the tattooing lines found on the faces of some of the Okvik human figures, and may have been intended to give harpoon heads and other hunting implements the magical power believed to be imparted in tattooing. The remarkable craftsmanship of these ivory pieces, compared to the heavier, rather cruder objects made in historic times, attests to a culture that was technically more advanced and artistically more sophisticated than that of subsequent Inuit epochs.

Okvik culture middens, both at St Lawrence Island and at East Cape, Siberia, have yielded scores of walrus ivory figurines. They are usually described as dolls, since most lack arms and legs but have carefully carved faces, suggesting that their rudimentary bodies were intended to be

called the Old Bering Sea style, which occurs at the same sites.

Dating from about AD 300, the Old Bering Sea style II is particularly noted for its elaborately carved harpoon heads and socket pieces, and for the mysterious, superbly carved 'winged objects', also of walrus ivory, that resemble massive butterflies. Were they stabilizers, like feathers on an arrow, attached to the butt end of a harpoon propelled by a throwing board? Some authorities say they were too heavy for this and the socket holes too small. Their ornamentation combined stylized animals with crowded geometric patterns of slanted or curving lines, like Melanesian tattoos and decorations.

The Old Bering Sea style III brings us to about the year AD 1000; its ivory carvings are sparser and more elegantly simplified than their predecessors. On harpoon heads, for example, circles and ellipses are so arranged in relation to the blade slot as to suggest the mouth and eyes of a minimalist bird.

The Ipiutak culture

Far to the north, at the site called Ipiutak, near Point Barrow on the North Alaskan coast,

covered with clothing – yet even as 'dolls' they may have played a magical role in shamanistic ceremonies. Some are clearly female figures, with small raised breasts or circles, and a well-defined genital area. But the faces of all these figurines bear a strong stylistic resemblance: elongated heads, long narrow noses and narrow chins, small mouths and carefully incised eyebrows, sometimes with tattoo marks on the cheeks or chin.

The finest of these figures, a landmark in Inuit art, is the 'Okvik Madonna', 6⅔ in. (17 cm) tall, representing a woman carrying or nursing a child. The arms and hands are carved in low relief; the torso is decorated with bands of incised lines and the female sex organ is clearly indicated. A very similar figure, though without a child, was discovered on St Lawrence Island in 1972.

The Old Bering Sea style

In some chronologies Okvik art is regarded as the first phase of an evolving three-stage culture

the remains of more than six hundred semi-subterranean houses were discovered, deployed along the crests of five old beach ridges. Begun in 1939, the excavations turned up one spectacular find after another. The most extraordinary grave contained a skeleton with realistically carved ivory eyes inlaid with pupils of jet, ivory nose plugs finely carved to represent birds, and an ivory mouth cover.

No less astonishing were the composite ivory masks consisting of separate elements that had once been lashed together and affixed to some sort of skin backing. One such mask-assemblage was found lying on the breast of a child skeleton, but the most remarkable was found in a heap by itself, not associated with a skeleton; besides being elaborately carved and decorated with stylized designs, the pieces contain eighty sockets cut into the surfaces that were evidently inlaid with jet, for eleven jet inlays remained intact.

Another special feature of the Ipiutak culture

Above: Walrus. The Ipiutak culture, *c.*AD 500. A vividly stylized carving.

Above: Spirit mask shown in colour on page 288.

Above: Ivory mask shown in colour on page 293.

were the many openwork ivories, unlike those at other sites, that may have had no functional purpose: chains, swivels and link ornaments – evidently a case of ivory imitating iron – and curiously twisted, pretzel-like objects. The middens also contain long ornamental strips of ivory incised with geometric faces as well as a variety of small animal figures, some of recognizable animals, others of mythological beasts. One Ipiutak baby walrus must rank as an especially notable example of the Inuit genius for expressive stylization. It links Ipiutak not only to the Old Bering Sea styles but to the Scytho-Siberian civilizations of Iron Age Central Asia. An iron-pointed engraving tool unearthed at Ipiutak has led to speculation that, even at earlier stages, the Inuit had access to metal tools – not merely flint or jade knives – for carving their superb ivories.

The Pre-Dorset and Dorset cultures

In the Hudson's Bay region of the eastern Arctic, excavations of the prehistoric Dorset culture have yielded a number of notable ivories: a tiny mask, for example, found in a midden layer radiocarbon-dated to 720 BC; a harpoon head decorated with incised lines and a human face; a pair of swans in flight, produced about AD 500 by an artist of the middle phase of the Dorset culture. These pieces, however, are far less sophisticated and ornate than those of the Alaskan coast; while the Ipiutak carvers were working within a rigorously stylized tradition, the eastern and central Inuit were folk artists whose carving has a naïve, improvised quality.

The Punuk culture

The ornate patterns of the Old Bering Sea styles gave way to the very much simpler art of the Punuk culture, dating from about AD 500 to 1450, which archaeologists first uncovered in a midden on one of the Punuk Islands in the Bering Sea. It was a direct outgrowth of earlier Bering Sea traditions but also incorporated important new influences from Siberia. By this time small but significant quantities of iron were being brought across Bering Strait by native traders, and a

number of engraving tools with iron tips were found in Punuk sites.

These early Inuit artists worked with blades whose edges were carburized furnace steels, not meteorite or soft iron, and such imports must have been the product of Chinese, Japanese or Siberian metallurgical centres. Studies of the ivories themselves have shown that much of the work could only have been produced by tools with steel cutting edges, such as hook-shaped burins, curved knives, adze blades with acute edge-angles and so on. We lack better evidence about the blades used during the first millennium because corrosion has destroyed any steel tools buried in the middens.

The Punuk culture was sufficiently close to Siberia to adopt many other Siberian advances in tools and hunting equipment, such as bolas slings used for hunting geese and other wildfowl – the balls were sometimes made of ivory – as well as specialized bird darts, ivory wrist guards, armour made of bone slats, bow braces and sinew twisters for the sinew-backed bow, bone and ivory daggers, iron net sinkers, and so on. Over the centuries the Punuk peoples and those of the related Birnirk culture (about AD 500–1000), first discovered near Point Barrow, North Alaska, improved the living conditions and material technology of the Inuit living on the islands and along the Alaskan coast, establishing the basis of all subsequent Inuit culture from Bering Strait to Greenland.

The ivory carvings found in Punuk and Birnirk middens cover a wide range of typical Inuit artefacts, including harpoon heads, drills, picks, adzes, knives, scrapers, needle cases and ivory runners for hand-drawn sleds. The pieces themselves, however, are plainer and more rectilinear than those of earlier epochs; their surface ornamentation has become simplified by means of straight lines and nucleated circles, now drawn with the help of a compass – a striking example of the effect that even the most rudimentary technology can have on artistic practice. Some of the finest Punuk pieces are smooth, finely carved implements decorated with designs of single or double lines that emphasize the function of the object.

Peculiar to the Punuk tradition are the so-called 'turreted' objects in walrus or fossil ivory whose purpose has thus far eluded the archaeologists. Their form seems to have evolved from that of the Old Bering Sea 'winged objects', though their function may have been quite different. In the early Punuk stage they bear a strong resemblance to the winged objects, except that the wings have become more pointed and slender, but in the final stage the wings have been transformed into turrets that point upwards and join the centre of the object, like a kind of medieval crown.

The Thule culture

The so-called Thule culture that was to succeed the Birnirk phase emerged on the North Alaskan coast of the Beaufort Sea, among a people who specialized in whale hunting. Their patterns of life were to become the dominant culture of the Inuit until the beginning of the historic period and contact with European technology. The Thule people ranged the open sea in skin-covered kayaks and in fleets of the larger, open umiaks in search of the bowhead or baleen whale and other sea mammals; they had dog-drawn sleds, probably wore fur and caribou-skin clothing and boots, and lived in domed, semi-subterranean houses that had walls and roofs of sod supported by stone slabs laid over rafters of whale rib.

About AD 800 Thule peoples began to move eastwards along the Arctic fringe of the continent, where they absorbed the Dorset people and eventually reached Greenland by way of Ellesmere Island, roaming south as far as Labrador. *En route* they must have learned how to make snow houses from the Dorset people, since this extraordinarily efficient form of shelter is absent from the Alaskan version of Inuit culture. Unlike its predecessors the Thule culture is not noted for its carvings, for its craftsmen seemed to feel no compulsion to decorate the many implements they made of walrus ivory, but archaeologists may uncover an occasional and surprising art piece.

One such surprise is a Thule comb found in the Pelly Bay region of the Canadian Northwest Territories; carved from a walrus tusk, it combines an ingeniously stylized adaptation of the human face and body with freehand geometric lines and wave-like designs. No less remarkable is a drill bow found on Baffin Island, which is regarded as the Thule culture's most informative artefact. Its two long, flat surfaces are engraved with a series of interlocking scenes of Inuit life, including whale hunters armed with harpoons, caribou hunters in kayaks, a battle apparently taking place before summer tents with archers using compound bows, an old person in a hooded parka and carrying a cane, and an Inuit dog with an upturned tail. Recent excavations on St Lawrence Island have also yielded earlier Thule pieces of extraordinary quality – a headless hermaphroditic figure, for example, and the broken-off head of what may have been a staff or a shaman's doll. Even the relatively artless Thule tradition has thus produced some notable ivories.

European expansionism

Although Norsemen came into contact with the Greenland Inuit as early as the tenth century, and navigators such as Martin Frobisher and Henry Hudson had memorable encounters with the Canadian Inuit during the sixteenth and seventeenth centuries, it was the eighteenth century that brought the full impact of European expansionism to the American north and northwest. Vitus Bering's discovery of Alaska in 1741 marked the beginning of an accelerating process of exploration, trade and colonization that transformed the native cultures of the region. In essence, the Iron Age had at last encompassed the Stone Age cultures of one of the world's great unexplored regions. Among the Inuit, iron soon replaced ivory in such applications as harpoon points, fish hooks and clasps, and before long the gun had superseded the bow and arrow.

None the less, walrus ivory continued to be the dominant artistic material among the Inuit long after they had begun importing such alien products as rifles and steel knives. Throughout the nineteenth century their traditional hunting culture remained intact, and native materials were still used for everything that did not absolutely have to be of steel. Accordingly, most nineteenth-century ivories are as well made as earlier implements – drill bows, arrow-shaft straighteners, bag handles, snow knives, fat scrapers and so on. Some of their greatest art and ingenuity went into the harpoon rests that were fixed to the prows of the umiaks; they were normally pieced together from two segments of walrus tusk and often took the form of two seals facing in opposite directions, with other animals, such as birds and whales, engraved on the central portion. The hunters' hats and eyeshades were very lavishly

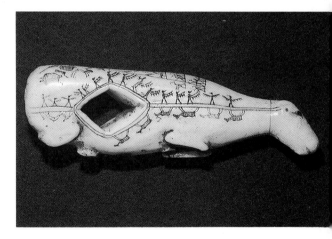

ornamented with abstract carvings and small seal or walrus amulets. One heavily decorated hat collected on Norton Sound in 1886 is half covered in such ivory ornaments.

A typical Inuit object was the ivory bilboquet they made for their version of the game of cup-and-pin, which they call *ajaqaq*. Inuit are still phenomenally skilled in the art of spearing a slippery bilboquet with a short stick, and just to make it more difficult they would drill several holes into the target piece, each with its own

Far right, below: Western Inuit arrow-shaft straightener. Made of walrus ivory engraved with shamans and animals.

Below: Inuit polar bears shown in colour on page 289.

Right: Thule comb. 4¼ × 1½ × ¼ in. (10.8 × 3.85 × 0.6 cm). Carved from a walrus tusk, it is an adaptation of the human face and body.

Opposite: Two men wrestling, from St Lawrence Island, off Alaska. Nineteenth-century; 2½ in. (6.4 cm). Carvers were inspired by photographs and illustrations in western magazines.

Below: Ivory cribbage board in the shape of a caribou, from Nome, Alaska. Late-nineteenth-century. Probably produced for the 'gold rush' market.

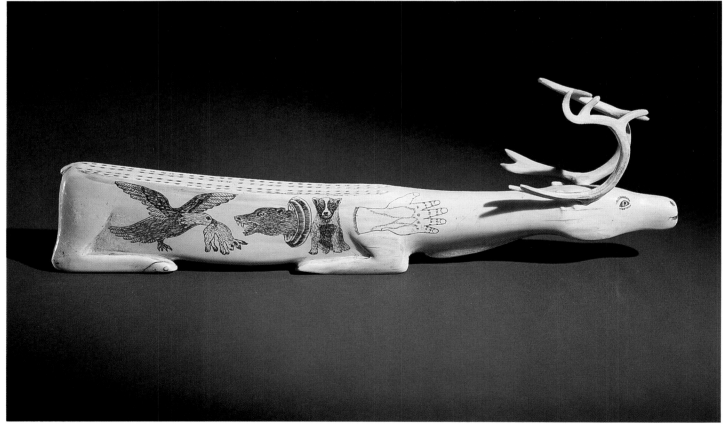

scoring value. Traditionally endowed with great magic, *ajaqaq* was played in the winter and early spring, since it was supposed to hasten the long-awaited return of the sun.

Among the Central Inuit virtually every object in daily use was still made of, or with, ivory – from sewing kits to hunting equipment and shaman's paraphernalia; some groups even lined the rims of their kayaks with ivory. Though harpoons now had steel points, the rest of the ivory fittings had not changed, and in some cases the shaft might still be a narwhal tusk. Small ivory fish or bear's teeth were used as lures in spearing salmon, and there were ivory snow knives for constructing igloos, ivory toggles for whale and seal hunting, and ivory goggles to prevent snow blindness. Even the smallest, most unassuming object usually had style: a toggle for managing the reins of a dog sled would have three seal heads carved on it in medium relief – elements of design that had the additional virtue of making the toggle that much less likely to slip out of the driver's hands.

But much of what the Inuit carved during the second half of the nineteenth century was no longer intended for their own use; they had begun making hundreds of souvenirs for the crews of the whaling ships that now appeared in the Arctic in large numbers. The whalers' demand for ivory mementoes led to the flowering of a new kind of Inuit art and a gradual change of style. The native carvers soon discovered that the American and European whalers were eager to purchase pieces engraved with scenes of Inuit life. Soon an ivory carving industry developed around Bering Strait and to the north, and the pictographic scenes of hunting and village life that had formerly embellished drill bows were now applied to pipes, cribbage boards and other saleable examples of 'market art'.

A noted authority on Inuit art, Dorothy Jean Ray, has identified a succession of pictographic styles in the Inuit engravings of the nineteenth century, beginning with the Old Engraving Style, in which the artist used 'a minimum of detail to create a maximum of action', by means of stick figures and schematic animal bodies. A journalist who accompanied an Arctic whaling voyage in the 1880s noted that with such figures an Inuit would 'keep a diary of his hunting trips by carving important events on a piece of ivory, showing his camps, shooting deer, walruses, seals or bears, or catching and drying fish'. These diaries were engraved on drill bows and other implements, and depicted caribou hunting, whaling, walrus hunting, village life, shamanistic ceremonies and so on.

The next stage was the Modified Engraving Style, exemplified by large ivory pipes and engraved walrus tusks sold as souvenirs in the St Michael area of Alaska between 1870 and 1900. Until then the Inuit artists had always applied their art to utilitarian objects, but now for the first time they began to work on whole walrus tusks for the souvenir market. As the available surface became larger, so did the human figures; the

Below: Detail from an engraved walrus tusk. Nineteenth-century. Western Inuit work, depicting a hunting scene.

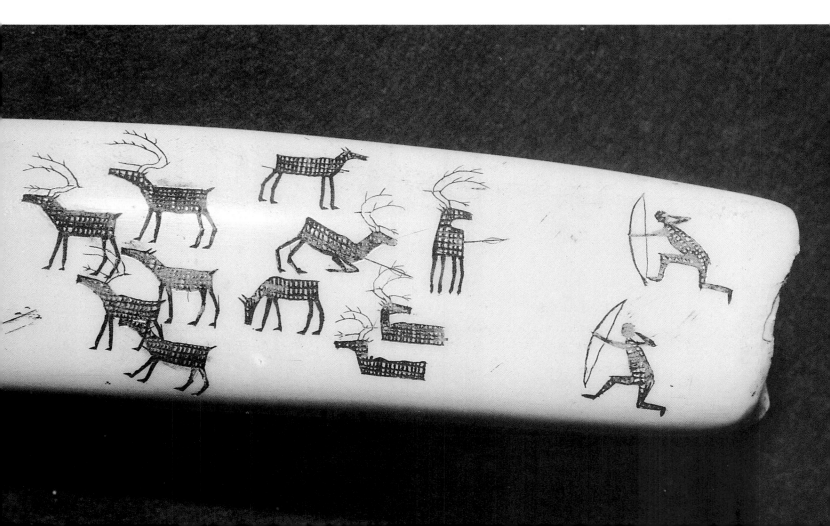

engraving grew more elaborate, and there was greater concern for shading and contrast, which were achieved by means of deeply incised lines filled with black to emphasize the contrast with the ivory background, and with vertical, horizontal and cross-hatched lines.

but lived as a hunter on Little Diomede Island until his feet froze on an expedition that left him drifting helplessly in the pack ice for nearly a month; he was forced to amputate a large portion of each foot, and since he could no longer go out to hunt he began to specialize in ivory carving.

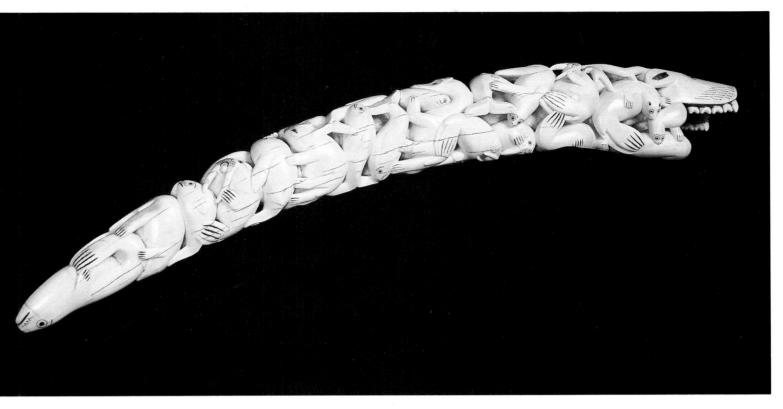

Above: Carved walrus tusk from Nunivak Island. 1930s; 27 in. (69 cm) long. Thirty-one animals – foxes, seals, walruses, whales, polar bears – are entwined along it. The larger terminal is a caribou or reindeer head, the smaller a sea mammal. Mouths, flippers and ears are red, eyes inset.

At the end of the century the Inuit carvers began copying from photographs and magazine illustrations to arrive at the Western Pictorial Style, designed to appeal to the gold miners who were pouring into Nome, Alaska. Though much of this did violence to the Inuit tradition, even at this late date the Inuit sculptors could still produce minor masterpieces of form wedded to function: a cribbage board in the shape of a caribou, for example, made for the Nome gold-rush market. It has a pair of souvenir-style engravings on each side – a bear attacking a walrus, an eagle holding a hare, etc. – yet despite these tattoo-parlour decorations, it is a superb example of applied design with its smooth, compact forms surmounted by a miniature pair of antlers of *trompe-l'oeil* exactitude. This is an art that has lost its primitive innocence but not its innate sense of form.

Modern Inuit art

'Modern times' in terms of Inuit art began with the emergence of Happy Jack, the first Inuit sculptor to be known by a name (his real name was Angokwazhuk, but he signed his work with his nickname) and not simply as an anonymous folk artist. He was born on Cape Nome, Alaska,

His work was so interesting that it attracted the attention of the American whalers in the 1890s; twice they took him on voyages as far as San Francisco.

When gold was discovered in Nome in 1900, he moved back to the mainland to sell his wares. His home on the Nome sandspit became a social centre for the Inuit and a meeting-house for Seventh Day Adventists. Other native carvers visited him, carved in his workshop and absorbed his techniques, which ranged from scrimshaw-like copies of the beautiful ladies pictured on soap wrappers (signed with a flourish by Happy Jack), to original hunting scenes drawn in a style that was half Inuit, half 'western'. Other Inuit artists, such as Guy Kakarook of St Michael, made a name for themselves at about the same time, and the tradition of carvers supporting themselves – albeit minimally – by selling souvenirs to outsiders became firmly established. Though the gold rush soon receded, the annual summer influx of tourists and traders kept Happy Jack busy turning out curios and works that were commissioned by special customers. He was the first, in 1909, to carve an ivory replica of a jolly kitsch figure called a billiken, which had just been

Above: Three examples of miniatures,
all painted on ivory, from the United
States. Early-nineteenth-century.
Top: Lovers' locket of a woman,
*c.*1835, in a Maine silver holder.
Left: Oil on ivory *c.*1820, in a wood
and gold-wash frame. *Right:* Portrait
of John Robinson of Philadelphia,
*c.*1817–29. See also page 313.

Opposite: American Indian carved
ivory. *Far left:* Tlingit ivory frontlet
with abalone teeth. Nineteenth-
century; 5⅔ in. (14.3 cm). *Left:* Tlingit
carved walrus tusk. Nineteenth-
century; *c.*13 in. (33 cm) long.
See also page 307.

Below: Fossil mastodon tusk with decoration by the Inuit sculptor 'Happy Jack'. *c.*1900; 11 in. (28 cm) long. His reproduction of a soap-wrapper is complete with beautiful girl and maker's name and slogan.

patented by a Kansas City schoolteacher, and which was destined to blossom into the Alaskan tourist souvenir *par excellence* and to be reproduced not only as a free-standing figure but on earrings, bracelets, letter-openers and whatnot, versions appearing even among the Siberians. Its immense and otherwise inexplicable success as a good luck charm may be due to its being little more than an Americanized version of the chubby Chinese god of good fortune. Inuit carvers turned out innumerable ivory billikens and probably breathed a collective sigh of relief when its vogue finally passed.

More interesting as art were the elaborately carved tusks produced by a group of gifted carvers on Nunivak Island, off western Alaska, during the 1920s and 1930s. These 'Nunivak tusks', made for the souvenir trade, are covered with deeply carved animals and birds that are interlocked rather like the human figures on the steles by the Norwegian sculptor Gustav Vigeland (1869–1943). Some of these tusks also enclosed cribbage boards, which remained the *pièce de résistance* of Inuit carvers throughout the Arctic until walrus tusks became too precious to be used for mere game boards.

When whaling declined the Canadian Inuit's contacts with the outside world became increasingly rare; for a time, life among the Inuit of the Polar north reverted to much of its erstwhile isolation. It was reported, in 1912, that ivory carving among the Inuit of Labrador was practically a lost art, the walruses having been driven northwards and the young men being uninterested in learning because the market was almost non-existent. Carving remained very much a male prerogative; for women, even painting was frowned on, though they might stitch designs into the fur parkas they made.

The Second World War and its aftermath – which saw the building of strategic installations throughout the Arctic – brought radical changes to the Inuit way of life. To make it worth their while practising their ancient skills as carvers, the Canadian artist James Houston began encouraging them to produce soapstone sculpture for the external market in 1948. Since then Inuit soapstone figures of men and animals have won wide international acceptance, though to purists these pieces represent the decay of a once-great tradition.

Although ivory was originally included among the materials that were carved for the art galleries of Toronto and Montreal, its increasing rarity made it unsuitable for commercial sculpture. Indeed, US laws passed in 1972 and 1973 effectively eliminated the importation or sale of items made from whale or walrus ivory, though some small pieces of contemporary walrus ivory carving do appear from time to time.

The Aleuts

The Aleutian Islands are strung out from the tip of the Alaskan Peninsula towards Kamchatka in eastern Siberia. To the north is the Bering Sea, to the south the Pacific Ocean. The Aleuts are closely related to the Inuit, though they have their own language. Like the early Inuit, they had access to 'fossil' ivory from Siberia and hunted the walrus, but unlike them, the early Aleuts rarely

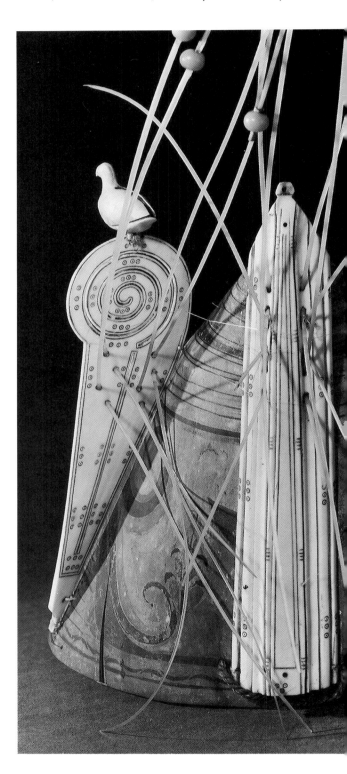

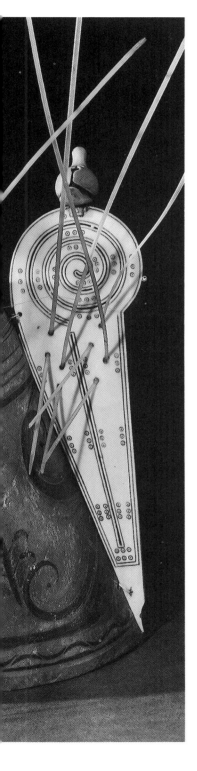

Below: Aleut hunting hat, made from driftwood. Carved ivory side-pieces and a strip of ornamental ivory are decked with waving, frond-like, sea-lion whiskers.

added ornamental carving to their bone and ivory implements. Of the thousands of prehistoric ivory artefacts that archaeologists have excavated in the Aleutians only a very small percentage is decorated: since the Aleuts had access to abundant supplies of wood they concentrated their carving skills on wooden masks.

They did, however, develop an extraordinary combination of wood and ivory that was to be found nowhere else in the world – the Aleut hunting hat, with its eye-catching accessories of walrus ivory and waving antennae of sea-lion whiskers. In its final, closed form the hat seems to have been an early-nineteenth-century confection, though centuries of development went into the bent-wood technology that made it possible. It was made from a single piece of driftwood (preferably California oak) scraped wafer-thin, bent into a sort of coal-scuttle cone and sewed together in the back with sinew. The front of the hat extended far out beyond the hunter's face and protected his eyes from the Arctic glare when he was out in his kayak. But it was also supposed to 'please the seals' with its clean silhouette, and the decorations were of the auspicious kind that brought good fortune in the hunt.

The stitches that bound the ends together were covered with an ornamental ivory strip that rose to the crown of the hat, where a kind of ivory thimble brought the whole arrangement to an ineffably elegant conclusion. There were two delicately carved pieces of ivory on either side, positioned like ears and voluted at the end – perhaps stylized bird beaks – that might also be surmounted by small figures of birds. The polished wooden surface of the hat was decorated with painted spirals and stripes of several earth colours, and occasionally with paintings of whales, seals, hunters, fishes. The long, elastic sea-lion whiskers held by the back strip were trophies of past hunts and had trade beads and feathers attached to them; like the feathers of a Sioux Indian bonnet they bobbed up and down in the breeze and with the wearer's every proud movement. Altogether it was a composition in wood, ivory, bristle, glass and feathers that would gladden the heart of the most aerodynamic of modern designers.

On his Pacific voyage of exploration in 1778, Captain Cook obtained from the Aleuts of Un-alaska Island seven small bird figures – apparently the only American ivories he collected. By then the Aleut culture was under threat. The fur trade, initially in Russian hands, invaded the Aleutian region in the eighteenth century and led to the forcible acculturation of the peaceful Aleuts. They were pressed into service as hunters for the Russian fur company in the great slaughter of sea mammals that in due course nearly exterminated the sea otter and the fur seal.

The Northwest Coast Indians

The eighteenth century brought the first written accounts of the North American cultures as seen through the eyes of sea-captains, naturalists and other emissaries of the European Age of Reason. In 1778 Captain Cook noted his findings at Nootka, off Vancouver Island. He was particularly astonished by the superb *objets d'art* produced by the Northwest Coast Indians, until then virtually unknown to the outside world, although the iron discovered by archaeologists at Cape Alava in Macan Indian territory, on the north-west tip of the state of Washington, must have reached the area a good many centuries before the arrival of the first European mariners. It resembles medieval Japanese iron and is thought to have passed from hand to hand through Aleut and Inuit intermediaries along the same trade routes – from Yakutat in Alaska to northern California – as were used by the Indians to obtain walrus ivory from Inuit hunters. Iron and walrus ivory both necessarily remained far scarcer among the Indians than with the Inuit. The most spectacular use of 'ivory' thus far discovered among prehistoric Northwest Coast Indian sites, also unearthed at Cape Alava, is a wooden sculpture of a killer whale's fin inlaid with 700 sea otter teeth in the form of a thunderbird.

Though the Indians employed only the most rudimentary tools, and had no knowledge of writing, money or agriculture, their arts and handicrafts compared favourably with the best eighteenth-century European workmanship. 'Everything they have', Cook noted, 'is as well and ingeniously made, as if they were furnished with the most complete tool chest ... Their invention and dexterity in all manual works, is at least equal to that of any other nation.'

Four years earlier, in 1774, the Spanish sea-captain Juan Pérez had brought back from Nootka Sound the first documented piece of Northwest American Indian ivory sculpture – a small, beautifully carved and polished amulet in the form of a duck, now in the Museo de America, Madrid. It sums up all the virtues of Northwest Indian art, combining realism and abstraction in a fashion that is unique to the North Pacific coast. Indeed, the typical totemic eye engraved on each of the duck's folded wings is proof that this was the work of an Indian rather than an Inuit artist, since such symbols are wholly absent from Inuit ivories.

For although the Northwest Indian cultures were also shamanistic, the purpose of such an object among the Nootka was not so much to heighten the hunter's power over his prey as to

Far right: Indian charms. Late-eighteenth- or early-nineteenth-century. *Top:* A Tsimshian dancing ornament which was hung around the neck. *Middle:* Tsimshian inlaid ivory charm. *Bottom:* Haida ivory charm, inlaid with haliotis shell.

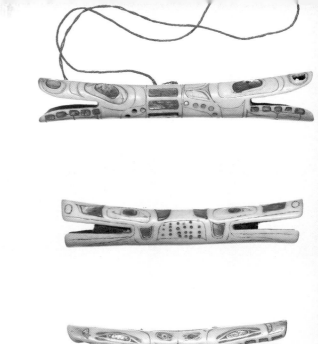

Below: Carved duck. Eighteenth-century. The first documented piece of Northwest Coast Indian art, it was brought from Nootka Sound in 1774.

establish the owner's relationship to an intricate totemic world inhabited by animals, spirits and men. The environment was far richer in natural resources and more temperate in climate than the lands of the Inuit. As a result the Indians had far more time for artistic pursuits; after centuries of experimentation – their culture is demonstrably more than 2500 years old – they had arrived at a brightly coloured totemic style that was, in its way, as informative as an advertising poster. The totem pole, with its imposing array of animal and human faces and bodies, symbolized a way of life and a mode of thought that dominated the coast from Vancouver Island to Yakutat Bay. Totem poles were not heathen idols but heraldic crests and images of memory, the Indian equivalent of a coat of arms.

Like every other European observer, Captain Cook failed to understand the myth-making functions of the totem pole, or the underlying conventions of this half-realistic, half-abstract art, which impressed him with its 'enormous deformity'. The smaller Indian sculptures, most of them in the form of applied art, were treated very much like totem poles in miniature, so that even utilitarian

poor design'. By the same token the ivory figures and other small-scale sculptures were collected as curios and exotic souvenirs, but not valued as art until the twentieth century, by which time countless treasures had been lost or destroyed. Nor were they thought sufficiently interesting for their provenance to be documented. Most eighteenth-century pieces now in public museums and private collections are catalogued simply as Northwest Coast Indian, 'tribe unknown'. Yet there is no doubt that many of the finest ivory artefacts, though of uncertain date and origin, are the product of eighteenth-century craftsmen working with their native tools. Their raw material came from the north, from the Inuit and Aleut walrus hunters, and from the south, from the hunters of sperm whales. With it they produced some of the world's finest and most magical ivory sculptures, in the form of shamans' charms, amulets, decorations for head-dresses known as frontlets, and 'soul-catchers', an indispensable device in psychotherapeutic treatments. These were the products of a high art and a centuries-old tradition; and as the Canadian writer George Woodcock has pointed out, they bring us 'most closely in contact' with the Indians' intellectual and spiritual life.

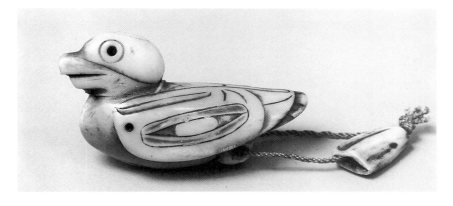

Opposite above: Two belt buckles, the one on the left in ivory and brass, the other ivory inset in leather. Nineteenth-century. *Opposite:* Selection of scrimshaw: whale's tooth and, left to right, ring, three pendants, cross-section of a whale's tooth. See also page 311.

objects such as spoons, knives, dance rattles and grease dishes bore the totemic symbols that haunted the imaginations, and determined the social and political status, of the Nootka, the Tlingit, the Haida and their various neighbours. Whereas the Thule Inuit developed a pictographic style with which they illustrated their lives on smoothed-down walrus tusks, the Indians used stylized totemic symbols whenever they carved a whole tusk or, more frequently, made charms and amulets from pieces of imported marine ivory.

The European artists who accompanied the explorers' expeditions had been trained to draw *d'après nature* with breathtaking verisimilitude, yet they were strangely unable to 'see' or reproduce Indian art. For well over a hundred years even the most sensitive Europeans regarded this art as crude and distorted. José Mariano Moziño, for example, the naturalist who came to Nootka in 1792, dismissed the totems as 'large figures of

The changes occasioned by the coming of the white man stimulated production of the region's traditional artefacts and the early nineteenth century was a golden age for Northwest Coast Indian art. The Indians could now trade sea otter pelts for axes and iron and make steel carving tools on their own forges – on which they also produced the impressive daggers which marked the zenith of Northwest steel sculpture; sometimes these fluted knives have pommels of bone or walrus ivory.

The sudden influx of wealth caused social upheavals whose after-effects were felt for the rest of the century and upset the tribes' traditional status relationships, leading to intense rivalries among the chiefs that could only be solved by means of lavish displays of gift-giving. For this purpose, more artefacts had to be produced than ever before. Moreover, the Canadian and American governments began to assert their authority and potlatch feasts gradually replaced violence as a way of settling disputes. 'When I was young I saw a stream of blood shed in war,' recalled an old Kwakiutl in 1895. 'Now we fight with our wealth.'

The Culture of the Northwest Coast

The Northwest Coast Indian culture was unlike any other on the continent. This civilization had developed independently of the rest of America because the Indian settlements were thinly scattered along a thousand miles of indescribably rugged coastline, cut off from the interior by a range of snow-covered peaks, or on a series of heavily wooded islands separated by a maze of sea channels. Here the Indians lived well on fish, molluscs, game and seal. The Nootka and the Quileute regularly went whaling in swift, seaworthy canoes.

In this generous environment they created a whole repertoire of beautiful objects that now fetch astronomical prices in the auction houses. They lavished their skill on mountain goat horn spoons, argillite grease dishes, cedarwood boxes inlaid with haliotis shell and snail opercula, whalebone 'talking sticks' and a whole spectrum of charms and amulets carved of bone, deer antler and marine ivory.

Working within their age-old totemic tradition they improvised continually new combinations of existing animal forms. It was an art of faces and eyes that went far beyond the European ideal of *physeos mimesis*, the imitation of nature, yet even the most abstract faces were remarkably alive. They prized realistic faces and heads but were curiously ambivalent about bodies; they 'saw through' the body with a kind of X-ray vision, passing (without a break in line) from depicting the outside of a whale – fins, eyes, mouth, tail – to the inside, with a cross-section of the bone structure and a catalogue of the contents of the stomach.

They made magnificent masks, closely observed from nature, for their flamboyant winter dances. 'Sometimes they disguise themselves with bear and deer skins and heads, or with wooden masks which represent a huge image of some aquatic bird,' noted the naturalist Monziño at Nootka in 1792. 'They try to imitate the movements of each animal, as well as those of the hunter who snares it ... so naturally and so

rhythmically in time with the music that they cannot help but excite admiration.' Some of the masks were intricately designed masks-within-masks – a giant bird's head whose two halves the dancer would suddenly fling open, revealing not his own face but an inner wooden mask of another mythic personage. The artists who carved these masks were among the greatest wood sculptors in the history of art, and there were so many of them that per capita, as it were, theirs may well have been the most art-conscious and artistically creative civilization that has ever existed.

The making and bestowing of artefacts played a central role in the social life of all the tribes whom anthropologists have called the 'people of the potlatch'. Sometimes a group would accumulate its worldly goods for several years only to give them away in one great splurge of gift-giving. A potlatch might be given to celebrate the accession of a new chief, the raising of a totem pole, the assumption of a crest or title. If the chief impoverished himself and his people in the process, so much the better, for he acquired unpurchasable prestige among his peers, who must then go one better at their next potlatch. In effect it was a preliterate form of investment banking.

Far right: Model of ceremonial dance on the Kuskokwim river, Alaska. Collected in 1890; model 15 in. (37.5 cm). Four slender pieces of bone support a square – possibly the smoke-hole. The benches are ivory. The fully dressed standing figure may be a trader. Beside him a man holds up a skin. The figure facing him wears a piece of red cloth. Figures on the benches hold drums, carved birds and (*centre*) the cords from which two oil lamps are suspended.

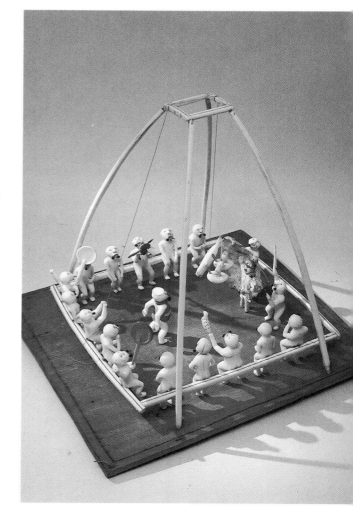

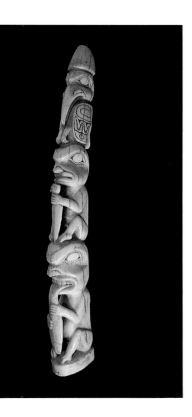

Above: Tlingit carved tusk shown in colour on page 300.

A major potlatch would last for several days and entail prodigious displays of eating and drinking, interspersed with singing, dancing, ball playing, dramatic performances and the conferring of honorific names. But the vital part of the occasion was the bestowing of gifts – bowls, boxes, baskets, blankets, canoes, ornaments – that the chief had collected among his people, from each according to his ability, and now distributed among his guests, to each according to his hereditary rank. It was not a democratic society. Indeed slaves might be clubbed to death at a potlatch in order to dramatize the host's contempt for his possessions.

In the latter half of the nineteenth century the slave-killing stopped but potlatching grew more and more reckless and extravagant. The Methodist missionaries succeeded in persuading the Canadian government to enact a law prohibiting potlatching. Henceforth the custom went underground, though it came out of hiding in the twentieth century after the ban was lifted. By then, however, conversion to Christianity had transformed Indian life.

Totemic art

So long as their basic institutions remained intact, the Indians continued to turn out the carefully finished artefacts that defined their culture, and their own place within it. The totem poles, looming above the 'big houses', provided an omnipresent model and frame of reference for every other work of art, since there was no sharp dividing line between sculpture and architecture, or between large wooden objects and small ivory carvings. A pole was a totemic narrative that could be read from top to bottom by anyone who had eyes to see. The 60-foot (18-m) Nhe-is-bik Salmon pole, for example – carved for a nineteenth-century Kwakiutl chief and now in Stanley Park, Vancouver – tells the legend of the coming of the salmon to Rivers Inlet. It is surmounted by a thunderbird with outstretched wings, the crest of the Raven clan to which the chief in the story belonged; beneath this is the figure of the chief himself; then other figures from the legend – the Salmon (abundance and prosperity), the Wolf (cunning), the Whale (spirit of the seas), the Grizzly Bear (chiefly power and authority) and, at ground level, Tsonoqua, the monster of the forests and spirit of the winds.

The Coast Indian sculptor could approach a walrus tusk in the same spirit and tell a story using three or four totemic figures of animals and men. The specific legend told on any one tusk may have been lost and can now only be surmised but like the large poles the ivory miniatures usually illuminate a mythological relationship that concerns the owner's, or carver's, membership in a group – perhaps under the aegis of a totemic bear, wolf or eagle. The ovoid shapes that are so characteristic of Northwest Coast art naturally lent themselves to being fitted into the slim, curved shape of the tusk. Often the result was a brilliant exercise in sculptural compression, in eminently tactile pieces whose shapes are rounded and organic, as though to illustrate Rodin's maxim that a work of sculpture ought to be able to roll down a hill without anything breaking off.

Shamanistic artefacts

Carvings of complete walrus tusks were rarely seen among the Indians south of the Alaskan panhandle because they had to be brought down from the Inuit country. Hence ivory was used sparingly, in small pieces, but for correspondingly important objects. The shaman's soul-catcher was a particularly significant implement: in time of war, it could be used to capture the spirits of the enemy; in time of peace, it was a curative, held to a patient's mouth so that the spirit of the dead shaman which was contained within it could enter the patient and expel the evil spirit causing the disease. Since soul-catchers had to be hollow, the form was intrinsically more suitable for bone than for ivory carving – traditionally the femur of a bear was the preferred material – yet some were made of walrus tusk, elaborately ornamented in bas relief and set with glittering pieces of haliotis shell. The soul-catcher is usually in the form of a Sisiutl, the double-headed sea monster, with an open mouth at each end, resembling the double-headed serpent motif found throughout the pre-Columbian cultures of the Andes and Mesoamerica as well as on the tombs of Han Dynasty China.

Occasionally a shaman's rattle might be made of ivory; a very fine Tlingit specimen, now in the Denver Art Museum, collected about 1870, is in the shape of a bird with a swan-like neck – an oyster-catcher – carrying a family of sea otters on its back. Since otters were thought to have the power to cause insanity, the rattle in question was probably used in the treatment of mental illness. The shaman was the tribe's spiritual leader, charged with supernatural powers. (There were women among them, though I here speak in masculine terms.) The shaman's curative amulets – necklaces and neck charms – represented the spirits which aided and protected him. A typical group of charms collected among the Tsimshian in 1879 consists of four small objects suspended from a leather thong: a killer whale, in stone; a human leg, in ivory inlaid with haliotis shell; a wolf and a lizard-like mythological beast, both with eyes of shell.

A shaman's charms usually depicted the beings he had seen in his power-seeking dreams and visions, and the most potent were attached to his necklace or dance cape, or worn as pectoral ornaments. There is a Tsimshian amulet that still retains all but one of its eighteen subordinate pendants – of birds, animals and serpent figures, among others – suspended from a central ornament of great power representing the spirits of the earth and the sky: two eagles' heads and a spirit face whose body has been symmetrically split in half. The shamans had wildly imaginative dreams, and their sculptural representation is one of the most fascinating aspects of Indian art. An amulet made for (and perhaps also by) a Tlingit shaman at Yakutat depicts a complex dream that includes what is probably a frog's head, a bear biting one man and holding another by the head, and a bird's head surrounded by the tentacles of an octopus, all presumably his spirit helpers.

Many amulets take the form of a killer whale, sometimes with a man riding on its back – a motif based on fact, not fiction, for one of the Nootka whalers' more spectacular feats was for a man to leap on the whale as it was harpooned and thrust a long knife into its back, staying with it as it submerged. A respected hereditary name among the Nootka means 'Stepping-on-a-whale'.

Most of these small ivories were carved from pieces of walrus tusk, with the design in high or low relief; others vary the pattern with openwork carving or figures in the round. Sperm whale teeth offered carvers a wider range of possible shapes. One unusual carving by a Haida sculptor, now in the Peabody Museum of Salem, Massachusetts, takes full advantage of the tooth's

volume by filling it out with a bulky woman in a tall rainhat: she is seated and holding a baby, and there are killer whale emblems engraved on the two sides. Female figures on ivory charms often assume the spraddle-legged squatting position known to anthropology as 'the shameless woman' – an ancient and ubiquitous fertility symbol that can also be found on every other continent.

There may be as many animal and human figures on these small pieces as on the large totem poles – and as many parts of the animal as possible will be shown at once, including the inner organs. Even ivory needle cases not much longer than a man's index finger were carved like tiny totem poles, for the Indian artist worked in a *horror vacui* style that rarely tolerated plain surfaces. The transformation of one being into another was a common theme; the tail of a killer whale amulet might end in a mask-like spirit face. Indeed, the relationship between beasts and men is usually shown to be one of kinship and close affinity. In the coast myths, as in many of the Inuit legends, animals constantly change into men and vice versa, and such transformations were one of the dominant elements of Northwest Coast culture. The thunderbird wore a human face on its breast, for example, to symbolize its dual personality. Tales of supernatural beings who conferred their power on humans were widespread: a Haida woman marries a bear and suffers agonies when her bear babies bite her breasts; a Tsimshian girl is tricked into marrying a dog in the guise of a man and bears canine offspring; the Raven plays a Prometheus-like role in liberating daylight for the benefit of mankind. But the core of these legends is usually a gift-relationship, since the supernatural animal, like the potlatching chief, bestows crests, privileges and special favours.

Some of the smallest, and finest, of these carvings are the ivory hairpins with which the shaman pinned up his long, snake-like locks. The pins, too, are carved to represent totemic animals, such as the land otter. The shaman would remove them during his rituals, to allow his thick locks to move of their own accord, as though they had a life of their own. The so-called 'talking sticks', usually of wood or whalebone, were also occasionally made of ivory. They served essentially the same purpose as a gavel, but rather more quietly; at tribal gatherings, only the chief holding the talking stick had the right to speak. An occasional pipe bowl would also be made in ivory and decorated with compact totemic figures that fitted comfortably into the smoker's hand.

Northwest Coast artists

Some of the small objects made in ivory, wood or bone are obviously the work of a master hand; others are quite crude, and evidently the product of a non-specialist. Unlike the Inuit, the Coast

Below: Carved ivory figure from the western Inuit. Nineteenth-century. Probably a shaman's charm.

Indians always had specialized, commissioned artists who produced sculptures for the upper class – the Northwest Coast was the only region in North America that supported a class of professional artists, though that did not prevent the non-professionals from decorating implements for their own use. 'Among our people,' recalled a Haida craftsman who talked to the anthropologist Marius Barbeau in the 1930s, 'the same carvers made the masks, the spirits (*narhnorh*) and the totems ... The art, however, was not the privilege of the common folk; it had to be inherited in high society. A carver had to train his successors to continue his work, but as long as he was able it was his exclusive right to carve. A carver of totems was a high man.'

Towards the end of the nineteenth century, however, events conspired to bring this great tradition to an end. More and more objects were being made for sale to the crews of visiting whaling ships and other outsiders to whom the totemic crests were meaningless, and as the Indians themselves were now at least nominally Christian, and industrial trade goods had replaced their handmade bowls, spoons and blankets, the art of carving fell into decline. Although several noted Indian artists, such as Charles Edensaw (1839–1924) and Tom Price, were still at work in 1900, the tribes as a whole had lost their totemic culture and had become 'modernized'.

Meanwhile a number of individuals and institutions were making serious efforts to collect what was left of the original art of the Northwest Coast. The most successful and important collector, George T. Emmons of the US Navy, had the single-mindedness of the great collector: he took it upon himself to raid old shamans' graves for the buried amulets and charms on which the reputation of the Tlingit ivory carvers now rests. The first Northwest Indian anthropologist, Franz Boas, the father of cultural anthropology, spent his most productive years among the Kwakiutl, learning their legends and studying their art.

Economically the Northwest Coast Indians have made adjustments to twentieth-century life. During the period when the coast tribes were becoming acculturated, a number of artists – following the example set by Charles Edensaw – continued developing and expanding their inherited idiom, creating important works of known authorship that are rooted in tradition but not copied from earlier models. But ivory was never abundant on this coast and since the early 1970s has been off-limits owing to new US laws protecting whale and walrus, though the superbly executed beaver made of Alaskan mastodon ivory by the Haida artist and goldsmith Bill Reid is one of the showpieces of the Koerner Collection in the University of British Columbia's Museum of Anthropology.

The United States

Scrimshaw

North American scrimshaw was a product of the nineteenth-century Yankee whaling industry, when long voyages, often lasting three or four years, left the crews to while away their time decorating sperm whale teeth. The name refers not only to the decoration but to the fact that this was a marine art.

Folk art

The scrimshoners began by smoothing the surface into a workable medium, using a file or knife, and sandpaper, sharkskin or pumice. Usually the irregular base was sawn off square to enable the tooth to stand upright. The scrimshoner would draw on his imagination or on printed pictures from various sources – such as *Godey's Lady's Book* – to work the design into the tooth. 'Some of them have little boxes of dentistical-looking implements, especially intended for the skrimshandering business,' writes Herman Melville in *Moby Dick*, drawing on his own experience in the South Seas. 'But in general they toil with the jack-knives alone; and with that almost omnipotent tool of the sailor, they will turn you out anything you please in the way of mariner's fancy.' Once the design was cut, gouged, stippled or scratched into the tooth, the engraving would be rubbed with lampblack mixed with spit, or with indian ink if available. An alternative to freehand carving was the 'pin-prick' method, whereby a pattern of some sort would be fixed to the tooth and its outlines pricked into the surface with a sail needle; later the dots were joined, and the scrimshoner would add extra details *ad libitum*. Alternative dyes were also available – sepia could be obtained with tobacco juice or a rust, green by means of copper oxide, and so on. Some artists stained the tooth itself with tea or tobacco juice to give it a more 'antique' finish, but most preferred their engraved designs to stand out boldly against the natural ivory, which was given a final polish and buffed with ashes to bring it to a high gloss.

Much of the earliest North American scrimshaw has a tentative, primitive quality; as yet there were no accepted standards and the self-taught engravers who produced it still had to feel their way towards an appropriate style. The idea of 'etching' on ivory came from the Inuit in the first place, and although Yankee subject matter was very different, the underlying documentary motive – to make a lasting record of one's prowess as a hunter – was often identical. Certainly the scrimshaw artist rarely missed an opportunity for whimsical self-advertisement of the sort exemplified by a tooth in the Mystic

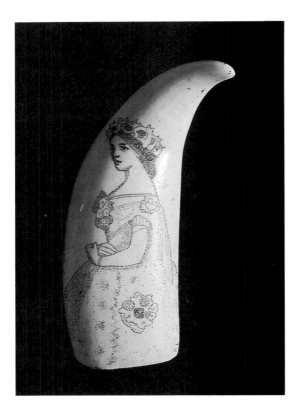

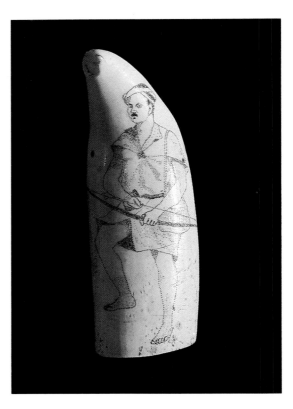

Right: An example of North American scrimshaw. Nineteenth-century; 6 in. (15 cm). Engraved with the figure of a pretty girl.

Far right: Another example of nineteenth-century American scrimshaw, showing 'Robin Hood'.

Seaport Museum in Connecticut. 'Remember,' the whaleman-author engraved on this memento, roughly carved in the shape of a whale, 'Never is heart more brave and free/Than he who hunts the whale at sea.'

Other artists liked to emphasize the hardships and hazards of their life at sea. A 'Whaleman's Woe' tooth depicts a whaleman minus a hand, an arm and a leg; he wears a patch over one eye and an understandably grim expression, since the weight of a three-masted ship is pressing down on him from above. More bloodthirsty and sanguine sentiments appear on a tooth engraved 'Off the coast of Japan' in the 1820s: 'Death to the living, Long live the killers, Success to Sailors' Wives, and Greasy Luck to Whalers.'

The sailors' wives and sweethearts figured prominently in the history of scrimshaw, both as a motive for doing the work and as a subject for illustration. Indeed, a large proportion of the ivory souvenirs carved on shipboard were intended as gifts for the patient womenfolk of Nantucket, New Bedford, Sag Harbor, *et al.* A tooth engraved 'Off Samoa' in 1847 bears the self-portrait of a young sailor and a plaintive verse expressing the pain of separation that prompted so much of this art:

> When I'm away on the restless sea
> I hope my love, you'll think of me.

Still, after two or three years away from home it was also possible to take a more ironic view of the matter. A tooth with a hoop-skirted lady on one side and a South Sea island girl in a sarong on the other bears the legend: 'To our Wives and Sweethearts. May they never meet.' A favourite whaleman's heroine was the female pirate Al-wilda, dressed in semi-male costume and with an upraised cutlass; her story first appeared in *The Pirate's Own Book* of the 1830s. But most of the women pictured on whale's teeth were of a more conventional kind, in bonnets and hoop skirts; the figures were drawn, for the most part, from the fashionplates that appeared in such magazines as *Harper's Weekly* and *Ballou's Pictorial Drawing Room Companion.* To turn such an anonymous lady into the object of one's longing it sufficed to add 'Jane' or 'Emily' by way of identification.

On rare occasions a scrimshoner might venture into uncharted waters and decorate a tooth with something approaching erotica, though such pieces are relatively rare. In July 1843, in the Indian Ocean, a whaleman from Mystic named Washington Foster fashioned a whale-tooth club for killing elephant seal on which he engraved a half-nude woman bound to a ship's rail and pleading: 'HELP HELP HELP IS THERE NOWON TO SAVE THE FAIR DAMSLE FROM THE FREEBOOTERS LEWD EMBRASE.' Most of the women shown on teeth, however, were carefully 'pin-pricked' copies of printed illustrations, and the engravers would let their imagination roam only as far as turning some of these fashionplates into mermaids by the addition of scales and a tail.

Historic personages – Washington, Lafayette, Napoleon – and foreign royalty provided additional grist for the scrimshoner's mill, as did American Indians, the harbour scenes of home and famous buildings. One well-known tooth depicts the US Capitol (in line, stipple and relief engraving) as it looked before the completion of the new dome in 1851. Patriotic American motifs always loomed large in the whaleman's repertory. Some of them might have been copied from tattoos – a tooth sporting the American eagle, for example, and *E Pluribus Unum* with a shield and cannons, and much else, together with a man-of-war under full sail and a banner with the legend, *Success to Our Navy*.

Understandably the scrimshoner was usually happiest on home ground, with three-masters running before the wind, and whales being hunted in the tropics or the Arctic. It is in this area that scrimshaw performs its most valuable function as a folk art and a documentary record, for here they were not afraid to work freehand, and to use their first-hand knowledge of rigging and whaling practice to illustrate the hunt. One matched set of three teeth engraved about 1855 depicts the highlights of the whaleman's otherwise monotonous existence: 'There She Spouts', 'Cutting In' and 'Stowing Down'. On such subjects the whalemen brought their art to the peak of perfection,

... take a very high place in an exhibition of turnery, though never a lathe was near it.'

Pastry cutters, or rather pie crimpers, were often a *tour de force* of ivory carving technology. Some were shaped like birds, others like towers or pieces of fantastic machinery incorporating 'ball in a cage' work; there is even one particularly ingenious Yankee pie cutter whose heavy wheel spells out 'GOOD PIE WELL MADE' as it rolls along. The list of household items and other utilitarian pieces of scrimshaw is a long and honourable one: thimble cases, crochet needles, spool holders, needle holders, jewellery boxes, rings, clock stands, wick picks, spoons, toothbrush handles, clothes pins or pegs, bird cages, latticework sewing baskets, teething rings, children's toys, dominoes, napkin rings, rolling pins, letter-openers, powderhorns, ink stands, bodkins and so on. The most spectacular item regularly produced on shipboard was the ivory and whalebone swift, a complex umbrella-like device used for winding yarn from a skein into a ball.

But the most intimate keepsake that a whaleman could make for his sweetheart was a whalebone busk – a flexible slab of bone, lovingly

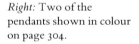
Right: Two of the pendants shown in colour on page 304.

creating what has been called 'the only important indigenous folk art' of North America – apart from that of the Indians and Inuits, of course.

In addition to drawing pictures on whale's teeth, and on the odd walrus tusk, the sailors would while away the time producing a vast range of useful ivory and whalebone objects. In *The Cruise of the Cachalot*, Frank Bullen recorded how the ship's carpenter started work on half a dozen walking-sticks. 'A favourite design is to carve the bone into the similitude of a rope, with "worming" of smaller line along its lays. A handle is carved out of a whale's tooth, and insets of baleen, silver, cocoa-tree, or ebony, give variety and finish . . . The work turned out would

engraved, that served as the front stay of a woman's corset. One poetry-loving scrimshoner engraved these memorable verses on a busk made from the panbone of a whale:

> Accept, dear Girl this busk from me;
>   Carved by my humble hand.
> I took it from a Sparm Whale's Jaw,
>   One thousand miles from land!
> In many a gale
> Has been the Whale,
>   In which this bone did rest,
> His time is past,
> His bone at last
>   Must now support thy brest.

Latter-Day work

Scrimshaw, as a folk art, did not survive the death of the American whaling industry early in the twentieth century, but a few artists have attempted to continue or revive its traditions, though not actually working aboard ship. One artist always mentioned in this connection is William Perry, a self-taught but non-seagoing scrimshoner from New Bedford, Massachusetts, who worked from the 1920s to the 1960s, carving ships and whaling scenes on to sperm whale teeth, which were then still plentiful. (Until Congress banned their importation and sale, sperm whale teeth were available from the Japanese, who maintained an active sperm whale fishery and exported tons of whale ivory to the United States.) Some of Perry's pieces are signed and have acquired a kind of post-hoc authenticity; the Mystic Seaport Museum had nine identified Perry pieces at last count, both tusks and teeth, and two probables.

Below: Two ivory jaggers or jagging wheels; American. Eighteenth-century.

Ivory products

If the stories are true, ivory's beginnings in the New World could not have been humbler. According to one local history, elephant tusks were used as ballast in the old sailing ships and dumped on the shores of towns along the Connecticut river. It was not long, however, before the early New England settlers discovered that ivory could be cut into combs. By the late eighteenth century, several ivory works had been established in Connecticut, where ivory continued to be cut up to the 1950s. The most prominent of these firms, Pratt-Read, aptly located in Ivoryton, operates today as a hardware manufacturer, and also hosts what is said to be the world's only ivory museum.

By and large, in the nineteenth-century United States, ivory combined decorative and utilitarian purposes. Most prominent perhaps was its use as a handle on everything from umbrellas and canes to handguns, mirrors, drawers, dinner bells and hair brushes. Fine crafts companies like Tiffany's and Gorham's employed their own ivory carvers – many of them descendants of European ivory craftsmen – to work the handles on their more elaborate dinnerware. Umbrella and cane handles were also sometimes intricately worked, and occasionally stained with tea for an 'old' look. So many objects were either adorned with or made from ivory that to list them would almost be to catalogue nineteenth-century life. They included hand seals; long buttonhooks or 'button handles', used for fastening footwear; glove stretchers (inserted in a wet glove to help it dry); pastry wheels; swifts for winding yarn; furniture inlay; letter-openers and desk sets; back-scratchers; judge's mallets or gavels; jewellery boxes; tea caddies; combs for the hair and the moustache, and 'nit' combs for head lice. Sewing implements – thimbles, embroidery punches, knitting needles, needle cases, and tape needles (for winding ribbon through lace) – were all made from ivory. So were electric-insulating buttons, collar buttons, cufflinks, dominoes, screws and 'flour triers' (essentially paddles or spatulas to use when checking flour for bugs). Among the more curious objects were 'Congress Letter Folders' – strips of ivory, of varying lengths, used to crease thick sheets of paper; 'gentlemen's toothpicks' – a precursor of the Swiss army knife, with three toothpicks, and sometimes a nail file, swivelling out from a little case; and 'date books', consisting of seven thin sheets of ivory fastened on an eyelet (a damp cloth served as an eraser).

Ivory was also a favourite with makers of musical instruments. Guitar nuts and saddles were made from ivory, as were the plates on organ stops. The making of piano keys, a particularly complicated process, began with 'junking' – sawing cross-sections of the tusk into 4-in. 10-cm) strips, which were then marked according to

Above: Whalebone swift. Nineteenth-century; extends to 30 in. (76 cm) diameter.

Above: One of the portraits shown in colour on page 301.

European models. Miniature portraits, however, in oil or water-colours, were frequently painted on ivory and set into gold frames. Carved ivory cameos were also popular, and could be hung on the wall or worn as a brooch or a pendant. In the 1920s, department stores sold imitation ivory miniatures set into frames made from recycled piano keys.

With the banning of the importation of elephant tusks in the 1950s, large-scale ivory production came to an end. Since 1958, when Pratt-Read received its last shipment of ivory, the company has manufactured from plastic everything it once made from ivory. Carved ivory stocks for custom-made pistols are still furnished by Colt, though at a high price.

Hawaii

Hawaii produced the most diversified corpus of ivory carvings in the South Seas. Ivory runs through the whole of Hawaiian art. Single teeth, polished but uncarved, were worn as pendants. Mushroom-shaped food pounders were used to prepare taro for *poi*. Ivory was used for inlay on carved bowls and furnished innumerable useful, yet ornamental, articles such as bodkins, needles, mesh gauges and netting needles, fish hooks, and spear rests for canoes.

There can be no doubt that ivory jewellery reaches its zenith on Hawaii. The caprice of the wearers was only equalled by the skill and patience of the carvers. The *lei niho*, or royal necklace, pendant worn by aristocratic women was a hook-shaped pendant of ivory about 4½ in. (11.5 cm) long. It was supported by a U-shaped cable of braided human hair, whose elasticity must have minimized the discomfort when the wearer walked or moved.

Even more impressive, from a technical point of view, are those necklaces where the whale's tooth has been laboriously whittled down to form miniature teeth, for beads about 1 in. (2.5 cm) long. Other beads took the form of long, tapering spikes or feather-shaped blades. Ivory ornaments were also made in the shape of turtles, or cleverly representational marine shells.

Not content with painstakingly shaping the ivory with stone saws, abrading it with sharkskin or coral, and then laboriously polishing it with wood ash, the Hawaiian carver developed a process for colouring it. The ivory ornaments were laid on a fire of charcoal, on top of pieces of sugar cane, and after steaming for hours, they acquired a rich dark colour.

The 'royal necklaces' all predate the nineteenth century. Captain Cook's expedition reached the islands in 1776 and Cook there acquired some whale's-tooth hook pendants and ingenious boar's tusk bracelets. Within a generation or so, the traditional way of life was destroyed.

the grain and cut into keys, water playing on the blade throughout to keep the ivory from burning; the keys were bleached with peroxide, and set to dry in the sun. Keeping waste to a minimum, the Yankee manufacturers sold the ivory sawdust as fertilizer.

Billiard balls and pool balls had to be cut from the dead centre of the tusk in order for them to roll properly. A tiny black dot – the nerve that runs through the tusk – can be seen on either side of a billiard ball. The makers soon learned that ivory from the female elephant, whose nerve runs straight through mid-tusk, was preferable to ivory from the male, whose nerve tends to veer off to the side.

Purely ornamental uses of ivory seem to have been fairly limited. What figurines and religious carvings were made were mostly imitations of

8
Central and South America

The ritual importance of bone and its recognition as a significant medium and object of elaboration are well founded in prehistory. Techniques for its working evolved gradually among the cultures of South America – the Maya, the Huastec, the Mixtec, the Aztec – and formed the basis of the technical mastery of carving and sculpting bone which was to yield results as fine as those achieved in ivory elsewhere in the world.

Above: Examples of Peruvian bone sculpture.

Opposite: Detail of a peccary skull from the
ceremonial centre at Copán, Honduras.
See also page 317.

Little documented, little illustrated, the tradition of bone carving in South American aboriginal and later cultures has remained an obscure subject among the otherwise rich, even exuberant literature on pre-Columbian and colonial arts. The different styles derived from a wide variety of cultural traditions, drawn from the simple societies of Lowland Amazonia to the high civilizations of the Andes and Central America, appear to have been used to decorate instruments of a not dissimilar purpose and to share certain general symbolic motifs.

The recognition of bone as a medium for plastic expression was made as far back as the Pleistocene period, ten thousand years ago, or more. The land bridge which connected Siberia to Alaska meant that large mammals, such as the mammoth and the mastodon, crossed over what later became the Bering Strait and began to populate the Americas, gradually moving down the continent to the more southerly latitudes. The remains of mammoth and mastodon have been found in excavations in the central valleys of Mexico and the Andes. Such large animals were not only prized as a source of food by the early hunters who pursued this prey, but their bones were also used to make tools and to create ritual artefacts.

The earliest recorded tools manufactured from bones were discovered from Tequixquiác, north of Lake Texcoco, where some twenty implements were found among the rich Upper Pleistocene fossil beds dating from 10,000–8000 BC. The dating of this site is roughly coterminal with the nearby lakeside site of Tepexpán, where the earliest evidence of man's occupation of Mesoamerica was found. Bone implements found in other sites on the shores of Lake Chapala in western Mexico attest to a similar antiquity. The tools manufactured from bone were used to work obsidian, to perforate hide and to aid in basketry. Of relatively common occurrence are the notched shoulder-blades of deer, rasped by a wooden stick to produce a distinctive noise which might have accompanied ritual celebrations. Far surpassing these pieces, which have little aesthetic appeal and do not testify to any art in the utilization of bone, is the worked sacrum bone of a now extinct species of llama which was also found in the valley of Mexico. This pelvic bone with its two deep cavernous openings has been further stylized to produce a mask which resembles a coyote. Sculptured and used nearly 10,000 years ago, it is similar to bone masks used today in the village of Mochitlán, Guerrero, which are worn during the Mojiguanga procession.

The civilizations of Central and South America – the Maya, the Huastec, the Toltec, the Mixtec, the Aztec – with their shared recognition of the ritual importance of bone, were to evolve their own characteristic styles of elaborating the medium.

Central America

The Maya culture: Mexico, Guatemala, Honduras, Belize

The Maya were a prehispanic people who inhabited the tropical rain forests of the Yucatán Peninsula, parts of the southern Mexican states of Tabasco and Chiapas, much of present-day Guatemala and a section of Honduras.

In the period between AD 600 and 900 the flourishing of Maya mathematics, astronomy, art and architecture, all to a religious end, enabled them to surpass and then assail all the other indigenous cultures of the Americas in the degree of their mastery of, and sophistication in, the accoutrements of civilization.

Very little evidence of the use of bone has been found in the Highland regions but unfavourable environmental conditions are not conducive to the preservation of the material. Most opinion favours the widespread use of bone implements and the utilization of carefully inscribed and sculptured artefacts for ritual and ceremonial occasions. Most of the extant pieces of sculpture and carving have been extracted from priestly or royal tombs in the Lowland ceremonial centres and it may be inferred that they were intimately related to their office; some authors even suggesting that the Maya were divided into lineages, each associated with a particular animal, whose powers and associations were made manifold by the priest or head guarding the appropriate bones. The bones found in burials, and which have been the subject of embellishment and the medium of sculpture, are of a limited variety and taken from animals that had a sacred significance for the Maya. They are from the jaguar, the peccary, a wild boar, and deer, but many objects exist in the form of inscriptions on or carvings from human bones: a material which the totemic argument fails to explain.

Among the earliest objects in bone from this area are the carved human femurs found at Chiapa de Corzo, in southern Mexico. The find consisted of two pairs of human femurs, each taken from the same subject, and laid together, in two separate places. Each pair consisted of one elaborately carved bone and one which although.cut and polished to similar dimensions was not decorated. The designs are carved in low relief whose contours are accentuated by deep incisions. Although no traces remain, the grooves may have been coloured with cinnabar, as was common throughout the area, to produce a greater clarity of the carved figures.

Both the carved bones are decorated with figures that represent a Saurian-type monster and a feline animal. Bone One depicts the Saurian to the left making swimming motions through an aqueous medium, while the feline rears upwards. The design on Bone Two illustrates what appears to be the emergence of these same beings from a substance like water or perhaps the earth. This rendering has carved the Saurian from a perspective looking down, while another similar creature with long stringy hair and a prominent skeletal-like jaw is shown to the right. The face of the feline, decorated with a head-dress, is all that is visible. The composition suggests that the pieces and the tomb in which they were found share a similar date, about AD 100.

The Saurian creature represents the Maya earth monster, Imix, the literal conception of the earth itself, associated not only with fertility and vegetative germination, but with water. The feline, identified as a jaguar, is also related to the earth, conceivably as an underworld deity closely associated with rain. The bones were probably containers for water used in baptismal or puberty ceremonies.

Not only does much of Maya carving use jaguar bone, but the animal itself is a commonly depicted subject. It appears as a seated underworld lord on a peccary skull from the ceremonial centre of Copán and as a mask attached to the back of a head-dress on a statuette of a priest from the Tabasco area. Both are later than the Chiapa de Corzo bones and date between AD 600 and 700.

The Copán skull represents another extraordinary example of the Maya achievements in bone carving. Depicted in the middle of the lozenge-shaped centre are two Maya lords seated by an altar by which stands a stele. They are richly adorned with necklaces, ear flares and bracelets, suggesting aristocratic status, and wear elaborate head-dresses, one decorated with a macaw-type bird, the other with what appears to be a skull. Below these personages a crouching grotesque which combines elements of the jaguar with skeletal details holds a conch shell in his left hand. He is surrounded by creatures such as deer, the monkey, the jaguar and a flying bird, while on the left three peccaries are shown in rapid movement. The piece illustrates a charming balance between the reposed Maya lords and the underworld deity in the centre and the animation of the beasts which surround them. The remaining cartouches and the glyphs have not been identified.

Some of the animal figures carved on the Copán skull appear again incised on the cache of bones found in another classic ceremonial centre of the same period, the Temple of the Giant Jaguar at Tikal. The carvings not only depicted mythological scenes and historical personages, but contained a large corpus of hieroglyphic inscriptions, the majority of which remain undeciphered. Perhaps among the most expressive scenes are two bones which show a number of persons and animals voyaging in a canoe. On the first of these the vessel is carried by an even tide, but on the second it is half submerged in the waves. The animal figures – the iguana, the spider monkey, the macaw and the peccary – have their hands raised in beseeching while their open mouths appear to shout for pardon, and the human figure seated with his head bowed washes a tear from his eyes. The steersman's slightly grotesque facial features and his crossed eyes suggest that he may be the Sun deity.

A peculiar characteristic of much of the incised bonework found at Tikal is that individual pieces are paired with mirror images which represent the same scene in reverse. Where they contain hieroglyphic texts these are given in identical sequence and clearly convey the same inscriptions.

Sculpture in the round is much less common than the carving and incision work described above, but the Tikal burial has yielded some examples. The first of these examples is of a monkey, crudely rendered with little more detail

Below: Peccary skull from Copan. AD 581; 8 in. (21.5 cm) long. Two lords are depicted sitting on each side of an altar, wearing jaguar skin skirts. Cinnabar pigment was rubbed into the incised design. See page 314 for detail.

than the form represented. The piece has articulated arms and legs to allow free movement and stands only 5 in. (12.5 cm) in height. The second piece is an exquisitely carved profile of a Maya lord or priest. The profile, carved within the open medallion-shaped upper part of a bone, tapers to a long stem, the top of which is decorated with minute carvings. Other notable pieces of sculptured bone, although eroded and not so well preserved, have been found in the nearby site of Rio Azul, a centre which fell under the influence of Tikal. Two sculptures which depict a human face emerging from the jaw of a monster-like creature were found carved from half a peccary mandible. Like the incised bones found at Tikal, these were matching mirror images and retained traces of a red pigmentation. In the same burial was found a pendant of a man whose expression and poise convey a strong sense of serenity. Believed to be a portrait figure of the entombed noble, it was surrounded by several tubular bone beads all of which were strung together to form a necklace. The pendant and the beads had been made from the bone of a deer.

Undoubtedly, the most outstanding example of bone sculpture from this area and period is the unprovenanced figure of a Jaguar priest (recently stolen from the National Museum of Anthropology in Mexico City). The figure which measures 3 in. (7.5 cm) in height depicts a solid standing figure with his hands resting on his hips, wearing a tunic fashioned from the pelt of a jaguar, and a jaguar-head mask at the back of his plumed head-dress. The figure is mounted on a hollow pedestal which was probably attached to a wooden staff. Drilled cavities suggest that at one time it was decorated with precious or semi-precious stones. Traces of pigment indicate that it was once coloured red. The sculpture was undoubtedly an important cult object, perhaps the staff of office of one of the Jaguar priests, who were high-ranking officials in their respective communities. No similar piece, in form or quality, has been found in Mesoamerica.

The distinct style so characteristic of classic and early Maya civilization, with its well-defined tradition of bone carving and the corresponding repertoire of subjects, fragments after 900 as external influences manifest themselves and the preponderant position which the civilization held is assailed by conquest from the north, the result of Toltec incursions. Many of the classic ceremonial centres, such as Tikal, Palenque, Copán, Yaxchilán and Piedras Negras, were abandoned, while other centres, such as Chichén Itzá and Mayapán, rise in stature, extending their polity after fortifying their ruling élite from Toltec stock. These profound changes coincide with a cruder style of bone carving and a rather inelegant, stocky and badly proportioned style of bone sculpture which lacks the lucidity of line easily discernible in the classic pieces.

Bone carving and sculpture persisted but as a result of Toltec conquests the style assumed more foreign conventions of representation.

Many of the same figures continued to be depicted, suggesting that central religious notions remained unaltered. An example of this is found in the carved bone tube which was recovered from a burial in Lamanai in Belize. Although dated to 1400–1530 and executed in a cruder style than sculpture from the classic period, its macaw head-dress reminds us of that worn by the Maya lord on the Copán skull and of the animal seated in the canoe from Tikal. This suggests that there is a limited and clearly defined cast of characters which were considered appropriate for depiction on bone and that the material was invested with peculiar symbolic values which associated it with these figures and the events associated with them while distinguishing it from more common mediums used for plastic representations such as ceramics and stone.

The Huastec culture: eastern Mexico

Although geographically isolated from the Maya centres of civilization, the Huastec of the eastern Mexican states of Veracruz, Tamaulipas and the Potosí highlands belong to the same linguistic family and are believed to have migrated from the south in very ancient times.

They shared with the Maya a developed and refined art of bone carving and sculpture, although their stylistic conventions are distinct. The carvings are lighter and usually more stylized with an exuberance of detail, with every available space filled with geometric designs. Some pieces reveal traces of red or, during later epochs, black pigmentation used to colour the incisions. Two examples, now in the British Museum, depict three serpents, their bodies imposed one on the other, and a later piece which shows a marked Toltec influence.

Few sculptured pieces of bonework have survived but their subjects are consistent with the preoccupations of the Maya. A notable example is a necklace of beads, each in the form of a skull, which comes from the Pánuco river area of Veracruz.

The Huastec examples of sculpture underwent marked transformations in style following the rise of the Toltec culture. For approximately two hundred years, 1100–1300, the bone artefacts share similar characteristics in their mode of pictorial representation with the conventions of Toltec art, while after that the denser style and trend towards geometric abstraction of peripheral elements of the central designs are reminiscent of carved bonework found in the Mixtec area of Oaxaca.

The Mixtec culture: south-eastern Mexico

The largest cache of bonework from the period 1100–1300 was recovered from a tomb at Monte Albáni, a ceremonial centre on top of a mountain which rises from the valley of Oaxaca. Although the tomb was originally constructed to house one of the Zapotec lords whose 'holy city' this was, it was reused following the Mixtec subjection of that kingdom after the former capital had been converted to a necropolis. The bonework dates from this later period.

The Mixtec were famed throughout Meso-america for their craftsmanship and mastery of a wide variety of materials of which bone was no exception. Similar stylistic conventions found in the Huastec region and the city states under the rulership of the Aztec and associated peoples attest to its diffusion which correspond to well-documented trade routes between these polities. The cache of thirty bones is not well documented and has been little studied, but the scenes depict mythological events and consist of a virtual men-agerie of animals and deities arranged in success-ive cartouches. A few of the carvings treat matters of dynastic succession and incorporate calendrical glyphs, but kingship was enshrined in a religious idiom, and no hard distinction should be drawn between myth and history. The founders of settlements were deified and successive rulers legitimated their authority by tracing their descent from them. The ideograms depicted on these bones are similar to the Mixtec pictorial style and

Below: Detail showing Ilzcuintli (dog) from the carved bone shown far right. Mixtec culture, AD 1400–1520. The carvings depict the thirteen day signs.

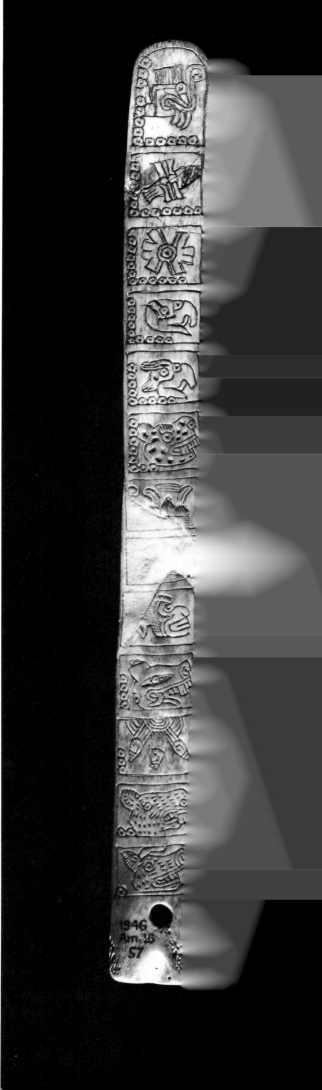

were painted with similar colours, which also emphasizes their glyphic relevance. Deities and rulers took their names from the day of their birth and since late-sixteenth-century documents from Oaxaca contain lists which relate these, together it is possible to identify some of the deities carved on the bones. All thirteen day signs can be found on one of the bones now in London.

As in other areas, the carvings are made on jaguar and human bones, although there are some executed on deer. The ideograms are small and compact and are arranged horizontally and vertically. In the bones from Monte Albán the incisions are rather deep, but others, and those found at sites such as Zaachila, have lighter outlines. Some of these carvings were encrusted and filled with semi-precious stones, such as turquoise, which can still be seen in some examples.

The Aztec culture: central Mexico

The art forms of the Mixtec-Puebla region appear to have been accepted by the Aztec, who colon-ized the central Mexican valleys from the fourteenth century and who perpetuated these traditions for their own ends. Close parallels exist between the style, symbolism and aesthetic criteria which the two regions and civilizations shared and which was reinforced by the presence of Mixtec craftsmen in Tenochtitlán, the capital of the Aztec world.

The most common bone objects which have been passed down to us from this period are bone rattles, two of which are in Berlin, one in Paris and another in Rome. The Berlin rattles are intended to be rasped and have handles shaped in the form of serpents, while the Paris rattle has the carved design of an eagle, which is believed to represent the soul of a warrior at whose burial it might have been used. It is thought that the use of the bone rattle was restricted to burial ceremonies where it would be played by slaves accompanying the funeral procession of a dignitary or warrior and later buried in his chamber. Although the pictorial style, the form and even the symbolic motifs associated with bonework had changed

after the period of the Maya decline, with the rise of the Mixtec, the material's association with the underworld and death rituals persisted.

The most spectacular and impressive objects made by the Aztec from a base of bone were undoubtedly the inlaid skulls which are preserved in the British Museum and the Berlin Museum für Volkenkunde.

The skull in the British Museum has its back cut away and its front encrusted with five bands which alternate between lignite and turquoise. Although the Mixtec used semi-precious stones to inlay some of the 'spatulas' found at Monte Albán, to the best of our knowledge it was only under the Aztec that this technique was used with three-dimensional works.

Mexico after the Spanish Conquest

It is not possible to assess at present the extent of the decline of indigenous bonework and its ultimate abandonment in and after the Spanish Conquest of Mesoamerica (1519–21) and the Andean

The early colonizers perhaps preferred ivory to bone and there emerged no demand for the manufacture of bone objects which could have substituted for the indigenous and now defunct market in that material. From the late sixteenth century onwards the Spanish trade regulations resulted in the importing of Philippine ivories, and towards the end of the century, ivory was also imported into Mexico, where workshops arose to carve small religious decorations, tablets and medallions. Most of these were established by monastic orders and the craftsmen were priests, resulting in a European style, sometimes much influenced by the baroque, but always readily distinguishable from those that had been imported.

Religious images derived from oriental workshops decorated many of the wealthier ecclesiastical buildings of colonial Mexico, but the political upheavals which accompanied the revolution in the first half of this century resulted in many of these being looted, often by pious

Below: Engraved horn from Mexico (*right*), said to have been obtained at the capture of Havana in 1792, and detail (*left*) of one of the designs, showing a Spanish galleon.

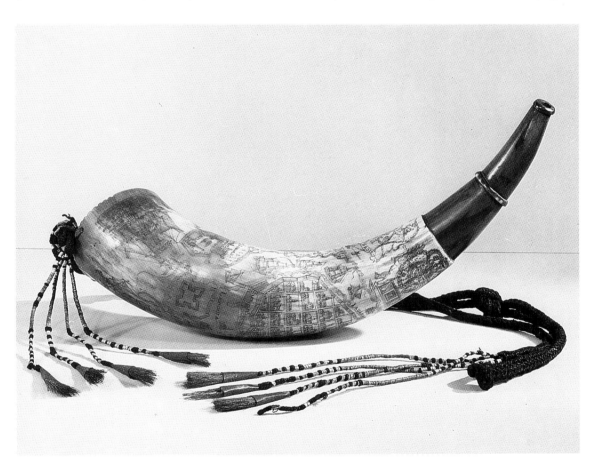

region (1532–5). A few beads are known from early colonial Mexico and a small carving of a skull, now in the British Museum, is not unlike those used for the Huastec necklace in earlier times. It was probably part of a reliquary and may have been made before Columbus set sail on his first voyage of discovery, in 1492.

peasants who prized them as objects for their personal veneration. The Jesuit convent of San Francisco de Javier in Tepotzotlán, just north of Mexico City, had over two hundred ivories looted from it during this period. Now converted into a museum, it houses one of the most important collections of colonial ivories in the world.

South America

Argentina, Peru and Brazil

Bone implements and instruments were used throughout pre-Columbian America from early times, but fragmentary source material for the areas south of the isthmus precludes any serious discussion of their provenance, dating or significance.

Seated and standing figures wearing elaborate head-dresses and sometimes carrying staffs have been found in Catamarca, Argentina.

The earliest recorded bonework from Peru dates to the Chávin culture (900–200 BC) and consists of spatulas, carved with abstract geometric designs which are sometimes surmounted by the sculptured figure of an animal, often a feline. During later periods llama bones appear to be the preferred medium for this type of work and seem to assume a similar importance to that which invested jaguar bones among the classic Maya. The Ica region of southern Peru (1090–1476) has yielded small figures of bone which belonged to the hand grip of staff-like weapons, and in the contemporaneous Chimu kingdom to the north of the Ica, the beams of market balances were carved from the same material. These sometimes had complementary figures sculpted at either end.

Flutes carved of bone from the Lowland Amazon area were used from early times and continue to be made today, and are associated with shamanistic rites. However, with little exception the tradition of carving and sculpting bone does not seem to have persisted much after the Spanish Conquest (1532–5) and the techniques used must be regarded as a lost art which died with the civilizations that sponsored them. That there are few known examples which postdate the conquest perhaps indicates the deep compromise of some of this art with ritual ceremonies which were suppressed by the Spanish. Once the religious demand for bone artefacts disappeared and their symbolic language became ineffectual, their manufacture came to an end.

Left: An example of Peruvian bone sculpture covered with incised designs which incorporate shamanic elements. They may represent a blood-letting ceremony and the consumption of ritual beverages. 4½ in. (11.4 cm).

Right: Bone implement from Ecuador, made from a human femur, surmounted by a monkey head. AD 1000–1479; 9 in. (22.8 cm). The eyes are silver and there is a monkey motif around the top band.

Below: Carved bone gouge from Peru, with inlaid shell or stone beasts. AD 200–400; 7½ in. (19 cm).

9

Contemporary Carvers

The rewards and challenges of working in ivory
still draw craftsmen throughout the world to this
unique material, even though legislation has
restricted supplies and much of the ivory used
today is either recycled or taken from small quotas
of Alaskan walrus or elephant tusks when available.
Most contemporary carvers are self-taught, learning
their skill not by lengthy apprenticeships but by
trial and error.

Above: 'Pirate Captain', scrimshaw by
William Gilkerson (United States).
Opposite: Elephant; netsuke by Michael Birch
(Europe). 3½ in. (8.8 cm).

Europe

In Europe ivories are still produced at Erbach in Germany, traditional home of Franz I's guild of ivory workers, and at Dieppe in France, where the Colette family create intricate ivory ships.

The United Kingdom is home to a number of exceptional carvers – among them Gwynneth Holt, who works from her Cotswold home and whose carvings are highly sought in the United States.

Michael Webb and Michael Birch, though British, take their inspiration from Japan and carve netsuke, though each develops the form from a different angle.

Michael Webb is a former director of Sotheby's and his professional interest in netsuke led him to take up carving himself. He makes use of both wood and ivory to create animals or insects. His carvings are unrivalled in their capacity to capture the essence of the subject, an essence enlivened by an intriguing movement or a textured feel to the fur.

An abstract, almost literary approach is taken by Michael Birch, who works without preliminary drawings and only rough marks on the uncut ivory. He brings a background of spectacle and art school training to his art and like many contemporary carvers makes full use of mechanical tools: dentist's drill, rotary brushes and buffers. This has a particular effect on texture, bringing a tactile quality to the carving, making it as interesting to the touch as to the sight.

Right: Macabre carving, in bone, by Roberto Ruiz (Mexico).

The United States

The United States is more fortunate than most countries in possessing a group of talented and productive carvers and many enthusiastic collectors.

William Gilkerson is regarded as one of the foremost scrimshoners in the world. Like his nineteenth-century counterparts, he spent his formative years at sea and has maintained a nautical connection for most of his life, restoring and sailing ships. His love of the sea and its history is deeply bound up with his scrimshaw, which depicts the great warships of the past in full sail and the pirates who once captained them. A chance encounter with a barman in North Beach sparked his interest and provided his first piece of ivory, a whale's tooth.

Though best known for his scrimshaw, Gilkerson's talent extends to three-dimensional carving. One of his most powerful creations includes a group of whale ivory polar bears, seemingly disturbed by an intruder, on an elephant ivory ice-floe. He is adept at carving heads and skulls, the hallmark of a good craftsman; many of his works are self-caricature.

Gilkerson works mainly in whale ivory. This is one of the toughest of all ivories to handle; its hardness is further complicated by an awkward colour change at the root of the tooth. But with his heads, and even a powderflask for a Colt revolver, Gilkerson has shown himself equal to its demands.

Garry van Ausdle and Lesley Harris are both self-taught. Van Ausdle, an ex-construction worker, first became attracted to ivory after buying a carving from a Long Island store. His first project, an eagle's head, took over a hundred hours of delicate cutting and shaving to complete; with astonishing detail it depicts every feather. Four years later, this meticulous approach won him great acclaim at the International Gem, Mineral and Jewelry show in Washington DC, where he submitted an exquisitely carved toad.

His use of power tools has enabled Van Ausdle to create unusual effects and indulge his taste for the grotesque. From a billiard ball he has fashioned an eagle claw grasping a skull; his other works include minute cameo heads with apocalyptic faces, and mysterious robed busts made from walrus teeth less than a forefinger in length.

Lesley Harris draws her inspiration from her native California and the natural world around her; her subjects include pelicans, flowers and other natural forms. Much of her ivory is used in jewellery.

Alaska is rapidly attracting ivory carvers. Homer Hunter and Earl Mayac are two of the

Above: Bear-man, by Earl
Mayac (United States).
c. 3½ in. (8.8 cm) long.
Mayac is one of a
number of Alaska-based
carvers.

most prominent. Although Earl Mayac now lives in Anchorage, he was born on King Island and continues the traditions of his Inuit forefathers, carving tiny pieces of walrus ivory; many contemporary Inuit have been forced to take up elephant tusk or soapstone instead.

Mexico

Most of the carvings in bone produced in Mexico today are intended for the mass market and are neither technically nor artistically demanding. However, the outstanding exception to this is Roberto Ruiz, who has achieved an extraordinary virtuosity of detail and clarity of line in his various sculptures and has encouraged a whole generation of new carvers.

Ruiz began his career carving wood before successfully transferring to bone. He acknowledges two direct influences on his work: the miniaturist tradition for form and style and the work of the popular engraver Jose Guadalupe Posada for subject and content. Posada's illustrations for ballads and satires transformed brides, musicians and other figures into skeletons and it is these macabre images that can be seen in Ruiz's carvings, together with historical scenes from Mexico's past. Ruiz works at the Instituto Nacional Indiginista.

China

Mainland China, once a great producer of ivory carving, still boasts some remarkable contemporary craftsmen. The foremost of these is Yang Shih-hui. He has worked for sixty years, producing some 1600 articles to date including brushpots, snuffbottles and animals. But since the 1940s he has been best known for his figure work, which ranges from recent historical subjects like Stalin and Mao Tse-tung to figures in the archaic Ming and Tang styles. He has also produced commemorative work and 'Ch'eng to Kunming Railway', carved from a tusk weighing 141 lb (64 kg), is now on permanent display at the United Nations headquarters in New York. In 1979 he was awarded the honorary title 'Handicraft Master'; the only ivory carver to be so honoured in China.

Yang credits much of his success to the collectivism of craftsmen in China, where ideas and techniques are freely shared. He himself has trained more than fifty apprentices and introduced his own children to the craft.

Another prominent carver from China is Lo Yang-tsing, whose favourite subjects are beautiful girls in long flowing robes, and multi-tiered pagodas. He is particularly notable for his use of antique and bright colour, combined with gold decoration.

Chang Gon-eng comes from Shanghai and brings the technique of micro-carving to ivory, creating characters that are literally the breadth of a single hair. The ivory is inked over and then the image scratched into it. Most people have to use a magnifying glass to view the completed work satisfactorily, though Chang does the carving without any visual aid.

Japan

In neighbouring Japan, Masatoshi has gained an international reputation and his work is well known through exhibitions, though the bulk of his output is contained in one private collection in the United States.

He was born in 1915, descended from a long line of carvers specializing in Buddhist images. After training from his father in this form of ivory sculpture, he chose instead to carve netsuke. He draws on traditional Japanese sources for his work: legends, Immortals and animal life. In each case he strictly obeys the rules of netsuke.

Two other Japanese carvers who concentrate on netsuke are Kodo and Bishu. Kodo was born in 1940 and is mostly modern in his conception and execution, contrasting markedly with Masatoshi. Many of his pieces are too fragile to function as netsuke; they are inspired by flowers, pebbles and sea life.

Bishu, a few years younger than Kodo, focuses mainly on animals. Through skilful carving and design, he is able to inject a restless, sinuous quality into his netsuke, giving them a tremendous vitality and life. He rarely uses stain, leaving the ivory with a high polish or finely textured with hair and inlaid eyes. Like Masatoshi he rarely departs from the ideals imposed by the medium.

It is hard to speculate what the future has in store for ivory; a substance so elastic and versatile, yet subject to fashion.

It is difficult to imagine such a stimulating material ever being far from creative art. Picasso, Brancusi, Archipenko, Derain, Pompon and Giacometti were all inspired to create modern sculpture by primitive ivories. This process continues today with new techniques and tools for working ivory being absorbed all the time. The unprecedented popularity of Chinese and Japanese works of art has once more kindled interest in and love of ivory. For carvers, all over the world, the future seems healthy.

Opposite: 'Priest', a netsuke by Masatoshi (Japan). *c.* 2 in. (5.2 cm). The descendant of a long line of carvers, he draws on traditional Japanese sources for his work.

Glossary

The entries and cross-references are in **bold** type for quick reference. Chinese entries are in Pinyin, with the traditional spelling, which you may still find in reference books, in brackets.

abaya-mudra
Buddhist gesture of reassurance, with the hand raised in blessing; a common pose in carved ivory *Bodhisattvas* (saints) all over the Far East, together with other *mudras* (hand gestures).

akshas
Indian term for the solid tip of the elephant's tusk; usually exported for the making of billiard balls. There was a huge demand for what was called 'billiard ball scrivelloe' in Victorian Britain; this was **turned** on a lathe, while being sprayed with water to prevent cracking.

ancien régime
French expression for the monarchy, political organization and culture which preceded the revolution of 1789. Its disappearance caused difficulties for ivory carvers, both through lack of patrons and through political censorship of such items as the king on a chessboard. The term is also applied to other parts of Europe at the same period.

Anglo-Saxon
English people and English culture from the seventh century to the Norman Conquest of 1066, when the Anglo-Saxon started to give way to the **Romanesque**. Anglo-Saxon carvers were supreme in **walrus ivory** and during the second half of the tenth century their techniques were closely linked to manuscript illumination, which was dominated by the **Winchester style**. They were not isolated from the Continent and their work shows **Carolingian** influence, but with a more linear and less naturalistic emphasis.

antique
The culture of classical Greece and Rome, predominantly from 500 BC until the fall of Rome in AD 410. The period is dominated at its beginning by the huge **chryselephantine** statues of Phidias and at its end by the Roman consular **diptychs** which continued, in Constantinople, into the **early medieval** period. These civilizations gave inspiration to the Renaissance and to **neo-classicism**.

arabesque
Abstract decorative motif, based on flowing plant forms, scrollwork and split **palmettes**; in the west, humans and animals are included. Originally from the **Hellenistic** cultures of Asia Minor, it was taken up enthusiastically by Islamic painters and carvers for whom figurative art was usually – but not always – forbidden.

Art Deco
European and American style, mainly of the 1920s and 1930s, which took its name from the Exposition internationale des arts décoratifs et industriels modernes, in Paris in 1925; typified by a sleek and streamlined modernism and geometric shapes. Together with Art Nouveau, which had preceded it, the movement saw a great output of **chryselephantine** figurines which – despite a new admiration for industrial design and mass production – were hand-finished.

Art Nouveau
Decorative style of the 1890s, characterized by sinuous lines and stylized flowers, leaves, etc. Ivory was often combined with gilt bronze to create **chryselephantine** statuettes and used, with precious metals, stones and enamels, in jewellery.

Asuka
Japanese period, AD 552–645, which saw strong Chinese Buddhist influence; sculpture of the period is mainly in wood and bronze.

bachiru
Carving or engraving technique, predominantly Chinese, using a curved tool to cut out a design in dyed ivory; sometimes the background was coloured in after the carving. The style was popular in the **Tang** dynasty.

baleen
See **whalebone**.

bamboo ivory
The hollow shaft of an elephant's tusk. It is approximately the same proportions as the human wrist and thus often used for bangles; other carvers make use of the shape for small circular boxes. The curve

of the shaft, and the need to conceal the pulpy core, led to the 'swaying stance' of figure carving in the **Gothic** and other periods.

baroque
Exuberant and theatrical style of mainland Europe in the seventeenth century, acting as propaganda for the Counter-Reformation and the absolute monarchies; the name comes from *barroco*, a Portuguese term for irregularly shaped pearls. Architecture, painting, sculpture and the decorative arts strive for grandeur and a vital sense of movement and contrast. The term is also applied to some Indian carving of the post-**Gupta** period.

Begram
Capital of the Kushan empire which stretched over north-western India, Pakistan and Afghanistan from the first to the late fourth century AD; near modern Kabul. It gives its name to the magnificent collection of ivories found there, most of which are now in the Kabul Museum. They are some of the best surviving Indian art and are mainly delicate and sophisticated carved plaques, probably applied to furniture, depicting voluptuous court ladies. The carving is deeply incised and has traces of colour. They are thought to date from the first or second century AD.

Biedermeier
German and Austrian style, *c.* 1820–60; characterized by exaggerated curves, realistic animal carvings and decorative flowers and fruits. Ivory pieces included back-combs, hairpins and elaborate fans.

blazon
Heraldic shield or banner.

Bombay boxes
Indian boxes elaborately **inlaid** with stained ivory, silver and horn.

bonbonnière
French term for small decorative box used for sweetmeats or other delicacies; from French *bonbon*, 'sweetmeat'; frequently carved in ivory.

bone carving
A common substitute for ivory, particularly in Central America and in the various **shamanistic** cultures. Various types of bone are used, from the llamas and jaguars of South America to the human skulls of Tibetan **kapalas**. French prisoners during the Napoleonic wars carved ships in bone from their rations. Bone is less fibrous and less easily torn than ivory, but its lack of natural gelatine makes it dead under polish.

braiding
Plaiting effect in carving; usually used in borders.

cabochon
Method of cutting gemstones with a rounded convex surface, polished but unfaceted; from the French *caboche*, 'head' or 'pate'. It is generally used for opaque and opalescent stones, and was the earliest method for stones set in jewellery. The semi-precious stones inlaid into ivory are commonly cut *en cabochon*.

Carolingian
The culture of the Holy Roman Empire from the crowning of Charlemagne in AD

800 until the early tenth century. There was a great revival in ivory carving, inspired by the naturalism of classical art and the Christian traditions of the late Roman Empire; some **antique** ivories such as consular **diptychs** were reused. Typical of the style are the early-ninth-century ivory book-covers made for the Lorsch gospels, now in the Victoria and Albert Museum, London.

chevron
Upturned V-shape; originally a beam or rafter; a common motif in all decorative art, often in the form of a zigzag pattern in moulding and carving.

chinoiserie
Western art which has been influenced by Chinese decorative styles; first seen in the sixteenth and seventeenth centuries, after early contacts, but at its peak in the eighteenth century, when it is allied to the **rococo**. It appears in wallpaper, porcelain, furniture and even, in England, in landscapes. Furniture is often **inlaid** with ivory.

chryselephantine
The combination of ivory with gold or gilt-bronze; from the Greek *chrysos*, 'gold', and *elephas*, 'ivory'; a popular technique for statues and figurines from the earliest times, usually with the flesh of ivory and clothes and hair of gold. In the very large statues of Athena in the Parthenon and Zeus at Olympia, made by Phidias in the fifth century BC, the ivory was bent over a wooden base and subsequently kept moist with oil or water. Chryselephantine statuettes were again very popular in the Art Nouveau and **Art Deco** styles.

churi
Indian term for the bangles, often of ivory, worn by many Hindu and Muslim women and frequently covering the

women and frequently covering the whole arm; carved from the central section of the tusk called the *chunibar* and either decorated with engraving or left plain and stained red, green or black. They were often given as Hindu wedding presents and worn for the first year of marriage before being replaced by silver or gold.

codex
Manuscript volume, usually of the Bible or an ancient text. To serve as the hinged outer covering of Roman books of this sort was an original function of the **diptych**.

coffret
Small coffer or strongbox in which money or valuables were kept; used especially as jewellery boxes. Beautiful ones in ivory were carved in the Byzantine world and these were widely copied in nineteenth-century Russia and France.

comb
One of the commonest ivory objects in virtually every culture; some of the first ivory pieces are combs found in early Egyptian tombs. In the **Gothic** era they were often very large and double-sided with a ceremonial and liturgical purpose. The laborious nature of their construction, requiring many different sizes of saws, files and rasps, made them an early candidate for industrialization and the first comb-cutting machine appeared in 1808.

crocket
Small ornament on the sloping side of gables, pinnacles, etc.; usually a bud, curled leaf or comma design; a feature of **Gothic** architecture, which was then transferred to the tops of book-covers, altarpieces and **diptychs**.

Daoism (Taoism)
Chinese religion, whose central principle is to 'do nothing' (*wu-wei*) against 'the

way' (**dao**); ranks second to Confucianism, which was more staid and official, and beside which it often coexisted in a domestic context. Its rivalry with Buddhism often caused persecution for both religions. Its mystical nature gave rise to great artistic expression and Laozi, its legendary founder, was a popular figure in ivory carving, as were the Eight Immortals and various longevity symbols.

diaper
A repeated pattern used as surface decoration, often based on square, grid or lozenge shapes; very popular in the Chinese **Qing** dynasty, particularly in the carving of eighteenth-century ivory fans.

diptych
Two-leaved, hinged writing-tablet, carving, painting or altarpiece; originally used to cover a Roman **codex**. Their convenience and portability led to their use as ostentatious greetings by the nobility of Rome and Constantinople. In AD 384 Theodosius limited their use to consuls, and consular diptychs became a major art form of the late antique and early medieval world, as well as a form of cultural exchange; they were carved in ivory or wood and had a message in wax on the inside. Their low-relief carving enabled them to be reused by the

Carolingians. Carved ivory diptychs were also popular as **Gothic** altarpieces. See also **polyptych, triptych**.

early medieval
From *c.* AD 400 to *c.* AD 1200. Artistic highpoints include the **Tang** dynasty in China, the Byzantine and Islamic cultures, and in western Europe the **Carolingian** and **Ottonian** Renaissances. From the seventh century the spread of Islam gradually reduced the supply of ivory to northern Europe, where the **Romanesque** culture which dominated the end of the period tended to rely on **marine ivory** for carving.

Edo-Tokugawa
Japanese period, 1615–1868; takes its name from the new upstart city of Tokyo, which began to rival the then capital Kyoto, and from the warlord Tokugawa Ieyashu (1542–1616), who started a regime after winning the power struggle which followed the death of the warlord Hideyoshi. During this period Japan forcibly isolated itself from the West until the arrival of Commodore Matthew Perry in 1863. Japan's finest colour prints were produced notably by Katsushika Hokusai (1760–1849). Lacquers and metalwork were **inlaid** with ivory, but the most important ivory artefact was the **netsuke**.

Embriachi
Northern Italian family of carvers in the late fourteenth and early fifteenth centuries, led by Baldassare degli Embriachi; specialized in the use of **hippopotamus tooth** in vertical strips side by side carved in curved reliefs. These decorated marriage caskets and chests or were built up into large complexes to form altarpieces. The process leads to rather stultified design.

encrustation
Overlaying or ornamenting a surface with a more precious material, an example being the ivory silhouettes sometimes seen on wooden boxes.

Fatimid
Political and religious dynasty which dominated Egypt and North Africa from the tenth to the twelfth century AD; claimed descent from Muhammad's daughter, Fatima. Their art is regarded as the most beautiful in Islam, particularly

in metalwork and ivory. Some work is abstract and linear in the usual Islamic style, but the high-relief plaques inherit the realistic figurative tradition of Mesopotamia.

floriated
Decorated with floral ornaments; seen at its most dominant in the **arabesque**.

fossil ivory
The preserved tusks of prehistoric **mammoths** and mastodons, and occasionally the **walrus**; used for carving by many cultures, particularly the Inuit and Chinese; it is brittle, sometimes mottled, and yellows quickly. In the nineteenth century large deposits were found in Siberia and Alaska. It was often used for the **veneer** of piano keyboards, but much of it was useless except for charring to become **ivory black**. The source seems now to be exhausted.

Garzean
Period of Egyptian culture, at its height *c.* 3300 BC; named after El Garza, where important remains were found. The most interesting ivory artefacts are the handles of flint knives, carved with hunting scenes.

Goanese ivory
Indo-Portuguese work, sixteenth century and after, following the

Portuguese discovery of the sea route to India in 1497 and the subsequent colonization of Goa. It is a hybrid of eastern and Christian culture; ivory is used for **inlaid** boxes and cabinets and for carved madonnas, angels and saints which have the details incised and stained.

Gothic
Dominant European style of the **late medieval** period; received its impetus from the **Île de France** in the middle of the twelfth century. The architectural language of pointed arches, pinnacles, tracery and strongly emphasized verticals was transferred to other media, including carving. Ivory was used for miniature altarpieces and **tabernacles** as well as emotional figures such as Pietàs, which were used for private as well as public devotion. The influential Virgin and Child of La Sainte Chapelle (*c.* 1250–60), whose curving pose was dictated by the shape of the tusk, was widely copied in materials where the curve was in fact unnecessary.

Gravettian
European culture of the **Palaeolithic** period, approximately 20,000 years ago; fine carvers of **mammoth** ivory. Their art was mainly representational, such as small female figurines in ivory, which were probably linked to fertility beliefs. Examples of ivory jewellery have been found in graves, in which the dead were buried fully clothed.

Guanyin (Kuan Shih Yin)
Chinese goddess of mercy, the name meaning 'who hears the cry of the world'; originally the *Bodhisattva* Avalokiteśvara, who was turned back by the cries of the suffering when about to enter Buddhahood; depicted as a male by Chinese carvers until the twelfth century AD, thereafter as a female. She was a frequent subject for ivory carvers and after the onset of western influence was often portrayed with a child, like the Virgin.

gui gong qui
'Devil's work balls'; a series of concentric spheres with openwork carving one inside the other; one in the Peabody Museum in Salem has twenty spheres. By the nineteenth century they were mainly being carved as tourist attractions

for the 'foreign devils', but in the Ming dynasty they were made for the home market as well, though none have survived.

guilloche
Decoration with two or more curved lines or bands twisting over each other in a spiral.

Gupta
Indian dynasty lasting from the fourth to the sixth century AD, which controlled the Ganges Valley and northern India; the Golden Age of Indian culture in which Buddhism flourished, decimal notation was introduced and the great Sanskrit epics were written. Political stability brought artistic unity and decorative carving has a vigour and delicacy of execution.

Han
Chinese dynasty 206 BC–AD 220; roughly contemporary with the Roman Empire; period of the great early emperors. The dynasty saw the beginnings of both porcelain and Buddhism. Major art forms were bronze, jade, silk-painting and pottery, which began to be patronized by the gentry as well as the nobility. The style could be both dynamic and dignified.

Harappan
'Indus Valley Civilization', *c.* 2300–1750 BC; named after a city in the Punjab. The major art form was carving in limestone and terracotta. Not a great deal of ivory has been found and what there is tends to be small objects – jewellery, hairpins, kohl-sticks and combs, frequently decorated with a circle-dot motif.

Hellenistic
The culture formed by the fusion of Greek civilization with surrounding, mainly oriental, elements; covers approximately the area conquered by Alexander the Great and the period 323–27 BC, ending with the conquest of Egypt by Rome. Carving is divided into two main styles – Alexandrian, which is naturalistic with landscape backgrounds and dominates the west, and neo-Attic in the east, which is more formal and symmetrical with plain backgrounds.

himotoshi
Hole (often two of unequal size) in a

Japanese **netsuke**, through which the cord holding the *inrō* (seal-basket) passed before being attached to the **ojime** (bead fastening). In the carved *katabori* **netsukes** it was often cleverly incorporated into the design by means of a leg or tail. After the onslaught of western culture and dress in the late nineteenth century the evolution of the netsuke from practical use to display object (**okimono**) is marked by the gradual disappearance of the himotoshi.

hippopotamus tooth
Good-quality ivory, weighing up to 30 lb (13.5 kg), which is obtained from the incisor and canine teeth; the thick outer enamel must be removed with acid; the inside is pure, white and hard but can crack with age. This ivory was used a great deal by the **Embriachi** in Italy.

hu
Chinese curved ivory tablet, originally of the **Tang** dynasty but imitated later; had a ceremonial use for imperial officials; could be plain or inscribed with poems or official symbols; also decorated in **bachiru** style. (Not to be confused with the Wade spelling of *hu* – a bronze vessel of the **Shang** and **Zhou** dynasties.) See also **yuan**.

Huguenot
French Protestant, many of whom fled to England after Louis XIV revoked the Edict of Nantes in 1685; brought with them many commercial and artistic skills, such as the ivory carving techniques of **Dieppe**. Particularly notable were the carved ivory portraits, plaques and medallions of Cavalier and Le Marchand.

Iconoclasm
Opposition to, and breaking of, holy images; particularly a movement of eighth-century Byzantium whose power lasted from the Emperor Leo III's edict in AD 726, ordering the destruction of religious images, until the Council of Constantinople restored Orthodoxy in 843. In England the doctrine was powerful long before the Reformation; in 1389 a Wycliffite wrote: 'Hit semes that this offrynge ymages is a sotile cast of Anti-christ and his clerkis for to draw almes fro pore men . . . certis, these ymages of hemselfe may do nouther gode nor yvel to mennis soules but thai myghtten warme a man's body in colde, if thai were sette upon a fire.'

Île de France school
The Île de France saw the origins of the **Gothic** style in the mid twelfth century and by the thirteenth there was a flourishing ivory carving industry there, whose heyday was 1230–40. Large numbers of objects, often for private devotion, were carved, including small **diptychs** and **triptychs**. Popular subjects were the Passion and the Virgin and Child.

inlay
Creation of an ornamental design by inserting one material into the depressed ground of another using adhesive or pegs; ivory is used both as inlay and as a host for other materials. Chests and gaming boards inlaid with ivory were found in the tomb of Tutankhamun (*c.* 1330 BC), and the technique is particularly popular in many cultures for the decoration of furniture.

intarsia
Technique of **inlaying** wood, ivory and ebony in a boldly contrasted mosaic, often using tiny pieces; thought to be introduced into Islamic culture by the Mamluk dynasty, who were originally military slaves, in the thirteenth century AD, but also popular in the Renaissance and **baroque** periods. The Islamic style includes scrolls, **arabesques**, pointed hexagons, plaques and koranic inscriptions.

ivory
Calcareous matter in the form of teeth, as opposed to **bone**; classically comes from the upper incisor (tusk) of the elephant but is also obtained from the **hippopotamus**, boar, warthog, and the various forms of **marine ivory**; popular carving material because of its workability; colour varies from pale white to deep red, particularly if oil is absorbed from the human body. The African elephant is larger than the Indian and its tusk can be 6 ft (1.8 m) long and 100 lb (45 kg) in weight. Ivory can be green (from the live animal), dead, cured (dead but well preserved) or **fossil**, which is the preserved remains of the prehistoric **mammoth** and mastodon.

ivory black
Artist's pigment; the best quality is made from charring ivory chips (often reject **fossil ivory**) in a closed oven; mixed with cadmium yellow it produces a range of bright greens. 'Black ivory' was eighteenth-century commercial slang for the slave trade and reflected the value of both commodities.

Jahangir
Indian period, which takes its name from the Mughal emperor who ruled 1605–28. There was religious tolerance and Jesuits were allowed to preach, which resulted in cultural exchange with the West. The emperor was a great patron of the arts, and carvings of the period show knowledge of **Carolingian** techniques.

kabinettsplastik
German expression for small and valuable objects intended for display in cabinets. Particularly popular were the seventeenth-century carved ivory tankards. Closely allied is the term *kleinplastik*, which is applied to small pieces for private enjoyment as opposed to monumental public sculpture.

kagamibuta
Form of **netsuke**; metal disc in an ivory dish.

kakihan
Scrolling monogram used by the carvers of Japanese **netsukes**; often emphasized in red lacquer once the netsuke became a display object (**okimono**) for sale to the West.

kapala
Tibetan drinking-bowl carved from a human cranium; from Sanskrit for 'skull'. They rested on triangular

pedestals (representing fire) on Buddhist altars and were used in ritual to offer wine (blood) and dough (flesh). The interiors were often handsomely decorated with semi-precious stones and *mantras* (prayers).

khatam-khar
Iranian technique of mosaic marquetry, used since the **late medieval** period. Sticks of wood, ivory, etc., triangular in cross-section, are tied in bundles into star patterns; these are then sliced and built up into intricate geometric patterns. The technique is popular for the decoration of musical instruments.

lambrequin
French term, originally for material hanging from a helmet and thus for any form of pendent draperies; now applied to a decoration based on a formalized representation of this in a jagged or scalloped outline; common in low-relief borders of the **baroque** period.

Lamu chairs
Wooden chairs with geometric ivory **inlay**; the name comes from an island off the Swahili coast of East Africa.

late medieval
From 1200–1500; dominated in Europe by the **Gothic** style which was ended by the Renaissance and the Reformation; first direct contacts with China, then ruled by the Mongol **Yuan** dynasty.

maeanda (meander)
Ornamental pattern of winding lines with right-angled turns and intersections; usually associated with Greek pottery but found in ancient art all over the world. It commonly represents water, but in China it is a cloud or thunder pattern (*lei wen*) and forms the background for the dragon which is the rain spirit.

Magdalenian
European culture of the **Upper Palaeolithic period**, 10–17,000 years ago; period of great cave paintings. Bone tools were often engraved with animal images and a **mammoth ivory** figurine was found at Lourdes.

maîtresse branche
French term for the outside leaves of a fan, the part most commonly carved in ivory; often the carver would make a

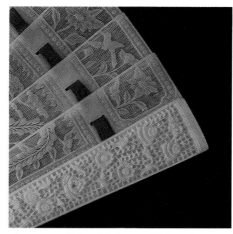

plaster model, which would then be copied by a **practicien** (assistant). By the eighteenth century the Chinese were making ivory fans, with lattice, trellis, or **diaper** designs, for the western market; these increased in size and angle as the century progressed.

makara
Indian mythical animal, like a cross between a crocodile and a dolphin; has a trunk and teeth, and its tail is often represented as a **foliated** scroll.

mammoth
Large tusked animal (*elephas primigenius*) with long reddish-brown hair; about five times the weight of an African elephant; now extinct. It flourished during the Pleistocene period (2,500,000–10,000 years ago) and was the source of early European ivory, but it had disappeared by 17,000 BC and ivory had to be imported from Africa and the Near East. It was reused later in the form of **fossil ivory**, which the Chinese thought to be from a giant mole.

manju
Flat, circular Japanese **netsuke**; the name means 'bean-curd cake'. There are either two cord holes in the *manju* or a metal ring at the back (**himotoshi**). It is thought to be an earlier form than the carved *katabori* **netsuke**.
See also **ryusa**.

mannerist
European style, usually applied to painting, which flourished between the High Renaissance and the **baroque** (*c.* 1520–1600). It features emotional poses with exaggerated perspective and bright colours. Typical artists are El Greco and Tintoretto.

marine ivory
Substitute for elephant ivory among all the maritime nations and throughout northern Europe when the ivory supply was interrupted by the spread of Islam; obtained from **whalebone** and **walrus** and **narwhal** tusks; used above all others by the Inuit.

Mauryan
Indian period *c.* 321–185 BC; dominated by an empire won after the death of Alexander and centred on modern Patna. The Emperor Asoka's enthusiasm for Buddhism led to the great stupas of 272–232 BC. He also commissioned some of the finest Indian art, which shows **Hellenistic** and Iranian influences. Carving tended to be in stone rather than ivory.

minbar
Islamic pulpit; used both for the preaching of sermons (*khutbahs*) and as a symbol of a caliph's authority. Some had elaborate ivory carvings.

Ming
Chinese dynasty, AD 1368–1644; means 'bright'; roughly contemporary with the Renaissance. It is the period of the great Chinese literature and the blue and white porcelain – and of the last indigenous elephants. Ivory carvings of **Daoist** figures show the same curving pose seen in European **Gothic**. Furniture was inlaid with ivory and many small objects such as hairpins were carved, but the use of ivory for calligraphers' wrist rests and brush pots was considered decadent by scholars; many such objects thought to be **Ming** are in fact **Qing** imitations. The Ming style is still used today.

Momoyama
Momoyama (or Azuchi-Momoyama), Japanese period AD 1568–1615; dominated by the warlord Hideyoshi. The power started to devolve from the samurai to wealthy merchants and the greatest art is the wall-paintings. The first pictures of western visitors appear, but these foreigners were driven out in the **Edo** period.

Morse
See **walrus ivory**.

mosaique
French term for an ivory technique used in **Dieppe**; the background of a carving

was decorated with a pattern of regular perforations. Dieppe declined in the nineteenth century, but the technique was imitated in Russia, using netting and lace patterns to surround portrait medallions.

Mosan
Regional school of the **Romanesque** style in the eleventh and twelfth centuries; centred on the river Meuse; mainly illumination, metalwork, enamelwork and ivory carving. The style has a rounded naturalism and is seen typically on the Notger ivory, mounted on a book-cover now in the Curtius Museum in Liège.

Mughal (Mogul)
Muslim dynasty which ruled India from the sixteenth to the eighteenth centuries, after which it was gradually supplanted by the British; started in 1526 after the conquests of Babar the Turk, a descendant of Genghis Khan. The Mughals were great patrons of the arts, particularly of the school of Indian miniature painters. Court objects, such as fan and fly-whisk handles, were made in ivory. The last emperor was deposed in 1858.

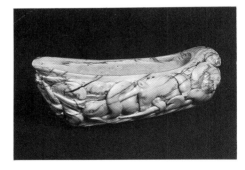

narwhal
Arctic porpoise with a straight, spirally grooved tusk which was used as a form of **marine ivory** but is now protected; the tusk is 6–8 ft (1.8–2.4 m) long and partly hollow, giving a hard, dense, white ivory. It was often thought to be from a unicorn and to have magical properties. It was carved in northern Europe, in Japan, and by the Northwest American Indians and the Inuit, who used it for harpoons.

neo-classicism
European style of the late eighteenth and early nineteenth centuries; a return to the restraint and balance of classical art. It

was partly inspired by republicanism, but was chiefly a revolt against the excesses of **rococo** which it had supplanted by 1780 in all but Germany. Its ideals were those of Winckelmann's *History of Ancient Art* (1764), which recommended 'noble simplicity and calm grandeur'. Ivory carving replaced the scroll with a more severe, rectilinear design, as did furniture – which made it ideal for ivory **veneer**.

neolithic
New Stone Age, *c.* 5000–750 BC; stone tools were shaped by polishing and grinding as opposed to the chipping method of the preceding **palaeolithic** period.

netsuke
Carved button-like object or toggle worn by the Japanese; means 'root-attach'. As the kimono had no pockets a nest of boxes (*inrō*), usually made of lacquer, was hung from the waistband (obi) by a cord which passed through two holes (**himotoshi**) in the netsuke, which held it in place under the obi. The most common form is the **katabori**, a sort of miniature sculpture which was at first made of wood but increasingly of ivory; the eighteenth-century ivory netsuke is a major collector's piece. With the nineteenth-century arrival of western dress it became an elaborate display object (**okimono**) rather than functional. See also **manju**, **obihasimi**, **ojime**, **ryusa**, **sashi**.

North Syrian
School of ivory carving in the first millennium BC. Unlike the contemporary **Phoenician** school the work had little Egyptian influence and was normally found close to home. Lions and winged sphinxes are common motifs and the carved circular boxes were often held by lions or a human hand.

obihasimi
Form of **netsuke** with a hook; uncommon.

ojime
Japanese term for a small sphere which held and tightened the cord which had been passed through a **netsuke**; sometimes in ivory, but usually of a lighter material.

okimono
Japanese term for a display object, often in ivory; the concept was originally foreign to the Japanese but developed as the **netsuke** became larger, less practical, and sought after by western buyers. The pieces were often decorated with red lacquer signatures.

oliphant
Obsolete form of 'elephant'; now used to mean carved ivory trumpets or drinking horns. The most famous were made in Mesopotamia between the tenth and thirteenth centuries and are decorated with scrolling vine-leaves.

Ottonian
German cultural Renaissance of the tenth and eleventh centuries; centred on Trier

and named after Otto the Great of Saxony, who was crowned Holy Roman Emperor in AD 962. It developed from the **Carolingian** style, but the figures on Ottonian ivory plaques and panels are stiffer and more upright with ornate backgrounds.

ovolo
Convex moulding, receding downwards, based on a quarter-circle or ellipse.

palaeolithic
Stone Age (c. 2,500,000–10,000 years ago); period when primitive stone tools were chipped rather than polished; many palaeolithic ivory objects have been found, made from **mammoth** tusks.

palmette
Decorative motif based on the fan-like arrangement of a palm frond; in the **arabesque** it is frequently split, with the outer part lobed and the inner long and curling. It is common in Egyptian, Classical, Byzantine and Islamic art.

Phoenician
School of ivory carving created in the first and second millennia BC by the trading people of what is now the Lebanese coast. The style is elegant and sophisticated with applied colour and many Egyptian features. It is found all over the Mediterranean.

pointillist
Technique used in **scrimshaw**, using a dotted line to etch designs in ivory with a sail needle; it was often used in copying magazine illustrations.

polyptych
Five or more hinged panels, decorated by painting or carving; often ivory; used as altarpieces in the **Gothic** period.
See also **diptych**, **triptych**.

practicien
French term for an artist's assistant or apprentice. Instead of 'direct carving' the master would make a model which his *practicien* would transpose on to the ivory. This work is less valuable.

pre-Columbian
The culture of the Americas before the arrival of Columbus in 1492 and the resultant European influence. Mayas and

Aztecs used bone rather than ivory for carving.

pricked style
Carving style of **early medieval** Germany; placing small notches in lines of drapery.

pyx
Christian vessel for consecrated bread; usually a small circular box with a conical lid; very often carved in ivory.

pyxis
Cylindrical ivory box; carved from the hollow section of a tusk (see **bamboo ivory**); often used for incense and called *arca turalis*. Pagan *pyxides* were frequently converted for Christian use in the Middle Ages, while retaining their secular decoration.

quatrefoil
Four-lobed decoration; often used in stone tracery or carving in the **Gothic** period.
See also **trefoil**.

Qing (Ching)
Last Chinese dynasty, 1644–1912; founded by the Manchus; noted for its high-quality jade and ivory carving. In 1680 the Emperor Kangxi set up workshops for ivory and other crafts; the Jesuit influence was notable. There was a prodigious output in a wide field, including wrist rests, brush pots and accessories for opium smoking and snuff taking. Relief carving and pierced work were popular.

reducing machine
Invented in 1828 by Benjamin Cheverton (1794–1876); used for making three-dimensional copies of sculptures or

carvings. It moved round the ivory using many rotary files and was powered by a foot-treadle or engine.

retable
Frame or shelf, with a series of decorative panels, above the back of an altar; could enclose ivory, wood, stone, metal or a painting.

rococo
Florid and highly ornamented style of art prevalent in Europe c. 1730–80; from the French *rocailles*, the artificial grottos of Versailles. It used scrolls and serpentine shapes for furniture-legs, etc., which meant that any ivory **veneer** had to be highly skilled.

Romanesque
Artistic style of Roman-influenced Europe from around 1025 until it was supplanted by the **Gothic** in the late twelfth century; increased in England after the Norman Conquest of 1066; the architecture features rounded arches, thick walls and small windows. Carving remained linked to styles of illumination but became more solid and sculptural rather than decorative. **Morse** and whalebone were used and the leading centres were Italy, Spain, Britain and the Rhineland.

ryusa
Form of Japanese **netsuke**; like a **manju** but with the background of the design pierced to reduce weight; suitable for holding a light lacquer *inrō*.

sashi
Thin elongated form of Japanese **netsuke**; pushed under the obi and decorated only at the top; uncommon.

scrimshaw
Generally a nautical term for sailors' handicrafts at sea; specifically engraved

ivory objects made by windjammer sailors of the eighteenth and nineteenth centuries. All the materials were at hand; marine ivory was etched with sail needles, stained with lampblack, ink or tobacco juice, and polished with sharkskin. Many objects, such as cane handles, bracelets and dominoes, were made for sale, but others, like the **stay busk**, were made for wives or sweethearts.

Sea ivory
See **marine ivory**.

sgraffito
Cutting or etching through a layer of colour to expose a different background; originally a Renaissance term in stucco decoration; now particularly used to describe **scrimshaw** techniques using lampblack, etc.

shaman
Witch-doctor or spiritual leader; originally from the northern tribes of Asia but applied to all cultures in which good and evil spirits could be approached only through the shaman, particularly the Indians of Northwest America. Shamans often used carved ivory for charms.

Shang
Bronze Age Chinese dynasty (1600–1030 BC); also known as Yin; the elephant was domesticated at this time. It is difficult to distinguish ivory from bone in Shang remains, which include weapons, fish hooks and slender beakers. A popular motif was a stylized animal shape called taotie.

Sherbro
Style of ivory carving done by the people of the coast of Sierra Leone and Guinea; centred on Sherbro Island, to which the original tribe had been driven in the fourteenth century. The main artefacts were magnificent *salieri* (salt-cellars) which were made for Portuguese patrons and decorated with geometric designs, coats-of-arms, lizards, etc.

Song (Sung)
Chinese dynasty AD 960–1278; its first period is called the Northern Song; after 1126, when the north had been conquered by invaders, it moved south and became the Southern Song. The

period was peaceful and prosperous but little ivory carving is attributed to it.

spandrel
Triangular space between the shoulders of two arches, or between one arch and its rectangular framework; often decorated with **trefoils**, etc.

staining
A more common process with ivory than is always apparent, the stain having been worn off in many older pieces. It is commonly done before etching, in techniques such as **bachiru** and **scrimshaw**. Green is a popular colour, especially among the Chinese in imitation of jade. Ivory worn next to the skin absorbs body oils and attempts may be made to fake this antique effect with tea or tobacco juice.

stay busk
The slightly curved flexible plate which strengthened the front of a corset; decorative ones carved in **whalebone** were a major item of **scrimshaw** made by sailors for wives and sweethearts.

strapwork
Ornamental motif of connecting units all in the same plane, as though a decoratively cut strap had been applied to a flat surface; uses scrollwork and shields; prominent in the **mannerist** and **rococo** styles.

striations
Linear marks on a surface; either ridges or furrows.

stupa
Buddhist tumulus or reliquary; originally a simple burial mound but ranges from the enormous edifices of northern India to the ivory miniatures of Thailand.

Sui
Chinese dynasty, AD 581–618; short but important as it reunified China and laid the foundations for the Golden Age of the **Tang**.

tabernacle
Canopied structure, usually ornate and containing an image; miniature altarpiece; often with folding wings for protection during travel. Carved in ivory in the **Gothic** period, they frequently depicted the Virgin.

tabletier
French term for maker of small luxury items, such as chessmen, which were often made of ivory and ebony.

Tang
Chinese dynasty, AD 618–907; the Golden Age of Chinese art; founed by Li Shih-min; Buddhism established. There were many beautiful small ivory pieces, and **Hellenistic** influence is apparent. **Bachiru** was popular.

Tempyo
Japanese style prevalent in the late Nara period (724–94); a highpoint in Japanese art. There was a greater realism in carving, particularly in facial detail. Many Chinese ivories from the **Tang** dynasty have survived in the *Shoso-in* storehouse, completed in AD 753.

tiki
Totem figure central to Maori art; human image based on a primeval ancestor; often carved in **whalebone**, sometimes as a pendant (*rei tiki*).

Transitional
West European style of the last quarter of the twelfth century; a link between the **Romanesque** and **Gothic**. It had many international influences, using Byzantine naturalism to react against **Romanesque** symbolism.

trefoil
Decorative motif using three leaves or lobes on a single stem; much used in the tracery of **Gothic** arches.
See also **quatrefoil**.

triptych
Three pictures, carvings or writing-tablets side by side, often ivory. Used as altarpieces or for private devotion; often hinged, with the smaller side-pieces folding on to the centre for easier travel.
See also **diptych**, **polyptych**.

turning
Technique of shaping ivory (or other material), using a lathe to rotate the article against a cutting tool; originally worked by hand or treadle but now by machine. In the seventeenth and eighteenth centuries much ivory was turned for domestic articles, musical instruments and chess pieces, which would then be finished by hand-carving.

By the nineteenth century, turning had become a popular hobby for the nobility.

veneer
Thin sheet of precious material such as ivory, cut into decorative shapes and applied with glue to another surface, often furniture; it can then be further ornamented with **inlay**. Veneer was particularly suitable for the rectangular shapes of the **neo-classical** style. Ivory was originally sliced by laborious sawing, but by the nineteenth century a machine could cut larger pieces by continuous peeling. Piano keyboards were veneered in ivory, hence the music-hall expression 'tickling the ivories'.

walrus ivory
Also called morse ivory; has a yellowish colour with a marbled effect when carved; oval in section, sometimes called 'fish-teeth'. From the tenth to the thirteenth centuries the Islamic conquests, interrupting trade, made it more common than elephant ivory in northern Europe. It was much used by the **Anglo-Saxons** and Inuit. Some cultures thought it could detect poison and staunch blood.

whalebone
Also called baleen; comes from the horny plates on the roof of the mouth of the sperm whale which are used for straining plankton; the rough furrowed outer surface has to be removed with a rasp. It

is a popular substitute for ivory from the Arctic to the South Seas and all over northern Europe in the **early medieval** period, being both hunted and found beached. It is the most common material for **scrimshaw**, where it is often decorated with whaling scenes, and strengthened many nineteenth-century objects such as corsets, crinolines and umbrellas.
See also **marine ivory**, **stay busk**.

white-on-black
Chinese decorative technique of ivory carving; inked-in background with incised design; similar to **bachiru**. It was a **Tang** style which was copied by the **Qing** dynasty.

Winchester style
English style of manuscript illumination and ivory carving, *c.* AD 1000. It was richly ornamented (often with acanthus leaves), deeply engraved with linear designs and less three-dimensional than continental carving; drapery had fluttery edges. Its influence was felt in Normandy and Flanders.

Yuan
Chinese dynasty, AD 1260–1368; established by the Mongols. Its cosmopolitan court had the first direct contacts with the West (including Marco Polo). Another visitor, in 1253–5, Friar William of Rubruck, described the use of the ivory **hu**: 'Moreover their principal messenger coming into the Tartar's court had a table of elephant's tooth about him of a cubit in length and a handful in breadth, being very smooth. And whensoever he spake unto the Emperor himselfe, or unto any other great personage, hee always beheld that table, as if he had found therein those things of which he spake . . . Yea, going to and fro before his Lord, he looketh nowhere but on his table.' Although the Mongols were very fond of ivory carving most knowledge of their styles is speculation.

Zhou
1. Chinese dynasty of the Bronze Age, *c.* 1027–256 BC; noted for abstract decoration and sacred jades; changed from the western dynasty to the weaker eastern in 770 BC.
2. Technique of **inlay** in the late **Ming** period; many rich and coloured stones and jade inlaid into ivory or wood.

Collecting Ivory Objects

The advice to anyone fired with enthusiasm to make a collection of ivory is to buy nothing for a lengthy period while visiting as many auctioneers, dealers and collectors as possible. With ivory as with most forms of applied art, constant handling seems to lead to absorbing the subject through the fingertips and this with continual questioning is an irreplaceable schooling. Museums are less satisfactory as it is not possible to touch the ivories; books, while they give a good technical and historical background, are more valuable later.

Handling develops the best possible way of recognizing the resin reproductions of all forms of ivory carving, netsuke and scrimshaw which are now flooding the market. Made in a flexible rubber mould which picks up every fine detail of engraving, cracking and wear, they are correct in weight, colour and polish. Vast numbers are on sale in respectable museums, sometimes at very low prices; others appear in country auctions, 'antique' fairs and shops and are invariably labelled in a way that suggests, but does not actually state, ivory.

Because ivory is dense, it conducts the heat of the hand away and seems to feel cold; plastic in contrast feels warm. Once the genuine and reproduction have been compared, the difference is obvious. This is a vital lesson. A more dramatic – if often impractical – test is to heat a pin in a match-flame held in pliers or tweezers and push it into an inconspicuous part of the suspect piece; if it is resin, this will result in smoke smelling of burning plastic. Ivory will not be marked; there will be no smoke, only the smell of a drilled tooth.

If an object is ivory, how is it possible to be certain that it is a genuine Ming Immortal, a medieval roundel, or an eighteenth-century netsuke? Although experience is the easy answer, that is no help to a novice.

The first point to remember is that the forger has one overwhelming drawback: *he is not an artist.* If he were, he could make a better, safer living by producing original works of art. All he has is a technical facility to reproduce – and even this is likely to apply to one aspect of the original rather than to the piece as a whole: he may evoke the feel of the genuine piece, the overall form, proportion, weight and movement, but be poor in executing the shape of a leg, arm or face; able to shape the limbs beautifully but a failure at the finely engraved detail, the hair, the finger-nails, the eyes or the signature.

The piece itself contains clues. A genuine example has salient features that forgers try to bring out to convince unwary buyers. Most forgers overdo things. If a genuine piece is tall and thin, the forger's is taller and thinner; if the genuine tends to have large hands, the forger carves frog-flippers; if the dress should have engraved flowers, the reproduction has a veritable garden. It is always worth bearing in mind that it is easier to master the skills of minute detail than of overall conception. By concentrating on the latter rather than the virtuoso skill of the finishing, it is often possible to recognize a forgery.

Ivory is a natural material that changes as it ages, becoming darker and more brittle. Forgers who attempt ageing, either try staining, a superficial treatment which cannot reproduce the deep overall tone of an ancient piece, or heat and smoke it as the Chinese do. This is invariably overdone, producing great black chasms and a sepia brown colour, and leaving the ivory so delicate it may break up spontaneously. Wear is an invaluable guide to authenticity, but, once

again, recognizing the right kind of wear requires experience. A forger may be an extremely skilled carver, but rarely has the time or intelligence to reproduce centuries of wear in the right places. A few simple questions may well produce correct answers. Are the holes of a netsuke worn? The weight of the *inrō* would be here . . . is the wear on the correct side of the hole? The side of the netsuke next to the body would have received more wear . . . has it? An ivory figure has many protruding parts, yet the damage is in an area which would be difficult if not impossible to reach. Has the forger done the damage on purpose, but not been able to bring himself to break an obvious part which would affect the value too greatly? A domestic sculpture would be handled when being cleaned or examined . . . is the wear in a logical position?

When all else fails . . . ask. Very few dealers will deliberately lie when confronted by straightforward questions. What is it made of? When was it made? Who made it? What condition is it in? If all the answers are satisfactory, make sure these points are recorded on the receipt. Auction law makes it dependent on the purchaser to satisfy himself as to the description in the catalogue; there is no come-back if the piece proves to have been incorrectly described. The major auction houses try to make absolutely sure that their lots are correct and some give a guarantee against forgery.

Finally, there is the often insurmountable problem of customs regulations when pieces are bought abroad. Most western countries are signatories to Wildlife Protection Acts and implement these more or less strictly. Check before you leave that you will be able to bring your purchase back.

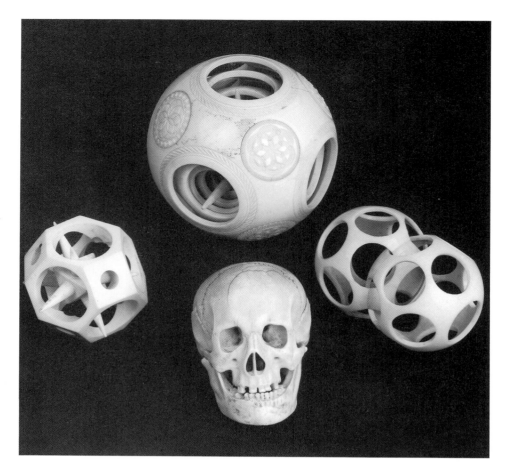

Right: Intricately carved ivory objects like these were exported in great quantities from China during the eighteenth and nineteenth centuries. Genuine ivory feels cold when handled; plastic feels warm.

Below: 'The Rape of the Sabines', by van Bossuit. Forgers are often skilled carvers, but they lack the artistic talent that is immediately obvious in a work of this calibre.

Care and Repair

The more you learn about ivory, the clearer it becomes that all but the simplest repairs (see below) are jobs for the professional. This is a case where D-I-Y, unless you are unusually talented, can all too often mean Destroy-It-Yourself. For the average amateur collector, the wisest course is to heed the time-worn but apt cliché, 'An ounce of prevention is worth a pound of cure.'

Contradictory as it may seem, both ivory and bone are at the same time unusually fragile and remarkably durable. This is especially true of ivory which, although it is the more brittle of the two, is also denser and harder and thus much longer-lived. Carved ivory exists that dates back to prehistoric times; pieces from biblical days are not infrequent, and medieval examples are almost commonplace. But even more recent antiques from the eighteenth and nineteenth centuries, even twentieth-century pieces, are likely to have incurred some damage – to have become cracked, broken, warped, discoloured.

Treasure them as they are, or take them to an expert.

Whatever their condition, they need tender, loving care. They are made of 'living' substances and, like the creatures they were once part of, react to heat and cold, to wet and dry, to light and dark. They expand and contract, swell and shrink. So sensitive to warmth and damp is ivory that if you lay a small thin piece in your palm – a side that has become detached from a snuffbox, for instance – you can actually see it begin to warp.

Display

Valuable items are best kept in glass-fronted cases, where temperature, light and humidity can all be controlled, providing protection from extremes and sudden changes, as well as from dust,

smoke, fumes and other pollutants. Museums, for the most part, maintain an average temperature of 18°C (65°F) and a relative humidity of about 55 per cent. But you need not freeze in your own home. Heating up to 20 or 21°C (about 70°F) and a slightly lower humidity – say, down to about 45 per cent – will do no harm. You can keep pieces in a cabinet comfortably humid with a tumbler of water set in an inconspicuous corner. Better too damp than too dry. Here, however, a word of caution: overmuch humidity can create mould, particularly on sensitive ivory miniatures painted in water-colour.

Whether in cabinets, on open shelves or hanging on the wall, precious bone and ivory must be sheltered from too much light. Harsh sunshine can cause blotchy bleaching and dangerous dryness. Strong electric light will do the same, or worse. And the heat of a light bulb in close proximity can bring about violent cracking.

Collectors' prizes such as Japanese netsuke should be housed in specially designed cabinets (*tansu*) with drawers lined with silk or velvet. Miniatures, if they are to be hung at all, should be grouped in protective shadow-boxes and placed on a dry wall where they are not subject to condensation; but they are really better off in drawers or under covers in cabinets.

Yet here is another contradiction: too much darkness makes ivory go yellow. So keep the piano open to give the keys natural light. Leave chessmen, tea caddies, letter-openers, bookmarks, combs and brushes out. And hang your antique fans where they can be seen, spread open, but with their fragile sticks and ageing fabric safeguarded behind glass.

Under no circumstances place anything made of bone or ivory near an open

fire or a radiator, in a direct draught, or next to a damp wall.

Never soak or wash cutlery that has bone or ivory handles in the dishwasher. These are open invitations to disaster. Both materials will swell, warp or crack if they get too wet, and ivory may separate into its intrinsic layers.

Storage and transport

If, as many collectors do, you like to vary the pieces you put out, you probably always have a few stored away. Wrap these in crumpled sheets of acid-free tissue paper, but loosely, to allow air movement, which discourages mould. Never use anything coloured, and avoid fabric, cotton wool or any other material that attracts dampness.

If you are moving house (and thus your entire collection) or perhaps lending carvings or statuettes to an exhibition, enclose each piece in acid-free tissue plus an outer layer of plastic bubble-wrap.

The most pernickety of all bone and ivory objects to safeguard, both on show and in transit, are model ships. They are complex, delicate, delightful dust-catchers and tragically accident-prone. They must always be kept in dust-free glass cases and, according to the *National Trust Manual of Housekeeping*, 'advice should be sought before any form of packing or transport is considered'.

Prevention

Ivory beads, bangles, etc., will ultimately absorb oils from the skin and discolour. Avoid direct contact with perfume, hand cream or face creams, hair lacquer and such products, as these will stain.

Cleaning

The strictures against cleaning are almost as severe as those against D-I-Y repairs. If in doubt, don't! But dusting is safe for uncomplicated pieces. An old, soft shaving-brush or a baby's hairbrush are probably the most efficient means. Work lightly. Carvings require a deft, gentle flicking with a small sable brush.

It would be foolhardy to attempt to dust a model ship or to clean the frame or the glass of a miniature. For the latter, no more than a puff of your own breath and a gentle wipe-over with a chamois.

There is a fair amount of argument among specialists about the washing of bone and ivory. Some diehards condemn it totally and expert restorers do not recommend it. If, however, you decide to try it, check first that the object is not cracked, or, of course, painted. Assuming that it is not, use lukewarm water. Detergent or soap would remove the natural polish and dry out the natural oils, but you can add a few drops – no more than that – of ammonia. Wiping the object with a damp cloth or cotton wool is better than immersing it. Rub quickly and very lightly. For more stubborn dirt, you could perhaps try a soft toothbrush. Many specialists counsel nothing harsher than a sponge and, for carvings, an artist's brush. Rinse with clear, cool water. Dry thoroughly and at once. Although it is tempting to give a finishing rub with oil or wax, to bring up the mellow gleam, oil will penetrate the surface, ivory being absorbent, and leave a patchy stain, and wax will clog the surface and attract dust.

For extremely thin and delicate ivory, try equal parts of water and alcohol (to keep it from curling as it dries). You can also try cotton wool lightly soaked in pure methylated spirit, which will evaporate almost immediately on contact, for cleaning piano keys, combs and brushes and the like. When cleaning the ivory escutcheons around keyholes, take care not to splatter the surrounding wood; and when you polish the metal of the keyhole itself, be meticulously careful to avoid the bone or ivory surround.

If more drastic cleaning is required – the removal of heavy accumulations of grime, or of stubborn spots – take advice. Palliatives strong enough to do the trick may also do considerable harm.

Pieces that are badly cracked or that have been painted or highlighted with indian ink may be dry-cleaned by a gentle rub with a soft eraser or with crumbs of eraser or soft white bread. A solution of spirit soap in white spirit or trichloroethane, removing every trace of the solvents, is another suggestion. But these techniques may remove some of the natural gloss. A soft polishing cloth and the natural oils of your own hands may eventually revive some surface gleam, but only professional polishing will restore the lustre that is removed by chemicals and detergents.

Bleaching

Connoisseurs prize the mellow patina of antique ivory in carvings and other works of art. Never try to bleach anything that is antique or valuable. Bleach strips the surface and leaves a powdery white, 'dead' look.

If you prefer to see less valuable items, such as piano keys or cutlery handles, looking pristinely white, they can be bleached – but with care! Wearing rubber gloves, give the object a wipe with mild peroxide on cotton wool. Wipe it off immediately with a clean, damp cloth. Dry thoroughly. You may then let the piece stand in sunlight for about an hour; the ultraviolet rays have a bleaching effect – indeed, you might try a sunlight 'bleach' first, and so avoid the peroxide altogether. Don't try to substitute a strong light for natural sun as this will not help and might cause cracking.

Be wary of over-bleaching. It can produce a parched, arid look. Never bleach anything that has been painted, tinted, or decorated by staining or burning.

Repairs

Remember that bone and ivory expand and contract – 'breathe', almost. Cracks are frequently caused by too much heat over too long a period – sun, spotlights, display lighting, central heating, etc. – or by too dry an atmosphere, or by immersing the object in chemicals, detergents, etc. If a piece cracks under heat, it is possible that by removing it to stand for a few weeks in a cooler, damper atmosphere you may find that a minor crack will 'close' of its own accord (though it can never be totally masked except by professional restoration). Precious, antique or badly damaged pieces should be turned over to a carver, who will fill the crack with slivers of matching ivory or with a cement made of ivory dust and gum arabic.

Some experts flout all the accepted rules and instead of avoiding damp, soak the damaged piece and/or wrap it tightly in a wet cloth to make it swell and close the gap; others believe this will simply encourage the crack to spread along the natural grain of the material. Experiment with a 'junk' cutlery handle.

Breaks in ivory are usually clean, following a lamination line, and can be glued, though the glue will eventually dry into a darker line so the join will show. Keep the separate pieces in the same place for several days, so that they attain the same degree of humidity and will shrink and swell at the same rate. Choose the glue with care; it too should shrink and swell, so you want one that is at least moderately soluble. Old-fashioned fish or animal glues are ideal. Avoid all modern, fast-bonding, miracle glues. You might like to experiment with certain cellulose adhesives, or polyvinyl acetate emulsions again on 'junk' items first. Such relatively flexible glues should also be used for resticking panels or pieces of marquetry. This too takes considerable skill.

Bear in mind that if you glue the repair badly, and have to turn to a professional, the specialist will have to clean off all the old glue and deal with any glue stains before starting work again.

Cutlery handles

The loosening of bone and ivory handles (and, for that matter, of mother-of-pearl, horn and wood) is the most common of all household casualties and, fortunately, the easiest to put right.

Antique cutlery – anything before 1900 – will almost certainly have been glued with animal adhesives, which are easy to remove. More recent resins and cements, too, will have worn partly away with many washings, but it takes a little more effort to clean off all their residue. Pull off the handle (you may need the help of a glue remover) and, with a skewer or knitting needle, scrape the inside. For a final cleaning, use a tiny bottle brush dipped in solvent.

With the same solvent, thoroughly clean the spike of the knife-blade, fork or spoon. Rinse both sections and, when they are completely dry, fill the cavity in the handle with epoxy resin and force the spike down into it.

If the fit is loose, make a paste of the glue mixed with marble dust or fine whiting. Let the join set for at least twenty-four hours.

Bibliography

Early Civilizations, Rome and Eastern Europe

Barnett, R.D., *A Catalogue of the Nimrud Ivories with other examples of Ancient Near Eastern Ivories in the British Museum*, second edition, London, British Museum Publications, 1975.

Barnett, R.D., *Ancient Ivories in the Middle East, Qedem*, Monographs of the Institute of Archaeology, The Hebrew University of Jerusalem, No. 14, 1982.

Beckwith, J., Early Christian and Byzantine Art. Pelican History of Art, Harmondsworth, 1979.

Bernard, P., 'Sièges et lits en ivoire d'époque hellénistique en Asie Centrale', *Syria* 37, 1970, pp. 327–43.

Bron, C., 'Les ivoires sculptées d'Avenches', *Bulletin de l'Association pro Aventico* 29, 1985, pp. 27–47.

Buitron D., and Oliver, A., 'Greek, Etruscan and Roman Ivories', in Richard H. Randall, Jr (ed.), *Masterpieces of Ivory from the Walters Art Gallery*, New York, Hudson Hills Press, 1985, pp. 54–79.

Cameron, A., 'Pagan ivories and consular diptychs', *Seventh Annual Byzantine Studies Conference*, Boston, Mass., 1981, pp. 54.

Cameron, A., 'A note on ivory carving in fourth century Constantinople', *American Journal of Archaeology* 86, 1982, pp. 126–9.

Collon, D., 'Ivory', *Iraq* 39, 1977, pp. 219–22.

Cutler, A., *The Craft of Ivory: Sources, Techniques, and Uses in the Mediterranean World: A.D. 200–1400*, Washington, D.C., Dumbarton Oaks Research Library and Collection, 1985.

Delbrueck, R., *Die Consulardiptychen und verwandte Denkmäler*, Berlin, 1929.

During Caspers, E.C.L., 'The Indian ivory figurine from Pompei – a reconsideration of its functional use', *South Asian Archaeology*, 1979.

Francis, E.D., and Vickers, M., '"Ivory tusks" at Al Mina', *Oxford Journal of Archaeology* 2, 1983, pp. 249–51.

Goldschmidt, A., and Weitzmann, K., *Die byzantinischen Elfenbeinskulpturen*, Berlin, 1930–34.

MacGregor, A., *Bone, Antler, Ivory and Horn, the Technology of Skeletal Materials since the Roman Period*, Beckenham, Croome Helm, 1985.

Özgüc, N., 'An ivory box and a stone mould from Acemhöyük', *Türk Tarih Kurumu Belleten* 40, 1976, pp. 555–60.

Weitzmann, K., *Catalogue of the Byzantine and Early Medieval Antiquities in the Dumbarton Oaks Collection 3: Ivories and Steatites*, Washington D.C., The Dumbarton Oaks Center for Byzantine Studies, 1972.

Winter, I.J., *North Syria in the Early First Millennium B.C., with special reference to ivory carving*, Columbia University, University Microfilms International, Ann Arbor, Michigan, 1973.

Europe: Middle Ages

Anderson, A., *English Influence in Norwegian and Swedish Figure Sculpture in Wood 1220–70*, Stockholm, 1949.

Beckwith. J., *Ivory Carving in Early Medieval England*, London, 1972.

Dalton, Q.M., *Catalogue of Ivory Carvings of the Christian Era in the British Museum 1909.*

L'Europe Gothique XIIIe XIVe Siècles, Paris, 1968.

Gaborit-Chopin, D., *La Vierge à l'enfant d'Ivoire de la Sainte-Chapelle*. Bulletin Monumental 130, 1972, pp. 213–24.

Gaborit-Chopin, D., *Ivoires du Moyen Age*, Fribourg, 1978.

Goldschmidt, A., *Die Elfenbeinskulpturen, Vols. I–IV*, Berlin, 1914–26.

Hoffmann, K., *The Year 1200*, Metropolitan Museum of Art, New York, 1970.

Kitzinger, E., *Early Medieval Art in the British Museum and British Library*, 1983.

Koechlin, R., 'Les Ivoires Gothiques Français', Paris, 1924, 3 vols.

Lasko, P., *Ars Sacra 800–1200*, Pelican History of Art, Harmondsworth, 1972.

Little, C., *Ivoires et art Gothique*, Revue de L'Art 46, 1979, pp. 58–67.

Monroe, W.H., 'A French Gothic Ivory of the Virgin and Child', Museum Studies of the Art Institute of Chicago, 1978, pp. 7–29.

Morey, C.R., *Italian Gothic Ivories: Medieval Studies in memory of A. Kingsley Porter*. Cambridge Mass., 1939.

Natanson, J., *Early Christian Ivories*, London, 1953.

Pope-Hennessy, J., *An Ivory of Giovanni Pisano*, Victoria and Albert Museum, 1971.

Porter, D., 'Ivory Carving in Later Medieval England', Ann Arbor Ph.D. Thesis, 1984.

Randall, R., *Masterpieces of Ivory from the Walters Art Gallery, Baltimore*, Baltimore and London, 1985.

Les Trésors des Eglises de France, Paris, 1965.

Williamson, P., 'Medieval Ivory Carvings', Victoria and Albert Museum, 1982.

Young, P.A., 'The Origin of the Herlufsholm Ivory Crucifix Figure', Burlington Magazine 119, 1977, pp. 12–19.

Europe: Sixteenth, Seventeenth and Eighteenth Centuries

Bever, G. van., *Les Tailleurs d'Yvoire de la Renaissance au XIXe Siècle*, Editions du Cercle d'Art, Bruxelles, 1946.

Grünenwald, E., *Leonhard Kern*, Schwäbisch Hall, 1969.

Longhurst, M.H., *English Ivories*, London, Putnam's, 1926.

Longhurst, M.H., *Catalogue of Carvings in Ivory*, Victoria and Albert Museum II, London 1929.

Philloppovich, E. von, *Elfenbein*, Braunschweig, 1961.

Randall, R.H., *Masterpieces of Ivory*, ibid.

Tardy, *Les Ivoires, Evolution Décorative du 1er Siècle à nos jours*, Paris, 1966.

Theuerkauff, C., *Die Bildwerke in Elfenbein des 16.–19. Jahrhunderts*, Staatliche Museen Preussischer Kulturbesitiz, Berlin, 1986.

Theuerkaulff, C., 'Der Elfenbeinbildhauer Adam Lenckhardt', Jahrbuch der Hamburger Kunstsammlungen 10, 1965.

Theuerkauff, C., 'Unrecognized Ivory Carvings by Jacob Dobbermann', Burlington Magazine, 108, 1966.

Theuerkauff, C., 'Der »Helffenbeinarbeiter« Ignaz Elhafen', Wiener Jahrbuch für Kunstgeschichte, XXI, 1968.

Theuerkauff, C., 'Baroque Ivory Sculpture – New Attributions to Adam Lenckhardt and Dominicus Stainhardt', Antichitá Viva 2, 1971.

Theuerkauff, C., 'Justus Glesker oder Ehrgott Bernhard Bendl? Zu einigen Elfenbeinbildwerken des Barock', Schriften des Historischen Museums Frankfurt/M., XIII, 1972.

Theuerkauff, C., Georg Pfründt, *Anzeiger des Germanischen Nationalmuseums*, Nürnberg, 1974.

Theuerkauff, C., 'Zu Francis van Bossuit (1635–1692), »Beeldsnyder in yvoor«,' Wallraf-Richartz-Jahrbuch, XXXVII, 1975.

Theuerkauff, C., 'Jacob Dobbermann und Joachim Hennen – Anmerkungen zu einigen Kleinbildwerken, Alte und Moderne Kunst 24, 162, 1979.

Theuerkauff, C., 'Ein künstlicher Bildschnitzer im kleinen . . . Kunst und Antiquitäten, 1981.

Theuerkauff, C., 'Einige Bildnisse, Allegorien und Kuriositäten von Johann Christoph Ludwig Lücke (um 1703–1780)' I, Alte und Moderne Kunst, 174–75, 1981.

Theuerkauff, C., Fragen zur Ulmer Kleinplastik des 17./18. Jahrhunderts, I, David Heschler (1611–1667) und sein Kreis, Alte und Moderne Kunst, 190/191, 1983.

Europe: Nineteenth and Twentieth Centuries

Arwas, V., *Art Deco Sculpture*, New York, St. Martin's Press, 1975.

Becker, V., *Antique and Twentieth Century Jewellery*, 1980.

Beigbeder, O., *Ivory*, Weindenfeld and Nicolson, 1970.

Burack, B., *Ivory and Its Uses*, Charles E. Tuttle, 1986.

Darmstadt, Hessisches Landemuseum, *Moderne Elfenbeinplastik*, 1960.

De Vere Green, B., *A Collector's Guide To Fans Over The Ages*, Frederick Muller, London 1975.

Erbach Im Odenwald, *Elfenbeinkunst des 19 und 20 Jahrhunderts*, 1971.

Flaydermann, E.N., *Scrimshaw and Scrimshanders*, New Milford Conn, N.E. Flaydermann, 1972.

Graham, F.L., *Chess Sets*, Studio Vista, 1968.

Freeston, E.C., *Prisoner of War Ship Models, 1775–1825*, Nautical Publishing Co., Lymington, Hampshire, U.K., 1973.

Gilkerson, W., *The Scrimshander*, Troubador Press, San Francisco, 1975.

Hughes, G.B., *Mechanical Carving Machines*, Country Life, Sept. 23, 1954, pp. 980–81.

Mackett-Beeson, A.E.J., *Chessmen*, Weindenfeld and Nicolson, 1968.

Milet, A., *Ivoirerie De Dieppe*, 1904.

Parker, I., *Ivory Crisis*.

Rapin, H., *La sculpture décorative moderne*, 2 Vols, 1925.

Ritchie, C.I.A., *Ivory Carving*, Arthur Barker, London, 1969.

Ritchie, C.I.A., *Scrimshaw*, Sterling, New York, 1972.

Williamson, G.C., *The Book of Ivory*, Frederick Muller, London 1938.

Wyatt, H.D., *Industrial Arts of the Nineteenth Century at the Great Exhibition*. Day and Son, London, 1851.

Africa

Bassani, E., 'Antichi avori africani nelle collezioni Medicee I and II, *Critica d'Arte*, 40:143, 144, 1975.

Blackmun, B., 'Reading a Royal Altar Tusk', in *The Art of Power, The Power of Art*, ed. P. Ben-Amos and A. Rubin: 59–70. (Los Angeles: University of California, Museum of Cultural History Monograph Series no.19), 1983.

Ben-Amos, P., *The Art of Benin*, London, Thames and Hudson, 1980.

Cornet, J., *Art of Africa: Treasures from the Congo*, London, Phaidon, 1971.

Dark, P., *An Introduction to Benin Art and Technology*, Oxford, Clarendon, 1973.

Ezra, K., *African Ivories*, New York, Metropolitan Museum of Art, 1984.

Fagg, W., *Afro-Portuguese Ivories*, London, Batchworth, 1959.

Fagg, W., *Yoruba: Sculpture of West Africa*, New York, Alfred Knopf, 1982.

Fisher, A., *Africa Adorned*, London, Collins, 1985.

Northern, T., *The Art of Cameroon*, Washington DC, Smithsonian Institution, 1984.

Nzekwu, O., 'Ivory Ornaments: Ibo,' *Nigeria Magazine* 77, 1963, pp. 105–16.

Ryder, A., 'A Note on the Afro-Portuguese Ivories,' *Journal of African History* 5, 1964, pp. 363–5.

The Near East, India

Atil, E., *Renaissance of Islam: Art of the Mamluks*, Washington, D.C., Smithsonian Institution, 1981.

Basham, A.L., *The Wonder That Was India*, London, 1954.

Barrett, D., *A Group of Medieval Indian Ivories*, Oriental Art, Vol. 1, No. 2, London, 1955

Beckwith, J., *Caskets from Cordoba*, London, Victoria and Albert Museum, 1960.

Binghamton University Art Gallery, *Islam and the Medieval West*, Binghamton State University of New York, 1975.

Birdwood, Sir G., *The Industrial Arts of India*, South Kensington Museum, London, 1880.

Chandra, M., *Indian Ivories*, London and Edinburgh, 1978.

Cott, P.B., *Siculo Arabic Ivories*, Princeton, 1939.

Diamond, M.S., *A Handbook of Mohammedan Decorative Arts*, New York, 1930.

Dwivedi, V.P., *Indian Ivories: A Survey . . . from the Earliest Times to Modern Times*, New Delhi, 1976.

Gluck, J. and S.H., *A Survey of Persian Handicrafts*, Tehran, New York, London, Ashiya, 1977.

Irwin, J., *Art and the East India Trade*, exhibition catalogue, Victoria and Albert Museum, London, 1970.

Kipling, J.L., *Indian Ivory Carving*, Journal of Indian Art and Industry, Vol. I, No. 7, London, 1985.

Kuhnel, E., *The Minor Arts of Islam*, Ithaca, N.Y., 1970.

Kuhnel, E., *Die islamischen Elfenbeinskulpturen, VIII–XIII Jahrhundert*, Berlin, 1971.

Lane-Poole, S., *The Art of the Saracens in Egypt*, London, 1886.

Van Lohuizen de Leeuw, J.E., *Indian Ivory with Special Reference to a Throne Leg from Orissa*, Ars Asiatiques VI, 3, 1959, pp. 195–216.

London, Hayward Gallery, *The Arts of Islam*, London, 1976.

Migeon, G., *Manuel d'Art Musulman*, Vol. I. *Arts plastiques et industriels*, Paris, 1927.

Rice, D.T., *Islamic Art*, London 1965.

Skelton, R., (ed.), *The Indian Heritage: Court Life and Arts under Mughal Rule*, exhibition catalogue, Victoria and Albert Museum, London, 1982.

The Far East, South-East Asia

Barber, R., and Smith, L., *Netsuke*, British Museum, 1976.

Bishop, C.W., *The Elephant and its ivory in Ancient China*, Journal of the American Oriental Society XLI, 1921, p. 290.

Bodrogi, T., *Oceanian Art*, Corvina, Budapest, 1959.

Boger, H.B., *Traditional Arts of Japan*, W.H. Allen, London, 1964.

Bushell, S.W., *Chinese Art*, London, 1905.

Chinese Ivories from the Shang to the Qing, Oriental Ceramic Society and British Museum Exhibition, British Museum publications, 1984.

Cox, W.E., *Chinese Ivory Sculpture*, New York, 1946.

Crossman, C.L., *The China Trade*, Princeton, 1972.

David, Sir P., *Chinese Connoisseurship*, London, 1971.

Dodd, E.H., *Polynesian Art*, Robert Hale, 1969.

Earle, Joe, *Introduction to Netsuke*, Victoria and Albert Museum, 1980.

Eastham, B.C., *Chinese Art Ivory*, J.E. Paradissis, Tientsin, China, 1940.

Howard, D. and Ayers, J., *China for the West*, Sotheby Parke Bernet, New York, 1978.

Hurtig, B., *Masterpieces of Netsuke Art*, Weatherill, New York and Tokyo, 1975.

Irons, N.L., *Fans of Imperial China*, Hong Kong, 1982.

Jenyns, R.S., *Chinese Carvings in Elephant Ivory*, Transactions, Oriental Ceramic Society, No. 27, 1953.

Jenyns, R.S. and Watson, W., *Chinese Art: The Minor Arts*, London, 1965.

Laufer, B., *Ivory in China*, Field Museum of Natural History, Chicago, 1926.

Lazarnick, G., *Netsuke and Inro Artists and How to Read their Signatures*, Reed, Honolulu, 1982.

Linton, R., and Wingirt, P.S., *Arts of the South Seas*, Simon and Schuster, New York, 1946.

Masatoshi and Bushell, R., *The Art of Netsuke Carvings*, Kodansha International Limited, Tokyo, New York and San Franscisco, 1981.

Mead, S.M., *Exploring the Visual Arts of Oceania*, University of Hawaii, 1979.

Riddell, S., *Dated Chinese Antiquities*, London 1979.

Ueda Reikichi, *The Netsuke Handbook*, Charles Tuttle, Rutland, Vermont and Tokyo, 1977.

North America

Barbeau, M., Haida Carvers in Argillite, National Museum of Canada, 1957.

Coe, R.T., *Sacred Circles* (Exhibition Catalogue): Two Thousand Years of North American Indian Art, London, 1977.

Collins, H.B., *The Far North* (Exhibition Catalogue): Two Thousand Years of American Eskimo and Indian Art, National Gallery of Art, Washington, 1973.

Feder, N., *Two Hundred Years of North American Indian Art*, Praeger Publishers, New York.

Harrison Matthews, L., *The Whale*, London, 1968.

Kaeppler, A.L., *Artificial Curiosities*, Bishop Museum Press.

Laguna, F. de., *Under Mount Saint Elias: The History and Culture of the Yakutat Tlingit*, Smithsonian Institution Press, Washington, 1972.

Miles, C., *Indian and Eskimo Artifacts of North America*, Bonanza Books, New York.

Munzing, J., *Die jagd auf den wal*, Heide, 1978.

Scoresby, W., *An Account of the Artic Regions*, 2 vols, Edinburgh, 1820.

Tyler Davis, R., *Native Arts of the Pacific Northwest*, Stanford University Press.

South and Central America

Arginier, P., *The Carved Human Femurs from Tomb 1, Chiapa de Corzo, Chiapas Mexico*, Papers of the New World Archaeological Foundation No. 6, Orinda California, 1960.

Caso, A., *Sobre una figurilla de Hueso del Antiguo Imperio Maya*, Anales del Museo Nacional de Arqueologia, Historia y Etnografia, Tomo I, Mexico, 1934.

Franco, J.L., *Objetos de hueso de a epoca pre colombina*, Museo Nacional de Antropologica, Mexico, 1968.

Joyce, T.A., *The Southern Limit of Inlaid and Incrusted work in Ancient America*, American Anthropologist, Vol. 10, No. 1, 1908.

Museums

Belgium
Brussels Royal Museum of Art and History

Canada
Churchill Eskimo Museum
Ottawa National Museum of Man
Vancouver University of British Columbia: Anthropology Museum and Koerner Collection

China
Beijing Imperial Palace Museum

Czechoslovakia
Prague The National Museum

Denmark
Copenhagen The State Art Museum; National Museum of Denmark

East Germany
Dresden State Art Collections: Historical Museum

Egypt
Cairo Egyptian National Museum; Museum of Islamic Art

France
Dieppe Château Museum
Paris Cluny Museum; National Library; Museum of Man; Louvre; Guimet Museum
Reims The Cathedral
St-Omer Henry Dupuis Museum

Germany
Cologne Schnütgen Museum and Cathedral Treasury
Essen Cathedral Treasury
Hamburg Museum of Arts and Crafts
Frankfurt Historical Museum
Munich Bavarian National Museum
Nuremburg German National Museum
Stuttgart Linden Museum
Ulm Ulm Museum

Great Britain
Durham Cathedral Treasury
Kingston Upon Hull Town Dock Museum
Liverpool Merseyside County Museum
London Museum of Mankind; British Library; Windsor Castle; Museum of London; Courtauld Institute; Sir John Soane Museum; Wallace Collection; British Museum; St James Palace; British Museum; Victoria and Albert Museum
Norwich Castle Museum; University of East Anglia – Sainsbury Collection
Oxford Ashmolean Museum
Powis Powis Castle – Clive Collection
Sheffield Graves Art Gallery – Grice Collection

Greece
Athens American School of Classical Studies; National Historical Museum

India
Bombay Prince of Wales Museum of Western India
Calcutta Indian Museum; Asutosh Museum of Indian Art
Hyderabad Salar-jung Museum
New Delhi National Museum of India

Iraq
Baghdad Baghdadi Museum

Israel
Jerusalem Aqsa Mosque

Italy
Florence Pitti Palace – Palatine Gallery; Archaeological Museum; National Museum
Milan Museum of Ancient Art, Sforzesco Castle; Cathedral Museum
Monza Cathedral Treasury
Naples National Archaeological Museum
Pisa Cathedral
Ravenna Archaeological Museum
Rome Vatican Library
Salerno Cathedral Museum
Venice Archaeological Museum

Japan
Tokyo National Museum

Nepal
Kathmandu National Museum of Nepal

Norway
Oslo Museum of Applied Arts

Portugal
Figueira da Foz, Dr Santos Rocha Municipal Museum

Spain
Madrid National Archaeological Museum
Pamplona Diocesan Museum
Tortosa Cathedral Museum

Sri Lanka
Dedigama Archaeological Museum

Sweden
Stockholm Museum of Mediterranean and Near Eastern Antiquities; Museum of Far Eastern Antiquities

Switzerland
St Gallen Historical Museum
Avenches Roman Museum

Syria
Damascus National Museum

Thailand
Bangkok National Museum; Suan Pakkad Palace

Turkey
Istanbul Museum of Turkish and Islamic Art; Topkapi, Palace Museum

USA
Anchorage Historical and Fine Arts Museum
Baltimore Walters Art Gallery
Cincinnati Taft Museum
Cleveland Museum of Art
Connecticut Mystic Seaport Museum
Denver Art Museum
Detroit Institute of Art
New York Museum of Primitive Art; Museum of the American Indian; Metropolitan Museum of Art: Rockefeller Collection
Portland Museum of Art – Rasmussen Collection
Richmond Virginia Museum of Fine Arts
Salem Peabody Museum
San Francisco Asian Art Museum – Avery Brundage Collection
Seattle Art Museum – Pan Asian Collection
Toledo Museum of Art
Washington Smithsonian Institution; National Gallery of Art; Dumbarton Oaks Museum

Russia
Leningrad State Hermitage Museum
Moscow Museum of Fine Arts

Index

Acknowledgements

Alaska State Museum 299; Alaska University 21, 291, 292; Alvins Antiques, Devon/Don Nicholson 218br; American School of Classical Studies at Athens, Agora Excavations 54bl; Archivo Fotografico Bresciano, by courtesy of Brescia Civic Museum of Art and History 20, 56, 57l, 57r, 60, 65; Archivo Fotografico Sacro Convento, Assisi 104b; Ashmolean Museum, Oxford 25lt; Ashmolean Museum, Oxford/ Werner Forman Archive, London 35bl, 35r; Asian Art Museum of San Francisco, the Avery Brundage Collection 246; Benin Museum, Nigeria/Werner Forman Archive, London 178t, 180; Joel Berger 31r, 327; Berlin State Museum, Dahlem 26l, 50, 62bl, 116; Bonhams, London/ Bridgeman Art Library, London 139, 149; Boyle Collection, 31bl, 186; Bridgeman Art Library, London 141l, 188, 214; by courtesy of the British Columbia Provincial Museum, Victoria 4, 289, 295tl, 300, 307; The Trustees of the British Museum, London 5, 33, 41, 42l, 47, 63, 70–1b, 82b, 83tr, 88, 91l, 95tr, 96br, 105, 197bl, 204, 207l, 238l, 255bl, 337t, 339l; British Museum, London/Bridgeman Art Library, London 34; British Museum/Photoresources, Canterbury 80, 183l; 298, 308; British Museum, London/ Werner Forman Archive, London 27l, 172l, 173, 177t; Odile Cavendish, London/Don Nicholson 169, 183r, 231, 260r, 280; Christie's, London 91r, 112, 113, 115r, 118l, 120, 122–3b, 341t, City of Kingston upon Hull Museums and Art Galleries, Town Dock Museum 144, 146, 153, 313t, 337br; Cleveland Museum of Art, Ohio 106b, 23t; Cluny Museum, Paris 84t, 100tr, 100tl, 111t; Courtauld Museum of Art, Conway Library, London 101r, Curtius Museum, Liège 87r; Dean and Chapter of Durham Cathedral 23l, 70tl; David Della Ratta 301t, 301l, 301r, 311, 313b; Deutsches Archäologisches Institut, Athens 42–3; Dieppe Museum/Don Nicholson 117t, 117b, 127t, 132l, 132r, 133l, 133r, 135, 136, 145, 160; Dumbarton Oaks Research Library and Collections, Washington D.C. 54bl; East Lancashire Regiment Gallery, Blackburn Museum 29l, 182b, 184–5; Editions Graphique, London 69, 164, 166, 167; Egyptian Museum, Cairo/Werner Forman Archive, London 35l; Eskimo Museum, Manitoba 23l, 296t; Fotomas Index 67b, 77, 83l; by courtesy of the Freer Gallery of Art, Smithsonian Institute, Washington D.C. 24r, 206l, 209; Freide Collection/Werner Forman Archive, London 18b; Garrard Jewellers, London 338l; Germanisches Nationalmuseum, Nürnberg 86t; William Gilkerson of Rochester, Massachusetts 325; Guimet Museum, Paris/Photographie Giraudon 203; Halcyon Days, London/Don Nicholson 7, 125t, 125b, 140b, 152; Robert

Harding 10, 11, 174b, 176b; Institut Royal du Patrimoine Artistique, Brussels 71t; by courtesy of the Israel Department of Antiquities and Museums 39; Simon Kwan Collection 237r, 240, 247t, 247b, 248t, 248b, 250, 255br, 258b; Lauros/ Photographie Giraudon, Paris 339br; Linden Museum, Stuttgart/Ursula Didoni 175, 176tr; Liverpool Museum 320, 321; Lloyd's Register of Shipping, London 154; Los Angeles County Museum of Art 237l; Louvre Museum, Paris 24bl; 74, 75, 97bl, 101l, 107; Mallet at Bourdon House, London/Don Nicholson 134, 140tl, 140tr, 141r, 142, 148b, 155r, 207r, 215r, 219br; Mansell Collection, London 64l, 64r; Metropolitan Museum of Art, New York 23r, 191t, 191b, 233; Metropolitan Museum of Art, New York, gift of George Blumenthal in 1941, 1; Metz Museum 85l, 85r; Middle East Photographic Archive, London 194l, 194r; Musée de l'homme, Paris 172br; Museo de Américo, Madrid 27r, 305l, 305r; Museo Arqueólogico Nacional, Madrid 86br, 87l; Museo Arqueólogica National, Madrid/Werner Forman Archive, London 79; by courtesy of the Museum of the American Indian, Heye Foundation, New York 29r, 296b, 297; Museum of Ancient Art, Milan 58r; Museum of applied Arts, Oslo 90; Museum of the History of Art, Schweizerhof Treasury, Vienna 68, 85t; Museum für Islamische Kunst Staatliche Museen Pressisher Kulturbesitz Berlin (West) 92l, 92r, 193l, 193r; Museum für Islamische Kunst Staatliche Museen Pressisher Kulturbesitz Berlin (West)/Werner Forman Archive, London 333t; Museum of London 96l; Museum of Mankind, London 302–3, 327br; Museum of Mankind, London/Don Nicholson 315, 318l, 318r, 322, 323; Museum of Natural History, New York/ Werner Forman Archive, London 294t; Museum of Turkish and Islamic Art, Istanbul 196tl; Mystic Seaport Museum, Connecticut 302l; National Museum, Damascus, Syria 22, 36, 38; National Museum of Denmark, Copenhagen 338r; National Museum of Denmark, Ethnography Department 208b, 241, 243; National Museum of Man, Ottawa/Werner Forman Archive, London 293, 294b; Naval Museum, Istanbul 197l; Peabody Museum, Harvard University, Massachusetts 251, 314, 317; Phillips Auctioneers, London 129, 339t; Photoresources, Canterbury 76, 295; Pratt-Read Corporation, Connecticut 332l; Private Collections 12, 15, 31t, 148t, 165, 215, 251l, 269, 271, 276t, 276b, 277tl, 277tr, 277bl, 277br, 279t, 287, 288, 295bl, 304l, 304t, 304b, 310l, 310r, 324, 329; Rhode Island School of Design, Museum of Art, Helen M. Danforth Fund 208t; Rosenberg Castle Museum, Copenhagen 130;

Royal Academy, London 151; Royal Ontario Museum, Toronto 45; Schindler Collection/ Werner Forman Archive, London 179, 181; Seattle Art Museum 206r; Sheldon Jackson Museum, Alaska 306; Shoso-in Treasure House, Japan 232, 266l, 266–7b; by courtesy of the Trustees of Sir John Soane's Museum, London 168–9; Sotheby's, London 62r, 150, 155l, 156–7, 162, 163, 189, 192, 196bl, 197, 211b, 219t, 220–21, 222, 223, 267t, 272, 273, 274, 275, 282, 283t, 283b, 284, 330l, 331r, 334, 336tr; Spink and Son Ltd, London 6, 14, 18t, 25l, 226, 235, 236, 238–9, 239r, 242, 244–5, 249t, 252t, 252b, 252–3, 256, 257, 258t, 259, 261, 262–3, 264, 332r, 333b, 335; Stiftsbibliothek, St Gallen, Switzerland 331b; St James's Palace, reproduced by Gracious Permission of Her Majesty the Queen 26r, 28, 177b, 182t, 215bl, 217; Jacob Stodel Antiques, London 118t, 124; Taft Museum, Cincinnati 100br; Versailles Museum/Robert Harding 121; by courtesy of the Victoria and Albert Museum, London 13l, 58l, 67t, 82t, 84b, 100bl, 103, 106t, 111b, 115l, 118r, 119, 122l, 137, 198–9, 201, 205, 213, 249b, 278, 331l, 336br; Victoria and Albert Museum/Bridgeman Art Library, London 126–7b, 128t, 128b; Victoria and Albert Museum, London/Photoresources, Canterbury 72–3, 227, 336l; Virginia Museum of Fine Art, Richmond 210, 212; Eric Van Vredenburgh, London 131, 336b; The Walter's Art Gallery, Baltimore 51, 53, 55t, 95b, 97, 104l; Werner Forman Archive, London, 8, 32, 93, 174t, 187l, 187r, 211t, 216; Winkler Collection/Robert Braumüller 116, 341b; Ulmer Museum, Ulm, West Germany/ Bernd Kegler 170, 178b; University of Philadelphia/Werner Forman Archive, London 174b, 176tl, 176b.

We would also like to acknowledge the following: Inge Meyer Antonsen; Arxiu Mas, Spain; Pierre Bazin; Isobel Beattie; Michael Birch; Bluett and Sons Ltd; David Combe; Anne-Marie Comert; Paul Cornish; Paul Davidson; Barry Davies; Lucy Dexter; P. Fawcett; Geza Fehervari; Roger Flint; Gulf International; Julia Harland; Nigel Hollis; Jose Hurst; Sara Jones; The London Library; Peter Lowe; John Mack; Madame A. Madec; The Mexican Embassy, London; Carol Morris; Ralph Pinder-Wilson; Nicola Redway; Ellen Rosenbush; Royal Society of Miniatures; Clarence Shangraw; A.J. Speelman; Stair and Company Ltd; Prudence Sutcliffe; Tuana Tan; Christian Theurkauff; Tortoiseshell and Ivory House Ltd; The Wallace Collection; Reiner Winkler; Stephen Wolff; Laura Wood-Homes; Harriet Wynter, London, Ltd.